Leisure Programming
Concepts, Trends, and
Professional Practice

Leisure Programming
Concepts, Trends, and
Professional Practice

Second Edition

Christopher R. Edginton
University of Northern Iowa

Carole J. Hanson
University of Northern Iowa

Susan R. Edginton
University of Northern Iowa

WCB Brown &
Benchmark

Book Team

Editor *Chris Rogers*
Developmental Editor *Scott Spoolman*
Production Coordinator *Deborah Donner*

 Brown &
Benchmark

A Division of Wm. C. Brown Communications, Inc.

Vice President and General Manager *Thomas E. Doran*
Executive Managing Editor *Ed Bartell*
Executive Editor *Edgar J. Laube*
Director of Marketing *Kathy Law Laube*
National Sales Manager *Eric Ziegler*
Marketing Manager *Pamela S. Cooper*
Advertising Manager *Jodi Rymer*
Managing Editor, Production *Colleen A. Yonda*
Manager of Visuals and Design *Faye M. Schilling*

Production Editorial Manager *Vickie Caughron*
Publishing Services Manager *Karen J. Slaght*
Permissions/Records Manager *Connie Allendorf*

Wm. C. Brown Communications, Inc.

Chairman Emeritus *Wm. C. Brown*
Chairman and Chief Executive Officer *Mark C. Falb*
President and Chief Operating Officer *G. Franklin Lewis*
Corporate Vice President, Operations *Beverly Kolz*
Corporate Vice President, President of WCB Manufacturing *Roger Meyer*

Cover, interior design, and copyediting by *Carnes-Lachina Publication Services*

Library of Congress Catalog Card Number: 91–72513

ISBN 0–697–12199–2

Printed in the United States of America by Wm. C. Brown Communications, Inc., 2460 Kerper Boulevard, Dubuque, IA 52001

10 9 8 7 6 5 4

Contents

v

Preface

The provision of high-quality, ethically sound, creative, relevant, and meaningful leisure experiences is the most critical challenge facing leisure programmers today. Customer perceptions concerning the quality of their leisure experiences, as well as other factors, are central issues in leisure program management. All leisure service organizations are in the service business. Those organizations that focus on service excellence as the cornerstone of their operations will outperform others that are focused elsewhere. This book is about creating and delivering leisure experiences with excellence. It is focused on issues related to providing leisure experiences, positive customer/leader interactions, quality, value, and other elements that contribute to excellence in service delivery.

Leisure programming encompasses the elements of direct-service delivery (customer/leader interactions or face-to-face leadership), program planning and organization, and program management. Direct-service delivery involves the ability to plan, organize, and conduct and/or facilitate leisure experiences. As such, direct-service delivery represents the front line work of any leisure service organization and fundamentally it is most important. Program planning must include an understanding of and the ability to apply the methods and procedures used in assessing customer need, designing leisure programs and services, and evaluating their impact. Program management addresses the need to analyze and implement policies and supervise staff in order to provide services through the utilization of diverse program strategies, program formats, program areas, program settings, and other resources.

This book addresses all three levels of leisure programming. While previous efforts have focused exclusively on either direct-service delivery (leadership) or program planning, few have attempted comprehensively to integrate all three components, including program management. Also, the book includes more contemporary material that defines the ways in which leisure service organizations can become excellent. Service excellence is not a mere by-word, it is a demanding force which influences all levels of organizational management. We hope that those who read and review this text aspire to higher levels of performance in creating and distributing leisure services. In the leisure service industry, excellence involves becoming more anticipatory, resourceful, prompt, and courteous in meeting the leisure needs of customers.

This second edition of the book reflects a much more comprehensive approach to leisure programming than that of the first edition. We have attempted to focus on the service delivery aspects of programming as a way of heightening students' and professionals' awareness of the need to place the customer at the focal point of their efforts. We also feel that creating and delivering leisure experiences is a management responsibility. We believe strongly that leisure managers need to acknowledge the work of front-line leaders. Such individuals are charged with the responsibility of implementing programs, thus satisfying customer needs. Too little emphasis is placed upon the recruitment, selection, orientation, and remuneration of front-line leaders. If leisure service organizations are to be successful, a much greater effort must be undertaken to ensure excellence in this area. It will require a greater investment of time, energy, and organizational resources to effect any meaningful change.

The authors would like to gratefully acknowledge the enthusiastic support and endorsement for this project by our editors at Wm. C. Brown—Chris Rogers and Scott Spoolman. Chris and Scott are among the best in their business. They provided the necessary stimulation and gentle prodding that is required to complete a project of this magnitude. They were simply great cheerleaders, providing the encouragement necessary to complete this endeavor. We enjoyed working with them greatly.

We would also like to acknowledge the contributions of a number of leisure service professionals to this project. Several individuals were instrumental in providing support materials concerning the ways in which leisure service programs are planned, organized, promoted, implemented, and evaluated. Among the individuals we would like to thank for their contributions to our effort include: Sylvia Harvey, Administrative Assistant, Parks and Recreation, City/Borough of Juneau, Alaska; Ray Coca, Recreation Supervisor, Parks and Recreation, City of Grand Junction, Colorado; Rose Marie Mancusa, Assistant Researcher, Parks and Recreation Department, The Corporation of the City of Thunder Bay, Ontario, Canada; Janet Barnett, Division Chief, Department of Recreation, Parks and Cultural Activities, City of Alexandria, Virginia; Marie Sales, Public Affairs Specialist, Superior National Forest, U.S. Forest Service, Duluth, Minnesota; John J. Callen, Director of Recreation, Sheraton Savannah Resort & Country Club, Savannah, Georgia; George Bailey, Director of Public Relations and Advertising, The Niagara Parks Commission, Niagara Falls, Ontario, Canada; Sergio Felicetti, Recreation Program Coordinator, Parks and Recreation Department, The City of Niagara Falls, Ontario, Canada; Susie Daly, Parks & Recreation Director, City of Ketchikan, Alaska; Nancy Carroll, Director of Parks and Recreation, Ames Parks and Recreation Department, Ames, Iowa; Daniel J. Starn, Administrative Assistant, Department of Recreation, City of Battle Creek, Michigan; Maureen Durand, Park Research Planner, Minneapolis Park & Recreation Board, Minneapolis, Minnesota; Dan Plaza, Superintendent of Parks and Recreation, Lottie Poe, Marketing Assistant, and Pat Lewis, Administrative Secretary, Willamalane Park and Recreation District, Springfield, Oregon; Brian Cousineau, Supervisor— Income Facilities, Parks and Recreation Department, Burnaby, British Columbia, Canada; Steve Howland, YMCA of Columbia-Willamette, Vancouver, Washington; Jack Gordon, Morale, Welfare, and Recreation Director, U.S. Naval Station, Long Beach, California; Steve Motchnik, Recreation Director, Morale, Welfare, and Recreation Department, U.S. Navy Air Facility, Atsugi, Japan; Linda Trzyzewski, Youth Development Specialist, Community, Family, and Soldier Support Command—Korea, Eighth United States Army, Seoul, Korea; and Glenn McLay, Assistant Superintendent of Parks and Recreation Department, Cranbrook, British Columbia, Canada.

In addition, several leisure service organizations and other agencies and businesses assisted us by providing information concerning their programs and services. We wish to acknowledge the contributions of the following organizations to our endeavors and thank them for their assistance. The organizations include: the Bureau of Parks and Recreation, City of Portland, Oregon; Seattle Mariners Professional Baseball Club, Seattle, Washington; Girls Clubs of America, Inc., New York, New York; Parks and Recreation Department, Indianola, Iowa; American Red Cross, Washington, D.C.; Horizon Air, Seattle, Washington; Parks, Recreation, and Cultural Services Department, City of Eugene, Oregon; Department of Parks and Recreation, City of Petoskey, Michigan; Black Hawk County Conservation Board, Cedar Falls, Iowa; U.S. Army Corps of Engineers, Kansas City District; Hawkeye Valley Area Agency on Aging, Waterloo, Iowa; Hennepin County Parks, Plymouth, Minnesota; Parks and Recreation Department, Chapel Hill, North Carolina; Lake States Interpretive Association, International Falls, Minnesota; Courage Center, Golden Valley, Minnesota; Orange County Department on Aging, Chapel Hill, North Carolina.

The authors would like to thank the individuals who reviewed the manuscript and provided critical and insightful responses. These individuals were Thomas Gushiken, University of Wisconsin–LaCrosse; Sandra Little, Illinois State University; and John Schultz, University of Minnesota. The authors also express their appreciation to Dawne Dougherty, Mary Grannan, Lynnette Gagnon, Eve Seyler, Marie Dodd, and Barbara Elliott for their assistance in typing, taking dictation, and transcribing the text. Without their diligent efforts, this book would not have been completed in a timely and professional manner. We are very thankful for their efforts and support for our endeavor in preparing this manuscript.

Finally, the authors would like to acknowledge the efforts of Deb Donner, Production Coordinator for Wm. C. Brown Publishers. She was particularly supportive in terms of allowing us the flexibility to make changes and adjust our scheduled timeline.

Christopher R. Edginton
Carole J. Hanson
Susan R. Edginton

Leisure Programming
Concepts, Trends, and
Professional Practice

1

Leisure in Contemporary Society

Learning Objectives

1. To help the reader develop an understanding and awareness of *the role of leisure in contemporary society.*
2. To help the reader understand the basic *concepts associated with leisure, recreation, and play.*
3. To provide information useful in developing a *philosophy of leisure programming.*
4. To help the reader understand the *relationship between leisure services and the benefits sought by customers.*
5. To help develop an *awareness of the leisure experience as a service.*

Introduction

We live in a society in which leisure is valued and sought after. Indicators used to measure the quality of life of North Americans invariably reflect the availability of leisure, discretionary income, aesthetic variables such as natural beauty and urban beautification, and leisure programs and services. The demand for leisure is continual and increasing, as reflected in the growth of expenditures for leisure goods and services over the past several decades. Today people seek a society and lifestyle in which they are given the opportunity to freely pursue their intellectual, social, physical, and spiritual development as individuals.

Professional positions involved in the creation and distribution of leisure programs have as their focus the creation of leisure experiences. *Leisure service programming* is the creation of a leisure experience with consequent benefits. The programming of leisure experiences provides a means for individuals to seek novelty, variety, pleasure, challenge, renewal, and growth in their lives. The work of the leisure programmer is one of understanding individual needs, wants, and desires in order to create opportunities for individuals to take part in meaningful, creative, and ethically sound leisure experiences.

The cultural diversity, gender and ethnic differences, generational value orientations, varying family structures, income stratification, and technological advances that exist in North American society today all provide dynamic and diverse challenges to leisure programmers. The task of leisure programmers today is one of meeting the challenge of providing high-quality, high-impact services that are responsive to the needs of individuals. People today want and demand quality and value in service delivery. The leisure service programmer must be responsive in providing leisure experiences that are relevant, meaningful, ethical, and that maintain a high degree of excellence.

Concepts of Leisure, Recreation, and Play

The definitions, interpretations, and meanings associated with leisure, recreation, and play are as value-laden and personal as emotional commitments, moral behavior, and spiritual beliefs are. Often the terms leisure, play, and recreation are used interchangeably, but in fact are not synonymous. There are a number of sources that provide possible definitions of these terms, and a basic understanding of these concepts can be useful in developing a personal and professional philosophy for programming.

What Is Leisure?

Leisure is an extremely difficult term to define precisely. It means different things to different people. However, central to most definitions of leisure is the notion of *freedom*. Leisure suggests freedom to pursue those things of interest to an individual. Leisure is derived from the Latin *licere* which means "to be free." From this word came the French word *loisir* which means "free time." To the Greeks the word *scole* or *skole* was used to define "leisure." This word led to the Latin word *scola* and the English word *school*. Thus it could be implied that for the Greeks there was a close relationship between leisure and intellectual, physical and spiritual development.

Today, we usually define leisure from five primary orientations—as *free time;* as an *activity;* as a *state of mind;* as a *symbol of social class;* and *holistically.*

1. *Free Time*—Leisure can be viewed as an unobligated block of time, or *free time,* when we are free to rest or do what we choose. Time can be divided into existence, subsistence, and discretionary time.
2. *Activity*—Leisure can be defined as the activities in which one participates.
3. *State of Mind*—Leisure is a style of behavior or an attitude that can occur in any activity. The emphasis is focused on one's state of mind or condition.

4. *Symbol of Social Class*—Leisure is defined by the desire to demonstrate one's ability to have leisure and to consume leisure goods and products.

5. *Holistic*—Leisure is a combination of some of the above definitions of leisure, with particular emphasis on the individual's perceived freedom in relation to the activity and the role of leisure in helping the individual achieve self-actualization. In this model everything has potential for leisure.

Brightbill (1960), Kaplan (1975), Dumazedier (1974), Nash (1960), Murphy (1974), Grey (1972), and Butler (1976) all provide perceptions on how leisure can be viewed. In defining leisure, Brightbill included several dimensions of an individual's existence. He examined leisure in relation to time, work, play, and recreation. He contends that leisure, in its relation to time, "is a block of unoccupied time, spare time, or free time when we are free to rest or do what we choose" (1960). Time may be divided into three segments: existence—the things we must do biologically to stay alive; subsistence—the things we must do to make a living (through work) or to prepare to make a living (through school); and discretionary time—the time that may be used according to one's own judgment. Though these types of time are used in very different ways, they are interrelated. Each segment of time is highly flexible, and each may be increased or decreased depending on individual circumstances. Included in the definition of leisure as time are the concepts of "true leisure" and "enforced leisure." "True leisure" is not forced upon a person; "enforced leisure" refers to leisure time that we do not seek—such as time spent in illness, time laid off or dismissed from a job, or time in forced retirement.

Defining leisure in relation to the concept of work may appear to dichotomize work time and leisure time. This is not necessarily the case. Work may be a time for personal involvement, cre-

ativity, purposefulness, and usefulness. The use of time for amusement, entertainment, participation, and creativity is often called "recreation." Traditionally, society has suggested that recreation takes place during what we call "leisure time," and therefore it is closely associated with the concept of leisure.

Kaplan has described several traditional concepts of leisure that he says are basic to an understanding of the subject (1975). The concept that Kaplan calls the "humanistic" model describes leisure as an end in itself, a state of being, or a positive condition of human beings. The "therapeutic" model, he suggests, shows leisure as a means, an instrument, or a control. In this way it may be instrumental as a therapy, as a social control, and perhaps as a status symbol. The "quantitative" model describes leisure as being the time left over when the work that is necessary for maintaining life is finished. This concept appears to be the most widely referenced and utilized. The "institutional" concept distinguishes leisure from other social values and behavior patterns such as religious, educational, or political involvement and commitment. The "epistomologic" concept relates activities of leisure to aesthetic and analytic expressions of understanding of the world in which we live. The "sociologic" concept has as elements of the definition of leisure the view that leisure is an antithesis to work and a voluntary activity—including a range of possibilities from highly creative tasks to total withdrawal from involvement. From the sociologic view, "nothing is definable as leisure per se and almost anything is definable as leisure, given a synthesis of elements . . ." (Kaplan 1975: 19).

Another often-cited leisure theorist is Joffre Dumazedier, who has suggested four broad definitions of leisure based on contemporary sociology. His first definition proposes that leisure is a style of behavior. As a behavior, leisure may occur in any activity—work, study, play; and any

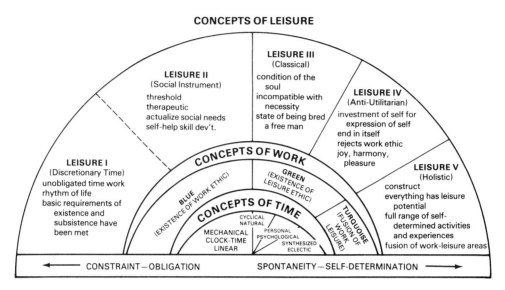

CONCEPTS OF LEISURE

LEISURE III
(Classical)
condition of the soul
incompatible with necessity
state of being bred a free man

LEISURE II
(Social Instrument)
threshold
therapeutic
actualize social needs
self-help skill dev't.

LEISURE IV
(Anti-Utilitarian)
investment of self for expression of self
end in itself
rejects work ethic
joy, harmony, pleasure

LEISURE I
(Discretionary Time)
unobligated time work
rhythm of life
basic requirements of existence and subsistence have been met

LEISURE V
(Holistic)
construct
everything has leisure potential
full range of self-determined activities and experiences
fusion of work-leisure areas

CONCEPTS OF WORK

GREEN
(EXISTENCE OF LEISURE ETHIC)

BLUE
(EXISTENCE OF WORK ETHIC)

CONCEPTS OF TIME

TURQUOISE
(FUSION OF WORK LEISURE)

CYCLICAL
NATURAL

MECHANICAL
CLOCK-TIME
LINEAR

PERSONAL
PSYCHOLOGICAL
SYNTHESIZED
ECLECTIC

CONSTRAINT—OBLIGATION   SPONTANEITY—SELF-DETERMINATION

Figure 1.1   Toward a Dynamic Conceptualization of Leisure. (From Murphy, J. F. (1975). *Recreation and Leisure Service.* Dubuque, Iowa: William C. Brown Company Publishers, 6.)

activity may become leisure. This concept has a psychological basis and refers to the attitude of some individuals rather than to the common behavior of all people. Leisure, in this context, does not define a specific sphere of activities and does not denote a measure of time. The second definition advanced by Dumazedier views leisure specifically in relation to work, suggesting that leisure should be equated with non-work. This view ignores other kinds of commitments and obligations that take place within a structure of time, such as family responsibilities. Yet another definition of leisure offered by Dumazedier covers the sociospiritual and sociopsychological obligations that influence the individual. This concept would seem to embrace heterogeneous realities—those of individual rights and institutional duties. Control by religious institutions over free time has receded greatly—perhaps freeing time for individually chosen activities for pleasure, possibly hedonism (Dumazedier 1974: 37). Sociopolitical activities may give the individual satisfaction through participation, but they are the "democratic duty" of the individual. Dumazedier's preferred definition is that leisure is

a concept of time that is oriented toward a person's "self-fulfillment as an ultimate end." This concept of time evolution is not determined by the individual but is a product of economic and social evolution, with the individual retaining the right to dispose of it as he chooses.

Murphy has shown leisure in relation to the two concepts of work and time (1974: 6); Figure 1.1 depicts leisure within the constructs of discretionary time, as a social instrument, in the classical tradition, as anti-utilitarian (an antithesis to work), and as a holistic approach. These conceptual descriptions are not drastically different from those suggested by Kaplan.

Nash (1960: 89) viewed the use of leisure for specific activities on four levels: passive, emotional, active, and creative involvement. Figure 1.2 illustrates man's use of leisure time with a progression of leisure activities. In addition it attaches a value to the kind of involvement and use of leisure time, as the levels move from the bottom to the top of the pyramid. Those involvements referred to at the base of the diagram are essentially negative in value and deemed undesirable.

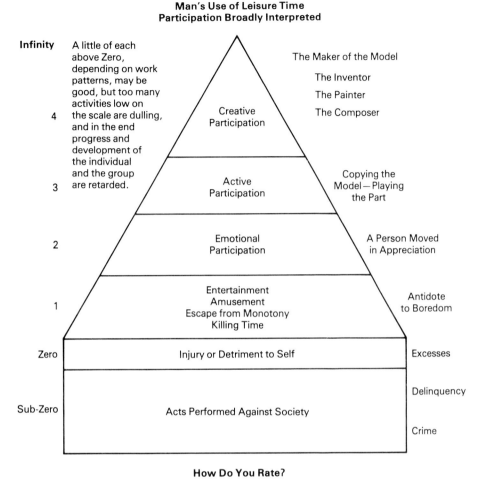

Figure 1.2   Nash Conceptualization of Man's Use of Leisure Time. (From Nash, J. B. (1960). *Philosophy of Recreation and Leisure.* Dubuque, Iowa: William C. Brown Company Publishers, 89.)

In concluding our brief discussion, there appear to be five basic orientations to leisure. The first views leisure as a block of time. This orientation suggests that an individual's time can be broken into segments for existence, subsistence, and leisure. Another orientation suggests that leisure should be viewed in terms of the activities in which one actually participates. A third approach suggests that leisure should be viewed in terms of the effects of one's leisure involvement.

Thus, the emphasis is focused on one's "state of mind" or condition of existence. Next, leisure is viewed as related to one's status. Leisure activities, apparel, events, and goods can be used to reflect a person's status in society. Finally, leisure is perceived in a holistic sense, incorporating all of these orientations.

The conditions of the leisure experience   To understand leisure, it is important to try to define and measure conditions of the leisure experience. Some of the critical questions to be asked are: How do we measure leisure? Can it be measured? How can we determine if one is at leisure?

Social psychologists who study the interactions of the individual have concluded that several criteria can be identified in order to define and measure the leisure experience. There are three basic criteria that are central to the leisure experience—*perceived freedom, intrinsic motivation,* and *perceived competence.*

1. *Perceived Freedom*—When a person does not feel forced or constrained to participate and does not feel inhibited or limited by the environment, we refer to this as perceived freedom. Perceived freedom is measured in terms of the concept of *locus of control.* The greater the internal locus of control, the greater the perception that the individual has control or is responsible for personal actions or behavior.
2. *Intrinsic Motivation*—Involvement in leisure pursuits that are initiated by the individual for personal feelings of satisfaction, enjoyment, and gratification are said to be intrinsically motivated. Extrinsically initiated participation reduces perceived freedom.
3. *Perceived Competence*—A person must perceive him- or herself to have developed a skill or a degree of competence when engaging in a leisure activity. Whether this perception exists in reality or not is irrelevant. It is the person's perception of his or her competence that is critical.

In a sense, the work of the leisure programmer should be focused on creating the conditions that enable individuals to successfully experience leisure. It is interesting to note that most leisure experiences occur in "casual" settings. Samdahl (1988) has conducted research that indicates that for most of us, leisure "just occurs" and is not often characterized by special activities or events. We give great attention to planning, organizing, and implementing leisure activities but, as Samdahl suggests, these might

be ". . . relatively rare and exotic leisure occasions." Perhaps the challenge in programming is to focus not only on the creation of the rare and exotic, but also facilitating and influencing the casual and "just occurring" life events that have potential for leisure. This can be done by recognizing that the conditions of a leisure experience—perceived freedom, intrinsic motivation, and perceived competence—can be facilitated by programmers in a variety of life spaces.

Elements in creating the leisure experience
Creating a leisure experience essentially involves arranging or assisting the placement of an individual in a *social, physical (man-made),* or *natural environment.* This may involve the functions of planning and organizing, assembling of materials and supplies, arranging for the use of facilities, providing for leadership, and/or other actions that lead to the creation of opportunities for leisure.

1. *Social Environment*—The creation of the social environment may involve the planning and implementation of such activities as rock concerts, festivals, and so on, that result in benefits such as aesthetic awareness, fantasy, fun, enjoyment, excitement, and social contact.
2. *Physical Environment*—Man-made facilities might include golf courses, swimming pools, fitness centers, tennis courts, parks, and other areas. Participation in these types of facilities bring the individual a sense of status, physical conditioning, and skill acquisition.
3. *Natural Environment*—There are many natural areas suited to outdoor recreation—ocean beaches, mountains, rivers, and so on. A feeling of awe, beauty, spiritual awareness, challenge, and solitude are all benefits that can be found in this type of environment.

Figure 1.3 illustrates the relationship between various environments that can be created by the leisure programmer and some of the potential

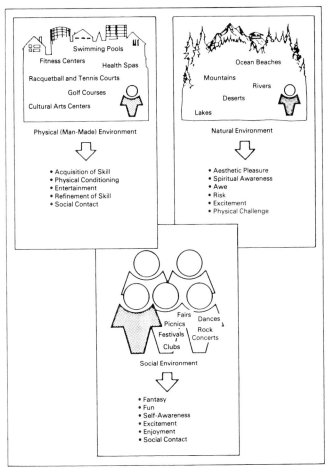

Figure 1.3   Leisure Environments. (From Bullaro, J. J., & Edginton, C. R. (1986). *Commercial Leisure Services.* New York: MacMillan.)

outcomes or benefits from each type of environment. The topic of benefits will be discussed in depth in the next section of this chapter. Although this figure is a simplistic portrayal of the environments in which the programmer creates and distributes services, it does reflect the concept that programming involves the organization and manipulation (to be viewed in a positive sense) of different elements to produce leisure experiences of value and benefit to a customer.

What is Recreation?

Traditionally, the term *recreation* has been thought of as a process that "restores or re-creates" the individual. It stems from the Latin word *recreatio* which means "to refresh." Thus, the historic approach in defining recreation has been to consider it as an activity that renews the individual for work. This approach to defining recreation has several limitations, one of which is the fact that many individuals do not view recreation as an element related to work or used to enhance an individual's job performance.

Most definitions of recreation focus on it as a form of activity. Neumeyer and Neumeyer (1958: 261) suggest that recreation involves:

> Any activity pursued during leisure, either individual or collective, that is free and pleasureful, having its own immediate appeal, not impelled by a delayed reward beyond itself or by any immediate necessity.

Hutchinson (1951: 2), while corroborating the activity approach, introduces an additional element of social acceptance:

> Recreation is a worthwhile, socially accepted leisure experience that provides immediate and inherent satisfaction to the individual who voluntarily participates in an activity.

Kraus (1971: 261) presents several other definitions promulgated over the past years, including those detailed below:

1. Recreation is widely regarded as activity (including physical, mental, social, or emotional involvement), in contrast to sheer idleness or complete rest.
2. Recreation may include an extremely wide range of activities such as sports, games, crafts, performing arts, arts, music, dramatics, travel, hobbies, and social activities. These activities may be engaged in briefly or in a sustained way, for single episodes or throughout one's lifetime.
3. The choice of activity or involvement is completely voluntary and not due to outside pressures.
4. Recreation is prompted by internal motivation and the desire for achieving personal satisfaction, rather than by "ulterior purpose" or other extrinsic goals or rewards.
5. Recreation is heavily dependent on a state of mind or attitude; it is not so much the activity one pursues as it is the reason for doing it and the way the individual feels about it, that makes an activity recreational.

6. Recreation has potential desirable outcomes; though the primary motivation for participation may be personal enjoyment, it may result in intellectual, physical, and social growth. This is not to say that recreation is automatically desirable; it may consist of activities that are dangerous, undesirable, or degenerative to the personality. However, when engaged in as part of a program of community recreation services, it is assumed that recreation is designed to provide constructive activity.

Thus, as one can see, recreation tends to be defined as purposeful, wholesome activity. Recreation, from a contemporary standpoint, is viewed as assisting individuals to have positive leisure experiences that help renew their spirit, restore their energy, or rejuvenate them as individuals. Recreation also often is linked with specific types of activities, such as games, arts, crafts, outdoor recreation, and others. The assumption is if people are participating in such activities, they are "recreating."

What is Play?

Play is viewed, generally, as a positive form of human behavior. Many definitions of play have been offered during the last 100 years. There are no definitive concepts that are universally accepted. Kraus (1971), writing in *Recreation and Leisure in Modern Society*, has suggested the following definitions for play.

1. Play is a form of behavior which is generally regarded as not being instrumental in purpose.
2. Play is often carried out in the spirit of pleasure and creative expression.
3. Play can be aimless, disorganized, and casual, or highly structured or complex.
4. Play is commonly thought of as activity engaged in by children, but adults also play.
5. Play stems from an instinctive drive, although much play behavior is culturally learned.
6. Play is regarded as voluntary, pleasurable, and non-serious, although it may involve risk and intense commitment.

7. Play appears to be found in all cultures.
8. Play is linked to important social functions such as law, religion, warfare, art, and commerce.

Developing a Philosophy of Programming

Understanding various definitions of leisure, recreation, and play can provide a basis for beginning to build a philosophy for leisure programming. A philosophy asks us what we value, what we believe in. We can think of a philosophy of leisure programming from the perspective of this question "What promise does leisure hold for people?" Is it a gift to be enjoyed, resulting in happiness? Should leisure programs be accessible to all? Should the leisure experience result in specific ends, or should it be unrestrained? These are questions to ponder in developing a philosophy of leisure programming.

On what is a philosophy of programming built? It first starts with the acknowledgment of a basic set of beliefs and values. These are then shaped into tenets, which guide the development of a philosophy. In turn, the adoption of a set of tenets will influence the operational methods selected by the professional to create and distribute services. Table 1.1 lists a set of tenets proposed by the authors to guide the professional in the formulation of a philosophy. These tenets should guide the professional in developing a philosophical basis for programming. The true test of one's convictions and goals will occur when the leisure programmer is asked to operationalize his or her philosophy—in other words, to develop and conduct the program.

What Do People Seek from Leisure?

What do people seek from their leisure? What do they value and seek as benefits from the leisure experience? According to Driver and Peterson (1986), it is important to clarify succinctly what is meant by "values and benefits." These authors note that values and benefits refer to preferred

TABLE 1.1 Tenets for Building a Philosophy of Programming

1. Every customer has the right to pursue recreation and leisure in the manner that satisfies the individual.
2. The programmer should have an understanding of the wants, needs, desires, and expectations that the individual has in relation to the recreation and leisure experience and organization.
3. The programmer should provide programs that appeal to a full spectrum of potential participant groups.
4. Leisure is freedom—freedom from the bondage of time and physical toil and to explore and express one's self.
5. Every customer must be viewed as having an equal opportunity to pursue and fulfill the leisure lifestyle.
6. Inherent in the leisure experience is the "pursuit of happiness"—the seeking of a sense of joy, wonder, accomplishment, and creativity.
7. The program should afford every customer a quality leisure environment that is safe, accessible, affordable, and environmentally pleasing.
8. Customers in recreation and leisure must be viewed in a holistic sense—not as a commodity to be quantified.
9. Every customer has the right to be treated in a dignified manner, with full respect for their heritage, age, sex, religion, condition of life, and ability.

conditions. They state that ". . . by benefit is meant an improved condition or desired change of state" (Driver and Peterson, 1986: Values—1). A value, on the other hand, is much more difficult to define. Values can be thought of as preferences or ideals that people have toward a particular idea, custom, object, or thing. In other words, values are ideals that people hold as being desirable.

Do people value leisure in North American society? Do they seek leisure? A long-standing goal of humankind has been the pursuit of happiness, freedom, and enjoyment of life. Early philosophers such as Aristotle, Cicero, and Seneca all espoused the importance of the pursuit of happiness. Aristotle, in particular, wrote that happiness was the most desirable state of life. Discussing Aristotle, Simpson (1989: 4) writes, the ultimate goal in life ". . . for which all other ends were means . . . was happiness." Simpson (1989: 5) goes on to note that, in defining leisure, Aristotle maintained that ". . . the freedom from having to be occupied, was the necessary condition or activity for happiness."

Recently, Sylvester (1987: 184) has written that ". . . included among the great ideas affecting the fabric of human existence are such notions as love, beauty, justice, goodness, freedom, and leisure." Thus, one can see that leisure, in the broadest possible context, is sought as vigorously as the other great ideals or values of humankind. Sylvester notes that ". . . leisure is a creation of the human intellect, an idea that gives meaning to experience." What we as human beings perceive to be of value and benefit shape, guide, and mold our existence. Leisure is an ideal that is valued in contemporary North American society. We seek the benefits that can be derived from participation in leisure events, activities, programs, and services.

Leading popular newspapers, such as the *Wall Street Journal,* and newsmagazines, such as *U.S. News and World Report, Time,* and *Newsweek,* have devoted considerable space to describing and discussing the leisure values and preferences of Americans. Noting the changing values of Americans, an article in *U.S. News and World Report* (1981: 58) asserted that "Not only is leisure a central part of America's pursuit of happiness, but more and more, people use leisure as a way of identifying who they are—a sports enthusiast, an opera buff, a craftsman, a lover of adventure." Schellhardt and Hymowitz (1986: 6D), writing in the *Wall Street Journal*, note that ". . . the leisure business is going to continue to grow. There should be more free time, holidays, and vacations—and discretionary income—to enjoy leisure."

Benefits Sought from the Leisure Experience

There are numerous specific benefits that can be sought in leisure. North American culture places great emphasis on individual choice and preference. This factor influences what people value in their leisure and what benefits they seek from leisure experiences. Individual preferences are

measured not only in the types of experiences sought in leisure, but also in the intensity with which individuals pursue a given leisure experience. Thus, even though one can identify broad societal leisure benefits and values, it is important to keep in mind that every individual expresses his or her values in different ways and with different degrees of intensity. As a society, we may seek "happiness" through leisure; however, the pathways to achieving this end will vary from individual to individual, community to community, and region to region.

There has been a considerable attempt to identify the benefits sought from leisure experiences. Benefits, according to Driver and Peterson (1986: 2), can be measured in two ways—economic and non-economic. *Economic benefits* sought in the leisure experience refer to the economic value of beneficial changes that occur as a result of involvement in leisure experiences. There are two ways to measure the economic benefit of leisure experiences—efficiency and equity. When measuring economic benefits using an efficiency perspective the worth of services is calculated and its impact in dollar terms is assessed. Equity is concerned with whether or not leisure services are dispersed in a fair manner. Questions of equity are ones that require political, social, and moral judgments.

Non-economic measures of the benefits of leisure are concerned with the behavioral values sought by individuals pursuing leisure. For example, the outdoor recreation adventurist pursues leisure activities that provide opportunities for risk, challenge, physical development, aesthetic appreciation, spiritual renewal, and so on. The individual seeking these values and benefits in a natural environment has the opportunity to change his or her behavior momentarily or on a long-term basis. These values and benefits are behavioral conditions that people seek. They are often difficult to quantify and measure. As a result, such benefits are often difficult to create consistently, posing a major challenge to leisure service programmers.

What then, are the non-economic benefits of the leisure experience? Some of the potential personal benefits of leisure experiences follow.

1. *Personal Development*—This type of benefit refers to changes in attitudes, values, and skills. There are many possible benefits from participation in leisure experiences that can be obtained; some of these are improved self-concept, greater confidence, spiritual growth, creativity, learning, self-reliance, and self-actualization.

2. *Social Bonding*—Leisure experiences provide opportunities for individuals to interact with one another socially. Leisure activities and events often provide opportunities to meet new people, establish new friendships, support family unity, engage in group cooperation, and develop stronger bonds with friends and other associates.

3. *Physical Development*—Certainly many leisure activities can contribute significantly to fitness and physical well-being. Enhanced fitness, in turn, can result in better health, greater energy level and strength, improved coordination and balance, and increased stamina, as well as an improved sense of self-worth and well-being. Leisure activities that are fitness-oriented can help individuals improve their self-image and dramatically influence their self-concept.

4. *Stimulation*—Leisure experiences provide individuals with opportunities for increased stimulation. In addition, they provide opportunities for individuals to use their curiosity and to expand their life horizons. Leisure experiences often provide individuals with new and novel situations that break the routine of their lives.

5. *Fantasy and Escape*—North Americans seem ever bent on engaging in activities that offer opportunities for escape and fantasy. Leisure experiences help individuals escape the daily routine of life. Often individuals will use their leisure to escape into their own personal space. For many, the quickened pace of life produces the desire for tranquility and/or escape from the roles that they occupy in their professional work lives.

6. *Nostalgia and Reflection*—Leisure provides individuals with an opportunity to reflect upon and appreciate previous life experiences. Reflection upon past life events is often reinforced through

participation in leisure experiences such as family reunions. Much of the pleasure that we experience in life comes from recalling and reliving experiences that provided joy, satisfaction, and pleasure.

7. *Independence and Freedom*—Characteristic of leisure activities is the individual's sense of perceived freedom and independence. A measure of perceived freedom provides individuals with an opportunity to express themselves, away from the constraints of daily living. This freedom can serve to energize an individual, promote creativity, and provide an outlet for the use of one's untapped potential.

8. *Reduction of Sensory Overload*—Leisure experiences may provide an individual with an opportunity to handle the sensory overload that comes from one's work, family life, and/or personal relationships. In this sense, the benefit of leisure would be to provide an individual with an opportunity to reduce tension, noise, confusion, and complexity.

9. *Risk Opportunities*—Leisure experiences may provide an opportunity for individuals to engage in risk-taking behavior. Many recreation activities require that individuals extend themselves to their fullest capabilities. Further, many leisure activities provide challenges that are adventurous, producing an element of risk. Exposing oneself to risk appears to be a way of expanding one's capabilities, coping with boredom, and increasing the exhilaration of life.

10. *Sense of Achievement*—One of the major benefits of the leisure experience is that it provides people with an opportunity to feel that they have achieved something. Leisure activities can be organized in a competitive way, and/or they can be organized to promote the personal best of each individual. By learning a new skill, climbing a mountain, painting a portrait, running a race, making a new friend, or participating in an exercise program, one develops a sense of achievement. This often fosters pride, and, in turn, builds self-confidence and self-esteem.

11. *Exploration*—Another potential benefit of leisure experiences is that of exploration. Many leisure experiences enable individuals to learn about new concepts and ideas. The leisure experience is an ideal way to examine and dis-

cover. Exploration can also refer to the idea of traveling to different locations for the purpose of discovery during one's leisure. Think of the child who attends summer resident camp and has an opportunity to learn facts about nature and the environment, as well as to work with others.

12. *Values Clarification/Problem Solving*—Leisure provides an opportunity for individuals to examine and clarify their perspectives, beliefs, or values. Often, the leisure setting offers an opportunity to view concepts and ideas from a different perspective. This perspective can enable individuals to see new patterns of thinking, new ways of approaching problems, and new ways of interacting with others. Further, leisure environments also present individuals with opportunities to use their problem-solving abilities to successfully negotiate challenges. Participation in games is often a means for individuals to clarify values related to winning and losing, teamwork, cooperation, sensitivity toward others, and so on.

13. *Spiritual*—Some important benefits that can be sought from leisure experiences are spiritual ones. Many leisure activities provide opportunities for contemplation, reflection, devotion, and spiritual renewal. For example, being outdoors and experiencing the grandeur of nature can present a person with feelings of awe, beauty, and humility. In fact, the natural environment has been described by Rolston (1986:Values 103) "as a cathedral." He further says that ". . . an encounter with nature is the cradle of spirituality."

14. *Mental Health*—Because many leisure experiences are chosen freely and usually result in positive outcomes and associations, they can contribute to an individual's well-being, including mental health. This is particularly the case in the use of leisure to relax, associate with other individuals, and/or engage in new and creative activities. It is often said that people should seek balance in their lives in order to promote good mental health. In fact, leisure programs and services are often used as therapeutic or healing strategies to help individuals improve mental health.

15. *Aesthetic Appreciation*—Closely associated with spirituality is the idea that leisure experiences promote aesthetic appreciation. Aesthetics focuses on beauty in art, nature, and other aspects of human existence. Leisure experiences provide opportunities for individuals to create and/or focus on activities that are pleasing to them from an aesthetic standpoint.

Thus, as one can see, there are many benefits that can be gained from participation in leisure programs and services. Undoubtedly, there are a number of other potential benefits that can be gained from leisure services. Grey and Greben (1979) have provided a list of these benefits, shown in Table 1.2. Often, a given activity will produce multiple benefits for the customer. It is important to remember in developing leisure services that individuals focus on benefits. People will purchase a service if they have been made aware of the predicted benefits, and if these benefits are consistent with their needs, wants, and desires.

Leisure Programming and Benefits

Leisure programs can be thought of as the vehicles that professionals use to deliver benefits to customers. We might think that a facility, an activity, or an event is "leisure." However, none of these contain the elements that are central to experiencing leisure. It is by focusing on benefits and arranging physical, social, and natural environments in such a way as to facilitate leisure that we, as professionals, produce leisure. The first step in the process of creating leisure experiences for our customers is to understand the importance of benefits.

Customers do not buy facilities, activities, or services. They buy benefits or expectations of benefits. Benefits sought by individuals in today's society are varied and ever-changing. Leisure is not a static state; it is dynamic in nature, providing challenges to programmers. The leisure service programmer is in the business of identifying and creating benefit packages that can lead the customer to a satisfying leisure experience.

Also, it is important to remember that the customer's expectations for a leisure activity can have a great deal of influence on the success or failure of the program. If the leisure service programmer claims that the benefits of a program will include fun, joyous, exciting, and pleasurable activities, but the program design does not produce these outcomes, then the individual participating will be disappointed, discouraged, and disinclined toward future participation. The expectation of benefits draws people to programs and services.

Leisure service organizations that view themselves in a broad context are far more flexible and have the ability to maneuver their resources to meet the needs of individuals. For example, it has been suggested that if the Union Pacific Railroad, in the mid-1800s, had seen itself as being in the transportation business, rather than the freight business, they might have put the first man on the moon. Charles Revlon, of Revlon Cosmetics, once noted that ". . . in the factory we make cosmetics, in the store we sell hope." The AT & T Corporation recently changed its focus in terms of the way it interprets its benefits to customers worldwide. They note that they are in the ". . . communications business, rather than in the business of making telephones." These organizations have focused their work on benefits to be provided in a broader context.

A good example of a leisure service that has attempted to define its benefits structure is the *Camp Adventure*™ program. This service involves providing contracted recreation programs to dependents of military personnel, residing on overseas military installations. The motto of the program captures the essence of the benefits structure promoted by *Camp Adventure.*™ It reads, "*Camp Adventure*™ will be an environment of magic and delight, joy and laughter, wonder and discovery, fellowship and friendship, learning and sharing, and pride and achievement." This benefits structure shapes the development and implementation of the program design, and also influences the promotional activities of the service. From a more intuitive standpoint it also shapes the expectations that are established in building transactional and transformational relationships between children served by the program and the camp directors, camp counselors, aquatics instructors, and other leaders.

The Leisure Experience as a Service

Most people think of the delivery of leisure experiences as a service; that is, most organizations and businesses providing leisure services fall within the service sector of society. Service industries, including leisure services, have grown dramatically during the past several decades. In fact, today, the service/ information sector of our society constitutes nearly 75 percent of all jobs in North America. Surprisingly, manufacturing accounts for only 13 percent of the work force and jobs related to agriculture only 3 to 4 percent.

What are the major characteristics of the service industry? How can service industry functions be separated from those of the manufacturing, agriculture, or information industries? First, let us consider the other components that make up the work force in North America today. The manufacturing industry is primarily concerned with transforming raw materials or refined resources into finished goods for resale. Certainly, there are many businesses that are involved in the creation of leisure goods, such as bicycles, bats, balls, skis, boats, exercise equipment, and leisure apparel. The agriculture industry is concerned with the production of food commodities. The information industry focuses primarily upon the exchange of knowledge and facts between parties. On the other hand, service industries focus on transactions *between people*. In other words, service-related activities involve exchanges that often require dialogue, empathy, creation of a mood, motivation, and personal interaction.

TABLE 1.2 Benefits of the Leisure Experience

Accomplishment	Family unity
Achievement	Feeling at home with my environment
Acquired use of the senses	Feeling better about one's self
Aesthetic experience	Feeling of belonging
Alienating boredom	Feeling of security in inner resources for one's life-style
Anticipation	Feeling of self-worth
Appreciating needs of others	Finding new talents
Appreciation of new values	Friends
Awareness of spiritual, physical, and cultural aspects of the human sphere	Frustration
	Fun
Belief in a future for society	Growth
Better citizen participation	Growth of interpersonal skills
Better idea of where to go from here	Happiness
Better perspective on life	Health
Body achievement	Healthy relationship with mind and emotions
Body awareness	Helping others
Breakdown of minority and racial barriers	Improved capacity of people to affect quality of their lives
Bringing all people together	Improved capacity to relate to children and young people
Broadened social feelings	Improved community
Challenge	Improved confidence in government and public service
Challenges	Improved perception of own rationality
Challenging one's habitual patterns of mental and physical action to new experiences	Improved self-confidence
	Improved self-image
Changes in self-esteem	Improved sense of "community"
Community working together	Improved skills
Community spirit	Improvement of mental health
Concept of what kind of city (environment) I want to live in	Improving my city and neighborhood as a place to live
	Increased imagination
Confidence	Increased self-worth
Coming down from an emotional or physical peak	Intensified skills
Competing, struggling, overcoming challenges	Interpersonal relations
Creative experience	Involvement
Creative expression	Inner peace
Cultural sharing	Joy
Developing ability to be innovative	Knowledge
Developing ability to lose	Learning
Developing ability to win	Learning about environment
Developing avocations	Learning about one's self
Developing new skills	Less destruction to our facilities
Developing personal expressiveness	Lessening tensions
Developing teamwork values	Making a contribution
Developing unique personal identity	Making friends
Development of friendship	Management of risk
Development of "skills of living" in a pleuralistic society	Mastery
Diversity and pleasurable experience for all	Mental achievement
Energizing the entire being	Mental exhaustion
Enhanced communication	Mental health
Enjoyment	Mental stimulation
Entertainment	More joy in personal and family life
Excitement	Motivation
Exercise	Muscle tone and coordination
Exhaustion	Mutual trust
Expanded awareness	New adventure
Expanded awareness of life	New experience
Expanded perspectives or views	New friendships
Expanded understanding of people	Oneness of body and mind
Exhilaration	Opportunity for interaction
Exploring relationships	Opportunity to identify enjoyable activities by trial and error
Exposure to new items	

TABLE 1.2 Benefits of the Leisure Experience—*Continued*

Outlet of emotions	Self-esteem
Participation with others toward common goals	Self-expression
Peer group relationships	Self-fulfillment
Physical fitness	Self-image
Pleasure from beautiful and well-kept surroundings	Self-satisfaction
Positive feedback	Self-testing
Positive relationships	Self-worth
Promoting feeling of belonging	Sense of achievement
Providing channels for creative self-expression	Sense of control of one's destiny
Providing interrelationships to improve racial skills	Sense of human fellowship
Providing socially approved models	Sense of reward
Recreated mind, body, and spirit	Separation from the mass
Re-creating	Service to people
Recreation leadership which provides bridge between people's good ideas and actual achievement of ideas	Shared experiences
	Simplicity in a complex/crowded urban life
Reducing tension by venting emotional drives	Skills development
Refined cultural horizons	Skills in personal relationships
Reflection	Socialization
Refreshed spirit	State of mind
Rehabilitation	Status
Rejuvenation	Stimulating interests
Relaxation	Stimulating occupational goals
Release valve against pressure of living in poverty, ignorance	Stimulation of educational goals and objectives
	Social skills
Relief and tension	Strengthened personal competency
Relief from the anxiety of fighting for self-image	Success
Risk	Teamwork
Sanity	Testing of body capabilities
Satisfaction	Thrills
Seeking and finding challenges and excitement	Understanding how I can help others
Self-actualization	Understanding of other human beings
Self-confidence	Understanding of potential to success
Self-confidence	Use of time in interesting ways
Self-discovery	Wider range of vision and comprehension of life

(Grey and Greben 1979: 23)

What are the characteristics of a leisure service? There are numerous definitions as to what makes an enterprise a "service." Some of the more common characteristics of a leisure service follow.

1. *Transaction Between People*—A leisure service involves a transaction between individuals. It often involves a leader working directly with a customer by providing instruction, interpretation, direction, coaching, or some other form of exchange.

2. *Services Are Not Tangible*—A leisure service is not a tangible item; you can't touch it. It is an experience that is created by both the leisure service programmer and the individual experiencing leisure.

3. *The Customer Must Be Present*—Because the leisure experience is a personal one, the customer must be present in order to partake in the service. Leisure experiences, unlike leisure goods, cannot be stockpiled or warehoused.

4. *The Service Cannot Be Created in Advance*—The leisure service cannot be created in advance since it occurs at the moment of delivery. It is dependent upon the direct involvement of the customer. Because it is delivered instantaneously, it cannot be experienced in advance of the event or recalled. As a result, quality assurance must occur *before* the service is rendered.

5. *Leisure Services Are Labor Intensive*—Because leisure service requires interaction between individuals, it is very labor intensive. This means that the success of such services depends, almost exclusively, upon having an adequate number

of well-trained, highly qualified, "people-oriented" individuals to plan and implement the service.

Many leisure service organizations view themselves in the context of being service-oriented. In this sense, they perceive themselves as being focused on people. They are cognizant of the need to manage the transactions that take place between the providers of services and the customers they serve. The management of such transactions may very well spell the success or failure of an organization.

A good example of a focused service orientation is that of the Eighth United States Army's Community, Family, and Soldier Support Command—Korea. This organization provides morale, welfare, and recreation services to military personnel and their dependents assigned to army installations in the Republic of Korea. Its motto is "People are our business." This organization sees its role as one of serving people. It has clarified its service orientation from the customer's viewpoint. Although this is an abstract concept, it helps focus the organization on benefits that are valuable to the customer.

Another example of a leisure service organization that has developed a service orientation is that of the YMCA of Columbia-Willamette, located in Vancouver, Washington. This voluntary agency focuses its services on people by building its image around the motto "The People Company." This suggests a people-oriented organization that is focused upon the needs of those whom it serves. The concept of being a "people company" permeates not only this organization's stationery, brochures, fliers, and other promotional materials, but also directly influences its value structure in terms of interaction with the customers it serves. It is focused on people and their needs as its primary organizational orientation (see Figure 1.4).

Figure 1.4 "The People Company" Logo, Promoting the Value Structure of the YMCA of Columbia-Willamette, Vancouver, Washington.

Effective leisure service organizations can be differentiated from those that are ineffective by the extent to which they have developed a service orientation. An important component of any leisure service organization is the *image* that it projects—not only to the customers it serves, but also to the broader community within which it operates. There is an old adage, "You are only as good as your name." When we hear the word image, as it relates to leisure service organizations, several things come to mind—goodwill, excellence, people orientation, credability, honesty, ethics, consistency, quality, value, and integrity. These are all factors that can impact on the image of a leisure service organization. From a service perspective, the term *image* can be thought of as the managed perception of the way that the leisure service organization does business. Those organizations that *manage their image* are more successful than those organizations that do not.

Another key factor in building a successful service orientation is the development of a *customer-friendly* system. Customer-friendly means that the programs and activities and systems used to deliver these services are organized for the convenience of the customer and not the organization and its members. To be customer-friendly means that the organization keeps the needs of the customer at the forefront of the work of the organization at all times. Often, this involves developing specific processes that can be managed or scripted for delivering a service and then ensuring that these procedures are carried out in a convenient, consistent, and courteous manner.

Often it is the little things that make a difference in service delivery, though every aspect of an organization's services should be addressed, from the primary services to those services that support, complement, or add value to the work of the organization. Successful leisure service organizations are ones that develop strategies for the following: (1) program and activity interactions, (2) telephone interactions, (3) information exchange, (4) registration interactions, (5) office interactions, and (6) casual conversations. These are more fully described in Chapter 12. All of these interactions can be scripted out and produce the desired benefit. Scripts that describe forms of interaction between the organization's staff and the customer help cue individuals to different elements in the environment and contribute to the creation of successful leisure experiences. Individuals can be cued in by positive acknowledgments, and by friendly, courteous, and informed interactions.

All of the above procedures can, and should, be addressed in written form. That is, they should be scripted out in writing in a detailed fashion. For example, at Disneyland and Disney World, interactions between customers and the "cast" are scripted out in minute detail. The Jungle Safari Tour illustrates this point. Guides are meticulously trained in the narrative to be used in each of the journeys taken by guests participating in this attraction. Even acceptable deviations from the script are written out and must be strictly adhered to. The point is, nothing is left to chance in terms of creating positive relationships between the customer and those providing services.

The last major component in building a strong service orientation is ensuring that the organization has customer-oriented, front-line people. Without question, it is people that make a difference in an organization. Front-line people must be customer-oriented people. The critical interface that takes place between the customer and the leisure service leader, host, guide, interpreter, coach, or instructor is fundamental to ensuring a successful leisure experience. Every transaction that takes place between the customer and the leader may result in the creation of a positive leisure experience. There are many moments of "truth" and these moments can and must be anticipated and managed effectively.

It is important for front-line people to know that each individual must be treated as if he or she is a unique person. Each individual must be dealt with in a courteous manner and with a great deal of care and support. People are often turned off if they are made to feel as if their needs are being handled in a routine fashion. Individuals requesting information, registering for a program, or participating in an activity need to be made to feel as if they are the most important customer served by the leisure service organization.

It is interesting to note that critical front-line positions in leisure service organizations are often viewed as the least important within the agency. Part-time and seasonal employees often make up the bulk of individuals actually delivering services. Individuals occupying such positions often receive minimum wages. Further, the resources invested in their training and development is low. With such a low investment, it is no wonder that there is a great turnover in individuals occupying these types of positions. Better strategies for promoting the value and worth of front-line staff must be developed if leisure service organizations are to effectively respond to the needs of customers.

A key element in improving the performance of front-line staff is building an awareness of the need to serve the customer in an attentive, courteous, and supportive fashion. This can be done by focusing the attention of front-line staff on the need for positive customer relationships. Positive relationships are built on the desire to serve people by being helpful, sincere, genuine, supportive, courteous, and competent. For example, one way of being helpful to a customer is to be sure they are provided with accurate, up-to-date, and factual information in a timely way. In order for this to occur, front-line staff members must be provided with accurate information on a daily basis. They must also be trained to seek and verify information they need from appropriate sources. Front-line people should be encouraged to solve problems, react with spontaneity and flexibility, and be able to recover from adverse situations with poise. Most of all, positive customer relationships are generated when front-line people are encouraged to show care and express concern for the welfare of others.

Summary

Leisure is an important indicator of quality of life to North Americans. Increasingly, individuals occupying professional positions as leisure programmers are influencing the leisure behavior and values of others. Leisure programmers are challenged to provide services that are linked to consumer needs and result in desirable benefits for those toward whom services are directed.

A key factor in succeeding as a leisure programmer is to understand the basic concepts of leisure, recreation, and play. Knowledge of these concepts is a fundamental building block in developing a philosophy of leisure programming. Leisure has been defined from many orientations. It has been defined as (1) an unobligated block of time, (2) an activity, (3) a state of mind, (4) a symbol of social class, and (5) a holistic concept that suggests everything has potential for leisure. Recreation is usually thought of as a wholesome activity pursued during one's leisure. Play is thought of as a positive form of human behavior that does not necessarily serve instrumental purposes. It is pleasurable, and can be aimless or disorganized on one hand, or structured or complex on the other.

The benefits that people seek from a leisure experience should guide the work of the programmer. There are numerous possible benefits—both economic and non-economic. Economic benefits are concerned with the worth of services from both the standpoint of dollars generated and from questions of equity. Non-economic benefits focus on the behaviors demonstrated or sought by individuals. Some non-economic benefits of the leisure experience include personal development, social bonding, physical development, stimulation, fantasy and escape, nostalgia and reflection, independence and freedom, reduction of sensory overload, risk, achievement, exploration, values clarification, spiritual enhancement, enhancement of mental health, and aesthetic appreciation.

The delivery of leisure experiences is usually referred to as a "service." The creation of a leisure service often requires the development of a mood, an atmosphere, and is usually dependent upon some personal interaction between a leisure programmer and a customer. Leisure services are not tangible but are personal in nature. For a leisure service organization to be effective, it must be service-oriented. It must be customer-friendly and encourage positive front-line staff behaviors. An important part of developing a service-oriented strategy is managing the image of the leisure service organization so that it represents the values that promote effective delivery of leisure experiences.

_____ **Discussion Questions and Exercises** _____

1. What roles do leisure programmers play in contemporary society?

2. Define leisure. Present five different orientations to leisure, citing specific examples of each.

3. Define recreation. What makes recreation different from leisure?

4. Define play. Do leisure programmers promote play?

5. What tenets would you build your leisure programming philosophy upon? How are these tenets linked to your own personal values and beliefs concerning leisure?

6. What are benefits? What are values? How does focusing on benefits rather than on services apply to the creation and delivery of leisure services?

7. Identify fifteen benefits sought by customers participating in leisure experiences. Cite specific examples of how these benefits may be created by leisure service organizations.

8. What is a leisure service?

9. What are the characteristics of a leisure service? How can they be differentiated from leisure products?

10. What elements are necessary in building a service-oriented strategy or leisure service delivery system?

_____ **References** _____

Brightbill, C. K. 1960. _Challenge of leisure._ Englewood Cliffs, NJ: Prentice Hall.

Bullaro, J. J. and C. R. Edginton. 1986. _Commercial leisure services._ New York: Macmillan.

Butler, G. D. 1976. _Introduction to community recreation._ 5th ed. New York: McGraw-Hill.

Driver, B. L. and G. L. Peterson. 1986. Benefits of outdoor recreation: An integrating overview. In _A literature review: The president's commission on Americans outdoors._ Washington, DC: Superintendent of Documents.

Driver, P. L. and P. J. Brown. 1986. Probable personal benefits of outdoor recreation. In _A literature review: The president's commission on Americans outdoors._ Washington, DC: Superintendent of Documents.

Dumazedier, J. 1974. _Sociology of leisure._ New York: Elsevier.

Grey, D. E. 1972. Exploring inner space. _Parks and Recreation_ 7(12) 18–19, 46.

Grey, D. and S. Greben. 1979. Wanted: A new word for recreation. _Parks and Recreation_ 9(3):23.

Kaplan, M. 1975. *Leisure theory and policy.* New York: John Wiley.

Murphy, J. F. 1974. *Concepts of leisure: Philosophical implications.* Englewood Cliffs, NJ: Prentice-Hall.

Murphy, J. F. 1975. *Recreation and Leisure Service.* Dubuque, IA: Wm. C. Brown.

Nash, J. B. 1960. *Philosophy of recreation and leisure.* Dubuque, IA: Wm. C. Brown.

Rolston, H. 1986. Beyond recreation value: The greater outdoors preservation-related and environmental benefits. In *A literature review: The president's commission on Americans outdoors.* Washington, DC: Superintendent of Documents.

Samdahl, D. (in press). Leisure in our lives: Enhancing the common leisure occasion. *Journal of Leisure Research.*

Schellhardt, T. and C. Hymowitz. 1986. Visions of the future. *Wall Street Journal* April 21, 1986: 6D.

Simpson, S. 1989. Aristotle. In H. Ibrahim, *Pioneers in leisure and recreation.* Reston, VA: American Alliance for Health, Physical Education, Recreation and Dance.

Sylvester, C. 1987. The ethics of play, leisure and recreation in the twentieth century, 1900–1983. *Leisure Science* 9(3):184.

U.S. News and World Report. 1981. "Our endless pursuit of happiness."

2 | Programming Concepts

Learning Objectives

1. To help the reader *define programming* and programming concepts.
2. To assist the reader in gaining a knowledge and understanding of the *strategies used in the organization of leisure services*—political/governmental, voluntary, and market systems.
3. To help the reader identify and define *steps in the social-planning process*.
4. To help the reader gain knowledge of the *process of community development*.
5. To provide the reader with an understanding of *social marketing*.
6. To help the reader identify and define the *process of social action*.
7. To provide the reader with information concerning *theories of programming* as identified in the literature of our field.

Introduction

Although it would be easy to say that programming is the raison d'etre of any leisure service organization, such a statement would not be accurate. It is important to remember that people and their *leisure needs* are the reasons for an agency's existence and should be considered the focal point of its services. Programs are the tools of the leisure service professional—the vehicle for service delivery. Through the use of programs, values are formed, skills are developed, processes are learned, and leisure is experienced.

What is a program? The recreation and leisure program concept may have different meanings for different people. What constitutes a program? Is it a park? A playground? A knitting class? A hobby show? A mobile zoo? Or is it all of these things? Does a program have to have the appearance of activity, or can it occur simply through the exchange of information between people? Is it possible for the participant to be passive? Broadly, a program can take almost any form within the framework of one's definition as to what constitutes a leisure experience.

A useful perspective on the concept of programming is provided by Rossman (1989). Rossman notes that the ultimate goal of programming is to assist individuals in achieving leisure. He suggests that the act of programming and what programmers do is to help individuals achieve leisure. The process of programming, according to Rossman, "Is the development of leisure opportunities by manipulating and creating environments to maximize the probability that participants will find the satisfaction they seek" (Rossman 1989: 4).

Consistent with this idea is the notion forwarded by Bullaro and Edginton (1986). They note that provision of leisure services is a process that helps individuals attain leisure experiences that they perceive to be beneficial. According to these authors, "Creating the leisure experience involves arranging for or assisting people to be placed in a social, physical (man-made), or natural environment. This may involve planning and organizing, assembling materials and supplies, arranging the use of facilities, providing leadership, or other actions that lead to the creation of opportunities for leisure" (Bullaro and Edginton 1986: 12).

Strategies Used in the Organization of Leisure Services

The way in which a leisure service organization chooses to allocate resources and/or make decisions depends on what it values. From a very simplistic standpoint, what we value will influence the types of strategies we use in organizing and delivering services. In general, there are three approaches to providing service—the *political/governmental system,* the *voluntary system,* and the *market system.* Following is a description of these approaches.

Political/Governmental System (Public)—The political decision-making process is a collective one in a democratic society. It often subordinates individual choice to the collective desires of the whole. In meeting leisure needs, *governments or political bodies draw resources from society and attempt to meet the needs of a culture.* Sometimes governments use a rational, logical, and systematic approach to making decisions. Other times governments are influenced greatly by special interest groups, pressure groups, and/or influential individuals. In some societies all of the resources of the culture are concentrated in government. In other societies this is not the case. In the United States vast amounts of resources are concentrated in government at the local, state, and federal levels. Approximately $5 billion is spent annually for park, recreation, cultural, and environmental services (see Table 2.1).

Voluntary System (Private nonprofit)—North Americans have been and are strongly committed to *the notion of giving time and talent on a voluntary basis to better community life.* Over the years the result of this value system has been the emergence of literally hundreds of thousands of organizations, agencies, and institutions that provide leisure programs and services as a way of enhancing the community's well-being. These organizations are funded primarily by contributions, gifts, memberships, and most importantly by the contribution of the time and talent of community members. Some voluntary organizations target their services to the community as a whole. Other organizations focus on specific target groupings, segmented by age, gender, or other variables. Many voluntary agencies promote specific values, that are linked to religious, social, environmental, or other concerns. It is estimated that expenditures by the voluntary system in the United States exceeds $14.5 billion (see Table 2.2).

Market System (Commercial)—The market or free enterprise system is built upon the assumption that the basis of decision-making is the individual. In the case of leisure, the customer uses his or her discretionary funds to purchase goods and/or services that meet his or her needs. *The*

TABLE 2.1 Leisure Service Delivery: Governmental/Political System (Public)

Local	State	Federal
• Municipal (City) Parks & Recreation • Township • County • Conservation Districts • Special Recreation Districts	• Parks • Forests • Waysides • Game & Fish • Conservation • Tourism • Hospitals • Prisons • Universities; Colleges	• National Park Service • U.S. Forest Service • Bureau of Land Management • U.S. Corps of Engineers • Dept. of Defense • Tennessee Valley Authority • U.S. Fish & Wildlife • Bureau of Reclamation • Bureau of Indian Affairs • Soil Conservation • Veterans Administration • National Endowment for the Arts • National Endowment for the Humanities

TABLE 2.2 Leisure Service Delivery: Voluntary (Nonprofit)

National Collaboration for Youth	Disaster Organizations	National Health Council
• YMCA • YWCA • Camp Fire • Girl Scouts of the USA • Boy Scouts of America • Boys/Girls Clubs of America • Big Brother/Big Sister • 4-H • Junior Achievement • Boys & Girls Clubs of Canada	• American Red Cross • Volunteers of America • Salvation Army	• Volunteer hospitals • Health education training
Philanthropic Intermediaries	**National Nonprofit Professional Associations**	
• United Way • Black United Givers • Hispanic Voluntary Contributors	• National Recreation & Park Association • Association for Volunteer Administration • American Camping Association • American Alliance for Health, Physical Education, Recreation, and Dance	

individual rather than the collective whole determines what to produce, how much to produce, and what the cost will be. In addition, the individual customer decides what to consume, how much to consume, and what he or she is willing to pay. The market system, as conceived by Adam Smith in the classic *The Wealth of Nations,* is one in which an invisible hand guides supply and demand. The market system in America today is responsible for producing over $290 billion in leisure goods and products. As it relates to leisure in the United States and Canada, the action is clearly in the market place (see Table 2.3).

Political/governmental systems, voluntary systems, and marketing-oriented systems will necessarily use different strategies for creating and distributing leisure programs and services. There are four major strategies that have been employed by leisure service organizations over the past several decades in varying degrees to provide programs and services. They are: *social planning, community development, social marketing,* and *social action.* All four of these strategies are employed by political/governmental organizations. Businesses use marketing procedures predominantly. *Social planning* is a task-oriented strategy that is directed toward solving problems. *Community development* is a process-oriented strategy directed toward helping individuals identify their own problems and assisting them with resources necessary to solve them. *Social marketing* is a strategy directed toward meeting anticipated consumer needs by directing services to them while at the same time meeting the organizational goals. *Social action* is directed toward changing the basic distribution of resources by forcing the existing power structure to change its priorities and policies.

A leisure service organization may employ several of these strategies at one time. An organization must consider carefully the conditions that it is confronted with and wisely choose the

TABLE 2.3 Leisure Service Delivery: Market (Commercial)

Participatory Facilities	Entertainment Services	Outdoor Facilities	Hospitality Facilities
• Tennis or racquet clubs	• Racetracks; raceways	• Ski resorts	• Convention centers
• Ice rinks	• Sports arenas; stadiums	• Marinas; beaches	• Self-contained resorts
• Health spas or clubs	• Rodeos	• Campgrounds	• Hotels; motels
• Fitness centers	• Circuses	• Camping resorts	• Guest houses
• Dance studios	• Nightclubs	• Resident camps	• Bed & breakfast inns
• Ballrooms	• Movie theaters	• Ranches	
• Bowling alleys	• Theme & amusement parks	• Sports resorts	
• Movie theaters			
• Roller skating rinks			
• Miniature golf; driving ranges			

Food Services	Retail/Shopping
• Restaurants	Places:
• Cafes and coffeehouses	• Shopping malls
• Food and beverage shops	• Conventional stores
• Fast food establishments	• Specialty shops
• Concession stands; refreshment services	Products:
• Catering	• Recreation vehicles
	• Sports equipment
	• Clothing
	• Toys & games
	• Home entertainment
	• Hobby supplies
	• Boats, canoes

strategy or strategies that best fit the particular community needs. For example, the rights of the disabled are often best championed by assuming a strong advocacy posture. The social action strategy might be the best approach to ensure the organization and delivery of leisure services to this population within a community. These strategies are presented below and their application in the provision of leisure services is highlighted.

Social Planning

Social planning, as previously indicated, is a task-oriented process directed toward rationally and logically distributing leisure services. It is a process of using the knowledge and expertise of professionals to plan, organize, and deliver services. We often refer to the process of social planning as *direct service delivery*. Basically, it involves the collection of pertinent information and data by physical and social planners. The analysis of this data provides information to individuals in decision-making roles. To succeed as a social planner, one must often have the ability to work within large bureaucratic structures.

What is the role of the professional using the social planning strategy with the individual or individuals receiving the service? Basically, social planners look upon individuals within a community as the customers of their services. Their job is to understand and know the customer well enough to provide meaningful services. Conversely, customers also view their role as one of consumer. They are the recipients of the process of social planning. They may or may not be interested in becoming involved in the planning, organization, and promotion of services (see Table 2.4). According to Howard (1984) the major factor influencing them is convenience of the service.

Leisure service professionals as social planners are involved in a number of tasks—technical, political, and social. Although there is no general consensus as to the specific tasks in which social planners should be involved, Lauffer (1974: 353) has identified eight approaches to the

TABLE 2.4 Social Planning as a Strategy for Delivering Leisure Services

Social planning is a task-oriented strategy directed toward rationally and logically distributing community resources. It is a process of using the knowledge and expertise of professionals to plan, organize, and deliver services (direct service delivery).

Goals	Problem-solving orientation to community needs, service
Basic Strategy	Fact gathering followed by rational decision making regarding the distribution of resources
Professional Roles	Program planner, fact gatherer, analyst, program implementer
Sector	Public, quasi-public, or private
Conception of Population Served	Consumers (we are the experts; people consume what we diagnose is good for them)

social-planning process. He suggests that the work of the planner can be viewed as the following:

1. A way of concerting community influence toward achievement of a common goal.
2. A rational method of problem solving.
3. A process in which policy determined by a separate political process is translated into a set of operational orders for the execution of that policy.
4. A systematic ordering of the near future; a designing of the future.
5. Rational, goal-directed behavior seeking the optimum adaptation of means and ends as guided by a limiting set of social values.
6. A process whereby the planner feeds more information into the decision-making system.
7. Program development based on a process of goal selection and the progressive overcoming of resistances of goal attainment.
8. A means of directing social change through some form of coordinated program in order to further social well-being by attacking social and community problems.

Social planning is a multistep process (Figure 2.1). The initial step is the development of a philosophical/ideological framework. This often

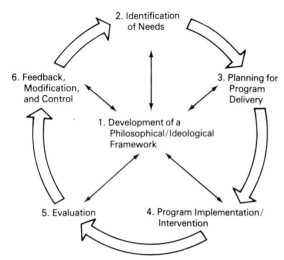

Figure 2.1   The Process of Social Planning.

refers to the vision or mission of the organization—its value orientation. This is followed by the identification and assessment of customer needs; this is a fact-gathering and analysis process. The next step is planning for program delivery. This involves acquiring and transforming the resources necessary to produce services. Following this is the actual program implementation. We usually think of our services as falling into one of three categories—activities, places, or information. The next step is the evaluation of the program. There are two different approaches to this—formative and summative. The former is ongoing evaluation, the latter is evaluation conducted at the end of the program. Last, there is a need for some tie or feedback, modification, and control. This is a logical, rational, systematic approach to delivering leisure services.

One final note concerning social planning. No matter how logical and rational the process is intended to be, it is important to recognize that the resources of an organization are finite. That is, they have definable limits. Even though the process of planning may be well organized and carefully thought out, it is impossible to meet all of the needs of all of the people all of the time. Thus, we challenge our organization leaders as well as our leisure professionals to make difficult decisions regarding the distribution of scarce resources.

Community Development

We can think of community development as enabling or *indirect service delivery*. It rests on the basic assumption that individual customers can be partners in the process of determining their own leisure destiny. In fact it suggests that individuals can learn the processes necessary to plan, organize, and implement their own leisure services based on their perception of their own needs. Basically, community development is focused on helping people help themselves.

Community development is not new to the leisure field. In the late 1800s and early 1900s, recreation and leisure services were social agency-oriented and resulted primarily as a by-product of community concern for the welfare of the poor. Leisure services initiated through the developmental efforts of settlement houses represented one of the earliest attempts to improve the general welfare of the community and, as such, was one of the earliest forms of community development. Furthermore, early leaders of the play and recreation movement were not trained in play or recreation leadership but viewed themselves as social activists engaged in the process of community development. Contemporary recreation and leisure theorists have rekindled interest in the process of community development. They argue that the task-oriented approach to the organization of recreation and leisure services is less effective in the face of rapid and constant change and the emergence of humanism. Discussing the development of the recreation movement, Murphy (1975: 51–52) has written:

> The recreation movement has passed through several stages of professional development, including a phase dominated by the concern of

park professionals for pleasant, passive surroundings in which people could enjoy leisure
at their own pace; a period of time which included the propagation of an egalitarian "recreation for all" principle, which stimulated an
almost compulsive concern for programs and
activities, and the legitimatizing of local government responsibility for recreation and leisure
service; a tumultuous period of social upheaval
and social unrest which brought the movement
back to issues of social concern and commitment to the provision of recreation designed to
meet important social needs; and most recently
a human developmental phase, which focuses on
the individual and the need to build and nurture
human services responsive to his needs. An eco-
logically based perspective, this evolving stage
of the Recreation Movement is concerned primarily with the interrelationships among people
in their physical and social environment and the
way these relationships contribute to or hinder
their ability to realize their human potential. The
Recreation Movement, then, grew out of hu-
manitarian concerns, and it appears that it has
now come full circle, to an era which again is
focusing on the individual. Recreation opportunities are increasingly being fostered with the
intent to build and nurture arousing situations
which are responsive to human needs. They are
not seen as trivial, but as fundamental to the developing individual.

Thus, we see the reassumption of the community development role as a strategy to be used
in the organization of recreation and leisure services. At the heart of this shift in strategy is the
recognition of the need to support alternative
values in our society. The formulation and acceptance of alternative lifestyles are factors influencing the development of new forms of
service delivery. There has also been an increased concern for the involvement of individuals in those decisions affecting their lives.

The role of the leisure professional involved
in the community development process can be
described in many ways. The professional can be
viewed as a resource to individuals and community groups, providing valued information and

insights. The professional can also be viewed as
a teacher or coach, helping people to clarify their
values as well as instructing individuals in the skills
necessary to work in groups. Also, the community developer can be a coordinator linking various resources together within a community to
assist individuals or groups in attaining their goals
and objectives. Still further, a community developer can be a friend or encourager to individuals
and groups, serving as a source of inspiration.

The community development process should
be viewed as a collaborative process. The community developer works directly with individuals
on a face-to-face basis, encouraging them to
identify and solve their own problems. The relationship between the community developer and
the participating individuals is one that requires
a great deal of mutual confidence, trust, and respect. The community developer does not try to
"diagnose" the clients but helps them develop
their own diagnostic skills and abilities. In this
sense, the community developer can be thought
of as a sharer and an activator in the process of
an individual's or group's development.

It is important to draw a distinction between
the work of a community developer and the work
of a social planner. Perhaps the most important
difference concerns the view that each has of the
customer. The social planner views the customer
as a consumer of his or her services. The role is
to isolate individuals with needs and then intervene directly with services. The community developer, on the other hand, views participants as
customers with whom he or she engages in an interactive process of problem solving. The social
planner is primarily involved in fact gathering in
an effort to determine the needs of the individuals being served. Once the appropriate information has been gathered, it is used in the
decision-making process to develop a rational
plan for the distribution of available or acquired
resources. The community developer, however,
maintains a basic strategy of change in which the
role is to help through collaborative efforts. The
community developer works with individuals and

small groups, whereas the work of the social planner is primarily carried out in large bureaucratic organizations. The skills needed by the social planner are primarily those of management and administration; the community developer's skills should be particularly strong in the areas of communications and small group behavior.

Specifically, community developers carry out four functions:

1. Community developers work toward stimulating individuals to think about and participate in not only their own personal development but also the development of the community in which they live.
2. Community developers work to develop the leadership capabilities of those with whom they work.
3. Community developers assist individuals by supplying information about the methods and procedures that an individual or group can use to bring about change within a community.
4. Community developers assist individuals in the formulation of values and the appropriate mechanisms with which to evaluate their progress toward the attainment of these values.

A good example of the community development process in action occurs when a leisure service agency works with a special interest club. In this situation, the agency attempts to organize information rather than activities and acts as a resource to the club, helping it evaluate its progress. There are numerous programs that could be shifted from a pattern of direct service delivery to an indirect program. In these days of financial constraints, this might be a useful pattern to explore. For example, why should a public service organization operate an adult softball league when the adults themselves have the ability to plan, organize, and implement the program? The staff resources saved in this area could be used in other program areas. How many leisure service organizations are prepared to let go of services in order to expand their community offerings? (See Table 2.5)

TABLE 2.5 Community Development as a Strategy for Delivering Leisure Services

Community development rests on the basic assumption that individuals can be partners in the process of determining their leisure destiny. It suggests that individuals can learn the processes necessary to plan, organize, and implement their own services based on their perception of their own needs. Community development focuses on helping people help themselves.

Goals	Self help, teaching process skills, promotion of democratic values, service
Basic Strategy	Assisting individuals to determine and solve their own problems
Professional Roles	Enabler, catalyst, coordinator, teacher, value clarifier
Sector	Public, quasi-public
Conception of Population Served	Partners

Communications and community development   The ability to communicate is a prerequisite to effectiveness as a community developer. It is essentially an exchange process that exists between people. Communication takes place only when the meaning of the message transmitted is clearly and accurately received by the recipient. Often people believe that communication has occurred because they feel that they have articulated their views clearly; however, it is important to remember that there is not only a sender in the communication process but also a receiver. If the receiver fails to grasp the meaning of the intended message or misinterprets it, then the communication process breaks down.

Because the community development process is a sharing process, the community developer not only must be an articulate sender but also must be able and willing to receive and understand the message transmitted by those with whom he or she works. The effective community developer double-checks the messages received to ensure that they have been received correctly; conversely, he or she checks to make sure that the messages communicated have been received as intended. The community developer doesn't build facilities or create activities but provides information and counseling in the broadest sense to individuals and groups. His or her raison d'etre, as an expert in the communications area, is to ensure that the process of individual and collective development is achieved without communicative hindrance.

The community developer should also have an understanding of group dynamics, especially small group behavior. Since much of the community developer's work takes place in small groups, it is advantageous for him or her to be aware of the type and quality of interactions that are possible in such settings. This requires an awareness of the subtleties of individual behavior that may take place in group situations. The role may be one of positive manipulations of the individuals within a group in order to help them identify and solve their particular problems. This may be accomplished by tactfully addressing the dysfunction created when antigroup roles emerge and by being supportive of those roles which are supportive of the group and are task-oriented. Essentially, the role is to make the group experience a positive one. If a group is experiencing difficulties, the community developer should be able to use his or her skills to manipulate group behavior in such a way as to propel the group into a more positive direction.

Operational assumptions of the community developer The community development process is not a value-free process. There are a number of ideas or values that may affect the interactions of people and, as such, may affect the role relationship that occurs between the community developer and the participant. Perhaps the most articulate statement of assumptions concerning the role of the participant and the community developer in the community development process is the following, developed by Biddle and Biddle (1965: 60–62):

1. Each person is valuable, unique, and capable of growth toward greater social sensitivity and responsibility.

    a. Each person has underdeveloped abilities in initiative, originality, and leadership. These qualities can be cultivated and strengthened.
    b. These abilities tend to emerge and grow stronger when people work together in small groups that serve the common (community) good.
    c. There will always be conflicts between persons and factions. Properly handled, the conflicts can be used creatively.
    d. Agreement can be reached on specific steps of improvement without destroying philosophical or religious differences.
    e. Although the people may express their differences freely, when they become responsible they often choose to refrain in order to further the interest of the whole group and of their idea of the community.
    f. People will respond to an appeal to altruism as well as to an appeal to selfishness.
    g. These generous motivations may be used to form groups that serve the welfare of all people in the community.
    h. Groups are capable of growth toward self direction when the members assume responsibility for group growth and for an inclusive local welfare.
2. Human beings and groups have both good and bad impulses.
    a. Under wise encouragement they can strengthen the better in themselves and help others to do likewise.
    b. When the people are free of coercive pressures, and can then examine a wide range of alternatives, they tend to choose the ethically better and the intelligently wiser course of action.
    c. There is satisfaction in serving the common welfare, even as in serving self-interest.
    d. A concept of the common good can grow out of group experience that serves the welfare of all in some local area. This sense of responsibility and belonging can be strengthened even for those to whom community is least meaningful.
3. Satisfaction and self-confidence gained from small accomplishments can lead to the contending with more and more difficult problems, in a process of continuing growth.

4. Within the broad role of community developer, there are several sub-roles to be chosen, depending upon the developer's judgment of the people's needs:
   a. Encourager, friend, source of inspiration, and believer in the good in people.
   b. Objective observer, analyst, truth seeker, and kindly commentator.
   c. Participant in discussion to clarify alternatives and the values these serve.
   d. Participant in some actions—not all.
   e. Process expert, advisor, conciliator, expeditor of on-going development.
   f. The prominence of the community developer is likely to be greater in the early stages, then taper off toward a termination date, but it may increase temporarily at any time.

Finally, in summary:

5. When community developers work on a friendly basis with people, in activities that serve the common good;
   When they persist patiently in this;
   When their actions affirm a belief in the good in people;
   When the process continues, even in the face of discouragement;
   Then people tend to develop themselves to become more ethically competent persons;
   Then they may become involved in a process of self-guided growth that continues indefinitely.

Knowledge of these operational assumptions can be useful to the community developer in guiding individuals and groups, since they serve to illustrate a potential philosophical framework and role definition from which the community development process can take place. The assumptions made by Biddle and Biddle are not unlike the philosophical values that we hold in the recreation and leisure field. We, too, are concerned about creating opportunities for self-improvement, self-expression, and self-initiative.

Social Marketing

Over the past several decades marketing has become a very popular topic in the leisure arena. We like the term social marketing. We choose this term for two reasons. The first is that *social marketing connotes an emphasis on the delivery of experiences rather than tangible products.* Most leisure experiences fall within the context of what can be thought of as "social services." The second reason is that the primary thrusts of the leisure service movement—wise use of leisure, promotion of an environmental ethic, and enhancement of human dignity—take precedence over efficiency, profit, or other goals. However, this does not mean that we ignore other desired ends, but rather have developed a priority structure that finds leisure professionals operating with a "social conscience." For example, profit is a goal sought in commercial outdoor recreation businesses. The social context that an outdoor vendor may operate in suggests a strong value orientation directed toward preservation and conservation of the environment. Marketing is built upon the basic assumption that an organization should have as its basic strategic objective meeting customer needs. It is a way of aligning resources with needs; supply with demand. *Marketing is a philosophy that focuses the work of the entire organization on satisfying the customer* (see Table 2.6).

According to Kotler (1972: 64), ". . . the true meaning of marketing is not hucksterism, making it possible to sell persons on buying things, propositions, or causes they either do not want or which are bad for them. The real meaning is the concept of sensitively serving and satisfying human needs. Perhaps the short-run problem of business firms is to sell people on buying the existing products, but the long-run problem is clearly to create the products that people need. By this recognition that effective marketing requires a consumer orientation instead of a pro-

TABLE 2.6 Social Marketing as a Strategy for Delivering Leisure Services

Marketing is built on the assumption that an organization should have as its basic strategic objective meeting customer needs. It is a way of aligning resources with need; supply with demand. Marketing is a philosophy that focuses the work of the entire organization on satisfying the customer.

Goals	Satisfying customer needs, profit
Basic Strategy	An analysis of needs. Integration and initiation of marketing mix to meet these needs.
Professional Roles	Analyst, planner, implementor, promoter
Sector	Discrete target markets
Conception of Population Served	Customers, consumers, guests

duction orientation, marketing has taken a new lease on life and tied its economic activity to a higher social purpose. . . ."

According to Rubright and MacDonald (1981) marketing involves a number of characteristics. These characteristics seem to apply in all sectors—marketing, voluntary, governmental/political—where leisure services are created and dispersed. The characteristics that appear to apply to all areas in which leisure services are delivered include the following:

Aggressiveness—An organization must have the capacity to seek new business instead of merely reacting to competition and then taking necessary action. An aggressive organization keeps up with new developments in its industry and takes risks if it can comprehend the ultimate benefits that may accrue to itself and its constituents.

A Continually Positive Attitude—If the overall agency attitude is characterized as mainly negative, cynical, or sour, it is almost impossible to achieve a positive climate for marketing.

Contrariness to Tradition—Marketing makes things change because its presence means doing things differently, taking chances, discarding old habits, making or seeking new friends.

Initiative—An organization inclined to market cannot wait for clients to come to it; it can't assume that, just because it exists, it has no obligation to plan and develop its future.

Responsiveness—A marketing-oriented organization succeeds if it correctly perceives its targets; if it meets the needs of referrers, users, and staff members; if it knows its constituents' psychosocial underpinnings. The organization's response to impacting forces must not be reactive or arbitrary, but deliberate and calculated.

Planning—The organization must make this a major characteristic of its operation. Marketing is the study of the future, some say, and any bright future involves the ability to do sound planning (Rubright and MacDonald 1981: 11–12.)

There are essential differences in the marketing of services as compared to the manufacturing and the delivery of products; whereas products are tangible items, services are intangible, usually involving contact between one human being and another. Products can be seen, held, studied, tried on, tasted, or felt before using; in other words, the customer can sample the product before purchasing. Services, on the other hand, are more difficult to experience before actual consumption. In fact, in order to effectively meet the needs of individuals, a customer must perceive and anticipate the potential benefit to be gained from the service. Thus, services require a great deal more interpretation and closer interaction with the leisure professional to present the value of the leisure experience to the customer.

Some of the unique characteristics of service transactions are as follows:

1. Consumption or use is not possible without the participation of the seller.
2. Services are sold, then produced and consumed simultaneously.
3. The capacity to produce a service must exist before any transaction can occur. Services can't be stockpiled.
4. Universal performance standards are difficult to attain. "Not only do performance standards vary from one service seller to another, but the quality of a single-service seller may vary from buyer to buyer."
5. Since most services are paid for after they are performed and cannot be repossessed, service providers are very dependent on the good faith of the buyer (Rathmell 1974: 6–8).

One of the misconceptions that is often made concerning marketing is that it involves selling. Marketing is more than just selling or promoting. Kotler (1982), a noted author in the area of the application of marketing concepts to non-profit organizations, has suggested that selling finds an organization focusing inwardly on its programs and services. Its primary goal is to achieve large numbers in terms of participation. The marketing orientation, on the other hand, is focused on consumer needs, wants, and desires. The work of the organization using a social marketing orientation is directed toward producing customer satisfaction. In contrast to the hard-sell approach, the marketing orientation is a process that involves integrating five components—the product (service/program), the place, the price, the way the product is promoted, and how the product is packaged—to produce customer satisfaction (see Table 2.7 and Figure 2.2).

Central to the idea of marketing is the identification of target markets. These are also referred to as "market niches." One of the central features of marketing is that an organization, to be successful, cannot be all things to all people. It must carefully determine what business it is in and what population it can best serve. In order to identify a target market, an organization will usually undertake the process of segmenting markets to understand specific customer needs to which it can effectively relate. Market segmentation usually is done by demographic and psychosocial variables. Demographic variables such as age, gender, and income are useful and psychosocial or lifestyle variables such as propensity or desire for risk, need for status, and others can be used to segment markets.

One of the interesting concepts to emerge in the marketing literature is that of the "product life cycle." This concept suggests that leisure programs have a definable life span (Figure 2.3). This life cycle can be viewed as having successive stages. When a service is first introduced, its acceptance by the marketplace is usually low. Over a period of time, if the service is successful, acceptance grows and reaches a point of maturity or saturation. At some point, adjustments need to be made in the way the service is packaged, promoted, and/or priced in order to accommodate changing environmental conditions. This must be done in order to ensure that the service remains viable over an extended period of time.

Leisure activities tend to have short life cycles. One could speculate that the novelty aspect of a

TABLE 2.7   The Marketing Mix

1. Product. The product refers to the type of service that is produced by the leisure service organization. There are five types of products—areas and facilities, activities, information, leadership, equipment, and supplies.
2. Price. The value of a service is often related to its price. There are multiple approaches to pricing.
3. Place. The time and location of a service is a critical factor in the marketing mix. Convenience is extremely important.
4. Promotion. Promotion is a process of communication between the organization and the customer. Promotional efforts let people know what is available and its cost, location, time, and benefits.
5. Package. Different programs and services can be packaged in different ways. This is referred to as the program format. The form can vary, yet the content remains the same.

Figure 2.2 Social Marketing Mix.

new leisure program is an integral part of its attractiveness. Ellis (1973) suggests in his book *Why People Play* that novel, complex, and dissonant events elevate an individual's arousal and move an individual to an optimum level that is accompanied by pleasure. This pleasure is sustained for a relatively short period of time. Csikszentmihalyi (1975) suggests that individuals must be constantly challenged; otherwise they will become bored. Therefore, it would appear that new leisure programs challenge individuals for a short period of time; eventually, people master the skills necessary to participate and move on to other more challenging activities.

A final note on marketing: As previously indicated, marketing is concerned with consumer satisfaction. Thus, the focus of marketing activities is to determine what benefits individual customers perceive to be desirable. This is a dramatic shift from a focus on activities or facilities. Using this orientation, one could broadly suggest that we are in the "life satisfaction" business, not just in the business of providing facilities and distributing leisure programs.

Social Action

Social action is a strategy that is not widely considered to be a part of the repertoire of skills of most leisure professionals. *It presumes that there is a disadvantaged population, great social injustice, and a need to force the system, institutions, organizations, and agencies to change the ways they are distributing resources, hence services.* The individual using the social action strategy operates outside of the system. To be a part of the system would be inconsistent with the concept. However, we all see injustice in the way in which resources are

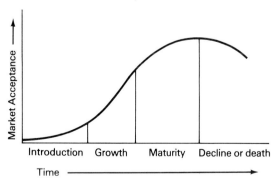

Figure 2.3 Product Life Cycle.

distributed and, therefore, are not able to distance ourselves from either the need to be involved or the effects of social action (see Table 2.8).

The social action strategy has been used successfully in advocating for the rights of the disabled, for promoting the environmental movement in North America, and for pursuing civil and human rights. In this latter case, the right to leisure opportunities is seen as an important human right as recognized by the Universal Declaration of Human Rights.

The roles of the leisure professional when using a social action strategy are numerous and varied. Perhaps the most common role is that of the advocate. The advocate is a person who serves to champion or promote the rights of others. Often the person in this role helps identify the issues and organize people and resources to impact upon the concern. Other roles that often are found are those of activist or agitator. Further, it is not unusual for the social action strategy to find an individual operating in the role of a negotiator or broker. These roles are not what we traditionally define as leisure professional roles. However, they certainly have the capacity to impact tremendously on the delivery of leisure services.

The social planning strategy and the marketing strategy view customers as consumers. Community development views the customer as a collaborator in the process. Social action views customers as individuals who are victims of society. As a victimized population, those engaged in social action attempt to redress the power structure. It is often done through conflict or confrontation. It often requires direct action to get the attention of decision makers in the form of public protest and other expressions of concern.

If, as a professional, you are confronted by individuals using the social action strategy, what should your response be? These groups and individuals can provide additional information and insight into problems with which they are concerned. On the other hand, certain individuals

TABLE 2.8   Social Action as a Strategy for Delivering Leisure Services

Social action is a strategy that presumes that there is a disadvantaged population, great social injustice, and a need to force the system, institutions, and organizations to change the ways they are distributing resources, hence services. To be a part of the system is inconsistent with the concept.

Goals	Shift of power and resources
Basic Strategy	Confrontation, crystallization of issues, identification of enemy targets
Professional Roles	Advocate, broker, agitator, negotiator, organizer
Sector	All sectors of society
Conception of Population Served	Disadvantaged, victims

and groups act as pressure groups promoting ends that may not be in the interest of the entire community. The professional must assess needs and apply resources within economic and political realities accordingly.

Advocacy   Advocacy can be thought of as *a process that is directed toward the support of an individual or group viewpoint, program, or ideological position.* The purpose of the advocacy posture is to ensure that the individuals in decision-making positions are aware of and understand the program or service being proposed by the professional leisure planner. Discussing the relationship of advocacy to recreation, Nesbitt and Edginton (1973) have offered the following information:

> Advocacy is a process directed toward improving the quality of goods and services rendered to consumers and an advocate [is] the person who generates and sustains the advocacy process. Functions include analysis, critique, planning, organizing, informing.

Thus, according to Nesbitt and Edginton, the advocacy mechanism is used not only as an informational tool but also as a means of improving the quality of services available to participants. In other words, the advocacy process is value-laden. It is directed toward substantially improving, via direct intervention, the welfare of individuals and groups addressed by the social activist.

Corey (1971) has identified *five basic types of advocacy:* (1) *inside non-directed advocacy,* (2) *outside-directed advocacy,* (3) *educational advocacy,* (4) *ideological advocacy,* and (5) *indigenous-liberation advocacy.* In *inside non-directed advocacy,* the individual carrying out the advocacy process works within the bureaucratic organization that is providing services. The advocate's role is to represent not only his or her own viewpoint but also that of the customers represented. In other words, the professional in this case is advocating "for" people. In *outside-directed* advocacy, the professional plans "with," rather than "for," the customers he or she serves. The professional actively aligns his or her viewpoints with those of individuals (or a group) processing similar viewpoints. *Educational* advocacy involves the teaching of advocacy mechanisms, so that others might carry out the process on their own. The fourth type of advocacy, *ideological,* finds the advocate focusing on ideals rather than on the actual felt or expressed needs of the customers. There are many ideological advocates whose advocacy work bears little or no relationship to the real or felt needs of those being advocated for. Nonetheless, the ideological advocate serves to facilitate initial exploration of alternative approaches for solving problems. The last type of advocacy, *indigenous-liberation* advocacy, involves the performance of the advocacy function by an independent group outside the realm of the social planning agency.

Edginton and Compton (1975) have identified and defined several roles that are carried out by people involved in the advocacy process. In the context of advocacy and special populations, the roles they identify are; (1) *initiator, planner, strategist, or organizer;* (2) *investigator or ombudsman;* (3) *mediator, arbitrator, or negotiator;* (4) *lobbyist;* (5) *counselor;* (6) *technical or resource*

assistant; (7) *educator;* and (8) *critic, analyst, or evaluator.* They define functions of each of these roles as follows:

The role of *initiator, planner, strategist, or organizer* might come from within the special populations group or may be an outsider who specializes in such advocacy activity. This is a critical phase in the advocacy process, as the initial planning and strategies are usually the cornerstone of any movement. Sound planning and strategies usually yield success if followed by those carrying out the advocacy process.

The *investigator or ombudsman* role is one in which individuals engage in fact finding, data gathering, and legal clarification in support of the rights of the members of our special populations. The role also includes identifying the current state of the art with respect to recreation, leisure, and cultural activities for special populations. In addition, it may involve preparing material for class action suits.

The role of *mediator, arbitrator, or negotiator* is often placed in legal or governmental hands, but may also be handled by persons outside the two negotiating factions. This role is one which comes to the forefront when issues have been identified, requests for action have been clarified, and no subsequent response has come forth from the recreation, leisure, or cultural activity delivery system.

The role of *lobbyist* is one that can be assumed by appointed and paid individuals, organizations, or other collective bodies. A lobbyist's function is to inform, gain attention, and persuade those making decisions about goods and services for a particular constituency. Particular attention must be paid to local ordinances, charters, state and federal laws, and regulations that directly affect the special populations consumer.

The *counselor role* is one which may be undertaken by an individual, either a consumer or an advocate. Counseling and guidance with respect to the quality and quantity of recreation, leisure, and cultural services is generic to efficient consumerism and advocacy. The counselor may work with one individual or a group. The counselor's job is to simply match resources with the individual or group needs.

The role of *technical or resource assistant* is involved with various functions such as financing, logistics, data gathering and compilation, identification, interpretation, and administration. This role may shift daily as the advocacy process emerges.

The *educator* role implies that there is an educational component to the advocacy process. Education, as an advocacy, focuses on the creation of societal awareness for the needs of the clientele represented. Working towards social reform, the object of this particular approach is to work within the existing political structure to represent the needs of special populations. The role of the advocate is to sell and/or educate each member of the society to be receptive and responsive to the pressing needs of those he or she represents. This approach has proved to be an effective and efficient method of bringing about change within our society. However, this method has also been viewed skeptically, as the interests of all the members of society are not inherently met.

Finally, the role of *critic, analyst, or evaluator* is one which is critical to any advocacy process. In order for the individual or organization to realize whether or not it has attained its objectives, the process of analysis or evaluation must take place. This process might be undertaken by a formal group which monitors progress toward stated objectives or may be an ongoing process which aids in identifying the quality and quantity of goods and services (Edginton and Compton 1975: 27–29).

Program Theories

In the leisure literature, authors have detailed a number of theories concerning the way in which program services are developed. Knowledge of these program theories can be useful to both the student and the professional. They can help the student gain an understanding of the processes and procedures that professionals use in the development of activities, facilities, and other services. An understanding of these theories can be useful to leisure service professionals by en-abling them to appraise their own methods of developing and selecting services. Ultimately, the professional might also be able to relate these theories to the type of organizational strategy selected for use within his or her agency.

Danford's and Shirley's Approaches

Interestingly, Danford and Shirley (1964) have set forth a number of commonly used but unsound approaches to programming. Although these methods may be useful as an integrated part of a comprehensive model for program planning, Danford and Shirley stress that these individual approaches should not be relied upon solely by the leisure service professional. The four approaches—*traditional, current practices, expressed desires,* and *authoritarian*—are summarized by Danford and Shirley as follows:

Traditional approach   This approach to program planning finds the leisure service professional *determining what services have been offered in the past by an organization and relying upon this same format for future programming.* In other words, the professional makes no attempt to relate his or her present program offerings to actual needs but maintains the program posture that has worked for him or her in the past. This approach is based on the mistaken notion that the environment and the people within it will remain absolutely constant. This is not to suggest that past history is not a great teacher; however, the leisure service professional should learn from the past and make modifications in the delivery of program services to accommodate an ever-changing and dynamic environment.

Current practice approach   This method of program planning suggests that the professional *identify current trends within the field and apply these practices to his or her own situation.* For example, a current trend in the park and recreation field is high-adventure and high-risk leisure service programming; the professional literature abounds with articles concerning this topic. However, current practices and trends may not be applicable to all communities. Planning should be location-specific; what may work in one community may not work in another.

Expressed desires approach   This approach relies on the use of a method to measure the program interests and needs of people. The assumption inherent in this method is that *the customer should share in the processes involved in the formulation of an organization's program.* This approach can be useful in developing interest in an organization's activity. It can also be a valuable tool for the planner, enabling him or her to collect and analyze data concerning the leisure, attitudes, behavior, and interests of the individuals he or she serves. However, sole reliance on this approach may hinder the effective use of professional knowledge and expertise. According to Danford and Shirley (1964): (1) The recreation interests and desires of people are limited by their experiences; and (2) one of the most important functions of leadership is to lead the people from where they are into new interests and new activities which will enrich life beyond anything they have known before.

Authoritarian approach   The professional who employs the authoritarian approach to program planning uses only his or her knowledge and expertise in determining what programs ought to be offered and where and when they should occur. The customer is denied any involvement in the planning process. This approach is likely to occur in organizations in which *the chief executive officer is unwilling to share with others in the decision-making process.* He or she may adhere to a given philosophy of leisure and be unwilling to adapt it, even to meet evident needs. Application of this method in the leisure service field has made it difficult for organizations to move from an activity-based, playground-oriented philosophy to an eclectic humanistically oriented service model (Danford and Shirley 1964: 107–109).

Kraus's Sociopolitical Approach

Kraus (1985) has suggested a program planning theory which he terms "the sociopolitical approach." Representing a desirable stance on the part of the professional, it may be summarized as follows:

The *sociopolitical approach to program planning acknowledges the influence of social and political pressure upon the professional.* It recognizes that professionals working in the governmental arena are subject to political pressures and are influenced by various societal factors. Special interest groups and pressure groups will affect the work of the professional, as will such societal factors as crime, poverty, and delinquency. Shifts in the economic cycle will influence the demand for services and will also generate rules and regulations, through the political process, that affect the provision of leisure services. The private entrepreneur will also be affected by such factors. Leisure service professionals do not operate in a vacuum; they must be responsive to conditions that occur as a result of fluctuations and changes in the sociopolitical structure in which they operate.

Tillman's Approaches

Tillman (1974) suggests that program planning be viewed as an orderly process that enables the professional to predict the results of his or her actions. He suggests that there are three plans that are used by practitioners to develop programs—*the reaction plan, the investigation plan,* and *the creative plan.* Tillman's ideas are summarized below.

Reaction plan   The professional who uses this approach to program planning does not make an active effort to gather facts concerning the participant's interests and needs. Rather, he or she responds to the demands of those individuals or groups who are in a position to influence the decision-making process of the organization. Simply stated, *the professional waits and reacts to demands generated by others.* Since the professional does not attempt to actively influence the leisure behavior of people, the formulation of professional values is of secondary importance.

Investigation plan The investigation plan *involves the use of fact-finding methods to more accurately determine the behavior and needs of participants.* Using a survey or other mechanisms for collecting information, the success of the investigation plan is dependent upon the professional's ability to accurately interpret the information collected via these processes. A weakness inherent in any survey-type information gathering is the gap between people's expressed opinions and their actual feelings. Individuals may answer questions in terms of the way they wish to be perceived or in terms of their perceptions of the interviewer's expectations. As a result, this process falls short of its goal of enabling the professional to plan with extreme accuracy; however, it is a relatively easy mechanism to employ and does offer an indication of the characteristics, behavior, and opinions of the participants with whom the practitioner is involved.

The creative plan This last approach to program theory suggests that the practitioner link the two above approaches together in the program-planning efforts. In other words, *an interactive relationship between the customer and the professional* is perhaps the most sound approach. The professional should use his or her own expertise and actively seek the views of the customer.

Murphy's Planning Models
Two additional program planning models have been set forth by Murphy (1975)—the *cafeteria approach* and the *prescriptive approach.*

Cafeteria approach As its name suggests, the leisure service professional using the cafeteria approach *establishes many program opportunities and allows the customer to choose from among these services.* Similar to food service in a cafeteria, the customer peruses the program "menu" and selects items that appeal to him or her. The cafeteria model is widely practiced in community park and recreation departments and, as an approach to programming, maximizes the consumer market model. However, the programs offered in the cafeteria approach do not necessarily result from efforts by the practitioner to determine the needs or interests of customers. It can be criticized, therefore, as an inefficient method for providing services since the resources (human and material) that an organization uses to create and provide unused services are wasted.

Prescriptive approach This approach to program planning follows closely the social-planning notion of intervention—in which *leisure services are used to move a person from a dysfunctional state of being to a functional one.* The role of the practitioner is to diagnose the needs of the customer, then provide services accordingly. Immediately the question arises, however, as to whether the professional can prescribe leisure services that have reliable outcomes, or whether the outcomes of programming can even be measured. Another drawback to this model is the lack of consumer involvement; the prescription of services is usually based solely on the professional's expertise and knowledge.

Edginton and Hanson's Theories
Seven program planning theories have been delineated by Edginton and Hanson (1976), including the trickle down, educated guess, community leadership input, identification of need, offer what people want, indigenous development, and interactive discovery theories. These operational models have been integrated with one another to varying degrees by recreation and leisure service organizations. A brief description follows:

Trickle down theory This theoretical approach to leisure program development is commonly practiced by leisure service delivery systems. *Programs are initiated at various levels within a given bureaucratic structure and trickle down through the organization to consumers.* A distinct advantage of this method is that it minimizes the organizational resources used in program development. Although it is a very efficient approach, it has been criticized for its inability to meet consumer needs and interests in an effective manner. It is basically a one-way process.

Educated guess theory   Similar to the trickle down theory, *activities are planned, organized, and implemented on someone's hunch that they will meet community and individual needs.* The efficiency of an organization is at stake when this type of approach is used to determine programming. It is foolhardy to consume organizational resources without a fairly accurate indication of the needs to be met. There is also a lack of predictability within this approach, which places the leisure services professional in a tenuous position. This is not to infer that professionals should not take calculated risks (based on various informational data). However, if the profession is to be successful in meeting community and individual needs, it must rely upon more effective and efficient methods than an "educated guess."

Community leadership input theory   It has been suggested that the success of any leisure service program is dependent upon consumer input. One method for determining consumer needs and interest is the *use of advisory and policy-making boards that represent the concerns of the public at large.* This approach assumes that each individual's interest will be represented by a select group of people and is based upon the premise that there is a need to improve communication between the providers and consumers of service. There are several problems inherent in this approach. It is unwise to assume that a select group of individuals will be able to represent the needs of all persons within a given service area. However, this form of community interaction with the providers of services is based on sound demo-

cratic principles and undoubtedly has merit. It represents the most common approach to opening channels of communication between providers and consumers of services.

Identification of need theory   *This approach involves gathering demographic and other information in order to analyze consumer needs.* It should include: demographic data—such as age, sex, marital status, education, income, occupation, place of work, family size, grade placement, allowance and earning, and time use; leisure behavior, in terms of programs attended and other activities; and information concerning psychological factors—most notably, those relating to Maslow's hierarchy of needs (see Chapter 5). This type of information is usually obtained by reviewing records (including those of attendance at and participation in leisure activities), by surveys and questionnaires, and by direct communication with the consumer. The advantage of this approach, in terms of program planning, is that ideally the consumer's interests and needs become evident to the provider of services, enabling him or her to plan more effectively. However, this method has several drawbacks. First, the individuals involved in interpreting the data may not be competent to do so. Leisure service professionals may misread consumer needs and plan inappropriate programs. Second, consumers often misrepresent their own needs for a variety of reasons, such as a desire to please.

Offer what people want theory   This approach to leisure service planning involves *interaction and communication between providers and consumers of services in order to design programs that reflect "what people want."* There are both strengths and weaknesses in this approach. On the one hand, it is desirable to have consumer input. On the other hand, the most vocal individuals may not be concerned with an equitable distribution of community leisure services; they may direct their efforts toward obtaining resources for a narrow segment of the population. Further, this approach presumes that people are aware of the program options available to them and the potential benefits to be derived from such opportunities.

Indigenous development theory Indigenous development is a process that *attempts to help people discover and use grassroots program opportunities* which utilize innate capabilities and are directed toward individual needs. This approach to leisure program planning should be encouraged. It insures that the consumers of services are involved in the planning process and have control over program offerings. However, this type of planning is demanding in that it requires the professional to meet with individuals on their own "turf." For example, an outreach worker might go directly to his or her clientele to provide services, or a center director might work with a neighborhood group.

Interactive discovery theory An extension and continuation of the indigenous development theory, this approach is *based on the assumption that people can work together to help each other grow and develop.* It assumes that there is no subordinate or superior relationship between involved individuals; rather, one individual's knowledge, skills, and abilities can be used to meet another's needs without necessarily superimposing a value system or set of expectations. Crucial to this approach is the formation of a relationship of trust, based on open and effective communication and creating avenues for exchange. Essentially a people-to-people program, the interactive discovery theory caters directly to individual needs of clients. Individuals involved in face-to-face leadership can be especially instrumental in initiating relationships of trust with clients and in creating noncoercive and nonthreatening environments in which to operate; they are in a key position to help clients discover their needs and capabilities.

Rossman's Symbolic Interaction Theory

Rossman (1989), building on the work of Blumer (1969) and Denzin (1978), has applied the symbolic interaction theory to leisure programming. Basically, Rossman states that leisure experiences occur in a social context. He notes that human interaction in the leisure experience is built on four assumptions. These assumptions are as follows:

1. Social reality is produced by individuals developing their own definitions or situations through interaction.
2. Humans are assumed to be capable of shaping and guiding their own behavior and the behavior of others.
3. In interacting, individuals carry on conversations with themselves and others.
4. Meaning arises out of interaction.

Basically, this concept *suggests that leisure experiences are created by participating individuals through interactions with objects in social settings.* From a programming perspective, the work of a programmer is to configure an environment in such a way that the leisure can occur. This is done by manipulating or organizing the elements that exist within any social occasion. Some of these elements include:

1. Interacting people who fill the occasion.
2. The physical setting itself.
3. Social objects that fill the setting and are acted on, including physical objects, abstract objects, and other people.
4. Rules that guide interactions within the setting.
5. Existing relationships that bind the participants to each other.
6. Animation of the event, which moves it through time.

Using the theory of symbolic interaction, the role of the programmer is to identify the unique configuration of elements necessary to produce a desired leisure experience. The service professional's task is one of anticipating how a series of events or actions making up a program that leads to leisure experience will unfold. Programming becomes a process of visualization. The role of the programmer is to anticipate the needs of the customer and plan the leisure experience in such a way that his or her effort is an unobtrusive intervention. By vicariously experiencing the potential outcomes of a leisure experience in advance, the leisure service programmer is able to anticipate and predict outcomes.

The value of this theory is that it can help leisure service professionals more clearly understand the relationship between the process of program planning and the creation of a leisure experience. The symbolic interactionist theory as adapted by Rossman (1989) to leisure programming provides an important framework for predicting outcomes. This enables the professional to operate more efficiently, clarify roles, and understand the consequences of his or her actions in creating leisure experiences.

Mixing Organizational Strategies and Program Theories

Is one organizational strategy more appropriate than another? Is there one "best" program theory that the professional should use in his or her development of organizational services? The use of organizational strategies and program theories should be situationally or culturally specific. In other words, leisure service organizations must select a strategy or program theory appropriate for their organization's particular needs and goals. The pragmatic professional should use any options available that will help him or her effectively and efficiently fulfill organizational responsibilities.

Figure 2.4, the program continuum, illustrates the relationship between the organizational strategies of social planning and

community development and the Edginton/Hanson operational program theory paradigm. This figure suggests that organizational strategies and program theories can be viewed as existing on a continuum. At one end of the continuum is the social-planning strategy of organizing recreation and leisure services. Related to this end of the continuum are the "educated guess," "trickle down," "community leadership," and "identification of needs" theories of program development. Generally speaking, the professional operating at this extreme of the continuum uses primarily his or her own expertise in the development of services. He or she may or may not consult the customer. The role is to organize direct services (that is, activities or facilities) and, in some cases to provide information. The social-planning strategy of organizing recreation and leisure services, resulting in direct service delivery, is task-oriented and professionally controlled. The professional is viewed as an expert; the customer is viewed as a consumer of services. The professional attempts to use his or her knowledge and perceptions of consumer needs to intervene with services. Services created via this approach tend to meet instrumental and utilitarian needs, comparable to Maslow's lower order needs. Levy (1971: 51) has written that fulfillment of these needs only serves ". . . to reduce pain, tension, fatigue, or boredom, they do not directly lead to growth, nor do they provide for growth."

Satisfaction from this type of recreation and leisure experience is dependent to a large degree upon the actions of others; it is "other-directed." The professional determines the course of events—the behavioral outcomes expected, the norms of gratification, and so forth. As a result, there is a tendency for the customer to become dependent upon the professional for leisure gratification rather than be self-reliant. The community development strategy of organizing leisure services is found at the other ex-

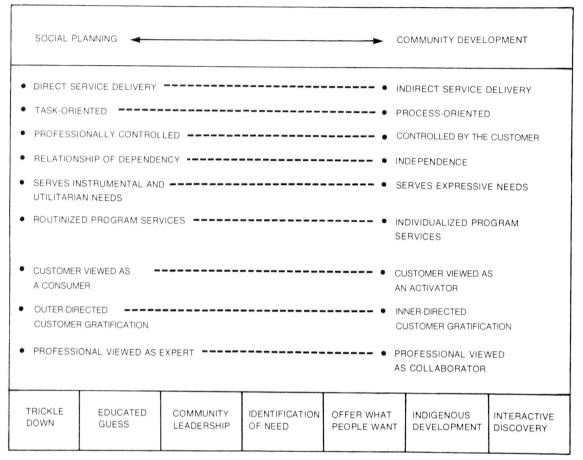

Figure 2.4   The Program Continuum.

treme of the continuum. This strategy can be aligned with the "indigenous development," "offer what people want," and "interactive discovery" program theories of the Edginton/ Hanson paradigm. The professional using a community development strategy encourages the independent functioning of the customer. He or she is viewed as a collaborator (with the customer) and, as such, is involved in indirect service delivery. The role of the professional community developer is to share his or her knowledge with the customer and help the customer define and attain leisure needs through his or her own efforts. The community development

process serves to individualize program offerings; whereas the social-planning approach concentrates and focuses on mass recreation and leisure experiences. Services tend to become routinized when the social-planning model is employed.

At the community development end of the continuum, opportunities meet man's expressive needs, i.e.,

. . . those which have to do with the uniquely human push toward self-realization, or very simply, to be psychologically more than one was yesterday. Since psychological growth can only be achieved through successful completion of meaningful tasks, only the factors having to do with the expressive aspects of one's life can influence these inherent growth needs (Levy 1971: 42).

Although we have dichotomized the relationship between the two organizational strategies (community development and social planning) in our discussion, in reality this is not the case. Many organizations mix these strategies and theories in order to accommodate the specific and varying needs of those customers whom they serve. For example, an organization might initiate interaction between customers with the professional in a dominant role, and gradually develops the relationship into one that facilitates the independent functioning of customers. It is also possible for individuals or groups operating within the framework of the community development strategy to influence an organization involved in direct delivery of services. A neighborhood association, for example, might organize itself around a given concern (i.e., the desire for a community center or skills-oriented programs) and join with the local parks and recreation department in its development. In other words, the community development and social-planning strategies may, in certain circumstances, complement one another; the most effective approach may involve the use of both strategies in varying proportions.

Summary

There are four basic strategies to use in the organization and delivery of leisure services. They are social planning, community development, social marketing, and social action. The strategy or strategy blend used by the professional will have an effect on the planning process and the program experience of the customer. The professional who employs the social planning strategy uses his or her professional expertise and knowledge to identify customer needs and to plan

programs accordingly. Thus, the locus of control in the process of program development remains essentially with the professional. Social planning is task-oriented. Another strategy, community development, demands grassroots participation and development. It is a process-oriented program strategy. The work of the professional who uses a community development strategy is aimed at enabling the customer to assume the initiative for his or her own self-development. Consequently, the locus of control is not found within the organization but rather is located with the customer. Whereas the social planning method often results in a "customer-dependent" relationship, the community development strategy fosters customer independence.

Still another strategy used by the professional in leisure programming is that of social marketing. Social marketing is a philosophical strategy directed toward meeting customer needs. This strategy involves integrating five components—the product, the place, the price, the promotion, and the packaging—to produce customer satisfaction. In other words, the social marketing effort is directed toward meeting customer needs and implementing the leisure experience while producing a strong degree of satisfaction. Another strategy that can be employed to develop leisure services is that known as social action. Social action presumes a disadvantaged population. The leisure professional works to advocate on behalf of disadvantaged groups, encouraging the redistribution of resources. Social action is often found in settings where there are disabled, disadvantaged, or deprived population groupings. As indicated in the text of the chapter, the strategies can be blended in various ways to suit the needs of particular situations.

In the leisure literature, numerous theories have been offered in the area of program development. In this chapter we have described some of the more relevant theories and have incorporated them into a paradigm. Essentially, the model (Figure 2.4) delineates the results that are likely to occur with use of either the social-planning or community development approaches to program planning and aligns relevant program theories along the continuum presented. The model attempts to point out that there are many ways to organize leisure services within these two basic strategies.

Discussion Questions and Exercises

1. What constitutes a leisure program?

2. Identify and discuss the differences between the political/governmental, voluntary, and market systems of leisure service delivery.

3. Select an agency from one of the categories listed in Table 2.1, Table 2.2, and Table 2.3. Schedule an interview with a professional engaged in the delivery of programs in each of these agencies and determine the following:
   a. The scope and types of program services offered.
   b. The type of professional leadership utilized.
   c. Methods of promotion.
   d. Strategies used to deliver services.
   e. Methods of program evaluation.

4. Define social planning. Identify the steps in the social-planning process.

5. Define community development. How does community development differ from social planning?

6. Define social marketing. What does the term "social" marketing mean in the context of the development of leisure services?

7. Contrast selling with marketing. What are the characteristics of marketing?

8. Define social action. What does the concept of advocacy imply?

9. Identify and discuss at least ten leisure program theories found in the literature.

10. Discuss how social planning and community development could be used simultaneously by a leisure service organization.

References

Biddle, W. W. and L. J. Biddle. 1965. *The community development process: The re-discovery of local initiative.* New York: Holt, Rinehart and Winston, Inc.

Blumer, H. 1969. *Symbolic interactionism.* Englewood Cliffs, NJ: Prentice Hall.

Bullaro, J. J. and C. R. Edginton. 1986. *Commercial leisure services: Managing for profit, service and personal satisfaction.* New York: Macmillan Publishing Company.

Corey, K. E. 1971. A framework for advocacy planning. Paper presented at the Annual Conference of the American Institute of Planners, San Francisco, (October 25).

Csikszentmihalyi, M. 1975. *Beyond boredom & anxiety.* San Francisco: Jossey-Bass Publishers.

Danford, H. and M. Shirley. 1964. *Creative leadership in recreation.* Boston: Allyn & Bacon

Denzin, N. K. 1978. *The research act.* 2nd ed. New York: McGraw-Hill.

Edginton, C. R. and D. M. Compton. 1975. Consumerism and advocacy: A conceptual framework for the therapeutic recreator. *Therapeutic Recreation Journal* 9(1):27–29.

Edginton, C. R. and C. J. Hanson. 1976. Appraising Leisure Service Delivery. *Parks and Recreation* 11(3):27, 44–45.

Ellis, M. 1973. *Why people play.* Englewood Cliffs, NJ: Prentice-Hall.

Howard, D. R. 1985. An analysis of the market potential for public leisure services, *Journal of park and recreation administration* 3(1).

Kotler, P. 1982. *Marketing for nonprofit organizations.* 2nd ed. Englewood Cliffs, NJ: Prentice-Hall.

Kraus, R. G. 1985. *Recreation program planning today.* Glenview, IL: Scott, Foresman and Company.

Lauffer, A. 1974. *Social planning in the United States.* In Fred M. Cox, John L. Erlich, Jack Rothman and John E. Tropman. *Strategies of community organization: A book of readings.* Itasca, IL: F. E. Peacock Publishers, Inc.

Levy, J. 1971. "Recreation at the crossroads." *Journal of health, physical education and recreation* 42, (September): 51.

Murphy, J. F. 1975. *Recreation and leisure service: A humanistic perspective.* Dubuque, IA: Wm. C. Brown.

Nesbitt, J. A. and C. R. Edginton. 1973. A conceptual framework for consumerism and advocacy in parks, recreation, leisure and cultural services. Unpublished paper presented at Montclair State College, Upper Montclair, NJ: (January 11).

Rathmell, J. M. 1974. *Marketing in the service sector.* Cambridge, MA: Winthrop Publications, Inc.

Rossman, J. R. 1989. *Recreation programming: Designing leisure experiences.* Champaign, IL: Sagamore Publishing.

Rubright, R. and D. MacDonald. 1981. *Marketing health and human services.* Rockville, MD: Aspen Systems Corporation.

Tillman, A. 1974. *The program book for recreation professionals.* Palo Alto, CA: National Press Books.

3 | The Leisure Service Programmer

Learning Objectives

1. To provide the reader with knowledge of the *criteria used in defining professional work*.
2. To identify and define *responsibilities of professional practice* for the reader.
3. To provide the reader with an understanding of the *concept of leadership*.
4. To help the reader gain insight into, and appreciation for, various *theories and empirical studies concerning leadership styles*.
5. To discuss the *relationship between professional values and leadership*.
6. To explore the various *roles of the leisure service programmer*.

Introduction

Individuals occupying professional positions in leisure service organizations play a key role in the successful planning, organizing, and implementing of activities and events. Such individuals are often referred to, in a generic sense, as "leisure service programmers." The range and variety of activities in which leisure service programmers engage throughout the entire profession is broad. The work of a leisure service programmer may vary from supervising a given program area to managing a facility. Leisure service programmers may engage in direct front line face-to-face service delivery or they may find themselves serving as supervisors in more of an administrative capacity. The point is, the work of leisure service programmers is varied, situation-specific, but always concerned with the development of leisure experiences.

Leisure service programmers are primarily concerned with organizing, promoting, implementing or facilitating in some way the leisure experience for customers. The work of the leisure service programmer may involve actually leading the program, or organizing all, or many, aspects of a service. Further, the leisure service programmer may serve as a facilitator, counselor, information provider, or developer of ideas, process skills, and strategies. Leisure service programmers are pivotal to an organization's success. Their creativity, enthusiasm, competence, drive, and vision provide, in large part, the thrust that allows a leisure service organization to effectively meet and exceed its customers' anticipated needs.

In this chapter, the leisure service programmer as a professional will be examined, including the leadership styles that he or she might use and the roles that he or she might assume. Specifically, the terms "professional" and "leadership" will be defined. In addition, the responsibilities of the professional and the importance of leadership to the leisure service field will be discussed. Included will be a number of significant research studies and models that deal with the subject of leadership.

The Programmer as a Professional

Professionals play a key role in North American society, and professional status is widely sought by a large number of occupations. Leisure services, as an occupation, strives toward professionalism; therefore, it is important to understand what constitutes a profession and why professional status is desirable. In this section, we will explore and attempt to explain the necessary components of a profession, relating this information to the leisure service field. Furthermore, we will determine to what extent the leisure service occupation meets the criteria of a profession as established by a number of noted authorities.

Primarily, the efforts of a professional are directed toward service rather than simply financial remuneration. In other words, the professional works to enhance the well-being of given individuals, motivated by altruistic values. The professional works with people because he or she is concerned with their development and growth rather than their potential as a commodity to be manipulated or coerced.

Occupations can be viewed as existing on a continuum between the two extremes of "professional" and "nonprofessional." Certain factors influence an occupation's status on the continuum. For example, the more recognition and status that an occupation is accorded by the public, the closer it will be to the "professional" end of the continuum. Edginton (1976) has described some of the other factors that affect the status of an occupation:

> *Discretionary Risk.* The status and recognition accorded an occupation is usually related to the amount of risk assumed by an individual practitioner in the process of intervention on the

consumer's behalf. It may be suggested that the high status accorded to the medical profession is a direct result of the risk involved in protecting human life.

Consumer Knowledge. The prestige of an occupation usually corresponds to the amount of knowledge that the public has of that given area of expertise. Simply stated, people are more in awe of that which they know little about. The omnipotence of professional practice in those occupations in which little consumer knowledge exists is evident.

Customer Values. Customers are more willing to accord professional status to those occupations which it values highly. If people value their leisure time more highly, greater status will be accorded the movement. If not, the prestige of the occupation will remain relatively stable. As the value of leisure time experiences increases, the status of the profession will increase (Edginton 1976: 85).

Common Elements of Professions

There are common elements found in all professions. Four common elements that all professions possess are: (1) *an organized body of knowledge;* (2) *organizations and institutions that exist to transmit professional knowledge;* (3) *creation of professional authority as a result of public sanction;* and (4) *a code of ethics and standards to guide professional practice.* These four elements represent areas in which the leisure service occupation can endeavor to improve in order to enhance its status and recognition as a profession. A discussion of each of these areas and the degree to which they have been achieved in the leisure service field follows:

An organized body of knowledge   One of the primary prerequisites of a profession is that it serve society in a unique way. In order to perform a unique function, a profession must have a distinct set, or body, of knowledge. We refer to the body of knowledge in the leisure service field

as *professional knowledge.* Our professional knowledge is composed of three areas. The first area includes *information drawn from the scientific disciplines* such as sociology, psychology, anthropology, biology, and botany. This information provides us with our basic theoretical notion of man, his environment, and the ways in which these interact with one another. The next component of professional knowledge is drawn from the *values we profess and to which we subscribe.* In the leisure service field, for example, such values might include the right of all individuals to have access to leisure experiences, the wise use of leisure time, promotion and protection of human dignity, and conservation and preservation of the environment. Professional values sometimes act as a filter, coloring any knowledge that is presented and influencing the extent to which we accept or reject even empirically verifiable scientific knowledge. The third area within our body of professional knowledge concerns *applied or engineered skills.* These are skills that the professional must have in order to perform his or her job. In the leisure service field, engineered and applied professional knowledge would include such skills as leading an activity, understanding the mechanics of the budget process, and knowing how to use public media to promote leisure programs.

The uniqueness of the body of knowledge of the leisure service field results from the blending of the resource areas around the phenomenon of leisure. The relationship between general scientific knowledge and professional practice is a linear one. As new bodies of knowledge are produced, the applicable or useful knowledge is incorporated into a professional framework (sometimes with modifications due to professional values). This process results in the development of quasi-theories of professional knowledge.

Professional knowledge is largely found in books, magazines, journals, manuals, technical and research reports, and statements by professional associations, agencies, and individuals. But is it systematically organized? The body of knowledge in the leisure service field has an existing organizational framework, but the organization of knowledge in the field has recently begun to center on such sub-areas as park and recreation administration, therapeutic recreation, outdoor recreation, program planning, and the social psychology of leisure.

Organizations and institutions that exist to transmit professional knowledge   The next criterion that we will apply to our discussion of leisure services as a profession is that of existing organizations and institutions for the creation, exchange, and transmission of professional knowledge. Institutions and organizations provide the means by which knowledge can be verified, recorded, and passed "officially" between individuals and organizations in a systematic manner. Furthermore, once an area of study has gone through this process ("institutionalized"), it is generally accepted as a routine service, integral to the public welfare. Institutions and organizations allow us to formalize our commitment to a given concern—in this case, the provision of leisure services.

At the present time, there are over 400 colleges and universities in the United States and Canada that have programs in parks, recreation, leisure, tourism, and natural resource management. Development, at the college and university level, of formalized curricula dealing with training in parks and recreation began in the late 1930s. Preceding the development of such programs were numerous career institutes and classes designed to train play leaders, including those organized and offered by Harvard University and the Playground and Recreation Association of America. The phenomenal increase of the number of curricula offered resulted in both a dramatic growth in the number of trained practitioners and some acceptance of the occupation as a profession (Stein 1975).

In the United States, the American Institute of Park Executives (1904), Playground Association of America (1906), and the American Recreation Society (1938) were some of the forerunners of the National Recreation and Park Association. The National Recreation and Park Association (in the United States) and the Canadian Park/Recreation Association serve as major professional organizations for the gathering and transmission of professional knowledge. Each of these organizations, in their respective countries, draft and advocate positions or policies relating to leisure service. In addition, these organizations encourage the exchange of professional knowledge through the organization of conferences, institutes, and workshops, and the publication of various magazines, journals, and technical reports. Other organizations that are involved in the transmission of professional knowledge include the American Alliance of Health, Physical Education, Recreation and Dance, the Resort and Commercial Recreation Association, the World Leisure and Recreation Association, and the National Employee Services and Recreation Association. The publication of magazines, journals, and books by these and other organizations transmits information and knowledge regarding the leisure service profession. Some of the most visible periodicals in the leisure service field include: *Journal of Leisure Research, Leisurability, Leisure Sciences, Leisure Today, Employee Services Management, Leisure Studies, Therapeutic Recreation Journal, World Leisure & Recreation, Tourism Management, Annals of Tourism Research, Journal of Travel Research, Journal of Park and Recreation Administration, Parks & Recreation, Recreation Canada, Management Strategy,* and *Recreation Research Review.*

Creation of professional authority as a result of public sanction   The notion of professional authority may be viewed from two perspectives. First, an occupation may be granted authority by the public at large to intervene on behalf of, or in concert with, the customer without assuming full responsibility for its actions. If this is the case, the occupation is said to have the sanction of society. The occupation is given full authority to carry out its activities with limited interference. This is primarily because (1) society assumes that the professional has had extensive and thorough training; and (2) the customer has only limited knowledge of the occupation and the way in which it functions. Second, as an occupation achieves full professional status, it monopolizes services. Thus the profession gains considerable authority, since it is the only occupational group with acknowledged ability in a given area of demand. To recapitulate briefly, professional authority is created and exists when an occupation is sanctioned publicly.

Licensure, certification, and voluntary registration serve to document the fact that society accepts the authority of a profession—i.e., that the profession has the sanction of society. A license, certification, or registration program sets forth the rights and privileges of the professional and establishes the boundaries and limitations of authority. For example, a license will grant an individual privilege to practice a profession but also will stipulate certain boundaries that, if disregarded, constitute malpractice or breach of confidence. In the park and recreation field in Canada and the United States, licensing has not occurred to any great extent. However, there is an increasing number of well-developed professional certification programs at the state and provincial level. In fact, the National Certification Board of the National Recreation and Park Association (NRPA) has developed a nationwide professional certification program requiring a written examination. Further, there is a well-developed professional certification program requiring testing for therapeutic recreation professionals operated by the National Council for Therapeutic Recreation Certification (NCTRC).

It would seem that the professional authority of leisure professionals has not been widely recognized and established in the United States and Canada. As leisure service professionals, we have not monopolized services; nor has the work of the leisure practitioner been sanctioned to any great extent.

Code of ethics and standards to guide professional practice Professional organizations establish a set of ethics or standards in order to govern the relationship that exists between the professional and those he or she serves. There is a need to establish norms of behavior by which the professional can exercise self-discipline because of the monopolistic nature and autonomy of professional practice. The leisure service field has been lethargic in the enforcement of behavioral standards. It was not until 1960 that the American Recreation Society (a forerunner of NRPA) established a code of ethics. Few professionals are aware of the content of this document and even fewer use the code as a mechanism for self-control. However, a large number of public park and recreation departments have adopted policies and procedures that serve to guide the behavior of employees. The area of ethics and standards in the park and recreation field needs further development. This is especially true in light of its evolution to a more humanistically-oriented philosophy as found within the contemporary leisure service literature and as demonstrated by the current practice of the profession. It is important to remember that it is not enough simply to have a written code of ethics; there also must be commitment to the ideals presented in the document. The leisure service profession would do well to promote the existing code of ethics and to be more fully aware of the ideals expressed therein.

Even though an occupation may satisfy all of the above criteria, it still may not achieve the level of status or recognition that some feel is appropriate. Even though we might have extensive professional preparation programs, a large body of knowledge, and a well-written code of ethics, certain other factors involving recognition may not apply to the leisure service field (such as risk, perhaps), thereby affecting the level of professional status attainable.

The Responsibilities of Professional Practice

As professionals, leisure service people must meet a number of responsibilities in order to operate in a "professional" manner. The guidelines presented here delineate responsibilities that, if fulfilled, can contribute to the development of individual and collective professional posture. They by no means represent the only factors of which the professional must be cognizant, but should be viewed as elements on which the professional can build. The ten points presented are based on the authors' practical experience; specifically, the direct application of these precepts in leadership, supervisory, and administrative positions in the leisure service field.

Placing the needs of the customer first   The most important responsibility of the professional is serving the needs and interests of the customer. This responsibility should carry over into all aspects of the professional's practice—planning, budgeting, and personal interaction. It should be an attitude that he or she not only practices but also conveys to subordinates so that the entire organization is directed toward meeting this goal.

Commitment to the ideals of the leisure service movement   The actions of the professional (resulting in program services) should be consistent with the philosophical aims of the leisure movement. It is his or her responsibility to promote the highest ideals of leisure and the productive use of leisure time. No single factor contributes to the regression of the movement more than the gap that exists between professional philosophy and ideals and the actions of "unprofessional" practitioners.

Protection of the customer's rights   The relationship that exists between a professional and those he or she serves should be one of trust, mutual respect, and confidence. The professional should protect the rights of the customer regarding privileged information or communication. Furthermore, the customer should have access to any information that affects his or her well-being.

Acquisition of adequate and appropriate knowledge prior to engaging in professional activities   The professional should have sufficient education and work experience to enable him or her to carry out the responsibilities of the job effectively. In addition, the professional should thoroughly research endeavors that he or she intends to pursue. There is nothing more frustrating to customers and other professionals than the individual who is ill-prepared and who has not adequately investigated the program area in which he or she is involved.

Practice of the highest standards of professional service   The professional should endeavor to provide each customer or group with the highest possible quality of professional service. He or she should attempt to maintain consistent quality. This consistency of service will enable the professional to enjoy a reputation for dependability in terms of the quality of services provided.

Continuous upgrading of professional knowledge, skill, and ability   In order to maintain high standards of professional service, the professional must continuously seek out and acquire contemporary knowledge. He or she must keep abreast of current trends, issues, and concerns. Frankly speaking, the professional who does not aggressively pursue new knowledge fails to serve his or her customers in the most effective and efficient manner possible.

Operating ethically and equitably   The leisure service professional has the responbility to be honest, forthright, and direct in his or her dealings with the public. He or she should not attempt to mislead individuals through false publicity and information; nor should he or she discriminate between users or show favoritism to any individual or group. Professionals should not allow themselves to be coerced, bribed, or compromised.

Maintaining a collaborative relationship with the customer   Once an occupation has achieved full professional status, it is said to have monopolized services. When this occurs, the amount of control that the customer is able to exert over the profession is dramatically reduced. In fact, the customer's desires and concerns are often minimized, and the relationship that develops between the professional and the customer finds the latter in a subordinate role. Obviously, this is unacceptable in the leisure service field. Leisure service professionals should strive for a collaborative relationship in which they and the customers are in complementary positions. Collaborative interaction involves dialogue—a *two-way* exchange of information. This type of approach is necessary to effectively translate the customer's interests and needs into tangible services or to assist the customer in the organization of programs.

Self-regulation   It is the responsibility of the profession as a whole to establish standards for professional performance and to monitor its members in regard to these expectations. It is the responsibility of the individual to use these established professional standards as guidelines and to control and regulate his or her behavior accordingly.

Contributing to the development of the profession and other professionals   The professional has a responsibility to share any special knowledge, skills, and abilities with others and to contribute his or her talents to the development of the profession as a whole. This can be accomplished through involvement in local, state, provincial, and national organizations, through the professional media, or through personal encounters. Established professionals should promote and encourage the development of younger, inexperienced professionals. The hallmark of a mature professional is the desire to share knowledge and experience enthusiastically with others. Such professional involvement contributes to the continuity and development of the leisure service movement.

Characteristics of Superior Leaders

What are some of the characteristics of superior or excellent leisure service programmers? Seemingly, this is a difficult question to answer. Kouzes and Posner (1987: 16) have studied the characteristics that followers most admire in leaders. They have looked at more than 225 different values, traits, and characteristics. Table 3.1 presents a ranked list of the characteristics of superior leaders as noted by over 2600 individuals in industry. This table shows that the four highest-ranked characteristics were, in order, "honest," "competent," "forward-looking," and "inspiring." These findings were corroborated by other studies conducted in the public sector. These four characteristics can provide a basis for the work of leisure service programmers. Following is a discussion of each of these variables.

> *Honest.* Operating with honesty or integrity is absolutely critical to establishing one's credibility as a leisure service programmer. Basically, a person's credibility is established in moment-to-moment, day-to-day interaction with others. We earn the trust and respect of others by operating in a way that is truthful, ethical, and principled (Kouzes and Posner 1987:18). Customers and other colleagues will follow an in-

TABLE 3.1   Characteristics of Superior Leaders

Characteristics	U.S. Managers (N = 2,615)	
	Ranking	Percentage of Managers Selecting
Honest	1	83
Competent	2	67
Forward-looking	3	62
Inspiring	4	58
Intelligent	5	43
Fair-minded	6	40
Broad-minded	7	37
Straightforward	8	34
Imaginative	9	34
Dependable	10	33
Supportive	11	32
Courageous	12	27
Caring	13	26
Cooperative	14	25
Mature	15	23
Ambitious	16	21
Determined	17	20
Self-controlled	18	13
Loyal	19	11
Independent	20	10

From Kouzes, J. and B. Posner (1987). *The Leadership Challenge.* San Francisco: Jossey Bass, p. 17.

dividual who they feel operates with integrity. We appreciate people whom we trust and in whom we can have confidence.

Competent. Competence refers to the leisure service programmer's ability to perform the role that he or she has been assigned. Competence may refer to a person's technical, conceptual, or human relations skills. All of these skills focus on the ability of an individual to get things done within a leisure service organization. An individual's technical skills provide him or her with the specific knowledge or details of a program area or format. Conceptual skills refer to an individual's ability to grasp and organize larger, broader issues associated with programming. Finally, human relations skills refer to one's ability to interact successfully with others in a manner that moves the organization forward. As Kouzes and Posner note," . . . the abilities to challenge, in-

spire, enable, model and encourage . . . must be demonstrated if leaders are to be seen as capable" (1987: 19).

Forward-Looking. Forward-looking refers to the leisure service programmer's visionary or future perspective. Again, as Kouzes and Posner have written," . . . we expect our leaders to have a sense of direction and a concern for the future of an organization . . . Whether we call it a dream, vision, calling, goal or personal agenda, the message is clear: admired leaders must know where they are going" (1987: 20). Forward-looking, visionary leaders are able to translate their ideas, concepts, and dreams for tomorrow into a reality that is understandable, acceptable, and achievable.

Inspiring. To be inspiring is to be enthusiastic, energetic, and encouraging of the best efforts of others. Superior leisure service programmers are those that can inspire the best efforts of others. They are individuals who can transform average talent and skill into outstanding performance. Sharing enthusiastically the potential impact of the leisure experience with others is often a key factor in the success of the programmer. The programmer's behavior has to convey to others the desired level of excitement, energy, and dynamism of the experience. We have all been associated with individuals who, because of their inspiring efforts, draw others to them and compel them to work or play with a greater degree of intensity, energy and enthusiasm.

What is Leadership?

Leadership is the pivotal force behind successful organizations (Bennis and Nanus 1985: 3). Our assumptions about leaders and the leadership process has gone through a great transformation during the past decade. It is a process that encourages the best that is possible from each individual. It involves working with individuals within the organizational context to achieve the goals of the agency. As Bennis and Nanus have stated, there is a greater focus on the work of professionals as leaders rather than managers.

They note, "Managers do things right, leaders do the right thing."

A definition of leadership can be viewed from a number of different perspectives. Some of the more contemporary leadership definitions found in the management literature are as follows:

> The very essence of leadership is that you have to have a vision. It's got to be a vision you articulate clearly and forcefully on every occasion. You can't blow an uncertain trumpet (Hersburgh 1987).
>
> The essence of leadership is found in a person's ability to move an organization from state A to state B, that is, to a higher level of performance (Hitt 1988: 6).
>
> Leadership is what gives an organization a vision and its ability to translate that vision into reality (Bennis and Nanus 1985).
>
> Leaders must encourage creativity, freedom of action and innovation among their subordinates, so long as these efforts are consistent with the goals of the . . . [organization] (Roberts 1990: 62).
>
> Challenging the process, inspiring a shared vision, enabling others to act, and encouraging the heart: These are practices that leaders use to get extraordinary things done in organizations (Kouzes and Posner 1987).

In the leisure service field, Edginton and Ford (1985: 9) have defined the concept of leadership as " . . . the process employed by the leader to assist individuals and groups in identifying and achieving their goals." They note that," . . . leadership may involve listening, persuading, suggesting, doing, and otherwise exerting influence on others." Danford and Shirley (1964: 80) suggest that leadership in recreation and leisure service organizations can involve many activities, including securing facilities, equipment, supplies . . . teaching basic skills, social and moral behaviors, and group strategies . . . providing information . . . establishing a friendly work atmosphere, within which members can work cooperatively. Kraus (1985: 20–21) notes that

leadership is a term " . . . used to describe the act of guiding or directing others in a mutual enterprise." Leadership is " . . . a function, a relationship, a phenomenon in group life, an ability, a form of interpersonal influence, and . . . a process."

Russell (1986) has suggested that leadership is a process of influence. According to Russell, leadership influence refers to that process whereby individuals guide or direct the thoughts, feelings, or behavior of other individuals (1986: 16). Russell has further noted that the influence may be direct or indirect. She writes " . . . [leadership] influence may be direct, such as a leader who relates as a director to others, or this influence may be more indirect, such as a leader who relates as an enabler with others (1986: 16).

In all of the above definitions of leadership, the emphasis is on establishing a vision and influencing the behavior of others. Leadership is a process in which participants and/or other professional staff members are moved toward a set of individual and/or organizational goals. Leadership is often viewed as an exercise of authority, a process of decision making and dynamic interaction. Leadership involves nourishing and enhancing others as well as persuading and influencing their behavior. It is a collaborative process that involves interaction between the leader and followers in a group setting. It often involves and results in cooperation and achievement among group members themselves.

Kraus (1985: 77–79) has written that leadership, as it relates to leisure service programming, involves four important elements. They are as follows:

> *Program Planning and Implementation.* This type of leadership involves the planning, organizing, implementing, and evaluating of leisure activities and events. In other words, the leisure service programmer exercises leadership by managing all phases of the program planning process.

Direct Activity Leadership. This type of leadership involves the actual conducting of program activities, including providing activity leadership, group leadership, and counseling or enabling activities.

Provision of Related Program Services. This type of leadership involves working with other organizations to provide leisure services or related activities. These types of cooperative leadership experiences find leisure service programmers working to coordinate the resources of various organizations to meet the needs of individuals in a more holistic fashion.

Supervision of Special Facilities. Many leisure service programmers serve as leaders supervising, managing, or actually leading programs and services at various types of leisure areas and facilities. Most notable is the work of individuals at outdoor recreation sites or special activity facility sites. Leadership in this type of setting may involve coordinating registrations, overseeing admissions, and providing general supervision.

Leadership Studies and Models

Over the past several decades there have been a number of leadership studies conducted and models developed to explain leadership styles and functions. These studies have emerged primarily from the areas of social psychology and business. They have provided an insight into the components of leadership style and situational variables that may impact upon the process of leadership. This section will highlight a number of the more important studies and models to date.

The Lippitt and White Leadership Studies

One of the earliest empirically based studies of leadership style was conducted by Kurt Lewin, Ronald Lippitt, and Ralph K. White in the 1930s at the University of Iowa. These researchers were interested in determining *the effects of different leadership styles on groups of boys involved in a variety of activities.* Lippitt and White organized two experiments to determine the effects of leader-

ship style on group behavior. Specifically, they were interested in determining the following:

> What underlies such differing patterns of group behavior as rebellion against authority, persecution of a scapegoat, apathetic submissiveness to authoritarian domination, or attack upon an out group? How many differences in subgroup structure, group stratification, and potency at ego-centered and group-centered goals can be utilized as criteria for predicting the social resultants of different group atmospheres? Is not democratic group life more pleasant, but authoritarianism more efficient? (1939: 271)

In the first study, two activity clubs of ten-year-olds were established. The leader of these activity groups used an authoritarian leadership style with one group and a democratic style with the other. The researchers found that aggression as well as hostility was more prevalent in the autocratically led group than in the democratically led group. In addition, they found that aggressive behavior within the group environment was directed toward others within the group and not toward the autocratic leader. This experiment raised a number of questions and prompted the researchers to conduct a second, more extensive experiment.

The second set of experiments conducted by Lippitt and White involved the organization of four new activity clubs composed of boys of the same age as in the previous study. In this experiment, four individuals were selected as leaders. "Every six weeks, each group had a new leader with a different technique of leadership, each club having three leaders during the course of the five months of the experimental series" (Halpin 1954: 20). In addition, a third leadership style was added—laissez-faire. The three styles are defined in Table 3.2. In this second experiment, it was possible to make comparisons among the methods used by each of the different leaders and the resulting reaction of the given group. The general atmosphere that prevailed within the groups, in terms of certain styles of leadership, was also compared and evaluated. Four of the five groups of boys showed apathetic behavior toward autocratic leadership. It was concluded by the researchers that this lack of aggressive behavior was due to the repressive nature of the authoritarian leaders. Most of the boys reported liking the democratic and laissez-faire leaders more than the autocratic leaders. Though these studies are valuable as representing the first scientific investigation of leadership styles, one must be careful in applying the findings of these studies generally. No effort was made in these experiments to relate leadership style to the effectiveness of the groups in the tasks being performed. Also, the study was limited to a very narrow segment of the population—ten-year-old boys involved in voluntary club activities.

It is interesting to note that the implications of this research study have been far-reaching in regard to the leisure service profession. Many texts on leisure service leadership include a discussion of these leadership styles and, based on the finding of this very limited sample, suggest that a democratic leadership style is most desirable and effective in all situations. However, the ideal leadership style will vary according to the needs of a given situation, as will become evident with the study of other investigations into leadership styles. Nevertheless, the Lewin, Lippitt, and White study is an important contribution to the understanding of leadership styles and resulting group behavior.

Ohio State Leadership Studies

In an attempt to identify various dimensions of leadership behavior, the Bureau of Business Research at Ohio State University established a series of leadership studies in 1945. The research staff developed the Leader Behavior Description Questionnaire (LBDQ) to help them

TABLE 3.2   Characteristics of Different Approaches to Leadership

Authoritarian	Democratic	Laissez-Faire
1. All determination of policy made by the leader.	1. All policies a matter of group discussion and decision, encouraged and assisted by the leader.	1. Complete freedom for group or individual decision without any leader participation.
2. Techniques and activity steps dictated by the authority, one at a time, so that future steps are always uncertain to a large degree.	2. Activity perspective gained during first discussion period. General steps to group goal were sketched; and where technical advice was needed, the leader suggested two or three alternative procedures from which to choose.	2. Various materials supplied by the leader, who made it clear that he would supply information when asked. He took no other part in work discussions.
3. The leader usually dictated the particular work task and work companions of each member.	3. The members were free to work with whomever they chose, and the division of tasks was left up to the group.	3. Complete nonparticipation by leader.
4. The dominator was "personal" in his praise and criticism of the work of each member but remained aloof from active group participation except when demonstrating. He was friendly or impersonal rather than openly hostile.	4. The leader was "objective" or "fact-minded" in his praise and criticism and tried to be a regular group member in spirit without doing too much of the work.	4. Very infrequent comments on member activities unless questioned, and no attempt to participate or interfere with the course of events.

From Kurt Lewin, Ronald Lippitt, and Ralph K. White: "Patterns of Aggressive Behavior in Experimentally Created Social Climates." *Journal of Social Psychology*, S.P.S.S.I. Bulletin, Vol. 10 (1939), p. 271.

determine how leaders carry out their work. The LBDQ was administered to a variety of groups— e.g., pilots and airplane bomber crews; navy personnel (officers, non-commissioned personnel, and civilian employees); and school superintendents, principals, and teachers. The LBDQ instrument was arranged in a multiple-choice format. The responder was to describe his or her leader's behavior concerning an item presented on the questionnaire by choosing one of five adverbs—always, often, occasionally, seldom, or never. The following statements are from an LBDQ administered by Halpin to airplane bomber crews:

1. He tries out his new ideas on his crew.
2. He rules with an iron hand.
3. He gets crew approval on important matters before going ahead.
4. He does personal favors for crew members (Halpin and Winer 20).

Various forms of the LBDQ were developed and tailored to the different groups tested by the Ohio State research staff.

The LBDQ contained a number of items that pertained to the dimensions of leader behavior called *consideration* and *initiating structure*. Initiating structure refers to the leader's behavior in defining a role relationship between himself or herself and the members of his or her group. More specifically, initiating structure involves the leader's delineation of the role that each group member is expected to play, the establishment of well-defined patterns of organization and channels of communication, and the formation of methods for completion of tasks (Halpin 1959: 4). The dimension of leadership behavior termed "consideration" involved actions indicative of friendship, mutual trust, respect, and warmth in the relationship between the leader and staff members (Halpin 1959: 21). In other words, initiating structure refers to leadership behavior

that is directed toward the completion of a task, and consideration refers to the personal relationship that develops between the leader and the group.

Hersey and Blanchard have created a visual illustration showing the relationship of the consideration dimension to the initiating structure (Figure 3.1). The figure presents leadership behavior as bi-dimensional rather than uni-dimensional. According to the Hersey and Blanchard model, there are four quadrants that provide four combinations of initiating and consideration leadership behavior.

Michigan Studies on Leadership Styles

The University of Michigan Survey Research Center in 1947 began a study to *determine principles of leadership behavior that contributed to both*

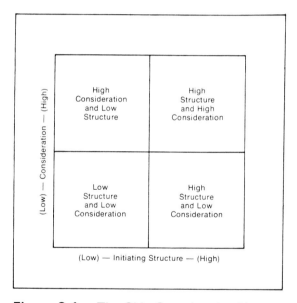

Figure 3.1   The Ohio State Leadership Quadrants. (From Hersey, Paul, and Blanchard, Kenneth H.: *Management of Organizational Behavior: Utilizing Human Resources.* 3rd Ed. Englewood Cliffs, N.J., Prentice-Hall, Inc., 1977.)

the productivity of a group and the satisfaction that a group derived from participation. In turn, these variables were applied to measures of performance. Within the study, the researchers exerted a high degree of control over specific factors such as type of work, working conditions, and work methods. Generally speaking, this research group viewed leadership behavior as existing on a continuum (see Figure 3.2). At one end of the continuum, the leader's behavior was employee-centered; at the other end, it was production-centered. An individual who used an employee-centered leadership style was concerned with people and with establishing good human relations between himself or herself and his or her employees. On the other hand, the production-oriented leadership style found the individual concerned with the completion of a task. Relating this concept to leisure service activity, the production-oriented leader would be more concerned about the customer's accomplishments of a given skill, whereas the people-oriented leader would be more concerned about the sociopsychological growth and development of the customer. Often the objective of a leisure program is the acquisition of a given skill; however, the opportunity for social interaction as well as other factors is as important—or perhaps even more important—to the customer. The leader style employed will influence the outcome of participation. The leadership styles emerging from this set of studies can be viewed as moving from one end of the continuum to the other. The basic ideas of task orientation and relationship orientation are consistent with the Ohio State studies; however, the relationship between the two variables is different. In the Ohio State studies the two variables could be mixed, as indicated in Figure 3.1. The Michigan continuum does not allow for the mixing of the two variables. It suggests that the more employee-centered a leader is, the less productivity-centered he is.

Another important feature of the Michigan Studies on Leadership Behavior was the attempt of investigators to identify effective leadership styles. In other words, they were interested in determining the variables that contributed to, or were associated with, outstanding leader performance. (In the Ohio State studies, there was no attempt to determine whether the leader's behavior was or was not effective. The researchers were interested in identifying the dimensions of leadership and the dominance of one dimension over another in a given situation.) In order to carry out their investigation into the variables associated with effective leadership style, the Michigan group identified high and low productivity sections within an insurance company and studied the leaders of the two categories. With control over variables that would bias the study, these researchers were able to determine that leaders in high-producing sections were more likely:

1. To receive general, rather than close, supervision from their superiors;
2. To like the amount of responsibility and authority they have in their jobs;
3. To spend more time in supervision;
4. To give general, rather than close, supervision to their employees; and
5. To be employee-oriented, rather than production-oriented (Fiedler 1967: 38).

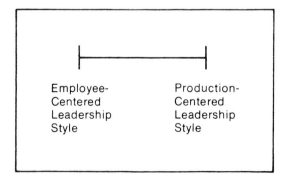

Figure 3.2 The Michigan Studies Leadership Style Continuum.

The Michigan Studies on Leadership Styles provide support for human relations–oriented leaders. They suggest that the more effective leadership style is one in which people are the major concern of the leader; subordinates are treated in a mature manner, are given responsibility and authority to conduct their tasks, and are not closely supervised (or, in a sense, coerced to complete their work activities). These studies also pointed out another important factor influencing leadership—that of the leader's superior. The leader behavior of the superior influenced the section leader's behavior toward his or her subordinates. There obviously are links between all levels of leadership in an organization, which ultimately affect the productivity of a group. One last point that emerged from the Michigan studies was that worker satisfaction was not found to be directly related to completion of tasks but to other factors. Perhaps the sociopsychological relationships that develop between individuals in a work group are of greater importance, in terms of satisfaction, than the material outcomes produced.

Fiedler's Contingency Model of Leadership

The Contingency Model of Leadership, developed by Fred Fiedler, *relates an individual's leadership style to the performance of his or her group;* hence, it indicates the leader's effectiveness. This model of leadership advocates a situational approach to the study of leadership behavior. The underlying premise of this approach suggests that different situations require different leadership capabilities and styles.

Fiedler developed several instruments and statistical procedures to measure leadership style. Two scales, the Least Preferred Co-Worker (LPC) and the Most Preferred Co-Worker (MPC), were created to allow individuals to describe people in their work environment. The use of these instruments for measuring interpersonal relationships was based on the assumption that "the way in which one person perceives another will affect

his relations with [the] other . . ." (Feidler 1967: 143) and, as such, will affect the leader's effectiveness. In addition, Fiedler developed a score to indicate the difference between an individual's LPC and MPC perceptions. He called this the Assumed Similarity Between Opposites (ASO) score. This measurement was obtained by determining the differences between the MPC and LPC scores, then squaring it. Fiedler hypothesized that different situations required different leadership styles. To test this hypothesis, he developed his Contingency Model of Leadership Effectiveness.

The model suggested that the selection and utilization of an effective leadership style was dependent on the favorableness or unfavorableness of the situation. The favorableness (or unfavorableness) of a situation was determined, according to Fiedler, by three factors. The first factor was the leadership relationship. This variable is perhaps the most important determinant of favorableness of a given situation to a leader. According to Fiedler, "A leader who is liked, accepted, and trusted by his members will find it easy to make his influence felt" (Feidler 1967: 150). The second factor affecting the favorableness of a situation was the *degree of task structure* present. The task structure refers to the activities that are required of a group to fulfill their own goals or obligations as a sub-unit within a large organization. The last and least important of the variables affecting situational favorableness was the *power position* of the leader—his or her status within the organizational hierarchy.

Combining the information on situational favorableness with the results of the ASO and related scores, and the concepts of task-oriented and relationship-oriented leadership, Fiedler described three situations and determined which leadership style could be implemented most successfully in each of them. Figure 3.3 indicates the leadership styles appropriate for various group situations. The first situation finds the leader in a favorable leadership situation and suggests that

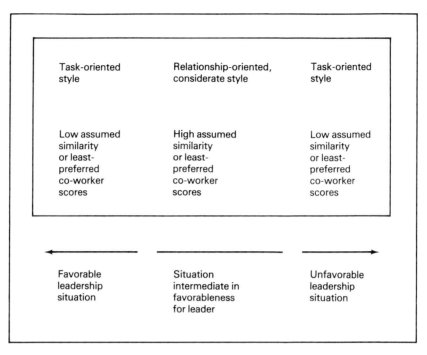

Task-oriented style	Relationship-oriented, considerate style	Task-oriented style
Low assumed similarity or least-preferred co-worker scores	High assumed similarity or least-preferred co-worker scores	Low assumed similarity or least-preferred co-worker scores
Favorable leadership situation	Situation intermediate in favorableness for leader	Unfavorable leadership situation

Figure 3.3 Fiedler's Contingency Model of Leadership. (From Fiedler, Fred E.: *A Theory of Leadership Effectiveness.* New York, McGraw-Hill Book Co., 1967, p 14.)

a task-oriented leadership style will be most effective. The middle situation is one of intermediate favorableness for the leader and calls for a relationship-oriented leadership style. The third situation described by Fiedler finds the leader in an unfavorable situation and indicates that a task-oriented leadership style, again, is most appropriate.

To empirically test the contingency model, Fielder conducted four investigations: one was a field experiment conducted in collaboration with the Belgian Navy; another was a study of three industrial and business organizations; the third and fourth ones were laboratory experiments. In all four studies, the group situations were ranked on the basis of favorableness for the leader. Based on the evidence provided by each of these studies, the task-oriented leader tends to perform best in situations that are very favorable, while the

relationship-oriented leader tends to perform best in situations intermediate in favorableness. Three of the studies also indicated that the task-oriented leader is relatively more effective in very unfavorable situations (Feidler 1967: 150).

The concept of contingency leadership challenges the assumption that there is one "best" style of leadership. It suggests, in fact, that there may be several appropriate leadership styles, depending upon the needs of a given situation. Furthermore, Fiedler suggests that it may be more effective to identify situations that fit the leader's style (and place him or her accordingly) than to invest large amounts of organizational resources on training or developing a leader to fit into a specific existing situation.

Although Fiedler's model is useful in furthering our awareness of leadership styles and behavior, it can be criticized from several perspectives. First, his model views leadership styles as being either task-oriented or relationship-oriented and does not allow for a blend of the two (as does the Ohio State study). Second, his model is based on the supposition that people are rigid and fixed in their styles of leadership—that they cannot be flexible in their leadership styles and thus react appropriately in a variety of situations. This essentially denies the entire notion of human resource development in organizations.

Path-Goal Theory of Leadership

The Path-Goal Theory of Leadership is the most recent approach to the study of leader behavior. Like the Contingency Model, this theory *attempts to identify the variables that influence the effectiveness of a given leadership style.* It offers four leadership approaches that can be used, in a situation-specific manner, to produce certain behaviors. According to House (1971), the theory involves the application of the following leadership styles:

1. *Directive Leadership*—This style is similar to the Lippitt and White authoritarian leader. Subordinates know exactly what is expected of them, and specific directions are given by the leader. There is no participation by subordinates.
2. *Supportive Leadership*—The leader is friendly and approachable and shows a genuine human concern for subordinates.
3. *Participative Leadership*—The leader asks for and uses suggestions from subordinates but still makes decisions.
4. *Achievement-Oriented Leadership*—The leader sets challenging goals for subordinates and shows confidence in them to attain these goals and perform well (House 1971: 321–338).

In discussing the relationships between leadership styles and the task to be performed, House suggests that highly structured tasks require a different leadership style than relatively unstructured ones (Hersey and Blanchard 1977: 103). He maintains that a high/low relationship leadership style is the most effective one when tasks are relatively unstructured. However, when individuals are performing highly structured tasks, the most appropriate leadership style is one that is very supportive or relationship-oriented. When a task is highly organized and regimented, there is little need to reinforce task-oriented activities. Such tasks preclude the opportunity for individual creativity and flexibility; therefore, the worker must derive satisfaction from sources other than task performance. The major role of the leader, then, is to create a satisfying work environment in which workers can derive gratification from leader-member relationships (as opposed to gratification from task involvement and completion).

Tannenbaum and Schmidt Continuum of Leadership Behavior

Robert Tannenbaum and Warren H. Schmidt have *depicted leadership styles as existing on a continuum that ranges from authoritarian task-oriented leadership to democratic relationship-oriented leadership.* Figure 3.4 illustrates this concept. As a leadership style along the continuum is applied by a given individual, the role of the leader—and the way in which this role is carried out—varies accordingly. An authoritarian leader is one who "makes decisions and announces them," as opposed to the democratic leader who presents problems, solicits suggestions, and then makes decisions, or who defines limits and asks the group to make decisions. In Figure 3.4, one can see that as the leadership style employed moves from authoritarian to democratic, the amount of subordinate freedom increases proportionately. Conversely, the leader's use of authority decreases as the style moves from authoritarian to democratic. As with other leadership models and theories, this continuum from Tannenbaum and Schmidt recognizes the existence of the two leadership components—one directed toward the completion of tasks and the other toward relationships between individuals. This model has been adapted by Frye and Peters

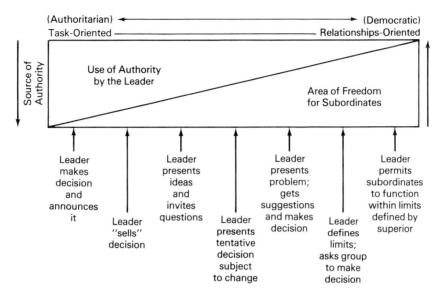

Figure 3.4 Tannenbaum and Schmidt Continuum of Leadership Behavior. (In Hersey, Paul, and Blanchard, Kenneth H.: *Management of Organizational Behavior: Utilizing Human Resources.* 3rd Ed. Englewood Cliffs, N.J., Prentice-Hall, Inc., 1977, p. 92. Adapted from Robert Tannenbaum and Warren H. Schmidt, "How to Choose a Leadership Pattern," *Harvard Business Review* (March-April 1957), pp. 95–101.)

(1972) to describe leadership behavior and customer involvement in the area of therapeutic recreation.

Tri-Dimensional Leader Effectiveness Model

The Tri-Dimensional Leader Effectiveness Model is an extension and elaboration of the basic work carried out at Ohio State University in the 1940s. The assumption behind this model is that *an effective leader's behavior is a result of the application and influence of three dimensions—task behavior, relationship behavior, and effectiveness.* Task behavior is similar to initiating structure; task behavior and relationship behavior can be defined as follows:

> *Task behavior* is the extent to which leaders are likely to organize and define the roles of the members of their group (followers); to explain what activities each is to do and when, where, and how tasks are to be accomplished; charac-

terized by endeavoring to establish well-defined patterns of organization, channels of communication, and ways of getting the job accomplished (Hersey and Blanchard 1977: 104).

> *Relationship behavior* is similar to consideration. It can be defined as follows: the extent to which leaders are likely to maintain personal relationships between themselves and members of their group (followers) by opening up channels of communication, providing socio-emotional support, "psychological strokes," and facilitating behaviors (Hersey and Blanchard 1977: 105).

The third dimension, *effectiveness*, suggests the presence of certain situational demands that require a different style of leadership behavior. In other words, there may be situations that call for an authoritarian style of leadership—a style with a high task orientation and a low relationship orientation; on the other hand, there may be situations in which a more humanistic or democratic leadership style would be appropriate. In the leisure service profession there are a variety of situations, calling for the application of different styles of leadership. Consider, for example, the leadership behavior required of an umpire or referee officiating at a sports program. The leadership required in this situation is highly task-oriented and authoritarian. The official cannot ask the teams to vote with him in making a decision on a call regarding rule violations and completion of plays. On the other hand, the leadership behavior most appropriate in a senior citizen's center would be quite different. In such a situation where social interaction is desirable, the most effective leadership style would be one emphasizing relationship behaviors and a democratic approach to leadership. Switching the application of either one of these styles into the other situation would be inappropriate. As Hersey and Blanchard have written:

> When the style of a leader is appropriate to a given situation, it is termed effective; when the style is inappropriate to a given situation, it is termed ineffective (Hersey and Blanchard 1977: 105).

The Hersey and Blanchard Tri-Dimensional Leadership Effectiveness Model is presented in Figure 3.5. As can be seen in the model, the two

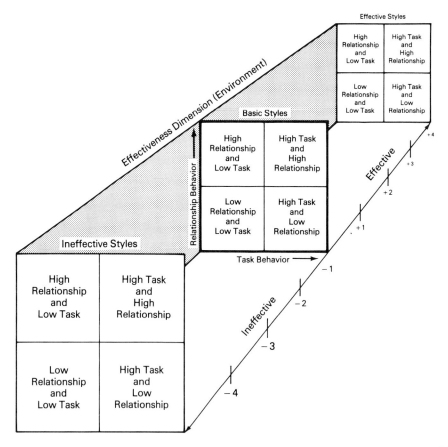

Figure 3.5   Tri-Dimensional Leader Effectiveness Model. (From Hersey, Paul, and Blanchard, Kenneth H.: *Management of Organizational Behavior: Utilizing Human Resources.* 3rd Ed. Englewood Cliffs, N.J., Prentice-Hall, Inc., 1977, p. 106.)

dimensions—relationship behavior and task behavior—yield four basic leadership styles. These styles are high task and high relationship, low relationship and low task, high relationship and low task, and high task and low relationship. When the effectiveness dimension is added to the basic styles, eight styles emerge. Four leadership styles, when applied in inappropriate situations, are known as "ineffective." The other four styles result from the application of the basic styles in an appropriate situation, and, therefore, are "effective" leadership styles. Thus, the role of the leisure service programmer is to diagnose the situation and apply the appropriate leadership style. As Danford and Shirley (1964: 82) state, "the difference between effective and ineffective styles is often not the actual behavior of the leader, but the appropriateness of the behavior to the environment in which it is used."

Table 3.3 presents the ways in which each of the four styles might be perceived in the context of effective and ineffective utilization. This model takes into account the situational variables that are absent in other models. As such, it is a con-

tingency model that emphasizes the use of a variety of leadership styles rather than the "one best" approach.

Theories of Leadership

The most important leadership models and research investigations into leadership have been fully described. However, there are several general theories and approaches to the study of leadership that are worthy of mention. One of the earliest theories of leadership is known as the *Trait or Great Man Theory*. Another theory widely used in the study of leadership behavior contends that leadership behavior is a *Function of the Group*. A third theory is known as the *Situational Theory of Leadership*. We will discuss each of these general theories briefly and describe their relationship and applicability to the empirical investigations already cited.

Trait or Great Man Theory

This theory sets forth two conditions on which leadership can be based. First, *individuals born to*

TABLE 3.3 How the Basic Leader Behavior Styles May be Seen by Others When They are Effective or Ineffective

Basic Styles	Effective	Ineffective
High Task and Low Relationship	Seen as having well-defined methods for accomplishing goals that are helpful to the followers.	Seen as imposing methods on others; sometimes seen as unpleasant, and interested only in short-run output.
High Task and High Relationship	Seen as satisfying the needs of the group for setting goals and organizing work, but also providing high levels of socio-emotional support.	Seen as initiating more structure than is needed by the group and often appears not to be genuine in interpersonal relationships.
High Relationship and Low Task	Seen as having implicit trust in people and as being primarily concerned with facilitating their goal accomplishment.	Seen as primarily interested in harmony; sometimes seen as unwilling to accomplish a task if it risks disrupting a relationship or losing "good person" image.
Low Relationship and Low Task	Seen as appropriately delegating to subordinates decisions about how the work should be done and providing little socio-emotional support where little is needed by the group.	Seen as providing little structure or socio-emotional support when needed by members of the group.

From Hersey, P. and K.H. Blanchard. (1977). *Management of Organizational Behavior.* 3rd ed. Englewood Cliffs, NJ: Prentice-Hall, p. 107.

a high station in life are destined to become leaders, and, second, some individuals are born possessing specific characteristics or traits that "automatically" enable them to emerge as leaders from any given situation. Most of the scientific investigations in this vein focused on identifying leader personality traits. After years of investigation, no conclusive results emerged. Therefore, research turned from study of the leader to study of those being led.

Leadership as a Function of the Group

This theory maintains that *the function of the leader is to facilitate or encourage the work of the group.* In order for group goals to be achieved, there must be positive interaction between the group and leader. As stated by Danford and Shirley, the role of the leader within this context involves:

> . . . the performance of such acts as helping the group to establish goals, assisting it to achieve the goals, creating a friendly climate within which the interactions among members will be improved, providing the group with the facilities, equipment and supplies necessary for the attainment of its goals, and building a feeling of group unity and solidarity (Danford and Shirley 1964: 84).

Essentially, this theoretical approach was emphasized in the Ohio State and Michigan studies, which focused on group perceptions of leadership behavior.

Leadership as a Function of the Situation

The situational approach grew out of the inadequacy of the trait and group theories. The basic premise of the situational theory is that *there are several variables that influence both the leader and the group in terms of performance, motivation, and satisfaction.* Fiedler's Contingency Model of Leadership Effectiveness represents an effort to scientifically investigate this theory, and the Tri-Dimensional Leader Effectiveness Model is a sit-

uational model (emphasizing the need to respond to the environment when selecting a leadership style).

Discussing the application of the situational theory to leisure, Kraus and Bates have written:

> Since the competencies required in a leader are determined in large degree by the demands of the situation in which he is expected to function as a leader, the recreation administrator should study the situation carefully before assigning a leader to a specific task. He should ask himself this question: "Do the qualifications of this leader prepare him to meet the demands of this particular situation better than any other leader in our department?" At least an equal emphasis should be placed upon appraisal of the situation as upon appraisal of the leader. An individual might prove to be an excellent leader of a teenage club and a total failure of a club for the aged (Kraus and Bates 1975: 178).

A Word About Professional Values and Leadership

As previously indicated, one of the components of an occupation's professional knowledge is its values and ideals. These values influence the provision of services. This is especially true in the leisure service field. An example of the way in which professional values can influence provision of service can be found in the playground manual of a Western municipal recreation department. In spite of the information we have gained from empirically-based scientific investigations, this organization has chosen to emphasize subjective professional values above all. Table 3.4 sets forth a list of leadership qualifications that are desirable according to this particular agency. These guidelines were presented to the entire staff as the basis for their actions. Some guidelines are appropriate; others may be questionable. The manual excerpt illustrates the way in which sociopsychological theories can be modified or bypassed because of adherence to subjective professional ideals. Particularly noteworthy is the statement "Is democratic" (relative to a quality necessary to being a good leader). Compare this thought with the many studies mentioned in this chapter.

Roles of the Programmer

What does the leisure service programmer do? This question can be answered on both conceptual and operational levels. Conceptually, the programmer is involved in two basic types of service—*direct and indirect.* To implement direct program services, the programmer uses the social-planning model of community organization. This approach (discussed in Chapter 2) suggests that the role of the programmer is to use his or her professional training and knowledge to diagnose the needs of the environment and to intervene in order to provide services. The second type of service (indirect) is based on the application of the locality development model of community organization. The role of the programmer in this strategy is to enable or encourage customers to assert their own skills in the initiation of programs and services that they feel will meet their needs. The purpose of this approach is to encourage self-help through collaboration between the professional and the customer. The customer has the ability to guide his or her own leisure destiny without the intervention of social welfare agencies.

Operationally, three professional roles result from our conceptual paradigm—the *activity leader, the program coordinator* and *the community developer.* Because the strategy employed by activity leaders and program coordinators usually emphasizes their professional expertise, they are essentially involved in a direct service role. Community developers fall into the indirect service category because of the strategy of community organization employed and the fact that they do not directly provide structured activities or facilities. In the remainder of this chapter, these three operational roles will be discussed in-depth.

TABLE 3.4 Professional Values' Influence upon Leadership Behavior of the Recreation Leader

It may be true that to many Recreation Leaders, the art of leadership has come "naturally"; however, the majority of them, by far, are made—not "born." In other words, to be a good Recreation Leader takes not only a strong yen to be one and a keen love of good fun but also conscious, plugging effort and some self-examination.

Ask yourself which of the following qualifications, which are needed for a good leader, you can claim or can develop:

LOVES FUN and radiates the spirit of fun to the group.

LIKES PEOPLE and deals with them kindly and considerately.

IS DEMOCRATIC and gives the group a chance to share in making decisions.

IS GROUP-MINDED. Feels that individuals are important, but getting them to participate happily in the group is the job of a Recreation Leader.

IS PREPARED. Checks over information, tries out ideas, and rounds up more than enough material.

IS CREATIVE. Works under all kinds of conditions; can improvise and encourage others to do so.

IS HUMBLE, though confident. If not so confident, can be apprehensive or "just plain scared."

HAS FAITH in mankind. The best leader, whatever the goals, is attempting to bring more abundant life to those with whom he or she works.

Every leader finds that in attaining his or her goal, there are certain devices or techniques that bring better results than others. The "how-to-do's" are the skills and tools of the Recreation Leader's trade!

Activity Leader

The face-to-face activity leader is one of the professional roles found within leisure service organizations. The number of full-time, face-to-face positions has declined over the years, and most of these positions today are part-time or seasonal; nevertheless, the professional must realize the function and importance of the type of role that the face-to-face leader plays in leisure service organizations.

What factors are involved in effective face-to-face leadership? This is a very difficult question to answer. The face-to-face leader may be involved in a variety of situations, calling for a large variety of skills in order to fulfill his or her professional responsibilities. Because the leader works directly with customers, the factors that influence the patterns of interaction among individuals within groups are extremely important. The behavior among individuals in the group context is called "group dynamics."

Group dynamics can be described as the character and quality of interaction that takes place among individuals within a group and between individuals and other groups. How can the leader promote effective group dynamics? First, he or she can contribute to the effective functioning of the group by creating, promoting, and maintaining a positive group atmosphere. He or she can positively influence group atmosphere by being supportive of the group membership and by arranging the physical environment in such a way that individuals will feel secure. In addition, he or she can establish acceptable levels of behavior for the group and employ methods that secure and maintain that behavior. The leader should insure that effective communication patterns exist within the group and work toward establishing a feeling of esprit de corps within the group.

Although different situations require different leadership styles, the innate personality or behavior of the leader is an important factor in the development of his or her leadership style. Kraus and Bates (1975) have written that the leisure service leader's personality has great bearing upon his or her ultimate success:

> He [or she] should be enthusiastic and lively in his presentation, so that his [or her] warm interest in the activity is communicated to group members. He [or she] should be well organized, and be able to help them enter into participation with a minimum of delay or confusion. He [or she] should be able to present the activity with the utmost clarity and efficiency. He [or she]

should know it thoroughly, and have all the materials and equipment needed for participation ready. He [or she] should have control over the group, in the sense that its members look to him [or her] for help and direction (Kraus and Bates 1975: 178).

There are numerous situations and settings that require the application of general face-to-face leadership skills. Playgrounds, recreation centers, camps, youth centers, senior citizens centers and programs, parks, nature centers, and athletic fields are a few of the facilities, areas, and settings in which this type of leadership is presented. As a face-to-face leader, the leisure service professional comes into direct contact with the customers receiving the service; it is through the process of exchange between the leader and the customer that many leisure services are delivered.

Broadly speaking, leaders who perform the general face-to-face activity leadership function are called *leisure service leaders*. Leisure service leaders are responsible for the organization and direction of activities and for the general supervision of facilities. Table 3.5 and Figure 3.6 represent two of the applied or engineered techniques used by the leisure service leader to lead activities. Table 3.5 focuses on the process of leading an activity; Figure 3.6 demonstrates the proper position of the leader relative to working with different group formations and activities. The general leisure service leader is expected to possess a broad knowledge of leadership skills and techniques (as opposed to a narrowly defined area of expertise). He or she must be able to direct games, lead contests, teach various skills, and supervise other activities.

The *leisure service specialist* is another kind of face-to-face activity leader. A person in this role functions within a very precise area of expertise and usually possesses a good deal of knowledge or training about a particular program area, population, or age group. When his or her expertise involves a specific program area, the leisure service specialist is usually involved in

These diagrams show the proper position of a leader when conducting activities in the following formations or conditions.

X—Represents the leader

Single-line formation

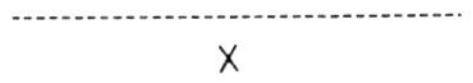

Double-line formation

Relay formation

Single circle

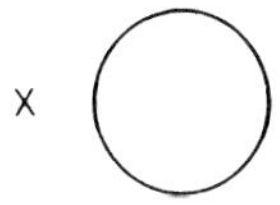

Two separate circle formations

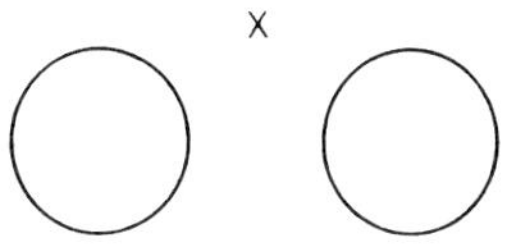

Double-circle (inside) formations

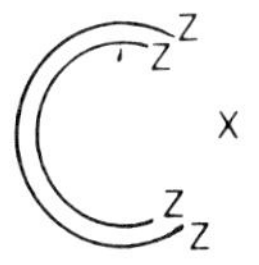

NOTE: During the explanation, the two circles break with Junior Leaders (represented by Z). This gives all participants a view of the leader. Join hands, re-form circle to start game.

Square or rectangle areas

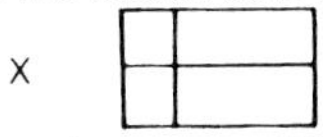

Stay in front of the group; never place yourself in middle of group. Always have group in front of you; do not allow participants to be behind you during explanation.

Figure 3.6 Proper Positions in Conducting Activities—An Example of Engineered or Applied Skills.

TABLE 3.5 Organizing and Teaching Games—An Example of Engineered or Applied Skills

1. Get attention of everyone.
2. Use a warm-up before starting explanation procedures.
3. Give directions of game first, then announce the *NAME*.
4. *DEMONSTRATION* rather than *EXPLANATION*.
5. Get group into formation before giving demonstration and explanation.
6. If the rules are complex, first have a trial demonstration and then ask questions.
7. Avoid repetition in your explanation.
8. Explanations *should not* be made in center of circle—too difficult for everyone to hear.
9. Coach while refereeing—try not to stop game.
10. Announcing scores stimulates interest.
11. Use relays to teach skills.
12. To insure success in games, teacher should be "IT" first.
13. Competing teams should be arranged equally in terms of skill and strength.
14. Avoid eliminating children from game when tagged; instead, give opposing team a point and allow those tagged to continue play.
15. Avoid monopolizing the game by re-tagging one another.
16. If child delays game by not attempting to reach base, have the group count slowly to five; if he is not on base at the count of five, he is considered out.
17. Avoid frequent changing of formations.
18. Avoid large groups; divide them into smaller groups to give children an opportunity to participate.
19. Gain attention by calling names or numbers.
20. Avoid situations where boys and girls are asked to *choose* partners.

IMPORTANT STEPS TO REMEMBER WHEN PRESENTING A NEW GAME ARE:
1. Explain the game.
2. Demonstrate the game.
3. Ask for questions.
4. Do the game.
5. Evaluate the game.
6. Be enthusiastic.

teaching. An individual hired by a leisure service organization to teach tennis, for example, would most likely be hired as a leisure service specialist. Such a person would be expected to have detailed knowledge of the rules, history, and procedures of the game. Often, he or she will have mastered the game itself. But most importantly, the individual would be expected to have developed the ability to transmit or teach the given skill or knowledge to customers. Another example of a role that the leisure service specialist might assume is the position of manager of an aquatic facility. An individual engaged in this type of work often not only possesses the technical knowledge (for example, familiarity with the pool filtration system) but also is certified as a lifeguard and swimming instructor. This person interacts with individuals on a face-to-face basis, insuring that they have an enjoyable and productive leisure service experience. A leisure service specialist also may have expertise in working with specific population groups—for example, a therapeutic recreation specialist. The therapeutic recreation specialist uses a specialized knowledge of the etiology of disabilities as well as various procedures and techniques to provide programs and services for individuals with given disabilities.

It is important to realize that the face-to-face activity leader (whether possessing general leisure service leadership skills or more specialized recreation skills) is the main conduit through which the organization comes in direct contact with those who are consuming its services. Therefore, it is important to have activity leaders who are well equipped to handle the assignments they are given and who are well versed in the policies, practices, and procedures of the organization. Face-to-face activity leaders are hired for their technical skill and ability, not for their conceptual knowledge. In order to assure a smoothly operating organization, the face-to-face activity leader should be made aware of his or her role in the organization and in relation to organizational goals. As stated by Graves (1977), "Beyond this, he [or she] should be able to view the activity, not just as a single event or experience taking place at a given time, but as a part of a continuing series of exposures and involvement in leisure pursuits for customers."

Neipoth (1983) has identified a number of roles which activity leaders may fill. These roles are diverse and may be situation-specific. Some of the roles include serving as a *leader* or *teacher, group facilitator, advocate,* or *referral worker.* To this list, we would add serving as a *counselor or outreach worker, host/guide,* or *coach.* Following is a discussion of these roles.

Leader   As mentioned above, we often find leisure service activity leaders involved in general leadership roles. Leaders, in this sense, are individuals who provide direction, influence, and organization in a leisure service setting, often within a discrete program area, program format, or facility. Leisure service activity leaders are involved in leading and directing activities in such areas as arts and crafts, drama, sports, and so on. They are often involved in working directly with target groups such as children on playgrounds or older adults.

Teacher   Leisure service activity leaders often provide instructional services. Teaching leisure skills to individuals often involves identifying competencies, creating a comfortable learning environment, and encouraging others. Also, the teacher will want to select an appropriate method to convey information to individuals. The instructional format can be either formal or informal. More formal instructional environments in leisure service settings often involve the teaching of specific skills, knowledge or values. The leader as an instructor uses various methods to communicate the desired skills, knowledge, or values to the customer.

Group facilitator   Often leisure service activity leaders work with groups to facilitate positive group interactions. There are numerous associations, clubs, special interest groups, and other types of groupings with whom leisure service activity leaders interact. Activity leaders in this situation help groups define goals, process information, develop identities, and establish and maintain procedures and methods for interaction.

Advocate   The leisure service activity leader as an advocate works to promote the interests of those individuals and/or groups that he or she represents. The advocacy function can involve representing others within an organization and/or providing information to individuals so that they may advocate on their own behalf. As Niepoth notes, " . . . advocacy is the effort of a staff member to get changes made that will benefit others . . . The staff member attempts to cause other people to make changes . . . that will benefit the people for whom the staff member is concerned" (1983: 233).

Referral worker   As a referral worker a leisure service activity leader is involved in helping individuals get to services that are needed but that are outside the scope of the direct services provided by a given leisure service organization. A leader must be perceptive enough to identify a person in need and then to be able to effectively identify those services which might meet that need. Leaders, in this sense, must be sensitive to individuals, and must also be resourceful in helping them identify and make contact with appropriate organizations.

Counselor   Often, leisure service activity leaders, especially those working in therapeutic recreation settings, engage in counseling. Counseling is usually directed toward helping individuals modify selected behaviors. Often counselors work to help individuals clarify values and to develop problem-solving and conflict-resolution skills. Leisure counseling (leisure education) often involves helping individuals identify resources, develop skills, modify or enhance leisure lifestyle perspectives, and solve leisure-related concerns.

Outreach worker   Outreach workers, according to Edginton and Ford (1985: 132), are also known as roving leaders, youth counselors, street club workers, and street gang leaders. The outreach worker provides assistance in programs to individuals and groups in their own locale. In other words, he or she takes the service out of the facility and brings it directly to the customer's own turf and on the customer's own terms. The outreach worker attempts to provide services to individuals as an extension of the work of an organization. The best example of an outreach function is the "Meals on Wheels."

Host/Guide   The host/guide, as a leisure service activity leader, carries out a variety of different functions. Serving in this capacity, the leader may be charged with making customers feel comfortable, providing information, leading tours, and, in general, helping to make the leisure experience pleasant and satisfying for customers. The host/guide must have knowledge of an organization's functions, the ability to meet and communicate with customers in an effective and articulate manner, and the ability to anticipate and meet the needs of customers.

Coach   Coaching, as a form of leisure service activity leadership, involves a variety of different functions. Coaching entails not only enthusiastically encouraging and inspiring others, but also involves teaching and framing strategies for different game situations. Coaches promote and encourage values such as sportsmanship, fair play, and teamwork.

The Program Coordinator

The role of the *program coordinator* or the *leisure service supervisor* is essentially one of middle management. In many organizations, it involves the actual creation and distribution of program services. Consequently, we may find the program coordinator involved in planning, organizing, promoting, supervising, and evaluating programs. The process followed by the program coordinator in his or her work is depicted in the program-planning model presented in chapter 2. The work of the program coordinator is diverse, challenging, and exciting. For example, on a given day a program coordinator could engage in a variety of work activities—appearing on a local television show to promote organizational activities, purchasing supplies and equipment necessary for the summer playground program, or supervising activity leaders at several sites. The program coordinator serves many functions in the office, community, and numerous special locations. This position is the major full-time entry-level position available to individuals graduating from colleges and universities with a degree in leisure studies.

The responsibilities of the program coordinator within the leisure service organization can be administratively grouped together as follows: (1) *program area*, (2) *facility*, (3) *population group*, (4) *geographical area*, and (5) *a combination of one or more of these.*

Program area   In many leisure service organizations, the program coordinator is given the responsibility for developing and implementing all services within a given program area. In a municipal parks and recreation department, there might be a sports supervisor who is responsible for organizing all sports activities for youth and adults. This could include competitive activities, such as leagues, tournaments, and playdays; instructional programs, such as skill classes, clinics, and demonstrations; and organization and club activities, such as a swim-for-fitness club, a jogging club, or a soccer club.

Facility   A program coordinator may be given the responsibility for managing one type of facility or a variety. For example, the program coordinator might be involved in the operation of a sports complex, a theater, a museum, a recreation center, an aquatic facility, an ice rink, a park, or other facilities. Usually a person who manages a given facility is charged with the coordination of physical maintenance, program development, and general supervision (including control of drop-in use). The coordinator of a multiservice senior citizen facility, for example, might be responsible for structured programs, drop-in activities, medical and social services, transportation, meal programs, fund raising, concessions, and maintenance. Leisure service organizations often have invested large sums of money in the development of physical resources. It is therefore vital that program coordinators have expertise in facility management.

Population groups   The work functions of a program coordinator also may be organized according to population groups. This finds the programmer responsible for providing a complete and well-rounded offering of program services to a given population group (as defined by age, gender, or some other special characteristics). For example, if organizing the work functions of a program coordinator around the factor of age, one would expect to see such activities as preschool programs, children's programs, youth activities, and adult services emerge. A program coordinator may also be assigned the responsibility of developing services for men or women, coordinating coeducational activities, or organizing program services for special groups (such as the physically or mentally disabled).

Geographic areas   Especially in larger communities, responsibilities for program coordination may be distributed geographically. This is usually done in an effort to maintain neighborhood cohesiveness and promote grass-roots development. In addition, there is a movement toward decentralization of services in order to bring those with decision-making powers closer to the recipients of services in a given geographic area. The decentralization of program services promotes accessibility of services and allows for the individualization of program offerings. The program coordinator operating within the decentralized model assumes many of the responsibilities just described—i.e., those associated with facilities, supervision, age group programming, and so forth.

Combination of work functions   As previously indicated, work functions within an organization are grouped together for administrative decision-making purposes. The structure of an organization—hence, its work assignments—is a reflection of its purpose or goals and the resources it has available to achieve these goals. In an ideal sense, it might be appropriate to classify the work activities of a leisure service organization according to one of the four classifications previously mentioned. However, in reality, an organization blends together its resources in the most efficient manner possible to achieve its goals. Therefore, we often find the work of a program coordinator organized around a combination of the previously described functions. For example, one of the authors, while serving as a recreation supervisor in a municipal park and recreation department of a middle-sized community, was responsible for the management of five community centers, summer playground programs, youth sports leagues, teen programming, and community-wide special events. Another of the authors, working in a community of similar size and organization, had the responsibility for all programming for children, women, and senior citizens (including year-round programs in sports, after-school activities, playground activities, and craft classes).

Although there are different ways to classify work functions, the actual kinds of tasks that are carried out by program coordinators are similar. A program coordinator must plan and organize the services for which he or she is responsible. This may involve determining customer needs, establishing objectives, hiring staff, and locating appropriate facilities and equipment. Once the service has been organized the program coordinator must promote the program through use of the media and public relations resources. When the program becomes operational, the coordinator supervises the individuals he or she has hired to implement the service—providing both human and material support, encouragement, and assistance. Finally, the program coordinator must audit and evaluate not only the efforts and work of his or her subordinates but also his or her own efforts.

Obviously there is a certain amount of glamour and excitement in organizing and implementing a successful program. It is truly a gratifying experience to see the results of one's efforts as a program coordinator being well received. However, it takes commitment and dedication to be successful. Often the program coordinator will carry boxes, make coffee, move furniture, sweep water off ball diamonds, and do other assorted tasks that are commonly absent from job descriptions in order to insure the success of his or her programs.

The Community Developer

The role of the leisure service professional as a community developer is not a new one. At the turn of the century, leisure service programs were primarily encouraged by social agencies. Many leisure services resulted from early attempts to improve the "general welfare" of the community, especially for the poor. As such, the efforts of social workers in this area represented one of the earliest forms of community development. The massive formalized growth of governmental intervention did not occur until the 1930s. Early leaders in the leisure service movement were not trained as play leaders; they were social activists, social organizers, or community developers. There is a movement afoot within the leisure service field to again pursue the role of community

developer and encourage people to take the responsibility and initiative for their own leisure concerns.

The adjectives used to describe a community developer are numerous. He or she has been called an enabler, a catalyst, a facilitator, a teacher, a change agent, a consultant, a stimulator, and a helper. We prefer the word "encourager" as the clearest description of the role of the leisure service professional operating as a community developer.

The leisure services professional as a community developer works primarily with community groups or associations that have been formed in response to an immediate concern or issue, such as the need for a swimming pool and community center or the rehabilitation of deteriorated park areas. These groups tend to be short-term, organized to solve specific problems. There is a tendency to try to include these groups as an official or quasi-official unit of government. However, when a relationship between a community group and the developer has matured, the community developer should avoid co-opting the primary purposes of the organization. The relationship should be one of cooperation—a relationship in which the two bodies work together constructively, complementing each other's aims. Neighborhood and community associations may be involved in the management of services as well as in the execution of advocacy functions.

The encouragement of self-help and local initiative through the community development process is useful from several standpoints. First, it encourages citizen participation and, as such, makes governmental bodies and voluntary organizations more responsive to the needs of people. Second, the cost of providing services, especially innovative and creative new services, is becoming prohibitive and the community development process increases available resources to the organization. At the same time, it attempts to share the responsibility of the development of services with the customers.

TABLE 3.6   Role and Function of a Community Worker

Qualities Required by the Community Worker:
1. Ability to establish relationships to demonstrate and create confidence.
2. Accessibility to all members of the community and to representatives of organizations across social and political barriers.
3. Flexibility in adapting to many situations.
4. Sensitivity, patience, and ability to work at the pace of the group.
5. Capacity to work toward long-term objectives.

Knowledge Required in Community Work:
1. Local social and political structures, services, facilities, and sources of support.
2. Processes of group interaction, methods of communication, and educational methods.
3. Organization—e.g., procedures in committees and at public meetings, processes in referrals, office administration (including finance).
4. Program development, supervision of group activities and management of premises.

Content of the Job:
1. Study of the community in all aspects, using both statistical and factual information and the feelings of people in a continuous process of interaction.
2. Reconnaissance and analysis, surveys, diagnosis, prognosis, review of progress, and achievements.
3. Problem solving, helping a group to clarify issues, decision making, adoption of a strategy, planning of tasks.
4. Working as a member of a team, helping groups to form and to work toward their aims, understanding the roles of other workers and agencies.
5. Cooperation with voluntary and statutory bodies and influential individuals and groups, acting as a link to provide information, advice, guidance, and referral.
6. Mediation between conflicting interests, personalities, and groups.
7. Administrative and secretarial work with and for groups (including minutes, records, accounting, fund raising, negotiations with statutory bodies).
8. Training indigenous leaders, on-the-job training for helpers, student supervision.
9. Public relations, speaking, broadcasting, editing and publishing, press liaison conferences, exhibitions, campaigns, protest meetings.
10. Working with uninvolved people in detached work or, where membership and support is poor, recruitment of volunteers.
11. Political involvement in advocacy in helping to meet community needs.

From Routledge and Kegan, *Current Issues in Community Development,* 1973.

The reviving of the community developer role in leisure service organizations requires the acquisition of a new and different set of knowledge and skills. A shift in the nature of services, from a structure in which the professional serves as a direct provider to one in which he or she plays an indirect role as an encourager, changes the basic technology that is used in the leisure service profession. The role of the programmer, rather than emphasizing diagnostic skills and the methods and procedures used to provide services, becomes one requiring social skills in order to serve as a resource for individuals and groups. In other words, his or her work is not focused on the technical aspects of creating and distributing services but on the process of helping people to help themselves. Table 3.6 lists the various roles and functions of a community worker (developer).

Summary

In this chapter we have examined the role of the leisure service programmer. We view the programmer as a professional. As such, he or she is involved in service to humanity. The professional performs his or her work in such a way that the needs of the customer are placed first. The relationship between the programmer and the customer is a collaborative one in which the programmer draws basic work gratification from the satisfying leisure experiences of the customer. The professional programmer has usually attained a unique set of skills and knowledge through extensive college or university training. This unique information prompts society to recognize his or her authority and expertise in the area. As a professional, the programmer has certain obligations, responsibilities, and duties. These are usually found in the profession's code of ethics or standards in the professional literature.

All programmers are leaders. Knowledge of leadership techniques, skills, and theories is essential to the programmer. Leadership can be thought of as a process of influence that, when properly directed, helps a group or organization achieve its goals. The leadership style of the programmer is a key element influencing his or her success. There are several leadership theories (e.g., trait, group, and situational). Contemporary scientific investigation has determined that a contingency approach to leadership is the most effective. In other words, leadership styles should be situation-specific. There is no "best" leadership style; the most appropriate style will vary with the situation involved.

Finally, in this chapter we have discussed, conceptually and operationally, the roles of the programmer. There are two conceptual roles that are identified—the direct service role and the indirect service role. The direct service role implies structure and the use of professional knowledge in meeting people's needs. The indirect approach to services involves providing assistance to the customer and encouraging community initiative and indigenous leadership. Three operational roles that can be assumed by the programmer are also identified. Those individuals employed on a full- or part-time basis to perform the face-to-face leadership are called activity leaders. They are the prime conduit through which an organization interacts with its customers. Program coordinators are those individuals who serve as middle managers in leisure service organizations. They are responsible for planning, organizing, and implementing services—e.g., employment of staff, public relations (via mass communication), and acquisition of facilities and equipment. Community developers represent another operational role. The community developer can be thought of as an encourager—an individual who works with people at the grass-roots level.

Discussion Questions and Exercises

1. What are the four common elements that all professions possess?

2. Discuss the professional status of leisure occupations.

3. What is professional knowledge? Cite examples of the types of knowledge that are involved in its development.

4. What is leadership? What are the levels at which leadership occurs within a leisure service organization?

5. Identify and discuss four different characteristics of superior leisure service leaders.

6. What is the difference between direct and indirect services?

7. Identify and define four operational roles performed by leisure service professionals.

8. Identify and discuss how the responsibilities of a program coordinator can be grouped administratively within leisure service organizations. Locate an organizational chart for a public leisure service organization and analyze it in light of these administrative groupings.

9. What are some of the specific roles that leisure service activity leaders play? Provide an example of each of these roles in an actual leisure service organization.

10. Discuss the work of the leisure service programmer as a community developer.

References

Bennis, W. and B. Nanus. 1985. *Leaders.* New York: Harper & Row.

Danford, H. G. and M. Shirley. 1964. *Creative leadership in recreation.* Boston: Allyn & Bacon.

Edginton, C. R. 1976. Consumerism and professionalism. *Parks and Recreation* 11(9).

Edginton, C. R. and P. M. Ford. 1985. *Leadership in recreation and leisure service organizations.* New York: Wiley.

Fiedler, F. E. 1967. *A theory of leadership effectiveness.* New York: McGraw-Hill.

Frye, V. and M. Peters. 1972. *Therapeutic recreation: Its theory, philosophy, and practice.* Harrisburg, PA: Stackpole Books.

Graves, S. 1977. *The community development process.* Waterloo, Ontario, Canada: University of Waterloo.

Halpin, A. W. 1954. The leadership behavior and combat performance of airplane commanders. *Journal of Abnormal and Social Psychology* 49.

Halpin, A. W. 1959. *The leadership behavior of school superintendents.* Chicago: Midwest Administration Center, University of Chicago.

Halpin, A. W. and B. J. Winer, in Ralph M. Stogdill and Alvin E. Coons. *Leader behavior: Its description and measurement.* Columbus, OH: Ohio State University Bureau of Business Research. n.d.

Hersburgh, T. 1987. *Time.* (May).

Hersey, P. and K. H. Blanchard. 1988. *Management of organizational behavior.* 3rd ed. Englewood Cliffs, NJ: Prentice-Hall.

Hitt, W. D. 1985. *The leader-manager.* Columbus, OH: Batelle.

House, R. J. 1971. A path-goal theory of leadership effectiveness. *Administrative Science Quarterly* 16.

Kouzes, J. and B. Posner. 1987. *The leadership challenge.* San Francisco: Jossey Bass.

Kraus, R. G. 1985. *Recreation leadership today.* Glenview, IL: Scott, Foresman & Co.

Kraus, R. G. and B. Bates. 1975. *Recreation leadership and supervision.* Philadelphia: W. B. Saunders.

Lewin, K., R. Lippitt, and R. K. White. 1939. Patterns of aggressive behavior in experimentally created 'social climates'. *Journal of Social Psychology* 10.

Linkert, R. 1977. *Organizational behavior.* 2nd ed. New York: McGraw-Hill.

Neipoth, E. W. 1983. *Leisure leadership.* Englewood Cliffs, NJ: Prentice-Hall.

Roberts, W. 1990. *Leadership secrets of Attila the Hun.* New York: Warner.

Russell, R. V. 1986. *Leadership in recreation.* St. Louis: C. V. Mosby.

Stein, T. A. 1975. Report on the state of recreation and park education in Canada and the United States. Arlington, VA: Society of Park and Recreation Educators.

4 | Understanding Customer Behavior

Learning Objectives

1. To help the reader better analyze how to understand *customer leisure behavior.*
2. To help the reader clarify how the relationship that develops between the individuals served and the professional is affected by *how participants are labeled.*
3. To identify *factors that influence customer decision making related to leisure.*
4. To help the reader gain an understanding of *the behavioral sciences and their application to leisure.*
5. To gain knowledge of *lifestyle variables and their impact upon leisure.*

Introduction

Understanding customer behavior is important to success as a leisure service programmer. When the customer is viewed in proper perspective, a leisure service organization is positioned to effectively meet individual needs. There are many factors that influence the behavior of customers. Values, motives, lifestyle, and personality are all individual characteristics that can influence the decision to pursue one leisure experience versus another. Further, social influences, such as family, reference group, and the community can also have a dramatic impact on the decision-making behavior of an individual.

Our knowledge of customer behavior is drawn from many different disciplines. Psychology, sociology, and anthropology, as well as areas of study such as marketing, provide a backdrop for organizing information concerning customer behavior. In the broadest possible context, the study of human behavior provides insight into those factors that motivate individuals and influence their decisions to participate in various leisure activities and events.

The task of analyzing human behavior and its relationship to leisure is a complex and imposing one. The study of human behavior is not as concrete as other areas of study, such as the physical sciences. For example, it is difficult to manipulate and control human subjects in an investigative effort, the way that one can exercise control in chemistry. However, it is essential that the leisure service programmer have some knowledge of how people pursue leisure through the lifespan, as well as other factors that may influence their decision-making behavior.

In this chapter, we will investigate some of the factors that influence customer behavior as it relates to leisure. We will first focus on the labels that are attached to individuals participating in leisure experiences by professionals. The purpose of this discussion will be to help clarify how the relationship that the professional establishes with the participant is dependent upon perceptions and assumptions about the nature of the interaction. Next, the chapter will provide a discussion of the factors influencing decision making regarding leisure activities and events. In addition, we will discuss the implications of demographic information and life cycle variables as they influence leisure choices.

What's in a Label?

The relationship that is established between a professional and the individuals that he or she serves is often reflected in the label that is attached to the person receiving the services. There are many common labels attached to an individual and/or group in the leisure service field. Some of the more common ones are *participant, patron, customer, client, member, user, visitor, guest,* and *consumer.* The use of one particular label versus another will have a direct bearing and impact upon the association that is established. In fact, it may infer degrees of freedom, dependence and independence, responsibility, patterns of communication, privilege, and/or acknowledgment of expertise or value assigned to either the leisure service professional or the person served by the organization.

The use and acceptance of terms describing the relationship between the professional and the person served by the organization should not be taken lightly. Why is this the case? Our work as professionals can be greatly affected by how we view others and our assumptions and expectations. Do we direct people or do we enable others? Are those we serve victims or helpless individuals who require our expertise, skills, and methods of intervention to improve their lives? Or are they capable of exercising discretion and independent judgment, and of making choices in meeting their own leisure needs? These are indeed difficult questions that have far-reaching implications for the nature of our work and its relationship to people.

An exploration of a number of labels that can be assigned to individuals served by leisure service organizations can be useful. Two graduate students at the University of Oregon, Stoll and Wheeler (1989), have explored this concept in a paper presented in a class entitled "Leisure Service Program Development." They write:

> As service providers we must be aware of categorizing people and its effect on services rendered. We are both enabled and limited by the words we use. Our service posture is related to our expectations of behavior, our communication patterns, and presumptions about the needs of those served. The labels we assign to people many times define the opportunities for service delivery and the way in which services are provided.

Some of the common labels often associated with the professional practice in the leisure service field as related to people served follow.

Client

A client can be thought of as an individual who *passively receives recommendations of the programmer.* The client/programmer relationship is one in which individuals subordinate their own personal choices and defer to the expertise of the programmer. A client/professional relationship is one that infers a relationship of dependency; that is, individuals receiving the services are dependent upon the application of the knowledge, skills, and values by the programmer to meet their leisure needs. The methods of treatment, the types of services and the strategies used to deliver services are tightly controlled by the programmer.

The role of the programmer in this type of relationship is to diagnose the needs of the individual and then intervene with those services he or she feels are appropriate based on the use of professional expertise and judgment. In a client/professional relationship the professional exercises a great deal of discretion in making decisions about what services would be useful or valuable to the individual. Thus, it may be implied that the professional in this relationship exercises a great deal of discretionary risk. Decisions about which programs, strategies, or services to be used are often not shared between the client and the professional. Communication is often one way. At best, an illusion of perceived freedom is applied to create the feeling that choice actually exists. Because the individual defers to the expertise of the professional their relationship often requires strict confidentiality.

Consumer

A consumer can be thought of as an individual who uses services. In economic terms, a consumer is thought to be someone who uses goods or services in order to meet his or her needs. Consumers, by definition, engage in a process of exchange. They exchange something of value (e.g., time, money) to receive a service. The role of the programmer in this process is straightforward. The programmer creates and disperses a service and the consumer absorbs the experience. A consumer does not have to subordinate his or her interests to the professional if he or she chooses not to. *The consumer is free to choose, to decide what services best meet his or her needs and whether he or she is willing to pay the cost of such services.* In this relationship the consumer retains control over the decision to participate.

Within this context, a movement has emerged to protect the consumer from unsafe, unhealthy, and poorly organized services. It is known as *consumerism.* It is directed towards having consumers influence the quality and value of services provided. Consumer activities in this arena often result in the establishment of regulations that protect their interests. A consumer/provider relationship can be a two-way relationship. The provider of services, in an attempt to more effectively meet the needs of the consumer, can discover ways of more effectively organizing services.

Customer

We can think of a customer as *an individual who participates in a service on a regular basis.* Customers often develop relationships with providers that are mutually beneficial. The assumption is that if an individual is returning on a regular basis to a leisure service organization, his or her needs are being met. Stoll and Wheeler (1989) have written:

> The term customer implies a relationship based on needs satisfaction and loyalty in which benefit accrues to both the provider and the customer. Communication is assumed to be interactive in the sense of evolving some form of needs assessment (either formal or informal) and some form of evaluative feedback (as in "The customer is always right"). Expectations are that the customer will seek the provider's service for the satisfaction of a perceived need. The success of that transaction will be dependent upon such factors as the perceived quality and value of the experience, its timeliness, and price.

As one can see, customer/programmer relationships are two-way relationships built upon developing satisfaction, trust, and loyalty. Because of the interactive nature of these types of relationships, the communications process is two-way. The provider of services must be willing to respond to felt and expressed needs of individuals. To be customer-oriented means that the leisure service programmer develops a mutually beneficial relationship that considers the needs of the customer a central theme in the development of services.

In this book we have chosen to use the label customer because of its focus on needs satisfaction and the establishment of interactive relationships with individuals. Further, customer relationships require attention to quality, value, and convenience. Leisure service programs built around these themes are often successful. In a sense, using the term customer weds the leisure service programmer to the needs of the individual. A needs-focused leisure service organization will out-perform one that is other-focused on a consistent basis.

Guest

A guest can be thought of as a party that is valued. Guests are often viewed in terms of behaviors that we as programmers exhibit when they come into our environments. A guest is *an individual who is treated courteously, respectfully, given special care and attention, and, in general, made to feel welcome in an environment.* Because we often associate the term guest with inviting individuals into our homes, we are assuming that such individuals are treasured, valued, and important to us. When an individual is considered a guest, the assumption is that the person will be treated with great dignity, and that every attempt will be made to satisfy his or her needs. Thus, the professional takes a pro-active stand in attempting to meet the needs of the guest. This stand requires two-way communication and a desire to fulfill the needs of others.

The best illustration of this concept in the leisure service field is found in the relationship that is established between guest and service provider at Disney World and Disneyland. At Disneyland individuals are treated as guests, but the word guest is spelled with a capital "G". The reputation for positive relationships that exists between the staff (actually called the *cast*) and individuals attending either one of these two theme parks is legendary. Much of the success of Disneyland and Disney World can be attributed to the establishment and maintenance of positive guest relations.

Member

Membership in an organization implies a sense of exclusivity. Thus, a person who is a member of an organization (like the YMCA or YWCA) is *an individual who has been given special privileges because the person has paid dues and/or been inducted in some fashion into a group or organization.* What kinds of unique privileges are accorded to an individual who has membership in an organization? In the context of leisure services, privileges might take several different forms. First, being a member of an organization might provide a person access to facilities and services that are unavailable to others. Membership may also enable an individual to associate with a prescribed group of people. Further, membership in an organization may result in greater individual attention, care, and service. The relationships that may evolve between members and professional staff may be more personalized, focused, and directly related to the unique needs of the individual.

Being a member of an organization is often a two-way relationship. By becoming a member of an organization, an individual often embraces the philosophy, values, and goals of that agency. Membership in an organization generally requires active as opposed to passive interaction. Thus, the relationship that often emerges between members and providers of services is two-way, requiring active involvement. This sort of interaction may result in the member influencing and perhaps controlling the types, levels, costs, and so on of services provided. The point is that individuals who hold membership in leisure service organizations may exercise control over their leisure experiences or destiny.

Participant

The label of participant has been used over the years as a term to denote individuals served by leisure service organizations. However, *to participate means to share or take part in an activity or service.* Thus, a participant viewed as "one who shares" is an individual who is actively participating in the process. An individual may share in the successful implementation of a leisure activity by cooperating, providing social and emo-

tional support to others, demonstrating teamwork, contributing ideas, engaging in problem solving, and other behaviors that contribute to the successful implementation of a leisure activity. In actuality, the participant is a collaborator with the leisure service programmer. This collaborator relationship must be one built upon the basis of trust, two-way interaction, and respect.

From the perspective of the leisure service programmer, to view an individual as a participant means that the professional must be willing to encourage sharing, open the process of decision making, and establish meaningful ways of involvement. This suggests the building of ownership, a sense of responsibility and desire for a positive outcome. Participation implies shared control and assumes that the leisure service programmer will act in a two-way mode.

Patron

The term patron has recently been applied to the area of leisure programming by Rossman (1989). A patron can be thought of as an individual who buys services on a consistent or regular basis from a leisure service organization. In other words, to be a patron suggests that there is a certain amount of loyalty between the person receiving the service and the organization. In most definitions, the idea of being a patron means that the person participates regularly or consistently within the organization. In a sense, a patron is much like a customer. *There is a relationship of satisfaction that has been developed between the provider of the service and the patron that results in a continuing interaction.*

Obviously, in viewing individuals as patrons, the leisure service programmer is seeking regular, continuous involvement. To encourage such involvement, the programmer must provide high-quality services that consistently meet the needs of the individual. This must occur in order to meet the needs of the individual on a continuous basis, which is the foundation for building loyalty. When individuals patronize a particular leisure service organization, a relationship of mutual respect often is developed. In fact, the word patron comes from the Latin *patronus* which means "a person to be respected."

User

The term user is often applied to individuals who consume leisure services. To use something means to avail oneself of a service. Users are individuals who are thought to involve themselves actively in a program or service on a regular basis. In other words, the concept of the term user suggests a consistent pattern of involvement in leisure services, rather than irregular use.

What is the relationship that emerges between the individual user and the leisure service professional? *A user/professional relationship is one of need, dependency, and dependability.* The leisure professional works to provide the service continuously in such a manner that the individual's needs for achievement, risk, spontaneity, and so on are met. To be a user does not necessarily suggest a relationship of two-way interaction with the professional. Nor does it necessarily suggest a relationship of cooperation, trust, mutual respect, but rather one that is built upon the self-interests of the individual. In other words, the person "uses" a leisure product or service for his or her own ends.

Visitor

Another term associated with leisure service delivery is visitor. A visitor can be thought of as *an individual who visits an area or facility or participates in a program.* Generally speaking, a visitor is thought to be an individual who comes to an organization's service, facility, or site. Such visitors may be invited, or their visits may occur more informally or spontaneously. Further, such participation may be regular or infrequent.

The status accorded to visitors is similar to that accorded guests. The expectation is that the visitor will be valued, treated courteously, and perhaps entertained, educated, or enhanced in some manner. The relationship that often develops between a leisure service programmer and a visitor is one of mutual respect, positive interaction, and support. The visitor often comes to see and/or participate in a unique geographic, cultural, or historical activity or site. Visitors often must be provided with support services, and must be made to feel as if their participation is valued.

Customer Decision Making

How do customers make decisions concerning leisure? What are the factors that influence their leisure preferences? This is, indeed, a complex and difficult question to answer. Only within the past several decades have researchers studying decision making in the field of marketing begun to develop a body of knowledge concerning this topic. Further, in the study of how people make decisions about leisure, there has been even less research. The application of decision-making theory to leisure has only emerged within the last few years.

Purchasing Patterns of Customers

Decision making concerning leisure activities and preferences will vary in terms of intensity and motivation. *Some decisions are made in a routine fashion, whereas others require extensive problem solving and investigation.* Take, for example, the following three scenarios. Each requires a different level of decision making on the part of a customer because of the potential effects resulting from the decision.

1. Dennis and Lyn are considering the purchase of a $30,000 recreation vehicle to be used during weekend and summer vacation months for excursions to the Oregon Cascade Range and the Oregon Coast.
2. Ron and Paula are considering vacationing at a new coastal location this summer. For the past ten years they have vacationed at Salishan Lodge, but now are considering moving their vacation site to Driftwood Shores.

3. Bob and Sally must replenish their supply of golf balls. They have purchased *Titleist* brand golf balls for the past seven years and intend to purchase the same brand when they go to their local athletic supply store.

These three situations point out the difference in complexity of decision making related to leisure. The first decision involves a major purchase. It requires in-depth investigation. Often the purchaser will compare other products to determine their comparable quality and value. This approach to decision making can be thought of as *extended/information search*. Because it is a major purchase, the customer is required to weigh the benefits of comparable products and engage in extended problem solving. Such a purchase is usually made once in an individual's lifetime and not in a routine fashion.

The second situation illustrates another level of decision making. In this case, the couple is switching between comparable vacation sites. Perhaps they are seeking novelty in their vacation experience and have decided to try another resort. Just as easily as they have sought the new location for their vacation, they could switch back to their former site. We call this approach to decision making *product, service, or brand switching*. It involves limited problem solving. The decision making is less complex than in the first situation, but nonetheless requires some search and problem solving.

In the last example, Bob and Sally's purchase of golf balls represents a minimal investment of time and effort in the decision-making process. They are simply buying a product that they have previously purchased and with which they have been satisfied. This process of decision making is labeled *routine/repeat decision making*, or routine problem solving. They know that they like the product and that it will meet their needs. It is a simple decision to make and often occurs out of habit. They do not have to engage in conscious decision making. In fact, they are very loyal to the *Titleist* brand because it has met their needs

in the past. Further, the actual cost of golf balls is low and, as such, represents a small investment.

These concepts are illustrated in Figure 4.1, entitled "Decision Making Complexity as Related to Costs of Leisure Products and Services." This model presents two continuums—one related to decision-making complexity and the other related to the financial risk of the leisure purchase. The horizontal continuum for decision-making complexity places routine decision making at one end and extended decision making at the other end. The vertical continuum places low financial risk at one end and high financial risk at the other.

As one can see, when viewing the model, there are four sections that result from the intersection of the two continuums. The four sections are *routine/low risk*, *extended search/low risk*, *routine/high risk*, and *high risk/extended search*. The decisions discussed in the scenarios above can be placed in one of the four sections of the model. For example, in the case of Dennis and Lyn's decision regarding the purchase of a recreation vehicle, there is a large financial commitment to be

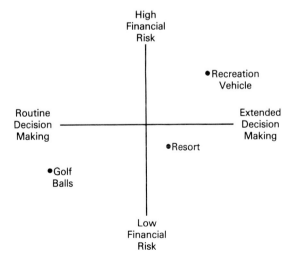

Figure 4.1 Decision-Making Complexity as Related to Cost of Leisure Products and Services.

made. Therefore, this decision would fall into the high risk/extended search category. In making this decision, they will shop carefully and spend considerable time and effort comparing the benefits of various vehicles.

In the second example of making a decision to switch to another resort, Ron and Paula have less of a financial stake, but will engage in some comparison and decision making. Thus, their decision would fall into the extended search/low risk category. There is not as much financial risk in their decision making and their investigation into their purchase will not be as thorough as that of Dennis and Lyn.

The last example, involving the purchase of golf balls, falls into the routine/low risk category. In this instance, Bob and Sally will not spend time researching the product they are about to purchase; it is a routine decision based on past satisfaction with the product. It involves little financial risk and they know that the product that they are about to purchase will meet their needs.

Why is this information regarding purchasing patterns useful to us? The point is that customers use information to make decisions. The complexity and intensity of decision making may vary from one situation to another, but nonetheless individuals process information and use it in order to choose between one service and another. The needs and lifestyles of individuals will greatly influence the information that they seek. Knowledge of such decision making patterns is extremely useful to leisure service organizations that are attempting to communicate the benefits of their services effectively to their customers.

Variables That Have an Impact on Customer Decision Making

There are three important variables that have an impact on customer decision making. These are known in the marketing literature as *involvement, differentiation,* and *time pressure.* The concept of

involvement refers to the extent to which a service or product reflects pertinence and relevance to the individual. In other words, involvement, as reflected by a particular service, tells us whether or not it reflects an individual's self-image, attitude, or selected set of behaviors. Such reflections on the part of an individual can influence decision making. For example, if a person perceives that a particular leisure product or service reflects or exemplifies their lifestyle, they may be moved to purchase.

Differentiation deals with the availability of leisure products and services. There can be many similar leisure services and products available in the marketplace. However, each of these services and products can be differentiated from each other in some way. Customers often look for these subtle, unique features that distinguish one leisure service or product from another. They will make decisions based on those subtle differences.

The last variable that affects decision making is that of time pressure. In certain situations, we are under constraints when making decisions concerning leisure products and services. Time pressures influence decision making in such a way that convenience and location may become major determinants influencing the selection of a service. For example, it is often easier to travel to a fitness club that is closer to one's home than to go to one across town that is more fully equipped and less expensive. Customers often go to the one that is convenient because of time constraints.

All of these variables interact with each other. For example, convenience may, in fact, be a subtle way of differentiating one service from another. Factors such as this motivate and shape the decisions that people make regarding purchase of leisure products and services. Attention must be given to the potential impact of each one of these variables in designing leisure activities and events and, also, in communicating their potential benefits to individuals.

Behavioral Sciences

To understand customer behavior it is necessary for the leisure service professional to apply knowledge from the behavioral sciences. Behavioral sciences are concerned with the systematic scientific investigation of behavior. The work of the behavioral scientist essentially involves the analyzing of human behavior in order to understand it. The goals of behavioral science are not unlike those of other scientific disciplines–i.e., understanding, explaining, predicting, and controlling the behavior of organisms (in this case, people). To this a fifth goal may be added in the area of the leisure services profession: the effort to improve the quality of life for individuals.

The behavioral sciences basically consist of three disciplines—anthropology, sociology, and psychology. *Anthropology* can be defined as the science of man. Anthropologists study all aspects of man and his experience. The information generated from the anthropologist's investigation generates a wealth of data. The problem for the leisure programmer becomes one of abstracting the general information and concepts and applying them. *Sociology* involves the study and investigation of human society and social behavior. Obviously, understanding man's behavior in a societal context can contribute greatly to the ability of a leisure programmer to plan for groups of people, organizations, and communities. For example, a knowledge of the sociological profile of a given group would enable a leisure professional to meet more effectively and efficiently the needs of this group in terms of relevant programming, involvement, and development. The *psychologist* studies the mind, emotions, feelings, desires, actions, traits, attitudes, and thoughts of human beings and, where applicable, animals. Psychologists are concerned with how organisms cope with and relate to their environment and to each other.

A working knowledge of these three behavioral sciences can provide the leisure professional with invaluable aid and insight and enable him or her to plan most effectively for those individuals being served. The following discussion will summarize the major thrust of each of these disciplines and the ways in which they can be applied to the leisure services field.

Anthropology

Anthropology is aptly defined as the study of humankind. It encompasses all aspects of the human existence as we know it. Holistic and comparative approaches are basic to anthropology. It can embrace a variety of disciplines such as history, sociology, economics, biology, physiology, and linguistics. The uniqueness of anthropology is derived from its broad scope and the fact that it includes the study of all men, in all periods of history, and in all aspects of life.

Not only do anthropologists study all aspects of humankind in all periods of history and all aspects of life, but also they attempt to broaden their approach by cross-cultural comparisons. Human populations have similarities and differences, both biologically and culturally; the anthropologist explores various populations and attempts to point out these similar and dissimilar factors. He or she uses cross-cultural analysis in order to discover differences and similarities in beliefs, customs, and biological traits. The basic philosophy behind this approach is the anthropologist's belief that one cannot make generalizations about other cultures from one's own culture without first making a careful investigation.

The comparative approach to the study of anthropology allows the individual to view his or her own culture in perspective—that is, he or she is able to identify the distinguishing factors that occur as a result of physical or cultural differences between peoples. There is a tendency for North Americans to view their culture from an ethnocentric viewpoint, giving little attention to the cultural diversity of individuals within our society. Much is written in the literature about integration into the melting pot or the mainstream of our way of life. Yet little is written regarding the protection of the heritage and integrity of different cultures within our society.

In organizing and delivering leisure programs, there is a tendency to isolate one or two physical or cultural traits and use these as the sole determinants on which to base the provision of a service. The holistic approach enables the leisure professional to have a broader perspective of the persons whom he or she is serving. By conceptualizing the needs of an individual while considering all of the aspects of his or her existence, the professional is better able to understand and meet the needs of the individuals. The holistic approach to anthropology emphasizes the relationships and interdependency of all factors of a person's experience and existence, culturally and biologically. Consideration of and application of this approach to the leisure field enables the professional to serve the individual in the most effective manner possible.

Psychology

Psychology can be useful to the leisure programmer in terms of helping him or her understand human motives, identify and appraise the leisure interests and abilities of the customers he or she serves, and to personally benefit through self-knowledge. It is difficult, if not impossible, to adequately define psychology or its sub-fields (such as clinical, experimental, social, and developmental psychology) as one usually defines and breaks down an area of study. Psychology has roots that have sprung from numerous sources, intertwining with one another to form the field as a whole. Basically, psychology is concerned with the behavior of humans.

Perhaps psychology more than the other behavioral sciences has the potential for enriching the process of providing leisure services by helping the leisure professional understand people's needs. Many areas within psychology can provide the professional with information to assist him or her in the role of manager, supervisor, face-to-face leader, therapeutic recreation

specialist, or leisure program planner. For example, the process of learning, which has been studied in-depth by psychologists, affects every aspect of human existence—including leisure behavior. The knowledge and skills that are needed in order to engage in a leisure activity (such as a game) are learned. The values or attitudinal components associated with the game are also learned. The process of learning illustrates the difficulty that arises in trying to view psychological processes separately. The learning process is not complete without consideration of the factors of motivation and performance. Learning will not take place in the absence of a motivation.

Motivation can be thought of as an inner drive or state that occurs in behavior that is directed toward a goal. Motivation, as previously indicated, interacts with other psychological processes such as learning. The basic motivation cycle can be thought of as: need → drive → goal. *Need* can be best thought of in terms of deficiency. When an individual has a physiological or psychological imbalance, needs are created. It is known that children seek activity that is self-stimulating. Therefore, a need will be present when the child is in an environment that does not provide adequate stimulation, and he or she will seek to meet that need. A *drive* can be defined as "deficiency with direction." It is the heart of the motivational process. For example, when an individual is lonely, his or her need (for an "unlonely" state) is translated into a drive for interaction and companionship with others. *Goals* are placed at the end of the motivational cycle. Attainment of one's goal provides a reduction or alleviation of needs and drives, thus completing the motivational cycle. Again, the goals of the individual striving to diminish loneliness will be accomplished when he or she interacts with friends. The motivational cycle can be extremely simple or complex, depending on the needs, drives, and goals involved.

Learning and motivation are just two of the many areas of interest within psychology. Even a brief discussion of the major areas of psychology and the specializations within them would be too lengthy for the purposes of this text. However, some of the areas of psychology applicable to development and delivery of leisure programs and services are listed here. For example, the face-to-face leader, the program supervisor, and the leisure service manager could all achieve a greater understanding of the needs of customers by acquiring knowledge in such areas as developmental psychology, social psychology, and learning and motivation. The professional involved in management might find such areas of study as organizational psychology, personnel psychology, and motivation particularly useful in dealing with the members of his or her organization in a productive manner. The individual involved in the area of therapeutic recreation would, of course, benefit from the areas of study already mentioned in regard to the supervisor and the face-to-face leader (developmental psychology, social psychology, learning, and motivation). He or she might also gain insight into the needs of the participants through such courses as psychological aspects of disability, motivation problems in rehabilitation, and abnormal psychology.

Sociology

Sociology is the study of human society and social behavior. More specifically, sociologists focus on groups, institutions, and social organizations in their scientific investigation. They seek to understand society, social systems, norms of behavior, customs, roles, and patterns of change in order to better understand the social behavior of man. Sociological investigation can be classified into several specific study areas—for example, group behavior, differentiations within societies, trends in demography, collective behavior, institutions, and social change. The study of leisure in a sociological context can take place within any of these primary areas of study. Sociologists, when selecting an area for investigation, usually specialize in one problem or content area (like

leisure) and choose one specific aspect of, or approach to, the content area. For example, a sociologist might focus on the leisure behavior of individuals in institutions. Following is a brief discussion of each of these six areas of study and their application to the leisure field where applicable.

Group behavior   Although in North American society we emphasize individual behavior, the interaction that takes place within groups is man's primary vehicle for social existence. The group is the most influential social unit in terms of behavior; one's personality and basic attitudes toward life are to a large extent determined by association with groups. Family, peer groups, work associates, and religious affiliations, for example, are very powerful influences on behavior.

The study of groups is important to the study of leisure behavior, since it is in group situations that leisure opportunities often occur. Sociologically, there are two types of groups—primary and secondary. *Primary* groups are characterized by a feeling of personal involvement—e.g., family, schoolmates, and friends. *Secondary* groups are more formal and less intimate than primary groups. These groups may include teachers, service providers, work and business associates, and social and community groups and organizations. The feeling of anonymity is often associated with secondary groups. More and more, today, secondary groups are dominating our lives. Because leisure-oriented groups often take on the characteristics of primary groups, they offer primary group experiences for many individuals who exist mostly in secondary settings—for example, those working in large corporations or living in highly populated urban areas.

Differences and variations   Another area of sociological study is that which concerns the differences existing between groups within society. In discussing the differences between groups, the two most common areas investigated by the sociologist are (1) the variations of groups through social stratification, and (2) the variations in lifestyle and opportunities for development among societal groups from different ethnic, racial, and social backgrounds. The social stratification of groups involves the classification of individuals according to status levels, roles, and social classes. There is considerable debate over the validity of the social class system within society. North American society is an open class society in which individuals occupy different levels according to ability and merit. In other words, an individual has the opportunity to be ranked in the social system (social status) based on his or her knowledge, skills, and ability.

Sociologists are also interested in studying differences that occur between ethnic and racial groups. They investigate differences between peoples as they relate to development or adaptation within the environment. Of interest to the leisure professional are the phenomena of prejudice and discrimination against social, racial, and ethnic groups. Prejudice occurs when one group of people feels that it is superior to another group; the result is discrimination. A humanistic philosophy, as it relates to the delivery of leisure services, cannot be practiced where prejudice and discrimination occur. If we are to recognize the worth and dignity of each individual whom we serve, we will plan to meet the needs of all individuals regardless of their status, race, or sex. The study of social stratifications can aid the recreation and leisure professional in determining the best course of action to encourage humanistic values in his or her organization.

Demography   Sociologically, the study of demography centers upon the investigation of populations in regard to size and the groups that they encompass, as well as the changes and distribution of populations. The study of demography can assist the leisure professional in planning for the future, enabling him or her to foresee shifts in population and other demographic variables

that may affect the scope of services to be offered. He or she also should be aware of the distribution of populations in the area being served. Certain areas will, of course, require more facilities and programs than others. The organization's services should be geared to the types of groups within the area being served, in order to provide meaningful leisure experiences for them.

Collective behavior   Collective behavior may be described as the mass actions that occur within a society. This type of behavior is usually very spontaneous and rapidly changing. Fads, social movements, and demonstrations are all forms of collective behavior. The term collective behavior can be used to describe the actions of the masses before those actions lead to changes in behaviors and social practices.

Two forms of collective behavior that are relevant here are mass culture and mass leisure. *Mass culture* (as distinguished from high culture—the culture of the elite) is simply the culture of the majority. It is often based on the mass media and the concepts and products these media disseminate. *Mass leisure* refers to the leisure activities typically engaged in by the mass of society—that is, the activities most often sought and desired by the largest number of individuals. A knowledge of mass leisure trends can serve the professional as an indication of the activities that might be desirable to the individuals he or she serves and of the trends that are likely to become "needs" to his or her consumers. However, the professional must be aware that mass culture and leisure may not always reflect the needs of his or her participants.

Institutions   Within all societies, there exists a demand to respond to the most widespread needs of people in a standardized way. In order to do this, societies create institutions. The study of institutions forms another important area of sociological investigation. An institution comes into being when a society directs its attention toward a particular issue or set of values. For example, in the late 1800s and early 1900s—when the welfare of children became of greater public concern—one result was the creation of local public playground departments, which provided clean and healthy play environments for children. At the national level, the concern for preserving unique environmental areas within the United States resulted in the creation of the National Park Service. These are examples of institutions that were created in response to society's belief that the issues and values involved demanded governed patterns of social action. There is an interrelatedness between society and its institutions—they necessarily affect one another. Society determines the issues and values of sufficient importance to demand the creation of institutions; however, once the institution is an entity, it may well have considerable influence over the behavior of members of society.

Social change   The last area of sociological investigation to be considered here is that of social change. The accelerated rate at which change takes place in today's society requires people to be flexible and have the ability to adjust. Sociologists study groups, institutions, and other social organizations in order to determine how they affect and are affected by change. In the study of social change, the sociologist focuses on factors that influence change and resistance to change. Among the factors that influence change are those which are within human control and those, such as physical calamity and weather, which are not. Factors that are subject to the control of society are such things as inventions and the diffusion of knowledge within a culture or between cultures. Inventions should be thought of in very general terms. They not only encompass scientific technological advancements but also involve the creation of new social ideas.

Individuals and groups are not always in favor of new ideas and technological changes. They may actively or passively oppose such innovations—in order words, they demonstrate a *resistance to*

change. Resistance to change occurs because of two reasons: (1) people are uncertain as to the effect that the change will have upon their lifestyle; and (2) habit conditions the individual to follow a predetermined behavioral response. Since leisure is a by-product of technological innovation, resistance to leisure-oriented values is a societal concern. The leisure professional not only must be cognizant of the changing environment but also must act as an agent or facilitator of social change among those he or she serves. By studying social change as it relates to the phenomenon of leisure (from a sociological perspective), the professional may be better equipped to guide participants into situations involving change.

Lifespan Variables

Leisure service customers include individuals across the whole lifespan—from infancy to old age. The knowledge/understanding that the leisure service provider has about various age groups and cohorts in our society is crucial to the provision of programs and activities to meet the leisure needs and interests of our society. Behavioral scientists for generations have studied the human being to determine how individuals develop and function as they do. Because the field of leisure services must know as much as possible about individuals and groups of individuals, it is necessary to focus on the whole lifespan of human beings.

The sub-discipline of developmental psychology, which focuses on lifespan development, examines and investigates a broad range of *factors that influence the development of human beings*. Included as areas of study are physiology, genetic inheritance, psychosocial history, education, religion, family, home, community, socioeconomic status, and culture, as well as other disciplines. Figure 4.2 is an illustration of the determinants that influence human growth and development. While the three ''conventional'' areas of investigation—physiological,

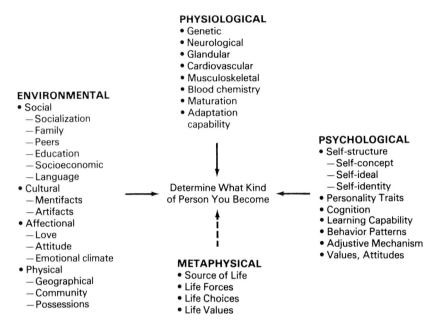

PHYSIOLOGICAL
• Genetic
• Neurological
• Glandular
• Cardiovascular
• Musculoskeletal
• Blood chemistry
• Maturation
• Adaptation
  capability

ENVIRONMENTAL
• Social
  —Socialization
  —Family
  —Peers
  —Education
  —Socioeconomic
  —Language
• Cultural
  —Mentifacts
  —Artifacts
• Affectional
  —Love
  —Attitude
  —Emotional climate
• Physical
  —Geographical
  —Community
  —Possessions

PSYCHOLOGICAL
• Self-structure
  —Self-concept
  —Self-ideal
  —Self-identity
• Personality Traits
• Cognition
• Learning Capability
• Behavior Patterns
• Adjustive Mechanism
• Values, Attitudes

Determine What Kind
of Person You Become

METAPHYSICAL
• Source of Life
• Life Forces
• Life Choices
• Life Values

Figure 4.2   Determinants of Human Growth and Development. (Kaluger & Kaluger.)

psychological, and environmental—are described, the area of metaphysical study is also included. The philosophical area of metaphysics is generally more speculative in scientific research than the other areas of focus. It is included in this figure to acknowledge "the possibility of the existence of principles that underlie the study of the nature of humankind and its place in the universal scheme of things" (Kaluger and Kaluger 1984: 70).

Developmental psychologists suggest that neither people nor their behavior remains constant. Throughout the lifespan, individuals change from year to year, from month to month, and even from day to day. Developmental psychology attempts to explore lifelong changes. Unlike child and/or adolescent development, or adult psychology, the developmental scientist examines the entire life cycle. Kaluger and Kaluger (1984: 2) indicate that "as life advances and experiences increase, both internal and external phases of behavior and growth change constantly." Traditionally, attention has been strongly focused on the growth and development of the young (chil-

dren and youth). However, only "one-fourth of an individual's life is spent growing up. Three-fourths of a person's life is spent in adulthood, growing older" (Kaluger and Kaluger 1984: 473). Therefore, the importance for the leisure service professional to focus on the human lifespan is evident.

Human development is a multi-faceted experience. It is the integration of age-graded internal biological (physiological) and psychological processes, with external social (environmental) influences that occur for cohorts (generational groups). Knowledge and understanding about both internal development and maturation, and external experiential differences, are important to the leisure service professional for needs identification and assessment, program development, and the delivery of leisure activities and services to the leisure customer.

Age-Related Phases

Table 4.1 illustrates a chronological approach to human development. It should be especially noted that developmental scientists Kaluger and

Kaluger (1984) and Turner and Helms (1983) focus on the several life stages of adulthood as well as the earlier stages of life from infancy to adolescence. In presenting theories of human development, previous behaviorists examined stages of life from infancy to adulthood (Freud 1917; Sullivan 1947, 1953) with no differentiation of adulthood ages. Havighurst (1972) examined human development from infancy to adulthood, but not specifically beyond sixty years of age (Table 4.2). Chronological age is only one measure of maturation. Turner and Helms (1983) have noted, as chronological age increases, age becomes a poorer criterion to use for comparative development.

Aging (the passage of years through all of life) involves developmental changes in definitive areas of life. Table 4.3 summarizes a multifaceted approach to human development. Physical development, mental development, and personality and social development by the individual integrates varied stages of growth and development. Developmental traits provide a basis for leisure program planners in designing leisure experiences. Program planning can be enhanced when the leisure service professional understands age-group characteristics in relation to human behavior (Table 4.4).

TABLE 4.1 Human Development: A Chronological Approach

Life Stage[1]	Age Approximations	Life Stage[2]	Approximate Time Period*
I. Prenatal		1. Prenatal period	Conception to birth
Conception	—	2. Infancy	Generally the first 2 years
Zygote	7 to 10 days	3. Toddlerhood	of life
Embryo	10 days to week 8	4. Early childhood	2–3 years of age
Fetus	Week 8 to birth	5. Middle childhood	Generally 3 or 4 to about
			age 5
II. Infancy*			Either 6–9 or 6–12,
Neonate	First 2 weeks		depending upon the usage of
Infant	To 2 years		the terms ''late childhood'' or
			''preadolescence''
III. Childhood		6. Adolescence	Generally the teenage
Early	3 to 5 years		years (13–19)
Middle	6 to 8 years	7. Young adulthood	19–30
Late	9 to 11 years	8. Middle adulthood	30–50 or 60
		9. Later adulthood	50 or 60–75
IV. Adolescence		10. Old age	75+
Early	12 to 15 years		
Middle-late	16 to 18 years		
Emerging adulthood	19 to 21–23 years		
V. Adulthood			
Early adulthood	23 to 40–45 years		
Middle adulthood	43 to 60–65 years		
Early old age	65 to 75–80 years		
Late old age	80 and over		

*As the individual matures, chronological age becomes a progressively poorer criterion to use.
[1]From Kaluger and Kaluger (1984).
[2]Time and Life stage. From Turner and Helms (1979).

TABLE 4.2 Theories of Human Development

Stage/Age	Birren (1964)	Bromley (1963)	Erikson (1963)	Havighurst (1972)	Peck (1968)	Freud (1917)	Sullivan (1947, 1953)
Prenatal	—	Zygote Embryo Fetus	—	"Developmental tasks"	—	—	—
Infancy	2	18 months	Basic trust vs. mistrust (0–1) Autonomy vs. shame, doubt (1–2)	(0–5, 6)	—	Oral (0–18 mos.)	Birth to articulate speech
Preschool to early childhood	(2–5)	(18 mos.–5 yrs.)	Initiative vs. guilt (3–5)	(0–5, 6)	—	Anal (18 mos.) –3 yrs) Phalic (3–5)	Childhood (2–6)
Middle childhood	(5–12)	Elementary (5–11 or 13)	Industry vs. inferiority (6–puberty)	(5 or 6 to 12 or 13)	—	Latency (5–12)	Juvenile (6–8½)
Preadolescence	—	—	—	—	—	—	Preadolescence (8½–11)
Adolescence	(12–17)	Puberty and jr. h.s. (11–16) Late adolescence (15–21)	Identity vs. role confusion (adolescence)	(12 or 13 to 18)	—	Genital (puberty)	Early adolescence Late adolescence
Early adulthood	Early maturity (17–25)	(21–25)	Intimacy vs. isolation	(18–35)	Adjustment tasks Valuing wisdom vs. valuing physical powers Socializing vs. sexualizing	Adulthood	Adulthood
Middle adulthood	Maturity (25–50)	(25–40)	Generativity vs. stagnation	(35–36)	Cathectic (emotional) flexibility vs. cathectic impoverishment Mental flexibility vs. mental rigidity	—	—

TABLE 4.2   Theories of Human Development—*Continued*

Stage/Age	Birren (1964)	Bromley (1963)	Erikson (1963)	Havighurst (1972)	Peck (1968)	Freud (1917)	Sullivan (1947, 1953)
Late adulthood	Later maturity (50–75)	(40–60)	Ego integrity vs. despair	(60+)	Ego differentiation vs. work-role preoccupation Body transcendence vs. body preoccupation	—	—
Old age	(75 and over)	(70 and over, then senescence)	—	—	Ego transcendence vs. ego preoccupation	—	—

Table from *Lifespan Development* by J. S. Turner and D. B. Helms, © 1979 by Saunders College Publishing, a division of Holt, Rinehart and Winston, Inc. reprinted by permission of the publisher.

TABLE 4.3   Multi-faceted Human Development

	Physical Development	Mental Development	Personality and Social Development
Infancy & Toddlerhood	Rate of physical growth is most rapid during first three years of life Physiological maturation which allows performance of tasks, i.e. locomotion, grasping, coordinated hand-eye movement and dominant handedness.	Cognitive abilities begin to be developed—thinking, perceiving and understanding. Beginning of sensorimotor skills—reaction, mental images, objects. Developmental patterns of speech and language.	Emotions emerging—fear, anxiety, and later anger and frustration. Prefer solitary activity (play) begin to investigate their environment.
Early Childhood	By fifth year birth length is doubled and birth weight has increased by five times. Muscular growth and development results in coordination abilities and gains in small and large motor skill activities.	Thought is characterized by ego-centrism/self-centeredness. Cognitive abilities develop in relation to people, objects, events. Language acquisition enables multi-word sentences and construction of ideas.	Self-concepts develop through interaction with family and peer groups. Expression of emotions verbally—resentment, anger; displays of jealousy, sometimes sibling rivalry. Activity becomes more socially oriented; active play, imitation, imaginary companions.
Middle Childhood	Advancement in motor-skill abilities—large-muscle movement and refined coordination. Sense of physical self and awareness of bodily changes in efficiency of varied motor skills.	Emerging intuitive thought and comprehension; organization of information and problem solving. Advancement in language skills; developing ability to understand and adapt to environment.	Interaction with peers influences socialization. Emerging self-image, self-esteem, sex-role identification. Emotional maturity evolving, influenced by the individual's personality.

TABLE 4.3 Multi-faceted Human Development—*Continued*

	Physical Development	Mental Development	Personality and Social Development
Adolescence	Pronounced growth spurt is experienced as children enter puberty. Maturation of primary sex characteristics. Continuing development of motor skill and coordination	Intellectual growth; past learning experiences contribute to higher-level thought processes. Cognitive advancement includes the ability to apply reasoning and exercise insight.	Struggle to attain satisfying sense of identity. Factors influencing self-concept include value system, standards of conduct and sexual identity. Desire for individuality and independence. Peer group becomes important agent of socialization.
Young Adulthood	Physical growth and development virtually completed. With maturation gradual declines begin to occur—height, fatty tissue, sense of hearing, sense of sight.	Intellectual maturity reaches a high level of function, both quantitative and qualitative. Mental ability is maintained throughout life, but is influenced by intellectual function and individual idiosyncrasies.	Emotional security, extension of self, relating warmly to others, realistic perceptions and establishing a philosophy of life. Adults learn to overcome irrational childhood notions and parental dependencies.
Middle Adulthood	Modest decline of physical abilities and noticeable bodily changes. Changes in sensory capacities. Some behavioral changes in both men and women.	Continued use and stimulation of intellect maintains adequate function. Ability to draw upon previous experience demonstrates wisdom.	Stability of adult characteristics. Acceptance of self and others. Interest in striving for self-actualization. (In all areas: physical, mental and social development there is the influence of the "mid-life crisis.")
Later Adulthood	Metabolic changes and slow down in physiological processes. Older adults have the same diseases as younger age groups, but recovery may be slower or may not occur. Decrease in efficiency of sensory function in hearing and vision.	General knowledge and vocabulary tend to remain constant. Long-term memory remains constant with some change in short-term memory. (Individual variations in memory exist throughout the life cycle.)	Successful aging appears to be satisfactory psychological (inner) and socially oriented (outer) adjustment. Variety in personality type influences adjustment to old age.
Old Age	Life's final developmental change—facing death. Death can and does occur at any age, but elderly people are more aware of its imminence.	Fear of the unknown. Sorrow from losses.	Loneliness. Sometimes loss of identity.

Adapted from Turner and Helms (1983).

Included on page 102 are projected population figures for 1995 (Figure 4.3) that indicate to the leisure professional the potential configuration of age groups in the population. The United States has an aging population. In other words, it is projected that in 1995, approximately 74 percent of the population in the United States will be over the age of eighteen and nearly 6 percent of the population will be over the age of seventy-five, which is the average of life expectancy for both males and females. The number of males under the age of eighteen will

TABLE 4.4 Age-related Human Behavior

Group	Age	Characteristic
Preschool	Under 4	Dependent on others, short attention span, self-centered, major motor development, and desire for immediate reward.
Primary	5–7	Developing social relations and additional motor skills, imagination and exuberance, develops self-control, and becomes industrious.
Intermediate	8–12	Perseverance, diligence, and competency develop; play is serious business.
Early Adolescence	13–15	Rapid physical growth, onset of puberty, sometimes awkward, and self-conscious.
Youth	16–19	Develops individual identity, discovers talents. Strong likes and dislikes, group memberships, sets goals, and strives for independence.
Young Adult	20–29	Seeks meaningful relationships, makes commitments, career choices, and uses a variety of recreation activities in the courtship ritual, may pursue outdoor and risk activities to test competency.
Adult Years	30–49	Major productive years, child-rearing responsibilities and other social obligations. Looks to recreation for activity, diversion, status, and autonomy.
Pre-retirement Adult	50–64	Reduction of intensity of some needs, generally secure, enjoys social outings, provides leadership in social-spiritual-civic and volunteer organizations.
Early Retirement	65–79	Recreation often replaces work as reason for being. Can be active or passive, depending on health. General physical decline and more difficult to stimulate.
Later Maturity	Over 80	Contingent upon health, can be a rewarding but semi passive way of life. Research has revealed that those who prepare for retirement and later maturity can prevent the despair associated with the loss of independence, isolation, and a lonely wait for death.

From Patterson (1984).

be slightly higher than the number of females; however, over the age of sixty-five there will be substantially more females in the population than there are males.

Traditionally in the leisure service field there has been much emphasis put on the planning and provision of services for children and youth. In addition to continuing to serve the young age groups in the population, leisure service organizations must enlarge their focus to meet the needs of adult population groups to a much greater extent. The leisure service provider must have comprehensive knowledge about demographic factors (described in this chapter), to be familiar with the interests, levels of health, financial abilities, family structures, cultural diversity, personality differences, and gender expectations of leisure customers in order to attempt to understand their leisure behavior and meet their needs.

Cohorts

A cohort is a group of *individuals who were born in the same time interval* (a range of five, seven, or ten years) and therefore share the same major experiences throughout their lives. Cohorts are faced with specific sets of life conditions during important and impressionable periods in their lives. In other words, cohorts (generational groups) have lived during the same time period and have experienced the same historical, social, economic, and political conditions during their lifespan.

Basic value creation is influenced and formed in early life. Primary influences on value development include family, friends, school, religion, and geographic place of residence, among other factors. By the age of four, an individual's basic personality is developed. Up to the age of seven is the time of *imprinting*. The human influences

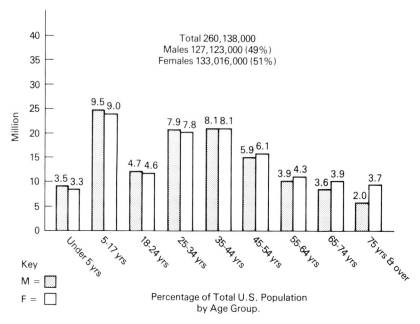

Figure 4.3 Projected Population in the United States in 1995. (From Statistical Abstracts of the United States (1989), Washington, D.C.: U.S. Government Printing Office.)

and the life events that have occurred have imprinted on and are a permanent part of that individual. Early formation of values, modeling, or exhibiting behaviors, matures during the ages of eight to thirteen. The values that were earlier imprinted may at this point be evident in the person's behavior and lifestyle. Socialization, being with others and seeking the approval of others for individual behavior, occurs during the teen years, fourteen to twenty. By the time an individual reaches twenty years of age, his or her value system is strongly in place.

Cohort groups also experience personal life events—starting school, graduating from high school or college, finding a job and beginning a career, getting married, raising a family, reaching retirement—at about the same time. Focus on cohort groups infers that major specific societal, cultural, and personal experiences have affected and influenced the lives and development of the individuals in the group in a unique way, as compared to other cohort groups (Table 4.5).

Adult cohort values often are reflected in orientation to social structure, perception of political process, attitude toward the work place, preference of lifestyle, and in leisure needs and choices of leisure activities. What is "good," "right," and/or "normal" is different for different cohorts. Interests in specific areas of leisure programming or choices of particular activity formats are related to cohort values. Although a cohort seems to express common interests, which is important to the leisure professional, leisure service providers must remember that groups are made up of individuals, and individuals may differ in personal interests and leisure preferences.

Differences among individuals within a cohort result from individual experiences. Major events that occur in a person's life, whether they are labeled life change units (LCU) or significant emotional experiences (SEE) (Table 4.6), may occur with greater frequency for some individuals than for others. When these events do occur for individuals it makes them different from others in their cohort. Experiential differences, individual intelligence, temperament and personality, social class, cultural influence, level of education, job and income, and racial and ethnic differences all contribute to forming the individuals who are our leisure service customers.

Demographics

The leisure phenomenon is extremely complex. Murphy, et al. (1973: 85) observed that " . . . the reasons for different individual expressions of (leisure) behavior are interrelated and exceedingly complex." It is necessary for the leisure service provider to examine individual behavior in relation to a variety of factors. Differences such as *age; gender; personality; education, occupation and income; race and national identity; health; and marital status and family* are several of the factors that have an impact on an individual's lifestyle and leisure behavior.

Age   As has been described previously in this chapter, primary influences related to age are physiological and psychological as well as social. Physiological characteristics include fine and gross motor skills, coordination, endurance, and level of acquired skill. These factors influence participation for individuals of all ages. Physical skills develop at varying rates across the lifespan and begin to decline as the person grows older. In addition, psychological development is related to age. The desire to function alone in activities as young children changes to the ability to be involved in cooperative activities and competition. Choice of leisure activity based on age is also influenced by the cohort that the individual is a part of and by the social and cultural expectations that exist.

Gender   Individuals become "socialized" by the society in which they live. In other words, certain expectations of leisure activity choices and behaviors are anticipated based on gender. However, in recent years, the differences have decreased and the involvement in similar leisure activities by both males and females (at all ages)

is expected and accepted. For example, sport competition (individual, dual, and team) is available for both sexes, co-ed leisure activities are accessible, and the creative arts and high-risk activities are pursued by both sexes.

Personality   Who we are influences what we do. Personality is an expression of interests, values, and capabilities. Personality is affected by personal variables such as age, gender, education, and others. Within an individual's personality are the components that indicate preference for structure or spontaneity in life activities, active or passive behavior, aggressiveness and interest in competition or preference for vicarious involvement, or cautious preference for familiar activities instead of interest in high-risk challenges.

Education, occupation, income   Generally accepted is the suggestion that the higher the level of education an individual has, the broader the base of leisure knowledge, skills, and experiences he or she has. As level of education increases, the opportunity for exposure to a broader range of opportunities and activities exists. Educational level is closely related to *occupation* and *income*. The kind of occupation and thus the potential for income are both influenced by the educational experiences an individual has had. Further, cultural expectations exist in relation to some occupations. Specific leisure activity choices may be anticipated or expected of individuals in particular occupational groups. Another variable that relates to occupation and leisure is the time factors that persons in different occupational groups must deal with. Self-employed and professional workers may have long working hours, while individuals who work more specifically structured hours may have more discretionary time. Available personal income may either limit or allow leisure activity choices. Spending for leisure may require a significant amount of money to initiate an activity or it may be spread over a long period of time.

TABLE 4.5 Cohorts and Generational Events

Decades of Cohorts	Historical Events	Business and Technology	Social and Media Events	Music and Dancing	Famous People
Old Age 1900–1909	Turn of century Spanish-American War McKinley assassinated	Severe unemployment Trolley cars Model T Ford Electric light bulb	First airplane flight First radio message First World Series Yellow fever epidemic	"Let Me Call You Sweetheart" "Home on the Range" "Sweet Adeline" The turkey trot	William McKinley Teddy Roosevelt W. H. Taft Henry Ford Orville and Wilbur Wright Charlie Chaplin Carrie Nation Isadora Duncan
Later adulthood 1910–1919	First woman in Congress World War I Communism started	Federal income tax Telephone invented Vitamins discovered Use of electricity	Panama Canal opens Halley's comet Titanic sinks	"Alexander's Ragtime Band" "When Irish Eyes Are Smiling" "Over There" The fox-trot	Susan B. Anthony W. H. Taft Woodrow Wilson Thomas Edison Buffalo Bill Cody Jack Dempsey Jane Addams Emma Goldman
1920–1929	Prohibition Act Harding's Teapot Dome Scandal League of Nations	Child labor laws Oil replacing coal Mechanical cotton picker Wall Street collapse	Bootlegging Lindbergh's Atlantic flight Empire State Building	Vaudeville "Yes, We Have No Bananas" "Old Man River" The Charleston	Woodrow Wilson Warren Harding Calvin Coolidge Herbert Hoover Babe Ruth Andrew Carnegie Margaret Sanger
Middle adulthood 1930–1949	Great Depression New Deal Social Security Act	Bank panic WPA—public works Color movies	Amelia Earhart solo across the Atlantic John Dillinger: public enemy no. 1 Hindenburg explosion	WPA orchestras "Brother, Can You Spare a Dime?" "I've Got You Under My Skin" The big apple	New York Yankees Bing Crosby Mickey Mouse Babe Didrikson Greta Garbo Amelia Earhart
1940–1949	World War II United Nations GI Bill of Rights	Taft-Hartley Act 40-hour week First electric locomotive First atomic bomb	Pearl Harbor attack First black major league baseball player—Jackie Robinson Country of Israel	Big band sounds "In the Mood" "White Christmas" "When You Wish Upon a Star" Jitterbug	Franklin D. Roosevelt Harry Truman Winston Churchill Joseph Stalin Bob Hope Frank Sinatra Eleanor Roosevelt Katherine Hepburn Clare Booth Luce

Period					
Young adulthood 1950–1959	Korean War Cold war Truman fires MacArthur	Minimum wage 75¢ per hour AFL–CIO merger First earth-circling satellite Salk antipolio vaccine	Racial segregation banned School desegregation Development of television Two monkeys in space	Hit Parade "Rock Around the Clock" "My Fair Lady" Twist; rock and roll Elvis Presley	Harry Truman Dwight Eisenhower George Meany Grace Kelly Perry Como Rosa Parks Julius & Ethel Rosenberg Marilyn Monroe
1960–1969	Civil Rights Act Assassinations of J. F. Kennedy Robert Kennedy Martin Luther King, Jr. Vietnam War	Minimum wage $1.25 per hour Affluent economy Men on the moon Birth-control pill	Fifty-star flag Beatniks, hippies, Woodstock Student demonstrations Drug culture	Beatles "Hello, Dolly" "Moon River" Rock	J. F. Kennedy Lyndon Johnson Richard Nixon Warren Burger Martin Luther King, Jr. Neil Armstrong Golda Meir Jackie Kennedy Martha Graham Rachel Carson Diane Arbus
Adolescence 1970–1979	End of Vietnam War Watergate scandal 18-year-olds vote Israel-Egypt accord	Minimum wage $2.65 Oil embargo Inflation increases Test-tube baby	Nixon resigns Women's lib Two popes die within 40 days.	Rolling Stones Country-western Punk rock Disco dancing "You Light Up My Life"	Richard Nixon Gerald Ford Jimmy Carter Muhammad Ali Hank Aaron Pittsburgh Steelers Gloria Steinem Billie Jean King Barbara Walters Patty Hearst
Children Early 1980's	Hostage crisis in Iran President Reagan shot Israel-PLO war in Lebanon	Major recession Energy crunch subsides Inflation slows down Industry and business in transition Artificial heart	Prince Charles marries Princess Grace dies Home computers are big items E.T.: The Extra-Terrestial Star Wars series	Rock subsiding Country rock Barry Manilow Dolly Parton Flashdance "Gloria" Michael Jackson	Ronald Reagan Pope John Paul Sally Ride Jesse Jackson John McEnroe Jane Pauley Geraldine Ferraro Christa McAuliffe
Preschool Mid 80's into the 90's	Challenger disaster US miliary action in Panama Fall of Berlin wall Operation Desert Storm	Acid rain VCR's Minimum wage $4.25 Professional baseball salaries Nintendo	"Batman" "Teenage Mutant Ninja Turtles" Children in daycare outside of the home	Rap music "Dirty Dancing" MTV	George Bush Mikhail Gorbachev San Francisco 49ers Norman Schwarzkopf Madonna Boris Yeltsin

*Cohort differences are influenced by the major events that occurred during significant periods in a person's life.
Adapted from Kaluger and Kaluger (1984).

TABLE 4.6 Life Change Units (LCU)

Events	Scale of Impact (LCU)	Events	Scale of Impact (LCU)
Death of spouse	100	Son or daughter leaving home	29
Divorce	73	Trouble with in-laws	29
Marital separation	65	Outstanding personal achievement	28
Jail term	63	Spouse begins or stops work	26
Death of close family member	63	Begin or end school	26
Personal injury or illness	53	Change in living conditions	25
Marriage	50	Revision of personal habits	24
Fired from work	47	Trouble with boss	23
Marital reconciliation	45	Change in work hours or conditions	20
Retirement	45	Change in residence	20
Change in health of family member	44	Change in schools	20
Pregnancy	40	Change in recreation	19
Sex difficulties	39	Change in church activities	19
Gain in new family member	39	Change in social activities	18
Business readjustment	39	Mortgage or loan less than $10,000	17
Change in financial state	38	Change in sleeping habits	16
Death of close friend	37	Change in number of family get-togethers	15
Change to different line of work	36		
Change in number of arguments with spouse	35	Change in eating habits	15
		Vacation	13
Mortgage over $10,000	31	Christmas	12
Foreclosure of mortgage or loan	30	Minor violations of the law	11
Change in responsibilities at work	29		

Modified from Holmes, T. H., and Rahe, R. H. Published with permission from *Journal of Psychosomatic Research, II,* The social readjustment rating scale, © 1967, Pergamon Press, Ltd.
From Kaluger and Kaluger (1984).

Choices of expenditures for leisure may be influenced strongly by the individual's personal survival needs.

Race and national identity Preservation of cultural heritage may be a strong influence on leisure choices made by individuals. Cultural attitudes in relation to social behaviors, competition, performing arts, and ethnic practices may pervade the involvement by minority groups in the general leisure activities of the community. Previous opportunities and experiences by groups of people in the general society will affect the leisure attitudes and behaviors demonstrated by those individuals.

Health The overall health condition of individuals at any age will limit or allow leisure activity involvement. Pursuit of leisure activities may also contribute to the continuing good health of the leisure customer. However, therapeutic in-

volvement in leisure activities can be an avenue to improving health conditions. On the other hand, onset of health problems may contribute to the necessity for individuals to change their leisure behaviors and lifestyle.

Marital status and family The home and family are the earliest influence on an individual's leisure choices and behavior. The structure of the family determines the opportunities for leisure involvement for both children and adults in the family unit. In society today, acknowledgment must be made of couples, couples with children, single individuals, single parents with children, extended families, and other living arrangements and family structures that people have. It is significant within the context of family today that greater numbers of children, youth, and older adults are with caregivers outside of the home for greater periods of time than they are within the family unit. Family unit activities, as well as independent activities for individual family members, impact the leisure service delivery system in the community.

Place of residence and mobility   Single family dwellings, high-rise apartment buildings, condominiums, and other kinds of residential living, influence the accessibility to leisure programs and facilities for leisure customers. The distance, traffic arteries, and availability and modes of transportation have a definite impact on the ability of customers to use leisure services. The primary means of "public transportation" in our society for many urban and rural residents alike is the private car. It is obvious that some groups of leisure customers are more affected by place of residence and mobility than others. These groups include children, young teens, individuals with special needs and disabilities, and older adults who have never driven a car or those who are no longer driving.

Leisure Behavior

As this chapter has discussed, lifespan leisure behavior is affected by numerous social and cultural forces, social agents (other people), and individual experiences. Iso-Ahola (1980) conceptualized the development of leisure behavior as shown in Figure 4.4, which he has labeled the "process of leisure socialization." The figure illustrates the interaction of components that contribute to overall leisure behavior.

The leisure activity skills needed by the leisure customer, across the lifespan, have been articulated in the "leisure skill assessment" offered by Navar (1980). By designing programs that contribute to developing the following competencies, the leisure service provider will contribute to the physical, mental, and social well-being of the leisure customers being served.

1. Physical skill that can be done alone.
2. Physical skill that can be done with others regardless of skill level.
3. Physical skill that requires the participation of one or more others.

4. Activity dependent on some aspect of the outdoor environment.
5. Physical skill not considered seasonal.
6. Physical skill with carry-over value for later years.
7. Physical skill with carry-over opportunity that is vigorous enough for cardiovascular fitness.
8. Mental skill participated in alone.
9. Mental skill requiring one or more others.
10. Appreciation skill or interest area which allows for emotional or mental stimulation through observation or passive response.
11. Skill which enables creative construction or self-expression through sound or visual media.
12. Skill which enables the enjoyment or improvement of the home environment.
13. Physical or mental skill which enables participation in a predominantly social situation.
14. Development of leadership or interpersonal skill which enables community service.

The source of leisure behavior is both intrinsic and extrinsic. Leisure behavior is influenced by the leisure competencies that an individual possesses and is encouraged by the availability of leisure activities and facilities. The variety of specific behaviors that leisure customers exhibit have been described by Murphy, et al. (1973). The following is a synopsis of a broad range of these behaviors.

1. *Socializing Behavior*—relating to others in a social experience in a social environment.
2. *Associative Behavior*—gathering people around a common interest, sometimes in a formal structure like a club group.
3. *Acquisitive Behavior*—interest and participation in acquiring or collecting things, such as a hobby.
4. *Competitive Behavior*—within a structured set of rules and cooperative team work; interest in continuing to improve level of personal skill.
5. *Testing Behavior*—competition against the natural environment; mental activities of problem solving.
6. *Risk-Taking Behavior*—individual measures the risk and assumes reasonable chance of success and/or safety.
7. *Explorative Behavior*—discovering new environments or rediscovering past adventure; involvement may be highly active or intensely passive.

Process of Leisure Socialization

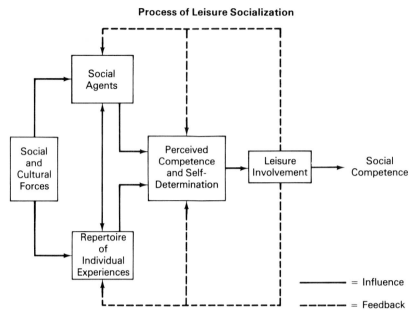

Figure 4.4   Development of Leisure Behavior. (Iso-Ahola, S. (1980), 132.)

8. *Vicarious Behavior*—involvement via viewing the participation, performances, or works of others.
9. *Sensory Stimulation*—experiences of intense sensory stimulation or manipulation of feeling, hearing, vision, or physical or emotional reaction.
10. *Physical Expression*—physical activities which emphasize personal expression without emphasis on competition.
11. *Creative Behavior*—creative expression through the arts and literature.
12. *Appreciative Behavior*—responding to the outcomes of creative behavior—your own or someone else's; response to the natural environment; aesthetics.
13. *Variety-Seeking Behavior*—diversion; a change from the normal routine, responsibility and involvement.
14. *Anticipatory and Recollective Behaviors*—participation includes planning and recalling in addition to actual involvement in an experience.
15. *Altruistic Behavior*—demonstration of concern for others results in satisfaction and pleasure.
16. *Spiritual Expression*—communion with others; expression of personal faith.

From the statistical description of leisure activity choices given in Table 4.7 and Table 4.8 one may conclude that several leisure behaviors can influence participation. Involvement in physical recreation and exercise activities can be related to physical expression, variety-seeking behavior, risk-taking behavior, testing behavior, or explorative behavior. On the other hand, a leisure customer's choice of arts performances and leisure activities may be related to socializing behavior, vicarious behavior, variety-seeking behavior or appreciative behavior. Several kinds of leisure behavior may be intrinsic in each leisure activity a leisure customer chooses. Although an individual may often select participation for one reason (i.e., competition, creative expression, or sensory stimulation) other behaviors are inherent in activity.

Summary

The relationship that is established between the leisure service provider and the person receiving the services is often reflected in the "label" that

TABLE 4.7 Adult Participation in Physical Recreation and Exercise Activities, 1987

Percent of population 18 years old and over who participated in each activity at least once in the previous 12 months.

Activity (Total Population)	Percent	Activity (Males)	Percent	Activity (Females)	Percent
Swimming	41	Swimming	43	Swimming	40
Bicycling	31	Fishing	42	Bicycling	32
Fishing	30	Bicycling	29	Aerobics, dancercize	24
Bowling	23	Pool, billiards	28	Bowling	23
Hiking	22	Basketball	26	Hiking	21
Camping	21	Weight training	26	Fishing	20
Weight training	20	Softball	25	Camping	19
Pool, billiards	19	Camping	24	Calisthenics	17
Softball	19	Hiking	24	Jogging, running	15
Jogging, running	17	Bowling	23	Volleyball	15
				Weight training	15

Statistical Abstracts of the United States 1989.

TABLE 4.8 Adult Participation in Leisure Activities and Arts Performances, 1985

Percent of population 18 years and over who participated in each activity at least once in the previous 12 months.

Activity (Total Population)	Percent	Activity (Males)	Percent	Activity (Females)	Percent
Reading (novels, short stories, poetry, or plays)	56	Reading (novels, short stories, poetry, or plays)	48	Reading (novels, short stories, poetry, or plays)	63
Visiting (art museums or galleries)	22	Visiting (art museums or galleries)	21	Visiting (art museums or gallery)	23
Attending Musical Plays	17	Attending Musical Plays	15	Attending Musical Plays	19
Attending Classical Music Performance	13	Attending Classical Musical Performance		Attending Musical Performance	14
Plays	12	Plays	11	Plays	12
Attending Jazz Performance	10	Attending Jazz Performance	10	Attending Jazz Performance	9
Attending Ballet Performance	4	Attending Ballet Performance	3	Attending Ballet Performance	5
Attending Opera Performance	3	Attending Opera Performance	2	Attending Opera Performance	3

Statistical Abstracts of the United States 1989.

is attached to the individuals being served. Some of the more common labels that are used in the leisure service field include participant, patron, customer, client, member, user, visitor, guest, and consumer. The label that is used may infer the level of dependence or independence, the expected patterns of communication, or the acknowledgement of expertise of both the leisure service provider and the person being served. The use of labels should not be taken lightly because it has a significant impact on how we view ourselves and others and on the assumptions and expectations made of each other.

Leisure customer decision making is influenced by three variables described in marketing literature as involvement, differentiation, and time pressure. Involvement describes the extent to which an individual finds relevance and interest in a particular leisure activity or leisure service. Differentiation relates to the multiple leisure opportunities that may be available from which the individual must choose. The third variable, time pressure, influences leisure choices based on both location and convenience of activities or services. Understanding leisure customer behavior across the lifespan is basic to successful leisure programming.

Individual differences based on life span variables, which include age, gender, cohort, leisure skills, leisure behaviors, and others, are the factors that the leisure service professional must consider when developing leisure programs and services. Leisure service customers include individuals across the whole lifespan and their leisure behavior has been influenced by individual experiences and social and cultural forces. The personal leisure interests, personal leisure skills, and personal leisure preferences of individual leisure customers determine the leisure behaviors that they exhibit.

Discussion Questions and Exercises

1. Discuss the physiological, psychological, and environmental determinants of human growth and development.

2. Examine the labels given to the persons for whom leisure services are designed. Describe the relationship between the leisure service professional and the person receiving the leisure service, that is inferred by each label—client, customer, guest, member, participant, patron, user, and visitor.

3. Leisure customer decision making may be influenced by three variables—involvement, differentiation, and time pressure. Describe how each of these may have an impact on leisure activity choices.

4. What is meant by a person being part of a cohort? Discuss the factors that influence generational differences among groups of people.

5. Demographics is a method of studying social factors that can be categorized. Discuss the way in which each of the following factors may have an impact on individual and/or group leisure behavior: age; gender; personality; education, occupation and income; race and national identity; health; marital status and family; and place of residence and mobility.

6. Describe the leisure activity skills needed by an individual that will contribute to the physical, mental, and social well-being of that individual.

7. Murphy, et al. described several leisure behaviors that may be exihibited by leisure customers through involvement in leisure activities. Discuss these behaviors and relate the behaviors to specific activities.

8. Discuss how changes throughout the lifespan have an impact on leisure behavior.

9. Interview at least two individuals in at least two different age cohort groups to determine how they approach their leisure.

10. Discuss the process of leisure socialization. What are some of the factors that may influence the way a person is socialized in their leisure?

References

Bammel, G. and L. Burrus-Bammel. 1982. *Leisure and human behavior.* Dubuque, IA: Wm. C. Brown.

Iso-Ahola, S. E. 1980. *The social psychology of leisure and recreation.* Dubuque, IA: Wm. C. Brown.

Kaluger, G. and M. F. Kaluger. 1984. *Human development: The span of life.* 3rd ed. St. Louis: Times Mirror/Mosby College Publishing.

Murphy, J. F., J. G. Williams, E. W. Niepoth, and P. O. Brown. 1973. *Leisure service delivery system: A modern perspective.* Philadelphia: Lea & Febiger.

Navar, N. 1980. A rationale for leisure skill assessment with handicapped adults. *Therapeutic Recreation Journal* 14(4): 21–28.

Patterson, F. C. 1987. *A systems approach to recreation programming.* Prospect Heights, IL: Waveland Press, Inc.

Rossman, J. R. 1989. *Recreation programming: Designing leisure experiences.* Champaign, IL: Sagamore Publishing.

Statistical abstracts of the United States. 1989. Washington, D.C.: U.S. Government Printing Office.

Stoll and Wheeler. 1989. Leisure service program development. Term paper, University of Oregon.

Turner, J. S. and D. B. Helms. 1979. *Lifespan development.* Philadelphia: W. B. Saunders Company.

Turner, J. S. and D. B. Helms. 1983. *Lifespan developments.* 2nd ed. New York: Holt, Rinehart and Winston.

5 | Needs Identification and Assessment

Learning Objectives

1. To help the reader understand the *process of needs identification.*
2. To help the reader gain knowledge of the *processes involved in needs assessment.*
3. To help the reader gain an awareness of the *differences between needs, wants, values, and attitudes.*
4. To provide the reader with specific information about *tools and techniques for needs assessment* that are available to the leisure service professional.
5. To help the reader gain an understanding of *need typologies.*
6. To provide *specific examples of needs identification and needs assessment tools.*

Introduction

Needs identification and assessment focuses on understanding the individual and collective behavior of the customers whom the leisure service professional serves. Through needs identification and assessment, the leisure service professional can become aware of people's interests, opinions, attitudes, habits, desires, and knowledge regarding recreation and leisure.

What people need and what they want can vary greatly. Perhaps a needs identification for recreation and leisure planning may result in the listing of more wants than needs. Wants are usually closely related to what people are knowledgeable about or things with which they are familiar. It is often easier for a person to express a desire for a specific skill or activity than it is to express or acknowledge a need for socializaion, novelty, or any enjoyment for which the activity is a means to an and—not the end in itself.

Needs identification involves the determination of habit patterns, especially those concerned with individual leisure lifestyle. In other words, what does a person do during his or her leisure time? What recreation facilities do individuals use—or, perhaps even more important, what don't they use? When and how often do they use them? In what organizations does a person have a membership? When does the person take a vacation?

Needs identification may be used to evaluate other factors relative to the delivery of leisure services and to determine the answers to such questions as: "What is the quality of leadership that exists?" "What facilities are available?" "What is the quality of maintenance and development of these facilities?" Identification and assessment of needs can reveal factors relating to both the customer (assessee) and the leisure service provider (assessor). When identifying needs, the leisure service provider must also be very cognizant of the varied base of the existing leisure opportunities and services available to the individual and to society in general in any given community.

Figure 5.1 proposes a set of categories of evaluative questions that can be used in the needs identification and needs assessment process. These are pro-active questions; that is, they are questions and considerations that must be reviewed prior to program design and implementation. In general, these questions ask: Who is to be served? What strategies should be used? How are programs and services to be organized and implemented? and, What results are to be achieved? The corollary to this approach of identification and assessment of needs is found in chapter 13. Figure 13.1 deals with evaluative questions such as: Were the strategies appropriate? Were the program elements configured correctly? and, What results were achieved?

Basic Concepts

When we speak of leisure needs, wants, and desires, it may appear to be easy to define these terms. However, understanding the differences among each of these concepts may in fact be complex and require close examination. In this chapter we will focus on the concepts of needs identification and needs assessment. These two terms, while seemingly the same, also have different meanings and carry different implications in terms of leisure service program planning and development. There are six basic concepts or terms that can be useful in developing strategies to plan programs more effectively, under the generic heading of "needs." These are: (1) *needs*, (2) *wants*, (3) *values*, (4) *attitudes*, (5) *needs identification*, and (6) *needs assessment*. Brief definitions of each of these concepts follows.

Needs

Needs can be thought of as a *physical, psychological,* or *social imbalance.* As Edginton and Ford (1985) have noted,

> When an individual has an imbalance—physically, psychologically, or socially—he or she has a need. Physiological needs are those deficiencies associated with biological drives, such as the

Categories of Needs Identification and Assessment Questions

Purpose	Goals	Strategies	Program Elements	Results
To Aid Decision Making	Who is to be served? What are their needs? What problems have to be solved if the needs are to be met? What funds are available for work in this area? What research findings have a bearing on problem solving in this area? What relevant technology is available? What alternative goals might be chosen?	Are the given objectives stated operationally? Is their accomplishment feasible? What relevant strategies exist? What alternative strategies can be developed? What are the potential costs and benefits of the competing strategies? What are the operating characteristics of the competing strategies? How compatible are the competing strategies with the system? How feasible are the competing strategies?	What is the schedule of activities? What are the personnel assignments? What's the program budget? What potential problems attend the design? What are the discrepancies between the design and the operations? What design changes are needed? What changes in implementation are needed?	What results will be achieved? Will they be congruent with the objectives? Will there be any negative side effects? Will there be any positive side effects? Do the results suggest that the goals, designs, or process should be modified? Do the results suggest that the project will be a success?

Figure 5.1 A Matrix for Identifying and Analyzing Evaluation Questions. (Stufflebeam, D. L. (1974). *Meta-Evaluation*, Kalamazoo, MI: The Evaluation Center: Western Michigan University, 18.)

need for food, water, sex, and sleep. Physiological needs reflect the desire of individuals to maintain an internal equilibrium. Psychological and social needs are more difficult to assess, but equally important. The need for companionship, social interaction, safety, love, self-esteem, self-worth, self-actualization, recognition, power, and achievement are all examples of psychological needs (Edginton and Ford 1985: 75).

In other words, needs reflect the discrepancy between the "ideal" state physically, psychologically, and socially, and the current condition of the individual and the environment within which he or she is functioning. We all have needs; we all act on these needs; and movement toward alleviating these deficiencies propels human behavior. Just as an individual has a "need state," so do communities, regions, nations, and whole societies.

It has been stated that play is a universal need. People have the need to play regardless of their social status, age, or psychological or physiological state. As George Bernard Shaw has written regarding play and age, "Man does not cease to play because he grows old—he grows old because he ceases to play." Another way of looking at need is that it is a state that is desired or necessary. A need occurs when something is lacking in one's life. Leisure needs occur when people lack the opportunity for play, access to leisure spaces, freedom, and the opportunity to choose, hence to experience leisure.

Wants

To want something is to desire it or to wish for it. Thus, we can think of a want as *something that is perceived* as being needed. Wants can be differentiated from needs in that they are desired by the individual, but not necessarily to sustain life. Wants are often based on an individual's previous experience and knowledge, whereas a need may be influenced more by an individual's physical demands. When a person expresses a "want" to participate in a particular leisure activity, he or she is expressing a preference or desire for engagement in an activity that he or she perceives will be beneficial. However, wanting to participate in an activity and actually having that experience meet a need are two different conditions.

Values

A value can be thought of as a *principle standard of quality that an individual, community, or society considers to be worthwhile*. We all make value judgments about our leisure preferences and experiences. These value judgments help us discern the relative worth of a leisure experience. Values can be thought of as assumptions that we make about what is or what ought to be.

People place strong values on their leisure pursuits. One's values related to leisure are often tied to status that is placed on a leisure experience. In addition, the value that a person places on a leisure experience often triggers an emotional response concerning its relative worth. Examples of ways in which people attach value to a leisure experience include how much they are willing to pay in relationship to the service they receive; the location of the experience that they choose (skiing in Aspen, surfing in Hawaii, or vacationing at Club Med in Mexico); and the types of people (socioeconomic status) that select the same leisure opportunity.

Values are difficult to measure. Although one can ask an individual what he or she values, it is often easier to draw conclusions from the way people act. Leisure values are an important factor to measure and/or study in the needs identification and assessment process. They represent an individual's psychological state and reflect psychographic (lifestyle) information that can be useful in the program planning process.

Attitude

An attitude is a *feeling or state of mind*. Leisure is often defined as a condition or state of mind. By understanding how people feel about their leisure, we can better understand what they would like to do during their leisure.

Leisure attitudes are more generalized in nature and much more complex than values. Attitudes can be thought of as a disposition to respond in a certain way. For example, individuals may hold the attitude that any form of participation in a leisure activity should be tolerated because it is an expression of freedom. To such individuals, freedom and individual license to engage in whatever behavior they see fit is synonymous with leisure. Contrary to this may be a prevailing societal value that certain restraints must be exercised in pursuit of one's leisure (e.g., off-road-vehicles should not have free access to all environments, but rather should be restricted to designated areas). As one can see, attitudes, like values, are emotionally charged, complex and sometimes not related to actual behavior or actions.

Needs Identification

Needs identification is a term used to describe the leisure service requirements that may exist in a given social or geographical area (Seigel et al. 1987: 71). Need identification strategies are designed to provide data that will enable program planners to determine the extent and kinds of needs in a specifically defined area. This process can be thought of as *a means of taking inventory of leisure wants, needs, behaviors, values, attitudes, and resources.* There are various ways to identify needs. We will discuss some of these later in the chapter.

The importance of the needs identification process is that it provides a basis for actual needs assessment. Before judgments can be made as to which needs and values should be addressed, and/or what leisure resources must be improved or created, one must know what the status or state of these variables is. The value of information collected in the needs identification process depends on its authenticity and reliability. The information must be as accurate and consistent as possible. In other words, every effort must be made to make sure that the information col-

lected accurately reflects the state of people's thinking and the status of resources that currently exist.

Needs Assessment

Needs assessment is the application of judgment to assess the significance of the information gathered in order to determine priorities for program planning and service development. In other words, once all of the relevant information has been collected, some *judgment is made as to the target groups to be addressed and the resources to be secured and delivered.* Further, the assessment process can be useful in making judgments on the continuance, the termination, or the development of programs and related resources.

What are some of the factors that can influence the assessment process? First, and perhaps most important, is the vision or mission of the organization itself. Although the needs identification process may uncover different needs, values, and attitudes, an organization may choose only to address those that are consistent with its mission. For example, a social welfare organization may differentiate its services and target more of its resources toward disadvantaged groups. A second factor is the availability of resources. It is important to realize that any leisure service organization must live within parameters or constraints. These parameters mandate careful descision making in the distribution of resources. Still another factor that may influence needs assessment is the broader community attitudes which may exist regarding the solving of the community problems. Even if a need exists and it appears to be a strong priority, it may be inappropriate because of prevailing social, political, or economic variables to create a viable program to meet the need. For example, think of the popularity of swimming in communities across North America. It is sometimes difficult to imagine that there are communities that do not have accessible swimming programs and/or facilities, because of the popularity of swimming.

Yet it may not always be feasible, based on the economic environment of a community, to decide to provide the needed swimming activities.

Although the needs identification process requires knowledge of a number of sophisticated strategies to collect information, it is in the assessment area that the professional expertise and judgment of a set of individuals comes into full play. It is one thing to have information available as a leisure program planner; however, it is another thing to know how to evaluate such information. It is still even more complex to organize information and subsequent judgments into an understandable and coherent plan that can be supported by the customers served by a leisure service organization. Judgments regarding the distribution of resources, directed at meeting needs, often require wisdom, experience, creativity, and vision. Further, once a course of action has been identified it often takes perseverance, determination, and drive to see that the program succeeds.

Making Assessments

What kinds of tools and techniques are available to the leisure service profession to engage in the needs assessment process? Most leisure service organizations use a combination of instruments in order to determine needs. It is often important to use a variety of instruments in order to produce different perspectives on needs. One instrument may be very useful at measuring one portion of a person's leisure needs, while another may provide a broader perspective of community needs.

Careful consideration should be given to the selection and development of the instruments used by a leisure service organization. If the instruments do not give an accurate measure (called *validity*) of the leisure deficiency being studied, or the instruments fail to give a consistent measure (called *reliability*) of the same phenomena, valuable organizational resources can be wasted.

Often the selection of inappropriate instrumentation results in the lack of correlation between the customer's needs and the services that the organization delivers to its customers. This problem can be a difficult one to remedy, not only because of the problem in selecting valid and reliable instrumentation, but also because of other variables. For example, a customer's understanding and willingness to participate in the needs assessment process can be a powerful factor in the success of the needs assessment process.

Most needs assessment processes engage a variety of approaches. Some of the common needs assessment procedures that can be employed in the leisure service field are *social indicators, social surveys, community group approaches,* and others. The following section describes these categories.

Social Indicators

Social indicators are quantitative measures that establish the need for a service. In other words, these types of measures involve *the development of standards and the correlation of the needs of a consumer group with these standards.* There are standards that have been established especially for determining needs in providing leisure facilities. For example, the National Recreation and Park Association (NRPA) and the federal government in the United States have developed documents that can be useful in helping communities determine facility availability and accessibility. Another approach that is often used in this area is the comparative approach. In other words, information can be collected from other leisure agencies or businesses and an analysis can be made to determine need.

Table 5.1 defines types and sources of social indicators that can have an impact on the delivery of leisure programs and services. There is a number of different types of information that can be collected in the needs assessment process. Normally this involves the use of what is known as secondary data—in other words, data that has

TABLE 5.1 Types and Sources of Social Indicators

Types	Sources
1. Standards	1. National organizations
2. Demographic information	2. State organizations
3. Socioeconomic variables	3. State and federal government
4. Health statistics	4. Census reports
5. Education trends	5. Government publications
6. Population density	6. Trade associations
7. Family characteristics	7. Political interest groups
8. Marriage patterns	8. Special interest groups
9. Housing characteristics	9. Religious organizations
10. Community participation	10. Futurist organizations and businesses
11. Delinquency rates	11. Others
12. Suicide rates	
13. Drug and alcohol use	
14. School dropout rates	
15. Others	

been gathered beforehand and not specifically for the expressed purposes of the current analysis. One might gather information from a variety of sources to shed light on a particular problem. For example, information might be gathered locally and then combined with other sets of data that have been obtained from national sources. The combination of these two approaches might yield insight and be useful in assessing need. There are many different types of information that can be collected or utilized. For example, knowledge of the amount of individual or family discretionary funds available could have an impact on the types of leisure activities that could be purchased by customers, or that might require a subsidy to insure access for customers. Some of the types of information that are often available include standards, demographic information, socioeconomic variables, health statistics, education trends, population density, family characteristics, housing characteristics, community participation, marriage patterns, delinquency rates, suicide rates, drug and alcohol use, school dropout rates, and others.

Much of this information is available from convenient and accessible sources. For example, census track data can be found at most public libraries. The federal government designates selected libraries throughout the United States which serve as repositories for government publications and documents. These are usually located in conjunction with major state colleges and universities. National organizations such as the National Recreation and Park Association (NRPA), the American Association for Leisure and Recreation (AALR), and the Canadian Parks/Recreation Association (CP/RA) all produce written documents that can be useful in the needs assessment process.

In recent years, futurist associations have provided composite information regarding social indicators in the leisure field. Such publications as *Leisure Watch* and *Leisure Industry Digest* provide summaries of leisure trends and expenditures in the leisure market. Trade associations such as Athletic Business and Recreation, Sports and Leisure often provide invaluable statistics concerning expenditures, trends and new developments in the leisure market. Other organizations including political interest groups, special interest groups, and religious organizations compile facts and figures in support of various issues and concerns they value. These types of organizations can be tapped. For example, the American Association of Retired Persons (AARP) annually produces a pamphlet entled *A Profile of Older Americans.* This document contains a wealth of information that has been researched and compiled by this organization and serves to illustrate the type of information available from special interest groups. A sample of the information is found in Figure 5.2.

Social Surveys

Social surveys are often used by leisure service organizations to assess need. Leisure service organizations use this strategy as a way of collecting information about individual and

Number of Persons 65 + : 1900 to 2030
Percentage of Total U.S. Population

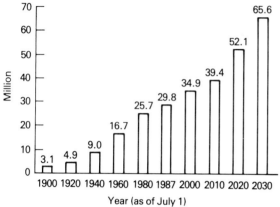

Year (as of July 1)

Note: Increments in years on horizontal scale are uneven.
Based on data from U.S. Bureau of the Census

Figure 5.2 Number of Persons 65 +
(1988). (*A Profile of Older Americans.*
Washington, DC: American Association of
Retired Persons.)

collective leisure preferences, opinions, and attitudes. Further, surveys provide *a method of collecting demographic information and provide the opportunity for correlation of such information with leisure preferences, etc.*

Information concerning expressed and felt desires can be translated into an analysis of a demand for leisure programs, services, and facilities. When we ask individuals to tell us what activities and facilities they currently participate in, and in which ones they would like to participate in the future, we are able to compare expression with the existing resources and forecast potential demand. Surveys can also be useful in providing the leisure service organization with information concerning the level and extent of services that a customer group might support. For example, in constructing questionnaires, we can determine whether or not taxpayers would be willing to support a referendum for facility

development or land acquisition. Still another example might be in the case of a youth serving agency asking its members whether or not they would support a membership fee increase. A leisure service business might want to survey its constituents in order to determine a need for expanded services.

Figure 5.3 outlines an eleven-step process used by the Bend (Oregon) Metro Park and Recreation District to conduct a needs assessment. The survey provided an opportunity for community involvement in the planning and decision-making processes of the district. Further, the study provided information useful to the Bend Metro Park and Recreation District Board of Directors and professional staff with empirically based information to assist in decision-making processes. Specifically, the survey involved the following goals.

1. Identification of the scope and depth of opportunities available for use for leisure in the public domain.
2. Identification of the activities in which individuals say they participate.
3. Identification of the activities individuals say that they currently do not participate in but would like to at some future date.
4. Identification of what additional leisure facilities and recreation and leisure programs should be developed by the Bend Metro Park and Recreation District.
5. Determination of what individuals believe is the present effectiveness and efficiency of the Bend Metro Park and Recreation District in providing services.
6. Determination of what factors influence initial and repeat participation in the services and facilities offered by the Bend Metro Park and Recreation District.
7. Identification and definition of barriers that prevent participation in services and facilities operated by the Bend Metro Park and Recreation District.
8. Identification of public opinions concerning future fiscal support for various programs and services of the Bend Metro Park and Recreation District.

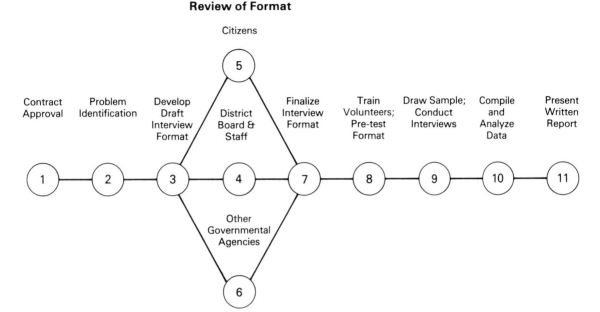

Figure 5.3 Format for Market Research. Bend (OR) Metro Park and Recreation District.

9. Identification of demographic information useful in predicting leisure behavior of District residents.
10. Identification of psychographic (lifestyle) variables useful in predicting leisure behavior of District residents.
11. Identification of the current time use of the residents of the Bend Metro Park and Recreation District with an eye toward understanding patterns of leisure time use.

The procedures employed in conducting this survey in Bend involved use of the personal interview format, conducted by telephone. A representative sample of the residents of the Bend Metro Park and Recreation District was drawn from the latest set of telephone directories, representing the telephone exchanges within the District. The number of telephone listings drawn from the entire population was done in a systematic fashion beginning at a random starting point. This was followed by the selection of every nth residential number listed. The total number of households selected was representative of the entire District population.

The interview format was developed by initially interviewing the professional staff, followed by discussions with:

1. The Bend Metro Park and Recreation District Board of Directors.
2. Community groups and individuals.
3. Other public agencies (governmental).
4. Other interested parties.

The final format was approved by the Bend Metro Park and Recreation District Board of Directors as recommended by the professional staff and the consultants. Individuals conducting the telephone interviews were trained in appropriate telephone interview techniques. The survey and telephone interview techniques were pretested to ensure reliability and validity. The interview process took place during the span of two days. Callbacks were attempted to make contact or to complete an interview where necessary.

The final report that was presented included:

1. A summary statement of findings.
2. Discussion of the purposes and objectives of the study.
3. Discussion of the methodology employed, with attention to the representativeness of the sample.
4. Discussion of survey findings with summary tables, reporting statistical information such as frequency distributions, percentages, mean scores, and median scores.
5. Recommendations for review by the Bend Metro Park and Recreation Board of Directors and professional staff.

The appendices of this book contain information concerning the telephone interview survey. As one can see, there are a number of questions dealing with activity participation, barriers to activity and facility use, and questions concerning opinions about future developments.

There are some drawbacks to using surveys. Often individuals do not respond as they really think and feel. Further, surveys measure the attitudes, interests, and opinons of people at a particular moment or period of time. Changes are often apparent when programs and services are actually implemented. Another factor is that much of the information collected using a survey yields quantitative information. However, leisure is a qualitative experience and the commitment that people make to a particular leisure event varies in intensity and in turn influences their commitment. Nonetheless, surveys are a very valuable method used in the needs assessment process and virtually every leisure organization uses this procedure.

One of the more recent uses of the survey format in leisure service organizations is using surveys to measure customer satisfaction. The Williamalane Park and Recreation District (Springfield, Oregon) conducts telephone surveys on a quarterly basis to assess, among other things, levels of customer satisfaction. According to Dan Plaza, Superintendent of Parks and Recreation, "Gathering marketing intelligence is fundamental to our work in understanding customer needs. One of the important elements in the process of marketing is determining the extent to which we actually satisfy the needs of those that we serve. This is an important yard stick we use in measuring our success."

Community Group Approaches

North Americans have a strong tradition of being involved in decisions that influence their lives. From a historical perspective, town hall meetings were one of the earliest forms of participatory democracy. These public forums were built on the assumption that all members of the community should have an active voice and opportunity to influence community affairs. This tradition continues today in some communities. This is especially true in the Northeastern portion of the United States where the major community decisions are still made at town hall meetings.

In more recent years the strategies and techniques employed in soliciting community input have become less informal, more sophisticated, and more fully developed, planned, and organized. In fact, in North America today there are a myriad of approaches or strategies that can be used by leisure service professionals to solicit and identify the ideas, opinions, and values of a community. The great value of many of these types of strategies is that they *provide community members or customer groupings with an active opportunity to express their opinions, to make their needs known, and to be involved in decision-making and planning processes.*

Generally speaking there are five community group approaches that have been identified in the literature. These are: *community forums, focus groups, nominal group technique, Delphi technique,* and *community impressions approach.* The following is a discussion of each of these strategies and their application in leisure service organizations.

Community forums   A community forum can be thought of as an open meeting. Although community forums may be called for discussion on a wide variety of topics or subjects, they also can be called to discuss specific projects, services, or problems that may warrant attention. In general, community forums allow for the expression of opinions by community members, customer groups, or groups with special concerns. In fact, community forums provide opportunities for unattached or unaffiliated citizens to express their viewpoints.

A community forum is usually called by the leisure service organization requiring input from customers. The role of the leisure service professional is to listen while at the same time communicating necessary information concerning proposed or existing projects, services, and programs. Most community forums involve a lively exchange with a free-flowing expression of opinions and ideas. Community forums that are misused often result in individuals feeling that they have been manipulated or used as pawns in order to induce customer acceptance of the work of professionals or politicians. On the other hand, community forums can provide an opportunity for coalition building and the development of a greater awareness of the projects, programs, and services of an organization.

Focus groups   Customer focus groups are another way of soliciting input concerning needs and wants. Such groups are established to provide a method of gauging customer reaction to a wide variety of concerns. Not only do focus groups have the ability to provide information concerning the types of services that may be desired, but they also can be valuable in assisting the leisure services professional in finding ways to promote activities, determine the prices, and assist in other areas related to program design and implementation. Further, customer focus groups can be a source of information about competitive services. Customer focus groups can alert the professional to changes that may be occurring in the marketplace and thus enable a leisure service organization to continue to maintain its competitive and/or cooperative activities.

One of the advantages of focus groups as opposed to other ways of collecting information about customers is that they can be set up to operate on a continuous basis. Further, customer groups can be established to focus on specific programs or facilities that a leisure service organization might operate. Several groups may function simultaneously. For example, a voluntary leisure service organization may have focus groups that deal with such diverse program areas and management concerns as youth activities, health promotion programs, resident camps, product sales, and facility use.

There are a number of challenges in forming and holding focus groups together. First is the danger of bias creeping into the recommendations made by groups because they are not representative of the customers served. Another difficulty is maintaining continuous interest in the work of the group. Of course, this can be alleviated to a certain extent by making sure that the recommendations of the focus group are listened to and implemented; their input must have impact. Focus groups can also be costly to establish and maintain. It often takes time to gain the trust of individuals in order to ensure that the concerns of the customer are of primary importance. This requires time, energy, and human resources; in effect, there is a real cost to an organization.

Howard (1989: 18) noted recently that the use of focus groups was especially valuable in the management of fitness and health centers. According to Howard, " . . . focus groups can be incredibly insightful in showing how members are experiencing a fitness center. Focus groups typically consist of six to nine people and a moderator who asks questions and records answers . . . focus group members are less inhibited about speaking their minds if their group meets at some place other than the fitness center and the moderator is a neutral third party. . . ." Focus groups are a way of developing feedback from customers to monitor the work of a leisure service organization and/or a specific leisure program or service.

Nominal group technique   The nominal group technique procedure is a model approach to program planning and program development. Basically, the nominal group technique is *a non-interactive workshop which is designed to maximize creativity and productivity and to minimize the argumentative style of problem solving and competitive discussion* (Siegel et al. 1987: 90). This technique involves a systematic process for defining problems, identifying barriers, and determining solutions. The nominal group technique involves the following steps:

1. *Problem Identification*—The first step in the process involves determining the problem or problems to be resolved.
2. *Ranking*—The next step involves the ranking of problems. This enables discussion of a wide variety of issues.
3. *Response of Critical Reference Groups*—Critical reference groups in this final step include customers, experts, and organization professionals.

Nominal groups consisting of eight to ten individuals are posed questions and asked to respond with ideas. These ideas are recorded and displayed for review by the entire group. Usually this is done in a round robin fashion with each member of the group having the opportunity to offer one idea until all of their ideas have been recorded. No comments are made during this period; this is to encourage idea generation. Following this procedure, idea clarification is pur-

sued during a discussion period. Then each member of the group is asked to identify and rank the five most important ideas. This allows for the prioritization of concerns without a competitive modality. As Siegel et al. (1987: 90) notes, " . . . It allows each member time for reflection and thought. It encourages the generation of minority ideas; it avoids hidden agendas; it imposes a burden on all present to work and contribute and to have a sense of responsibility for the group; it facilitates creativity; it allows for the airing of personal concerns; and . . . it does not allow any one person or point of view to dominate."

Delphi techniqiue   The Delphi technique is another strategy that can be used by leisure service professionals to gather information about needs. This procedure *allows for systematic input of information on specific areas of focus*. The Delphi technique procedure is usually used in areas having an impact on broad policy formulation. It helps in the process of making value judgments where decisions require broader, more expansive thinking. Basically, the Delphi process provides a format for exploring questions and opinions and then summarizing information.

Siegel et al. (1987: 90) have written that the Delphi technique involves five steps. These steps are as follows:

1. *Identification of Key Issues*—The first step in the Delphi procedure is to develop a questionnaire that identifies the key issues.
2. *Panel Experts*—The next step in the process involves giving the questionnaire to key individuals to complete and return to the initiators of the process.
3. *Tally Results*—Results of the returned questionnaires are tallied to summarize areas of agreement and disagreement.
4. *Items of Disagreement*—The panel of experts receives a second questionnaire containing items of disagreement and the reasons for the initial judgments that were made.
5. *Repeat of Process*—The first four steps are repeated until an agreement can be reached.

A major advantage of using the Delphi technique is that it provides a systematic way of allowing input by individuals on specific issues. In addition, the Delphi process is useful because it is methodical in nature. In other words, it is a way of ordering the process by which information is gathered within an organization. It provides focus on a set of specific issues or concerns and enables an organization to derive responses or opinions to issues that have been identified. Another major reason that the Delphi technique is useful is that respondents can maintain their anonymity. In other words, the identification of a particular customer can be held in confidence. The value here is that individuals are presumed to respond more freely and openly when their identity is not known. Thus, the Delphi technique is a controlled way of garnering feedback on issues related to need.

There are some drawbacks in using the Delphi technique. The major drawback seems to be the fact that there are no specific guidelines in the use of the strategy. For example, how many times must questions be returned to respondents in order to develop the final focus? Another problem lies in maintaining the anonymity of the participants. Obviously, the individuals responding to the questionnaire will be known to some parties. In fact, the question could be asked, should the respondents be anonymous? Often, people working in tandem or groups operate creatively, producing synergistic solutions to problems and issues.

A prime example of the application of the Delphi technique in the leisure service field was a survey of customer opinion of the " . . . operation, needs, and future directions of the Parks and Recreation of the City of Lake Oswego, Oregon." The study was aimed at forecasting future plans and developments, as well as ascertaining attitudes regarding current operations. The Delphi technique was used as a method for arriving at concensus and determining priorities directly related to the future direction of the organization.

The method used in this procedure by the City of Lake Oswego involved several steps. Initially, a questionnaire was mailed to a group of respondents who remained anonymous to each other. These participants gave short opinion statements that were synthesized into a second questionnaire. The second questionnaire was sent to the respondents who then ranked all of the concerns, their own as well as the others, and this data was compiled to make a third questionnaire. The third questionnaire had the rankings from the previous survey and allowed the respondents a chance to amend their prior rankings. From this process emerged a concensus of the entire group surveyed. Before explaining the procedures undertaken, they were justified. The reasons for specific procedures relating to the overall technique were then more evident.

The Delphi technique has, in the past, been used most frequently in situations where professional groups or narrowly defined populations were asked to give advice hinging on their professional expertise. The researchers' efforts were an attempt to serve the same purpose in the City of Lake Oswego. These individual respondents had ideas that were especially important in establishing future plans.

One of the main features of the Delphi is its "democratic" quality. Without having to bring people together, the Delphi brings opinion together in the same way as New England town meetings did. It also creates an equality of individual opinion, allowing each respondent to have equal say. The method acts as a communication medium as well as a fact gathering instrument. Each participant has the opportunity to review the generalized opinions of others, becoming better informed and at the same time seeing his or her own separate ideas within the context of the larger group. The Delphi also has a practical virtue. The results gained constitute a very usable reflection of opinion, from which substantive conclusions may be drawn and suggestions can be made.

To better understand the process of the Delphi technique, an outline of the specific procedures of the study in the City of Lake Oswego follows.

Date(s)	Action
October 9	Initial study team visited the community. Coordinated study plan with City Manager and staff. Agreement signed.
October 18	Letter sent to twenty individuals whose names were provided by the City. Each person was invited to participate and provide ten names of knowledgeable and concerned citizens who might enjoy participating.
October 23–29	Follow-up phone calls to those among the twenty who had not responded. Research and preparation of FIRST Delphi questionnaire.
October 30	FIRST questionnaire sent to 119 citizens—list provided by City and the "Snowball Sample." The FIRST questionnaire was deliberately open-ended, seeking (1) areas of satisfaction and/or dissatisfaction, and (2) suggestions for changes, additions, and/or improvements for the Parks and Recreation Department. The FIRST survey was designed to provide an information base for the development of the SECOND questionnaire.
November 10–20	Continuous follow-up phone calls
November 20–24	Fifty-seven FIRST questionnaires returned. Each specific response catalogued in card file which became the reservoir of opinion from which the SECOND questionnaire was constructed. Opinion correlated into subject topics and specific concerns which formed the outline of the SECOND quesionnaire.
November 26	The SECOND questionnaire sent to fifty-seven respondents who agreed to participate. Respondents asked to rank both topics and more specific concerns within the three broad areas of administration, areas and facilities, and programs. A ranking did not necessarily imply endorsement but simply an order of priority. The SECOND questionnaire was as precise as possible, without sacrificing any of the concerns raised in responses gathered in the FIRST questionnaire.
December 5–10	Follow-up phone calls to those who had not returned the SECOND questionnaire.

December 13–16	Forty-eight SECOND questionnaires returned, of which forty-three were usable. Tabulation of data, establishing both average and rank-ordered priorities. From these rankings the THIRD questionnaire was developed.
December 17	THIRD questionnaire sent to same fifty-seven respondents as the SECOND questionnaire. The THIRD questionnaire gave the rankings of the SECOND and asked respondents to reevaluate their earlier opinions and rank them again.
December 30–31	Follow-up phone calls to those who had not returned the THIRD questionaire.
January 7–10	THIRD questionnaire tabulated. Organization of data collected.
January 10–13	Report writing.
January 16	Review final draft with City representatives.
January 20	Presentation of Final Report to City.

Community impressions approach The community impressions approach to identification and assessment of needs finds the leisure service professional working with specific groups that have been identified as having the greatest level of needs. It is a strategy that is *committed to involving a group in the process to help reduce its own need.* Often the community impression approach involves key members in the community who can speak on behalf of and/or represent effectively the group in need. Leisure service professionals using this approach find themselves in a proactive role reaching out to customer groups in order to help them solve their problems.

Community impression groups are often organized as Special Interest Groups. For example, a neighborhood association may already exist that can provide information on needs in a given geographic location. A sporting group, like a softball association, may provide a nucleus of a group that could provide input into decisions concerning facility development and/or utilization. Special interest groups often are very vocal in advocating that their needs be met. They can be well organized, politically sensitive, and astute

in promoting their own self-interest. On the other hand, these types of groups may lack political sophistication, financial resources, and organizational know-how. In other words, within a community, these special interest groups run the gamut in terms of their levels of complexity and effectiveness.

It has been suggested that this type of community group is less expensive than other approaches to assessing community needs. However, the community group approach often involves the use of highly trained facilitators and is not necessarily efficient from a time perspective. It is often difficult to solicit meaningful input from customer groups within a prescribed time limit. When limits are established it often prevents a thorough discussion of ideas, concepts, opinions, and/or needs. Other problems associated with the community group process can occur when groups are over- or underrepresented. For example a domineering group of individuals can force its perspective on others, even the majority, if it is not properly handled within the context of the group process chosen. Despite some of these limitations, the community group process is found throughout North

America today. Although this concept emerged in the public and voluntary sector, it is not unusual to find customer focus groups working with leisure services businesses in the commercial sector to improve their product and service lines and methods of distribution, as well as their procedures for interacting with the customer.

Other Strategies

Bullaro and Edginton (1986: 215–217), discussing commercial leisure services, have suggested that there are a number of methodologies that can be employed by commercial leisure service organizations in identifying and assessing leisure needs. They suggest that there are several simple, inexpensive, and effective strategies to collecting market-oriented information related to needs. The strategies they suggest are as follows:

1. *One-on-One, Face-to-Face Interviews*—Basically this approach involves talking to people one-on-one and listening to what they have to say. Bullaro and Edginton note that leisure service professionals can contact people who would subscribe to or buy their services, in order to ask questions and engage in brainstorming.
2. *Telephone Interviews*—Another procedure for collecting information is to sample potential customers using a telephone interview format.
3. *Direct-Mail Questionnaires*—Direct-mail questionnaires that do not take more than five minutes to complete are an effective way of gathering marketing information concerning needs.
4. *Combination Mail/Telephone Surveys*—This approach to gathering information consists of sending the customer a questionnaire in advance and then following it up with a phone call. The result is that the customer is able to become familiar with the questions being asked and therefore is less suspicious of the motive or intentions of the needs assessment effort.
5. *Primary or Secondary Data Sources*—Another way of gathering information on needs is to use primary or secondary data sources. Public libraries, government agencies, businesses, and trade associations are all useful sources, as previously mentioned in this chapter.

6. *Trade Shows*—Trade shows are a valuable way of testing the market. Trade shows attract people interested in particular kinds of products to meet their customers' needs. The potential of a given product or service can be gauged to some extent based on the reaction of individuals attending the trade show.

Need Typologies

Perhaps the most often cited theoretical construct pertaining to human needs is that of Abraham Maslow. Maslow (1943) has suggested that needs are hierarchically ordered. At the base of the hierarchy are the primary physiological needs of the human being (e.g., food, sex, shelter), and at the apex of the hierarchy are those needs that are related to the psychological factors of self-actualization (sense of pride, sense of achievement, and so on). Maslow's hierarchy of needs is diagrammed in Figure 5.4.

In terms of the conceptualization of leisure needs, there are a number of problems in the application of Maslow's hierarchy. The first of these problems has to do with the hierarchical ordering of needs. Such life factors as food, shelter, sex, recognition, and creativity are not, in reality, divided into sectors but are often overlapping and occur simultaneously—although proportionately, there will be differences between them. For example, a person may have to reach a certain level of existence to be generally "self-actualized"; however, an individual can have experiences of self-actualization at all levels of the hierarchy. A second problem in using the hierarchy is related to its application to leisure services. The identification of needs as set forth by Maslow does not give any indication of the way in which these needs are expressed. It is somewhat difficult to operationally define how needs come into existence. Are they expressed by the participant, or have they come into existence as a result of the professional's diagnosis of the deficiencies of the participant? Traditionally, the problem has not been in recognizing the type of needs that Maslow has identified but in applying the model in an operational sense. Withstanding

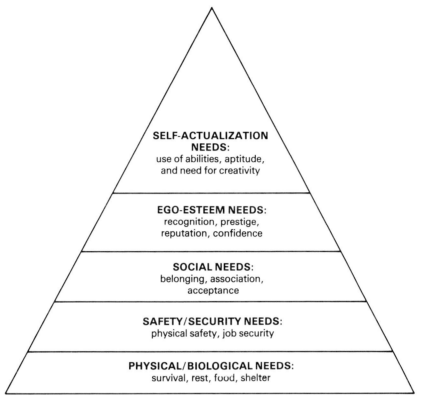

Figure 5.4 Maslow's Hierarchy of Needs.

these concerns, the hierarchy is obviously a useful way of identifying and categorizing the different types of needs that individuals have.

Another conceptual framework within which needs are identified is a holistic perspective. Figure 5.5 illustrates fundamental human needs as viewed in their integrated relationship to each other, in the five basic aspects of living: physical, emotional, social, intellectual, and spiritual (Brill 1973). Holistically, life is a dynamic process and therefore the needs and fulfillment of needs in each of these dimensions continually changes for every individual person.

Identification of need in each of these aspects as they relate to leisure is difficult for both the individual leisure service customer and the leisure service provider. The leisure service provider must be aware of the total individual and

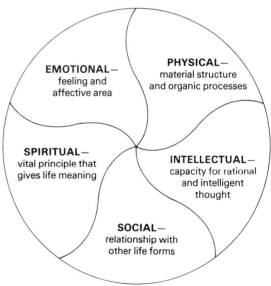

Figure 5.5 Total Man—the Continous, Dynamic Interaction of Five Vital Areas. (Brill (1973). *Working With People: The Helping Process.* J. P. Lippincott Company.)

attempt to facilitate opportunities for satisfaction at varying levels of development. It is also necessary for the leisure service provider to recognize and be sensitive to a large number of variables that have direct impact on individual needs. These variables include interests and abilities; wants, values, and attitudes; and gender, age, cultural background, and other factors.

A taxonomy of potential individual leisure expressions in these five aspects of living is given by Murphy and Howard (1977) in Table 5.2. This suggestion of perceived needs provides a base for creating leisure service environments that facilitate opportunities for fulfillment in all aspects of individual needs.

Bradshaw's (1972) conceptualization of needs is concerned with the opportunities and problems that arise in identifying different types of social needs. He suggests that there is more than one frame of reference or set of values that can be applied in the social service area and that the difficulty lies in making clear what is meant by a need. To alleviate this problem, he suggests that social needs be classified into four categories: *normative, felt, expressed,* and *comparative.*

Mercer (1973) and, later, Godbey (1976) and McAvoy (1977) have applied Bradshaw's con-

cepts of needs to recreation. According to Mercer, "The term 'need' is frequently encountered in the literature related to recreation research and planning, and yet only rarely is it defined with any degree of precision." Mercer's discussion was written to stimulate controversy and provide an exchange of ideas concerning needs. McAvoy (1977) used Bradshaw's and Mercer's ideas to discuss the relationship between the social taxonomy and the needs of the elderly. Both of these authors also suggest that the conceptualization of social needs must be translated into goals that can be measured. Godbey has expanded the number of classifications in the social needs model by adding a fifth category, *created* need. The five types of needs—*normative, felt, expressed, comparative,* and *created*—are discussed below.

Normative needs   According to Mercer, normative recreation needs can be defined as "more or less *precise and objective standards which are set up by experts* in various fields associated with recreation and leisure." In other words, normative needs represent value judgments that are made by professionals in the leisure service field (such as criteria for open space standards). There are

TABLE 5.2   Potential Recreation Outcomes

Physical	Psychological-Emotional	Social	Intellectual-Educational	Spiritual
relief of tension	anticipation	interpersonal relationships	mastery	ecstasy
relaxation	reflection	friendships	discovery	mind
exercise	challenge	trust	learning	expansion
motor skill development	accomplishment	companionship	insight	transcendence
rehabilitation	excitement	involvement	intensified skills	revelation
fitness	achievement	fellowship	new experience	release
coordination	aesthetic	communication	developing	contemplation
physical growth	appreciation	group and family unity	avocations	meditation
muscle tone	self-image	develop sense of	cultural awareness	wonderment
rejuvenation	introspection	community	learning about one's	
testing of body	security	compatibility	self-evaluation	
capabilities	pleasure	appreciation	synthesis	
	self-confidence	cultural sharing	problem solving	
	self-actualization	concern for others		
	enjoyment	belonging		
	exhilaration	interaction		
	self-expression			

Murphy and Howard (1977).

a number of standards used in the determination of normative needs, including the "desirable relationships between areas, population, user groups, time, distance, staff, sites, and so forth. . . ." These normative needs, stated as standards, are usually expressed in quantitative terms—for example, normative needs for park acreage in a community are usually expressed in terms of the amount of park acreage desirable per 1,000 population. For example, a community of 100,000 should have 1,000 acres of parkland.

The use of normative needs as a *single* determinant of need can be criticized on a number of points. First, the development of standards is usually based upon individual (or small group) value orientations. That is, the individuals involved in the determination of standards are influenced by such factors as their own socioeconomic status, cultural heritage, and so forth. As a result, these standards could not be applied, with any degree of validity, to the population as a whole. The next problem arises from the notion that services ought to be distributed equally throughout every community and neighborhood within each community. Different communities and neighborhoods may require different quantities and qualities of recreation and leisure services. All people do not have the same needs, desires, and interests; thus, the application of a universal set of standards can create problems.

In connection with the concern just discussed is the assumption that we can also define *normatively* the type of services that ought to be provided. Standards usually include the kinds of facilities that a public leisure service organization ought to provide (such as parks and playgrounds). Over-attention to these types of suggestions might preclude the possibility of meeting other types of needs that are not mentioned on the "normative" list.

Normative, by definition, refers to the standards that reflect the needs of the majority of the population. However, such a perspective may not reflect or cater to the needs of certain types of minority populations, such as the physically disabled. The Americans With Disabilities Act (ADA), 1990, is having a far-reaching impact on all human and leisure services, and facility and program accessibility. Until recently, government buildings (including many park and recreation facilities) did not allow for accessibility of the facility to the disabled.

Felt needs   Felt needs can be defined as the *desires that an individual has but has not yet expressed actively.* In other words, felt needs are based on what a person *thinks* he or she wants to do, rather than what he or she is actually doing or has done in the past. According to Mercer (1973), "Felt needs are, of course, very largely *learned* patterns. We generally want what we have become used to having" (p. 41). They are very often a reflection of the normative needs that have been defined by social agencies (e.g., governmental, leisure service organizations). Therefore, in many cases, felt needs are limited by the individual's knowledge and perception of available leisure service opportunities. However, mass communication has expanded the individual's potential for knowledge, perceptions, and experiences ordinarily outside his or her realm of existence. As a result, felt needs, on the one hand, are limited by an individual's perception of opportunities but, on the other hand, can be based on fantasy.

The concept of felt needs can be used by leisure service organizations in a number of ways. First, it enables the consumer to express his or her desire for those activities, programs, and services in which he or she would like to participate at some future time. This provides the leisure service organization with an indication of what the consumer would like to do, or plans to do, in the future. Such information can be useful in the planning, development, and distribution of resources within the decision-making framework of the leisure service organization.

Second, the use of the felt needs concept reduces the amount of cognitive dissonance that the participant experiences relative to his or her participation in organizational services. Cognitive dissonance may be broadly defined as two perceptions or pieces of information that have contradictory implications for one's behavior. In other words, if an individual has a desire to play tennis and instead is offered only other programs, he or she experiences cognitive dissonance. In such an instance, the participant will be motivated to alter the state of dissonance to one of cognitive harmony. Therefore, if an organization aligns its program services with the felt needs of the consumer, the cognitive dissonance of the consumer is reduced and, conversely, cognitive harmony is a likely outcome. According to Godbey (1976: 10), "Individuals will be happier participating in what they perceive they want to do during their leisure than they will if their leisure options are dictated to them by the professional."

The major limitation of using felt needs in a pure sense as the sole determinant of program services is that they are limited to the perceptual knowledge of the individual participant or participants. Another limitation of the utilization of felt needs as a guide to the distribution of resources is the fact that, from an idealistic standpoint, leisure service organizations would like to please everyone; however, from an organizational standpoint, the availability of resources limits the fulfillment of this idea.

Expressed needs   Those *activities in which individuals actually participate* are known as expressed needs. An individual playing, knitting, or swimming is engaged in the fulfillment of his or her needs. By actually participating in an activity, an individual provides the leisure service manager with knowledge as to his or her current leisure preferences, tastes, and interests. Expressed needs are felt needs "put into action." However, in order for an individual to express his or her needs, he or she must first be able to conceptualize what the needs are, and then visualize how

these needs might be fulfilled. For example, an older adult who is lonely and desirous of companionship may translate this feeling (felt need) into action (expressed need) by going to the senior center in his or her community.

If expressed needs are used as the sole determinant of an organization's planning process—hence, its distribution of resources—there are a number of problems that might occur. First, if programs and services are based on expressed needs (what people are doing), the practitioner precludes the initiation of new services and programs within his or her organization. There is an unstated faulty assumption on his or her part that the services presently available are meeting all of the needs of his or her consumer. However, the participants' behavior is limited by the specific programs that are available; their behavior must *necessarily* conform to the services that are offered. This presents a circular dilemma—the participants attend the services available, and the practitioner limits his services to the consumers' behavior; thus, the consumer continues to have his or her behavior defined and molded by the current service offerings of the leisure service organization. On the other hand, if an organization only provides activities that participants have previously attended, it will be certain of the reception that the offered programs and services will receive. Consequently, there will be little waste of resources or effectiveness. Efficiency—in regard to the *specific* programs attempted—will be maximized.

Comparative needs   Often *an individual or organization will compare itself with another individual or organization.* This may be done purely out of interest or curiosity, or it may serve to help the individual or organization identify deficiencies. When applying the same idea to program planning, this concept can be thought of as the *comparative* need approach to needs assessment in program development. The comparative need approach may be defined as a method whereby an organization compares the services it offers to a given population and the behavioral outcomes of these programs with similar populations and their services. In this way, an organization may be able to identify those areas in which it is deficient and can improve services to lessen such deficiencies. For example, a leisure service organization may want to improve services in order to overcome social or environmental dysfunctions in the community it serves. By comparing its program offerings with those of another community, which is effectively offsetting social problems, the leisure service organization may be able to identify services that could alleviate existing dysfunctions. Of course, the assumption here is that only communities with similar population characteristics will be compared. The comparative need process not only can be used to overcome dysfunctions, but it also can be viewed in a positive sense—enabling an organization to expose its population to beneficial experiences.

Another way to apply the comparative approach is to identify the differences in leisure experiences among groups in a community or neighborhood. For example, there may be differences in the services provided for special groups and those provided for the rest of the population. Assuming that people who fall within the categories known as "special groups" have the same rights to leisure services as others, an organization using the comparative need approach would be able to see the differences that occur in terms of services—and the results of those differences. The organization could then provide appropriate services to the individuals affected or could make special efforts to integrate them into existing programs in order that they might fulfill their leisure interests.

Care must be practiced when utilizing the comparative need method in needs assessment and program planning. It is faulty reasoning to assume that what works well in one situation will automatically be effective in another. Furthermore, it may be that the intensity of the service needed may vary a great deal among populations or groups within communities. Another problem to consider is the realty that each community may

not have the necessary resources to pursue the fulfillment of equal services. As a result, sometimes comparative needs assessment may serve as an ideal that communities may strive for rather than as an effective way of immediately dealing with dissimilarities that exist among population groups in communities.

Created needs Leisure service agencies and organizations exist to plan and offer programs to individuals in the community. These programs and services, as has been indicated throughout this section of the book, are based on several approaches to the identification of needs. Godbey (1976) has expanded on Bradshaw's taxonomy of social needs by adding a fifth need—*created need*. He suggests that the professional engaged in the program planning process must also consider the created need. The concept of created need implies the following:

> . . . Agencies can create leisure interests and values independent of what people do, [what] they want to do, or have supplied to them during their leisure. Created need refers to those recreation activities which [agencies and organizations have] . . . introduced to individuals in which they will subsequently participate at the expense of some activity in which they previously participated (Godbey 1976: 13).

In other words, created need refers to *those programs, services, and activities solely determined by the organization and accepted by the participant without question, desire, or prior knowledge.*

For example, a municipal park and recreation agency might initiate a day-care center for senior citizens (who live at home with their relatives), thereby creating a need in the community for such a service. Once the leisure service agency starts programs such as this, the community is awakened to a need heretofore unrealized; the community then will depend on the continuance of such programs.

The created needs approach to need assessment can be useful to the participant as well as to the organization as a method of defining needs. Many individuals are grateful to organizations for helping them identify an area of interest that they had not previously considered. In a sense, the approach is a form of leisure education that is an important component of many recreation and leisure service organization's philosophy. The organization also benefits by serving as an agency that creates opportunities for stimulation and enrichment. As a result, individuals may look to the organization as a vehicle for providing innovative experiences.

Implicit in the created need approach is the notion that the professional's knowledge is sacrosanct. It is wrong to assume that the professional is the only person with problem-solving abilities. The ability to deal with conflict and solve problems is distributed widely in our population—not just among professionals. It is important to recognize that the consumer also has the ability to diagnose his or her felt, expressed, and comparative needs. The professional should avoid using the created need approach at the expense of other approaches. As with the other approaches to need assessment, the created need method should be used in conjunction with all of the available tools for defining and interpreting need.

Summary

This chapter has focused on the concepts of needs identification and needs assessment. Understanding people's needs, wants, interests, values, and attitudes can have an impact on the provision of leisure programs and services. Needs identification is a term that describes the processes that leisure program planners use to de-

termine the extent and kinds of needs that are within a specifically defined social or geographical area. Needs assessment is the process of judging which of the needs will be addressed in a priority scheme within an organization. In other words, needs identification helps the leisure service professional understand what concerns must be addressed and needs assessment helps the professional prioritize their efforts.

There are a variety of different strategies that can be employed to make assessments. We usually think about making assessments by using a variety of different procedures and/or instruments. Some of the approaches that can be taken include identifying social indicators, using social surveys, and employment of several community group approaches including use of community forums, focus groups, nominal group techniques, Delphi technique, and community impressions approach. There are still other methodologies that can be applied, such as one-to-one interviews, telephone interviews, and direct-mail questionnaires.

There have been a variety of typologies developed to help understand needs. Perhaps the most consistently applied need typology is Maslow's hierarchy, which arranges needs from the most basic physiological needs to those factors dealing with the psychological needs of self-actualization. In the leisure service field, there have been a number of different frameworks or typologies developed to explain needs. Some of the categories include normative needs, felt needs, expressed needs, comparative needs, and created needs. Understanding these need typologies can be useful in helping identify consumer needs and responding with appropriate leisure services.

Discussion Questions and Exercises

1. Define needs identification.

2. Define needs assessment. How can you differentiate needs assessment from needs identification?

3. Define needs, wants, values, and attitudes.

4. How can social indicators be used in establishing the need for a service?

5. Organize a survey of a specific social grouping to determine its leisure needs. Develop a questionnaire similar to the one found in the Appendix.

6. What is a customer focus group? Identify how customer focus groups can be applied to the delivery of leisure services. Locate a focus group used in a leisure service organization, and describe its structure and operating procedures.

7. Compare and contrast the nominal group technique with the Delphi technique for assessing needs. Describe the conditions that would be favorable to the use of each of these strategies.

8. Discuss how Maslow's hierarchy of needs can be applied to understanding leisure behavior.

9. Discuss Mercer's typology of needs.

10. What are the limitations inherent in applying each of the categories of Mercer's typology of recreation needs?

References

AARP, 1988. A profile of older Americans. Washington, DC: American Association of Retired Persons.

Bradshaw, J. 1972. The concept of social need. *New Society* 19 (496):640–643.

Brill, A. 1973. *Working with people: The helping process.* Philadelphia: J. B. Lippincott Company.

Bullaro, J. J. and C. R. Edginton. 1986. *Commercial leisure service: Managing for profit, services and personal satisfaction.* New York: MacMillan Publishing Company.

Edginton, C. R. and D. M. Ford. 1985. *Leadership in recreation and leisure service organizations.* New York: Wiley.

Godbey, G. 1976. *Recreation and park planning: The exercise in values.* Paper presented at University of Waterloo, Waterloo Ontario (January).

Howard, D. R. 1989. Turning a member's bad experience into a good one. *Athletic Business* 13(13).

Maslow A. H. 1943. A theory of human motivation. *Psychological Review* (July): 370–396.

McAvoy, L. H. 1977. Needs of the elderly: An overview of research. *Parks and Recreation* 12(3):31–34, 55.

Mercer, D. 1973. The concept of recreation need. *Journal of Leisure Research* 5(1):37–50.

Murphy, J. F. and D. R. Howard. 1977. *Delivery of community leisure services: A holistic approach.* Philadelphia: Lea and Febiger.

Siegel, L. N., C. C. Attkisson, and L. G. Carson. 1987. Need identification and program planning in the community context. In Cox, F. M., J. L. Erlich, J. Rothman, and J. E. Tropman, eds. *Strategies of community development.* 4th ed. Itasca, IL: F. E. Peacock Publishers, Inc. pp. 71–97.

Stufflebeam, D. L. 1974. *Meta-Evaluation.* Kalamazoo, MI: The Evaluation Center: Western Michigan University.

6 | Establishing Direction: Developing Goals and Objectives

Learning Objectives

1. To provide the reader with information useful in *establishing direction within an organization.*
2. To help the reader gain *appreciation of the role that an organization's culture plays* in the provision of leisure services.
3. To help the reader understand the processes in *establishing vision and mission statements.*
4. To help the reader gain insight into the process of *establishing program goals and objectives,* including those related to program development, promotion and sales strategies, and financial strategies.
5. To provide the reader with information and strategies for *developing performance objectives* emphasizing desirable behaviors and levels of achievement.

Introduction

An important part of leisure programming involves the establishment of direction for the work of professionals. In a broad context, we can look at this on two levels. The first level is the direction that the organization establishes for itself overall. This broader philosophical direction will influence the types of programs and services an organization delivers, the target groups it serves, the benefits it promotes, and the values it encourages. The second level is the direction that is established for each individual program or service offered by the agency. We often refer to these types of direction statements as goals and objectives.

Why is it important for the leisure service programmer to have a grasp of the concepts related to the creation and maintenance of an organization's culture? As an employee within the organization the programmer must ensure that his or her goals and objectives are in line with those of the organization. Programs and services developed within an organization must reflect the broader intentions of the leisure service organization. Specific program goals and objectives must be related to and reflect the broader values of the organization.

Why is establishing direction for the work of a leisure service organization important? From an overall organizational perspective, the direction that an organization establishes helps define how its resources will be used. Also, an overall philosophical direction for an organization establishes the "culture" that exists within an organization. As Edginton (1987: 6) has noted, " . . . the culture of a leisure service organization may be the most powerful factor influencing its success or failure." An organization's culture may influence the work of employees, the quality of services, the transactions that take place with customers, and the image that it establishes with its public.

The culture of an organization may occur by happenstance or it may be planned and cultivated. Careful planning can produce desired organizational behaviors that result in superior levels of service, innovation, productivity, and positive public image. These are all hallmarks of successful organizations; organizations that are perceived as contributing in positive ways to society by providing valued goods and services. Leisure service organizations that reflect on their culture often are able to be more progressive and aggressive in adapting to change and building strong and lasting relationships with their customers.

When setting direction for programs or services, the establishment of program goals and objectives is useful in terms of linking the benefits to be produced with the procedures to be employed to accomplish them. Program goals and objectives allow us to define exactly what services we are going to create, how we will create these services, when we are going to produce them, and how we will measure whether we have produced them as intended. Program goals and objectives move the work of the leisure service organization from complex, broad, generalizable, and global patterns to more discrete, measurable, specific, and concrete actions.

There are a number of reasons why leisure service organizations must establish program goals and objectives. First, program goals and objectives link customer needs with organizational services. Second, they provide a mechanism for linking means and ends—means being procedures and ends being outputs. Third, program goals and objectives provide a basis for measurement and evaluation. Finally, they offer a way to focus resources so that priorities can be established and decisions made about concerns such as program equity, value, and quality.

This chapter will discuss the establishment of the overall direction of a leisure service organization and then present more specific information on the establishment of program goals and objectives. The success of a leisure service organization and its subsequent program efforts may very well depend on clear articulation of the intentions of leisure programs and services. Further, the work of an organization can be enhanced dramatically if there is common agreement as to the direction that the enterprise should take. With these two concerns in mind, the material in this chapter offers both theoretical and practical information that can be applied in various leisure service settings.

Establishing An Organization's Culture

The *culture* of a leisure service organization refers to the prevailing norms, customs, values, and behaviors that are exhibited by its members. This culture can have a great deal of impact on the work of an organization. For example, some organizations are guided by a strong service ethic, while others are not. Some organizations are profit-oriented, while others are nonprofit. Certain leisure service organizations direct their energies and efforts toward building the character of youth; some organizations emphasize leisure as a therapy treatment.

Culture Statements

The following statements have been derived from several different types of leisure service organizations, representing the different systems providing leisure programs and services—the political/governmental sector, the market sector and the voluntary sector. As will be seen in viewing each of these statements, the values being imparted establish the tone for the work of professionals within the organization. They represent attempts to establish the organizational culture—the norms, customs, values, and behaviors—of individuals within the organization.

The first statement is from the American Red Cross. In a statement by the chairperson of the American Red Cross (1986: 1) the values of the organization are clearly stated. The chairperson notes," . . . underlying all that we do, every service we provide, every new direction we undertake, are five basic values of the American Red Cross—values that drive us . . . that guide us . . . that instill all that we do with the unique Red Cross quality." The values promoted by the American Red Cross are *impartiality, volunteerism, humanitarianism, service excellence,* and *internationalism.* As this statement suggests, the American Red Cross is " . . . an organization filled with people for whom these values represent not just a corporate philosophy, but a personal way of life." These five values represent symbolically the values of the American Red Cross. They are its life's blood, providing the cornerstone for its efforts.

The next statement comes from a local park and recreation system—Willamalane (Springfield, Oregon) Park and Recreation District (1984). This organization has established a management philosophy to guide the behavior of its employees. This Gold Medal Award-winning organization has developed a written management philosophy as a way of communicating its shared values and expectations. Its management philosophy is built on five basic principles—*team unity, excellence in service, community involvement, dedication to productivity,* and *effective communications.* These principles were established to guide both the individual and collective actions and behaviors of professional staff members. According to the Superintendent of Parks and Recreation for the District, these value statements " . . . allow our organization to operate with unity and a sense of purpose, consistent with the District's overall mission and philosophy statements."

An example of service values related to the customer comes from the Sheraton Savannah (Georgia) Resort and Country Club. This hotel/resort complex provides comprehensive vacation and recreation facilities. A distinctive pattern of interaction with customers, as guests, has emerged. Guided by a set of "ten commandments" of the hotel business (see Figure 6.1), employees are encouraged to ensure that the customer comes first. The vision of Sheraton's Savannah Resort is to be a "first class, year-around resort of the finest standards."

The Community, Family and Soldier Support Command—Korea provides another example of an effort to develop a consistent organizational culture. The document entitled "Service Ethic" outlines standards of service and business responsibility to be followed by employees of this

Sheraton Savannah Resort & Country Club

SHERATON HOTELS, INNS & RESORTS WORLDWIDE
The hospitality people of ITT

THE TEN COMMANDMENTS OF THE HOTEL BUSINESS

I   Our guests . . .   are the most important people to us.

II Our guests . . .   are not dependent on us — we depend on them.

III Our guests . . .   are not an interruption of our work — they are
                        the purpose of it.

IV Our guests . . .   do us a favor when they visit our hotel — we
                        are not doing them a favor by serving them.

V   Our guests . . .   are not a cold statistic — they are flesh and
                        blood, human beings with feelings and emotions
                        just like our very own.

VI Our guests . . .   are not someone to argue or match wits with.

VII Our guests . . .   are people who bring us their wants — it is our
                        job to fill those wants.

VIII Our guests . . .   are deserving of the most courteous and attentive
                        treatment we can give them.

IX Our guests . . .   are the people that pay our salary no matter what
                        job or position we hold.

X   Our guests . . .   are the lifeblood of the Hotel Business.

Figure 6.1   The Ten Commandments of the Hotel Business.

organization. It addresses such concerns as "programs offered, service, facilities, community responsibility, fair trade practices, program development and profit." The statements reflected in Figure 6.2 provide an underpinning of values upon which employees base their actions.

The last statement is from *Camp Adventure*™. *Camp Adventure*™ is a successful model for providing contracted leisure services for children, youth, and teens. The "Values and Traditions" statement found in Figure 6.3 outlines the im-

portant organizational expectations for leaders, specialists, directors, and supervisors. These values and traditions are integral to the success of the program and every attempt is made to ensure that individuals not only understand, but also embrace, these precepts. The *Camp Adventure*™ management team is entrusted with the responsibility of maintaining the values and traditions of the organization as a way of ensuring the continued development of a high-quality, high-impact series of contracted leisure services for children, youth, and teens.

Service Ethic

As a member of the Community, Family and Soldier Support Command-Korea and in the spirit of the highest standards of service and business responsibility

We Hereby Pledge to:

Programs Offered	Provide value in all the morale, welfare, and recreation programs we offer our patrons.
Service	Maintain courteous, attentive, and efficient service in a pleasant atmosphere and maintain a professional attitude at all times.
Clean Facilities	Meet and maintain all prescribed standards of sanitation service and remain constantly aware of our responsibility to our patrons.
Community Responsibility	Earn the respect of the military community and contribute to command and community life by supporting the programs that enhance the quality of life in the military community.
Fair Trade Practices	Operate with integrity in all operations and engage in fair and open competition based on truthful representation of services offered.
MWR Program Development	Contribute through dedicated service to our patrons toward the growth and development of better morale, welfare, and recreation programs.
Profit	Maintain the ability to earn a reasonable profit so that facilities can be renovated and value to our patrons can continue to be a primary objective.

Figure 6.2 Service Ethic. (Community, Family and Soldier Support Command-Korea, Eighth United States Army.)

Not only is an agency's organizational culture related to the formal organization with corresponding rules and guidelines, but there is also an informal organizational culture "that may influence the behavior of employees. In other words, the norms, customs, and values of an organization are not necessarily found only on a piece of paper, but they are also found in the actions of leaders and others within the organization. In fact, at times there may be discrepancies

CAMP ADVENTURE™

"Values and Traditions"

"We Value Excellence"
- We strive to produce the impossible; our staff has few preconceived notions. If they believe it can be done, it happens.
- We value an individual's commitment, motivation and dedication.
- Excellence is an attitude that results in superior performance.

"We Care About Kids"
- Our bottom line is our front line leaders.
- We promote positive, caring child leader interactions.
- Sincerity, genuineness and caring are our hallmarks.

"We Are All Part of the *Camp Adventure* ™ Family"
- Teamwork, as reflected by caring, sharing, and helping one another is a hallmark of the program.
- Any group of people that work together as a team are far more successful than people operating individually.
- We protect one another by looking out after each person's interests, needs and respecting their personal concerns.

"Well-Planned Means Well Executed"
- We believe in complete and thorough planning as a prelude to program implementation.
- Our attention to detail reflects our commitment through planning.
- There is no substitute for planning; it is the keystone to success.

"We Create Magic Moments"
- Our goal is to create magic moments for children that last a lifetime.
- We strive to produce fun, joyful, exhilarating and treasured experiences.

"Today's Children Are Tomorrow's Leaders"
- Our staff members serve as positive role models for children.
- Positive, purposeful, play activities that develop leadership skills are our focus.

"Our Contractors Are Our Partners"
- We strive to produce mutually beneficial services.
- We value those we work with and seek their professional expertise and knowledge to enhance services.
- We strive to create a win/win situation with our partners.

"The *Camp Adventure* ™ Name Means Quality"
- Our name is a guarantee of quality services.
- Extensive planning and staff development produce quality experiences for our partners.
- We produce high quality, high impact services that make a difference in children's lives.

"Enthusiastic and Energetic Leadership"
- Our staff is dynamic, moving, energetic and committed.
- *Camp Adventure*™ staff are high on life, high on kids.

"*Camp Adventure*™ is Innovative and Creative"
- We believe our success stems from commitment to innovation.
- Creativity is encouraged in all of our spontaneous and planned programs.
- *Camp Adventure*™ is never the same from one year to the next; it is constantly evolving to meet the needs of kids today, as well as the needs of our partners.

"We Believe in the Power of Play"
- Play is enriching, it helps enhance and sustain life.
- Our social play environments emphasize fun and laughter, joy and delight, adventure and discovery.
- Play is a shared experience between children and leaders.

"You Have to Earn It to Wear It"
- Our staff earns the right to wear their *Camp Adventure*™ uniforms by affirming our values.
- They train diligently and must demonstrate a high level of competence.
- They must demonstrate their commitment to the ideals of the program.

Figure 6.3 The Values and Traditions of *Camp Adventure.* ™ (School of Health, Physical Education and Leisure Services, University of Northern Iowa.)

between what is stated in writing and what is actually practiced. However, the closer the informational culture is to the formal organizational culture, the greater the possibility that the organization will move forward in a positive and progressive fashion.

Vision and Mission Statements

The broad, overarching goals of an organization are usually reflected in vision and mission statements. The purpose of such statements is to reflect the value system of the organization. These types of statements provide philosophical direction to a leisure service organization. They can emerge from the cognitive as well as the spiritual or intuitive domain. They are usually written in such a way that they are bold, broad, and inspiring, giving direction to the efforts of individuals at all levels within the organization. They also serve as a way of communicating to customers the intentions of a leisure service organization.

Such statements are useful from a number of perspectives. First, they provide common direction for individuals within an organization. They are thus useful in guiding the daily behavior of employees. This is especially important in setting standards for the way employees will interact with customers. Second, such statements are often motivational and inspirational in nature. They inspire employees to achieve higher levels of performance because they become dedicated to an ideal and are able to channel their energies in prescribed directions. It enables them to develop a sense of purpose and value for their work efforts.

In addition, these types of statements are very useful in decision making. They enable an organization to understand its parameters, focal points, target population, and/or scope of service delivery. Such statements are also valuable in that they empower employee behavior. If the values of an employee are consistent with the values of an organization, the employee is capable of independent action. Finally, such statements provide for continuity of purpose over the years. This can be especially useful in retaining the focus of an organization during times of rapid change. The Girl Scouts of the U.S.A. may, for example, change their activities, reward structure, leadership methods, but they never lose the focus of their broader, more global intentions, such as character development of youth.

Vision statement   Vision can be thought of as the power of forward thinking. *Vision statements attempt to create a mental image of the future desired state of the organization.* Vision statements often are written in such a way that they focus on potential benefits to be gained by association with a particular leisure service organization. Vision statements should draw individuals to the organization and its services, and should inspire, motivate, excite, and stimulate them. Vision statements should project an image of the organization's worth to individuals, the community, and the region that the organization serves.

An example of a vision statement for a local park and recreation agency is found in Figure 6.4. This vision statement reflects a number of core values. The statement emphasizes the idea of "partnership, leadership, friendship, and enjoyment." It is an example of how a vision statement can guide the work of an agency toward a higher level of productivity and performance. It sets forth the benefits that can be derived from participation in the agency's services and/or association with the agency. Another vision statement is that of the Oregon Park and Recreation Society, Inc. (see Figure 6.5). Again, this statement, written in a compelling and inspiring fashion, outlines the benefits to be derived from association with this group.

In discussing the establishment of vision statements, Peters (1987) has written that there are a number of steps that should be employed in developing them. These comments serve as a guideline for individuals and organizations wishing to develop such statements. They are as follows:

1. Effective visions are inspiring.
2. Effective visions are clear and challenging—and about excellence.
3. Effective visions make sense in the marketplace, and by stressing flexibility and execution stand the test of time in a turbulent world.
4. Effective visions must be stable but constantly challenged—and changed at the margin.
5. Effective visions are beacons and controls when all else is up for grabs.
6. Effective visions are aimed at empowering our own people first, customers second.
7. Effective visions prepare for the future, but honor the past.
8. Effective visions are lived in detail, not broad strokes (Peters 1987: 401–404).

Willamalane's Vision

Willamalane Park and Recreation District is a *partnership* of people dedicated to the happiness, growth, and well-being of the residents. This dynamic partnership will be committed to enhancing the quality of life in Springfield and will be a source of pride to everyone. The human spirit will be emphasized in all Willamalane does, resulting in superior services and an atmosphere of cooperation, openness, trust, and inventiveness.

Willamalane will be a *leader* in the progressive development and care of attractive and hospitable places where people may enrich their lives. Willamalane will always treasure our heritage and natural resources and will preserve and protect priceless open spaces for the children of the future.

Willamalane will be a *friend* who will offer unique opportunities for people of all ages and abilities to enjoy friendship and laughter, the beauty of nature, and a sense of well-being. With Willamalane, people will have the chance to experience the joy of learning and sharing, the thrill of adventure and discovery, and the pride of achievement and service.

Willamalane is dedicated to the *dreams* of its residents. Willamalane's tomorrows will be built on the dreams of today.

Figure 6.4　Vision Statement. (Willamalane Park and Recreation District (1985).)

OPRS Vision Statement
Adopted by the Board of Directors, January 15, 1988

It is our belief, as members of the Oregon Park and Recreation Society, that we have the unique opportunity to create within our diverse communities, environments in which citizens in Oregon can experience human dignity and true quality of life through readily accessible leisure experiences. IT IS THEREFORE OUR VISION:

- That we share knowledge and expertise freely through an educational ethic that transcends all boundaries;

- That we cultivate a fundamental respect for Oregon's exceptional cultural and environmental heritage.

- That we are advocates for a service ethic which demands equity of leisure opportunities for all.

- That we instill in Oregonians the passion for affecting change in their own lives.

- That we consciously link our sense of purpose to the resolution of significant social/cultural issues.

By dedicating ourselves to this vision we are committed to leisure participation because of the joy, self-esteem and sense of belonging it brings; life's enhancement by enthusiastic participation; and the people's recreation through a playful and meaningful approach to life at its fullest.

Figure 6.5 OPRS Vision Statement.

Developing a vision for an organization or refining an existing one provides the leisure service programmer with a unique opportunity to shape the destiny or future of an agency. By relating program and service efforts to an organization's vision, individuals are linked to a far more compelling, challenging, and exciting effort. When operating as a part of the whole, consistent with the vision of an organization, the leisure service programmer is positioned to draw upon the resources and energy of the entire operation. Programming efforts become more satisfying, meaningful, and valuable when tied to a broader, stronger concept.

Mission statement Mission statements are often thought of as being synonymous with vision statements. Like vision statements, they provide overall direction to an organization's effort. They usually spell out the broad ends or aims that the organization attempts to achieve. However, there are some differences between vision and mission statements as they have been developed and applied within leisure service organizations.

The most apparent difference between vision statements and mission statements in the leisure service field is in the motivational aspect or tone of the statement. Mission statements tend to be direct, pragmatic, and focused in terms of the types of services to be provided and/or broad features related to potential benefits. Mission statements also tend to be much shorter and more direct than vision statements. Vision statements, as mentioned, attempt to be more motivational in nature, employing emotional terms and phrases to project the direction of the organization. Even though the differences between these two types of statements are subtle, they have a great deal of impact on the development and evolution of a leisure service organization.

Mission statements define the primary work of a leisure service organization. They help an organization define its scope and function in terms of services to be provided and benefits to be achieved. Mission statements may also focus on target groups or populations. Like vision statements, they are useful documents in not only shaping the work of an organization, but also communicating the organization's intentions internally and externally.

What are the characteristics of mission statements? There are a number of important elements found in most mission statements. They are as follows:

1. Mission statements are short and direct statements that are focused in terms of the work of an organization and its aspirations.
2. Mission statements often focus on specific types of services, markets, and benefits to be produced by the leisure service organization.
3. Mission statments may reflect a focus on quality and excellence and/or other variables that influence the way in which services are delivered.
4. Mission statements often reflect organizational values that provide direction to the overall work of the organization.
5. Mission statements are often difficult to measure and quantify because they are written in broad, global terms.

Mission statements serve as a basis upon which professional practice occurs. Ultimately, the goals and objectives of a leisure service organization are linked to its mission statement. Thus, mission statements provide a beginning basis for determining the direction of an organization and its areas of focus. In the delivery of local governmental park and recreation services, organizations often focus on the provision of "parks, leisure, and cultural services as a way of improving the quality of life" of those served. In a youth-serving organization like the YMCA, the focus of the mission statement might be to "improve and positively influence conditions which affect the quality of life for the people we touch." In a leisure service business organization, the mission statement might read, "to provide high quality services while at the same time earning a profit in order to return value to our customers."

Mission statements will vary greatly depending on the type of organization and its general purpose. Below are listed mission statements from various leisure settings. The examples presented represent several different types of leisure service organizations.

Eugene YMCA (Eugene, OR)—The Eugene Family YMCA is an association of individuals from this community and around the world—youth and adults of all ages, ethnic backgrounds, and faiths, united in a common effort to put Christian principles into practice, where the spirit of love for all people is shown through thought and deed.

Hennepin Regional Park District (Minneapolis, MN)—Hennepin Parks' mission is to provide opportunities for people to enrich their lives and increase their enjoyment and well-being through outdoor recreation and education in a natural resources-based park system.

Hartman Reserve Nature Center (Cedar Falls, IA)—The Hartman Reserve Nature Center is dedicated to the preservation and protection of this unique, natural area and to the promotion of a better understanding of our environment.

Courage Center (Golden Valley, MN)—The mission of Courage Center is to promote the maximum independence, personal responsibility, self-esteem, and dignity of people who have a physical or sensory disability, with primary emphasis on individuals with severe or multiple disabilities. Courage Center provides pioneers and promotes vital and caring programs in rehabilitation, independent living, and recreation at the appropriate regional, national, or international level.

Portland Bureau of Parks and Recreation (OR)—The mission of Portland Parks and Recreation is to create and promote recreational opportunities and to preserve and enhance Portland's parks and natural areas to enrich the lives of the citizens of Portland.

These five mission statments reflect many of the common characteristics noted above. They are short and to the point. They serve to focus the work of each of these organizations and/or programs. They identify the benefits to be pursued as a result of development of programs and services. Such mission statements are extremely important in the development of programs and services. They provide the philosophical underpinnings for the work of leisure service programmers. They are the basis upon which programs and services are created and distributed. They serve as broad guidelines that are useful in developing more specific goals and objectives.

Program Goals and Objectives

Most leisure service programmers are required to establish goals and objectives to be used as a part of the planning process in the development of programs and services. Establishing goals and objectives links the day-to-day work of the programmer with the broader philosophical direction of the leisure service organization for whom he or she works. This linkage legitimizes the work of the programmer. By linking program goals and objectives to the broader philosophical directions of an organization, the programmer is empowered to access the resources of the agency.

The programmer can bring to bear the influence and resources of the organization to develop and implement leisure program offerings.

Establishing goals and objectives allows the leisure service programmer to determine what results are desirable. Goals and objectives that are established in general terms are difficult to measure and to implement. Therefore, the more specific that goals and objectives become, the greater the probability that these goals and objectives can, in fact, be measured. Thus, when establishing goals and objectives, one of the first things that leisure service programmers must remember is that they must be specific and focused.

One of the steps that follows the establishment of goals and objectives is their communication to various individuals. Often, by communicating goals and objectives, leisure service programmers can build consensus for their efforts within an organization and to the target populations served by the agency. Effectively communicated, goals and objectives help build a common framework for action.

Setting Goals and Objectives: Areas for Consideration

Leisure service programmers may focus their goal-setting in several broad areas. Remember, it is important to recognize that there are many component parts to developing a program. The activity must be selected, the format developed, and the evaluation techniques chosen. Further, strategies for promoting the program must be developed and careful consideration must be given to the way in which the program is financially managed. In general, there are three broad areas that the leisure service programmer will want to consider when developing goals and objectives for a given program or service. They are *program development, promotion and sales strategies,* and *financial strategies.*

Program development At the heart of the goal-setting process is the establishment of goals and objectives for the program or service to be created and delivered. Goal and objective statements related to program development would focus on such questions as "Who are the recipients of services?" "What are the services?" "What leadership resources are required to execute the program?" "What will the content of the program consist of?" "Where will the program be located?" "What will be the length and duration of the program?" These and other questions form the basis for the establishment of goals and objectives in this area.

Promotion and sales strategies Another important area in which goals and objectives are established is that of promotion. In establishing goals and objectives in this area, efforts should be undertaken to identify ways of communicating with target markets. Goals and objectives statements in this area would focus on such questions as "What channels of promotion should be used in communicating with customers?" "What specific tools or methods of promotion (e.g., fliers, brochures) will be used?" "What time(s) should the information be disseminated or released?" Goals and objectives related to promotion may very well detail not only promotional actions, but how these actions relate to revenues desired.

Financial strategies Every leisure service program has a break-even point. The development of goals and objectives related to expected revenues and expenditures is extremely important. Basic questions here might include the following. "Should a profit be earned?" "Should the program be subsidized by the agency?" "What equity factors must be considered when developing fees and charges for programs?" "How are funds to be received and dispersed?" Financial management in leisure service organizations has become increasingly important. In public agencies tax dollars have become scarce and in the marketplace customer discretionary dollars have become scarce. Contributed dollars to voluntary organizations become more and more difficult to obtain. The establishment of goals and objectives related to careful financial planning has become increasingly important within leisure service organizations.

Goals and objectives are not established in a vacuum. Ideally, the leisure service programmer will work with a variety of individuals when developing goals and objectives. They should reflect the opinions and needs of both individuals within the organization and those external to the organization, since program goals and objectives are a way of linking customer needs to the work of the organization.

A key feature of program goals and objectives is the idea that they enable the programmer to *focus* his or her activities. Focusing on program goals and objectives creates a mechanism to guide the work of the professional. Rather than wallowing in uncertainty, leisure service programmers are able to clearly understand what they are trying to accomplish, how they are trying to accomplish it, and how their work will be measured. Likewise, this focus enables the customer to understand what services are to be produced, what benefits will be available, and what resources are to be employed. Thus, goals and objectives increase accountability for the programmer and help customers assess the extent to which their needs are being addressed.

Common Characteristics of Program Goals and Objectives

The terms *goals* and *objectives* are often thought to be synonymous. However, most definitions of goals suggest that they are broad statements, whereas objectives are more specific and measurable. When referring to program goals and objectives we might define these terms slightly differently. *Program goals can be thought of as broad statements that define the leisure services to be produced.* They are the aims or ends toward which the leisure service professional directs his or her activities. *Program objectives—can be thought of as specific statements that are measurable and have some dimension of time.* In developing program objectives, the leisure service programmer will usually consider what is to be done, how it is going to be

done, when it is going to be done, and how it will be measured. A program objective describes the way in which the accomplishment of a goal can be carried out and measured—just as program goals are linked to the mission of the leisure service organization.

Some of the common characteristics of both program goals and objectives are as follows:

1. *Specific.* Program goals and objectives are specific, clear, and concrete. They help put the vision or mission of a leisure service organization in operation.
2. *Measurable.* Program goals and objectives must be measurable. There must be some way to determine whether or not the desired results have been achieved.
3. *Pragmatic.* Program goals and objectives also must be pragmatic; that is, they must be attainable and reality-based.
4. *Useful.* Program goals and objectives must have worth; that is, they must be worth the effort needed to accomplish the end. They must be of value to the customers being served, to the leisure service programmer, and to the organization as a whole.
5. *Linked to Needs.* Program goals and objectives must be linked to the needs of customers and the organization's vision or mission.

Well-defined and articulated program goals and objectives make things happen within organizations. They not only provide direction regarding things that the leisure service programmer may wish to have occur, but their establishment often actually produces the momentum necessary to move the organization in a specific direction. As indicated, program goals and objectives help identify programs to be developed, ways of promoting activities and events, and financial strategies to be employed.

Most program goals and objectives are written in terms of benefits or outcomes to be realized by the customer; as a result, they are written as *performance objectives*. A performance objective has the same qualities and attributes as a program objective. However, in addition to the factors just described, *performance objectives are written in terms of the behavior that is to be demonstrated by the customer* as a result of his or her involvement in a program or service.

Since performance objectives refer to the actual behavior that is to be demonstrated by the customer, they must be stated in terms of what the consumer is to know and what he or she is to demonstrate. Essentially, the programmer attempts to change or maintain certain types of defined customer behaviors. He or she does this by directly intervening with a program or service or by providing assistance as an enabler to help the customer in his or her leisure pursuits. Performance objectives focus on the behavior of the customer rather than on the actions of the programmer. In other words, performance objectives are not written to include the programmer's actions (such as intervening, enabling, and the like). They are written only to identify and measure the behavioral changes displayed by the customer.

Another key characteristic of performance objectives is that the behavior learned by the customer must be observable in order to be measured. One cannot measure that which is not seen. An example of a psychomotor skill that could be demonstrated (by the customer), observed, and measured is a free throw in basketball. A customer in leisure program activities, in order to fulfill a performance objective related to a physical skill, would be expected to demonstrate a described level of proficiency. Using the example of free throws, one might achieve a level of proficiency with the successful completion of eight out of ten free throws. A leisure program customer might display a cognitive skill through the application of knowledge. For example, the knowledge that a sports official has gained or possessed can be evaluated in terms of his or her performance on a written test regarding the rules and regulations of the sport he or she officiates.

In another performance objective, the customer may be expected to demonstrate behavior in the affective domain—e.g., displaying an intangible such as enjoyment. What is enjoyment, and how can one measure such an intangible element? It is possible for the programmer to set standards and definitions for enjoyment that are based on his or her own specific interpretations, and perceptions, and then to measure enjoyment in this way. For example, the programmer might define enjoyment at a youth drop-in center as the number of smiling and laughing individuals, the length of time that the customers stay at the drop-in center, and the frequency with which they attend the center. In this way he or she can, at least theoretically, attempt to measure enjoyment. This, in turn, may help the programmer in the evaluation of activities for these types of programs because he or she has operationally defined intangible behavior in a tangible, measurable form.

Obviously, it is easier for the leisure professional and the customer to conceptualize the use of performance objectives in relation to tangible behaviors, such as the demonstration of a physical skill or the display of acquired knowledge. On the other hand, it is much more difficult to evaluate—hence, measure—feelings, values, and emotions. The difficulty in measuring intangible behavior and the comparative simplicity in measuring tangible behavior may account for the major emphasis on efficiency-oriented evaluative techniques (such as counting the number of customers) and for the dominance of programs that lend themselves to measurement by these types of performance objectives. In order to measure the essence of the leisure experience, increased emphasis should be placed on the quantification of intangibles such as enjoyment, social interaction, and excitement.

According to Edginton and Hayes (1976: 21), there are four factors involved in writing performance objectives:

1. What must be known or done by the customer?
2. How is the customer to demonstrate a specific behavior?
3. What are the factors or conditions that might affect the customer's acquisition and demonstration of a specific behavior?

4. What is the minimum level of acceptable achievement for the customer's performance of a given behavior?

In writing performance objectives, the leisure programmer must first state exactly what is expected of the customer. These expectations or behavioral outcomes can be referred to as terminal behaviors. Terminal behaviors are the ends, events, or actions that the customer will eventually demonstrate. The professional must state the terminal expectations using an action verb. For example, "To hit the ball" is an example of a desired terminal behavior, and the action verb describing that behavior is the word "hit." This is not an easy task for the programmer. In writing objectives, it is easier to focus on the actions of the programmer or on the process rather than on what the customer is expected to know or do. Edginton and Hayes (1976: 21) have indicated that "there is a tendency to focus on leisure activity as an end in itself rather than as a means to an end." It is important to remember that the customer must be aware of exactly what he or she is to know or do in terms of facts, ideas, physical movement, problems to be solved, and other factors that can be identified.

The next step in the process of writing performance objectives is to specify conditions or circumstances that may affect the acquisition of knowledge or demonstration of a skill. The objective should specify the form that the activity must take or the nature of the instruction that will be applied. In developing performance objectives, one is dealing with individuals or groups. Because individuals and groups vary in terms of values, interest, desires, needs, skills, and knowledge, each performance objective must account for these differences. Adaptations and modifications that might be considered as being based on individual and group differences include leadership styles, activity progression, game and contest rules, and the social and physical setting in which the activity takes place. Spelling out the special conditions or circumstances under which an action is to take place is especially important

in dealing with special populations. For example, disabled individuals in wheelchairs play basketball using modified game rules.

The final step in writing performance objectives is consideration of the level of achievement required by the participant. For example, it is not sufficient to describe only what the participant is to do or know (such as "hitting the ball"); one must also specify the level of proficiency to be achieved in hitting. This can mean the distance the ball must be hit, the accuracy of the hitter, or the number of hits per attempts by the hitter. By specifying the achievement level required of the participant, one can more specifically define the type of behavior expected. Likewise, we are quantifying the outcome in more precisely measurable terms. An example of the process is found in Table 6.1.

Identification of these four components serves both the customer and the organization. The customer benefits because he or she is able to visualize what it is he or she is trying to achieve through involvement in a recreation or leisure activity. The organization can benefit from the

TABLE 6.1 Writing Performance Objectives

Writing Performance Objectives
Step 1—State the performance objective with a *verb* that defines the accepted behavior: "The customer *will demonstrate* proficiency in skiing . . ."
Step 2—State the *method* of performance which the participant can demonstrate: *by traversing* a giant slalom course . . ."
Step 3—State those *factors or conditions* which may affect the attainment or achievement of the objective: "of 4,000 feet in *length,* with a *vertical drop* of 1,200 feet . . ."
Step 4—Indicate in each *performance* objective how it is to be *measured:* "covering the course in under five *minutes.*"

The customer will demonstrate proficiency in skiing by traversing a giant slalom course of 4,000 feet in length, with a vertical drop of 1,200 feet, covering the course in under five minutes.

Edginton and Hayes 1976.

use of performance objectives in terms of its accountability. In other words, the organization is forced to define exactly what it is trying to do in terms of behavioral changes in people. When questioned as to the purpose of their organization, many leisure service agencies respond, "We exist to provide recreation and leisure activities to all members of the community." By using performance objectives, an organization can go a step further and define not only in general terms the activities they offer but also in more specific terms the behavioral outcomes that can be anticipated for the individuals that participate in these activities.

At this point, we should also introduce some of the problems associated with performance objectives. First, they are extremely time-consuming to formulate. In addition, they require an organization to deal with people on an individual rather than a mass basis. Given the present structuring and financing of public recreation services, this may be difficult and considered inefficient. Performance objectives also require a precise degree of structure in their formulation and implementation. According to some individuals, this robs potential from a recreation and leisure experience. For example, spontaneity and freedom of interaction are two highly valued attributes of the leisure experience. By overstructuring, we may reduce the possibility that experiences featuring these attributes will be available. In the opinion of the authors, the problem is not one of overstructuring but of operationally defining terms such as spontaneity. Even in a modified form, it is strongly recommended that organizations and individual leaders employ the concept of performance objectives.

Learning taxonomies developed by Bloom (1956), Krathwohl (1964) and Bush (1972) can aid the recreation and leisure professional in the development of performance objectives. These taxonomies define different levels of learning within the *cognitive, affective,* and *psychomotor domains.* Application of the learning taxonomies to performance objectives allows the professional to conceptualize potential levels of behavioral outcomes. The professional should be able to develop an awareness of the needs of the individual as they relate to the types of services that may be made available by an organization.

Tables 6.2, 6.3, and 6.4 present the major categories in the cognitive, affective, and psychomotor domains. As indicated, they are hierarchically ordered—with the simplest form of learning presented at the top of each table, progressing to the more complex forms of learning at the bottom. The cognitive domain deals with the acquisition of knowledge, comprehension, and understanding. The affective domain involves feelings, values, and emotions. The psychomotor domain includes the acquisition of physical and neuromuscular skills. These taxonomies are hierarchically ordered; a person progresses from one level of knowledge, skill, and feeling to the next level. The taxonomies start with simple types of behavior and progress toward more complex forms. As an individual progresses from one level to the next, we suggest that he or she has experienced growth and learning.

If an individual came to an organization and was desirous of increasing his or her skill level in

TABLE 6.2 Cognitive Domain

Major Categories in the Cognitive Domain
1. *Knowledge*—Knowledge is defined as the remembering of previously learned material.
2. *Comprehension*—Comprehension is defined as the ability to grasp the meaning of material.
3. *Application*—Application refers to the ability to use learned material in new and concrete situations.
4. *Analysis*—Analysis refers to the ability to break down material into its component parts so that its organizational structure may be understood.
5. *Synthesis*—Synthesis refers to the ability to put parts together to form a new whole.
6. *Evaluation*—Evaluation is concerned with the ability to judge the value of material for a given purpose.

Bloom 1956.

TABLE 6.3 Affective Domain

Major Catgegories in the Affective Domain
1. *Receiving*—Receiving refers to the client's willingness to attend to particular phenomena or stimuli.
2. *Responding*—Responding refers to active participation on the part of the participant.
3. *Valuing*—Valuing is concerned with the work or value a client attaches to a particular object, phenomenon, or behavior.
4. *Organization*—Organization is concerned with bringing together different values, resolving conflicts between them, and beginning the building of an internally consistent value system.
5. *Characterization by a Value or Value Complex*—At this level of the affective domain, the individual has a value system that has controlled his behavior for a sufficiently long enough time for him to have developed a characteristic "lifestyle."

Krathwohl 1964.

TABLE 6.4 Psychomotor Domain

Major Categories in the Psychomotor Domain
1. *Imitation*—Imitation of some observed act usually lacking neuromuscular coordination.
2. *Manipulation*—Manipulation emphasizes skill in following directions.
3. *Precision*—Precision emphasizes accuracy, exactness, and control with reduction of errors.
4. *Articulation*—Articulation involves coordination of a series of acts—involves accuracy and control, plus elements of speed and time.
5. *Naturalization*—Naturalization occurs when the art has become routine, automatic, and spontaneous. Performance is natural and smooth.

Bush 1972.

a given area, the professional utilizing this model could first analyze the level at which the person was presently performing and then determine exactly what kind of instruction and involvement would be necessary to meet that person's need for more complex levels of learning. To illustrate this further, let us assume that an individual involved in tennis has demonstrated accuracy in using the backhand stroke and a degree of exactness in using the forehand stroke. However, he or she has not been able to coordinate the use of these strokes in a fluid manner during actual play of the game. In this instance, the professional might analyze the participant's ability as falling within the level of precision in the psychomotor domain. The task of the professional would be to develop a performance objective for the customer that conceptualizes the desired outcome and level of performance. This would involve planning a program that addressed itself to the level within the psychomotor domain known as articulation. It must be remembered that performance objectives are stated in terms of desired behavioral outcomes and not in the process involved in producing the outcome.

Murphy et al. (1973) have suggested that leisure experiences often incorporate elements found in each of the domains of learning. In many cases, a recreation and leisure experience combines these elements. In other words, there is an integration of these domains in many of the typical leisure organization programs and services. For example, when individuals practice basketball, they increase their knowledge (cognitive domain) of the game while, at the same time, improving their shooting technique (psychomotor skill) and increasing their desire (affective domain) to perform well. Thus in this particular activity, each domain plays an integral part in shaping the recreational experience of the individual.

The use of performance objectives allows the leisure professional to bridge the gap between means and ends in his or her development of program activities. By focusing on behavioral outcomes, the professional is able to realize not only what he or she is doing in terms of the delivery of leisure services but also in what way his or her actions are affecting and influencing the customers being served.

Summary

In this chapter we have discussed the importance of establishing direction for the work of the leisure service organization and that of the leisure service programmer. In a formal sense, the direction that an organization establishes is reflected in its vision statement, mission statement, program goals, program objectives, and performance objectives. The establishment of organizational goals is essential in the following: (1) establishing the final end toward which the organization and the programmer direct their resources; (2) providing an indication of how the intended result or end will be achieved; and (3) serving as a control indicating whether the desired ends have been obtained.

The culture of a leisure service organization is usually established by developing a vision statement. Vision statements are bold, motivating statements that reflect the values of an organization. A vision statement is useful in establishing the ideals that an organization wishes to pursue. It becomes an important mechanism to communicate the intent of the organization to its own employees internally, as well as those private groups it serves externally. Closely related to vision statements are mission statements. Mission statements in the leisure service field tend to be written in a shorter, more pragmatic, more direct, and more focused fashion than vision statements.

Program goals, program objectives, and performance objectives are methods for linking the work of the leisure service organization to its broader vision. They are much more specific than either mission or vision statements and they can be operationalized. Program goals can be thought of as broad statements that direct the work of the programmer. Program objectives are more specific, concrete statements that can be measured. Performance objectives have the same properties as program objectives, the only difference being that they are stated in terms of the desired behaviors to be demonstrated by the customer.

Providing direction to an organization is an important step in leisure service programming. By having a clear understanding of what one is trying to create, what behaviors one is trying to produce, or what outcomes are desirable, organizational resources are used more wisely. Further, the needs of the customer are more clearly linked to the work of the organization.

Discussion Questions and Exercises

1. Why is establishing direction for the work of a leisure service organization important?

2. What is meant by the culture of a leisure service organization? How does the culture of the leisure service organization have an impact on its programs and services?

3. What is the difference between a vision and a mission statement?

4. Write a vision statement for a leisure service organization or program area of your choice.

5. Define the difference between goals and objectives.

6. How might goals and objectives vary when developing them for: (1) programs; (2) promotion and sales strategies; and (3) financial management? Develop a set of goals and objectives for each one of these areas for a given leisure service activity.

7. What are some of the common characteristics of goals and objectives?

8. What are performance objectives?

9. What four factors are involved in writing performance objectives?

10. Develop a taxonomy of behavioral outcomes that can be used in writing performance objectives.

References

American Red Cross. 1986. 1985 Annual report.

Bloom, B. S. 1956. *Taxonomy of educational objectives: Cognitive domain.* New York: McKay.

Bush, P. 1972. *A program course for writing of performance objectives.* Chico, CA: North California Program Development Center.

Community, Family and Soldier Support Command—Korea. n.d. *Service Ethic.*

Edginton, C. 1987. Creating an organizational culture. *Management Strategy* 11(1): 6.

Edginton, C. R. and G. A. Hayes. 1976. Objectives in the delivery of recreation services. *Journal of Leisurability* 3(4):21.

Krathwohl, D. R. 1964. *Taxonomy of educational objectives: Affective domain.* New York: McKay.

Murphy, J. F., J. G. Williams, E. W. Neipoth, and P. D. Brown. 1983. *Leisure service delivery system.* Philadelphia: Lea & Febiger.

Peters, T. 1987. *Thriving on chaos.* New York: Alfred Knopf.

Willamalane Park and Recreation District. 1984. Management philosophy.

7 | Program Development

Learning Objectives

1. To provide the reader with an understanding of the factors involved in the *total program planning process.*
2. To help the reader gain an understanding of *program areas.*
3. To help the reader gain an understanding of *program formats.*
4. To help the reader understand how *the specific content of a program contributes to the development process.*
5. To provide information concerning factors related to the *timing, facility needs, supply and equipment needs, and cost of a leisure program.*
6. To provide the reader with information concerning the concept of *activity analysis* and its relationship to leisure programming.
7. To recognize the place of *risk management* in all program planning activities.

Introduction

The program development step in the total program planning process integrates the customer needs that have been identified and the goals and objectives that have been determined, and focuses on the factors that are crucial in constructing both individual programs and the total programs and services made available by the leisure service organization. The same elements in the development procedure may be applied in all situations where program construction takes place. In other words, whether the leisure service professional is organizing a swimming class, a softball tournament, a travelogue series, a ballet performance, or a community-wide weekend arts festival, the same methodology can be applied to the development of the activity. Whether the program being developed is for a small number of individuals, for several groups of people, or for a large number of leisure customers, there are common elements in the development process that are applicable to all situations.

Program Development Factors

Though not listed in rank order, the following factors are common to all program development situations. With the specific customer group(s) in mind the leisure service professional will focus on the program area, program format, program content, time factors, facilities, setting, equipment and supplies, staffing, cost, promotion, activity analysis, and risk management. The prominence and degree of influence of each factor in the development of the specific program will vary with the situation. For example, in one situation the cost of staffing and the resulting cost to the customer may be of primary importance. In another situation, securing the facilities and creating the setting may be most crucial to the development step, or developing and facilitating a program promotion plan may be of greatest importance to constructing a particular program or event. However, whatever the situation is and whatever the specific program is, all of the factors are important to the program development step.

Some of the following factors are considered in greater detail later in the book—specifically, program areas are discussed in chapter 8 and program formats in chapter 9. They are introduced here as a part of the program development step in the program planning process.

Program Areas

The term *program areas* refers to the way in which leisure program activities are categorized or classified in the context of this book. Chapter 8 provides a detailed discussion of the way in which leisure activities may be identified. The areas of programming included in this book are: *the arts— visual arts (including crafts), performing arts, new arts; literary activities; aquatics; sports, games, and athletics; outdoor recreation; social recreation; self-improvement/education activities; wellness activities; hobbies; travel and tourism; and volunteer services* (see Figure 7.1). Through needs identification and assessment and determination of goals and objectives, the leisure service programmer selects the area(s) of programming that will be the focus for development.

Program planners in leisure service organizations attempt to provide a broad spectrum of programming in a variety of program areas. Consideration must be given to the several customer groups for whom an agency plans. Further, leisure service program planners attempt to develop and maintain somewhat of a balance of programming in order to meet the greatest number of customer needs and interests. In other words, activities in several areas of programming can be developed by the leisure service organization. For example, sports, wellness activities, aquatics, arts and crafts, volunteer activities, travel and tourism, and hobby groups can all be included in the programming offered by a specific organization. At the same time, activities at several skill levels can be provided for customers. An example of this is in aquatic programming,

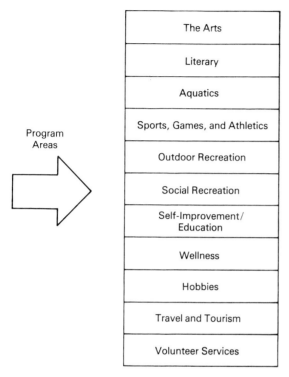

Program
Areas →

| The Arts |
| Literary |
| Aquatics |
| Sports, Games, and Athletics |
| Outdoor Recreation |
| Social Recreation |
| Self-Improvement/ Education |
| Wellness |
| Hobbies |
| Travel and Tourism |
| Volunteer Services |

Figure 7.1   Areas of Programming.

where often there are specific opportunities offered for beginning swimmers, intermediate swimmers, advanced swimmers, diving instruction, synchronized swimming, and life-saving courses. This variety of activities for different skill levels can be applicable in all programming areas.

The arts   Programs in the arts embrace all creative disciplines. *Visual arts* can be thought of as decorative arts, including both graphic and plastic forms. Activities could incorporate such mediums as oil painting; pen and ink drawing; stone, metal, and clay structuring; tapestry making; block printing; and wood carving. A *craft* may be distinguished from other visual arts in that it results in a product that serves a utilitarian purpose. Some examples might include leather craft, sewing, embroidery, tie-dyeing, candle making, pottery, snow and ice sculpturing, fly tying, furniture refinishing, and macramé. The *new arts* involve creative use of twentieth-century

technology. They may include computer art, photography, and music synthesizers. The *performing arts* involve artistic expression in which the individual is the mode of expression. Performing arts include such activities as acting, singing, and dancing. The participant must be actually involved in the activity, although it is of no consequence whether or not an audience is present. Modern dance, pantomime, puppetry, opera, barbershop quartets, symphony orchestras, and dramatizations are all examples of performing arts.

Literary activities   Literary activities are leisure opportunities that emphasize literary, mental, and linguistic activities. Literary activities facilitate communication through writing and speaking, and may include the study of English and foreign languages, creative writing and composition, oral reading of poetry, short stories, plays, etc., book reviews and discussion, and study of literature. In addition, this area of programming may encompass development of oral histories, storytelling, and study of family genealogies.

Aquatics   Though aquatics may fit well into the category of sports, games, and athletes, it is such a large area of programming by many leisure service organizations that it is included here as a separate category. This area of programming encompasses swimming, diving, aerobic activity in the water, water games, practices of life saving, aquatic instruction, and can also include other water-related activities such as canoeing and boating and the safety practices related to these activities.

Sport, games, and athletics   Any physiological activity that requires gross and fine motor muscle control may be categorized within this cluster. Swimming, track and field, rifle shooting, archery, golf, weight lifting, handball, badminton, volleyball, softball, and water polo are all examples of this classification.

Outdoor recreation Outdoor recreation and leisure activities are natural, resource-oriented. Some of the activities that strongly depend on the use of natural resources are sailing, fishing, camping, hiking, climbing, and hunting.

Social recreation Social recreation involves activities that are created in order to bring about interaction between individuals. Social recreation programs may involve the use of other areas (such as those already mentioned) to contribute to its objective. Generally speaking, the setting is most important in social recreation programming.

Self-improvement/educational activities Activities in this programming area can be broad in scope and interest. Discussion groups of all kinds may be included: current events, politics, financial planning, and home improvements, to name a few. There may be specific instructional opportunities included in this category that may focus on family life, child rearing, presenting a new self-image, interviewing skills, and interpersonal communication.

Wellness activities Wellness activities in leisure programming include physical fitness activities, changes in health behaviors such as weight reduction, cessation of smoking and chemical intake, dietary concerns and adaptations, and other preventative measures for good health. Wellness also includes social and emotional good health, and lifetime practices and activities that contribute to a positive lifestyle and living environment.

Hobbies A hobby is a leisure activity that is pursued with interest over an extended period of time. Two classifications of hobbies are collecting and creative. Examples of collecting hobbies are stamps, coins, guns, books, antiques, nature objects, dolls, and models. Creative hobbies include writing, composing, cooking, and gardening.

Travel and tourism As a program area, travel and tourism encompasses the movement of persons from their immediate surroundings and places of residence to other locations for the purpose of interacting with the physical and social environment. This may include viewing and interacting with natural physical features, manmade structures, and the human culture of the area.

Volunteer services Volunteer programs involve the utilization of one's skills and abilities during leisure time, with the purpose of giving to others. Whereas other individuals may receive satisfaction from directly participating in an activity, the volunteer receives his or her satisfaction from service rendered to others.

Program Formats

The program format is the way in which an activity is organized and structured for delivery to the customer. Obviously, the format used to organize an activity will have a great deal of influence on its appeal to the customer. To make an overall program attractive and desirable, activities within the program areas must be organized using creative and appropriate program formats. Individual programs within the several program areas should be formatted to cater to broad sections of the population in order to meet the needs and interests of a variety of groups of people. Leisure programming formats include: *competitive, drop-in, class, club, special event, workshop, interest group,* and *outreach* (see Figure 7.2).

A feature that makes leisure programming dynamic is that activities in many of the programming areas can be offered in a variety of formats. At the same time, formats can be mixed to add interest to activities that are provided. To illustrate the application of formats to program activities, sports can be used as examples. Basketball, volleyball, softball, or any other sports activities can be offered competitively through leagues and tournaments. Skill development in

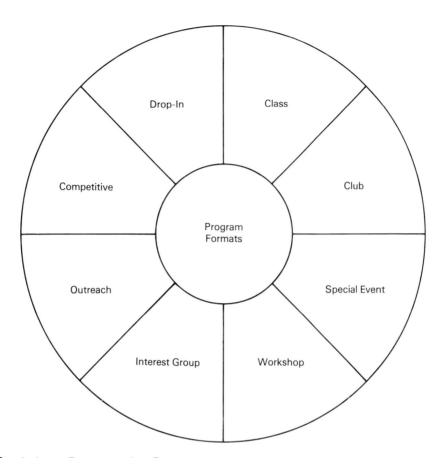

Figure 7.2   Leisure Programming Formats.

these activities may be facilitated through structured instruction in a class format. Open facilities with non-scheduled activities offer opportunities for drop-in participation, while workshops and seminars present opportunities for sports coaches and officials to be trained to lead the sports activities. Sometimes there is a fine line between formats used for a particular activity. For example, a sports tournament could be both a special event and a competitive event or just one of the two. A matrix which shows the application of formats to program areas is included in chapter 9.

Competitive   Many leisure activities, especially sports, games, and athletics, can be competitive in nature. Competition can stimulate interest and provide motivation among participants. This is not only true for sports, but also applies to other program areas. Leisure activities, which focus upon competition, should take into consideration the relative skills and abilities of the participants involved and correspondingly adapt the level or intensity of competition. Common methods used to organize program areas into competition include leagues, tournaments, and contests.

Drop-in/open   Drop-in/open formatted activities provide the participant with an element of freedom in contrast with activities that operate on rigidly fixed time schedules. Generally speaking, activities are arranged in a manner that allows them to be either ongoing or spontaneous. Utilization of a gymnasium track for jogging and use of a library for reading are examples of drop-in programming.

Class　Another method of organizing leisure activities is through instructional classes. Classes are generally very formal when compared with the drop-in approach. They usually involve the hiring of an instructor who teaches within a given subject area. Although the class setting may be formal in comparison with other program forms, the emphasis is one of individual concern and attention.

Club　A club consists of a group of people who are associated for a common purpose. The club membership usually provides its own leadership, organization, and perhaps finances. A club is customarily a self-contained unit unless facilities are needed to operate. Leisure service organizations often provide facilities to meet the interests of individuals within clubs. Furthermore, they can provide initial stimulation for the formulation of a club around a specific area of interest—e.g., organizing an introductory meeting or providing ''in-kind'' services, such as storage space or clerical help.

Special events　A special event is a method of organizing an activity in a unique manner. Ranging from simply executed activities to elaborate and lengthy productions, the special event is a method of stimulating interest. Special events include exhibits, parades, festivals, demonstrations, and carnivals.

Workshops/conferences　The workshop/conference is a method of organizing activities and people into a format that allows intense participation within a short period of time. The duration of a given workshop/conference is usually determined by the amount of material to be covered. However, they usually last a maximum of two weeks and, in many situations, are organized for much shorter periods of time. A conference is a meeting at which individuals with common interests gather to discuss issues, to disseminate information, and to make decisions.

Interest group　An interest group may have some of the characteristics of a club; however, such a program format is usually a collection of individuals that are formed around an activity issue or a program area. Special interest groups usually have their own leadership. The lifespan of an interest group may vary from meeting together one or two times to a more on-going existence. Several individuals may serve as resource people for the group according to the interest for which the group was formed. Groups may form in relation to social needs, social issues, community projects, leisure interests, etc.

Outreach　Many programs and services are organized around the utilization of facilities rather than around people and their needs. Outreach programs meet people in their own locale. Emphasis is placed on taking the activity to the participant rather than on having the participant come to the activity.

Program Content

Once the leisure programmer has identified the program area in which a service will be offered, determined the specific activity to be presented, and selected the format that will be used to implement the program, it is necessary to develop the specific content that the program will have. In order to have continuity in planning programs, a leisure service organization may wish to have a common format for program descriptions so that similar information will be included in all activity planning. Figure 7.3 illustrates a program description format that may be applicable to most planning situations. With a format to follow the planner can be more certain of including necessary and appropriate information for each activity that is developed.

Program Area:	Crafts
Program Format:	Class
Name of Program:	Holiday Crafts
Customers:	Adult Women and Men
Program Goal:	To provide a craft program for adults.
Program Objectives:	To offer an opportunity for individuals to see holiday craft ideas demonstrated.
	To teach skills in making craft items.
	To provide the opportunity to finish a project each week to take home.

Time: Tuesdays, 7:00–8:30 P.M., eight weeks

October–December

Content: Week 1 — Pine Cone Wreaths
          ˝ 2 — Wheat Weaving
          ˝ 3 — Counted Cross-Stitch Ornaments
          ˝ 4 — Ceramic Holiday Items
          ˝ 5 — Bread Dough Ornaments
          ˝ 6 — Evergreen Rope
          ˝ 7 — Candle Making
          ˝ 8 — Cookie Recipe Exchange

Figure 7.3 Program Description and Class Content.

Both long-range planning and short-range planning are necessary in order to bring a program to implementation. The long-range planning may include general information in regard to the program goals and objectives, the customers for whom the program is being planned, the time for the program to be offered, and the general content for the sessions that make up the program. Figure 7.4 is an example of a long-range program plan which includes a plan for offering the program over a two-year time period. A short-range plan, on the other hand, focuses on the individual sessions that will take place during the program. Figure 7.5 shows the plan that is applicable to each session. In other situations, a short-range plan may offer even greater detail than the example. In the case of an instructional (class) program, the short-range plan would describe in detail exactly the content that would be covered each class session, the materials necessary to carry out the session, and the anticipated outcomes from the session. There is an example of a detailed short-range plan in chapter 9, in the description of the class format.

Whenever long-range plans and short-range plans are being written, the leisure programmer and the activity leader must always keep in mind the specific customers for whom the activity plan is being developed. Knowledge and common sense must be exercised in all situations so that the goals and objectives are realistic, the contents are intrinsic to the program and the planned activities are age-appropriate and group-appropriate. For example, a leisure service organization might offer a beginning swimming class for young children and another one for adults. Although the desired outcomes of comfort in the water and beginning swimming skills are the same for both groups, the approach to accomplishing those outcomes would be different in working with the two diverse age groups.

Program Area:	Travel and Tourism
Program Form:	Drop-In
Name of Program:	Travel Adventures
Customers:	All Members of the Community
Program Goal:	To provide a variety of travel experiences through film, videos, slides, and speakers.
Program Objectives:	To enable individuals to "travel" the United States and the world.
	To bring the culture of distant places to the local community.
	To stimulate discussion and exchange of travel experiences among those in attendance.
Time:	Second Wednesday each month, September through June Two sessions each month; 1:30 P.M. and 7:00 P.M.

First Year:
"Around the World"

Sept. — North to Canada
Oct. — Mysteries of the Orient
Nov. — Exploring Spain and Portugal
Dec. — Christmas in Scandinavia
Jan. — Enchanting Egypt
Feb. — Secrets of the Soviet Union
Mar. — The South Seas: Tahiti and Samoa
Apr. — Intrigue of India
May — Winter in Australia
June — Ethnic Fest

Second Year:
"Exploring the USA"

Sept. — The Meandering Mississippi
Oct. — Cactus and Other Desert Flowers
Nov. — New England Winter
Dec. — Snow-Capped Mountains of the USA
Jan. — Romantic Cities: New Orleans
                              San Antonio
                              San Francisco
                              Minneapolis
Feb. — Southwest USA
Mar. — Lakes of the USA: Superior, Meade, Champlain, Crater
Apr. — Summer in Alaska
May — Festivals and Fun: Eugene (OR) Bach Festival; St. Paul (MN) Winter Carnival; Traverse City (MI) Cherry Blossom Festival
June — Heritage Days

Figure 7.4   Long Range Program Plan: Travel Adventures.

Generally speaking, individuals involved in the planning and supervision of leisure programming are not expected to teach or lead, or be involved in the face-to-face delivery of program activities. Their primary task and responsibility is to help identify the need for the activity and to pull together the resources (human, material, and monetary) that are necessary in order to implement the program. The leisure programmer secures (hires) qualified staff (full-time or part-time) in order to plan specific program content and carry it out. Further, the leisure programmer has the responsibility to reserve the facility and to coordinate the availability of the equipment and supplies that are necessary to implement and carry out the planned program. He or she also has the responsibility to make decisions about the budget for the specific program, both the potential disbursements for staff and materials and the potential of revenue from the customer and other sources.

Objectives for each session:
To provide an atmosphere of comfort.
To facilitate interaction between customers and speaker.
To encourage interaction among customers.

Equipment and supplies:
Chairs, coffee pot (and necessary supplies), refreshments, A/V
equipment — projector, screen, VCR, and TV.

Outcomes:
A positive social environment.
Customers interested in attending "Travel Adventures" another time.

Figure 7.5   Short Range Program Plan: Travel Adventures.

It is important to remember that the customer can make valuable suggestions regarding the content of the program. It has been suggested that individuals who are involved in the formulation of the learning experience will be more interested in the activity and more highly motivated; hence, more effective learning will take place. This practice can be applied in the leisure programming context. The leisure programmer and the activity leader should interact with potential customers and/or the individuals in specific programs in order to gain an understanding of their needs and attitudes. The customer, through dialogue with the program leader, can gain a better understanding of the goals and the methods that are to be employed in implementing the leisure experience. In certain situations, customers may want to design their own program content; in other situations, they may wish to interact with the leader to develop the experience. In the former case, a drop-in type of format may be most appropriate; in the latter instance, a more structured type of format may be more effective.

Time Factors

Time is an overriding factor in the program development process. The time factor both influences and is influenced by the other elements of program planning. For instance, determining the time to start planning, deciding the time the program will begin, and scheduling the time (day and time of day) that the activity will take place are all extremely important. Because of the importance of time in leisure program planning it is necessary to examine several components of the time factor.

Establishing a time line for planning will serve as a guide for the leisure programmer. The time line may be as long or as short as the planner decides to make it. It may be as detailed or as brief as the leisure programmer desires. For example, a time line for program planning may begin with the needs identification and assessment phase, move to the task of developing goals and objectives, then include the program development process and the program implementation stage, and conclude with program evaluation. On the other hand, a time line may be created only to guide the leisure programmer through the phase of program development; or a time line for the "life of the program" (implementation) may be written. A time line is an outline or list of tasks to be carried out, including people to contact, facilities to reserve, materials to secure, and promotion to be distributed; all of which will be designated with a specific time when the task should be completed. Figure 7.6 gives an example of how a time line may be prepared.

Other time factors that are a part of planning are time of day, time of week, week and month of year, and length/duration of each activity session or the whole program. These time decisions cannot be made in isolation from other factors.

Event: Community Concert

I. 12-16 weeks prior to event
  A. Reserve facility
  B. Sign contract with performer
  C. Determine budget

II. 9-11 weeks prior to event
  A. Order printing of tickets
  B. Order advertising
  C. Reserve necessary A/V equipment
  D. Contact radio and TV stations

III. 6-8 weeks prior to event
  A. Discuss all performance needs with facility management
  B. Know regulations at facility—security, fire, crowd management, etc.
  C. Release initial advertising and publicity

IV. 4-7 weeks prior to event
  A. Distribute additional advertising and publicity
  B. Monitor ticket sales—fill mail orders
  C. Continue in contact with facility management and follow up
     on equipment reservations

V. 1-3 weeks prior to event
  A. Continue to monitor ticket sales—hold mail orders for pickup
  B. Set up interviews with performer by local media
  C. Monitor all last-minute details

VI. Day of event
  A. Check with facility to know that all seating, concessions, equipment, etc., are in place
  B. Provide for the performer's convenience—motel, dressing room, food, etc.
  C. Monitor all necessary details
  D. Attend concert

VII. Immediately following event
  A. Pay all bills
  B. Return all borrowed equipment
  C. Write and send thank-you letters
  D. Write critique of strong and weak points of planning and implementation
  E. Close financial record and prepare report

Figure 7.6   Program Development Time Line.

These time decisions are influenced by the program area and specific activity that is being planned. The format that will be used to implement the activity influences time decisions. The customers for whom the activity is being planned and the facility where the program will take place also influence how the time factors are established. There is an interrelatedness of many elements in time planning.

Consider one program—swimming lessons for children—to illustrate the decisions that must be made in relation to time. There are several questions that must be asked and answered. What time of year is the program to be offered? If it is offered both during the school year and during the summertime, how will this change the time planning? How many sessions will be offered? How long will each session be? What time of day will the program be offered? How many times a week will the program meet? In order to answer these questions, the planner must keep in mind when the customers (children) are available. The planner must also know when parents or other significant adults are available to get the children to the program. During the school year, the times that children are likely to be available for participation is on weekdays after school into early evening and on weekends. During the summer, children would probably have greater flexibility of time and be available for longer periods of time. How frequently should the swimming sessions be offered? Once a week for ten weeks, twice a week for five weeks, five times a week for two weeks? Figure 7.7 is a suggestion of the variety of ways in which a given number of activity sessions could be structured.

Farrell and Lundegren (1983) have suggested that scheduling can be thought of in specific patterns. The first pattern involves the seasons of the year or natural annual time blocks such as holidays. These blocks of time may also include traditional program planning which falls into eight-to-ten-week time periods. This pattern of planning seems to accommodate the class format and structured competitive sports leagues, and facilitates a plan for periodic promotional and program registration activities. A second scheduling pattern may have more of a monthly or weekly focus. Ongoing programs, such as club groups that meet on a regular basis, weekly programs, special events, monthly themes fit into this type of pattern. This pattern of programming enables the leisure programmer to accommodate special interests and emphasize particular kinds of programming in concentrated periods of time. Further, this programming pattern may appeal to the drop-in customer more than other programming options. The third pattern for scheduling focuses on the lifestyle patterns of leisure customers. Days of the week are divided into time-use patterns.

Time Structure	Program Idea
Once a week for ten weeks	Creative Dramatics for Children
Twice a week for five weeks	Adult Aerobics
Five times a week for two weeks	Summer Swimming Class
Twice a day for five days	Cheerleading Camps
Two days, five hours each	CPR Training
One day for ten hours	Sports Official Re-Certification Workshop
Twice a month for five months	Square Dance Club
Once a month for ten months	Travelogue Series

ays

Figure 7.7 Varied Time Structuring for Ten Session Programs.

Daily time-use patterns have been divided into five blocks of time by Farrell and Lundegren (1983: 117–118). These five time periods include:

1. *Morning Session*—This time slot is a possible activity period for senior adults, preschool children, swing-shift workers, housepersons, and others. The activity rarely begins before 9:00 A.M. and is usually completed before noon, although a meal may be a part of the program activity.

2. *Early Afternoon Session*—This time period may well attract the same clientele as those listed above. The camp will incorporate a rest hour here, or the institution may choose this time period for special medication or treatments, such that immediately after the noon hour activity generally is at a lower level. After this normally slower period, it can be expected that activity periods will be popular.

3. *Late Afternoon Session*—This may be the busiest time during the school year in which children of school age will require programs and participate in recreational activities. During the summer months, however, this [may] not be a highly participatory time.

4. *Early Evening Session*—Aside from varying work shifts in the area, this remains a most popular time for recreational activity. There are many elements in a person's life that compete for this time of one's day. Television, part-time jobs, community service work, social clubs, family get-together time, school activities and studying, church work and fellowship groups, and socializing with peers; all tend to be competitors for activity during evening discretionary hours.

5. *Late Evening Session*—Depending on the bedtime habits or possible curfew regulations in the area, this time block could extend well into the early morning hours. Although this tends to be an adult time period, there are many areas of the country in which younger children are out until well past midnight.

To these five blocks of time we would add three more.

6. *Early Morning*—This is a time period popular with leisure customers who wish to "get into" their leisure activities before their workday or other daily activities begin. This time block may be 5:00–8:00 A.M. used by leisure customers at leisure facilities or on their own at home.

7. *Noon Hour*—In the "busyness" of people's schedules, this is a time that individuals choose to engage in leisure activities. Though it may not be a lengthy period of time, it is a busy time block at a variety of leisure facilities.

8. *Evening Dinner Hour*—This time period of leisure activity participation can be inserted between late afternoon and early evening. It may encompass primarily the time between 5:00 and 7:00 P.M., and may be included in the customer's personal schedule between daytime and evening commitments and activities.

Societal changes continue to have an influence on the way in which leisure programs are scheduled and on the times that leisure facilities are available to customers. Some work schedules may require longer workdays, but fewer workdays per week. Further, some places of employment may have employee work schedules that differ from week to week. Other places of employment may schedule a shutdown time at the same time each year when all employees have the same vacation time period. With the flexibility in work schedules that exists, leisure service organizations must build flexibility into program scheduling to serve leisure customers. Concentrating leisure activities into shorter periods of time, e.g., scheduling a workshop over a three-day weekend, instead of on three consecutive Saturdays, may be more attractive to the leisure customer.

The availability and usability of a specific facility also influences the scheduling of particular programs and services for leisure customers. Figure 7.8 is an example of the way in which the four primary physical activity areas are scheduled in a YWCA. Program planners may also wish to "group" activities so that a customer can be involved in more than one program during the time they are at the facility. For example, referring to the schedule in Figure 7.8, an individual could participate in four activities on Thursday

-----------------Clip and Save-----------------

BUILDING SCHEDULE
January 8 - March 24, 1990

Control Center Hours: M, T, W, Th, F: 6:30 a.m.-9:00 p.m.
Sat. 8:00 a.m.-3:00 p.m.

WD = Water Dynamics
LS = Lap Swim
OP = Open Plunge
AA = Adapted Aquatics Exercise
FP = Family Plunge

LS/OP = Lap Swim, Open Plunge
(Lap swimmers must yield to plunge participants)
OG = Open Gym

	POOL	WHIRLPOOL	GYM	BODY SHOP
MONDAY	6:30-8:00 a.m. LS 8:00-8:45 a.m. WD 8:45-9:30 a.m. LS 9:30-10:15 a.m. OP 10:15-11:00 p.m. AA 11:00-11:45 a.m. WD 11:45-1:00 p.m. WD 4:00-4:45 p.m. WD 5:30-6:15 p.m. WD	6:30-8:00 a.m. 8:45-10:15 a.m. 11:45-1:00 p.m.	6:30-9:00 a.m. OG Adult 12:00-1:00 p.m. OG Adult 1:00-3:00 p.m. Volleyball 6:45-9:00 p.m. OG Adult/Youth	6:30 a.m.-8:45 p.m.
TUESDAY	6:30-7:15 a.m. WD 7:15-8:00 a.m. OP/LS 8:00-8:45 a.m. WD 8:45-9:30 a.m. LS 9:30-10:15 a.m. OP 11:00-11:45 a.m. WD 11:45-1:00 p.m. LS 5:00-5:45 p.m. WD 5:45-6:30 p.m. LS 7:15-8:00 p.m. OP	7:15-8:00 a.m. 8:45-10:15 a.m. 11:45-1:00 p.m. 5:45-6:30 p.m. 7:15-8:00 p.m.	6:30 a.m.-4:30 p.m. OG Adult 8:00-9:00 p.m. OG Adult/Youth	6:30 a.m.-8:45 p.m.
WEDNESDAY	6:30-8:00 a.m. LS 8:00-8:45 a.m. WD 8:45-9:30 a.m. LS 9:30-10:15 a.m. OP 11:00-11:45 a.m. WD 11:45-1:00 p.m. LS 4:00-4:45 p.m. WD 5:30-6:15 p.m. WD	6:30-8:00 a.m. 8:45-10:15 a.m. 11:45-1:00 p.m.	6:30-9:00 a.m. OG Adult 1:00-4:00 p.m. OG Adult 6:45-9:00 p.m. OG Adult/Youth	6:30 a.m.-8:45 p.m.
THURSDAY	6:30-7:15 a.m. WD 7:15-8:00 a.m. OP/LS 8:00-8:45 a.m. WD 8:45-9:30 a.m. LS 9:30-10:15 a.m. OP 10:15-11:00 a.m. AA 11:00-11:45 a.m. WD 11:45-1:00 p.m. LS 5:00-5:45 p.m. WD 5:45-6:30 p.m. LS 7:15-8:00 p.m. OP	7:15-8:00 a.m. 8:45-10:15 a.m. 11:45-1:00 p.m. 5:45-6:30 p.m. 7:15-8:00 p.m.	6:30 a.m.-4:30 p.m. OG Adult 8:00-9:00 p.m. OG Adult/Youth	6:30 a.m.-8:45 p.m.
FRIDAY	6:30-8:00 a.m. LS 8:00-8:45 a.m. WD 8:45-9:30 a.m. LS 9:30-10:15 a.m. OP 11:00-11:45 a.m. WD 11:45-1:00 p.m. LS 5:30-6:15 p.m. WD 6:30-8:30 p.m. FP	6:30-8:00 a.m. 8:45-10:15 a.m. 11:45-1:00 p.m. 6:15-8:30 p.m.	6:30-9:00 a.m. OG Adult 12:00-5:00 p.m. OG Adult 7:00-9:00 p.m. Volleyball	6:30 a.m.-8:45 p.m.
SATURDAY	8:00-8:45 a.m. WD 12:30-1:30 p.m. LS 1:30-3:00 p.m. FP No Family Plunge on February 9	12:30-3:00 p.m.	8:00-8:45 a.m. OG Adult/Youth 1:00 a.m.-3:00 p.m. OG Adult/Youth	8:00 a.m.-3:00 p.m.

Figure 7.8 Building Schedule. (YWCA of Black Hawk County, Waterloo, Iowa.)

morning. The customer could work out in the gym beginning about 7:30 A.M., use the body shop at 8:00 A.M., participate in lap swim at 8:45 A.M. and enjoy the whirlpool at 9:30 A.M.

Another time factor that is a part of our society is the concept of "time deepening." Godbey (1985: 18) indicates that time deepening " . . . has three related aspects: undertaking an activity more quickly, undertaking more than one activity simultaneously, and using time more precisely." An activity undertaken more quickly may be to play racquetball over the noon hour instead of playing in a volleyball league in the evening. Watching television while eating, or having a business conference on the golf course is involvement in more than one activity at a time; and calling before 8:00 A.M. to schedule the tennis court at 4:40 P.M. illustrates using time more precisely.

Leisure customers must be understood for who they are and for the time segments that are a part of their lifestyles. The common ways in which we group individuals as older adults, employed people, home managers, college students, children, junior and senior high school students, singles, married couples, single parents, and families influence the way in which we schedule leisure opportunities for these groups of leisure customers. Not only must the leisure programmer be sensitive to the activity interests and needs of these groups of customers, but perhaps more important, to the time availability and restrictions that leisure customer groups have. Figure 7.9 presents a schedule for a community center's swimming pool. Attention is given to attempting to meet the varying needs, as well as the varying interests, of different age groups.

Facilities

Leisure service facilities, in this context, include both *buildings and land areas.* In other words, structures such as recreation centers and swimming pools and areas such as ballfields and golf courses are all included when referring to leisure service facilities. Numerous man-made facilities in addition to natural areas are crucial in the provision of leisure services, programs, and activities. The location, the design, the availability, and the accessibility of any facility is what contributes to its usability for both structured and spontaneous participation in leisure activities. For example, the proximity of facilities to those who wish to use them, the hours of the day and days of the week that they are open, and the convenience of parking personal cars or using public

Community Center Pool Fall Schedule   September 18, 1989 - February 4, 1990

Monday	Tuesday	Wednesday	Thursday	Friday	Saturday	Sunday
6-9 Lap Swim Daily Lifeguard Break: 7:30 - 7:35 a.m.						
9:15 - 10:00 Parent-Tot Adult	9:00 - 9:45 Arth. Aquatics	9:15 -10:00 Parent -Tot Adult	9:00 - 9:45 Arth. Aquatics	9-10 Open Swim	9-9:25 Parent-Tot / 9:30-9:55 Pre Sch	
10-11:30 Senior Swim	9:50 -10:35 Aquasize / 10:45 - 11:30 Open Swim	10-11:30 Senior Swim	9:50 -10:35 Aquasize / 10:45 - 11:30 Open Swim	10-11:30 Senior Swim	10:00 - 10:40 Beginner / 10:45 - 11:25 Adv. Beginner	
11:30 - 1:00 Lap Swim 11:30 - 1:00					11:30 - 1:30 Lap Swim	
1- 2 Maintenance	1-2 Special Pops Open Swim	1-2 Maintenance	1-2 Special Pops Open Swim	1-2 Maintenance	1:30-6:30 Open Swim	
2-3 W.E.B.	2 - 2:30 Maint. / 2:30-3 Pre Sch	2-3 W.E.B.	2 - 2:30 Maint. / 2:30-3 Pre Sch	2-5 Open Swim		
3-5 Open Swim	3:05 - 3:50 Beg/Adv Beg / 3:55-4:55 Int Swim BWS or EWS	3-5 Open Swim	3:05 - 3:50 Beg/Adv Beg / 3:55-4:55 Int Swim BWS or EWS			
5-6:30 Lap Swim 5-6:30					4 - 8 Free Admission	
6:30 - 8 Swim Team	6:30 - 7:15 Beg/Adult/B.Beg. / 7:15 - 8:00 W.Aerobics/Int	6:30 - 8 Kayak	6:30 - 7:15 Beg/Adult/A.Beg. / 7:15 - 8:00 W.Aerobics/Int	6:30 - 8 Swim Team	6:30 - 8 Lap Swim	
8-9 Masters / 9-10 Open Swim	8-10 Scuba or Water Safety	8-9 Masters / 9-10 Open Swim	8-10 Scuba or Water Safety	8-9 Masters	**Look for revised Schedule During the Holidays (Fall Break,Thanksgiving, Christmas)	

**Pool Closes at 5:00 pm on Friday 9/22/89

Figure 7.9   Community Center Pool Schedule.

transportation are all factors that make the use of leisure facilities possible for leisure customers.

Though many facilities in communities are designed and used for leisure services and programs, there are many other facilities that lend themselves to use for leisure activities. It is traditional that school facilities have often been primary leisure service areas in many communities. Schools have been built for educational purposes and therefore offer a wide variety of spaces for leisure use. Schools have gymnasiums, swimming pools, locker rooms, athletic areas, tennis courts, arenas, auditoriums, craft areas, meeting rooms, libraries, kitchens, dance studios, the-

aters, and parking lots, which make them desirable leisure service areas. Further, in many communities, public utility buildings, banks, churches, social and human service organizations, and shopping malls have meeting spaces, auditoriums, and in some cases gymnasiums and playing courts, which are available to organizations and community groups to use for leisure programs and activities. Commercial recreation facilities in communities, which may include bowling alleys, fitness centers and spas, movie theaters, ballrooms, and restaurants are sometimes available for use by outside groups for the delivery of leisure service organization programs and services.

Town of Chapel Hill
Recreational Areas & Facilities

	Lighted Tennis Courts	Picnic Area	Athletic Fields	Basketball Goals	Play Equipment	Nature Trails	Fitness Trails	Recreation Center	Swimming Pool	Free Play Open Space	Volleyball Courts
1. Hargraves Park	3	•	•	•	•			•	•	•	P
2. Umstead Park	*1	•	•	•	•	•	•	•		•	•
3. Oakwood Park	1	•		P	•					•	
4. Cedar Falls Park	6	•	•	P	•	•	P	P	P	•	P
5. Ephesus Park	6	•	•	•	•	P	P			•	
6. Legion Field		•								•	
7. Phillips Park	4	P									
8. Jones Park		•			•	•					
9. Westwood Park					•						
10. Lincoln Center				•☆				•			
11. Gomains Play Area		•			•						
12. Burlington Play Area		•			•					•	
13. Community Center Park		•		•☆	P			•	•☆	•	•

14. Plant Road Administrative Offices
15. N.C. Botanical Garden
16. Chapel Hill High School
17. Seawell Elementary School
18. Phillips Junior High School
19. Estes Hills Elementary School

20. Ephesus Elementary School
21. Carrboro Elementary School
22. Glenwood Elementary School
23. Frank Porter Graham Elementary School
24. Culbreth Junior High School

P Proposed Facility
☆ Indoor Facility
• Existing Facility
* Not Lighted

200 Plant Road, Chapel Hill, N.C. 27514 · 968-2784

Figure 7.10   Areas and Facilities Guide. (Chapel Hill (North Carolina) Park and Recreation Commission.)

The kinds of facilities and areas that a leisure service organization has available for use will obviously determine what kinds of programs and activities the organization can provide for its customers. For example, the list of areas and facilities in Figure 7.10 identifies the resources available to the customers served by the Chapel Hill (North Carolina) Parks and Recreation Commission. It is obvious that in order to offer aquatic activities in a community, there needs to be some kind of aquatic facility available in proximity to the potential customers. This is an example of a very specialized facility required for specific programming. On the other hand, there are many activities that could take place in a variety of spaces with some adaptability. The ideal place for tennis to be played is on a court designed for that purpose. However, tennis can be played on a grass surface, on a variety of hard surface areas such as a parking lot or a gymnasium floor, and in some cases, when there is shortage of space, the roof of a building that has been prepared for that purpose and that has a fence high enough to keep both the balls and the players on the roof.

The design and maintenance of any facility contribute greatly to the usability of that facility. Leisure service programmers may not always have had the opportunity to be involved in the design of an existing facility. In other words, some leisure service facilities may have originally been designed and built for a purpose other than their present use. Some school buildings are renovated to become recreation centers. Sometimes stores or other places of business have been converted to senior citizen centers. Creative imagination and good judgment are the attributes that a programmer must have to make maximum use of any facility that is available. Cleanliness, good lighting, comfortable temperatures, use of attractive colors on walls, ceilings, and window covers, appropriate floor surfaces, and monitoring and prevention of vandalism contribute to respect for property by the customers and the desire to use of the facility.

The question may be asked, "Is a leisure facility a leisure program?" A facility is not a program per se, but all leisure activities must have some kind of facility in order to happen. On the other hand, unless a leisure facility is put to its best and highest use with good programming, the facility is of little value. Therefore, the need for a facility in order to create a program and the need for a program in order to make use of a facility make these two factors crucial in program development and delivery.

Setting

Closely related to the areas and facilities for leisure programming is the setting in which the activity will take place. While areas and facilities may refer to the physical structure of buildings, sports fields, and parks, the setting encompasses the physical and social environment within these facilities. As referred to earlier, the design and maintenance of any facility contribute to its usability and the environment that it creates. Outdoor maintenance of a building is as important as the maintenance that is carried out inside the building. The degree to which there is maintenance of lawns, flower beds, bushes, and trees, as well as sidewalks, parking lots, outdoor lighting, walls, windows, and doors of any facility

make it either attractive to its users or invite abuse, vandalism, and sometimes destruction. The initial impression that a customer has of the physical environment of a leisure facility may help determine whether or not that individual continues to be a customer and whether or not that individual encourages or discourages others from being customers of a particular leisure service organization.

The physical environment inside a facility is also of extreme importance to the delivery of leisure services and programs. The setting (physical space and feeling) in which an activity takes place has a strong impact on the leisure experience for the individual. If there is junior high basketball taking place in the gym (with all its inherent noise) at the same time as there is a speaker for a group of senior adults in the meeting room next to the gym (where quiet is necessary), the physical environment for the senior adults would probably contribute to a negative leisure experience. How could this situation be avoided? Move the quiet meeting further away from the gym (because basketball cannot be moved from a gym), or perhaps schedule the two activities at different times if other planning can be done for either group. Other factors of the physical environment were also listed in the facilities section. Cleanliness, lighting, temperatures, colors, furniture, floor surfaces, and location of restrooms, drinking fountains, information areas, lounges, and waiting areas are extremely important elements of the physical environment.

The multiple uses of areas in a leisure service facility also contribute to the physical environment. It is obvious that many leisure activities need specific spaces in which to occur—for example, high ceilinged rooms (gyms) are necessary for volleyball and basketball. Further, there are some activities requiring special equipment that is best left out, instead of being put away after every use (free weights, stationary bikes, etc.) that make it necessary to set aside a special area for that activity only. On the other hand, many kinds of physical activities can take place in a gym, high ceiling or not. Games and relays, exercise programs and running, badminton and tennis, and cheerleading and gymnastics all are "at home" in the gymnasium. If necessary, discussion groups, craft classes, lectures, and meetings could also take place in the gym, if other spaces are not available. However, these activities would be better served by being held in meeting rooms or classrooms within a facility. Rather than not making a particular leisure activity available because the "ideal" space is not available, adapt the activity or adapt a space, or both, and create the most suitable setting in which the activity may take place.

Taking program activities out of traditional settings and carrying them out in new settings can add interest to programming. Moving a theatrical production off the elevated stage in an auditorium and offering it in a "theater-in-the-round" or "theater-in-the-park" setting may attract more and different customers to the program. Moving an after-school program for children from an established leisure facility to an elementary school may make the program more accessible for more customers because of the proximity of the activities to the children. Using the outdoors for outdoor activities, instead of taking them indoors, taking programs to locations closer to the customers, and adapting both the setting and the activity as suggested in the previous paragraph, will enable the leisure service organization to demonstrate more flexibility and variety in programming.

Social environments are as important to leisure experiences as the physical settings in which they take place. Although the physical setting contributes significantly to the social environment, the human factor in the leisure experience is the primary element in the social environment. The individual customer, the leisure service provider, the other individuals in the same leisure activity, and all other customers within the same facility have an influence on the outcome of the leisure experience. The leisure professional must consider many elements in the planning process.

Depending on the leisure activity that is being planned, the planner must decide who will be included in the program. If the program is for children, will it always be for both girls and boys, or is it appropriate to offer a program just for girls or just for boys? Sometimes separating groups of customers is good planning. Another necessary consideration is to be aware of what groups of customers may be using a facility at the same time. When there is open swimming at a pool, should all age groups be in the water at the same time? Maybe all customers would be better served if there were designated times in the scheduling for young children only, families only, or teens and young adults only.

Individual customers have individual preferences in regard to the social environments in which they choose to participate. How groups are structured, how many people there are in the group, how much individual attention a customer may prefer or wish to avoid, and how many and what kind of customers may be at a facility at the same time are factors that influence the participation choices that people make. The leisure programmer must be conscious of the "mixture" of both program activities and kinds of customers that are in a facility at the same time. Although leisure activities are broad in scope and many facilities are designed for multiple use and leisure experiences, the settings in which leisure programs take place must be selected with appropriate planning and good judgment.

The interaction between the leisure service providers and the customers in any setting is important to the social environment that is created. The leisure programmer, the activity leader, the custodian, the office manager, the locker room attendant, and the organization executive director and other organization staff are all a part of providing services to the customers of their organizations. It is the way in which each of these individuals interacts with or ignores the customer that will contribute to the quality of the leisure experience for that customer. Congeniality, concern, and accessibility, and providing service and caring about individual customers establishes the social environment in a leisure service organization.

Equipment and Supplies

In addition to facilities and settings, it is necessary to have equipment and supplies in order to implement leisure program activities. Equipment is generally thought of as those items that are permanent and/or reusable, while supplies are materials that are consumed during activities and cannot be reused. In other words, equipment can range from basketball backboards to tennis rackets, to scissors and easels, to record players and VCRs, to coffee pots and clip boards, and to tables and chairs. Supplies include the items needed each time a particular activity is carried out, such as craft materials, chalk for athletic fields, chemicals for swimming pools, award ribbons and trophies, and all other materials that are depleted at the end of the activity.

Attainment of equipment and supplies by leisure service organizations is primarily accomplished in three ways: wholesale or retail purchase, having customers supply the materials for themselves, or scrounging to acquire items at little or no cost from a variety of sources. Some organizations may use only one of these methods, while others may use all three. The cost of the necessary equipment and supplies, the availability of the materials, the ages of the customers involved, and the philosophy of the organization may be factors that determine the method(s) of acquisition that an organization uses.

Contributing to the availability of equipment for leisure programming may be the practice of sharing equipment. This can be accomplished in several ways. In leisure facilities where there is similar programming for a variety of groups, it is only practical to use the same equipment. In other words, if there is one volleyball league for men, one league for women, and a coed league, the use of the same nets and standards is logical. Use of the same volleyballs may also be possible, unless the level of competition by one group or the other dictates the use of a different quality

of ball. Another example of equipment sharing might be a situation in which several units within an institution use audio/visual equipment periodically. Rather than each unit having equipment that is seldom used, units could share use of the A/V equipment through a coordinated sign-out system. A third example of equipment sharing might be new softballs provided for adult softball leagues and then used for children's programming after they have been "broken in." Because most leisure service organizations must monitor expenditures and equipment inventory very carefully, multiple use of equipment for several programs is necessary.

The equipment and supplies needed for a particular program activity will have an influence on the cost of offering the program. If the activity involves equipment that has been or can be used repeatedly, the cost involved may be less than if supplies must be acquired each time the program is offered. The leisure program planner and the activity leader should have a plan of regular and ongoing maintenance and repair of the program equipment. In addition, there should be a structured system to monitor the inventory of supplies that the leisure service organization has or will need to secure.

Staffing

Staffing is the process of securing the human resources for program delivery. Personnnel and staffing decisions are an on-going activity in all leisure service organizations. At the same time, staffing decisions must be made in relation to each program that is planned. There are several considerations that must be kept in mind as activity staffing is resolved. The leisure program planner must determine the level of knowledge, skill, and ability needed by the activity leader, and in some cases the age of the leader in relation to the customers with whom the leader is working. Athough each of these factors will not be discussed in detail here, they are inherent in the process of selecting staff.

Traditionally, there are three levels of leadership in leisure service delivery (see Figure

7.11)—the administrative level, the supervisory level, and the face-to-face level of leadership. The program-planning activities within a leisure service organization primarily involve the supervisory level (programmer) and the face-to-face level (direct activity leader.) On the other hand, the

staffing of programs and services is a comprehensive activity within the organization. At whatever level and for whatever purpose staff is being secured, there are several procedures that are involved.

Planning, recruiting, selecting, training, supervising, evaluating, and compensating are all necessary elements in the staffing process (see Figure 7.12). Planning involves an analysis of the job, the determination of the tasks and responsibilities that the job has, and the qualifications required of the person to fill the position. A job description should be developed that includes information about both of these factors. Recruiting can be both internal and external to find applicants for the positions that are available. A leisure service organization may distribute information to current staff and/or customers, to community groups, to community organizations, to schools and colleges, to job placement departments, and to employment agencies. Leisure service organizations often use local media, such as newspapers, to recruit staff.

Figure 7.11 The Three Levels of Leadership.

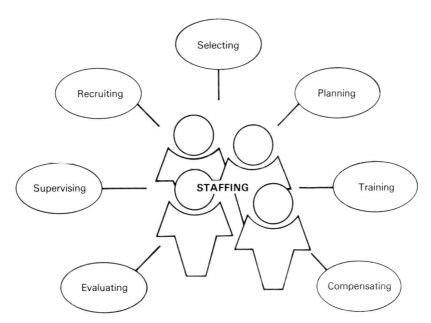

Figure 7.12 Elements of the Staffing Process.

Selection (hiring) of staff is generally accomplished through the application and interview process. Once individuals have been selected for program leadership, it is necessary to orient them to the organization for whom they are working and to train them for the position that they hold. Supervision of activity leaders is carried out by the program planner and takes place during the development and implementation phases of programming. Evaluation of all staff is an ongoing process. Formative evaluation contributes to the growth and development of the individual staff person, and the summative evaluation enables the person to know how well his or her job expectations have been accomplished. Compensation for work can be in the form of both monetary compensation and/or individual acknowledgement or public recognition.

In many leisure service organizations, the program activity staff is composed of part-time and seasonal employees, both paid and voluntary. As indicated earlier in the content section, leisure service professionals in the supervisory/ programmer role are often not the direct activity providers. However, the authors recognize that in many organizations the program planner also functions as the direct program provider. Also it is necessary to recognize that some leisure service organizations pay all of the personnel within the organization. In other organizations, there is a combination of paid and voluntary personnel; in some, professional paid staff supervise volunteers and/or volunteer leadership supervises paid professional staff and activity providers.

The place of the programmer in the leisure service organization was discussed in chapter 3. It is important to know that the role of each staff person within an organization is significant to that organization and to the customers that are served by the organization.

Cost

Determination of the cost of leisure program activities is based on both the program's expenditures and its potential for income. Program expenditures include staff salaries and wages, equipment and supplies, facility or physical space maintenance, promotion, and all other overhead costs that must be accounted for such as postage, facility rent, etc. On the other hand, program income may come from several sources. These include the organization's general budget, customer fees and charges, purchase of equipment and supplies from the organization by the customer, and special contributions from other sources.

Both the expenditures and income for leisure program activities are influenced by several factors. The overall nature of the program—area of programming, program format, setting, facility needed, equipment and supplies necessary, the level of specialization and expertise required of the activity leader, and the age of the customer, and the customer's ability to pay all influence program cost. In addition, the philosophy and practice of the organization in relation to funding has an impact on program cost. The organization may have a "pay as you go" system, a membership fee with additional program fees, a membership or service fee which includes all program participation costs, or the outright purchase of programs and services by the customer; the extent to which program cost is affected will depend on which system is used.

Chapter 11 will provide much greater detail about program cost, securing equipment and supplies, and will provide a discussion about determination of wages and salaries for program staff.

Promotion

Promotion is the communication of the leisure service organization with the leisure customer. Communication involves a communicator (the leisure service organization), a message (information about programs and services), channels of distribution (advertising, publicity, personal selling, public relations, and sales promotion), and an audience (the target group) that the organization wants to receive the message. Chapter

10 discusses promotion in great depth, but promotion is included here as an important element in the program development process.

All elements of the program development phase are crucial to providing program activities. However, the most dynamic planning and innovative programming will go for naught if there is not detailed planning and implementation of promotion. Although the development of promotion may be built into the program development time line, it may also be necessary to develop a time line for the program promotion element itself. To develop promotion, leisure programmers must avail themselves of resources of expertise that may exist within the leisure service organization as a whole or within the institution of which leisure services may be a part. It is also necessary for leisure service programmers to become familiar with persons and resources in the general community that will facilitate the promotion process.

The program planner must become involved in determining for what audiences particular promotional materials need to be developed. Channels and tools to distribute the information must be selected. As stated earlier, a time line for the promotion process should be set and adhered to. As in many of the phases of the program development process, several persons may be involved in the promotion process, and therefore adequate time to complete tasks must be anticipated and designed into the planning.

Activity Analysis

Activity analysis is the procedure of breaking down and examining the inherent characteristics of an activity. This process provides the means by which the leisure programmer and the leisure customer can determine whether the customer is capable of meeting the requirements necessary to take part in the activity. In addition, activity analysis shows whether the activity contributes to meeting goals and objectives for the customer.

When an individual is involved in an activity, behavior occurs in three domains—psycho-motor (physical/action), cognitive (intellectual/thinking), and affective (emotional/feeling). In other words, activities require the customer to use muscular or motor skills to perform an action or carry out a task, to demonstrate understanding, recall, and problem solving to accomplish an expectation, and to display feelings that reflect character.

The nature of each specific activity may emphasize one performance domain more than the other two. However, each domain of behavior is present to some degree in all activities. When a person is involved in swimming, the psycho-motor domain is most obvious, but at the same time the individual must cognitively make appropriate judgments about the safe behavior in the water and may affectively show satisfaction with improvement in a swimming skill. In another example, passive participation at a symphony concert emphasizes the affective domain of enjoyment, while some knowledge of the music or musical instruments contributes to the experience, and the physical action is getting to the concert.

Another area of behavior that is considered in activity analysis is the amount of social interaction or social skills needed to participate. Avedon (1974) described social interaction patterns. These patterns include:

1. *Intra-individual*—Action taking place within the mind of a person, or action involving the mind and part of the body, but requiring no contact with another person or object. An example of this social behavior might be day dreaming or twiddling ones thumbs.
2. *Extra-individual*—Action directed by the individual toward an object in the environment, and requiring no contact with another person. Walking, reading, or playing solitaire are examples of action.
3. *Aggregate*—Action directed by the person toward an object in the environment while in the company of other persons, but no contact or interaction with the other persons is necessary. This behavior might be playing bingo, attending a movie, or painting a canvas.

4. *Inter-individual*—Action of a competitive nature directed by two persons toward each other. This action might include playing badminton or board games.

5. *Unilateral*—Action of a competitive nature among three or more people, with one person being the "antagonist" or "it." A variety of games and activities with an "it" are examples of this social interaction.

6. *Multilateral*—Action of a competitive nature among a group of three or more persons, with no individual as the antagonist. This action might include card games, trivial pursuit games, etc.

7. *Intragroup*—Action of a cooperative nature by two or more persons attempting to reach a mutual goal. Music groups and drama groups are examples of cooperative action.

8. *Intergroup*—Action of a competitive nature between two or more intragroups. Competitive team sports activities are intergroup action.

Farrell and Lundegren (1983: 72) note that in addition to the behavioral domains and patterns of social interaction, the comprehensive activity analysis model also examines the level of leadership necessary, the equipment that is required, the duration of time for the activity, the facilities needed, the number of participants involved, and the age of the participants. The function of activity analysis is to provide the information needed to match the needs of the individual with the types of activities that will contribute to the successful accomplishment of goals and objectives. In so doing, activity analysis provides an accountable manner in which to provide activities. It seems ridiculous, but too often activities are offered with no consideration of their consequences. Activity analysis is based on preplanning to insure that appropriate activities are provided to the customers.

Risk Management

Risk management in program development is the anticipation of situations, not problems, and the exercise of reasonable care and judgment as a precaution to reduce and/or eliminate hazards and risks. Risk management is not limited to individual program planning within a leisure service organization; the management of risk is a comprehensive management tool in the total operation of the organization. It is applicable to total program development and individual program development at the same time.

Nilson and Edginton (1982: 35) have said, "The basic goal of a risk management program is to identify and evaluate risks with an eye toward reducing or eliminating the agency's financial loss." The sources of risk within a leisure service organization, according to Nilson and Edginton include contracts, programs, facilities, participants, employees, and equipment. Though finances are not listed as a source of risk, losses in any of the areas listed ultimately leads to a financial loss of some (sometimes severe) magnitude. Financial loss will occur whenever there is deterioration or destruction (vandalism) of property and equipment; negligence or dishonesty by staff; injury or the loss of life to customers; and catastrophic events, such as natural disasters or accidental occurrence such as fire.

The need for risk management in program development is to protect the leisure service organization, the organization's staff, and the customers that are served by the organization. According to Kraus and Curtis (1990), in order to minimize the risk of lawsuits common in society today, a leisure service organization must have a well-organized plan for risk management and accident prevention. The organization must be responsible for adequately maintained facilities and equipment at all times. There must be a specific plan for the routine monitoring and maintenance of all physical facilities and areas, and all equipment. Organization staff must provide appropriate accident prevention supervision for all services, programs, and activities. As a part of supervision practices, there must be a planned follow-up procedure when problems do arise. In addition, leisure customers need to be protected from their own ignorance in the use

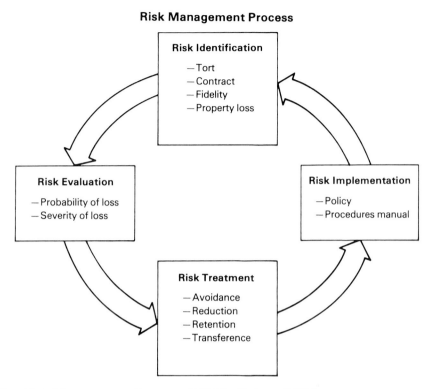

Figure 7.13 Risk Management Process (1986). (Kaiser, 229.)

of leisure areas, facilities, and equipment. The leisure service organization must use more sophisticated approaches to educating the public in regard to environmental values and criminal acts.

Figure 7.13 illustrates the process of risk management. Kaiser (1986) has indicated that to manage risks, they must be identified, evaluated, and treated (selected), and a management plan must be developed. Nilson and Edginton (1982) include a fifth step in the risk management process, the ongoing review and evaluation of the whole process itself. Kaiser focuses on risk treatment which he also refers to as risk selection. According to Kaiser (1986: 232), choosing the "method for risk treatment is based on the frequency of the occurrence and severity of loss."

Risk treatment methods are risk avoidance, risk reduction, risk retention, and risk transfer.

Risk avoidance is the possible elimination or cancellation of a leisure program or activity, or the closure of a facility by the leisure service organization. Making the decision of risk avoidance weighs the advantages of the activity or facility against possible undesirable results. Risk reduction practices attempt to lower the chance that a loss will occur and to reduce the severity if a loss does occur. It may be possible to reduce risk by developing safety rules for operation of facilities and equipment, conducting periodic safety inspections of facilities and equipment, aggressively using preventive maintenance, training staff in safety procedures, and developing emergency procedures (Kaiser 1986). These items will be considered in greater detail below.

The risk treatment method of risk retention means that the leisure service organization assumes a level of losses. Risk retention can be either passive or active. Passive retention means that the organization is not aware of the risk and therefore does not attempt to manage it. Active risk management occurs after identification of the risk and is the consideration of how to manage it. Kaiser (1986) indicates that risk retention, when coupled with loss prevention and an insurance program, has the greatest potential for the leisure service organization. Shifting the risk to another party is the method of risk transfer. This generally occurs when the risk may be of high frequency and/or carries the potential of high financial loss. It may be the shifting of the facility or program to another source or by transferring the risk of loss to another party, as in the case of coverage by insurance.

A systematic plan with control procedures is mandatory to carrying out risk management practices. Listed earlier were guidelines to reducing risk. Kraus and Curtis (1990) have considered these factors in some detail.

1. *Systematic Reporting and Record Keeping*—Reports and records are a means of monitoring trends and trouble spots within the leisure service organization. Systematic record keeping may also give an indication of where improvements in problem situations are occurring. Although reporting and record keeping is an orderly processing of information, there still are the possibilities of the unusual and unanticipated incidents occurring.

2. *Facilities Inspection and Hazard Abatement*—Inspection and hazard abatement is peculiar to each situation and setting in which it should be carried out. For example, on the playgrounds, all equipment must be inspected to ascertain that it is in proper working order and that all parts of the equipment are maintained and replaced when necessary. On the other hand, in leisure facilities, walks, steps, floor surfaces, lighting, storage spaces, exits, etc., must all be inspected and managed to reduce hazards.

3. *Participant Safety Briefing and Preparation*—The leisure service organization must exercise the responsibility of informing customers and helping them to understand the inherent risks involved in inappropriate behavior and incorrect use of leisure areas, facilities, and equipment.

4. *Staff Training and Goal Setting*—Risk management can be effective only when all staff members are aware of it and committed to maintaining a safe environment and program. Staff orientation and training provide an introduction to risk management, but focus on risk management must be continued at staff meetings, during personnel evaluation, and in other management procedures. Staff should be involved in setting risk management goals and objectives and in reporting and recording information to protect both the leisure customer and leisure service personnel. It should be noted that leisure service providers may be at higher risk for injury because they become involved in emergency and life-saving situations and procedures.

5. *Emergency Procedures*—Specific procedures for first aid, accidents, and other emergencies should be precisely laid out for all staff in a leisure service organization. Because leisure service providers function in such a variety of places and situations—from mountainsides to swimming pools, to sports arenas, to health care facilities, to bowling alleys—procedures for action must be clearly defined and understood. Emergency procedures should be regularly practiced at leisure areas and facilities, appropriate public relations procedures should be exercised in emergency situations, and necessary first-aid supplies and transportation arrangements should be available in all settings.

The reasonable approach in risk management suggests that leisure service providers should not dwell on all of the possibilities that could happen, but exercise appropriate planning for the probabilities that exist for hazards and problems. Kozlowski (1988: 58–59) advises that " . . . the most important element under the reasonableness standard is the concept of foreseeability . . . address the foreseeable hazards, rather than worrying about every conceivable mishap." Alleviate the hazard. This is common sense.

Summary

Program development is the integration of identified needs and the goals and objectives that have been developed. There are specific factors generic to all program development and applicable to any situation. The factors that have been discussed in this chapter include: program area, program format, program content, time factors, facilities, setting, equipment and supplies, staffing, cost, promotion, activity analysis, and risk management. The amount of emphasis given to all or to each of these program development factors is relative to the specific planning situation.

Program areas are the way in which activities are categorized, while program format is the way in which activities are structured for program delivery. Activities in all areas of programming may be formatted in a variety of ways to make programming more dynamic for the leisure customer. Program content includes goals and objectives and describes activities that will take place during a specific program, whether it is a one-time event or takes place in several sessions. Time factors in program development are inherent in the whole process. Time-use patterns of leisure customers and availability of facilities and settings influence the outcome of the leisure experience.

The leisure service environment which includes facilities, settings, equipment and supplies, and staffing is crucial in program delivery. The availability and accessibility of facilities, the physical and social environment of the setting, and the attainment of equipment and supplies contribute to the quality of the program. Staffing is providing the human resource to the program situation. In the programming process, the leisure programmer will work with activity leaders in implementing many of the leisure program activities. Program costs include both income and disbursements and are influenced by other factors such as staff salaries and wages, supplies and equipment, etc. Promotion of programs is the way by which the leisure service organization communicates with leisure customers. It is the development of information that is delivered to an audience using varied means of distribution.

Activity analysis in program development examines the inherent characteristics of an activity. It focuses on the potential psychomotor, cognitive, and affective behaviors of the leisure customer, as well as on the social interaction patterns of the activity. Risk management in leisure program development is the anticipation of situations and the exercise of reasonable care and judgment to reduce and/or eliminate risks. Managing risk is facilitated by the leisure service organization developing a specific risk management plan as a tool of operation within the organization.

Discussion Questions and Exercises

1. List the planning factors included in the development of leisure programs and activities.

2. Discuss the way in which emphasis on particular factors may vary in a variety of programming situations.

3. Explain the domains of behavior and social interaction patterns in the activity analysis procedure. What is the value of activity analysis in program development?

4. What is risk management? How can the management of risk be implemented within the leisure service organization?

5. Discuss the differences between facilities and settings. Explain the relationship between them.

6. (a) Write a time line for the development of a summer softball league, or (b) develop a time line for planning a day-long bus trip for older adults.

7. Explain the difference between equipment and supplies in leisure programming. Give several specific examples of each.

8. Take one program activity from a specific program and suggest how it could be offered in four different program formats.

9. What is the difference in the long-term plan and the short-term plan when developing program content?

10. Explain the purpose of promotion. What factors are included in the process of communication?

References

Avedon, E.M. 1974. *Therapeutic recreation service: An applied behavioral science approach.* Englewood Cliffs, NJ: Prentice-Hall, Inc.

Edginton, C. R. 1977. Expanding community services: A view of recreation programming. *Journal of the Association of Canadian Community Colleges* 1(1):56–58.

Farrell, P. and H. M. Lundegren. 1983. *The process of recreation programming: Theory and technique* 2nd ed. New York: John Wiley & Sons.

Godbey, G. 1985. *Leisure in your life: An exploration* 2nd ed. State College, PA: Ventura Publishing, Inc.

Kaiser, R. A. 1986. *Liability and law in recreation, parks, and sports.* Englewood Cliffs, NJ: Prentice-Hall.

Kozlowski, J. C. 1988. A common sense view of liability. *Parks & Recreation,* September: 56–59.

Kraus, R. G. and J. E. Curtis. 1990. *Creative management in recreation, parks, and leisure services.* 4th ed. St. Louis: Time Mirror/Mosby College Publishing.

Nilson, R. A. and C. R. Edginton. 1983. Risk management: A tool for park and recreation administrators. *Parks & Recreation* August: 34–37.

8 | Program Areas

Learning Objectives

1. To acquaint the reader with information concerning *program areas, including categorization and classification systems.*
2. To impart to the reader knowledge of *the arts* as a program area.
3. To help the reader understand *literary activities* as a program area.
4. To provide the reader with information concerning *aquatics* as a program area.
5. To enable the reader to understand *sports, games, and athletics* as a program area.
6. To offer the reader information about the *outdoor recreation* program area.
7. To provide the reader with a greater awareness of *social recreation* as a program area.
8. To help the reader understand the program area of *self-improvement/education.*
9. To help the reader gain an understanding of *wellness* as a program area.
10. To provide the reader with information concerning *hobbies.*
11. To help the reader understand *travel and tourism* as a program area.
12. To provide information concerning *volunteer activities.*

Introduction

In this chapter, the focus for discussion will be on the categorization and classification of leisure service program *activities*. There are a variety of ways in which leisure service activities may be classified. Activities may be grouped according to the amount and kind of involvement by the customer (i.e., passive or active); within physical, mental, and social contexts (i.e., high risk or low risk, structured or unstructured, planned or self-directed, individual or group); on the basis of the general environment in which the activity takes place (i.e, indoor or outdoor, or seasonal—summer, fall, winter, spring); and on the basis of facility or setting (e.g., courts, courses, fields, recreation centers, studios, parks, camps). Leisure activities may also be classified on the basis of the age and/or gender of the customer.

Another of the methods of classifying activities is based on types of activities. For example, Russell (1982) has identified activity areas as follows: sports and games, hobbies, music, outdoor recreation, mental and literary recreation, social recreation, arts and crafts, dance, and drama. Farrell and Lundegren (1983) offer the following categories: arts, crafts, dance, drama, environmental activities, music, sports and games, and social recreation. Sessoms (1984) classifies recreation activities as follows: music, dance, dramatics, literary activity, sports and games, nature and outings, social recreation, and arts and crafts. More recently, Rossman (1989) has suggested a classification system that includes sports, individual activities, fitness activities, hobbies, art, drama, music, and social recreation.

Another system by which activities may be categorized is based on goal structure. According to the goal structure of the individual involved, activities can be classified as competitive, individualistic, and cooperative. Sheffield (1984) has indicated that in the competitive structure, in order for one customer to accomplish his or her goal, other customers must be prevented from accomplishing theirs. In the individualistic goal structure, the customer's successful goal attainment is not related to any other customer's goal attainment—all may accomplish their goal, none may accomplish their goal, or some may accomplish their goal. Cooperative goal structure is a mutually inclusive goal and can be accomplished only when all customers involved accomplish their individual goals (Table 8.1).

Categorizing activities by partitioning, using statistical procedures like factor analysis, multidimensional scaling, or some other statistical method is another approach to classification. These typologies often focus on benefits or outcomes, or the reasons that people are motivated to participate in such activities. As MacKay and Crompton (1988) note, terms such as relaxation, achievement, intimacy, power, or socialization define clusters of activities.

MacKay and Crompton (1988) suggest six typologies to delineate leisure program activities based on *activity characteristics*.

1. *Nature of the Service Act* examines whether the program is directed at people or things, and whether the act is tangible or intangible.
2. *Type of Program Relationship* refers to formal relationship with customer such as membership, and whether the service delivery is continuous or discrete.
3. *Potential for Customization* illustrates the potential for tailoring programs to meet individual customer needs and whether or not there is high participant-provider contact or low participant-provider contact.
4. *The Nature of Demand for a Program* relates both to the supply or capacity to make a program available and the quality of the program that is offered.
5. *Attributes of the Program* describes the relative importance of people (providers) and facilities to the customers' perceptions of programs.
6. *The Program Beneficiaries* are often determined by the source of the programs and services—public or private, and by the level of use the customer may expect to receive at various facilities.

TABLE 8.1 Examples of Multiple-Option Programming

Activity	Competitive Goal Structure	Individualist Goal Structure	Cooperative Goal Structure
Swimming	Swim meets or water polo leagues	WSI/Life saving course or aquacise	Synchronized swim or water games, water ballet
Aerobics	Best original routine contest	Aerobic fitness class	Cumulative job or partner aerobics
Cooking	Chili cook-off	Cookbook of "my best" recipes	Clambake or fish fry
Birdwatching	Christmas bird count	Hunting with a camera outing	Establishing a bird sanctuary
Needlecraft	Needlecraft show with prizes	Folk art technique class	Commemorative or "city" quilt
Tennis	Challenge ladder	Practice board for solo usage	Tennis marathon
Cycling	BMX racing	Bike care class	May Day bike ride
Orienteering	Orienteering meet	Wilderness survival skills clinic	Partner/team orienteering
Creative Writing	Short story contest	Open workshop on creative writing	City history project
Flower arranging	African violet show	Plant care classes	Garden club
Wood working	Pipe carving contest	Auction "find a treasure" trips	Carve a totem pole
Painting	Juried show	Face painting at art festival	Town hall mural
Social Dance	Break dance contest	Aerobic fitness	World record/fund-raising dance-a-thon
Choral Group	All-city chorus tryouts	Musicians' hotline program	Community sing-alongs
Basketball	HotShot tournament	Weekend coaching clinic	All touch/no scoring/no standing

Sheffield 1984.

These classification systems are designed to facilitate generalizations about leisure activities and programs and to contribute to the development of theory in program development. The typologies illustrated here allow application of these concepts to a large variety of other related activities (see Figures 8.1, 8.2, 8.3, 8.4, 8.5, and 8.6).

For purposes of discussion in this chapter, the *program areas* are classified in the following way: *the arts: performing arts (music, dance, drama), visual arts (including crafts),* and *new arts; literary activities; self improvement/education; sports, games, and athletics; aquatics; outdoor recreation; wellness activities; hobbies; social recreation; volunteer services;* and *travel and tourism.* A brief description of each of

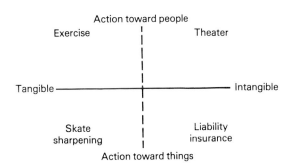

Figure 8.1 Nature of the Service Act. (MacKay, K. J., & Crompton, J. L. (1988). Alternative Typologies for Leisure Programs, *Journal of Park and Recreation Administration* 6(4), 52–64.)

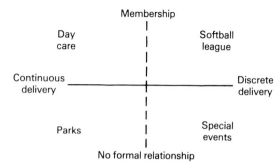

Figure 8.2 Type of Program Relationship. (MacKay, K. J., & Crompton, J. L. (1988). Alternative Typologies for Leisure Programs, *Journal of Park and Recreation Administration* 6(4), 52–64.)

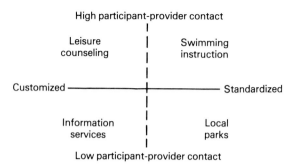

Figure 8.3 Potential for Customization. (MacKay, K. J., & Crompton, J. L. (1988). Alternative Typologies for Leisure Programs, *Journal of Park and Recreation Administration* 6(4), 52–64.)

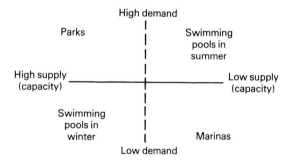

Figure 8.4 Nature of Demand for a Program. (MacKay, K. J., & Crompton, J. L. (1988). Alternative Typologies for Leisure Programs, *Journal of Park and Recreation Administration* 6(4), 52–64.)

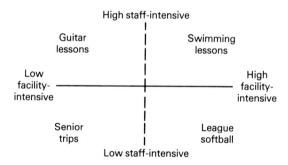

Figure 8.5 Attributes of the Program. (MacKay, K. J., & Crompton, J. L. (1988). Alternative Typologies for Leisure Programs, *Journal of Park and Recreation Administration* 6(4), 52–64.)

these program areas is presented in chapter 8. The authors recognize the interrelatedness of all program areas—for example, music and dance are as much a part of theatrical production as is the dramatic performance of the actor. Often there is no distinction made between sports and outdoor recreation. The person who has trained to become skillful in mountain climbing cannot be categorized only within the realm of outdoor recreation activity and not categorized in sports as well.

Chapter 9 will present a discussion of what this text calls *formats of programming*. A program format is the way in which an activity is organized for implementation. Formats of programs included are class, competitive, club, drop-in, special events, outreach, interest groups, and workshop/conference. Table 9.4 on pages 248–249 is a matrix illustrating the application of program formats to program areas to create program activities.

Program Beneficiaries

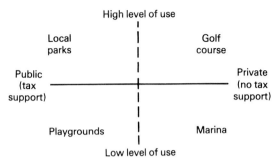

Figure 8.6 Program Beneficiaries.
(MacKay, K. J., & Crompton, J. L. (1988).
Alternative Typologies for Leisure Programs,
Journal of Park and Recreation Administration
6(4), 52–64.)

The Arts

Through the arts, the expression of national culture is highly visible. Art—a term that embraces all of the creative disciplines—can be manifested in leisure service activities in a number of ways. There are acknowledged divisions within the arts that designate more clearly the uniqueness of this program area. Broadly, the performing arts (in which the participant is the mode of artistic expression) include music, dance, drama, literature, poetry, and writing. The visual arts (also called fine arts) include painting, sculpture, architecture, engraving, etching, woodcutting, lithography, printing, and crafts. In the visual arts it is the product of the artistic expression that is important. The new arts—including photography, television, radio, films or cinema, and recordings—use a technological medium as the form of expression.

Performing Arts

Music.   Throughout history, music has been an integral part of human culture. Like all arts, music is a means of self-expression and communication. Corbin (1970: 235) writes, "Music is a form of human expression of pleasing and melodious combinations of tones. It is the language of the spirit and a release of thought that are inexpressible."

Ideas about music include the following:

> Music has been called the language that speaks in every dialect. Sound, whether organized into melodic phrases or recurrent rhythms, is one of the major communication sources . . . few human emotions exist that have not been expressed in sound (Arnold 1976: 97).

What is there about music that attracts so many people, engages so many in wholehearted participation, and holds their affection throughout a lifetime? What is there about people that makes music so much sought after, striven for, or when it comes without seeking, welcomed as a friend? What human needs or what capacities for enjoyment does music serve? (1963: 198).

> People vary a great deal in the values that they find in music. Enjoyment, a sense of well-being in relation to self and others, and beauty of the music itself are all derived from music. Enjoyment can be derived from both the melody and the rhythm of music—through the sheer pleasure of hearing, participating, feeling, and moving. Music is personal. What a person hears and the way in which reaction to music is demonstrated is uniquely personal. A sense of social well-being can be present in music, as can "a sense of being able" (1963: 198–199).

According to Arnold (1976: 199), "In music the unskilled person can reach the heights of artistry in a well-directed chorus singing first-rate music." Through music, one has the power of expression—the ability to express feelings such as joy, sorrow, and enthusiasm. Music enhances the feelings in experiences and associations familiar to us—such as holidays (Christmas and the Fourth of July) and athletic events. In describing the beauty of music as a value of music, we must recognize it for its own sake, without attaching a personal or social significance to what music is and what it can do.

There are numerous other values of music suggested by Danford and Shirley (1970: 237):

1. It is universally accepted as a highly desirable activity.
2. It can be enjoyed alone or in a group.

3. Music appeals to all ages.
4. Its cost ranges from nothing to whatever one wishes to pay.
5. It helps to create friendships and a sense of unity.
6. It provides emotional release and relaxation.
7. Of all the arts of communication, music is one of the most expressive.
8. A wide range of skill from the neophyte to the master is possible with a high degree of enjoyment accruing at each level.
9. It brings into the lives of people an element of refreshing beauty.
10. Music contributes to a developing sense of personal adequacy by providing reassuring experiences of success.
11. Music contributes to one's cultural development.
12. It contributes to the morale of both the individual and the group.

There are so many kinds of music within our culture that nearly everyone can relate to one form or another. There is classical, semiclassical, opera, popular, rock, soul, bluegrass, jazz, country and western, blues, and folk music. There are literally thousands of organizations, groups, and individuals involved in playing, singing, and producing music. The range of instruments and styles of singing are too numerous to be listed here. Instruments range from the homemade drum to the electronic synthesizer—and everything in between. Most instruments—strings, brass, woodwinds, percussion—not only can be used as they were designed, but also can be amplified or be electronic in design.

What about music as a leisure activity? It has a very important place in all leisure service organization programs. How does music in a recreation setting differ from music in other settings? If we choose to define a difference, perhaps music in the leisure setting is less formal. However, this does not preclude emphasis on skill development and the pleasing production of sound. Perhaps in the leisure program area "the overall aim is to show how much better and richer life can be through the influence of music rather than to produce polished musicians" (Danford and Shirley 1970: 236). The better a person understands something, the more he or she will enjoy and appreciate it, and so it is with music—the opportunity to listen, play an instrument, sing, or otherwise have a musical experience will contribute to a person's familiarity with music and increase the level of his or her interest. For example, an individual may find it easy to become involved in an athletic event, having experienced the same physical activity at an earlier time. Similarly, a person who has had a previous musical experience may be better able to relate to music. A taste for music can be cultivated through a gradual experiential approach. Obviously, not all people will like all kinds of music, but a person can better choose what musical sounds are most desirable to him or her after a broad exposure to various types of music.

There are numerous music activities that can be offered through leisure service programs. Table 8.2 describes the general classifications of musical activities in leisure settings. Leisure experiences in music can be carried out individually or in groups in many of the classifications. There also can be opportunities for individual lessons as well as for performances, in groups or solo. Table 8.3 suggests a number of musical experiences in recreation and leisure service programs (such as band concerts, guitar lessons, and variety shows).

Dance "Dance is a form of expression through movement" (1963: 40). Dance is a manifestation of the human need to move. It has been used to symbolize the activity of life by all peoples and cultures. Dance can express joy, sorrow, love, war, reverence, and other emotions. Arnold distinguishes between movement and dance this way:

> Movement is a conscious or unconscious non-verbal communication that comes from the inner being in response to some intrinsic or extrinsic stimulus. Dance is a spontaneous or artistic

TABLE 8.2   Classification of Music Activities

Singing	Playing	Listening	Rhythmic Movement	Creating	Combined Activities
Informal singing	Rhythm instruments	Incidental hearing	Purely rhythmic	Songwriting	Folk dancing
Community sings	Simple melody instruments	Records	Simple interpretive singing games	Other music making	Musical charades
Choruses	Simple harmony instruments	Radio and television	Play, party games		Shadow plays
Quartets and other ensembles	Fretted instruments	Live concerts	Folk dances		Festivals
Glee clubs	Bands				Seasonal and holiday programs
A cappella choirs	Orchestras				Caroling
Madrigal groups	Ensembles and chamber music groups				Community programs
Solos	Solos				Variety shows
					Talent shows
					Sports events
					Swimming, skating
					Park concerts
					Operettas
					Opera
					Workshops

The Recreation Program Book 1963.

TABLE 8.3   List of Music Programs

Accordian bands	Harmonica bands
Adult quartets	Kazoo bands
Band concerts	Listening groups
Children's choir	Minstrel shows
Choral groups	Music festivals
Combos for dance accompaniment	Old fiddlers' clubs
Country music groups	Orchestra groups
Creative music for children	Playground music and festivals
Drum and bugle corps	Rhythm bands
Folk singing	Rock bands
Glee clubs	String quartets
Group singing	Variety shows
Guitar lessons	Vocal groups
	Ukulele groups

Danford and Shirley 1970: 238.

(constructed) movement or series of movements that is an expressed reaction to an intrinsic or extrinsic stimulus.

The fundamental movements common to man are also the movements that are present in dance. These are jumping, darting, expanding, contracting, turning, raising and sliding (Arnold 1976: 71).

Dance has developed in many ways, but examining dance as a folk expression and as a structured performing art can enable us to understand its evolution. Early dances depicted such happenings as the disappearance of the sun and the rising of the moon, hunt scenes, and ceremonial events. In more recent history, American folk dance was fashioned around the culture of many nationalities and took place at social events such as barn-raisings, gathering of harvest, celebrating of new statehood, and many more (Arnold 1976: 73). Folk dances that have been taken from the folk art, advanced to a higher degree of skill and performance, have become "performing folk art"—ethnic dances. Participation in this activity took on a new form when scholars, dance masters, and musicians began to structure the performance and teaching of dance. As a result of this structuring, a very scientific study of dance and movement emerged, and dance began to develop as a structured performing art (Arnold 1976: 73).

Dance as a leisure activity has many values for the individual participant. Dance is a physical activity and is sufficiently active and vigorous to contribute to physical fitness. Involvement in dance activity can release tension, develop grace and control of the body, and may lead to body changes—toning and trimming. Dance also offers an opportunity for creativity. Many forms of dance lend themselves to self-expression and interpretation. Dance further offers an opportunity for social interaction. Tillman (1973: 168–169) lists other values of dance as a leisure program activity. He suggests that dance may enable the customer to develop an appreciation for beauty, recognize and understand one's culture, relax and escape, develop rhythm and coordination, and have an opportunity for a new experience.

There are many areas within dance that can be included in programming. Table 8.4 illustrates the classifications of dance. Kraus (1985) has presented a list of dance activities that are frequently found in the community leisure service organization (see Table 8.5).

Drama Drama reflects, interprets, and enriches life by enabling the individual to express his or her feelings and understanding of life. Drama is an imitation of life.

> Man has always been a storyteller. It is the most personal and direct way that he passes on his culture. More personal than the printed word, more direct than the symbolism of dance and music. He needs only his voice and body to create that pure self-expressive art called drama.
>
> It is self-expressive creativity because it allows man to interpret his environment and feelings to others with techniques and styles that not only communicate but entertain. Unlike dance, music, or literature, it must have an audience to sustain meaningful participation. Man can retire to solitude and talk to himself with music, dance, and crafts, but drama demands others to witness it (Tillman 1973: 281).

TABLE 8.4 Classification of Dance

Folk Dance
  American folk dance
    Square dance
    Round or couple dance
    Longways dance
    Circle dance
    Solo dance
  Folk dances of other lands
    Ethnic groups
Social Dance

Popular Dance

Dance Mixers

Creative Rhythms for Children
  Free rhythms
  Identification rhythms
  Creative fitness rhythms
  Dramatic Rhythms
  Rhythm games
    Singing games
    Simple folk dances

Modern Dance
  Conditioning and free exercise
  Art of movement
  Concert dance

Tap, Clog, Character Dance

Ballet

The Recreation Program Book 1963: 41,42.

Dramatics, as a performing art, encompasses two broad areas—formal and informal. Tillman offers the following descripton of formal dramatics:

> Formal dramatics involves a written script, lines to be memorized, a director who interprets the play and directs action, emphasis on staging and costuming, and major consideration given to the entertainment of an audience and its reaction to a finished product (Danford and Shirley 1970: 281).

Informal dramatics is a broad term that encompasses a wide variety of activities (imaginative play, make-believe, story dramatization,

TABLE 8.5 List of Activities in a Dance Program

Ballet	Tap and clog dance
Ethnic dance	Creative dance for children
Jazz dance	Folk, square, and round dance
Rock-and-roll dance	Modern dance
Disco dance	Social or ballroom dance

Kraus 1985: 168.

TABLE 8.6 List of Activities in a Drama Program*

Blackouts	Monologue
Ceremonials	Musical comedy
Charades	Observances
Children's theater	Operetta
Choral speech	Pageants
Community theater	Pantomime
Creative drama	Peep-box
Demonstrations	Plays
Dramatic games	Puppetry
Dramatizations	Script-in-hand
Festivals	Shadow plays
Formal drama	Shows
Grand opera	Skits
Imaginative play	Story reading
Impersonations	Storytelling
Light opera	Stunts
Marionettes	Symphonic drama
Monodrama	Tableaux
	Theater-in-the-round

The Recreation Program Book. 1963: 68.

*Because of the great variety and universal appeal of dramatic forms, it is difficult to compile a complete list. The most usual forms have been arranged in this table.

pantomime, impromptu work, extemporaneous presentations, shadow plays, puppetry). The emphasis in informal dramatics (also called creative dramatics) is on the person involved and not on the audience.

Values of participation and involvement in dramatics can be far-reaching and very personal. Participation in drama may extend the horizons of the participant by stimulating his or her imagination and by allowing an opportunity to momentarily be "someone else." Drama allows for interpersonal exchanges and group interaction

as well as personal expression. It is an important part of cultural life—a reflection of many lifestyles. Consequently, it enables persons to better understand their own lifestyle and to appreciate lifestyles different from their own. Because of the scope of drama, it can appeal to all age groups, both as direct participants and as spectators. Table 8.6 briefly illustrates the variety of dramatic forms and activities that may be found in leisure service organization programs.

The integration of the arts is as important as the expression of each art individually. Examples of integration are highly evident throughout the arts. For example, production of drama incorporates dance choreography, visual arts display (set construction), and decoration and costume design, as well as the performance of the actor. The performance of dance may inspire the artist to interpret the expression on canvas or in sculpture; the dancer interprets the music that may, in turn, be an interpretation of words, ideas, and feelings from literature and poetry. Relative to the various program areas of the arts, recreation and leisure service organizations should provide opportunities for the participant to develop an appreciation of the arts, in the passive as well as the active sense. In an active sense, it should enable participants to learn, develop, and apply skills within the arts.

The Visual Arts

When defining art within the context of the visual arts, we are speaking of the decorative arts—beautiful objects for their own sake—and crafts. Crafts can be interpreted to mean useful arts—beautiful objects for utilitarian use. It is obvious that arts and crafts cannot be understood as precisely different areas of involvement. Separately, or together, they are an outlet for human expression and provide a vehicle for the inherent desire of the individual to create. Crafts may be viewed essentially as the utilization of materials to produce items having a utilitarian value.

Art may be defined as utilizing materials in a graphic or plastic demonstration of a symbol or concept. Simply stated, a craft can be handled and used, while art displays a perception.

Communication is one of the primary values of arts and crafts. Through the development of craft objects, a person may communicate with others and the environment and express his or her personality and the culture that has contributed to the development of that personality. Individuals involved in using materials to create art display varying levels of skill, technique, and interpretation. However, the specific piece or production that is the outcome of the art experience is not as important as the satisfaction that the individual achieves through the creating experience.

Communication through arts and crafts can be viewed in various ways. It may take place through creativity, self-expression, or integration. Creativity involves the ability to change or modify existing components to produce a new or different end result. For example, an individual may see in a gnarled piece of walnut wood the possibility of a finished clock case; an individual may redesign a coat into a pair of slacks, a person may visualize pottery in a piece of clay, or see trees and a stream on a canvas. Self-expression can occur whenever the opportunity exists for the individual to demonstrate his or her feelings. In arts and crafts, this occurs when an individual shapes an object or creates a product that reflects his or her personality. The concept of self-expression is present in many areas of leisure service activity, but in arts and crafts, there is a visible object produced as a result of a personal emotional expression.

Specific art and craft activities can range from items of simplicity to those of great complexity. Crafts can include making bread-dough items and burlap flowers, crewel embroidery, leather tooling, knot tying, copper enameling, and so on. Art can include finger painting, drawing in charcoal, painting with acrylics, sculpting in clay and marble, etching on glass, or molding in silver or bronze. There are several categories within arts

and crafts in which activities may be grouped. Shivers and Calder (1974: 7) suggest the following: the graphic and manipulative types of art—printmaking, using papier-mâché, sculpting, casting, and handling mosaics or ceramics—and the types of craft—leather crafts, woodcrafts, metal crafts, weaving, sewing, nature crafts, rug hooking, crafts from recycled materials, and theater crafts.

Arts and crafts have gained prominence and increased participation as a result of the "culture explosion" in our society. Another reason for the popularity of arts and crafts as a leisure service activity is the desire of many people to "get back to the basics." Many people choose to make craft items as utilitarian products—making pottery, weaving, knitting, crocheting—rather than consume mass-produced items. Arts and crafts reflect the need to personalize one's lifestyle by creating and consuming objects that are unique. Leisure service organizations may be a vehicle for individuals to learn the skills of arts and crafts and to produce, demonstrate, display, and sell many of the items they create.

The New Arts
The new arts—in which an individual uses a technological apparatus of some kind to carry out an activity or produce an outcome—may include photography, computer programming, filmmaking, television production, and other media. For artistic expression, the person uses a camera, a computer terminal, a videocassette recorder or some other technological device as a vehicle.

Photography—whether it results in photographs, slides, videotapes or motion pictures—may be an artistic means of self-expression. Through photography, an individual may reveal feelings, attitudes, and interests which are visible in the subjects chosen and the ideas expressed. Informal photography may be a vehicle for capturing a mood, a motion, a situation, an event, or an object. Photography also may be an expression of color, motion, distance, shapes, and texture. The resulting pictures may express joy, sorrow, fear, contentment, weariness, love, and many other emotions. The individual's "knack" for creating pictures is displayed through techniques of slow-motion, animation, and stop-motion, as well as through various kinds of photographs, such as microphotography and telephotography. Furthermore, displaying the results of photography in panoramic views, close-ups, single or multiple screens, and dissolves may demonstrate the person's abilty to communicate with photographic visuals.

Radio and television are vehicles for expression, utilizing verbal and visual communication. An individual's inventiveness may be involved in the production of materials such as scripts and videotapes that are original in concept and treatment. Simulated radio allows planning of dramatization, writing and reading, performing music, or producing sound. Videotape systems are a means of recording performance, producing animation, and capturing action and sound. With television production, the person or persons involved may have immediate feedback and observation of results.

The use of computers allows artistic expression through the highly specialized involvement of an individual. With appropriate knowledge and skill, a person may design computer-generated animation through free-form sketching at a terminal; and images may be created through description in numerical or mathematical terms. A computer program such as MacDraw™, MacPaint™, and others provides a means through which the user may engage in creative expression.

A person's leisure expression in the new arts, as in all of the arts, can be as individual and creative as the person using the device allows it to be. As in all artistic expression, the limitations are controlled only by the individual's imagination.

In regard to the new arts, the availability of the technology needed to produce it has increased to make program planning and participant involvement more accessible. Some of the technological media (such as cameras) are readily available to individuals and organizations, while other devices (such as computers) may be available for use on a more limited basis.

Literary Activities

Numerous program offerings can be included within the area of literary activities. These activities can be grouped into categories such as writing, communication, reading, foreign studies, and discussion groups. Writing activities include the original writing of plays, poetry, short stories, novels, and even business and personal communications. Writing activities may lead to such experiences as sharing what has been written (e.g., through reading sessions) and performing the written material. Communication activities may take the form of public speaking, debate, broadcasting, group discussions, storytelling, recording tapes for the visually impaired, and other activities. Book clubs, great books seminars, and discussions of Shakespeare or American literature since 1900 are some of the reading activities that could be developed for recreation and leisure. Interpretive reading, book reviews, a magazine corner, and library visitations are other activities. Foreign studies may involve the study of language, culture, economics, and the social history of countries throughout the world; they might also encompass folklore, mythology, classics, and translations. Discussion groups within a recreation and leisure setting could cover any topic ranging from Peruvian art, philosophy, the Bible, or English poets. The categories that have been illustrated here in no way preclude the development of other activities. In all program areas, the potential activities are limited only by the planning capabilities of the recreation and leisure professional.

Self-Improvement/Education Activities

Of emerging importance in the leisure services field is a growing array of personal self-improvement activities and programs. Many of these literary, mental, and linguistic activities—which result in personal development and individual or group improvement—are generic to this category. Self-improvement activities are those in which the individual engages for the primary purpose of developing either cognitive, communicative, or affective skills. For example, a self-development activity may lead to a change in behavior that may result in the improvement of the individual as shown in his or her work, home, or leisure environments and relationships.

The primary sponsors of self-development activities have been individual specialized businesses, corporate schools, community and technical colleges, the voluntary sector, and churches. Also a number of book clubs provide specialty books and tapes featuring self-improvement. Religious organizations provide not only literature but also retreats and mass rallies to build spiritual values and positive lifestyles. For example, marriage and family encounters have become popular program responses to the rising divorce rates in North America. Another commercial venture in self-improvement is training programs organized by institutes and private enterprises such as the Dale Carnegie Institute.

The scope of programs in the self-improvement area is wide. It includes such diverse activities as continuing education, avocational sales promotions, marriage and family development, and intellectual development through games. Assertiveness training may enable an individual who has assumed a subservient role—whether in a work, family, or leisure setting—to gain a better sense of self-worth.

Women's needs, rights, and roles are other areas in which there has developed an array of programs and services. In keeping with the rapidly changing roles for women, a number of books and training programs have emerged to encourage positive personal development. The topics are broad, including such areas as management challenges and techniques, sexual behavior, gender definition, and total lifestyle management.

Marriage and family retreats have become extremely popular. Participation in these programs has been encouraged by religious and other organizations as a means of promoting positive relations within the home. The setting is usually a camp or outdoor area—a contrast to the regular living environment. These day or weekend programs are a way of restoring and shaping positive individual feelings as well as family relations.

Intellectual development through games is widespread. *Outburst, Trivial Pursuit, Scrabble, Word Yahtzee, Monopoly,* and other table games may improve one's intellectual skills. In addition, computer technology has spawned such intellectual challenges as Sim City (a simulation of a growing community), MacPaint, and other software innovations. There are local, state, regional, and national organizations that actively promote these activities through newsletters, competitions, and demonstrations.

Another activity that has become popular over the last several years is genealogy. This study of one's family history and lineage is a time-consuming activity. Individuals and groups spend hundreds of hours examining and clarifying their "roots" and family trees. In North America, this activity has been supported by the public libraries, where census information and other appropriate records (e.g., birth, death, business) are usually made available.

Sports, Games, and Athletics

A sport is an activity that demands a combination of physical skill, endurance, alertness, purpose, and enthusiasm. Performance of a sport represents an accomplishment for which the body has been trained and for which the person must work to become skillful. In most sport activities, the person uses a specifically designed piece of equipment (such as a ball, a racquet, a bat, or a wicket) and often carries out the activity on a field or area of a determined shape and dimension, on which there may be permanent equipment. Sports activities may take many forms and are defined in several catgories (see Table 8.7). A sport can be classified as an individual activity—that is, an activity that may be carried out by an individual without a partner, team, or opponent (such as golf, archery, gymnastics, swimming, track and field, and so on). Dual sport activities

TABLE 8.7   List of Individual, Dual, and Team Sports

Individual Sports		Dual Sports	Team Sports
Archery	Weight lifting	Tennis	Hockey
Golf	Trap shooting	Boxing	Crew racing
Bowling	Riflery	Wrestling	Basketball
Swimming	Hunting	Badminton	Volleyball
Diving	Fishing	Handball	Baseball
Gymnastics	Sky diving	Racquetball	Softball
Skating	Hang gliding	Squash	Football
Skiing	Surfing	Etc.	Soccer
Hiking	Etc.		Etc.
Track and field			

TABLE 8.8   List of Low-organized, Table/Board, and Mental Games

Low-Organized Games	Table/Board Games	Mental Games/Puzzles
Dodgeball	Checkers	Guessing
Tag	Chess	Construction puzzles
Two deep	Backgammon	Crossword
Run-for-your-supper	Kalah	Word games
Newcomb	Chinese checkers	Etc.
Four square	Box hockey	
Deck tennis	Battleship	
Relays	Aggravation	
Goal games	Card games	
Etc.	Dominoes	
	Etc.	

are those in which there must be at least two people in order to implement the activity. Such activities as wrestling, tennis, badminton, and fencing are dual sports. Team sports are those for which a group of people is needed to carry out the activity. Some team sports are soccer, basketball, football, baseball, volleyball, and hockey. There are numerous other ways of identifying sports by category. For example, there are combative sports—boxing, wrestling, karate, and judo. There are vehicle sports—auto racing, motorcycling, and snowmobiling—and other kinds of locomotive sports—sailing, yachting, horseback riding and horse racing, hang gliding, parachuting, tobogganing, bicycle riding, and sky diving. There are sports that rely on the environment as an impetus (such as mountain climbing and river rafting). Classification of sports may also be based on the kind of equipment used (such as ball games and net games) or the season (e.g., winter for skiing, sledding, and ice skating) or some other distinction (such as water sports—swimming, surfing, diving, water skiing, canoeing, and sailing). There are many other sport activities that perhaps fit best in a miscellaneous category, such as bowling, riflery, weight lifting, fly casting, and roller skating.

Games can have many different characteristics. They can be physical activities of low organization, often requiring only a low level of skill; usually these games have a few simple rules and are of short duration. Conversely, some games can be quite complex (Table 8.8). Games can be carried out in an individual, dual, or team situation. They can be active, as in dodgeball and tag, or inactive, as in guessing and word games. There are numerous board games in which it is necessary to practice the decision-making process by

TABLE 8.9   Profiles of Activities Denoted by Central Concepts

Determining Attributes	Play	Recreation	Activities Denoted By: Contest or Match	Game	Sport or Athletics
1. Activity exclusive of concerns and influences emanating from outside of contest of activity	X				
2. Existence of fantasy or make-believe	X				
3. Actor or actors commence activity at will	X	X			
4. Actor or actors limit act in space and time	X	X			
5. Actor or actors terminate activity at will	X	X			
6. Activity not necessarily utilitarian in project (may be devoid of economic, material, prestige, power, or status-achievement goals)	X	X			
7. Competition not a necessary component	X	X			
8. Activity characterized by a necessary degree of spontaneity (not restricted by formal or informal rules of procedure)	X	X			
9. Relevance of role restricted to boundaries of activity	X	X	X		
10. Individualistically focused and oriented	X	X	X		
11. Actor or actors involvement in activity necessarily voluntary	X	X	X		
12. No imperative formal hierarchical arrangement of roles and positions	X	X	X	X	
13. Physical exertion not a necessary component	X	X	X	X	
14. Preparation for participation in activity not a necessary component	X	X	X	X	
15. No formal stabilized history or tradition necessary	X	X	X	X	
16. Activity inclusive of concerns and influences emanating from outside of context of activity		X	X	X	X

solving complex problems. Three basic elements are usually present in game situations: luck (as in rolling the dice for a board game), physical endurance (as in running and playing tag), and skill (as in throwing darts or tossing rings).

> There is . . . [a] . . . difference between sports and games even more fundamental than the degree of organization. When children play games they quit when tired. The participant in a sport, provided he is truly an athlete, a competitor in the highest sense of the term, continues after he is tired, even to the point of complete exhaustion (Danford and Shirley 1970: 188).

There is perhaps a fine line of distinction between sports and athletics.

A sport may be either competitive or noncompetitive (swimming, for example); in the case of athletics, however, the definition is limited to the competitive aspect of sports. Whereas swimming may be engaged in as a sport for recreation, technically this sport becomes athletics when it is organized for purposes of competition (Donnelly et al. 1958: 3).

Sports or athletics may be defined in terms of the participant's motivation, or by the nature of the activity itself. Sport is a playful activity for some participants, while others place it in the context of work or an occupation. Moreover, the boundaries of sport as an activity blend into the more general sphere of recreation and leisure (Ball and Loy 1975: 12).

Contributing to the organization of a sport for competition are factors such as duration of play,

TABLE 8.9   Profiles of Activities Denoted by Central Concepts—*Continued*

Determining Attributes	Play	Recreation	Activities Denoted By: Contest or Match	Game	Sport or Athletics
17. Nonexistence of fantasy or make-believe		X	X	X	X
18. Actor or actors may not commence activity at will			X	X	X
19. Actor or actors may not terminate activity at will			X	X	X
20. Actor or actors do not have prerogative to limit activity in space and time			X	X	X
21. Activity utilitarian in product (emphasis on attaining economic goals, prestige, power status, self-esteem)			X	X	X
22. Competiton necessary component			X	X	X
23. Activity necessarily characterized by formal or informal rules, regulations, restrictions, or limitations that must be followed			X	X	X
24. Activity not necessarily voluntary; may be forced				X	X
25. Relevance of role not restricted to activity				X	X
26. Activity necessarily collective in character				X	X
27. Preparation for participation in activity necessary					X
28. Formal history; recognized records and traditions					X
29. Physical exertion a necessary component					X
30. Imperative formal hierarchical roles and positions					X

Edwards 1973: 58, 59.

accumulation of points, achievement of a pre-determined score, or completion of a specified course. In athletic competition, the primary object is to perform physically with strength, endurance, and agility, along with knowledge that gives one individual the advantage over his or her opponent. Table 8.9 delineates the characteristics of play, recreation, contests, games, sports, and athletics.

Edwards (1973: 59) suggests that as a person moves from play to sport, the following occurs:

1. Activity becomes less subject to individual prerogative, with spontaneity severely diminished.
2. Formal rules and structural role and position relationships and responsibilities within the activity assume predominance.
3. Separation from the rigors and pressures of daily life becomes less prevalent.

4. Individual liability and responsibility for the quality and character of behavior during the course of the activity is heightened.
5. The relevance of the outcome of the activity and the individual's role in it extends to groups and collectivities that do not participate directly in the act.
6. Goals become diverse, complex, and more related to values emanating from outside of the context of the activity.
7. The activity consumes a greater proportion of the individual's time and attention due to the need for preparation and the degree of seriousness involved in the act.
8. The emphasis upon physical and mental extension beyond the limits of refreshment or interest in the act assumes increasing dominance.

There is a tremendous potential for positive physical, social, and psychological growth as a result of participation in games, sports, and athletics. Games—whether they involve children or adults—can initiate various kinds of behavior and outcomes. Involvement in a game situation may enable a person to learn to take turns, to accept and follow directions and rules, to experience both winning and losing, to learn new skills, to develop abilities for decision making, to practice sportsmanship and consideration of others, and to feel the spirit of cooperation. The leader's role in the organization of games is to involve all participants as successfully as possible, to implement complementary group structures, and to encourage the participant to realize that the process of playing the game is more important than winning or losing.

The values acquired through participation in sports are as broad and varied as the number of individuals involved. Because the primary concern of a leisure service organization should be with the individual, certain values should be emphasized in individual and group sports participation. Sports have great carry-over value for a person throughout life. As with nearly all leisure activities, participation in sports need not be terminated at any time. Although it would seem that society has traditionally emphasized team sports, it is easier to continue involvement in individual and dual sports; this is because involvement can be continued on an individual basis or with one or two other people more easily than with one or more teams. Sports contribute to the individual's health and physical well-being and help one to develop a feeling of self-confidence, self-esteem, happiness, and personal satisfaction. Participation in sports enables the individual to function as a member of a group or team—fostering feelings of acceptance, camaraderie, and cooperation. Participants in sports learn to follow rules and to accept authority and the decisions of others.

Sports in our society have come to be a social institution, a tradition, and a reflection of our cultural and ethnic heritage. Social scientists have defined and analyzed sport in conjunction with other social institutions (such as education, health, religion, politics, and economics). The professionalization and commercialization of competitive athletics and sports have permeated our culture and social structure. Whether one is a spectator or a participant, sports touch nearly everyone's life.

Sports, games, and athletics—as a part of organized leisure services—are reaching the greatest number and the widest variety of participants of any program area or activity. Opportunity for personal involvement can be made available through organized recreation and leisure services—whether the participant is young or old, male or female, able-bodied or differently abled, large or small. Examples of some very basic modifications of sport activities that exist in order to broaden the opportunity for participation are slow-pitch softball, slow-break basketball, T-ball, and lightweight football. Adaptations of this type are made in order to allow greater numbers of persons to participate.

Aquatics

The program area of aquatics is an important dimension in the management of many leisure service organizations. Swimming is one of the most popular activities pursued by individuals in their leisure. Many leisure service organizations have built a large portion of their program effort around the idea of aquatics. For example, the Red Cross and the YMCA have developed instructional aquatic programs directed toward improving individual safety in and around the water. It is not unusual for an organization that emphasizes aquatics to employ a number of full-time aquatic program specialists and many part-time and seasonal staff members.

Most aquatic programs are built around three goals. The first is to have a safe aquatic experience, the second is to encourage individuals to have fun and enjoyment, and the third is skill development. Depending upon the facilities available, some aquatic programs will emphasize fitness, competitive swimming, and/or other benefits. An excellent example of a well-rounded aquatic program is that operated by the Willamalane Park and Recreation District. This organization manages two swimming pool complexes. One of the complexes (a leisure pool) features a wave-generating pool, a lap pool, a kiddie pool, a slide, and a jacuzzi that can accommodate up to fifty people. Their other pool, a more traditional operation, features opportunities for competitive swim, lap swim, water aerobics, learn-to-swim, and also features a water slide. Both swimming pool complexes are inviting and encourage participant involvement in a safe and enjoyable environment (see Figure 8.7).

There are a broad range of aquatic services that can be provided by a given leisure service organization. Most are dependent upon having adequate pool facilities; however, many locations can provide safe adaptations that extend their services by encouraging the creativity of their aquatics staff. Some of the programs often associated wth aquatics include the following.

Instructional Swim—Instructional swim lessons for all ages is a mainstay of many leisure service organizations. Both the American Red Cross and the YMCA have excellently structured, progressive programs in the learn-to-swim area. Most of these programs are focused on children, but adult swimming classes or even parent/infant classes are other possibilities.

Open Swim—The open swim format enables people to use the aquatic facility to swim or enjoy the aquatic environment. Drop-in swim programs often attract large numbers of individuals, requiring attention to appropriate safety procedures and methods.

Competitive Swim—Competitive swimming programs cater to individuals desiring a more intensive aquatic experience. Competition between teams promotes increased performance and can build esprit de corps among team members. Competitive swimming programs also are valuable in helping participants establish individual

standards reflected in their desired levels of performance. Competitive swim programs are often thought to cater only to elite swimmers, but a good program will provide entry points for individuals of many skill levels.

Aquatic Exercise Programs—Fitness-oriented programs, including water aerobics, lap swimming, and others, have become very popular. Aquatic environments provide low-impact resistance to force and, therefore, as a medium of exercise can be pursued comfortably by individuals of varying levels of fitness.

Small Craft Instruction and Safety—Learning how to maneuver small crafts in and around aquatic environments safely is another activity managed by leisure service organizations. Lessons in kayaking, canoeing, windsurfing, sailing, and so forth are all potential instructional areas available to leisure service organizations.

Aquatic Games—Numerous games can be played in aquatic settings. These can range from relatively simple activities such as low-organized games to more complex athletic events like water polo. Aquatic games can bring increased interest to this program area and stimulate fun, competition, and enjoyment. Aquatic games can also serve as a method of progressively teaching skills in a fun manner. They can also be used to promote fitness.

Social Activities In and Around the Water—Water is a magnet to many individuals. Combined with social recreation activities, it can provide a pleasant atmosphere for parties and other functions. Such programs should be organized to promote both safety and enjoyment. Many organizations will rent out their swimming pool complexes to groups for social functions. These rentals can be important sources of income for leisure service organizations.

This is by no means an all-inclusive list of aquatic activities. Aquatic programs operated by public leisure service organizations are used to generate enough revenues to pay for the operation of the aquatic programs and facilities.

Willamalane
Park & Recreation District

LIVELY PARK SWIM CENTER

6100 Thurston Road, Springfield, 747-WAVE

LIVELY PARK SWIM CENTER HOURS

Effective January 1 through March 25, 1990

➤ Refer to "SPECIAL HOLIDAY HOURS AND POOL CLOSURES" for schedule changes. Phone 747-WAVE anytime you have a question about Lively Park Swim Center Splash Play Swim and Adult Lap Swim schedules. Phone 726-2752 for all other program information.

SPLASH PLAY SWIM: WAVES AND WATER SLIDE
Mon., Wed., Fri., Sat........6:30-9:00 p.m.
Sat. & Sun.............12:00 Noon-5:00 p.m.

ADULT SPLASH PLAY SWIM: WAVES, WATER SLIDE, SPA
Tuesday & Thursday..............8:30-9:30 p.m.

ADULT LAP SWIMS
Monday - Friday............... 5:30-9:00 a.m.
Monday - Friday............Noon-1:30 p.m.
Monday - Saturday............6:30-8:00 p.m.
Saturday...........................9:00 a.m.-Noon

SWIMNASTICS AND PRENATAL EXERCISES
Monday, Wednesday,
& Friday.............................8:00-9:00 a.m.
Tuesday & Thursday.........8:00-9:00 a.m.

SENIOR SWIMNASTICS/LAP SWIM
Reserved for adults age 55 and over.
Monday - Friday................1:30-2:30 p.m.

SWIM FEES

SPLASH PLAY SWIM WAVES AND WATER SLIDE

Daily or Single Admission
Individual Admission.....................$3.00
Willamalane Resident.................$2.00

Coupon Book of 10 Discounted Tickets
Individual Coupon Book...............$24.00
Willamalane Resident................$16.00

Coupon Book of 5 Family* Discounted Tickets
Family* Coupon Book.....................$26.00
Willamalane Resident................$20.00
*Parents with children representing one household.

ADULT LAP/ADULT SWIMNASTICS SENIOR EXERCISE

Daily or Single Admission
Adult (18-54 years)......................... $2.25
Willamalane Resident..............$1.50
Senior (55+years) $1.50
Willamalane Resident..............$1.00

Coupon Book of 10 Discounted Tickets
Adult(18-55 years)..........................$18.00
Willamalane Resident............$12.00
Senior (55+years). $12.00
Willamalane Resident............$ 8.00

Coupon books make great gifts!!

SAFETY AT LIVELY PARK SWIM CENTER

Willamalane Aquatics staff members exceed the Oregon State Health Department requirements for lifeguards and take your safety very seriously. Please remember that any physical activity exposes the participant to risk of injury or impairment and observe these guidelines:

- Avoid injuries caused by running, shoving or rough play.
- Avoid injuries caused by diving into shallow water. Diving is prohibited in Lively Park Swim Center.
- Fitted, child-sized lifejackets provided for your use. Willamalane recommends that parents remain with young children using lifejackets.
- Willamalane recommends that children under six years of age not use the spa. 102° water slows the heart rate and dehydrates young children.
- Willamalane Aquatics staff reminds parents to provide prompt supervision for their children immediately after the swim session ends.

(over)

Figure 8.7   Flyer. (Lively Park Swim Center, Willamalane Parks & Recreation District, Springfield, Oregon.)

Willamalane
Park & Recreation District
Springfield, Oregon

FALL 1990
LIVELY PARK SWIM CENTER HOURS/FEES

LIVELY PARK SWIM CENTER, 6100 Thurston Road
747-WAVE (747-9283) or 726-2752

Effective Sept. 4, 1990, through Jan. 5, 1991

➧ Refer to "SPECIAL HOLIDAY HOURS AND POOL CLOSURES" for schedule changes. Phone 747-WAVE (747-9283) anytime you have a question about Lively Park Swim Center swim schedules. Phone 726-2752 for all other LPSC program information.

PLAY SWIMS

ALL AGES
Day: M-Sa Time: 6:30-9:00p
Day: Sa-Su Time: Noon-5:00p

FEES:
Daily or Single Admission
Individual Admission....................$3.50
    Willamalane Resident........$2.50
Family* Admission.........................$8.50
    Willamalane Resident........$6.50

Group Discounts
(Groups of 10 or More)
Individual Admission................$3.00 each
    Willamalane Resident...$2.00 each

Coupon Book of 10 Individual
Discounted Tickets
Individual Coupon Book................$28.00
    Willamalane Resident........$20.00

Coupon Book of 5 Family*
Discounted Tickets
Family* Coupon Book.......................$34.00
    Willamalane Resident........$26.00

*Parents with children representing one household.

ADULT SWIMS

ADULT LAP SWIMS*
(shared with simultaneous programs)
Day: M-F Time: 5:30a-3:00p
                 6:30-9:00p
Day: Sa Time: 9:00a-5:00p
                 6:30-9:00p

*18 & over

FEES:
Daily or Single Admission
Adult (18-54 years)..........................$2.25
    Willamalane Resident...........$1.50
Senior (55+years)..............................$1.50
    Willamalane Resident...........$1.00

Coupon Book of 10
Discounted Tickets
Adult (18-54 years)...........................$18.00
    Willamalane Resident........$12.00
Senior (55+years)..............................$12.00
    Willamalane Resident...........$8.00

WATER FITNESS

Session 1–Weeks of Sept. 17-Nov. 9
Session 2–Weeks of Nov. 12-Jan. 4
These are all registered classes. Registration begins at LPSC Sept. 10. Drop-ins also welcome, however health quaestionaires must be completed and approved.

AEROBIC WATER AND
PRENATAL FITNESS
M/W/F.................................8:00-9:00a
Cost: Session 1–$22
        Session 2–$21
M/W.....................................8:00-9:00p
Cost: Session 1–$14.50
        Session 2–$12

FLUID MOVEMENTS
EXERCISE CLASS
Tu/Th...................................5:30-6:30p
Cost: Session 1–$14.50
        Session 2–$12

SENIOR ADULT AEROBIC
WATER FITNESS
Instructor-led exercise program reserved for adults age 55 and over.
Tu/Th...................................11:00-Noon
Cost: Session 1–$10
        Session 2–$8

Figure 8.7   (continued)

However, in recent years, there has been a general decline in the revenue position of aquatics programs. Perhaps this is not due to a decline in the interest of people in aquatics, but rather to a lack of dynamically designed facilities that are in step with contemporary needs. Today, an aquatic facility must be more than just a body of water; it must be creatively programmed in order to effectively draw individuals.

Outdoor Recreation

Outdoor recreation programs, according to Jensen (1977: 8), are "those recreational activities which occur in an outdoor (natural) environment and which relate directly to that environment." He further suggests that activities can be classified as resource-oriented or activity-oriented.

> Resource-oriented recreation includes those forms that depend strongly on the utilization of natural resources, such as the study of botany and wildlife, camping, hiking, fishing, boating, and hunting. Activity-oriented recreation includes the performance or the witnessing of a performance such as athletics, dramatics, art, music, crafts, and so on (Jensen 1977: 8).

It is understood from this definition that the mere movement of activity-oriented programs into the outdoors does not make them outdoor recreation (resource-oriented). Many activities may certainly be enhanced by their being carried out in the outdoor environment, but only activities that depend on the natural environment for their occurrence are truly outdoor recreation. There are a number of objectives that should be considered in planning for outdoor recreation in our society. The majority of people in our urban society do not have opportunities for contact with the outdoors; therefore, there should be an opportunity for them to develop appreciation for nature in order to make them aware of the importance of preservation practices and sound

conservation. Participation in outdoor experiences leads to individual satisfaction and enjoyment. Outdoor recreation experiences also should provide opportunity for diversion and relaxation. Opportunity to develop physical fitness occurs in outdoor recreation through involvement in activities that are vigorous and taxing—moving participants beyond their usual levels of exertion. There is great emphasis on physical fitness in our society, and outdoor recreation allows many opportunities for fulfilling this need. "The fact that today's outdoor recreator must share his or her resources with many other people requires the development of desirable patterns of social outdoor conduct" (Jensen 1977: 8). Development of desirable behavioral patterns for life in the "crowded" environment should encourage a comfortable sharing of natural recreation resources and preserving of resources in an ecological balance.

The scope of outdoor recreation activities and experiences is as large as the environment itself. Outdoor recreation experiences can encompass such activities as sailing a yacht, paddling a canoe, walking in the park, climbing a snow-capped mountain, visiting a rose garden, touring the Everglades, studying the geology on the banks of a small stream, seeing geological formations in the Grand Canyon, planting a garden, observing the wildlife, smelling the rain in the forest, and viewing the sunset across a plowed field. Recreation experiences in the outdoors may involve physical activity, intellectual discernment, and aesthetic appreciation (1963: 238). Horseback riding, skiing, hiking and climbing, hunting and fishing, swimming, diving and boating, building fires, and outdoor cooking all involve physical activity. Intellectual discernment is evident in outdoor recreation activities such as visiting interpretive centers; hearing naturalists describe areas of a park (or of a forest, desert, or body of water); and studying and observing areas of natural, cultural, scientific, and historical significance. Aesthetic appreciation and awareness can be demonstrated through activities such as painting, photography, writing, recording of sounds, landscaping, and creating natural craft items. It is important to note that "one cannot provide outdoor recreation. . . . It is possible to provide opportunities for, or resources and facilities for, but it is next to impossible to provide outdoor recreation as such all neatly packaged and predigested" (U.S. Department of Commerce n.d. :10).

Outdoor recreation programs take many forms. For example, the Thunder Bay (Ontario) Parks and Recreation Department in conjunction with the Lakehead Region Conservation Authority operate a system of trails (see Figure 8.8) as a part of their outdoor recreation program. The Portland (Oregon) Bureau of Parks and Recreation in conjunction with the Audubon Society of Portland (Oregon) provides informational documents for observing different species of birds. Figure 8.9 presents information concerning the blue heron and its rookeries in the Portland area. The U.S. Forest Service runs a variety of outdoor programs. For example, its "Plant a Tree" program recognizes the contributions of individuals who plant trees for multiuse management in national forests (see Figure 8.10).

Several factors influence the significance of outdoor recreation in our society today. Population and urbanization, mobility, work and leisure, income, education, and technology are all elements that influence the direction and the existence of our rapidly moving society. The number of people living in a given area has a strong influence on patterns of utilization of natural resources. The growing urban areas, as well as the changing makeup of our society, concerns not only sociologists and demographers but also those responsible for the development and delivery of outdoor recreation and leisure services. The demand for space (green areas), clean air, and water resources for outdoor recreation is extremely critical. The primary public transportation system, which is the use of personal automobiles, exerts massive pressure on outdoor recreation providers. Development of sophisticated roads and highways for access to specific

Figure 8.8 Flyer. (Recreation Trails in Thunder Bay, Parks and Recreation Department, Thunderbay, Ontario.)

areas and provision of extensive parking areas for cars and recreational vehicles, boat trailers, campers, and motor homes consume large areas of land space. The ability of people to travel long distances to use resource-oriented recreation areas is a by-product of society's mobility. The decline in the amount of work necessary to earn

THE GREAT BLUE HERON

PORTLAND'S CITY BIRD

Even to the casual observer, the Great Blue Heron is a dramatic component of our urban landscape as it glides along the Willamette River or over Oaks Bottom Wildlife Refuge. Although it is truly a bird of rivers, sloughs and wetlands, with its six foot wingspan it can also be seen soaring past downtown skyscrapers.

The Great Blue Heron stands nearly four feet tall and is sometimes mistaken for the unrelated Sandhill Crane. The two birds are, however, easy to tell apart. The Great Blue Heron is distinguished by its habit of holding its neck in an s-shaped curve when in flight and by its long black and white plume and blue-gray plumage.

THE SPIRIT OF PORTLAND

The Great Blue Heron, adopted as Portland's official bird is a symbol of our quality of life. This link is expressed by William Stafford, Oregon's poet laureate, in his poem "Spirit of Place", written especially to celebrate Portland's Great Blue Herons.

SPIRIT OF PLACE

Out of their loneliness for each other
two reeds, or maybe two shadows, lurch
forward and become suddenly a life
lifted from dawn or the rain. It is
the wilderness come back again, a lagoon
with our city reflected in its eye.
We live by faith in such presences.

It is a test for us, that thin
but real, undulating figure that promises,
"if you keep faith I will exist
at the edge, where your vision joins
the sunlight and the rain: heads in the light,
feet that go down in the mud where the truth is."

- William Stafford

Figure 8.9 Flyer. (The Great Blue Heron, Portland (Oregon) Bureau of Parks & Recreation and Audubon Society of Portland.)

income for personal economic maintenance and for the production of goods has increased the average individual's amount of discretionary time. The amount and kind of work in which a person is engaged and the amount and length of leisure time he or she has available influence his or her leisure activity choices. These are important factors to be considered in planning for outdoor recreation.

Closely related to the concept of outdoor recreation (resource-oriented) activities is the area of outdoor education. Smith and colleagues (1963: 16) have stated that "Outdoor education is the term . . . used for the learning experiences in and for the outdoors." Figure 8.11 indicates the curriculum areas that can be applied to outdoor education. Although the word education and the concept of education have traditionally been limited within the realm of educational institutions (the schools), education is also the domain of other human services programs—including leisure service organizations. As demonstrated in Figure 8.11, education in the outdoors is an extension and application of school curricula. Education for the outdoors involves the development of skills and knowledge

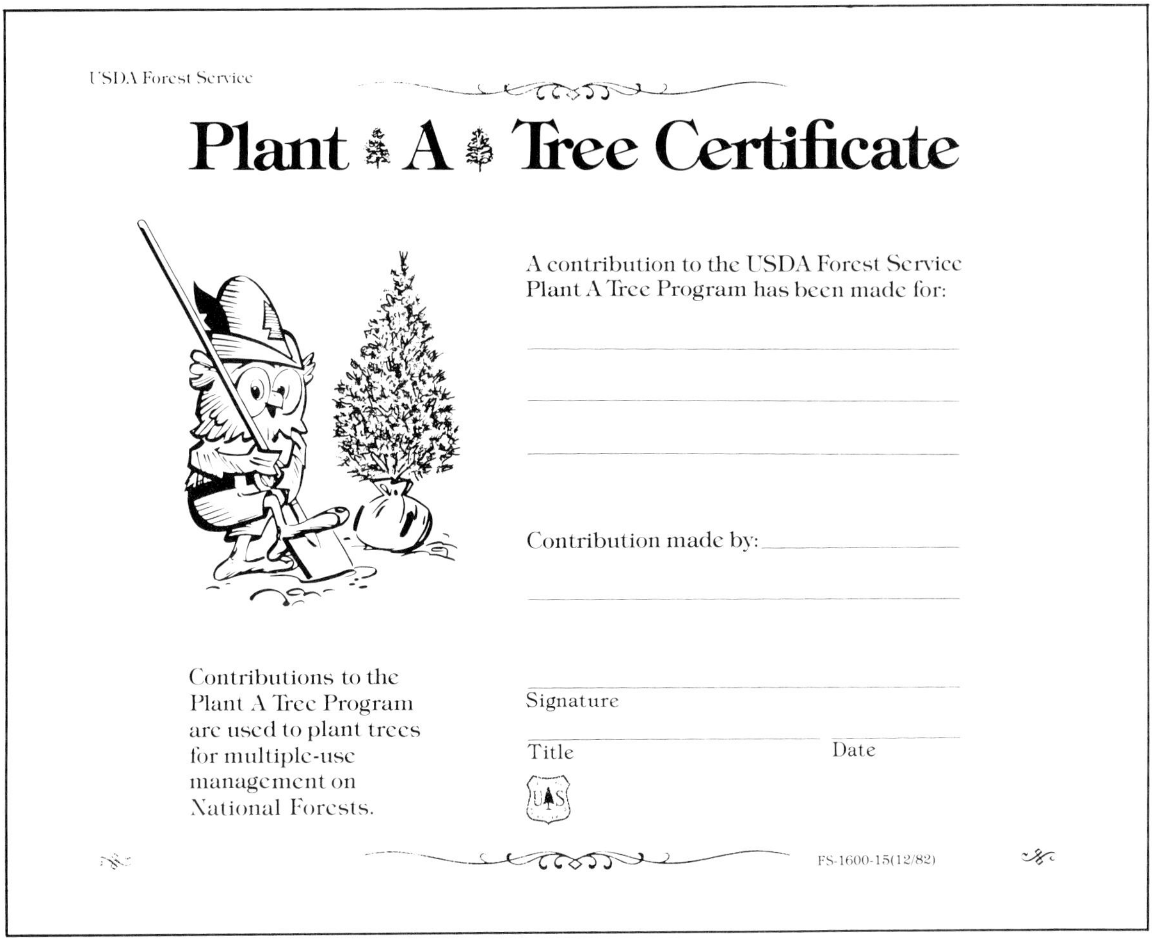

USDA Forest Service

Plant ❋ A ❋ Tree Certificate

A contribution to the USDA Forest Service
Plant A Tree Program has been made for:

_____

_____

_____

Contribution made by:_____

_____

Contributions to the
Plant A Tree Program
are used to plant trees
for multiple-use
management on
National Forests.

Signature
_____
Title   Date

FS-1600-15(12/82)

Figure 8.10 Plant a Tree Certificate. (U.S. Forest Service.)

concerning outdoor resources within the context of leisure programs. This kind of education should be the responsibility of leisure service organizations. Community leisure service organizations and educational institutions can contribute to outdoor education by cooperating to provide areas and facilities for outdoor education experiences and by exchanging personnel and services to develop education and leisure services.

Camping also is a part of the total leisure service program area of outdoor recreation. In camping—temporary living in the outdoors—

customers are able to interact with the natural environment and engage themselves in outdoor education by extending the "outdoor education academic curriculum"—thus acquiring skills and knowledge. Camping, obviously, can assume various forms. The resident camp offers an opportunity for the customers to remain in the camping area for a period of time—a week, or an entire season. Day camping involves only a brief period of camp time and usually does not include an overnight stay. Camping can be carried out in many ways—with peers or family, in a tent, a motorized home, or a cabin. The kinds of camps that

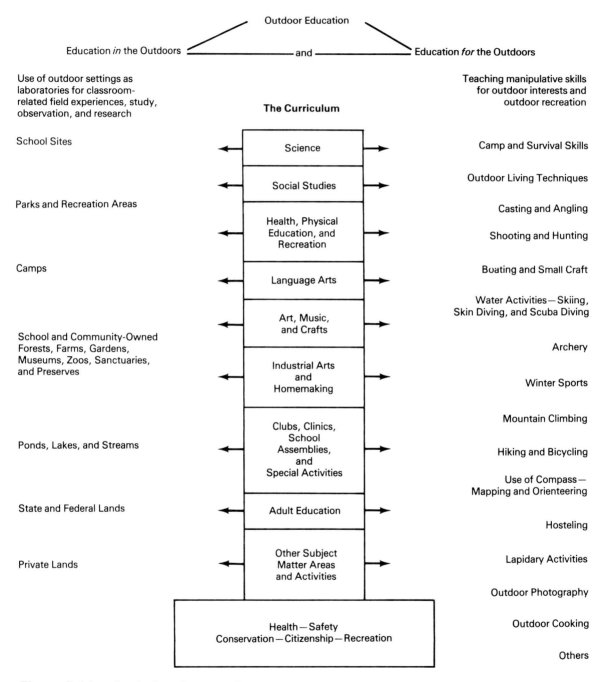

Outdoor Education

Education *in* the Outdoors ———————— and ———————— Education *for* the Outdoors

| Use of outdoor settings as laboratories for classroom-related field experiences, study, observation, and research | **The Curriculum** | Teaching manipulative skills for outdoor interests and outdoor recreation |

School Sites	Science	Camp and Survival Skills
	Social Studies	Outdoor Living Techniques
Parks and Recreation Areas		Casting and Angling
	Health, Physical Education, and Recreation	Shooting and Hunting
Camps	Language Arts	Boating and Small Craft
	Art, Music, and Crafts	Water Activities—Skiing, Skin Diving, and Scuba Diving
School and Community-Owned Forests, Farms, Gardens, Museums, Zoos, Sanctuaries, and Preserves	Industrial Arts and Homemaking	Archery
		Winter Sports
	Clubs, Clinics, School Assemblies, and Special Activities	Mountain Climbing
Ponds, Lakes, and Streams		Hiking and Bicycling
		Use of Compass—Mapping and Orienteering
State and Federal Lands	Adult Education	Hosteling
Private Lands	Other Subject Matter Areas and Activities	Lapidary Activities
		Outdoor Photography
	Health—Safety Conservation—Citizenship—Recreation	Outdoor Cooking
		Others

Figure 8.11 Curriculum Areas in Outdoor Education. (Smith, J. W., Carlson, R. E., Donaldson, G. W., & Masters, H. B. (1963) *Outdoor Education,* Englewood Cliffs, NJ: Prentice-Hall, 17.)

are most familiar have often been characterized by the sponsorship or activity—agency camps (4-H, Camp Fire, Boy Scouts, Girl Guides, Girl Scouts, or social services), public camps (local government or leisure service agencies), school camps, special interest camps (music, sports, special needs, ranches, elderly), private camps (business enterprise), and religious organization camps.

Leisure service organizations both in the private sector and at all levels of government have an increasingly important role in the area of outdoor recreation programs and services. The management of people along with natural resources is a primary contemporary concern (Jensen 1977: 45–46). Outdoor recreation areas should be identified and preserved for that purpose; the utilization of resources for recreation, conservation, and preservation should be a high priority. The leisure service movement must become more active in the area of ecology. We should assume strong positions in leadership and advocacy on behalf of and in cooperation with those individuals and groups concerned with ecological problems.

Wellness

A program area that has emerged over the past several decades has been that of wellness. Wellness programs operated by leisure service organizations have taken on increasing importance paralleling the rising interest in health, fitness, and well-being. Not only is wellness an individual concern, but it is also a concern of organizations. Increasingly, the health of an organization's employees is recognized as having a bearing on its effectiveness and efficiency. Organizations are concerned with the absenteeism, morale, and job performances of employees, as well as medical claims that are forcing increases in insurance rates. Today, many organizations are employing wellness specialists with the hope of reducing or minimizing these undesirable health-related factors.

The wellness program area is known by several terms. Wellness is an all-encompassing term that embraces many different kinds of activities. It is far broader than, for example, physical fitness. Another term that is often heard is *lifestyle management*. Lifestyle management is a broad term, like wellness, yet lacks focus. Another term that is often used is *health promotion*. Health promotion focuses on the promotion of positive health behaviors. Health promotion activities include any combination of educational or other interventions that produce healthier individuals.

What is wellness? Wellness is difficult to define; it means different things to different individuals. From one person's perspective, wellness may be viewed as a process that helps individuals enjoy their lives more fully. Schlaadt (1983: 20) has written that wellness is a lifestyle dedicated to following desirable health practices and to achieve optimal health. Another person may look upon wellness as a program of intervention focused on reducing the risks present in one's environment. Lawrence Green, former director of the Office of Health Information and Health Promotion, Department of Health and Human Services, has suggested that wellness is " . . . any combination of health, education, and related organizational, economic, or political interventions designed to facilitate behavioral and environmental changes conducive to health (Girdano 1986: 5–6). Wellness can also be viewed more narrowly: it can be focused on a single dimension of a person's life, such as physical, emotional or social well-being, or other kinds of well-being.

From our perspective, wellness is a broad concept that is tied to helping people formulate values and then act on them, through the provision of a variety of activities and services. As Behrens (1983: 1) has written, wellness " . . . begins with people who are basically healthy and seeks the development of community and individual measures to help them develop lifestyles that can maintain and enhance their state of well-being." *Wellness* programs (such as nutrition, physical fitness, leisure education, and stress management) are different from *health protection* (occupational safety, toxic agent control, and accidental injury control) and *preventative services* (high blood pressure detection, immunization, and family planning). Wellness programs are usually participated in voluntarily. They " . . . provide people with information, education, opportunities for behavioral change and/or incentives to help and encourage them to make the best possible choices about lifestyles they practice" (Behrens 1983: 1). Basically, a wellness program organized by a leisure service organization should deal with three elements. These are as follows:

Information—Leisure service organizations can provide individuals with information related to their well-being. This can include providing information concerning the ill effects of a poorly managed lifestyle and directing individuals to appropriate activities and services that can help them develop and maintain a greater sense of wellness and well-being.

Values Clarification—Another way that a leisure service organization can assist individuals is by helping them clarify their values related to wellness. In order to promote a permanent change in behavior, people must be motivated. Ideally, individuals ought to be able to see the value of a healthy life, but often are unable to motivate themselves even in the face of overwhelming evidence that would suggest that their present behaviors are unhealthy. People are influenced by societal factors and habits that lead them to focus on short-term activities that provide immediate gratification, rather than focusing on longer-term goals related to wellness.

Activities, Programs, and Services—An important contribution that leisure service organizations make is in the structuring of opportunities for participation in wellness programs and activities. Not only can leisure service organizations directly create activities that they plan, organize, and implement, they can also work with a variety of different community agencies to co-sponsor events. Also a leisure service organization can serve as a clearinghouse, helping to identify and refer individuals to other programs, agencies, and resources.

The above strategies suggest that leisure service organizations can potentially engage in a wide variety of wellness-related services. The diversity of wellness activities provided by leisure service organizations may address a variety of different health, lifestyle, and well-being concerns. In one community, a leisure service organization may be narrowly focused on one type of activity or service, such as a fitness program. In another community, a leisure service organization might have a broader approach, providing a more comprehensive wellness program that includes hydrostatic weighing, cholesterol screening, nutrition classes, counseling, and various fitness activities. Still further, some leisure service organizations operate programs and services for which they have contracted with a corporation or government agency to provide a comprehensive wellness service.

What kinds of activities, programs, and services are normally associated with wellness programs? There are a myriad of services that can be offered under the wellness umbrella. Following is a list of some of the more popular activities that are often associated with wellness/lifestyle programs as adapted from Behrens (1983: 7). They are:

1. *Physical Fitness*—Jazzercize, aerobic exercise, jogging, tai chi, flexibility training, discount or corporate memberships in a health club, healthy back, fitness equipment, showers and lockers, a gymnasium, and fitness evaluation and prescription.
2. *Nutrition*—Information on dietary guidelines, preparing heart-healthy meals, controlling fats, sugars, sodium, and cholesterol, and eating healthy for less money.
3. *Leisure Education*—Information on leisure activities, values, attitude states, boredom reduction, and leisure resources. Could include guidelines and procedures for choosing satisfying leisure experiences that promote healthy lifestyles.

4. *Weight Reduction*—Nutrition information, diet classes and monitoring, Weight Watchers, Take Off Pounds Safely, and diet support groups.

5. *Smoking Cessation*—Quit-smoking classes, self-help books, support groups, hypnosis, and biofeedback.

6. *Stress Management*—Relaxation training, biofeedback, yoga, avoiding burnout, coping with loss, coping with loneliness, death, and dying.

7. *Alcohol and Drug Awareness*—Wise use of prescription and nonprescription drugs, medication interactions, AA, Al-Anon, teen drinking and drug use, and non-alcoholic party drink recipes.

8. *Women's Health Issues*—Breast self-examination, working mothers, working while pregnant.

9. *Medical Self-Care*—Teach steps to take before calling a doctor, such as taking temperatures and blood pressures, how to determine when medical care is needed, and what information to have ready when calling a physician.

10. *Support Groups*—Jogging groups, former smokers groups, weight-loss support groups, stroke clubs, mended heart clubs.

Leisure service organizations often will work in conjunction with other community agencies to provide services. It is not necessarily realistic to think that a leisure service will have all the resources necessary to structure a comprehensive wellness program. Further, it may be that the strategy taken by the organization may be one of facilitating the work of divergent community groups to build a comprehensive community effort. Even if the leisure service organization is not the major motivating factor behind the provision of services, it will want to support the efforts of other organizations in building wellness programs. Many mutually beneficial relationships can be derived from working with the community resources that are in place. Some of these community groups may include the following:

1. *Voluntary Agencies*—Local heart, cancer, lung, diabetes, and arthritis associations can provide material, staff time, space, and consultation.

2. *Special Interest Groups*—The American Red Cross and the Y's are placing a national focus on health promotion and may have material, courses, or teachers available. Alcoholics Anonymous and Al-Anon may offer assistance in handling crises. Groups such as the safety and dairy councils have many useful materials. The National Retired Teachers Association's volunteers might provide "people power" for special activities or have individuals to teach courses.

3. *Hospitals*—A growing number of hospitals have lifestyle, occupational health, and employee assistance programs designed especially for implementation in local businesses and industries.

4. *Public Health Departments*—Many public health departments have health educators and some have developed special programs for worksites.

5. *Colleges and Universities*—Teachers and students may be able to offer assistance in planning and evaluation, determining training methodologies, and course content. Students may be able to develop and teach courses or research specific topics as part of their course work or to gain experience. Look especially for students in health education, public health, exercise physiology, nutrition, etc. Medical and nursing students also may be willing to help.

6. *Professional Organizations*—Local medical, dental, and hospital associations may have material and be able to direct you to people or groups that offer worksite programs or can offer consultation.

7. *Community Organizations*—Community organizations, such as the United Way, have been a valuable resource in the development of community-wide guides listing available health promotion programs. This kind of guide is useful to all local businesses and its development helps facilitate cooperation and information exchange among local businesses and program providers.

8. *Civic/Service Groups*—The Lions Clubs have a national program aimed at preventing blindness, and local groups may have a variety of resources to draw upon. Local Jaycees, Rotary Clubs, Kiwanis, and a wide range of other civic and service organizations may be valuable sources of volunteers, materials, and support.

9. *For-Profit Groups*—Groups such as Weight Watchers or Take Off Pounds Safely may schedule meetings at or near your worksite. Other organizations are eager to supply material or speakers for use in your employee health program. Many for-profit groups will provide a whole package of programs for your employees.

10. *Extension Services*—Most extension services have a nutritionist, as well as a health subcommittee, that could be helpful in developing in-house programs. Some also have services in other content areas. To find your local cooperative extension service office, look in the white pages of your phone book under county or city government.

Any or all of these types of organizations can provide invaluable information, assistance, and/or support for the development of a wellness program. Leisure service organizations should work actively to foster ties that are in the best interests of those whom they serve.

Wellness Program, City of Ames, Iowa, Parks and Recreation Department

An example of a wellness program for city employees developed by a parks and recreation department is that of the City of Ames, Iowa. This program is directed toward permanent city employees, spouses, and dependent children, with an objective of improving the health and fitness of employees, and it is organized by a Wellness Coordinator. The program has a variety of different types of activities and motivational schemes to encourage employees to take part. Some of the activities include a weight-loss support group, walking, racquetball, jogging, golf, hockey, football, softball, soccer, rope-skipping, rowing, skating, skiing, tennis, aerobics, aquatrim, volleyball, weight training, wellness seminars, and a health-risk appraisal. For participating in any or each of these programs, individuals earn "bucks" for exercising, playing sports, and attending wellness education seminars. These bucks can be redeemed for prizes such as free fitness sessions, T-shirts, socks, passes to activities, gift certificates, sweatshirts, and so on (see Figure 8.12).

Figure 8.12 Wellness Program. (Parks & Recreation Department, Ames, Iowa.)

Willamalane Park and Recreation District— Health Fitness Program.

Another example of a wellness program is the Health Fitness Program operated by the Willamalane Park and Recreation District, Springfield, Oregon (see Figure 8.13). This comprehensive health fitness program is available to all members of the community and includes the provision of a well-equipped fitness center. The program enables individuals to participate in an individualized fitness program (IFP) in which the fitness staff design programs for customers to meet their fitness and lifestyle goals. Other programs include hydrostatic weighing (see Figure 8.14), calisthenics, Swedish massage,

Figure 8.13 Health Fitness Program.
(Willamalane Park & Recreation District,
Springfield, Oregon.)

Figure 8.14 Hydrostatic Weighing.
(Willamalane Park & Recreation District,
Springfield, Oregon.)

aerobic dance, aerobic fitness, water fitness, aerobic water and prenatal fitness, and fluid movement (calisthenics in the water). Special events such as the "Willamalane Turkey Stuffer" are designed to engage customers in a holiday fitness run or walk (see Figure 8.15).

Hobbies

A hobby is an activity that an individual pursues over a period of time with intense interest, primarily for the pleasure it brings. This would seem

Figure 8.15 Turkey Stuffer. (Willamalane Park & Recreation District, Springfield, Oregon.)

to define many leisure activities; however, the area of hobbies is a discrete program area in the way it develops and is pursued. Perhaps it is the quality of the individual's interest in the activity—its intensity and longevity—that is especially characteristic of the hobby concept. Hobbies are usually separate from an individual's professional pursuits, although not necessarily so.

Hobby activities may be broadly classified in several ways, so that the scope of activities can be better understood (see Table 8.10). Any given hobby may fall within more than one classification; or the same hobby might be classified a certain way for one person and a different way for another person. The hobby classifications included within this section are, by and large, all-inclusive. These classifications include collection hobbies, creative hobbies, educational hobbies, and performing hobbies (1963: 182–187). There may be other terms or categories to indicate such

things as construction hobbies, learning hobbies, demonstration hobbies, or hobbies for sale; however, the four classifications (collection, creative, educational, and performing) should encompass most hobbies.

Collection hobbies are probably derived from man's natural tendency to gather or accumulate things. People collect just about anything and everything found in the environment—from glass doorknobs to celebrity signatures. Collectors often classify themselves according to what they collect (e.g., antique collectors, stamp collectors, art collectors, relic collectors, memorabilia collectors, firearms collectors, comic book collectors, and quilt collectors). With creative hobbies, there is a different type of involvement than with collection hobbies. People have a psychological drive to make, construct, and create; and they find pleasure and satisfaction in the resulting object or product. The need to be creative often is fulfilled through vehicles such as painting,

TABLE 8.10 Classifications of Hobbies

Collection	Creative	Educational	Performing
Phonograph records	Models	Astronomy	Dancing
Sheet music	Writing	Ornithology	Acting
Automobiles	Short stories	Meteorology	Singing
Placemats	Poems	Beekeeping	Sailing
Church bulletins	Plays	Archeology	Skiing
Autographs	Diary	Mineralogy	Horseback riding
Coins	Woodworking	Travel	Running
Recipes	Ceramics	Music	Chess
Dolls	Music	Drama	Backgammon
Postcards	Composing	Art	Checkers
Stamps	Singing	Crafts	Fencing
Christmas plates	Playing	Reading	Golf
Glassware	Cooking		Tennis
Medals	Metal work		Skating
Campaign buttons	Photography		Mountain climbing
Canes	Sculpture		
Matchbooks	Painting		
Marbles	Rug making		
Rocks	Macramé		
Scissors	Knitting		
Flat irons	Sewing		
Art	Carving/whittling		

writing, using a computer, composing, inventing, making craft objects, cooking, sewing, or dancing. Hobbies that emphasize the learning of skills and acquisition of knowledge are called educational hobbies. Incidental and experiential learning occurs in whatever we do—the experience of creating is educational; the practice of collecting can lead to many opportunities in which to learn more about the items collected. Performing hobbies are based primarily on the use of physical skills—in such activities as dance, sports, crafts, and musical performance. This kind of hobby involvement enables individuals to gain satisfaction from performing alone or with others.

As leisure service programs, hobbies have values that are different from those of many of the other program areas. Involvement in many hobby activities often requires the acquisition of few, if any, specialized skills by the participant. Although some skills may be involved, these usually can be developed by the individual when needed in order to progress in the hobby. On the other hand, some educational and performing hobbies require highly developed levels of knowledge and/or skill. Hobbies may require very little outside stimulation or demand in order to create and sustain lasting interest and continued pleasure. Individual involvement in hobby activities may also serve as a device for relaxation during limited leisure time and reduction of boredom, a means of compensation (by excelling in a hobby), a channel for development of interpersonal relationships and sociability (by meeting and being with other people involved in a hobby), an opportunity for youth to test interests for future career involvement, and a chance for adjustment by the older adult who has recently retired.

As we stated earlier, it is natural for a person to want to collect objects, pursue various new learning experiences, and to seek opportunities for creative self-expression. Therefore, involvement in hobbies is very much a part of cultural tradition. However, there may be factors that affect, to some degree, the pursuit of hobbies. Both the social and physical environment may determine, in some situations, what kinds of hobby involvement will be appropriate. Religious beliefs, educational opportunities, and family values may be strong influences on the development of a hobby. The physical environment has a great influence on the kinds of hobbies that people may be able to pursue in a given location; a large urban area may be more likely to offer better museum and library facilities to the person interested in studying European artists than a small community that is some distance from the urban center. Thus, it follows that it would be easier for the person who is interested in hiking if he or she had easy access to open fields, wooded areas, and country roads. The technological developments, level of affluence, and accessibility to resources will affect the knowledge and skills that the people within the society will contribute toward their involvement in hobbies. Leisure service organizations can provide opportunities for hobby development by making various program area activities available to participants for the development of skills and knowledge, and by making facilities available for such things as displays, demonstrations, sales, hobby shows, and exposure to different types of hobbies.

Social Recreation

In the social recreation program area of leisure activities, sociability is intended to occur as the primary function of the event and the setting. Social recreation uses all program areas to accomplish its objectives. It may include sports, games, drama, music, dance, arts, crafts, and outdoor recreation. The forms and kinds of activities may vary; however, the key factor is the reason for participation (social interaction) rather than the activity itself. Within social recreation, there is a de-emphasis on competition. Many of the activities may be competitive in nature, but socializing is more important.

Settings for social recreation activities vary greatly. Socializing may be the primary emphasis at conferences, workshops, campfires, clubs, parties, picnics, family reunions, and banquets. Emphasizing sociability in a social recreation sit-

uation is a prime way to accommodate a wide variety of ages, interests, and abilities within a group. Ford (1970: 134) has indicated that we view a group in one of two ways: either as a horizontal group or as a vertical group. A horizontal group is composed of people with similarities in age, experience, skills, interests, or knowledge. Examples of horizontal groups would be Girl Scouts, sororities, certain clubs, or associations of related professionals. A vertical group is composed of people with varied ages, skills, and interests. Examples of this kind of group would be a family reunion, a father-daughter banquet crowd, or a playground party.

Individuals participating in social recreation activities do not need to possess specific knowledge or skills prior to involvement in the given program. Most social recreation activities require only simple skills; they have few rules and can be used with various kinds of improvised equipment. Social recreation activities should include several general types of activities such as first-comers, icebreakers, mixers, active games, and quiet activities. First-comer activities are planned to involve all customers as they arrive for the event, so that they need not feel awkward or uncomfortable. A first-comer activity is one that can be entered into at any time without having to wait for a specific time to begin. It may be an activity that can be done individually or in small groups, and it may be competitive or noncompetitive. Icebreakers serve to involve all participants; the intention is to enable the shy, inhibited person to feel more comfortable. Icebreaker-type activities usually occur with everyone doing something similar for the purpose of mutual fun and sociability. Mixer activities are designed to provide participants with an opportunity to socialize with one another for the purpose of direct communication and as a means of getting acquainted. Active games involve team play of a more active physical nature than most other social recreation activities. These games may involve running, tagging, dodging, or throwing. Inactive games usually are played while most customers are seated; they may include dramatic games, creative actions, guessing games, and noisy games.

In planning social recreation events, certain factors should always be considered. Ford has suggested that a social recreation event should follow a "social action curve" (Ford 1970: 134). There should be a low level of excitement as the customers arrive for a social recreation activity; the event should build to a higher level of excitement about midway through the event (based on the activities that take place). Toward the end of the event, the level of excitement should decline. The social action curve shows a definite beginning and end for a social recreation event. Another pattern that should emerge in planning social recreation events is the progression from pre-event planning to carrying out the event and finally to a post-event evaluation. In many situations, there are specific procedures for participant evaluation immediately after the event has taken place.

There are many values inherent in social recreation events that are different from other forms and areas of leisure service activities. Social recreation events can be implemented in conjunction with other program activities (such as planning a banquet to follow a sports tournament, planning a social event in coordination with a dance recital or an art exhibit, or initiating a campfire at the end of each week at camp). Social recreation events can be planned for staff—as first-aid and safety training workshops for playground staff, values clarification retreats for agency staff, and pre-camp orientation for camp staff. Social recreation events (like all recreation events) are for the benefit of the participant. The social recreation group process can foster the development of group solidarity and feelings of loyalty and belonging. Often social recreation events can bring out special interests and latent talents of the participants.

The Chinquapin Park Recreation Center in Alexandria, Virginia, organizes birthday parties for customers ages three through teens. The package birthday party includes swimming, food, table decorations, and gift certificates. Figure 8.16 is a flier advertising this social recreation service.

LET US
ENTERTAIN
FOR YOU...
AND YOU'LL
HAVE
A REAL GOOD
TIME

Birthday Parties at Chinquapin for
Ages 3 - Teens

Package includes:
Swimming

Choice of hot dog, fries and drink
or
Pizza, salad and drink

Balloons for each person

Gift certificate for birthday celebrant

Table decorations

$6 per person
*Chaperones required – no fee

We can also provide at an additional cost:
Wallyball party (exclude swimming)
Big birthday decorated cookie
Decorated sheet cake
Party entertainment

Call 931-1127 for reservations
Minimum 6 persons

Parties at Chinquapin
3210 King Street
Alexandria, Virginia 22302
N-REC-0248

Figure 8.16 Parties at Chinquapin. (Chinquapin Parks Recreation Center, Alexandria, Virginia.)

Volunteer Services

> One of the highest forms of recreation is to use part of one's leisure to do something for someone else. This is facilitated by the volunteer program of the recreation agency . . . If the recreation agency does not have a program of volunteers it does not have a complete recreation program, for to many, volunteer service is a means of recreation (1963: 316).

A volunteer can perform various services, accomplish specific tasks, and carry out numerous responsibilities without remuneration. There is great variance in the number of volunteers, the use of volunteers, the necessity of volunteers, and the recognition of volunteers within leisure service organizations. However, there are three general areas in which volunteers function: *administrative, program-related,* and *service-oriented.*

Volunteers involved in *administrative* responsibilities work very closely with the professional executive staff in determining policies, supporting program areas, raising funds, and supervising expenditures. Often persons functioning as volunteers at the administrative level have been appointed by elected officials or elected by members of the organization. These persons serve as board or committee members within the organizations. For example, an administrative volunteer might serve as a member of the board of directors of a voluntary youth organization (e.g., the YMCA) or as a member of the board (or of a commission) within a municipal leisure service department.

Program-related volunteers deal directly with program activities, often in a face-to-face leadership capacity. Volunteers working within the area of program activities may have specific responsibilities in planning and implementing programs, in addition to directly carrying out planned program activities. The ways in which program volunteers can be involved in recreation and leisure service activities are literally endless. The primary determinant in the kinds of involvement possible for the volunteer is the type of leisure service organization with which the volunteer is associated. Numerous youth organizations within our society were created and have been traditionally maintained by extremely strong, effective, voluntary leadership. These organizations include the YWCA, YMCA, Boy Scouts, Girl Scouts and Girl Guides, 4-H Club, and Camp Fire. Most of the leadership within these organizations is voluntary—most visibly at the program level. Within public leisure service organizations (such as municipal agencies), volunteers at the program level can become involved as teachers, coaches, officials, program specialists, counselors, and leaders. Volunteers are sought to work in all program areas. Some volunteer involvement at the program level may be short-term (such as a week of counseling in a day camp) or long-term (such as teaching in the cultural arts program) or seasonal (such as coaching an athletic team).

Volunteers who function in a *service-oriented* capacity may have varied responsibilities, which can include typing, preparing large-scale mailings, making an inventory of equipment and supplies, repairing buildings, preparing campgrounds, and coordinating library and resource services. A service volunteer may also practice his or her professional skills to the benefit of the organization—for example, a doctor who gives assistance in a youth-sports program physical examination clinic; an attorney who gives legal advice; an accountant who audits the books of an organization; a person in public relations who designs publicity materials; or a dietitian who consults on meal planning for congregate meals. All of these responsibilities and tasks require specialized skills and professional knowledge.

Volunteers are recruited primarily on the basis of their value to the organization; however, the organization must never lose sight of the value that such an opportunity will hold for the volunteer. The organization can seek out volunteers through several sources. Sources for recruitment include former members or program participants in the organization, community volunteer bureaus, educational or religious organizations, service organizations, civic groups, youth clubs and organizations, and retired persons.

Although planning for volunteers and recruiting them are two crucial phases of volunteer program development, the selecting, orienting, training, and recognition of volunteers are also extremely vital. Volunteers should be selected in much the same way that staff persons are selected—on the basis of application, interview, and demonstration of skills and knowledge. It is important to know why the person has chosen to volunteer and if the volunteer is willing to accept supervision, direction, and guidance in carrying out responsibilities. Orienting the volunteer to organization philosophy, purpose, objectives, and policies should be followed with specific training as to the nature of the volunteer's tasks and how they are to be carried out. The volunteer should have a written job description to reinforce his or her training. In addition to preparing the volunteer to function appropriately and effectively within the organization, the leisure service professional must be able to function effectively in a supervisory capacity to accept the volunteer as part of the organization, and to provide appropriate reinforcement for services that are accomplished. Figure 8.17 is an example of the types of volunteer opportunities available in the Portland, Oregon, Bureau of Parks and Recreation. An application form for volunteers is found in Figure 8.18.

Voluntary service has value for the individual who volunteers and for the organization. Voluntary service enables some individuals to perform skills and demonstrate knowledge with which they are familiar and confident. For others, volunteering may offer an opportunity to discover latent skills and talents. Volunteering may be especially rewarding for individuals who are no longer involved in paid professional responsibilities (such as retired persons, homemakers and househusbands, or disabled persons), offering them an opportunity to extend their professional expertise. All volunteers are offered the enjoyment that comes from contributing. The

Figure 8.17 Volunteer Opportunities. (Portland (Oregon) Bureau of Parks & Recreation.)

value of volunteers to a leisure service organization is broad in scope. Through the involvement of volunteers, an organization strengthens its ties with the community that it serves. Volunteers can add enthusiasm to organizational plans and programs, and can contribute specialized skills and knowledge to enhance existing activities. Volunteers also offer additional human resources to carry out existing programs or to enlarge and extend services. Figure 8.19 and 8.20 are examples of recognition programs for volunteers operated by the Portland, Oregon, Bureau of Parks and Recreation.

PORTLAND BUREAU OF PARKS AND RECREATION
APPLICATION FOR VOLUNTEER SERVICE

NAME: _____ APPLICATION DATE: _____
First / Last

ADDRESS: _____
Number / Street / City / State / Zip

TELEPHONE: _____ _____ Can we call you at work? What is the best time to call?
Home / Work ☐ Yes ☐ No

BIRTHDATE: _____ / _____ / _____ _____
mo. / day / year

IN CASE OF EMERGENCY, PLEASE NOTIFY: _____
Name / Phone / Relationship

- -

EDUCATIONAL BACKGROUND: _____
_____

WORK EXPERIENCE: (Please describe your work history, listing current and past positions.) _____
_____
_____

VOLUNTEER EXPERIENCE: (Please list the organizations for which you have volunteered and the kinds of work you did for them.) _____
_____
_____

SPECIAL SKILLS, INTERESTS, OR HOBBIES: _____
_____

WHY DO YOU WISH TO VOLUNTEER FOR THE PARK BUREAU? _____
_____

If obtaining a volunteer job is a requirement for you, is there a special form or report that the Park Bureau will be expected to complete? ☐ Yes ☐ No

WHERE DID YOU LEARN ABOUT THE PARK BUREAU'S VOLUNTEER PROGRAM?
☐ From a friend or Parks volunteer   ☐ A Parks Bureau publication/Help Wanted flyer   ☐ The newspaper
☐ TV/Radio   ☐ Saw a flyer or poster   ☐ RSVP/Volunteer Bureau
☐ Other:_____

WHAT DAYS AND TIMES ARE GENERALLY BEST FOR YOU?
☐ Open/Flexible   Comments: (Are there any days/times that are especially good or bad for you? _____
☐ Evenings/Weekends   _____
☐ Weekdays

HOW LONG DO YOU ANTICIPATE YOU WILL BE AVAILABLE TO VOLUNTEER?_____

DO YOU HAVE YOUR OWN TRANSPORTATION? ☐ Yes ☐ No: Do you use ☐ bus ☐ bike ☐ other: _____

IF YOU HAD YOUR CHOICE, WHAT PART OF TOWN WOULD YOU PREFER?
(circle one) N   SE   NE   Westside   Downtown   Doesn't Matter

(over)

- -

Data entered _____ # _____ Mail Code(s) _____ Category _____

Figure 8.18 Application for Volunteer Service. (Portland (Oregon) Bureau of Parks & Recreation.)

There are lots of options for volunteering in the park system. The listing below is designed as a skills and interest index. Please review the list and select those activities which best match your skills and interests.

ARTS AND CULTURAL PROGRAMS
_____ Children's Museum Guide
_____ Costume Shop Assistant
_____ Sew Costumes
_____ Gallery Guide
_____ Music Librarian
_____ Music Performances:_____
                       (instrument/voice)
_____ Music Accompaniment:_____
                       (instrument)
_____ Pittock Mansion Guide
_____ Pottery Assistant
_____ Production Assistant: Theater
_____ Theater Technician: _____
_____ Theater Usher

MECHANICAL/TECHNICAL/ BUILD/FIX
_____ Carpentry
_____ Custodial
_____ Exhibit Construction
_____ Furniture Refinishing
_____ Glazier
_____ Indoor Signs/Lettering
_____ Outdoor Signs (Paint or Route)
_____ Painting
_____ Plumbing (must be licensed)
_____ Reupholstery
_____ Wiring (must be licensed)
_____ Woodworking/Cabinetmaking

PUBLIC RELATIONS/GRAPHICS
_____ Audio-Video Production
_____ Brochure/Newsletter Production
_____ Displays - Bulletin Boards
_____ Graphic Design
_____ Illustration/Cartooning
_____ Lettering/Calligraphy
_____ Media Events/Press Releases
_____ Photography
_____ Slide Show Production

COMMUNITY RECREATION
_____ Afterschool Activities
_____ Swimming Pool Checker (summers)
_____ Arts and Crafts Instructor
_____ Blood Pressure Screening
_____ Disabled Citizens - Bowling
_____ Disabled Citizens - Field Trips
_____ Disabled Citizens - General Programs
_____ Playground Aide (summer)
_____ Wading Pool Supervisor
_____ Preschool Aide
_____ Roller Rink Aide
_____ Seasonal Festivities
_____ Senior Citizens - Exercise Leader
_____ Senior Citizens - General Programming
_____ Storytelling
_____ Teach a class in: _____

SPORTS
(c = coach a = assist o = officiate)
(circle one)

c a o   Youth Baseball
c a o   Youth Basketball
c a o   Youth Boxing/Wrestling
c a o   Youth Football
c a o   Youth Gymnastics/Tumbling
c a o   Youth Soccer
c a o   Youth Softball
c a o   Swimming
        o   Volleyball
c a o   Tennis
        o   Track and Field
_____ Lead a sports activity:_____
_____ Supervise Open Gym
_____ Assist with sports administration:
_____

OFFICE/CLERICAL
_____ General Clerical
_____ Computer Data Entry
_____ Library/Catalog
_____ Reception/Phones
_____ Recordkeeping/Accounting

GARDENS, GREENHOUSE AND TRAILS
_____ Grounds Maintenance/Garden care
_____ General Horticultural activities
_____ Propagation
_____ Trail Construction/Maintenance
_____ Tree & Shrub Pruning
_____ Greenhouse/Nursery

INTERPRETIVE PROGRAMS
_____ Botanical Illustration
_____ Outdoor Guiding (Parks & Trails)
_____ Interpretive Writing/Editing
_____ Plant Label Production
_____ Mapping Grounds
_____ Plant Identification/Horticulture
_____ International Seed Exchange Program
_____ Field Survey and Label trees & shrubs
_____ Visitor Information Services

ADMINISTRATIVE SERVICES/ PLANNING
_____ Marketing and Promotions
_____ Board or Advisory Committee Member
_____ Resource Development/Grant Writing
_____ Surveys/Evaluations
_____ Landscape Architecture/Design

OTHER SPECIAL SKILLS
_____ First Aid/CPR - current
_____ Current WSI
_____ Fluent in another language: _____
_____ Sign for the deaf
_____ Have a chauffeur's license
_____ Willing to provide transportation on occasion
_____ Other special skills: _____

Any other thoughts or comments? _____

_____

_____

_____

Volunteer's Signature

CITY OF PORTLAND
BUREAU OF PARKS AND RECREATION
MIKE LINDBERG, Commissioner
CLEVE WILLIAMS, Superintendent
1120 S.W. 5TH, ROOM 502
PORTLAND, OREGON 97204-1976

Figure 8.18   (continued)

Travel and Tourism

How do we define the concepts of travel and tourism within the realm of leisure activities? According to Milne (1976: 76), "Travel is defined as the movement of people; and tourism concerns the entire business of leisure travel and related supporting activities." The U.S. Commerce Department (3, 7, 11), in the publication *Tourism and Recreation: A State-of-the-Art Study*, has suggested several definitions for the word tourist, such as the following:

> A tourist or pleasure traveler is defined to be anyone who has traveled away from home for pleasure purposes; . . . a person, not on business, who stays away from home overnight; [and a person who travels with] an element of recreation in mind.

The study suggests that the individual's motivation for or purpose in taking the trip would be the most important factor characterizing the tourist. Other terms defined by the Commerce Department Study in its report included the following: outing—"an occasion on which persons are away from home for the major part of the day"; trip—"an occasion on which persons are away from home at least overnight"; and vacation—"an occasion lasting four or more days" (9).

Is there a definable difference between the tourist and the leisure activity customer? The degree of difference between the tourist and the leisure customer will largely depend on the characteristics of the individual tourist. Just as leisure customers are involved in activities within their immediate vicinity, most tourists are involved in a variety of activities in the course of their travels, and both are participating in these activities in their leisure time. Consequently, the difference between the tourist and the leisure customer is more a matter of locale than anything else. The Department of Commerce Study suggests the following:

> Recreation is conceived of in the generic sense of the word, the 're-making' or 're-creating' of

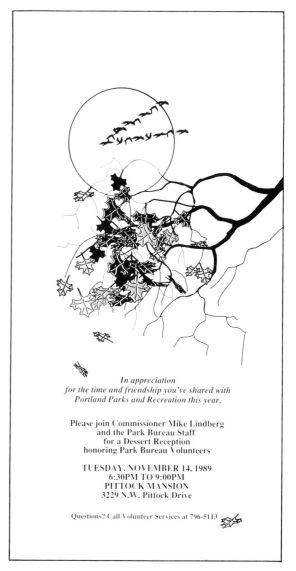

Figure 8.19 Invitation for Reception Honoring Volunteers. (Portland (Oregon) Bureau of Parks & Recreation.)

an individual through the use of leisure time in such a fashion as to restore or rebuild what has been depleted or exhausted in his makeup and to add to his knowledge and abilities with the purpose of a fuller, more satisfying life.

Both the tourist and the recreationer add to their stock or knowledge and experience as a result of their activities. The recreationer . . .

Rising Star Award

In recognition of a new volunteer whose demonstration of commitment to the Bureau of Parks and Recreation has made them an important member of the team and indicates great promise as a star of tomorrow, this award is presented to

_____
NAME

_____
DATE

_____
Commissioner of Public Affairs

CITY OF PORTLAND
BUREAU OF PARKS AND RECREATION
MIKE LINDBERG, Commissioner
CLEVE WILLIAMS, Superintendent

_____
Superintendent of Parks

Figure 8.20 Rising Star Award. (Portland (Oregon) Bureau of Parks & Recreation.)

frequently needs to acquire new skills, or new abilities in order to engage in a particular form of recreation . . . Tourism consists primarily of travel for pleasure purposes, it does not normally involve a large measure of physical exertion, nor does it involve the acquisition of new skills (10).

The Commerce Department Study suggests, interestingly, that it is possible to be both a tourist and a service customer—a tourist, being a person who is traveling from place to place for pleasure, may be called a recreationer when he or she participates in any activities at those places where he or she may choose to stay. In our sedentary society, there are many who travel to find an activity that is physically challenging—e.g., skiing, surfing, scuba diving, and mountain climbing. "With equal zest, others travel to find the challenges to the mind that appear in contrasting one's own feelings and actions against those of people in other . . . [areas] or . . . countries" (Milne 1976: 20).

The travel and tourism industry in the United States, Canada, and throughout the world has a major impact on the economy. Travel is one of the major industries of the United States, and in many countries of the world it is by far the major industry. In the coming decades, steadily increasing leisure time will make travel more important. The numerous kinds of services necessary to accommodate tourists (such as self-contained resorts, commercial lodging establishments, theme parks, eating places, auto service areas, and amusements) are supplied by private enterprise.

The program area of travel and tourism, under the auspices of the local community leisure service organization, can include both informative and participative activities. The organization could provide travel literature, travel films, "armchair" travel groups, and short- or long-term travel opportunities—involving a few hours, a short trip of several days, or extended travel experience here or abroad. Leisure service organizations can serve an especially useful function by providing opportunities for those who cannot ordinarily travel on their own or find it difficult to do. For example, the organization could initiate a ski trip for teens, a trip out of town to a major sports event for boys and girls, an excursion to a safari zoo for children, or a trip to Hawaii for a group of retired individuals.

Blank (1989) has identified a number of examples of tourist attractions. He notes that the list is far from being comprehensive but does define some of the elements that attract and hold tourists for a leisure experience. Among these are: (1) natural resources or a natural feature, (2) economic activity, (3) an ethnic/cultural makeup, (4) historic features, (5) climatic attractions, (6) religious attractions, (7) outdoor recreation, (8) specialty tourist attractions (e.g., stadiums, race tracks), and (9) events. Programmers can build on each of these attractions to create a comprehensive leisure experience. For example, a religious attraction may involve another type of tourist experience as well.

Discussion Questions and Exercises

1. What is a program area?

2. Identify at least three categorization/classification systems.

3. What is the difference between the performing arts and the visual arts? Provide specific examples.

4. What is a craft?

5. Distinguish literary activities from self-improvement/education activities.

6. What are the salient characteristics that distinguish games from sports and athletics?

7. Identify major aquatic services. What is meant by the statement, "The leisure service programmer must work creatively to program aquatic complexes in our contemporary environment"?

8. Identify four classifications of hobbies and provide examples of each.

9. What is social recreation?

10. What are the steps in organizing and implementing a volunteer service program? Why do you think volunteer services has been included as a program area?

References

Arnold, N. D. 1976. *The interrelated arts in leisure.* St. Louis: C. V. Mosby Company.

Ball, D. W. and J. W. Loy. 1975. *Sport and social order: Contributions to the sociology of sport.* Reading, MA: Addison-Wesley.

Behrens, R. 1983. Worksite health promotion: Some questions and answers to help you get started. Office of Disease Prevention and Health Promotion, Public Health Service, Department of Health and Human Services, August.

Blank, U. 1989. *The community tourism industry imperative.* State College, PA: Venture.

Corbin, H. D. 1970. *Recreation leadership.* Englewood Cliffs, NJ: Prentice Hall.

Danford, H. and M. Shirley. 1970. *Creative leadership in recreation.* 2nd ed. Boston: Allyn and Bacon.

Donnelly, R. J., W. G. Helms, and E. D. Mitchell. 1958. *Active games and contests.* New York: Ronald Press.

Edwards, H. 1973. *Sociology of sport.* Homewood IL: The Dorsey Press.

Ford, P. 1970. *A guide for leaders of informal recreational activities.* Iowa City, IA: University of Iowa.

Girdano, D. A. 1985. *Occupational health promotion.* New York: Macmillan.

Jensen, C. R. 1977. *Outdoor recreation in America.* 3rd ed. Minneapolis, MN: Burgess Publishing.

Kraus, R. G. 1985. *Recreation program planning today.* Glenview, IL: Scott, Foresman and Company.

MacKay, K. J. and J. L. Crompton. 1988. Alternative typologies for leisure programs. *Journal of Park and Recreation Administration* 6(4):52–64.

Milne, R. S. 1976. *Opportunities in travel careers.* Louisville, KY: Vocational Guidance Manuals, Inc.

The recreation program book. 1963. Chicago: The Athletic Institute.

Schlaadt, R. G. 1983. "Wellness or lifestyle management." *The ACHPER National Journal,* Winter.

Sessons, H. D. 1984. *Leisures Services.* 6th ed. Englewood Cliffs, NJ: Prentice-Hall, Inc.

Sheffield, L. 1984. Are you providing multiple-option programming? *Parks & Recreation:* May 56–57.

Shivers, J. S. and C. R. Calder. 1974. *Recreational crafts: Programming and instructional techniques.* New York: McGraw-Hill.

Smith, J. W., R. E. Carlson, G. W. Donaldson, and H. B. Masters. 1963. *Outdoor education.* Englewood Cliffs, NJ: Prentice-Hall.

Tillman, A. 1973. *The program book for recreation professionals.* Palo Alto, CA: National Press Books.

U.S. Department of Commerce. *Tourism and Recreation: A State-of-the-Art Study.* Washington, DC: Superintendent of Documents, Government Printing Office.

9 | Program Formats

Learning Objectives

1. To help the reader define and understand the *program format concept.*
2. To demonstrate the relationship between *program formats and customer satisfaction.*
3. To help the reader gain an in-depth knowledge of *various types of program formats* including competitive, drop-in or open, class, club, special event, workshop/conference, interest group, and outreach formats.

Introduction

A program format is another variable under the influence of the leisure service programmer. Selection of program format is important because different ways of structuring programs produce different types of experiences for individuals. In order to effectively implement various activities, a leisure service organization should make a concerted attempt to review the wide variety of available program formats. Individual customers may prefer some program formats to others and certain formats may be more effective as a means of implementing the program.

Ideally, customers should be able to choose from a variety of formats to meet their leisure needs. For example, one customer may be more interested in swimming in a more structured format such as a class, whereas another may prefer a more open or drop-in type format. Still further, another individual may seek a competitive experience. The formatting or structuring of an experience can have a direct impact on the satisfaction of a customer. As a result, careful consideration must be given to the structuring of activities.

In this chapter, we will discuss a number of factors related to the formatting of programs. First, a discussion of how program formats are defined will be presented. Included will be a discussion of various definitions as presented by leading program theorists in the field. The relationship between program formats and customer satisfaction will also be presented. Finally, various program formats will be discussed. Program formats to be covered include competitive, drop-in or open, class, club, special event, workshop/conference, interest group, and outreach formats.

What is a Program Format?

The way in which a leisure experience is structured and organized can be thought of as a program format. In general, one can think of a program format as its general makeup. The program format is the configuration or *the way in*

which experiences are sequenced and linked to one another in order to increase the likelihood that customers will achieve desired benefits. In certain program formats, different outcomes are emphasized. For example, in one situation, the leisure service programmer may want to emphasize the skill acquisition components of an experience. In another situation the programmer might want to emphasize the competitive aspects of an experience. Each of these examples would require the design of a different program format in order to achieve the desired outcome.

The idea of program formats has been addressed in the literature that deals with leisure service programming. Farrell and Lundegren (1983: 83) suggest that the term *program format* ". . . refers to the basic purpose for which a program is designed. . . ." It is the program's structure. According to Farrell and Lundegren, the program format chosen will be directly related to the experience desired for the customer. They suggest that there are five program formats: (1) education, (2) competition, (3) activity club, (4) performance or special event and (5) open facility.

A similar view is offered by Russell (1982). She says that a program format is the structure through which the activity is presented. Russell suggests that there are still other ways of structuring programs. She writes that some of the more frequent program formats that are available to the leisure service programmer include: (1) clubs, (2) competition, (3) trips and outings, (4) special events, (5) classes, (6) open facility, (7) voluntary service, and (8) workshops, seminars, and conferences. Each of these program formats varies in terms of its purpose and general characteristics. Some allow for a continuous, uninterrupted leisure experience, whereas others are short in duration, catering to lifestyles that require convenience (Russell 1982: 212).

Still another approach to categorizing program formats has been offered by Kraus (1985: 186). He suggests that the program format is the form that an activity takes in the planning and scheduling process to meet a customer's needs. Kraus identifies eight potential program formats

that may be employed by a leisure service organization. These are: (1) instruction, (2) free play or unstructured participation, (3) organized competition, (4) performances, demonstrations, or exhibitions, (5) leadership training, (6) special interest groups, (7) other special events, and (8) trips and outings. He suggests that within a given recreation activity, a diverse number of program formats may be employed and that the format selected by a given leisure service organization may be directly related to its philosophical orientation. For example, Kraus notes that an ". . . organization that bases its operation on the marketing orientation will concentrate on programs that yield revenue in one form or another . . ." (1985: 191). Kraus further notes that the selection of a program format should be completed through an intelligent process of planning and implementation, (1985: 191).

Thus, one can see that there are several different approaches to defining the format that a program will take. Such classification systems can be useful to the leisure service programmer in defining the ways in which a leisure experience can be structured and organized. The challenge to leisure service programmers is to link the most appropriate program format with the needs of the customer. Increasingly, efforts directed at segmenting needs in the marketplace have forced a more specific customization of experiences. Such a process of customization requires that the programmer be knowledgeable about the different structures that are available to deliver leisure experiences.

Program Format and Customer Satisfaction

One of the most compelling reasons for careful analysis of the type of leisure program format selected is the fact that it may be directly related to the satisfaction that individuals derive from a given leisure experience. In other words, there may be a direct relationship between the type of program format selected by a leisure services programmer and the satisfaction derived from the experience by individuals participating. Do

competitive programs deliver the desired outcomes we and those served seek to achieve? Do instructional programs produce the levels of satisfaction in the leisure experience that are sought by individuals? These types of questions must be confronted by the leisure service programmer in the program planning process.

One of the key issues that we, as a profession, are concerned with, is the satisfaction experienced by individuals participating in a leisure environment. We can think of leisure satisfaction as the pleasure that one derives from participation in an organized leisure service program. As Beard and Ragheb have written, leisure satisfaction can be thought of as ". . . the positive perceptions or feelings which an individual forms, elicits, or gains as a result of engaging in leisure activities and choices" (1980: 22). Rossman (1984) has suggested that program satisfaction can be discussed by identifying eight potential outcomes—achievement, physical fitness, social enjoyment, family escape, environment, economy, relaxation, and fun—and can be directly linked to leisure program formats.

Perhaps the most definitive study concerning the relationship between program format and customer satisfaction was conducted by Rossman (1984: 39–51). Rossman was involved in examining the impact of typologies for classifying leisure program formats and their impact on customer-reported levels of satisfaction. Studying a range of customers from eleven to eighty-nine years old, with a mean age of 35.5, he found that customer satisfaction was greater when leisure programs were organized in formats that related to certain benefits to be derived from a given type of experience. For example, in studying the satisfactions derived from consumer involvement in programs that were environmentally oriented, Rossman discovered that satisfaction is increased in the open facility and special event program formats. Satisfaction with the benefit identified as social enjoyment is most likely achieved in the special event program format and is least likely achieved in instructional classes.

Opportunities for family escape are most likely to be achieved in either directed programs and open facilities, and least likely to be realized in leagues and tournaments.

As Rossman points out, the implications of this study for leisure service programmers is clear. He notes ". . . it seems clear that when the manager selects a program format for structuring a program, he or she is predetermining the probability that some satisfactions will be realized by the participant while limiting the probability that others will [occur]" (Rossman 1984: 48). Thus, it seems apparent that the selection of a program format may have a great deal of impact upon the satisfaction derived from a leisure experience by a customer. Careful consideration must be given to linking the appropriate program format with the benefits to be achieved.

Another study focusing on the relationship of program format and participant satisfaction was conducted by Hupp (1985). Using the same model as Rossman, Hupp studied the impact of program format upon the leisure satisfaction of a sample of women fifty-five years of age and older. She found that leader-directed programs produced the lowest level of satisfaction. On the other hand, programs that were organized in a drop-in format provided a higher level of satisfaction. In her study, customers indicated that achievement, relaxation, and environment contributed significantly to their levels of satisfaction with programs.

Again, this study confirms the importance of the selection of an appropriate program format to produce desired outcomes. As Hupp writes, ". . . senior center directors and personnel involved with programming . . . could utilize these study findings in the planning and implementation of leisure programs" (Hupp 1985: 93). It could very well be that leisure programs for senior citizens could be formatted to produce the types of experiences and levels of satisfaction most desired by this population. It points out the need to consider the most important programs and formats that will produce satisfaction for customers.

Formatting Programs

As indicated, there are a number of ways that leisure experiences may be formatted. Knowledge of program formats can provide the leisure service programmer with information that can be useful in creating successful leisure experiences that meet the needs of customers. This portion of the chapter provides detailed information about eight different program formats. Specific information is provided concerning *competitive, drop-in or open, class, club, special event, workshop/conference, interest group,* and *outreach program formats.*

Competitive   In the competitive format of leisure activity, *a person's performance is judged in terms of established standards of performance or the performance of another person.* Competitive performance may be categorized in several ways. An individual may compete against himself or herself so that he or she may gauge his or her level of performance and work toward the further development of skill and improvement in performance. An individual may compete against an opponent—either in parallel performance or direct face-to-face competition; this latter activity may be accomplished as an individual, in dual performance, or as a member of a team against another team. An individual can also compete against nature or the environment; this type of competition is carried out in such activities as hunting and fishing, mountain climbing, skiing, canoeing in white water, and hang gliding. Competition in some activities, such as skiing, can involve both human and environmental opponents.

There are two fundamental modes of competitive behavior. First, competition may take place in the form of a *contest,* which is a comparison of ability in parallel performance. By parallel performance, we mean that opponents do not interfere with the performance of each other. Some examples of contests are dance contests, spelling contests, bowling contests, and archery contests. The performance of one opponent does not affect the performance of the other opponent. A *game* is another form of competition—one in which there is direct face-to-face opposition between competitors. The interference or strategy of one opponent or of a team directly affects the performance outcome of the other opponent(s). Obvious examples of game situations are tennis, softball, football, chess, and checkers.

> Contests differ from games in three significant ways. *First*, in a contest there is no interference with the contestant by his opponent(s), whereas in a game there is constant and deliberate interference with his [or her] plans and plays. *Second*, strategy and deception have no place in a contest, while games are full of unexpected situations, strategy, and deception—it is part of a game to outwit one's opponents and confuse them as to what one intends to do. *Third*, a contest presents few if any situations in which the player must exercise choice as to his or her moves, whereas games are filled with opportunities and emergencies calling for choice (Donnelly, Helms, and Mitchell 1958: 3).

There are several plans that can be used to organize games and contests for competition. One plan for competition can be a *meet*. In a meet situation, one's skills are matched against another's and individual scores are acknowledged; individual scores may also be combined for a total team score. Examples of this type of competition are a golf meet, swimming meet, or track meet. Another plan for competition is that of the organized *league*. In this plan of organization, all individuals or teams are scheduled to play an equal number of games against all other opponents in the league. A league is the plan of competition used for many team sports. Final standing is determined by the most number of wins or the greatest number of points by an individual or a team. *Tournaments* are another plan of organization for competition. This kind of competition can take several forms to determine the final winner or winners. The elimination tournament is the most common kind of tournament. There are both a single elimination tournament and a double elimination tournament. Contestants are drawn by lot and matched by pairs on a draw sheet. In the single elimination tournament (see Figure 9.1), the individual or team is eliminated after losing only one game in the tournament. The contestant remaining undefeated is the winner. In the double elimination tournament (see Figure 9.2), initial pairings are determined in the same way as in the single elimination, but a contestant must lose twice before he or she is eliminated from competition. The consolation tournament (see Figure 9.3) is also an elimination tournament, which is made up of contestants who have been defeated in the first round of play. They may continue playing in a bracket from round one and a contestant must be defeated twice before being eliminated. Still another type of tournament used in competition is the ladder tournament (see Figure 9.4). This is a popular form of tournament for individual and dual activities. In the ladder tournament, contestants' names are posted in rank order, and contestants may challenge those persons who are placed above them one or two rungs on the ladder. Winners move up the ladder to the place that the loser held. No

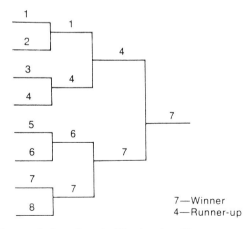

Figure 9.1 Single Elimination Tournament.

Winners' Bracket

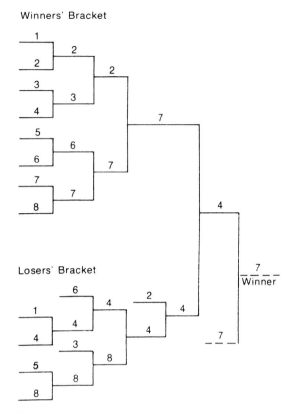

Figure 9.2   Double Elimination Tournament.

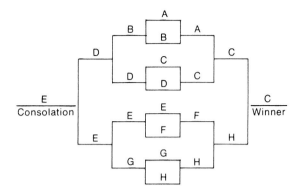

Figure 9.3   Consolation Tournament.

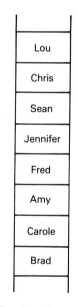

Figure 9.4   The Ladder Tournament.

one is ever eliminated completely from this type of tournament. Initial placing of contestants on the ladder may be accomplished by having the contestants sign up for competition on a "first come, first listed" basis. There are variations of the ladder (non-elimination) tournament that may be used for activity competition (see Figures 9.5 and 9.6.) A very popular kind of tournament, frequently used in leisure activities is the round robin tournament (Figure 9.7). In this type, each contestant plays successively every other contestant in the tournament (this is the kind of tournament often used in league play.) All contestants play the same number of games, and no contestant is eliminated from the tournament.

This kind of tournament is difficult to manipulate if there are many contestants. The solution to handling large numbers is to organize more than one league.

There are several factors that must be considered when employing competition in leisure service programs. Competition is perhaps one of the most commonly used as well as one of the most

Patrick		Susan
James		Michael
Todd		Kyle
Sara		David
Molly		Joanna
Zeke		Jessica
Ann		Deb

Figure 9.5 Challenge Tournament.

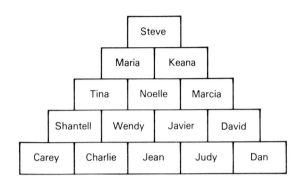

Figure 9.6 Pyramid Tournament.

Five Team Schedule

1–2	1–3	1–5	1–4	2–3
3–4	2–5	2–4	3–5	4–5
Bye	5	4	3	2	1

Six Team Schedule

1–2	1–4	1–6	1–5	1–3
3–4	2–6	4–5	6–3	5–2
5–6	3–5	2–3	4–2	6–4

Rotation System

	1	2	3	4	5	6
1	X					
2		X				
3			X			
4				X		
5					X	
6						X

Figure 9.7 Round Robin Tournament.

controversial forms of program activity. Although competition is an important part of leisure because of the values it has for both competitors and spectators and because of the place it has in our society, it is also very controversial since it has often been abused. Competition in leisure activities is a continuation of the competition met by most people in all life experiences, especially in education and work situations. Successful competition is thought to prove a person's worth. Competition has value in that it can be a motivator for continued performance and self-improvement on the part of the person involved. Competition also offers an opportunity for vicarious involvement on the part of spectators attending a competitive event. Competitors are often rewarded for their accomplishments; however, the importance of reward should not be emphasized.

The leisure service organization professional who plans competitive program activities must acknowledge all of the levels of skill and interest that program participants may exhibit. Competitive activities must be organized in such a way as to accommodate all persons who wish to participate. There are many ways of "equalizing" competition between participants. Within tournament competition, there may be seeding of players—in this case, for the assumed advantage of the better player who has proved himself or herself in competition. In some sports (such as bowling and golf), the score for the poorer player may be given a handicap. This means the poorer player's score has been made more equal to that of the better player. Some other sports activities, as mentioned earlier, have been adapted to offer more people opportunities for competition. These adaptations include slow pitch softball, slow break basketball, and teams organized according to the sizes of the players. Another equalizing factor that can be used is classification of teams according to the size of the city they come from or of the school they represent.

Drop-In or Open

Drop-in or open facility participation in leisure activities may take place at specific recreation facilities, such as community centers or tennis courts, or it may involve visits to libraries, museums, or botanical gardens. Because the nature of involvement in leisure is often spontaneous and not specifically planned, there must be opportunities and places for drop-in involvement. Drop-in participation may be stimulated by the desire to continue involvement in an activity after association with a class, team, or group is no longer possible or feasible. It may be engaged in by an individual who does not feel "ready" to associate with or make a commitment to a group for the purpose of regular involvement. *Drop-in activities do not have to follow a particular schedule and need very little supervision or leadership.* Equipment and materials may or may not be provided. This form of activity may be available in many areas of programming. When we consider the drop-in form of activity, we can often assume that there is a facility or area where the individual may participate. Drop-in opportunities may be available for all age groups, throughout the year—at times and places most accessible to the individual who will participate.

Within the community setting (such as a recreation center), gymnasium and game room facilities often are available on a drop-in basis. The swimming pool is frequently open for "splashes." Many kinds of craft room facilities (such as the ceramic potter's wheel, a drawing board, or an easel) may be available to the drop-in participant. Many times, facilities have supervisory personnel to maintain order and safety in the physical areas and craft areas and to provide information in response to questions concerning the activities and equipment. When people are using facilities during a drop-in time, they may be expected to supply their own equipment (for sports and games) or their own materials (for crafts). This makes it possible for the facility to be available at minimal or no cost to the customer. Driving ranges for golf, tennis courts, outdoor sports courts, and playing fields are easily available for drop-in use when not scheduled for other events and activities. Much of the participation that occurs at mobile units and locations is on a drop-in basis.

Drop-in activities do not require any commitment on the part of the customers, often dismissing the need for registration and roll taking. Since leisure time availability varies for many individuals, drop-in activities are valuable because they can complement varying schedules. In time slots such as the early morning, lunch hour, mid-afternoon, and late evening, the majority of customers may not be available for scheduled program activities, but others may find these to be convenient times to engage in leisure activities on a drop-in basis. Opportunities for drop-in participation in recreation and leisure activities also enable many persons to move more easily into structured programs after becoming familiar with what is available.

Class

The class program form used in leisure activities is a *highly structured teaching/learning situation*. A class can be defined as a group of persons meeting together to study the same topic over a specific period of time. Teaching and learning presumably occur through participation in all forms of activities. This we may call *incidental learning*. However, in a class situation, opportunities for learning are directed through predetermined content development. As a result, designated outcomes of learning can be more easily measured. Although most program formats in leisure settings tend to be open and informal, in a class situation there are certain elements of structure and organization that must exist. The class situation is a shared experience between the teacher (leader) and the learner (customer), but the teacher must assume specific responsibilities in developing the learning environment.

Included in the learning environment are such factors as the physical conditions and surroundings, the intellectual atmosphere, the emotional climate, and the social structure. The physical environment in a class situation includes location, size, and shape of the room; color and lighting; heating and ventilation; acoustics and furniture arrangement; and all equipment, supplies, and materials needed for the class. In order to comfortably accommodate class participants, the leader should take the characteristics of each given class into consideration. For example, a class for older adults should take place in an area or facility that offers easy access (preferably without steps), soft but adequate lighting, bright and pleasant colors, comfortable chairs and tables, easy access to restroom and telephone facilities, and audio/visual teaching aids that can be both easily heard and easily seen. When planning for children, the leader should realize that the use of furniture that is appropriately designed and sized will accommodate them most comfortably.

The intellectual atmosphere of a class situation includes the teaching materials that are used and the individually directed learning experiences that are available. General organization of the learning experience fosters a more comfortable feeling for the class member. The emotional climate in a class involves the sensitivity of the teacher in meeting individual needs of the students for security, acceptance, and emotional involvement. A desirable emotional climate encourages person-to-person relationships between individual class members and between individuals and the teacher. Social structure in a class situation refers primarily to the method of leadership that prevails. Is the class carried out in a democratic manner, with input from both teacher and learner? Is the class structured more loosely with little direction from the leader? Or is the class structured tightly, with little input from the customer? Appropriate integration of the elements within the learning environment into the class form of activity enables both teacher and learner to share alike in a dynamic learning experience.

There are several methods of presenting course content that can be employed in the class situation. In deciding which methods to use, initial consideration must be given to the size of the class group, the nature of the material being presented in the course, and the situation in which it is being presented. Some of the ways in which teachers may present information are through lecture, lecture with visual aids, use of videotapes and films, demonstration of projects and/or procedures, direct individual participation by the class members, and participation by class members in groups. All of these teaching methods may be employed within sessions.

It is the teacher's responsibility to practice good planning for his or her classes. Good planning takes into account the scope of the program activity to be covered, the goal that is to be reached, and the means of achieving that goal. A plan may be either a rigid design or a flexible arrangement, but the most effective planning seems to incorporate both specifics and alternatives. The effective teacher should understand why good planning is necessary. Both teacher and learner will reap the benefits of planning when a class (or session of classes) takes place.

It is necessary to develop both long-range and short-range planning. In leisure activities, class sessions often are planned to extend over a period of time. Classes may meet once a week for ten weeks or twelve weeks, or twice a week for four weeks or six weeks, and so on. Long-range planning, then, would cover the total number of weeks that the class will meet, and short-range planning, the content of each class period. In other words, the teacher would have a plan for the entire session as well as daily plans. The following illustrations demonstrate the way in which a plan might be drawn up for a six-week session, Children's Art Class in Painting.

Long-Range Planning

1. Name of class: Children's Art Class in Painting
2. Participants: Boys and girls, seven to ten years of age.

3. Length of time: Six weeks. The class will meet once a week for one hour.
4. Goal: To enable the child to become familiar with varied media and techniques related to painting.
5. Weekly sessions:
   a. Week 1—Finger Painting
   b. Week 2—Straw Painting
   c. Week 3—Squeeze Painting
   d. Week 4—Soapsuds Pictures
   e. Week 5—Sand Painting
   f. Week 6—Painting with Acrylics

Short-Range Planning
Week 1—Finger Painting

1. Objective: To allow the child to create a colorful painting without knowing how to paint.
2. Materials: shelf paper, scissors, spoon, sponge, finger paint.
3. Teaching procedure:
   a. Cover the entire working surface with newspaper.
   b. Cut the shelf paper to the desired size.
   c. Wet the paper with a sponge.
   d. Smooth the surface of the paper with your hand.
   e. With a spoon, drop some paint on the surface.
   f. With your hand, spread the paint over the surface.
   g. Using different parts of your hand, form a design (Shivers and Calder 1974: 117)
4. Outcomes:
   a. A happy participant.
   b. A visible object, a painting.

Week 2—Straw Painting

1. Objective: To enable the child to produce a painting without using his hands.
2. Materials: drawing paper, straw, paintbrush, paints.
3. Teaching procedure:
   a. Cover the work area for protection of the surface.
   b. Place a drop of paint on the paper.

   c. Hold the bottom of the straw 1/4 inch from the drop of paint and blow into the straw.
   d. Place another drop of paint on the paper.
   e. Blow the drop around the paper.
   f. Finish design (Shivers and Calder 1974: 119)
4. Outcomes:
   a. A fun and creative experience.
   b. A painted design to take home.

In the planning process for class implementation, the teacher (leader) confers with the program supervisor, plans for the customers as well as with them, and reviews and evaluates the outcomes. For many customers, the class form of program activity represents their initial exposure to the activity. It may determine whether or not that person continues into other classes involving that same activity. Consequently, careful planning and implementation are extremely important.

Club

People are gregarious and, as a result, seek opportunities to be together in congenial social situations such as those found within the club program format. A club consists of *a group of persons organized for some particular purpose.* Clubs in leisure settings are most likely to be formed on the basis of age group, activity interest, or for the exchange of information and ideas. For example, age group clubs in leisure service organizations often exist for older adults or for children. Many clubs are organized because of a special interest in activities such as foreign cooking, rugby, bridge, jogging, or quilting. Clubs initiated for the exchange of information and ideas might be based on discussion of current events, evenings at the theater, or operation of ham radios. The purpose here is not to try and categorize each type of club group but to indicate the variety that is possible.

As a form of program activity, the club can have value for both participant and organization. A club experience can be a very educational one. Being with other people in a situation of this nature may enable the individual to broaden his or her ideas and interests and encourage individuals to learn from one another. Congeniality and cooperation do not require total agreement from all members at all times; people can learn from differences of opinion. Within a club, individuals have an opportunity to learn both leadership and "followership." People may learn to lead intelligently, and followers may be taught not to follow blindly. There are also opportunities for individual specialization—more so than in many other forms of activity.

There are several principles of organization that should be considered when developing a club. Within a club—more so than perhaps other forms of leisure activity—customers function as a group, and there is a long-term association of the group members. A group that is organized into a club should establish objectives and purpose for the organization. The club itself exists for the members and not for the leisure service organization professional. Clubs that are organized should be appropriate for the community in which they exist, and membership in the club should not become cliquish and restrictive. This is especially true if the club functions within a public leisure service organization. Membership dues and financial commitments should not be excessive for the customers. The cost of belonging to a particular club will be greatly determined by the nature of the club and the interests and activities the customers pursue. A person who belongs to a group of Broadway theatergoers is going to spend more money than the person who is in a jogging group, and supplies for a gourmet cooking club will probably cost more than for the Saturday morning birdwatching club. Appropriate budget allowances on the part of the leisure service organization should be made for clubs, just as for other activities, so that the club members do not have to assume the entire cost of the club's existence.

Because clubs function in a different way than other forms of program activity, there must be internal organization among their members. Internal organization may be very formal or somewhat informal, but the pattern of organization should follow some order. The constitution and bylaws of a club are the written orders of organization, which clubs develop according to their intended purpose. "The Constitution lays down the fundamental principles on which the club is to operate. The By-Laws establish the rules of guidance by which it is to function. The By-Laws may be more easily amended and altered than the Constitution" (Milligan and Milligan 1942: 27). A constitution and a set of bylaws are given here in very brief outline form. The club supervisor or leader may wish to expand on these items. The source used most frequently as a reference for parliamentary procedure is *Robert's Rules of Order*.

Outline for Constitution

Article I—Name

Article II—Purpose

Article III—Membership

Article IV—Officers

Article V—Executive Board

Article VI—Meetings

Article VII—Amendments

Outline for Bylaws

I—Membership

II—Dues

III—Duties of Officers

IV—Executive Board

V—Committees

VI—Quorum

VII—Order of Business

VIII—Parliamentary Authority

IX—Amendment

The club format of activity within a leisure program attempts to accommodate some of the varying interests of the program participant. Clubs can be limitless in the kinds of participants that they serve and in the kinds of activities and interests around which they may be formed. In the club format, more of the leadership and program planning may be assumed by the participants in conjunction with the leisure service professional than in many other forms of program activity.

Special Event

Depending on the leisure service professional's interpretation of program areas and formats, the special event is sometimes considered a program area. We shall consider it as a program format—a way in which activities may be offered. Special events are "those *phases of recreation programs that depart from the normal routine and that require special planning and assistance*" (*The Recreation Program Book* 1963: 308). This source suggests that a special event "is the single most powerful means to impress people that recreation programmers have" (1963: 198). Special events may cover activities that do not fall within the other forms of leisure programs already suggested.

The special event should allow for the participation and involvement of all the individuals attending it. This factor should be considered in the planning of the special event. For example, if the special event is "Wild West Days" on the summer playground, there should be activities for boys and girls and for those age groups utilizing the playground. If the special event is a day of "Pioneer Life on the Prairie" for an entire community, everyone in the community should have some activity in which they can be involved.

Special events may be planned and implemented by leisure service organizations as an introduction to program activities. For example, a special event such as a parade may open the week of competition for youth drum and bugle corps. Or a community-wide square dance may be the culminating activity for a weekend celebrating early American history, with quilting, candle making, maple sugaring, and shoeing horses. Special events may be planned at any time during the program year to stimulate community interest or add interest to current programs. Events of this nature make a leisure service organization much more visible within the community; they also can service large numbers of community residents in a unique and attractive way.

In planning special events, the leisure service professional should capitalize on as many traditional bases as possible. For example, the seasons—winter fun, blossom time, lazy summer days, autumn leaves—are natural themes for special events. Traditional holidays and other days are standards for special event programming—for example, Fourth of July, Dominion Day, St. Patrick's Day, and Halloween. It seems easier—even for the seasoned leisure program planner—to list special events and let them describe themselves than to attempt to justify the importance and value of special events within any organization's program (see Table 9.1).

On an annual basis, the River Road (Eugene, Oregon) Park and Recreation District organizes, in conjunction with students from the University of Oregon's Department of Leisure Studies and Services, a Halloween-oriented special event. Recent celebrations have used the theme "Harvest Moon Festival," and have featured a variety of special events focused on family activities. Figure 9.8 depicts a flier that was used to publicize this event.

Workshop/Conference

The workshop/conference is another program format utilized by leisure service organizations. Generally speaking, a workshop can be thought of as *a program form with an intense content conducted over a relatively short period of time.* The workshop/conference can be used for instructional purposes or for problem solving. As an instructional vehicle, the workshop format allows individuals to focus on a number of specific topics that are of interest to the participant. As a means of organizing individuals or groups of people around a specific issue or concern, the workshop is an excellent way of arousing public interest and attracting publicity. Many different techniques for disseminating information can be used, ranging from the traditional lecture method to small group discussions. The planning methods used in organizing a workshop/conference, institute, seminar, clinic, or convention are similar.

What are the advantages in using the workshop/conference as a program form? First, it allows individuals to become intensely involved and to focus on specific topics, issues, or concerns in a relatively short period of time. In this way, an individual is able to concentrate his or her learning on a continuous, uninterrupted basis—an obvious advantage for the customer. In other forms used—especially in the class method—learning is often spread over an extended period of time with sessions of short duration, and the interruption that takes place between class sessions may detract from the learning experience. The second advantage is that workshops/conferences usually focus on small group interaction. As a result, there is opportunity for individuals to express themselves and to work in accordance with their unique purposes.

Figure 9.8   Flyer. (River Road (Eugene, Oregon) Park and Recreation District.)

TABLE 9.1   Examples of Special Events

Holidays and Special Days	The Arts	Ethnic and International	Animals
Christmas	Battle of the Bands	Spanish Night	Fishing Derby
Thanksgiving	Fiddlers' Contest	French Riviera	Dog Show
Easter	Barber Shop Singing	A Night in Venice	Cat Show
Valentine's Day	Art In The Park	Cinqo de Mayo	Pet Show
St. Patrick's	Hobby Show	Scandinavian Vikings	Farm Animal Show
Fourth of July	Craft Auction	Scottish Kilts	Horse Show
Washington's Birthday	Film Festival	Irish Sweepstakes	Unusual Pet Show
Lincoln's Birthday		British Jubilee	
Martin Luther King's	**Sports and Games**	Flight to Tokyo	**Instructionals**
Birthday		Midnight in Moscow	
Dominion Day	Punt, Pass, and Kick	Canadian Sunset	Workshops
Queen Victoria Day	Hit, Throw, and Run	Greek Islands	Clinics
Halloween	Junior Olympics	German Polka Day	Symposia
Ides of March	Table Tennis Tournament	African American Culture	Demonstrations
April Fool's Day	Gymastics Clinic	Day	Lectures
May Day	Marble Madness	Jewish Festival	Forums
Father's Day			Conventions
Mother's Day	**Special Days**	**Locomotion**	Conferences
Flag Day			
Arbor Day	Hobo Day	Tractor Pull	**Promotionals**
	Outer Space Day	Soap Box Derby	
Seasons	Wild West Day	Sports Car Rally	Open House
	Backward Day	Bicycle Derby	Master Demonstrations
Winter Carnival	Gay Nineties	Steam Engine Days	Exhibition Games
Spring Fling	Roaring Twenties		Sports Skills Contests
Summer Evening	Fifties Day	**Specialties**	Basketball Free Throws
Fall Frolic	Circus Day		Punt, Pass, and Kick
First Day of Spring	Clown Parade	Freckle Contest	Football
Midsummer's Night		Bubble Gum Blowing	Catch, Throw, and Run
		Contest	Baseball
		Watermelon Seed Spitting	Grand Openings
		Contest	Pep Rallies
		Pie-Eating Contest	
		Egg Throwing	
		Treasure Hunt	
		White Elephants	
		Scavenger Hunt	

We have suggested that the planning methods used in organizing workshops, conferences, institutes, seminars, clinics, and conventions are essentially the same. Yet each type of meeting has a somewhat distinct set of characteristics. It is best to keep in mind how each one varies in order to plan effectively. Table 9.2 illustrates six types of meetings—their various functions and general characteristics. In addition to these general types of meetings, there are a number of different small group meetings that may exist within the broader framework just presented (see Table 9.3). Each grouping can be seen as a mode of communication. Certain groupings facilitate one-way communication; others are useful in establishing a dialogue between individuals. The selection of

TABLE 9.2 Types of Meetings

Type	Usually Used For	Characteristics
Convention	Annual meetings	All general sessions and committee meetings—mostly for giving information and voting on official business. May use subgroups within general session
Work conference	Planning, fact finding, or problem solving	General sessions and face-to-face groups; high participation
Institute	Training	General sessions, some face-to-face groups; staff provides most resources
Workshop	Training	General sessions and face-to-face groups; participants are resources
Seminar	Group of experienced people, or resources share experience	High participation, usually face-to-face group; leader is discussion leader, not only content expert.
Clinic	Clinical exploration of some particular subject—participants usually in trainee role and clinic leaders in training role	Usually face-to-face, but may be general sessions and face-to-face

Bickhard 1956: 29.

a particular type of grouping will depend on the objective. For example, if a group is trying to resolve an issue or concern, it may be organized to encourage fact finding and problem solving through two-way communication. On the other hand, in a teaching-learning situation, each individual may function very independently toward completion of a work project (reflecting primary one-way communication).

To illustrate the application of the workshop/conference in the delivery of leisure service programs, we have included a program from a Community Conference on the Cultural Arts held in Fremont, California (see Figure 9.9). This conference was established to serve as an inventory of leisure interests in the community, to inspire interest, and to give people an opportunity to meet and address experts and community officials concerning the area of cultural activities. It was an attempt to link the social environmental planning with the community's physical planning. A number of nationally and internationally

prominent individual leaders in the cultural arts field spoke at the general sessions of the conference. In addition, discussion groups were organized around ten cultural arts areas covered by the conference. This is an excellent example of how the conference method of organizing a program can be used in a recreation and leisure service organization.

Interest Groups

Interest groups are very similar to clubs in organization and structure. We can think of an interest group as *a collection of individuals that has formed around an activity, issue, or program area.* Usually interest groups generate their own leadership and may exist in a less structured way than a club format, and the lifespan of an interest group may be shorter in duration than that of a club group. Kraus (1985: 188) suggests that leisure service organizations can be supportive of these types of groups by either sponsoring or encouraging their formation.

TABLE 9.3 Small Group Meeting Formats

Grouping	Kinds of Subject Matter	Group or Number of Participants
General sessions	Information giving Orientation Reporting to total group Voting Business meetings Demonstrations Speeches, lectures	Total conference group
Plenary sessions	General session with official action (business meeting, delegate assembly)	Total official group (voting members)
Work groups	Working with a problem or aspect of a problem to come up with action, recommendation, or finding; report usually expected; may meet once or several times	Usually not more than 20—to allow for maximum participation; group composed heterogeneously from conference groups
Special interest groups	Composed of people with common interests in a problem or with a common back-home job; exchange of opinions, experiences, ideas; usually no action required although finding may be produced	10 to 20 to allow for maximum participation
Occupation groups	Special interest groups built around back-home jobs of members	
Application groups	Designed to apply new learnings or information received to other situations of the members	7 to 15
Skills practice group	Found in workshops and institutes; designed to give members practice opportunities in subject being studied (leadership training, conference leadership)	12 to 18
Training group or process group	Specialized form used in some human relations workshops, where subject is study of group process and behavior in groups	12 to 20
Off-the-record groups	Small groups designed to give participants opportunities to react to the conference; no reporting required, but may become informal channel to conference staff for gripes, suggestions; an official conference bull session	5 to 10
Orientation groups	Small groups that meet once at beginning of conference for introduction and orientation	5 to 10

Bickard 1956: 29.

Over the past several decades, there has been a rise in the number of special interest groups that are organized around leisure concerns. Many of these are not only organized around specific leisure activities, but have been formulated to meet specific issues and concerns such as the preservation and conservation of the environment. Often, special interest groups will form in a neighborhood and be focused on issues and concerns that have an impact on that geographic area's social and physical amenities.

PROGRAM
SATURDAY OCTOBER 24

MORNING SCHEDULE
8:30 – 9:30
REGISTRATION .... REGISTRATION INFORMATION CENTER
GET ACQUAINTED COFFEE .... REFRESHMENT CENTER
EXHIBITS AND DISPLAYS .... EXHIBIT AREAS
9:30 – 10:15
GENERAL ASSEMBLY .... GYMNASIUM
KEYNOTE SPEAKERS
Mr. Tom Patterson – Originator of the famed Stratford
Shakespearean Festival in Canada
Dr. Robert Loper – Executive Head, Department of
Speech and Drama, Stanford University
10:15 – 12:00
INDIVIDUAL DISCUSSION GROUPS .... See Session Schedule on Next Page
Attend the Discussion Group of Your Choice
AFTERNOON SCHEDULE
12:00 – 1:30
CONFERENCE LUNCHEON .... LUNCHEON COUNTER
EXHIBITS AND DISPLAYS .... EXHIBIT AREAS
ENTERTAINMENT, 12:00 – 12:30 .... LITTLE THEATER
YOUTH TAP AND BALLET DEMONSTRATION
Joan Caldwell - Instructor
12:30 – 1:00 .... LITTLE THEATER
IMUA HAWAIIAN CLUB
Mrs. Donald Richie - President
1:00 – 1:30 .... GYMNASIUM
FREMONT PHILHARMONIC
Eugene Stoia - Conductor-Director
1:30 – 2:00
GENERAL ASSEMBLY .... GYMNASIUM
KEYNOTE SPEAKER
Mr. Martin Dibner – Executive Director, California Arts Commission
2:00 – 3:45
INDIVIDUAL DISCUSSION GROUPS .... See Session Schedule on Next Page
Attend the Discussion Group of Your Choice
3:45 – 4:30
GENERAL ASSEMBLY .... GYMNASIUM
CLOSING REMARKS
Mr. Tom Patterson   Mr. Charles Merrifield

CULTURAL ARTS FESTIVAL AND CONFERENCE COMMITTEE
Mrs. Richard Aston   Mrs. Raymond Gordon   Mr. Samuel Levine   Mr. Wes Peterson
Mr. Jim Bertino   Mrs. Walter Hartzell   Mr. Wayne Lucas   Mrs. Donald Tarr
Mrs. Lamar Bupp   Mrs. James Higgins   Mr. John MacDonald   Mrs. Gladys Williamson
Mrs. Allen Dailey   Mrs. Robert Lancefield Mrs. Charles McCrory Mrs. Henry Yezek
Mrs. A. W. Ebright   Mr. Charles Merrifield

RECREATION COMMISSION
Mr. Charles Bryant - Chairman
Mr. C. F. Giles   Mr. H. G. Clouser
Mr. Walter Davis   Mr. Howard Tom
Mr. Floyd Erickson   Mr. L. B. Harper

CITY COUNCIL
Mr. Don Dillon - Mayor
Mr. Carl Martineau - Vice Mayor
Mr. Gene Rhodes
Mr. Geoffrey Steel
Mr. William Van Doorn

Figure 9.9 Schedule of Events—Community Conference on Cultural Arts, Fremont, California.

Edginton and Ford (1985: 257–259) have suggested that there is a variety of different types of community groupings or special interest groups that can be addressed by leisure service organizations. Some of these types of groups include: (1) neighborhood associations, (2) sports associations; (3) youth groups; (4) cultural associations; (5) activity or program advisory groups; (6) advocacy associations; and (7) service, civic, or fraternal organizations. They suggest that the work of the leisure service programmer is one of helping individuals develop their own abilities, skills, and knowledge. The process that they recommend is that of enabling. *Enabling* is focused on helping special interest groups learn the processes that are necessary to conduct their own affairs. The work of the leisure service programmer involves the provision of guidance, organization, access to resources, and encouragement. Some of the roles in which a leisure service programmer might be involved in working with special interest groups include the following.

Networking Agent—In this role, the programmer links the special interest group with resources necessary to meet their needs. Such resources may include other people, funds, areas and facilities, information, supplies, equipment, and others.

Organizer—Helping special interest groups organize is a critical role for the leisure service professional. Organizing involves the selection of goals, objectives, and, in turn, the creation of a structure and roles for individual members of the group. Organizing may also involve helping a special interest group coalesce around specific concerns and issues.

Encourager/Coach—Working as an encourager or coach, the leisure service programmer provides motivation to group members, as well as feedback to help the group attain its goals. Often the leisure service programmer will serve as a sounding board for a special interest group. The idea here is that the programmer will use his or her knowledge and values to guide the group toward appropriate ends.

Facilitator/Process Expert—Perhaps one of the most important roles that a leisure service programmer will play in working with special interest groups is that of helping the group to learn process skills. How are meetings conducted?

How does a group become officially sanctioned? What kinds of rules, procedures or by-laws might be established to assist the group in governing itself? Facilitating involves working with groups to help them develop these types of skills so that they can operate independently in the future.

Much of the work of the leisure service programmer working with special interest groups involves interacting with from six to ten individuals. Helping these individuals understand processes involved in operations in a group becomes important. More than likely, participation in a special interest group has occurred on a voluntary basis. Keeping the special interest group together and operating in a smooth, responsive manner to individual group member needs can be a challenge. Often, special interest groups can become dominated by one or more individuals. Such cliques can affect group harmony and cohesion. The leisure service programmer can work with group members to help them to learn more effective processes of decision making as well as ways of helping them remain sensitive, responsive, and aware of the individual needs of others in the group. As Edginton and Ford (1985: 267) have noted," . . . two factors that often drive people from involvement in . . . [special interest] groups are the feelings of being under-involved or overwhelmed." Thus, the leisure service programmer can play a critical role in helping to nurture group cohesion by making special interest group members aware of their impact on one another. This can be effected by the interpersonal skills that are developed within the group. Such group process skills as sharing information, providing feedback to others, and decision making can be influenced by the work of the leisure service programmer with a given special interest group.

One of the process areas that can be especially critical in facilitating special interest groups is that of conflict resolution. Conflict is almost inevitable whenever two or more people interact with one another. People often disagree with one another, not only regarding the general goals of a special interest group, but also on the processes used to achieve desired ends. The leisure service programmer can assist groups by helping them understand ways of resolving conflict in a positive fashion. Such activities find the programmer working to help individual group members compromise and collaborate in a positive fashion with one another.

Outreach

In a society as mobile as ours, it is assumed that individuals can travel easily or move from one location to another in order to participate in leisure activities. Yet there are large numbers of individuals who—for economic, social, physical, or psychological reasons—cannot travel in order to avail themselves of leisure services. An emerging role within leisure service organizations and other social agencies is that of extending services to individuals outside traditional modes of delivery—a concept known as *outreach*.

In the leisure service field, many organizations limit their services to the facilities, areas, and structures developed for the purposes of delivering services. Traditionally we think of parks, playgrounds, recreation centers, swimming pools, and athletic fields as places in which services are provided to a community. In order to receive services or to participate in activities, the participant is required to travel to the given activity or service. Reliance on a facility-oriented approach for provision of services ignores the vast potential for leisure opportunities in the home, on the street, in churches, storefronts, and libraries, as well as other areas more accessible to the customer. *The outreach concept enables an organization to expand and extend its services to broader segments of a population.* In this way, an organization is able to reach out—meeting people on their turf, within their culture, and according to their particular needs, whether physical or social. "Simply stated, outreach work occurs when a social service agency reaches out and assists through personal contacts those previously excluded from, unaware of, or unreceptive to its services" (Bannon 1973: 33).

The outreach concept depends heavily on direct personal contact between the workers of an agency and the customers within the latter's environment; thus, leadership is an extremely important factor. Quite often, individuals employed as outreach workers come from the population group with whom they are working. This is especially true of the roving leader working with inner-city youth.

> Specialized training in recreation is not (necessarily) required and, in fact, the background and personal qualities of (outreach) workers are usually considered to be more important than formal credentials. Theoretical knowledge of group dynamics, . . . or social work is not as important as knowledge of the (social) milieu, personal experience, and character traits that are needed to work with (a given population) (Kraus and Bates 1975: 266–267).

This is not to say that specialized training in recreation cannot be extremely useful in these types of settings, but that the qualities mentioned are the most important qualities in working with outreach groups.

Our conceptualization of the outreach program is a broad one. It is viewed as a potential program format for working not only with the disadvantaged but also with the population as a whole. There are a number of ways in which outreach programs can be employed. For example, the "Meals on Wheels" program, primarily serving the elderly within a community, reaches individuals in their own homes. Another service of a similar nature is the congregate meal program for the elderly, which makes meals available to groups of persons in close proximity to their homes. In both cases, contact with the outreach worker (or with peers, in the latter case) may be of equal or greater significance than the meals themselves, at least in a psychological sense. Health and medical services can be delivered to the community through such outreach programs as visiting nurse services and neighborhood clinics.

The outreach concept has been used extensively throughout North America by organizations that are a part of the voluntary sector. Many traditional youth agencies make their programs easily accessible to their customers in locations such as schools, churches, housing developments, and community meeting places. Girl Scout programs during the lunch hour in a school, a Boy Scout meeting in the evening at a church, a Boys-Girls Club basketball league at a housing complex, and a Big Brother/Big Sister program meeting at a community center are examples of the outreach delivery system concept.

Public leisure service organizations have implemented the outreach concept through the use of mobile recreation units. Outreach programming through the use of mobile recreation units has enabled many organizations to extend their services significantly. Discussing the relationship between mobile units and the concept of mobility and outreach, Frieswyk (1966: 14) has written:

> (Urban conditions) require that programs and services be mobilized. Neighborhoods lacking basic play spaces, lacking institutional stability and cohesiveness, and lacking economic, educational, and other essential means and know-how are confronted with emergency situations which can only be met by the extension of mobile programs and services.

Mobile recreation units can be grouped into the following categories:

Bandwagons—built-in units for musical performances or talent shows.

Portable Shells—acoustical facilities for varied presentations.

Show Wagons—built-in facilities for dramatic performances.

Portable Stages—facilities for dance or drama.

Puppet Theaters—for either puppet or marionette shows.

Craftmobiles—for participation in art or craft activities.

Artmobiles—for display of art and craft objects.

Bookmobiles—traveling libraries.

Filmobiles—for presentation of motion pictures and slides.

Information and Counseling Mobiles—for dissemination of information on recreation and programs and services.

Playmobiles—transporting playground, game, and other equipment to playgrounds.

Sportsmobiles—transporting gymnastics and sports equipment and supplies to areas used by older teenagers and adults.

Hobbymobiles—transporting equipment and supplies for any hobby.

Mobile Swimming Pools

Living roomobiles—outdoor social centers, primarily for the elderly.

Mobile Roller Rinks

Mobile Ice-Skating Rinks

Circusmobiles—exhibiting circus acts and trained animals.

Naturemobiles—for exhibit and conduct of nature-related activities.

Zoomobiles—for exhibit and conduct of activities related to animals.

Sciencemobiles—for exhibit and conduct of science-related activities.

Aerospacemobiles—for exhibit and conduct of activities related to aerospace.

Starmobiles—for exhibit and conduct of activities related to astronomy (Frieswyk 1966:8–16).

An integration of program areas and program formats is presented in Table 9.4. Essentially, this demonstrates the application of the various program formats within the major program areas. It is a graphic illustration of the broad scope of program possibilities that can be implemented to suit the varying needs of customers.

TABLE 9.4 Program Matrix

Program Areas	Class	Competitive	Club	Drop-In
Visual Arts	Drawing Class	Pottery Contest	Miniatures Whittling Club	Visit to Art Museum
New Arts	Photography Class	Film Festival	Radio Club	Photography Lab
Performing Arts (Dance)	Tap Dance Class	Dance Marathon for Charity	Square Dance Club	Boom-Box Music for Dancing
Performing Arts (Drama)	Puppet Class	Debate Contest	Dinner Theater Group—Once a Month	Costume Design Shop
Performing Arts (Music)	Guitar Lessons	Battle of the Bands	Older Adults Kazoo Band	Classical Music Listening
Literary	Spanish Lessons	Topical Debate	Current Book Club	Library Reading Room
Sports, Games, and Athletics	Beginning Golf Class	Softball Tourney	Soccer Club	Tennis Court
Outdoor Recreation	Orienteering Class	Cross Country Obstacle Ski Club	Sierra Club	Picnics
Hobbies	How to Get Started on a Hobby	Matchbook Collectors Contest	Electric Train Owners Club	Hobby Shop Slot Car Racing
Travel	Reading Topography Maps	Sports Car Rally	Antique Car Club	Sightseeing
Social Recreation	Quilting Tips for Beginners	Pie-Eating Contest	Saturday Group	Conversation
Voluntary Service	Orientation to Working with Children	Taking a Sports Team to Play at Corrections Institution	Candy Stripers	Tutoring for Students
Wellness	Aerobics	Fun Run	Weight Loss	Open Gym
Aquatics	Water Aerobics	Swim Team	Masters Swim Club	Open Public Swim

Summary

In this chapter the topic of program formats has been reviewed. A program format can be thought of as the way in which an activity is structured or organized. The manipulation of program formats provides the leisure service program with another variable to control in the process of pro-gram planning and development. It is important to recognize that different program formats produce different benefits for individuals within a given leisure experience. The formats that a leisure service programmer chooses may have a direct impact on the success or failure of the

TABLE 9.4—*Continued*

Special Event	Outreach	Workshop/Conference	Interest Group
Art in the Park	Craft Sale at Residence for Elderly	Conference Teachers of China Painting	Arts Focus Group
Computer Art Display	Photography on Display in Mall	Conference on Television as Art Form	Photography Group
Black Dance Troupe Concert	Teen Dance at a Shopping Parking Lot	Workshop on Ethnic Dancing	Jazz Dance Group
Community Theater Production	Shakespeare in the Park	Creative Dramatics for Children	Mime Troupe
Barbershop Concert	Christmas Caroling	Master's Workshop	Choral Group
Rare Book Exhibit	Bookmobile	Workshop on the Works of Shakespeare	Library Advocates
5K Run	Rollerskate Mobile	Workshop for Youth Sports Coaches	Sports Boosters
Winter Carnival	Day Camp	Family Conference on Boat Safety	Gardening Club
Hobbyists Trade Show and Sale	Mobile Display of Stamps and Coins	How to Know the Value of Book Workshop	Hobby Interest Group
Driving Along the Autumn Trail	Travelogs	How to See Europe by Train Workshop	Senior Travel Program
Progressive Dinner	Friendly Visitors	Bridge Club Workshop	Partners Program
Recognition Dinner for Volunteers	Reading to Visually Impaired in Their Homes	Role of Volunteers in the Community Conference	Volunteers in Action
Health Promotion Fair	Health Exams/Check-up	Conference on Smoking Cessation	Walking Group
Swim Meet	Aquatics Mobile	Safety in Pool Clinic	Polar Bear Group

event. Therefore, close attention to choosing the appropriate structure for an activity must be given in order to ensure that customer satisfaction is achieved.

The idea of program formats has been identified and discussed in the recreation literature. Most authors support the view that a program format is the structure or form that the activity takes. The literature does not suggest consistency in identifying different types of program formats. However, many common structures used in organizing leisure services are identified by the authors surveyed. In this book, the program formats discussed have included competitive, drop-in or open format, class, club, special event, workshop/conference, interest group, and outreach formats. The format that a program takes is directly related to customer satisfaction.

Knowledge of program formats is essential in the work of the leisure services programmer. One of the common program formats found in leisure service organizations is that of competition. The competitive program format finds individuals pitted against themselves or others in a situation in which performance is measured. The drop-in or open facility format is one in which little or no structure or face-to-face leadership is provided. When a program is organized to emphasize educational or instructional objectives, it is usually called a class. The club program format is usually one in which leadership comes from within a group focused around a particular program area. Special events are usually high-energy programs of a short term duration. Workshops, conferences, and seminars provide an opportunity for an exchange of information in a short time and with intensity. Special interest groups are similar to clubs, and yet are unique in that they focus on issues and concerns rather than a program area like a hobby. Finally, the outreach program format is one in which the professional takes the services to the customers in their homes or neighborhoods.

Discussion Questions and Exercises

1. What is program format? Why are program formats important to the leisure services programmer?

2. What is the relationship between customer satisfaction and the format chosen for a program?

3. Describe and present examples of the competitive program format.

4. What responsibilities does the leisure service programmer have in planning and implementing an open facility or drop-in type format? What concerns for customer safety need to be taken into consideration when using this type of format?

5. Using the lesson plans described in the chapter, develop both a short- and long-term outline for conducting an instructional class in two different program areas.

6. Locate and analyze the bylaws from a recreation club sponsored by a leisure service organization.

7. Describe the characteristics of the special event program format.

8. What is the difference between the workshop/conference format and the class format? Develop a working outline for a workshop or conference dealing with managing one's leisure lifestyle.

9. How can special interest groups be distinguished from clubs? What are the similarities and differences?

10. How might emerging technology have an impact on program formats? How can new technological developments put program formats into effect?

References

Bannon, J. J. 1973. *Outreach: Extending community services in urban areas.* Springfield, IL: Charles C. Thomas.

Beard, J. G. and M. G. Ragheb. 1980. Measuring leisure satisfaction. *Journal of Leisure Research* 12, (4):20–30.

Bickhard, R. 1956. *How to plan and conduct workshops and conferences.* New York: Association Press.

Donnelly, R. J., W. G. Helms, and E. D. Mitchell. 1958. *Active games and contests.* New York: Ronald Press.

Edginton, C. R. and P. M. Ford. 1985. *Leadership in recreation and leisure service organizations.* New York: Wiley.

Farrell, P. and H. M. Lundegren. 1983. *Recreation programming.* 2nd ed. New York: Wiley.

Frieswyk, S. H. 1966. *Mobile and portable recreation facilities in parks and recreation.* Washington, DC: National Recreation and Park Association.

Hupp, S. L. 1985. *Satisfaction of older women in leisure programs: An investigation of contributing factors.* Unpublished doctoral dissertation, University of Oregon, August.

Kraus, R. G. 1985. *Recreation program planning today.* Glenview, IL: Scott, Foresman and Co.

Kraus, R. G. and B. J. Bates. 1975. *Recreation leadership and supervision: Guidelines for professional development.* Philadelphia: W. B. Saunders Co.

Milligan, L. R. and H. V. Milligan. 1942. *The club member's handbook.* New York: The New Home Library.

The Recreation Program Book. 1963. Chicago, IL: The Athletic Institute.

Rossman, J. R. 1984. The influence of program format choice on participant satisfaction. *Journal of Park and Recreation Administration* 2(1):39–51.

Russell, R. V. 1982. *Planning programs in recreation.* St. Louis: Mosby.

Shivers, J. S. and C. R. Calder. 1974. *Recreational crafts: Programming and instructional techniques.* New York: McGraw-Hill Book Co.

10 | Program Promotion

Learning Objectives

1. To make the reader aware of *the program promotion process* and its relationship to effective program planning.
2. To help the reader become aware of *the communication process and its relationship to program promotion.*
3. To provide the reader with knowledge of *five key channels for promoting programs and services.*
4. To provide the reader with an understanding of *the tools available for promoting programs and services.*
5. To provide *examples of program promotion tools* used by various leisure service organizations.

Introduction

Program promotion is a key element in effective program planning. "Promotion is communication that tells potential users about an agency's services and attempts to persuade them as to the benefits they provide, benefits that should satisfy customer wants and desires" (Rubright and MacDonald 1981: 159). If the customer is not made aware of what the organization is offering, and where and when it is being offered, there is very little chance that the program will succeed. Therefore, the effective employment of various promotional channels and tools is essential in order to support the efforts of the leisure service organization. Although program promotion involves a great deal of effort, it is also a very rewarding type of activity for the professional in that it involves creativity and resourcefulness and results in tangible evidence of success (e.g., media coverage). In this chapter, the importance of communication in the promotional process is explored, and both promotional channels and tools are identified and defined.

Communication Process

The successful promotion of a program basically hinges on the professional's ability to communicate effectively with people. *Communication can be thought of as an exchange between two entities (such as two individuals, or an individual and an organization) that carries meaning.* The exchange process is the vital link that enables an individual to express his or her needs to the organization and allows the organization to identify its program services. This communicative exchange can take place through verbal expression or visual stimuli. Communication can take place through the written word (brochures, news releases, annual reports, etc.), or can be non-written (slides, audiotapes, personal appearances, etc.).

The process of exchange that exists between the leisure service organization and the customer must be a two-way process. Effective communication means that the organization communicates *with* the prospective customer rather than *to* the prospective customer. That is to say, the communication process is not complete until the prospective customer acts upon the message that he or she has received. The customer digests and evaluates the information being sent and either accepts or rejects it, based on his or her own values, norms, interests, and needs.

The processing of information for promotional purposes can be conceptualized by viewing the model presented in Figure 10.1. This process has four elements: the communicator, the message, the channel of information distribution, and

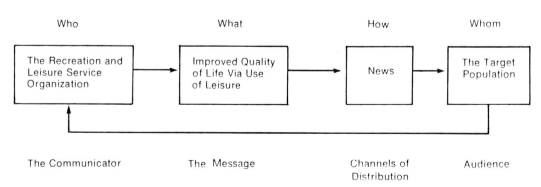

Figure 10.1 A Model for Processing Information.

the audience. The *communicator* is the leisure service organization—its professional staff and other associated members (such as persons in policy-making positions). In addition, program customers (current and prospective) can also serve as communicators. In general terms, the message to be communicatd by a leisure service organization is one of improving one's quality of life through the wise use of leisure. Specifically, the *message* communicated will depend on the particular activity and the values to be derived from involvement. For example, the message used to promote a jogging class will center on the value of physical fitness, isolation, physical and mental challenge, relaxation, and so on. *Channels* used to distribute information include advertising, publicity, sales promotion, personal selling, and public relations. These will be defined shortly. Finally, this model suggests that the communicator direct his or her message through various channels to a selected *audience,* or target population. In other words, the communicator asks the question,"Toward whom is the information being directed—an age grouping, a geographic area, a lifestyle clustering or interest group, or males or females?''

Through the communication process, information is targeted toward the prospective customer in an attempt to stimulate involvement in a particular program service. As the individual becomes aware of the information communicated to him or her, he or she may relate to it in terms of his or her own needs and view it as a way of fulfilling those needs. It is important to remember that the promotional process often is one that not only informs individuals but also persuades them. Frequently, the persuasion aspect is viewed negatively, with the assumption that promotional efforts are only for the benefit of the provider of the service. In some instances—few, we hope—this may be the case. It is probably more apparent in the area of commercial recreation enterprises, where profit may have a higher priority than the welfare of the customers. However, most leisure service organizations have a humanistic philosophy; as a result, they are interested primarily in the provision of services that are beneficial both to the customers and the organization. In this sense, the promotional effort is not directed toward the exploitation of individuals but toward the provision of services that are in the best interest of the consumer.

Channels for Promoting Programs and Services

As previously indicated, there are five channels that can be used in promotion of programs and services: *advertising, publicity, sales promotion, personal selling,* and *public relations.* These channels have some common characteristics—especially in terms of the media employed—and should be utilized simultaneously; however, they each serve distinctly different ends. In order to successfully promote a program, the professional should carefully design a strategy that incorporates each of the channels just mentioned in an effective manner. Promotional efforts should be well planned; the productive professional should avoid an ad hoc approach.

Advertising

What are the distinctive factors that characterize advertising? Nylen (1975: 4) has suggested that most definitions include three basic factors. He writes:

1. Advertising is a paid message, as contrasted, for example, with publicity, which is not.
2. Advertising appears in the mass media. (Mass media or public advertising carriers such as television, magazines, and newspapers.) By contrast, selling by a salesman is a public message that does not appear in a public medium.
3. Advertising has as its purpose informing or persuading people about a particular product, service, belief, or action. For marketers, the dominant use of advertising is to sell products and services.

Based on these factors, it might be concluded that *advertising is a paid message, delivered via the mass media, and aimed at persuading and influencing individuals to become involved in the consumption of a service* or to adopt a belief or idea. Basically, advertising is accomplished through the use of newspapers, television, radio, magazines, and other tools, such as billboards, placards on public transportation, grocery bags, and restaurant place mats.

Advertising is an important aspect of a leisure organization's promotional efforts in that it enables the organization to reach large numbers of people rapidly with its message. This channel of promotion has been used primarily by commercial enterprises as a mechanism to persuade individuals to join in various pursuits, and the principles and methods involved can be applied successfully to the public and nonprofit sectors. Advertising can be beneficial in a number of ways. It increases the customer's awareness of programs and services available. The individual also is able to make comparisons among the services offered—based on quality, cost, and location.

There are basically two types of advertising—direct action and indirect action. *Direct action advertising encourages the individual to act immediately on the information presented.* For example, direct action advertising might inform the prospective customer of the need to sign up immediately for swimming lessons at the local pool, or for day camp at the YWCA. *Indirect action advertising tries to create long-term interest in a service.* In other words, an indirect advertisement merely cites the availability of certain services or programs available from an organization. Special advertising for Park and Recreation Month in July, or Boy Scout Week in March are examples of this.

Publicity

"Publicity [may be] the most enduring promotional channel, the least expensive and perhaps easiest to use" (Rubright and MacDonald 1981: 169). It consists of *media coverage of the events, activities, and services of a leisure service organization.*

"Publicity embraces news releases and features, speakers' messages, and press conferences. Agencies find countless outlets for news releases in daily and weekly newspapers, in regional tabloids, in an ever-growing number of radio stations and in some television markets" (1981: 169). The organization that uses publicity effectively conveys information to various media sources in such a way that it is presented in a favorable light to the public. Newspaper coverage of a public meeting in which policy issues are discussed, a feature story highlighting the efforts of an individual within the organization, a picture of the winning junior softball team—these are all examples of productive and positive publicity. On the other hand, an exposé on ineffective management practices or an editorial condemning an organization and its efforts could wound an organization severely.

How does one develop a favorable publicity posture? There are many tools that can be employed—news releases, photographs, press conferences—to provide the various media sources with positive information. Basically, the professional must sell the media on the newsworthiness of the various events and activities of his or her organization. In order to accomplish this, the professional should actively cultivate sources or contacts within the various media. Obviously publicity is not paid for, so the organization is placed in a competitive position for space in the newspaper and for radio time and TV time. An organization should compete by exemplifying excellence and by extending itself courteously to the media.

Does the organization or professional create news? The answer to this question is definitely "yes." However, creating news does not imply the staging of news. News is created by providing programs, by informing the media of the programs, and by conveying to the media the human interest features of these programs.

Another primary kind of publicity that is generated by a leisure service organization is the brochures, fliers, reports, and newsletters that are distributed at various times and for various purposes to customers and potential program users.

Though there is cost involved in producing these publicity items, it is generally less expensive than the information delivered through advertising.

Sales Promotion

At times, an organization will want to stimulate consumer interest in a service beyond advertising and publicity. In order to generate this kind of interest, organizations will often organize special promotional activities. These types of activities are referred to as sales promotions. *Items for sales promotions are designed to promote and persuade potential and existing customers rather than to merely educate them.* Most sales promotion pieces ask for an immediate or decisive response or action from the customer. Sales promotion items may include special mailings, attractive application or survey forms, or special invitational materials that may be left in shopping malls, posted in public buildings, or distributed at churches, medical facilities, grocery stores, and other public places. The information distributed may invite immediate participation, allow opportunity to visit specific facilities or describe how to take advantage of the organization's services. Other sales promotion items may include pencils, notepads, buttons, T-shirts, frisbees, caps, and similar articles that present frequent and attractive reminders about the organization.

Other important tools that can be employed in a sales promotion campaign include sampling, use of coupons, contests, and demonstrations. Edginton and Williams (1978: 272–273), in defining each of these concepts and discussing their application to recreation and leisure service organizations, have written:

> *Sampling* is an attempt to presell the consumer. For example, an organization attempting to promote arts and crafts lessons for children might want to allow the children to participate in one class free of charge. This provides the child with the opportunity to sample the experience, with the idea that he will be influenced to participate in an entire series of lessons.
>
> The *coupon* concept has been greatly utilized in the promotion of products, but has yet to reach its full impact in the area of social services. The one area in which coupons have been effectively used in the delivery of leisure services is senior citizen participation. Many organizations provide reduced rates for senior citizens (often during a given time of day or day of the week) providing they have a special card or coupon. This senior citizens example is actually profitable to the organization in two ways. Not only does the organization attract a group of consumers who are ordinarily unavailable to it, but it also enhances the public image.
>
> *Contests* have also been used to stimulate consumer interest in a service. Participation in a contest may result in cash prizes, food, and so on for the winner or winners. An example of the constructive use of a contest in the delivery of leisure services is the traditional Easter egg hunt (oftentimes augmented with special prizes for locating certain items). Sometimes a competitive program form is used in the provision of the service. A flower-arranging contest will motivate people to participate in the activity. Using the contest is also a promotional method directed toward creating enthusiasm and interest in the activity.
>
> *Demonstrating* a service to the target market is still another method used in sales promotion. To create interest for a class in judo instruction, a demonstration might be arranged to take place at an intermission during a sporting activity, at a shopping mall, or at a school assembly. Essentially, this method allows the consumer to see the skills, attitudes, and other benefits that can be derived from participation in the activity.

Sales promotion activities, if successfully arranged, enable an organization to generate a great deal of interest and enthusiasm for their service. These types of activities represent short-term promotional efforts and should be used sparingly rather than on a continuous basis, or they will lose their edge.

Personal Selling

One of the most effective channels of promoting programs is that of personal selling. Usually, personal selling involves *making direct face-to-face contact with an individual or group.* One should not underestimate the potential of the direct personal contact. It is perhaps the most pervasive, effective form of promoting a program's service.

In leisure service organizations, personal selling is not directly identified as such. It most commonly occurs within the context of public speaking to various community groups. It also occurs when prospective customers make direct contact with organizational staff members for information or clarification. What makes a successful "salesperson" for the organization? Basically, an effective salesperson must be personable and able to relate to people. He or she must be aware of customer needs and how to communicate effectively the ways in which the services of the organization can meet those needs. This implies that a good salesperson understands not only people but also how the organization's service line can be employed to meet individual needs. The successful salesperson tailors his or her presentation to the audience, environment, and other relevant factors. "Personal selling is often one of the more pleasurable and self-rewarding channels of promotional communication. It permits organization personnel to experience the impact that the agency is making on its customers" (Rubright and MacDonald 1981: 170).

Public Relations

Public relations should be viewed as an important organizational tool. While in some circles public relations may not be considered as a channel of promotion, we include it here as a crucial aspect in the development of positive public attitudes toward the leisure service organization. Touching every part of an organization's operations, it deals with items such as the caliber of services, the manner in which the public is dealt with on the phone, the manner in which leaders interact with customers, and so on. Because public relations is involved in so many organizational areas, it should not be left to chance.

As a management process, *public relations efforts are directed toward engendering goodwill toward the organization and establishing an understanding*

of its operations. Public relations efforts seek to develop a positive rapport with the public served by establishing management policies and practices conducive to the public interest and well-being. Such policies might deal with the following topics, specifically delineating guidelines for staff and employee behavior:

1. Interactions with the public
2. Standards for dress and grooming
3. Standards for building and grounds maintenance
4. Rules regarding press release clearance
5. Clearance for special projects

The good name of an organization is its greatest asset. An organization should try to cultivate good community relations in order to attract customers. A negative public image will, obviously, seriously affect the ability of an organization to serve a community effectively.

Tools for Promoting Programs and Services

There are many tools that can be employed by the leisure service organization to promote its programs and services. In the remainder of this chapter, a number of such tools are detailed—including use of the newspaper, brochures, logo/emblem, awards and citations, annual reports, information and press kits, exhibits, displays and demonstrations, novelty items, public speaking, fliers, newsletters, stationary advertising, radio and television, use of the telephone, and videotape and slide presentations.

To be successful and productive, promotional tools should have several characteristics. Rubright and MacDonald (1981: 160–162) have listed the following: Tools are written or prepared for specific targets and communication channels, reflect or suggest program and service benefits, may indicate organizational missions and goals, have an acceptable tone, style, and character, are concisely written and edited, persuade or inform, elicit some action or participation by the customer, and have a distribution plan. "Tools must direct the customer from unawareness in order to convince an individual to try the service, repeat its use, and recommend it to others."

Further, in the development process for promotional tools, Rubright and MacDonald (1981: 162) list several factors that must be considered and decided upon in order to determine the most appropriate tools for disseminating information. The process must include determination of the specific purpose of the tool, what promotional objectives are to be reflected by the tool, the target group to be reached by the tool, methods of distribution, designation of the individual to prepare the tool, designation of how production will be accomplished, and decisions regarding how the tool will be evaluated.

Newspapers

One of the most important tools for the delivery of information is the newspaper. The majority of leisure service organizations are based at the local and neighborhood levels and, as such, they depend greatly on distribution of information via one or more newspapers. Basically, there are five classes of newspapers: national, daily, weekly, shopping guides, and special audience newspapers. The local daily community newspaper is most frequently used by leisure service organizations in the promotion of their services.

1. *National Newspapers*—National newspapers such as *USA Today, Christian Science Monitor, The National Observer, The Wall Street Journal,* and *The Sporting News* are papers that are aimed at a broad cross section of individuals and do not focus on a particular geographic area. This type of newspaper can be used to draw national attention to an organization's unique programs and services. If the thrust of a leisure service organization is national in nature—such as the national offices of local youth agencies—use of this type of media presentation can be particularly effective.

2. *Daily Newspapers*—The daily newspaper usually originates in a specific locale; thus, its primary news thrust is on the locality or geographic area it serves. It is not unusual for a daily newspaper to assign one of its reporters to cover the activities of a local leisure service organization. The impact and potential of working with a local daily newspaper cannot be overstated.

3. *Weekly Newspaper*—The fastest growing type of newspaper is the weekly. Weekly newspapers are often found in suburban areas surrounding a large city. Often the weekly newspaper is simply the Sunday edition of the major city newspaper or newspapers, subscribed to by residents in a wide geographic area around the city. In working with a weekly newspaper, the professional must be much more careful and precise in his or her planning. One must be careful to release information appropriately time-wise. This is a bit more tricky when a newspaper comes out just once a week; one does not want to release information too soon so that it loses its impact, or too late so that individuals are prohibited from planning ahead to any degree.

4. *Shopper's Guide*—Shopper's Guides are usually distributed on a weekly or monthly basis, with the main focus being that of sales of items and services. These papers usually contain little editorial or news commentary. The professional should, however, pursue the shopper's guides that are distributed in his or her area to determine their formats and whether or not they might be conducive to dissemination of information regarding recreation and leisure services.

5. *Special Interest Newspapers*—Newspapers are not necessarily organized only on a geographic basis. Often, especially nationally, newspapers are specialized around a particular interest population. For example, if one were to organize a special event such as a coin or stamp hobby show, one could potentially utilize regional and national newspapers that cater to individuals with these types of interests. There are many publications for individuals interested in such activities as table tennis, swimming, or track and field.

It is important that the professional build a good working relationship with the newspapers. Whether one is seeking coverage of news-making items, seeking to disseminate public service information, or purchasing advertising, it is important to be aware of the methods and procedures that are necessary to facilitate the specific coverage desired. This involves knowing who to contact and how to deliver information in the most appropriate manner to the newspaper. Newspaper personnel should be viewed as allies. If they perceive the professional to be an honest, efficient, and competent manager, they will in turn be likely to act in a similar manner. The professional should be cognizant of the newspaper's deadlines, limitations, and interests. One of the things that irritates any newspaper is misinformation. The professional should double-check all information emanating from his or her department to ensure that it is accurate as well as concise, brief, and to the point.

Often, newspaper personnel are taken for granted and do not receive support, positive feedback, or other evidence of recognition for their efforts. The leisure service professional should be appreciative of the support he or she receives from newspaper reporters. Members of the press should always be viewed as invited guests. They should never be asked to purchase tickets or pay admission. Complimentary tickets to activities are a standard rule of thumb in dealing with the press. It is also beneficial to send a note, expressing your support and appreciation, from time to time. The occasional thank-you note should be a part of organizational etiquette.

The news release   Releasing information to the newspaper is often done via a formal news release format. A newspaper does not have the resources to write all of the organization's stories, and, in some cases, it would not be to the organization's advantage. Thus, it becomes incumbent upon leisure service professionals to prepare news releases. A news release can be thought of as the assembling of facts and information into a coherent written statement.

How do you write a news release? Very carefully! It must be written in a very concise, factual, and direct manner. When preparing news release copy, one asks the questions "Who, What, When, Where, Why, and How?" The standard for preparing a news release is to use the inverted pyramid format, as illustrated in Figure 10.2. The first paragraph is the *lead paragraph* and should answer the most important of the "W" questions. The lead paragraph is one sentence in length. The second paragraph may be called the "bridge" paragraph and is a transition to the detailed information in the news story. The next few short paragraphs should provide the reader with additional factual information, in descending order of importance. If it is necessary for the news release to be edited, it is usually the practice for the news professional to edit from the bottom up, so the order of information in the news items is important.

It is important to keep in mind some writing tips when preparing news releases. Ryan (1988) indicates that news releases should be written with short sentences, short paragraphs, and short words. Be very concise and factual when including times, places, phone numbers, people's

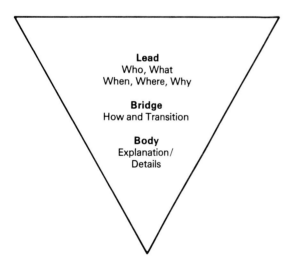

Figure 10.2   From: Ryan, Katrine Fitzgerald. (Summer 1988.) Getting the word out to the media through news releases and news advisories. *Voluntary Action Leadership.*

names and other program information. A news release should be written as an objective report and is not the place for subjective, descriptive adjectives, such as "wonderful," "very good," or "enjoyable."

Whenever possible, one should create an official form on which the press release will be written. Why should this be done? Newspapers receive literally hundreds of news items per day. When your news is received at the newspaper's office it should be distinctive, recognizable, and easily distinguished as a press release.

Type the news release on the agency news release form. Leave a margin on all sides of the typed copy. Type all releases double-spaced and on one side of the paper only. If you need to go to a second page, type the word "more" at the bottom of the first page. Try not to split a paragraph at the bottom of a page—end the page with the end of a paragraph and start the next page with a new paragraph. Be sure that your organization's name is at the top of the page. At the end of the release, type "-30-" or "###." These symbols mean "the end" to a news editor. You may wish to put a title on your news release so that the news editor can quickly know the subject matter of the release. Do not spend undue time writing the title; the news editor will write a headline for your story according to space, type style, layout, and production. Your news release form should include the name of your organization, a phone number, and the name of a contact person. Make it as easy as possible for the newspaper to contact you. This will contribute to ensuring that your news will be used and that it will be published as accurately as you want it to be.

Figures 10.3 and 10.4 are examples of press release forms used by the Indianola, Iowa, Parks and Recreation and the Juneau, Alaska, Parks and Recreation Department. Figures 10.5, 10.6, 10.7 and 10.8 are examples of short news releases that have been published in a local newspaper. Each of these provides information about upcoming events, programs or services offered by various leisure service organizations.

News features News features deal with information concerning a person, an activity, or an idea. News feature stories are not generally written and submitted by the leisure service organization itself, but because newspaper organizations are looking for human interest stories, the leisure service organization can suggest ideas for feature stories. It is not unusual for leisure service organizations to be involved in interesting and meritorious activities or events. Newspapers also are interested in issues and may want to run a feature on an issue that concerns the recreation and leisure service organization. Often the leisure service organization will have several special events during the year, and frequently these can serve as the subject for a feature story. A news feature article does not usually have to appear on a specific date; thus, it is more flexible, in regards to time constraints, than the press release.

How do special news features come to be written? A news story of interest or significance to the community will be picked up by one of the reporters on the staff of the local newspaper. Large leisure service organizations often employ individuals whose responsibilities include public relations. These individuals are often involved in the organization of feature stories to be inserted in the newspapers. As indicated, it is not often that the public relations officer or leisure service professional will actually write a feature story; rather, they are usually employed in facilitating its development—gathering facts, organizing them, and choosing relevant photographs.

The news feature entitled "Marketplace Shoppers Relive History" is a feature that discusses a special event staged by Carole Edginton, Promotions Assistant for the 5th Street Public Market, Eugene, Oregon (see Figure 10.10). This event, "Celebrate the Century," was tied to Historic Preservation Week in Eugene, Oregon, and

Indianola
Parks and Recreation

301 W. 2nd Ave.   Box 299   Indianola, Iowa 50125

OFFICE
515/961-9420

Glen Cowan
Director of
Parks & Recreation

Marie Ware
Recreation Superintendent

Tim Van Essen
Park Superintendent

ATTENTION: _____   DATE: _____

PAPER SECTION: _____ News   _____ Sports

FROM: _____ Glen Cowan   _____ Marie Ware   _____ Tim Van Essen

PHOTO STATUS: _____ None with this News Release
                _____ Black & White 500 Film Exposure Attached
                _____ Photo taken by Newspaper Photographer

EVENT NAME: _____

EVENT DATE: _____

DO NOT PRINT NEWS RELEASE IF AFTER: _____

- FOR IMMEDIATE RELEASE -

"WE TAKE FUN SERIOUSLY"

Figure 10.3   News Release Form. (Indianola (Iowa) Parks and Recreation.)

Figure 10.4   News Release Form. (Parks and Recreation Department, Juneau, Alaska.)

Hearst Center seeks volunteers

CEDAR FALLS — The Hearst Center for the Arts is developing a volunteer corps.

Tour Associates are needed to assist with school tours at the Center. Volunteers will assist tour guides and help with related art activities during tours. Interested persons may attend a training session from 2 to 3:30 p.m. Monday at the Hearst Center for the Arts, 304 W. Seerley Blvd.

Figure 10.5 Free Publicity Used to Recruit Volunteers. (*Waterloo Courier,* Waterloo (Iowa), January 19, 1990.)

UNI baseball camp is set for Sunday

The University of Northern Iowa baseball camp is scheduled for Sunday starting at 8:30 a.m.

The camp for ages 7–12 is from 8:30 a.m. to noon while ages 13 through junior in high school is from 12:30 p.m. to 4 p.m.

Campers should report to the south deck of the UNI-Dome and bring a glove. Registration fee is $10.

All indoor facilities, including the batting cage, will be used. The camps will be divided by age and skill level and UNI players will serve as coaches.

Those wishing to pre-register may send their name and age along with the $10 fee to Baseball Office, Upper NW UNI-Dome, University of Northern Iowa, Cedar Falls.

For more information call UNI baseball coach Gene Baker at 273–6223 during the day or at 266–1327 at night.

Figure 10.6 A News Story Promoting an Upcoming Event. (*Waterloo Courier,* Waterloo (Iowa), January 16, 1990.)

Two Super Bowl workshops available

Get ready for the Super Bowl with two new workshops at the Waterloo Recreation and Arts Center.

Instructor Susan Lantz will demonstrate how to plan the ultimate Super Bowl party and make several tempting treats that will score points with guests at the Super Bowl Hors d'oeuvres Workshop Tuesday from 7–9 p.m. The workshop fee is $7.

Discover what the game of football is all about at Armchair Quarterback School with instructor Don Erusha. Explore the object of the game, rules, player positions and penalties. The workshop is on Tuesday and Wednesday from 7–9 p.m.. Fee is $9.

Registrations may be made at the Waterloo Recreation and Arts Center. For more information, contact the Center at 291–4491.

Figure 10.7 This Event Gets Free Publicity. (*Waterloo Courier,* January 14, 1990.)

Sunday, January 14, 1990 Waterloo Courier Page D3

Home Show, Taste Fest to be Feb. 8-11

It's time to mark your calendars and plan to attend the 39th Annual Eastern Iowa Home Improvement, Taste Fest and Garden Show.

The event will take place Feb. 8–11 at the Five Sullivan Brothers Convention Center, sponsored by the Waterloo Exchange Club.

Hours are 5 to 10 p.m. Feb. 8; 4 to 10 p.m. Feb. 9; 10 a.m. to 9 p.m. Feb. 10; and 11 a.m. to 5:30 p.m. Feb. 11.

Trends, ideas and products for the '90s will be spotlighted at this year's show. Exhibits will feature the American Society of Interior Designers showcase, home exterior and interior remodeling, contractors, furniture and home, lawn and garden upkeep and more.

Figure 10.8 News Story, Free Publicity. (*Waterloo Courier,* Waterloo, Iowa, January 14, 1990.)

featured gold panning for kids, antique quilts, antique cars, a historical display, and period music. Such news features can promote an interest in an organization and its activities. Figure 10.9 is the header in the front section of the newspaper for this event, calling the reader's attention to the inside news feature. Such headers further highlight and add emphasis to the credibility of an organization or agency.

Editorials and letters to the editor Editorials or letters to the editor often have no middle ground. Either the person writing the editorial or letter to the editor is very much in favor of or is very much opposed to certain aspects of the work of the leisure service organization. The primary source for letters to the editor is the community at large, while editorials are generated by the newspaper organization. Although it is not often practiced, a leisure service organization itself can initiate editorials or letters to the editor. Sometimes newspapers can be encouraged to support interesting activities or projects in the form of an editorial. The leisure service organization does not write its own editorial; rather, the local newspaper is encouraged to investigate a given subject. A leisure service organization may wish to have a local newspaper editorialize on the

need for constructive playground environments. The leisure service organization can accomplish this by gathering statistics and other relevant information, plus examples concerning the value to children of well-organized and well-supervised play areas, and presenting them to the editor of the local paper. Of course, ultimately, the editor will decide whether the subject reflects his or her interests and those of the paper and whether the subject is one that he or she wishes to elaborate on in an editorial.

Letters to the editor that concern the leisure service organization, written by other parties, can be either positive or negative. The letter to the editor found in Figure 10.11 is an example of a negative letter regarding park and recreation services, in this case ice skating. How should the professional respond to a negative letter to the editor? Although the professional might like to rationalize that individuals who write letters to the editor are cranks who should be ignored, that is not a productive way to deal with such opinions. Every effort should be made to investigate the accusations, determine their cause, and make contact with the individual or party concerned personally or in writing. Every effort should be made to correct any error or to satisfy the displeased individual.

SUMMARY

A.M.

HEADLINES

CITY/REGION

A display of old cars at Fifth Street Public Market kicks off National Preservation Week.

■ Panning for real gold is part of Historical Preservation week at Eugene's Fifth Street Public Market / **1C**

NORTHWEST

■ A group that bought the Columbia Gorge town of Bridal Veil plans to let the area return to nature / **1A**

■ Police along the Oregon Coast report an increase in thefts from vehicles as tourist season begins / **2C**

NATIONAL

■ Workers at a nuclear weapons plant claim the site's contractor forced them to work in unsafe conditions / **3A**

INTERNATIONAL

■ Syrian President Hafez Assad rejects a U.S.-backed compromise on a Mideast peace conference / **1A**

Figure 10.9   Front Page of the Newspaper Noting a Feature Story about a Local Special Event. (*Eugene Register Guard, Eugene* (Oregon) May 13, 1991.)

staff photo by Paul Carter

Seven-year-old Lindsey Wells of Eugene stands on tiptoe to glimpse the interior of a 1936 Plymouth convertible on display Sunday at Fifth Street Public Market.

Marketplace shoppers relive history

By CATHY PETERSON
The Register-Guard

Cars, quilts launch week of celebration

You could say Ed Ransom practices history.

He certainly looked the part Sunday in his flannel shirt, boots and felt hat as he demonstrated gold panning for onlookers at the Fifth Street Public Market.

Ransom was just one of several history and preservation enthusiasts who gathered at the market Sunday to "Celebrate the Century" — the theme of the day — and to kick off the beginning of National Preservation Week in Eugene.

Hunched over a Frisbee-sized plastic pan filled with water and sand, Ransom pointed to almost invisible flecks of gold, transferring each speck with his finger to a tiny vial filled with water.

"If you have the time to pick the gold out of the sand," he said to a passing couple, "I'll help you."

Ransom, a mechanic for Lane County, said he spends his weekends and holidays mining a claim on Sharps Creek in Cottage Grove as a hobby.

"Panning's part of our heritage," he said. "We should keep it alive."

As a barbershop quartet and fiddler kept tune, about 500 people were drawn to the market Sunday by displays of old cars, antique quilts, historical photographs and maps, celebration organizers said.

Vicki Carlile, a market employee who helped exhibit the quilts, said the collection included a quilt from 1856.

Another antique quilt called "Baskets," had one imperfect quilt square stitched intentionally into the pat-

Turn to HISTORY, Page 3C

Figure 10.10 Sample of a Local Special Event. (*Eugene Register Guard, Eugene* (Oregon), May 13, 1991.)

LETTERS TO THE EDITOR

Skater unhappy

CEDAR FALLS — For the past 20-plus years I have had the wonderful opportunity to figure skate during the winter months at our fine McElroy facility during public skating time.

The figure skaters would skate in the middle of the rink and do their jumps and spins, and the hockey and speed skaters would skate on the outside of the rink and do their thing. This seemed to meet everyone's satisfaction.

Now I am being told that there is no designated area for figure skaters and that I can no longer figure skate during public skating time because I may be endangering the safety of other skaters.

Why, after almost a quarter of a century, have those in charge of public skating decided to discriminate against figure skaters? I find this so hard to understand.

In all the years that I have figure skated at McElroy, I never caused an accident or have I ever seen an accident that was directly attributed to a figure skater.

I also feel this is an infringement of my right of freedom of expression, which is the core of figure skating.

I am asking those in charge of public skating to reconsider their current policy against figure skaters and come up with a solution that is acceptable for everyone.

JIM ZIMMER
3133 Tucson Drive

WRITE US!

The Courier welcomes letters on topics of general interest. Letters must include the writer's signature, address and phone number. Concise and legible letters are printed with the least delay. Letters should not exceed 300 words. All letters are subject to editing. Letters not meeting Courier policies will be returned with an explanation. Address: Letters to the Editor, Courier, P.O. Box 540, Waterloo, Iowa

Figure 10.11   Sample of Letter to the Editor, Which Results in Negative Publicity. (*Waterloo Courier,* Waterloo (Iowa), January 18, 1990.)

The letter-to-the-editor format can also be used by the leisure service professional to publicly thank individuals who have assisted his or her organization in terms of time or money. The work of leisure service organizations often goes unrecognized, and this is a relatively easy way to publicly express appreciation.

Sports and athletic news information   Information concerning sporting and athletic events is often handled in a slightly different manner than other news information. Sports editors frequently like to have a complete informational package concerning the organization's sporting event(s)—whether a league, meet, or contest—prior to the actual implementation of the activity. This often includes the presentation of complete team rosters or a list of contestants prior to competition. In addition, it is not unusual for a sports editor to request individual and team pictures prior to an activity. With this information in hand, the sports reporters of a given

Eugene Parks & Recreation
Fall Leagues
3x3
MEN

A RESULTS — Community Markets d Pushing "30" 30-11, 31-15. Kappa Sig d Sultan's Of Swish 30-13, 30-20. **A STANDINGS** — Community Markets 4-0, Fishers Farmers Insurance 2-1, Kappa Sig 2-2, Pushing "30" 1-3, Sultan's Of Swish 0-3.

B RESULTS — Over The Hill Gang 30-23, 32-17. Brokers d Lead Feet, forfeit. Bill, Andy, Jim & Steff 30-27, 30-28. Jones & Roth d Hackers 31-28, 30-24. **B STANDINGS** — Jones & Roth 3-0, Hackers 2-1, Brokers 2-1, Over The Hill Gang 2-1, Bill, Andy, Jim & Steff 2-1, Lead Feet 1-2, Ideal Steelers 0-3, Second Wind 0-3.

Eugene Parks and Recreation
Fall Leagues
FINAL STANDINGS
COED

B STANDINGS — Vise Squad 5-0, Summertime Brews 3-2, Selectemp Sluggers 3-2, Pecadilloes 2-3, Foul Play 2-3, Mr. Morton 0-5.

C-1 STANDINGS — Late For Dinner 5-0, Mary Kay Cosmetics 4-1, Tino's 3-2, G.W. Finishing 2-3, Bellair 1-4, Play It Again Sports 0-5.

C-2 STANDINGS — Charlie's Raiders 5-0, Sharp Shooters 3-2, Centaurs 3-2, Central Lutheran Demolanders 2-3, Commercial Air 2-3, Northwest Spirit 0-5.

D STANDINGS — Tecdus 4-1, Aco Wood Works 4-1, Guys & Dolls 3-2, The Mutants 2-3, Pounders 2-3, Helium Heads 0-5.

E STANDINGS — Relief Pitcher-Brew Crew 5-0, Great Harvesters 3-2, Good News Bears 3-2, New Way Electric 3-2, Ad-Art Design 1-4, Women's Care Associates 0-5.

F STANDINGS — Altair Slammers 4-1, Bohemia Axe-Kickers 3-2, Parcs Fools 3-2, Terminators 2-3, Artisan Automotive 2-3, OSL Players 1-4.

G STANDINGS — Gardners' Quicksilver 5-0, Aliens 3-2, Kerry's Mitt Wits 3-2, Liberty Savings 2-3, Sluggers 1-4, Knefights 1-4.

H STANDINGS — The Duck Heads 5-0, Beer Bellies 3-2, The Simpsons 3-2, Centennial Bank 2-2, Oregon Research Institute 1-4, Briles-Cascade Security 1-4.

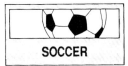

Lane Amateur Hockey Association
At Lane County Ice

LEAGUE RESULTS — Team Athletics 3, Shooter's Pub 2. Good Times 4, Cascade Medical 1. Angus Inn 7, Guido's-U of O 2. Good Times 7, Guido's-U of O 4. Angus Inn 7, Shooter's Pub 2. Team Athletic 3, Cascade Medical 2. **LEAGUE STANDINGS** — Angus Inn 2-0-0: 4 pts. Good Times 2-0-0: 4 pts. Team Athletic 2-0-0: 4 pts. Cascade Medical 0-2-0: 0 pts. Guido's-U of O 0-2-0: 0 pts. Shooter's Pub 0-2-0: 0 pts.

Lane Amateur Broomball Association
At Lane County Ice

LEAGUE RESULTS — Team Genetics 3, Sacred Heart 1. Whittier Mutant Warriors 3, Whittier Ravens 1. Russ Fetrow Engineering, Inc. 4, Weyerhauser Paper 0. **LEAGUE STANDINGS** — Russ Fetrow Engineering 1-0, Whittier Mutant Warriors 1-0, Team Genetics 1-0, Sacred Heart 0-1, Whittier Ravens 0-1, Weyerhauser Paper 0-1.

Emerald Valley BMX
At Eugene
AGE-GROUP RESULTS
Oct. 18

7-EXPERT — 1, Sean Zorn. 2, Leon Medart. 3, Keith Bowers. **11-INTERMEDIATE** — 1, Katie Burke. 2, Jacob Pipkin. 3, Shanna Adams. **11-EXPERT** — 1, Kaleb Watson. 2, Brett McAllister. 3, Joe Parrott. **12-EXPERT** — 1, Jeremy Cutright. 2, Jon Barron. 3, Marc Reed. **15-INTERMEDIATE** — 1, J.J. Lemasters. 2, Davis Crump. 3, Brady Morris. **16-EXPERT** — 1, Cris Marsh. 2, Jason Tanner. 3, Kari Saner. 12 **AND UNDER-CRUISER** — 1, Cris Marsh. 2, Marc Reed. 3, Katie Burke.

Oct. 20

5 AND UNDER-NOVICE — 1, Tyler Lyons. 2, Jason Wood. 3, Mark Medart. **6-EXPERT** — 1, Vance Tarusan. 2, David Oakes. 3, Steven Faver. **7-EXPERT** — 1, Sean Zorn. 2, Leon Medart. 3, Brad Smith. **9-INTERMEDIATE** — 1, Jacob Pipkin. 2, Jeff Moorehead. 3, Cory Elgin. **11-EXPERT** — 1, Joe Parrott. 2, Kaleb Watson. 3, Steven McCullam. **13-NOVICE** — 1, Chip Wilbur. 2, Craig Brown. 3, Jeff Davie. **13-EXPERT** — 1, Jeremy Cutright. 2, Devin Wolfe. 3, Jesse Howes. **15-NOVICE** — 1, W.C. Grover. 2, David Crump. 3, Brady Morris. **16-EXPERT** — 1, Scott Naive. 2, Jim Guynes. 3, Chris Lute. 15-16 **CRUISER** — 1, Scott Naive. 2, Chris Lute. 3, Cris Marsh. 7-8 **GIRLS** — 1, Lisa Biggs. 2, Krystal Vickers. 9-10 **GIRLS** — 1, Katie Burke. 2, Lisa Jackson.

Road Run Calendar

SUNDAY, NOVEMBER 4 — Dream of Roses, all-women's 10k and 2-mile fun run-walk & race-walk beginning at 10 a.m. at Chemeketa Community College. The entry fee is $4 by Oct. 27, $8 after; add $7 for long-sleeve T-shirt, $10 for sweatshirt. For more information, call Phidippides Running Store in Salem at 399-7057.

THURSDAY, NOVEMBER 22 — Willamalane Turkey Stuffer, 5k beginning at 8:30 a.m. at the Lively Park Swim Center, 6100 Thurston Road, in Springfield. The entry fees including custom shirt, pancake breakfast, turkey raffle and wave pool swim are $12 by Nov. 17, $15 after; $5 and $8 without shirt. For more information, call 726-4368.

Figure 10.12 Sample of Box Score Information. (*Eugene Register Guard,* Eugene, Oregon, 1990.)

newspaper can construct stories that are colorful, comprehensive, and accurate without actually being present at the event. Furthermore, it is not unusual for a newspaper to have a special form to record box scores for sports events that the leisure service organization is required to use when reporting these activities. If a form is not required, sports results may (in certain newspapers) be called in via the telephone. Figures 10.12 and 10.13 are examples of sports information standings and scores as they might appear in a local newspaper.

Photographs The statement may be trite, but it is true—"A picture is worth a thousand words." A picture can communicate actions, feelings, and events better than any written description. Pictures taken at intervals during a given program

NOTES/ANNOUNCEMENTS

WILLAMALANE BASKETBALL — The Willamalane Park & Recreation District will hold an organizational meeting at 7 p.m., Wednesday, Nov. 7, at the Memorial Building, 765 N. A St. in Springfield for all new teams planning to play in the winter basketball leagues. Team representatives should be present to discuss team fees, league format and registration procedures. For more information, call 746-1669.

KIDSPORTS VOLLEYBALL — Registration is available for the 1990 Kidsports volleyball program. Practice begins this week with the six-week season ending with a tournament on Dec. 7-9. The program is open to boys in grades 3-8, girls in District 4J grades 3-5 and girls in grades 3-8 in other school districts. The fee per player is $16. Registration forms are available at the Kidsports offices in Eugene (2190 Polk St.) and Springfield (1030 G St.). A late-night registration will be held from 5:30-7 p.m. Tuesday at Petersen Barn, North Eugene High School (Room 206), Sheldon High School and the Eugene-Springfield Kidsports offices. For more information, call 683-2373 (Eugene) or 746-0403 (Springfield).

KIDSPORTS FOOTBALL TOURNAMENT — The 1990 Swede Johnson Memorial Kids Bowl season-ending football tournament for tackle football will be held next Sunday. All games will be held at Autzen Stadium beginning at 1 p.m. Admission is $2 for adults, $1 for seniors age 55 and older and free for youths 18 and younger. For more information, call 683-2373.

EUGENE PARKS AND RECREATION BASKETBALL — Registration for Eugene Parks and Recreation fall basketball leagues begins Tuesday, with league play beginning in December and continuing through the first week in March. For more information, call 687-5333.

STORM THE STAIRS BENEFIT — Recreation and Intramurals (RIM) at the University of Oregon and Sacred Heart Hospital's U-Can Center are sponsoring a "Storm the Stairs" event from 10:45 a.m.-1 p.m., on Sunday, Nov. 11, at Autzen Stadium. Part of the National Collegiate Drive to Cure Paralysis, proceeds from the pledge-oriented event will go towards purchasing rehabilitation equipment for the U-Can Center. The idea will be to collectively set a "world record" for vertical distance by climbing stairs at Autzen Stadium. In addition to stair climbing, there also will be demonstrations and recreational activities. For more information, call RIM at 346-4113.

WILLAMETTE VALLEY BABE RUTH — Willamette Valley Babe Ruth is accepting applications for coaching positions in the 9-12 Bambino, 13 Prep and 13-15 Babe Ruth leagues to be formed in the spring of 1991. Send applications to Roger Boothe at 3215 Meadow Lane, Eugene 97402. An organizational meeting is planned for 7 p.m., Wednesday, Nov. 7, at the Marist High School cafeteria. For more information, call Roger Boothe at 689-3443 and 484-7080, or Thomas Westfall at 686-9041 and 484-9509.

HUNTER EDUCATION — The River Road Park and Recreation District will hold a hunter safety course on Nov. 6, 7, 8 and 12-15 at the district facility at 1400 Lake Drive. The cost is $1 for district residents and $1.50 for all others. For more information, call Michael DeRobertis at 688-4052.

BOYS' POWER VOLLEYBALL — The Columbia Empire Volleyball Association, the local affiliate of the United States Volleyball Association, is looking to form a local team for its boys' power volleyball program. Anyone interested in organizing a team, playing or coaching, call Jerry King at 684-3108 or Reuben Chong at (206) 687-4845.

Figure 10.13 Sample of Sports Notes and Announcements. (*Eugene Register Guard,* Eugene, Oregon, 1990.)

can show its progress. Pictures attract attention, while a caption may not. Although a number of different types of pictures will be discussed here, it is important to capture action, whenever possible. Most newspapers today do not want formal photographs and prefer to have informal photos—e.g., a team in action rather than in a lineup.

Photographs of individuals within the leisure service organization are often used by newspapers. There are two types of photographs that the organization might want to keep on file—the formal staff photograph and the action photograph. The formal photograph is taken by a professional photographer and can be used to complement any article concerning that individual. The action photograph, of course, shows the individual "on the move" within an organizational activity, program, or event. The organization might want to keep several of these action photographs of its employees on hand and update them to correspond with specific articles.

Group photographs or group action scenes are also often used by newspapers. Newspaper editors usually like horizontal photographs that result in a two-column illustration. These photographs should be submitted as eight-inch-by-ten-inch glossies where possible, although newspapers with excellent photographic and editorial staffs can use four-inch-by-five-inch photo without seriously affecting the clarity of the picture when it is reproduced in the newspaper. Generally speaking, it is best to use uncluttered backgrounds (unless a background is needed for perspective).

Photo captions should be included with each photograph submitted to a newspaper. One should not assume that a newspaper will be in a position to identify individual photographs. A photo caption can be typed on a separate piece of paper and taped to the back of the photograph. (The caption should not be written on the back of the photograph; this risks the transfer of felt-tip or ballpoint smudges to the front of the picture. Nor should a caption be taped to the front of the picture; this can cause damage to the image area of the photo. If the need to write something on the back of a photograph arises, a hard surface should be used to eliminate damaging impressions.) When the photograph involved is an individual's picture, the caption need only name the individual and organization or position. If the photograph is of a group, all names as well as positions and the event and date of the event should be listed. Sometimes the photograph itself will tell the story; other times, the professional will have to be more elaborate in his or her interpretation of the photograph.

Newspaper advertising As a vehicle for advertisement, the newspaper is important to profit-oriented as well as nonprofit leisure service organizations. For leisure services such as theaters, amusement parks, commercial bowling alleys, and other enterprises, the newspaper is utilized extensively. Nonprofit organizations occasionally purchase paid advertisements or have benevolent or public-spirited businesses in the community sponsor such advertising space in a newspaper.

There are several approaches used by newspapers to calculate advertisement cost. A newspaper, for example, may have a flat rate—that is to say, the newspaper charges the same rate per area unit for advertising regardless of volume or size of the advertisement or the frequency of the advertisement. Often a newspaper will charge a lower rate per unit for larger advertisements or advertisements that appear a certain number of times. The basic rate for advertisements is determined by measuring the proposed advertisement in terms of column inches or agate lines. (There are fourteen agate lines to the column inch.) Once the newspaper has determined this basic measurement, it will charge for space according to its own rates.

The process of creating an advertisement should be done in conjunction with the news-

paper staff. It is the role of the leisure service professional to provide as much information as possible to the advertising specialist about the service and the market toward which it is directed. Other than simply listing the activities of a leisure service organization in the newspaper, it is advisable to build an advertisement around a central idea or theme. The central idea concept can be thought of as the verbal or visual device around which the advertisement is written. Often the utilization of a theme helps to capture the attention of the newspaper audience the professional is hoping to attract. Figures 10.14 and 10.15 are examples of display advertising directed toward encouraging customers to participate in the leisure services of these respective agencies. Figure 10.14 is an example of one that is used by a travel agency to promote Alaskan vacations. The other one presents information about a special event offered by the Hilton Hotel

Figure 10.14 A Paid Display Advertisement. (*Waterloo Courier,* Waterloo (Iowa), January 14, 1990.)

Figure 10.15 A Paid Display Advertisement. (*Eugene Register Guard,* Eugene, Oregon, 1990.)

Wanted: camp counselors. Girl Scout resident camp near Dubuque is hiring staff for the period of June 17-August 4. Unit leaders, unit assistants, waterfront, naturalist, craft director, horse wranglers and assistant director are needed. Write to Little Cloud Girl Scout Council, Inc., c/o Program Services Director, P.O. Box 26, Dubuque, Iowa 52001 for an application.

Figure 10.16 A Paid Classified Advertisement to Hire Staff. (*Northern Iowan,* University of Northern Iowa, Cedar Falls (Iowa), January 26, 1990.)

in Eugene, Oregon. An example of a classified want ad for camp counselors is found in Figure 10.16.

Brochures

One of the most widely used and effective tools for disseminating information is the brochure. A brochure can be thought of as a printed work bound together in such a way that it highlights programs, areas, facilities, and activities or presents information that enables people to find desired leisure experiences. Brochures come in all sizes, colors, shapes, and designs. In many respects, they have been a mainstay in the promotion of many leisure service programs.

In creating a brochure, the professional recreation and leisure service staff member or members must deal with a number of basic questions including:

1. *Brochure Content*—To begin with, the leisure service programmer must ask himself or herself, "What is the purpose of the brochure? Are we promoting an activity, a set of activities, a facility, or are we disseminating information concerning other leisure opportunities?" The professional must be acutely aware of precisely what he or she wants to convey, in order to decide what a given brochure should contain.

2. *Timing*—The factor of timing basically deals with the question, "What is the most appropriate time to produce the brochure to insure timely distribution and maximum visibility and impact?" It may be best to produce a brochure on a seasonal basis when promoting the schedule of activities of a municipal park and recreation department; conversely, it may be more effective to have a brochure available on a continual daily basis when promoting the use of a given facility (e.g., a swimming pool, an ice rink, or a drop-in center). There is no universally accepted set of rules for the proper timing of various brochures. Obviously the timing of specific brochures for various events is crucial, but it is highly situational and must be dictated by the individual professional.

3. *Format and Design*—The manner in which information will be arranged and presented in a brochure is of great importance. Will the brochure contain pictures or graphic designs? What colors will be employed—will it be multicolored or limited to one color? Is the intent of the brochure to be striking and bold in appearance or more subtly persuasive? The type of design chosen will reflect on the material presented. For example, a bold design may indicate that the programs detailed will be bold in nature, whereas a soft approach may indicate to the public that the program involved is "relaxing," "classy," or "intellectual." What will the size of the brochure be? Will it be magazine size? A small booklet form? Folded in three panels?

4. *Distribution*—How does the leisure service professional intend to reach his or her target public? How will the public gain access to the information provided by the professional? Will the brochure be mailed? If so, to whom? If the brochure is to be made available to individuals visiting a facility, where should these brochures be located within the facility? Should the brochure be made available to service clubs, community organizations, the Chamber of Commerce, and groups within the community such as the Welcome Wagon? Should the brochure be distributed through the school system? These types of questions must be asked each time a brochure is disseminated.

5. *Cost*—Obviously the amount of money available to an organization for the production of brochures will affect the quantity and quality of its brochures. It is interesting to note that profit-oriented organizations spend a great deal of their budget for advertising and publicity, whereas in nonprofit and governmental organizations, this is not the case. However, it is becoming a more general practice for these organizations to sell advertising space in the brochure to finance production.

In the following discussion are a few helpful suggestions for putting together brochures. It is important to remember that the professional is attempting primarily to inform his or her target public. As such, the brochure should be instructive, informative, and eye-catching. Information written for a brochure should be concise and to the point. The informaton should be accurate—containing all necessary names, locations, and phone numbers. There is nothing more embarrassing to the professional than a brochure that contains an erroneous phone number or other misinformation.

The contents and format of a brochure will vary. For example, a brochure promoting activities will often include a description of the activity, its cost, the time of the activity, its location, and perhaps its instructor. This type of brochure may also contain application or registration forms and information, depending on the circumstances. Brochures describing facilities might include a description as well as a diagram of the facility involved. Often, pictures and designs are used to make such a brochure distinctive or to emphasize the attractiveness of the facility and activity to the customer. For example, in terms of communication within a brochure, a picture of children playing in a swimming complex may be far more effective than a written message. "Clip art" is frequently used and can highlight information and add attractiveness to the brochures.

The selection of a printer or design firm is important not only from the standpoint of cost but also in terms of production. Printing firms can often be very helpful to the professional in the selection of type—its size and most appropriate style. When laying out the brochure, it is important not to waste space or overcrowd the material. The printer can help the professional organize his or her material in an orderly fashion that will be clear to the individual reading the brochure. Once the decision has been made as to the content, the type of paper, the size of type, the number of pictures, and other designs to be used, the layout of the brochure can proceed.

In working with artists, typesetters and printers, the professional will be asked to provide the following information:

1. *Artist*—Most artists base their fee on the amount of time involved in designing the publication and the amount of preparation for the final camera-ready art required of them. A graphic artist may or may not be an illustrator as well. The artist will want to know:
   a. Type of design work required: basic conceptual design, layout, pasteup of a dummy, preparation of camera-ready art, illustrations, hand lettering.
   b. Number of pages of final product.
   c. Time: how soon the work will be needed.
2. *Typesetter*—Typesetters usually base their fee on the system of typesetting they use, the time it takes to set the material, and the number of manuscript pages. A typesetter will want to know:
   a. Number of manuscript pages.
   b. Typeface: for body copy, for headlines.
   c. Specifications: size of all type, leading (spacing) between lines, column widths.
   d. Anticipated number of author's alterations, if any.
   e. Time: how soon the work will be needed.
   f. Pasteup: will you want the typesetter's artist to do the pasteup?
3. *Printer*—Printers want to know paper stock specifications as soon as possible, so that they can order the paper early enough to meet time constraints. If possible, try and select a paper that is easy to obtain to cut down on delays. The printer will want to know:
   a. Size of publication (e.g., 8½ by 11 inches; 5 inches by 8 inches)
   b. Number of copies.
   c. Number of colors of paper or ink.
   d. Type of paper for both cover and text.
   e. Type of binding.
   f. Number of photographs.
   g. Any difficult registration jobs (a fine line running next to a color border, for example).
   h. Will you need a proof?
   i. Time: how soon the work will be needed.

Generally, leisure service organizations use four types of brochures. Brochures are used to identify and define activities, to provide information concerning the design and layout of areas and facilities, and to promote other recreation and leisure resources. Often, two or more of the above types of brochures are merged together into one brochure to create the fourth (combined) type of brochure. For example, seasonal brochures usually not only define activities of the leisure service organization, but also identify and provide information concerning its facilities. Furthermore, because of the dependent relationship of many activities upon a specific type of facility, often these two types of information are joined in a single brochure.

There are a number of brochures that are used to promote leisure services. One of the frequently employed brochures is the comprehensive seasonal program brochure. These are built around the seasons of the year and mailed to individuals or households on a quarterly basis. Figures 10.17, 10.18, and 10.19 provide examples of these types of brochures. Figure 10.20 is an example of a summer brochure for youth. Figures 10.21, 10.22, and 10.23 are examples of brochure cover designs for specific areas, facilities, or programs.

Fliers

Another widely used form of publicity in leisure service organizations is the flier. Fliers are used as an inexpensive communication tool for mass distribution. They provide the consumer with the vital details of the program, designed in such a way as to not only inform but also stimulate interest. Fliers are usually printed on a single sheet of paper and are designed to be read as individual units. The effective flier must be attractive and eye-catching in order to capture the attention and interest of the individual reading it.

The flier can be an elaborately produced item, or it can be relatively simple. A professionally designed and printed flier may be appropriate to

Figure 10.17 Program Cover Design. (Indianola (Iowa) Parks and Recreation.)

Figure 10.18 Program Cover Design. (Burnaby (British Columbia) Parks and Recreation and Burnaby (British Columbia) School District 41.)

Figure 10.19 Program Cover Design. (Battle Creek (Michigan) Recreation Department.)

CRAFTS ⊙ FRIENDSHIP ⊙ SUNSHINE
COOL ⊙ FITNESS ⊙ SPORTSMANSHIP
COMPUTERS ⊙ FANTASY ⊙ SHARING
CHALLENGE ⊙ FUN ⊙ SENSATIONAL
CREATIVE ⊙ FIELD TRIPS ⊙ SKILLS

COUNSELOR-IN-TRAINING

COMPUTER CAMP

CHEJUDO CHALLENGE

SPORTS/RESIDENT CAMP

CAMP ADVENTURE DAY CAMP

Figure 10.20 Program Cover Design. (Community, Family and Soldier Support Command—Korea, Eighth United State Army.)

Clinton Lake

Hiking Trails

US Army Corps
of Engineers
Kansas City District

How To Reserve a

PORTLAND PARK FOR YOUR PICNIC

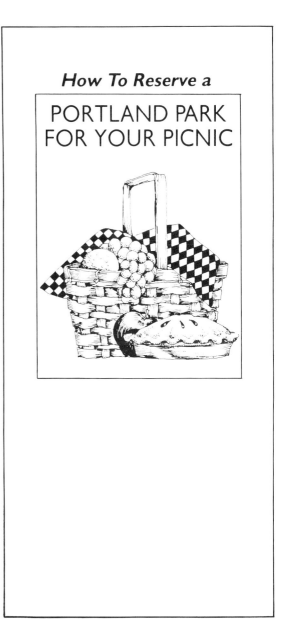

Figure 10.21 Brochure Design. (U.S. Army Corps of Engineers.)

Figure 10.22 Brochure Design. (Portland (Oregon) Bureau of Parks and Recreation.)

promote certain programs within an agency. On the other hand, a hand-written or typed flier produced on an organization's copy machine may be adequate in most cases. Regardless of the method of production, the flier must reflect an effective use of space in terms of layout, design, and color. Fliers should be kept simple and should be constructed around a central theme or idea. The central idea should directly convey the message that the organization wishes to promote. This is usually accomplished by use of an illustration and a headline to draw the reader's attention to the program. The fliers in Figures 10.24 and 10.25 each use this concept. They each contain a headline and accompanying illustrations, which convey to the reader the nature of the activity and what it is likely to entail. The information presented is uncluttered and easy to distinguish. It conveys to the reader the program to be implemented, as well as the location, time, date, and other relevant information.

Although it is important to include all relevant, accurate information about a given program or activity, this written information is actually secondary in importance to the visual impact of the picture or headline used in a flier. The reader is first attracted to a flier's main thrust, and if it catches his or her interest and attention, he or she will read the details. What specifically should be included in the flier format and, generally, in what order?

1. *The Name of the Event or Activity*—This might include a brief description of the activities or types of experiences that are to be gained by a customer. This message should be direct, simple, and conveyed in a few words.
2. *Identification of the Target Audience*—For whom is the program designed? One might want to identify the age grouping, sex, geographic location, competence/skill level, and perhaps leisure preference. For example, a flier might designate that a particular activity would especially interest the outdoor enthusiast.
3. *The Location, Date, and Time of the Event*—This might necessitate the inclusion of a map to specify location. When mentioning the date, one might want to further clarify it by mentioning the day of the week. The time should specify not

only the time the program starts but also the time the program will end. If the program is to extend over several days, it should be made clear what times the program will be in progress each day.
4. *The Sponsoring Agency*—Included should be not only the name, telephone number, and address of the agency sponsoring the program but also a contact person (where appropriate) in the organization.

Figure 10.23 Brochure Design. (Dorris Ranch, Willamalane Park and Recreation District, Springfield (Oregon).)

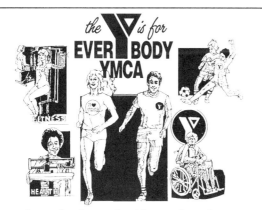

Figure 10.24 Flyer. (Eugene (Oregon) Family YMCA.)

The distribution of fliers can be carried out in several ways:

1. *The Individual Collection*—Individual parties within the distribution area pick up a number of fliers and distribute them or offer them for distribution. For example, the Chamber of Commerce might be involved in the distribution of fliers in this way.
2. *Mailing*—If the organization's budget allows, a leisure service organization can use the postal service to distribute fliers. The mailing of fliers usually involves selected populations. For example, one might mail fliers to given age group-

Figure 10.25 Flyer Design. (Battle Creek (Michigan) Recreation Department.)

ings (such as senior citizens to announce appropriate trips and activities).

3. *Displaying*—Fliers can be attached to a variety of surfaces. Often the professional will use a window, door, wall, bulletin board, or other surface. In this sense, they become mini-posters.

4. *Personal Distribution*—Perhaps the most frequently used method is personal distribution of fliers. The professional may hand out the fliers himself or herself or may convince schools, grocery stores, and clubs to distribute the fliers. Selection of the distribution points should complement the program involved. For example, a children's program can be effectively promoted by distributing fliers through the schools. A community-wide event, on the other hand, might be better publicized if fliers are distributed through community grocery stores.

Fliers are very useful and efficient tools for promoting leisure services and programs—an inexpensive way for the organization to communicate with prospective customers. Care should be given to choosing both the design and distribution methods. A poorly designed flier or one distributed at the wrong place or the wrong time will not be effective in promotion of programs; however, fliers that are "on target" in terms of these factors can serve the promotional efforts of the organization well. In any case, fliers are inexpensive enough that the organization can afford to experiment with design and distribution points in order to determine their most effective use.

Many leisure service organizations are using computers to design and print high-quality, innovative fliers on an in-house basis. The advent of desktop publishing, facilitated by laser printers, provides the necessary tools for developing professional-quality fliers at a reasonable price for distribution. For example, the Pagemaker software program used by Apple's Macintosh® Computer provides a wide array of options that can be used in designing fliers. Some of the options include creating text, importing text, importing graphics into text, wrapping text around graphics, creating different fonts/type styles, and creating different sizes of text. It is also possible to get clip art software programs for the Macintosh, to print in color with a color printer, and to create your own graphics with a graphics software program. In addition to Pagemaker®, Apple® has other programs, such as MacDraw™, MacWrite®, Letraset Design Studio®, Ready, Set, Go®, and QuarkXpress®. IBM also has several desktop publishing programs, such as Ventura Publisher® and Pagemaker®. Figure 10.26 is an example of a computer-generated flier.

Newsletter

A newsletter is a means of communicating with an organization's membership and constituents. It can be thought of as a tool for providing information in a more concise and brief manner than that of a newspaper or magazine. The newsletter is a direct means of communication. Similar to other tools used to promote a program, its major objectives are to inform individuals and to create a positive image of the organization. Newsletters may represent the viewpoint of the chief executive of the organization or may be indicative of the broader viewpoint of the organization's membership.

In developing a newsletter, Logan (1975: 22–25) has suggested that there are five major points of concern. First, one must consider the audience toward which the newsletter is to be directed. Is the newsletter going only to the members of the organization, or will it be distributed to the public as well? If distributed to the public, will it be distributed to a given geographic area or another type of population grouping? The audience that the newsletter is aimed at will dictate the type of news that it will include as well as the way in which the news is written (e.g., newsletters that are designed for an organization's members only may be written more specifically and might have a more personal orientation).

Size and format should also be considered in developing a newsletter. Size and format (and the sophistication of the format) can vary widely. The

WANNA BE CLOSER TO NATURE? WANNA
BREATH SMOGLESS AIR? IF SO, THEN
SIGN UP FOR TWO AND A HALF DAYS OF
ROUGHING IT WITH TANYA AND CRAIG.
THE TRIP STARTS FROM FRIDAY, AUG. 24
TO SUNDAY, AUG. 26. THE CAMPSITE
WILL BE PARIS LAKE. ALSO, YOU MUST
BE 13 YEARS OF AGE. SIGN UP BY AUG.16
NO EXCEPTIONS!!

* COST: $20.00   (BRING EXTRA $7.50 IF YOU WANT TO GO ON THE WATERSLIDE)
*TIME LEAVING: 2:00 PM FRI.
*TIME RETURNING: 6:00 PM SUN.
*COST INCLUDES MEALS, CAMPSITES, AND GAS.

Figure 10.26   Computer-Generated Flyer. (Morale, Welfare and Recreation Department, U.S.
Naval Station, Long Beach (California).)

newsletter format can be a mimeographed sheet of paper or an elaborately produced item (resembling a magazine format). The newsletter should, in any case, employ a format that is readable and attractive. The type of format that an organization employs will primarily be determined by the funds available to produce it. These funds can be enhanced by selling advertising space in the newsletter to outside business interests.

Central to the development of an effective newsletter is the organization of a newsgathering operation. Depending on the complexity and sophistication of the newsletter, this may involve an entire staff (e.g., in very large governmental organizations or commercial recreation and leisure organizations) or a single contact individual to whom articles for the newsletter are submitted. This individual may also seek out and report information relevant to the organizational newsletter.

The type of printing and method of distribution of a newsletter may also vary widely, according to its sophistication and the funds available. Printing involves the use of graphics, selection of type, color, and paper. Often, an organization may combine the printed form with the more economical typed and copied—having the heading printed commercially, then using a copy machine to run off the bottom of the front page and the remaining pages of the newsletter. This can be a shrewd approach in that the heading is bold and eye-catching—encouraging the attention of the reader—but it is still fairly economical and can be produced on a monthly or bimonthly basis. The Hennepin Parks (Minnesota) used this approach in their "Road Explorer News" (see Figure 10.27). This newsletter highlights various events and activities of the organization, while providing personal insights into employee activities and reinforcing departmental policies in a positive way.

Annual Reports

An annual report can be thought of as a year-end comprehensive summary detailing the financial status, program services, physical developments, and prospective changes in a leisure service organization. An annual report is a publication that is submitted to a governing body or board of directors, depending on the nature of the organization. It is designed to be graphically informative. An annual report can be a useful component of a leisure service organization's promotional activities. The annual report is a way of indicating the current state of affairs to the organization's present customers. Used as a promotional tool, the annual report can serve to entice potential customers. If done well, it will enhance the image of the organization. Kraus and Curtis (1990: 339–340) have noted that annual reports may include: (1) organization address and staff/directors names; (2) opening messages; (3) table of contents and acknowledgements; (4) organizational chart; (5) financial report; (6) major facility developments; and (7) program information, participation, etc. Figure 10.28 presents the cover design from an annual report for the Thunder Bay, Ontario, Parks and Recreation Department.

Information and Press Kits

Leisure service organizations should have material available that offers background information about the organization—its staff, programs, and facilities. Such information can be used to provide current and new community members with detailed information concerning opportunities for leisure participation. The same information may be useful to public officials and individuals who are becoming active volunteers and assuming leadership positions with the leisure service organization. In addition, information packets or "press kits" can be useful in enhancing a public speech about the organization. Quite obvious is the necessity to have a

ROAD EXPLORERS NEWS

HENNEPIN PARKS

Yours to Enjoy, Naturally.

Editor: John Jonassen
  Bicycle Coordinator
Coon Rapids Dam Regional Park

Fall 1989

Road Explorers Bike Club

The Hennepin Parks Road Explorers Bike Club is dedicated to providing a quality bike ride to people of all ages and cycling ability. Almost every Saturday throughout the cycling season the club offers day trips of varied distance throughout the state. Overnight weekend tours occur about once a month at places like the North Shore, Itasca, Lanesboro, and more. Special rides are also offered weekday evenings including Full Moon rides and a Halloween Program.

Many hours of research go into finding the very best route available. Route standards include a scenic route, little traffic, paved bike lane, and interesting rest stops. Every turn is marked with short life orange arrows, providing riders with an easy to follow route.

Each ride is provided with full support including a sag wagon equipped to handle repairs and deal with emergencies. The sag wagon locates lost riders, carries extra water for riders, rests tired riders, and will even carry lunches and extra baggage. The sag wagon provides overnight riders with the added luxury of transporting overnight gear.

Trained leaders in first-aid, CPR, and bike mechanics accompany riders along the route. Each leader is there to make sure that every rider has an enjoyable experience and return for more. Each trip is recreational and club leaders provide an un-hurried atmosphere, encouraging riders to go at their own pace.

Hennepin Parks keep costs on all trips very low. Day trips are free to members and $2 to non-members. The cost of the overnight trips are $10 for members, and $15 to non-members. The fee includes gear transportation, sag wagon, overnight accommodations, and the use of Hennepin County camping equipment, food and add-on activities are extra.

Reservations are required on all trips. Reservations can be made by calling the Coon Rapids Dam Regional Park at 757-4700. Reservations for the overnight trips should be made prior to the pre-trip meeting. The pre-trip meetings are scheduled the Tuesday prior to the ride. The pre-trip meeting covers information as to lodging, food arrangements, transportation, and equipment needs. While helmets are not required they are recommended for all rides.

Figure 10.27   Newsletter Design. (Hennepin (Minnesota) Parks.)

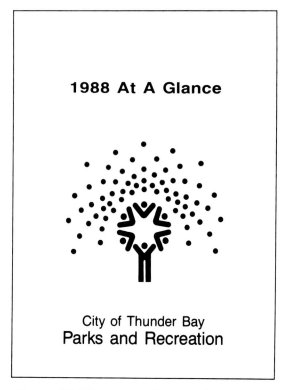

1988 At A Glance

City of Thunder Bay
Parks and Recreation

Figure 10.28   Annual Report Cover Design. (Thunder Bay (Ontario) Parks and Recreation.)

"press kit" on file with local newspapers, and radio and television stations. In general, whenever the organization is making professional contacts, the press kit can be an asset.

It is difficult to compile a comprehensive list of information packet contents that would apply to all leisure service organizations. However, the following list of suggested material should be somewhat helpful to the leisure professional:

1. A brief history of the organization.
2. An organizational chart.
3. Biographical sketches of staff members.
4. Organizational programs, services, and facilities.
5. The annual report.
6. Reprints of newspaper articles, editorials, or other media material.
7. Photographs of activities, services, and facilities.

A press kit can be assembled in a binder, folder, manila envelope or other organized form. For the sake of expediency and cost, the folder or manila envelope is probably the best method for presenting the press kit. A well-prepared and well-organized press kit can make a very positive and lasting impression and provide an individual with a good deal of insight into an organization. In addition, it is extremely important that an information packet be kept up to date with names of people, current photographs, accurate charts and maps, etc. Outdated or incorrect information about an organization may have a more negative effect than no available information at all.

Postage Meter Message
One of the techniques that is a useful promotional tool and that can be incorporated into brochure and flier distribution or used on other mailings or organizational correspondence is the postage meter message. Figure 10.29 as an example of a postage meter message used in Dundas, Ontario. The phrase "Your Leisure is Our Business" is affixed to all correspondence sent from this organization.

Logo/Emblem
Through logos/emblems, a leisure service organization can gain the public's awareness. The visual identity of a graphic design is very important to any organization. In essence, the logo/emblem is a communicative device. At a glance, it relates to the individual viewing it the presence of "the organization." In other words, it is a visual symbol that represents the organization. For example, some organizations with easily identifiable logos/emblems are the "Y", the Girl Scouts, the 4-H Club, professional sports teams (e.g., the "Seahawks" for Seattle).

Logos/emblems become representative of the organizations involved; as a result of this association, they are imbued with shades of meaning for the individual who views them. For example, the "Y" symbol conveys not only the reality of the organization (in terms of buildings and facilities) but also certain values, such as integrity,

Figure 10.29   Postage Meter Message. (Dundas (Ontario) Parks and Recreation.)

155 So. Seward St., Juneau, AK 99801 (907) 586(3300) ext. 226

Figure 10.30   Sample Logo Design. (Parks and Recreation Department, Juneau (Alaska).)

dependability, stability, and community service. When a logo/emblem is able to convey such a set of values, it is a valuable asset to any organization. Leisure service organizations have this potential—that is, their logo may come to be identified with values that are considered to be helpful to the organizational image. However, if an organization is involved in or associated with actions that are considered indicative of poor values, the logo/emblem can elicit those same connotations in the mind of individuals viewing it. Logos or emblems can be many things—geometric designs, organic objects, or animate or inanimate objects. Smokey Bear, for example, has long been a symbol for park fire safety and prevention. Ideally, a logo/emblem is simple in form and design. The colors, shapes, and objects employed and the manner in which these are blended and laid out will affect the impact of the logo design.

How and where do leisure service organizations employ logos/emblems? They can be used wherever they can be employed with taste—on stationery, business cards, fliers and brochures, posters, press release forms, annual reports, novelty items (especially T-shirts), organizational vehicles, uniforms, signs, and so on. The use of

a logo/emblem on organizational vehicles and uniforms can be especially useful in promoting the organization, since vehicles and uniforms are seen in all areas of a community. A distinctive logo that attracts attention—appearing on organization vehicles, which are seen in various parts of town on a fairly frequent basis—gives the appearance of a busy organization at work.

Ours is a visually oriented society; hence, the creation of a distinctive dynamic logo is an important aspect of an organization's overall promotional effort. Examples of designs used to promote leisure service organizations are found in Figures 10.30, 10.31, 10.32, and 10.33. These logos serve as visual symbols for the organizations represented. They suggest that the organizations involve people-oriented services. While some of the designs are more abstract than others, all are effective organizational logos that could become easily recognizable in a community.

Awards and Citations

There are many ways to recognize community organizations and groups for their contributions to leisure service organizations. Awards and citations are one way. They are primarily used as

Figure 10.31 Sample Logo Design. (Hennepin (Minnesota) Parks.)

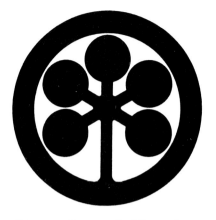

Figure 10.32 Sample Logo Design. (Portland (Oregon) Bureau of Parks and Recreation.)

public relations tools. Awards become meaningless if they are given too freely, but they should be presented—when they are deserved—to promote goodwill and support for the organization.

Not only are such types of recognition useful in promoting positive relations between the leisure service organization and community groups and individuals, but also the presentations of awards and citations are often newsworthy events and serve to promote organizational efforts. A picture in a newspaper accompanied by a news story serves as publicity for the organization and may arouse interest in the organization's programs and services.

What specific actions should the leisure organization recognize with such awards? There are a number of ways in which individuals and groups within the community can serve and support the leisure service organization, and which culminate in their recognition. First, and perhaps most important, is the contribution of time, energy, and creativity toward the promotion of the organization, generally or for a specific activity. For example, one might want to recognize a local service club that sponsors an activity (such as an annual Easter egg hunt), an individual serving as a member of a policy-making board (e.g., a park board), or a program volunteer. An award for this type of action is especially important in that it formally recognizes a contribution of service. The organization will also want to recognize tangible contributions—represented, for example, by gifts of cash, land, buildings, trees, play equipment, and so on. There are other meritorious acts, occurring during the daily workings of the organization, that do not fit easily into a category. The leisure services professional should have the insight to recognize such efforts and reward them as they occur.

What types of rewards and citations should the organization distribute? Wall plaques, framed certificates (see Figures 10.34, 10.35 and 10.36),

Figure 10.33   Sample Logo Design. (Lane County Ice, Eugene, Oregon.)

and desk sets are probably most often given as awards. In special circumstances, the organization may want to be a little more personal—awarding paintings, sculpture, or other items appropriate to the situation. Often, when an individual or group financially supports the building of a park or facility, plants a grove of trees, purchases a significant amount of playground equipment, or generously contributes to refurbishing a room or other leisure space, the organization will name it after the major contributor.

The organization should not neglect its own members and customers when they make special contributions or appear to be noteworthy in their efforts. Organizational morale is served well by awarding members of the organization with plaques, citations, and so on. However, as mentioned before, these should be given sincerely, or they lose their meaning to the individual or individuals receiving them.

Individuals participating in organizational programs have come to expect awards (certificates, ribbons, trophies, etc.) for activities in which competition is involved. Many leisure service organizations only give awards to customers for excellence—such as for winning a baseball tournament, placing first in a swim meet, and so on. Such awards usually take the form of trophies, ribbons, clothing, and certificates. However, an organization that wishes to promote participation may want to consider the distribution of some type of award to all customers. For example, all individuals participating in a cross-country run may receive a patch, T-shirt, or ribbon as recognition of involvement. The authors feel that this approach should be encouraged more in leisure services. This is not to discourage awards for excellence; rather, it is to encourage a blend of the two approaches—that is, a form of recognition for all customers as well as a distinctive award for excellence (e.g., first-, second-, and third-place finalists).

Novelty Items

Promotion can be accomplished through the use of novelty items such as buttons, decals, and banners. Individuals are often attracted by and enjoy participating in such forms of promotion; even though the professional may not think to employ such items and methods, they can be very effective in promoting programs, services, and the organization itself. For example, the use of a logo or phrase printed on T-shirts is effective in promoting programs with all customers; bumper stickers might be useful to the professional attempting to promote an upcoming event or project. Novelty items that can be employed by a leisure service organization include:

1. Decals and bumper stickers
2. Buttons and pins
3. Imprinting of matches, pencils, pens
4. Banners and flags
5. Postcards
6. Toys/sports equipment
7. Imprinted clothing
8. Patches

Figure 10.34 Certificate of Appreciation. (Indianola (Iowa) Parks and Recreation Department.)

Patience is Virtue Award

In honor of unusual patience, perseverance, and the undying faith that, in time, all good things can come to pass, this award is gratefully presented to

_____
NAME

_____
DATE

_____
Commissioner of Public Affairs

CITY OF PORTLAND
BUREAU OF PARKS AND RECREATION
MIKE LINDBERG, Commissioner
CLEVE WILLIAMS, Superintendent

_____
Superintendent of Parks

Figure 10.35   Patience is a Virtue Award. (Portland (Oregon) Bureau of Parks and Recreation.)

CERTIFICATE OF

PARTICIPATION

Life. Be in it.

BICYCLE SKILLS RODEO

This is to certify that _____
has been awarded this certificate for participation in the Chapel Hill - Orange County
Bicycle Skills Rodeo.

Signed _____   Signed _____

ORANGE COUNTY   CHAPEL HILL
RECREATION and PARKS DEPARTMENT   PARKS and RECREATION DEPARTMENT

Figure 10.36 Certificate of Participation. (Orange County (North Carolina) Recreation and Parks Department and Chapel Hill (North Carolina) Parks and Recreation Department.)

There are many other novelty items that can be utilized in promoting programs and services. Some of these are keychains, ribbons, blotters, calendars, badges, patches, armbands, and hats. Distribution of such items is most easily accomplished when people are massed together—e.g., in a sports activity, at a convention, or at special events. This type of promotion can create a feeling of a goodwill; the organization is paired with the act of giving, which is a positive association in the mind of a potential consumer. Often, commercial profit-oriented organizations will absorb the cost of novelty items if their logo or advertising message is paired with that of the public or nonprofit organization. This can be a mutually beneficial arrangement, both organizations accomplishing their promotional goals (see Figures 10.37 through 10.42).

Exhibits, Displays, and Demonstrations

Leisure service organizations can use the exhibit, display, and demonstration methods to highlight their program services and organizational efforts or to use for purposes of interpretation. Basically, the professional can use the methods just mentioned in two ways—as a part

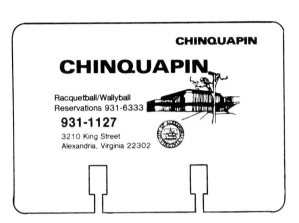

Figure 10.37 Rolodex Card. (Chinquapin Park Recreation Center, Alexandria (Virginia) Department of Recreation Parks and Cultural Activities.)

Figure 10.38 Sample Sticker. (U.S. Army Corps of Engineers.)

Figure 10.39 Bumper Sticker. (Thunder Bay (Ontario) Parks and Recreation.)

of a program service (e.g., a display in a museum) or as a vehicle to facilitate promotional efforts aimed at public involvement or support of a program (e.g., sale of a product like cookies).

Exhibits and displays have the same characteristics. A display is usually two-dimensional; an exhibit may often include three-dimensional objects. They both involve the use of inanimate objects and materials only. A demonstration, on the other hand, involves the use of organizational members or customers as "demonstrators." It is

Figure 10.40 Bumper Sticker. (Chinquapin Park Recreation Center, Alexandria (Virginia) Department of Recreation Parks and Cultural Activities.)

Figure 10.41 Logo on a Patch. (Ames (Iowa) Parks and Recreation Department.)

Figure 10.42 Lake Clean Up Patch. (U.S. Army Corps of Engineers.)

a dynamic approach to program promotion, featuring individuals who perhaps have participated in a leisure service organization's activities (e.g., a tumbling, ballet, or swimming demonstration). Although an interpretive exhibit may be confined to a specific location, displays and demonstrations used to promote an organization's services may be conducted in a variety of settings. A gymnastics demonstration during the half-time show of a football game, a mime troop performing on a street corner, and a bear cub from the local zoo at a shopping mall are all types of demonstrations. Exhibits used to promote the programs of an organization can be placed in a church, school, shopping mall, bank lobby, town square, or department store.

Stationary Advertising

Stationary advertising differs from other forms of advertising in that it is not delivered to the prospective consumer. As a result of this restriction, it is vital that stationary advertising be strategically placed, so that it is likely to be viewed by the prospective customer. Though exhibits and displays may also be classified as stationary promotional tools, they also are designed to be moved from location to location for specific purposes. The other types of stationary tools described here are generally intended to remain where they are—stationary. There are four types of stationary advertising used by leisure service organizations. These are bulletin boards, posters, billboards, and signs. A brief discussion of each of these forms of stationary advertising follows.

Bulletin boards   For the purposes of this discussion, a bulletin board can be thought of as any large, bordered surface used to inform through the display of announcements, schedules, projects, and other informative material. The bulletin board can be fixed or portable—enabling it, for example, to be carried from school to school or to various areas in a hospital. The material presented on a bulletin board should be ar-

ranged in a neat and orderly way and should employ the use of color and design to emphasize the information it is attempting to present. Bulletin boards can also be organized around a theme. For example, an activities center might want to emphasize the seasons of the year in a bulletin board format when promoting programs. Items attached to a bulletin board are usually temporary in nature, so that they may be changed in order to keep the bulletin board current and stimulating.

Posters   Posters are usually thought of as large advertisements appearing on posterboard (cardboard). The elements that are important in the design of a good flier are also relevant to the design and layout of an effective, dynamic poster. The poster, however, is usually more "finished" than the flier, since it is often professionally printed or silk-screened. The color choice for poster design may also be greater than that available for a flier. Posters can be displayed in store windows, on countertops, or on the sides of a counter and on bulletin boards in schools, churches, and recreation centers. It is important to be selective in the placement of posters, as they usually represent a greater investment than that for fliers. Also, one should be conscientious in placing posters; the posters that are distributed should ideally be picked up by the organization from the distribution points after they have served their purpose. The posters should not be displayed in places that do not complement the aesthetics of the environment—for example, on telephone poles, wooden fences, and so on. Figure 10.43 is a poster used to promote a community recreation activity, "Christmas on Ice." Figures 10.44 and 10.45 are posters promoting swim lesson registration and a concert series. Although the placement of the logo for the swim center on the poster in Figure 10.44 is subtle in nature, it is a logo used annually; thus, it is easily recognized and attended to by individuals in the community.

Figure 10.43 Poster Design. (Burnaby (British Columbia) Parks and Recreation.)

Billboards Billboards are large outdoor signs that are usually placed in key, heavily trafficked areas. Although billboards may come in a variety of sizes and shapes, they are usually about thirteen feet tall and forty feet wide. Illustrations and written messages are either pasted or painted on these advertisements. As in other forms of advertising, billboard messages are usually built around a central theme or idea. The copy and illustrated elements must be dynamic in nature, combining use of color and space. The billboard has a very limited amount of time in which to deliver its message. Cars traveling by a billboard may see it for a few seconds only; thus, it must be extremely pointed and concise in its message. Al-

though this avenue of advertising is used primarily by commercial enterprises, advertising agencies will often dedicate a selected number of billboards for free public use. A large facility (e.g, a public zoo) may erect one or more billboards to promote its services. Many public leisure service organizations may not be in a position to purchase billboard space; however, they can use this same concept on a smaller scale by installing relatively large "billboards" in shopping areas and public parks to publicize special events. For example, the Wooster, Ohio, Parks and Recreation Department designed and displayed two "billboards" (approximately four feet by six feet) in a downtown shopping square and on a busy street to publicize its annual "Art in the Park."

Figure 10.44 Poster Design. (Lively Park Swim Center, Willamalane Park & Recreation District, Springfield (Oregon).)

Figure 10.45 Poster Design. (Morale, Welfare and Recreation Department, U.S. Naval Station, Long Beach (California).)

Signs Signs can be used in several capacities. First, an identification sign can be used simply to provide individuals with information as to the location of a given building. An identification sign (such as one reading "The City of Denton Parks and Recreation Department") also indirectly acts as a form of advertising each time it is viewed by an individual. This is true of identification signs for such areas as parks, golf courses, and ski areas

as well. Consequently, such signs should not be underplayed; they should be nicely designed and maintained. Signs can be used in another capacity—to more specifically inform the consumer as to the proper use of services, facilities, and park areas. For example, symbolic signs in a park area might show silhouettes of individuals engaged in sailing, hiking, hunting, or picnicking. On the other hand, such signs might depict, for example, a picture of a bicycle with a red slash through it, indicating that bicycling is not allowed in the park.

Signs in parks can intrude upon the landscape if they are not designed to blend with the surroundings; thus, professionals should give due consideration to the symbols used and the shape of the sign, as well as its color, size, and style of lettering.

Radio and television   Use of television and radio to promote leisure programs and services is becoming increasingly important to a large number of agencies throughout Canada and the United States. Television reaches a large percentage of people nationwide. Radio, on the other hand, is more geographically oriented; in addition, its audiences are more specifically defined for given programs. Radio—perhaps more than any other medium—reaches youth.

Television and radio stations that cover local events are perhaps the best sources through which to promote a leisure service program. In addition to providing news coverage for the local leisure service organization's activities, these stations will often provide air time for free public service announcements to either public or nonprofit private community service organizations.

Thus, television and radio are publicity tools that should not be overlooked by leisure service organizations when they do not have the means to purchase advertising. There are a number of approaches that can be taken in using these media, including the following.

Advertising   There are two types of advertising that can be purchased—advertising that will sponsor an entire program, and advertising "spots." When purchasing advertising, one should consider the desired audience—remembering that television reaches a broad general audience and radio tends to reach more select geographically limited audiences.

Television and radio advertisements involve placing a proposition before the potential customer. This proposition must be attractively and

dynamically introduced in order to be effective. It may involve employment of actors, artists, producers, directors, some designers, and other personnel. Most radio and television advertisements are sixty seconds or less. Thus, one must get the message across quickly; this implies extreme selectivity in the amount of information presented. Since radio advertisments are not visual, an image must be created in the mind of the consumer.

Public service announcements   Public service announcements (PSAs) are similar to commercials. Basically, public service announcements are created to sell an idea or concept. Public service announcements can be made for fund-raising or charitable purposes, for educational or informational campaigns, and for sale of nonprofit organizational services. Often, the public service announcement format can be used to promote a special service event or convey an idea related to a theme, such as "plant a tree." Most television and radio stations prepare guidelines for organizations and are willing to help organizations produce professional-quality announcements. Spot announcements can range from ten to sixty seconds. Shorter announcements, in general, stand a better chance of being used on the air. Approximate word count to apply in preparing announcements are:

10 seconds = 25 words

20 seconds = 40 words

30 seconds = 80 words

60 seconds = 120 words

Whether a PSA is being prepared for radio or television, the "who, what, when, where" questions still apply. The same timing in the length of a PSA applies both to radio and television, but television gives the opportunity to appeal to both ear and eye. Consultation with television professionals is necessary to determine the type, size, and quality of visual materials that are best to use.

Talk show   One of the popular formats used in radio and television today is the talk show. The approach to this particular type of programming is usually a question and answer format. This type of format usually offers an opportunity for a more lengthy promotion of a given idea/service than a traditional PSA. It is also more casual in its approach. Generally speaking, these talk shows follow a given format. The person being interviewed is not given a script or set of prepared questions. He or she is interviewed spontaneously—although the producer or script person may ask for some background information prior to the show from which they may formulate various questions. Because of the spontaneity of the interview, it is vital for the leisure service professional to keep in mind the points he or she wants to make, so that the discussion does not wander too far afield. The professional should attempt to guide questions that are off the subject back to those items he or she is interested in promoting. The most important thing to remember when involved in a radio or television interview is to be yourself—avoid artificial posturing.

Television/radio news releases   News or radio releases can be designed for the community calendar-type format (strictly program/service information), or they can be intended for release as news items (e.g., to appear on the 5 P.M. news, with other information such as park board decisions). News releases to television and radio should be distinctive and should not merely duplicate corresponding releases to the newspaper.

Public Speaking

One of the most effective ways to promote a program is through public speaking appearances. The only cost involved (at least in terms of local speaking) is transportation and time. How important is effective speaking by professional staff members to an organization? The individual who has the ability (innate or developed) to present himself or herself well in a public speaking situation will also reflect well on his or her organization. He or she is adding a personal touch to communications with various individuals, organizations, and groups. Often newspapers cover such speeches and further publicize the organization and its efforts. However, the professional who does not have a gift for public speaking and whose presentations are likely to be weak, ineffectual, and boring will not serve the interests of his or her organization by inflicting himself or herself upon community groups.

What elements will a good speaker attempt to incorporate in his or her speech? Essentially a good speaker should enlighten, inform, and entertain the audience. In order to accomplish this, the speaker must first have a message that he or she wishes to convey. In other words, there must be a purpose to the speech. It is also vital that the speaker be in tune with his or her other audience not only in terms of topic, but also in his or her method of presentation. Another important factor to consider is the length of the speech. All people have a limited attention span, and the leisure professional should take this into consideration when determining the length of a speech.

One can view the actual presentation of a speech as ranging from a spontaneous delivery to one that is read from a manuscript. Ideally, the speaker wants to give the appearance of speaking extemporaneously—in other words, appearing as though he or she is communicating conversationally with the audience. Whether in a room of fifteen or 500 people, a speaker who is using the extemporaneous approach will appear as though he or she is speaking individually to each person in the audience. Whether or not the speaker is using a microphone, he or she must ensure that his or her voice can be clearly understood by those present. The speaker should also put animation and changes of pace in his or her voice. And while the message may be loud enough and excellent in content, the audience will tune it out if it is delivered in a dull monotone.

The speaker may enhance his or her speech with various materials such as a slide presentation, transparencies, flip charts, graphs, and photographs. These can be a valuable asset to any presentation, but the speaker should not attempt to hide behind such technology—they should complement the presentation, and not vice versa.

Using the Telephone

The leisure service professional often does not consider use of the telephone (telemarketing) to promote a program—probably with good reason. First, time is money and it can take a good deal of time to contact a large number of individuals by telephone. Organizational personnel would have to be paid for the time and effort involved in this type of promotion. Second, generally speaking, people do not like telephone solicitation. Consequently, such an approach not only might have limited effectiveness but also might actually engender hostility toward the leisure service organization. However, when used correctly and appropriately in terms of the situation involved, it is one of the most direct, personal, and effective tools of promotion.

When is it correct to use telephone solicitation? It is appropriate to contact individuals already involved in activities of the organization. Phone use can be simply a form of encouragement or a reminder to individuals who have prior knowledge of activities. For example, phone use is appropriate when the organization is attempting to contact members of a league, club, youth drop-in center, or senior citizens center concerning a special activity or an upcoming trip.

Once the decision has been made to use the telephone to contact individuals, certain telephone courtesy and protocol should be employed. The caller should begin his or her conversation by personally addressing the individual by name, then identifying himself or herself by name, title, and organizational affiliation. The caller should then describe the program or service involved in terms of location, date, time,

and activities that will occur. The benefits of participation should also be covered in a subtle way (e.g., "your presence would be greatly appreciated"). Needless to say, the caller should be very courteous—speaking politely, in a calm, inviting tone of voice. Although the caller may be very enthusiastic about his or her program or service, an ebullient approach can appear overbearing; it has been shown that the calm informative approach is more effective in phone promotion.

Another type of telephone-related service that leisure service organizations can provide is information/facilitation. A customer seeking information may use the telephone as a resource to obtain knowledge concerning programs, services, current activities, and facility locations. Whether an individual is calling the leisure service organization for specific or more general information, it is obviously an excellent way to promote the agency's services. Whether an organization formally addresses the need to provide information over the telephone (via the establishment of an information line) or whether telephone information dissemination occurs on an ad hoc basis, it is important that staff members be schooled in the appropriate use of the telephone.

It is not unusual for organizations to take or give information using taped messages. Use of such devices can extend an organization's resources and services to people, especially after regular working hours. However, answering machines offend some individuals by their impersonal quality. Nevertheless, a service providing information on an organization's current activities—including special events, facility hours, rates of programs, and especially information that may fluctuate daily (such as the ice safety factor of park ponds)—is indeed valuable.

Films and Slide Presentations

One of the most effective means of promoting a program is the use of visual aids. Videotapes and slides can be used as visual aids to complement other promotional efforts (e.g., a display or exhibit), or they can stand by themselves. Professionals, when appearing before civic groups or service clubs often use a slide presentation in conjunction with their verbal presentation. This enables the audience to visualize the topics, concepts, programs, and services that the professional is promoting.

Obviously, organizations will want to consider the production of their own videotape and slide presentations. However, there are opportunities open to the professional to use visual aids (available on a rental or purchase basis) that have been prepared by various national organizations.

The production of either a video or a slide presentation involves basically the same steps. The first step in the process is to identify the subject matter. What is the story that is to be told? Does the topic concern the organization's entire line of services? Is the organization attempting to promote just one aspect of its services (such as its aquatic program)? Is the organization putting together a presentation in support of an idea or concept, such as ecology? Another step in the process of production is the preparation of a script. Essentially, this involves the specific content of the story, the organization of the content, the narration, and so on. The script should be in tune with the visual presentation, it should be logical, and it should attempt to hold the attention of the audience throughout the entire presentation.

The actual videotaping or photographing of slides should be a representative and accurate portrayal of the subject matter to be covered. One does not have to shoot the video in sequence order; scenes that are geographically similar might be photographed at the same time. A video may be shot over a fairly short period of time; for a slide presentation, however, the organization may take slides throughout the year. It is necessary to accumulate a much larger number of slides than will actually be used, so that there are sufficient slides from which to make the best selections. Once the photographic work has been completed, the video must be edited and put together in an effective manner. This involves the selection of scenes—slides that best tell the story or convey the concept one is attempting to promote. If appropriate, music might also be included as a part of the finished presentation. Slide presentations have been effectively shown with accompanying music only and without narration of any kind.

Summary

In this chapter, the various channels for promoting recreation and leisure service programs have been discussed. Promotion involves the ability of the organization to communicate effectively with those it intends to serve. Communicating involves a two-way processing of information—with the leisure service organization (the communicator) providing a message through various channels of distribution to an audience or target population. This process attempts to persuade and stimulate the prospective customer into action (participation in programs/services) that will meet his or her individual needs.

Five basic channels of communication are used to distribute information—advertising, publicity, sales promotion, personal selling, and public relations. Advertising is a paid message distributed primarily through the mass media in what may sometimes appear to be an impersonal way. Publicity can be thought of as free media coverage generated by a leisure service organization—it is the news that an agency generates. Sales promotion is a way of creating interest in a program/service by employing special promotional techniques (such as sampling, use of coupons, contests, and demonstrations). Making direct, face-to-face contact with an individual is termed personal selling. Finally, public relations is a management function directed toward the cultivation of goodwill between an agency and the public it serves. There are numerous tools that an organization can employ within the five channels of program promotion—newspapers, brochures, fliers, newsletters, annual reports, information and press kits, postage meter messages, logos/emblems, awards and citations, novelty items, exhibits, displays, and demonstrations, stationary advertising, radio and television, public speaking, telephones, and video and slide presentations. These promotion tools, when well-developed and used effectively, can be very influential in communicating with the current and future customers of a leisure service organization.

Discussion Questions and Exercises

1. Discuss the process of communication of information in relation to the promotion of programs in leisure service organizations.

2. Define and identify five channels used by leisure service organizations to promote programs. Discuss how an agency might employ each of these methods in promoting their services.

3. Discuss and apply tools of promotion for the major channels of the program promotion process.

4. Identify the components of a press release. Write a press release describing a leisure activity for a public leisure service organization.

5. Locate a computer and graphics program and prepare a flier for a leisure service activity.

6. Describe the elements important to effective public speaking.

7. Identify the important elements involved in producing a brochure. Also identify and discuss methods of distributing them.

8. How can the use of the telephone be important in promoting a recreation and leisure service program?

9. Prepare a short public service announcement for a local television station promoting a leisure activity. Visit the television station and discuss with representatives the procedures they use in receiving and handling such requests for promotion.

10. Create a resource file of promotional activities. Collect one or more of each of the promotional tools described in the chapter.

References

Edginton, C. R. and J. G. Williams. 1978. *Productive management of leisure service organization.* New York: Wiley.

Kraus, R. G. and J. E. Curtis. 1990. *Creative management in recreation, parks, and leisure services.* 5th ed. St. Louis: Times Mirror/Mosby College Publishing.

Logan, D. 1975. "What's In a Newsletter?" *Trends.* Jan./Feb., pp. 22–25.

Nylen, D. W. 1975. Advertising. Cincinnati, OH: Southwestern. 4.

Rubright, R. and D. MacDonald. 1981. *Marketing health and human services.* Rockville, MD: Aspen Systems Corporation.

Ryan, K. F. 1988. Getting the word out to the media through news releases and news advisories. *Voluntary Action Leadership,* Summer: 18–19.

11 | Program Budgeting and Resource Attainment

Learning Objectives

1. To assist the reader in understanding the *importance of budgeting and resource attainment* in the process of leisure service programming.
2. To acquaint the reader with various *trends that have an impact on budgeting and resource attainment* in leisure service organizations.
3. To help the reader understand *how budgets and resource attainment plans assist the leisure service programmer.*
4. To assist the reader in differentiating between *cost (expenditures) and revenues.*
5. To help the reader understand the concept of budgeting and various *types of budgets.*
6. To help the reader analyze *budget worksheets* and other budget planning procedures and methods.
7. To help the reader understand the concept of resource attainment and various *strategies used to acquire resources.*

Introduction

The success or failure of many leisure service program endeavors depends on the programmer's ability to organize and implement a financial plan for the event or activity. The processes involved in financial management, although not exclusively, are generally known as budgeting. Budgeting involves the acquisition and distribution of financial resources. Central to the process of budgeting is the recording of financial transactions to ensure integrity, accuracy, and accountability. This chapter focuses on the topic of budgeting as it relates to leisure service programming. The intent here is to provide the reader with information of both a conceptual and practical nature.

Budgets should follow programs, not the reverse. This is not the case in most leisure service organizations today, however. There is a tendency for the budget to be the major controlling factor influencing the design of a program. In reality, a programmer should work to design a program of excellence and then determine appropriate methods to attain the resources that are required to support the endeavor. Many leisure service organizations are tied to the amount of financial resources that have been allocated to a program in the past. Although historical financial records can be useful as a basis for initiating program activities and/or developing new events, they should not limit the creativity, innovation, or imagination of the programmer. The secret to successfully developing a program and a financial resource base to support its implementation is to first plan the program and then develop an effective resource attainment plan to ensure that the activity or event can occur.

Drucker (1985: 185) has written that one of the major obstacles to innovation in the public sector is that most agencies are budget-based rather than results-oriented. Such an orientation reduces the probability that a leisure service organization will be innovative enough to respond to the dynamic changes that are occurring in the market place. Programmers must be flexible as

well as shrewd in developing strategies to support leisure service program endeavors. Increasingly in leisure service organizations the ability to manage financial resources is equated with individual and organizational success. Leisure service programmers who can identify and acquire key strategic financial resources will outperform their counterparts who are bound by conventional wisdom and tradition.

This chapter is organized into six major sections dealing with fiscal and other resource management issues as they relate to leisure service programs. The first section deals with the topic of trends in budgeting and resource attainment. The second section describes how a budget and resource attainment plan can assist the leisure service programmer. The next section is concerned with providing background information on cost (expenditures) and revenues. This is followed by a section which defines the concept of budgeting and identifies various budget types available to leisure service programmers. The fifth section of the chapter is concerned with the concept of the resource attainment plan. Finally, the chapter provides information concerning the pricing of leisure services.

Trends in Budgeting and Resource Attainment

Over the past several years, a number of trends and issues have emerged that have had an impact on the financing of leisure service programs. These trends and issues affect the scope and nature of the services provided by leisure service programmers. The increased complexity of environments in which leisure services are provided have placed greater demands on programmers to be responsive to fiscal operational concerns.

Several leading authors in the field have discussed some of the emerging changes in financial management that are having an impact on the provision of leisure service programs. Rossman (1989: 289) in discussing the work of programmers, has noted that they " . . . are no longer simply responsible for designing and producing program services. They must also be concerned with the cost of services and how to generate revenue for them." Crompton (1987: xi), discussing the role of individuals working in public recreation and parks, notes that the work of the professional has changed from that of being " . . . primarily concerned with the allocation of government funding to that of an entrepreneur who operates in the public sector with minimal tax support." Deppe (1983: 134) has suggested that leisure service professionals will be challenged to provide creative and imaginative leadership especially in the area of financing leisure services. He writes that organizations must be prepared to adopt appropriate strategies to deal with uncertain and changing financial conditions. Thus, as one can see, there will be a need for innovation, change, and the adoption of new strategies for leisure service programmers especially in the area of financing services.

Some of the trends that leisure service programmers are being challenged to deal with are as follows.

Agency Effectiveness, Accountability, and Responsiveness

A pervasive theme of the 1990s will be a continued focus on organizational accountability and effectiveness. Deppe (1983: 1) has suggested that leisure service organizations will have to focus their attention on fiscal economy and productivity. The desire for greater accountability has been reflected in the use of program and performance budgets over the past several decades.

Equity

The topic of equity has been referred to several times in this book. Equity issues relate to both social and economic concerns. Equity issues require leisure service programmers to make demanding and difficult decisions regarding the distribution of fiscal resources. At the heart of all equity questions are issues of societal, organizational, and individual values. This complex array of values often makes choices difficult.

Doing More with Less

It seems trite to suggest that organizations will have to do *more* with *less* today. Over the past decade, leisure service organizations have been challenged to become innovative and more entrepreneurial. Crompton (1987: xi) has written, " . . . many park and recreation managers have embraced this new role with enthusiasm."

Self-Supporting Programs

The idea of self-supporting programs is not a new one to the leisure service field. What is new is the percentage that public park and recreation agencies in particular are attempting to recover from program fees and charges. In fact, the goal of some agencies is 100 percent cost recovery. The term *target zero* refers to the attempt to produce a completely self-sustaining system and was noted in the literature as early as 1980 by Howard and Crompton in their text entitled *Financing, Managing and Marketing Recreation and Park Resources.*

Pricing Philosophy

Rossman (1989: 289) has written that " . . . pricing program services has not been systematically approached by many leisure service agencies." Pricing will affect accessibility of programs to customers as well as customers' perception of the value of the service. Pricing decisions may well be at the heart of the survival and stability of given leisure service organizations. Successful decisions will enable organizations to return value to their customers, whereas inappropriate decisions may prove to be detrimental to an organization.

Social Cost/Economic Cost

Economic costs of programs are relatively easy to calculate. Social costs are more difficult to calculate. There is a trend today in viewing fiscal practices in public leisure service organizations to link social and economic costs together. Stronger consideration in the future will be given to aligning these two variables when determining leisure services offered by a given organization.

The economic cost of one program may be higher than another, but the lack of a particular program may produce higher social costs. This will have to be calculated in making decisions about services.

Risk Management/Liability Concerns
A major factor in the financial management of leisure services is that of risk management. We live in an increasingly litigious society—people are bringing more and more lawsuits against individuals, organizations, and institutions. At the same time people are demanding more opportunities for risk in their leisure experiences. Thus, the result is that while people clamor for more risk, they also are exposing themselves and the agency providing such services with greater risk. Financial demands occur as a result of the cost of insurance or considerations for the safety of customers.

Technology
The computer is having a dramatic impact on the types and amounts of financial information that can be made available to programmers. The computer allows the storage of larger amounts of information and its quick retrieval. Financial calculations become more routine via the use of the computer, thereby enabling the programmer to react more responsibly and accurately to changes in the market place.

These trends and issues provide challenges to leisure service programmers. Further, the rate and speed of change also means that there will be many emerging trends that will have to be addressed in the coming years. There will undoubtedly be economic, political, environmental, and cultural changes that will have an impact on the delivery of leisure services and the work of programmers. Careful and thoughtful responses will be required to ensure successful leisure programs in the future.

How the Budget and Resource Attainment Plans Assist the Programmer

Budgets and resource attainment plans for leisure service activities and events are valuable tools that the leisure service programmer uses to create leisure service experiences. They can provide the leisure service programmer with systematic and analytical information that supports the program in process. Budgets provide information that enables the programmer to determine the size and scale of the endeavor and to evaluate the success of a program in terms of economic costs. Budgets and resource attainment plans also enable the leisure service programmer to link economic costs with broader program goals and objectives. In a sense the budget and resource attainment plan provide a basis for equating broader social goals with fiscal resources.

Budgets and resource attainment plans can be useful to the leisure service programmer in several ways. Some of the ways a budget and resource attainment plan assist the leisure service programmer follow.

Contributes to the Planning Process
Perhaps first and foremost, a budget and resource attainment plan enable the leisure service planner to engage in the process of planning. They enable individuals to determine how many leaders will be necessary to conduct a program; what types and numbers of supplies and materials will be required; and what other associated services such as transportation, rental fees, advertising, etc., that are often used in creating and implementing a leisure experience, will be needed. Detailing a budget requires the leisure service programmer to think about all of the resources necessary to ensure that a program is successful.

The budget requires that the resources necessary to create and implement a leisure experience are stated in financial terms. In other words, the programmer must translate the actual costs for leaders, materials, supplies, and other services into dollars and cents. This enables the programmer to understand exactly what is required to organize the program. The budget and resource attainment plan, if carefully constructed, can serve as an important pre-implementation plan, outlining detailed program requirements. The greater attention given to planning an activity or event, the greater the likelihood that it will succeed. Therefore, as one can see, the more attention given to the budget and resource attainment plan, the greater the probability that the program will be successful.

Supports the Implementation of Leisure Services

Once the budget is in place, the leisure service programmer has the fiscal resources to create a leisure experience. In other words, the budget places at the disposal of the leisure service programmer the resources necessary to "make things happen." The programmer can hire leaders, purchase supplies, and locate other resources to make the leisure experience a reality. As such, programmers working in professional positions are able to expend funds that can result in positive outcomes for participants.

Perhaps one of the most exciting parts of operating as a leisure service programmer is being given the responsibility to develop and implement a program area. With the responsibility comes the opportunity to expend as well as earn fiscal resources. This is the heart of the work of a professional. The budget and resource attainment plan are thus the cornerstone of the professional's operations. The program is the budget and the budget is the program. The program is reflected in the budget and it allows the implementation of the desired activities and events.

Provides a Reference Point for Controlling the Expenditure of Fiscal Resources

With the responsibility of developing programs and expending resources comes the responsibility to account for the use of resources. A budget serves as a reference point that allows the leisure service programmer to determine whether funds are being expended in an appropriate fashion. The budget is a benchmark. Wide variations in expenditures or unexplained deviations from budget act as a signal to the programmer that there may be problems.

By reviewing expenditures in the budget periodically the leisure service programmer is able to take corrective action. As a control mechanism the budget provides the programmer with information on the extent to which resources are being used. Further, the budget provides a measure of the extent to which resources are addressing the goals established by the programmer and the customer. By controlling the use of fiscal resources wisely, the programmer is better able to provide the customer with services of higher quality and greater value. In turn the organization benefits not only by having a satisfied customer, but also by increasing its profitability and/or extending its service capabilities.

Translates the Program Concept into Economic Reality

When a program idea is created in the mind of an individual, it is an ideal, a dream, or a vision. This idea must be translated into economic reality. Simply stated, it requires fiscal resources to produce programs. Whether the resources are taxpayer funds, user fees, entrepreneurial capital, or membership fees, or even if they occur through the volunteer efforts of others, they require the commitment of a fiscal unit that can be measured or accounted for in some way. The expression of the cost of a program in financial terms occurs through the creation and implementation of a budget. The budget is the management instrument that the leisure service organization uses to turn the ideal, concept, or vision into a tangible expression of value.

One caveat regarding the budget as a management document relates to program development. Because the budget takes the abstract and makes it real, there is a tendency for a budget to be viewed as the source of program inspiration. However, a programmer should guard against seeing only the budget as a source of inspiration. It is important to remember that inspiration, innovation, and insight come from the leisure service programmer. The budget is a tool that helps us translate what we believe can be done and present it in a document that allows for clarity, concreteness, and that defines the confines of the resources available to a leisure organization.

Establishes Program Priorities

The budget and resource attainment plan are also very useful tools in helping the leisure service programmer establish program priorities. No organization has an infinite amount of fiscal resources. All organizations are constantly challenged to make decisions concerning the use of their fiscal resources. The budget provides an avenue to compare the cost/benefit of an individual program with another one. In this way, leisure service programmers are able to make decisions and establish priorities in terms of the use of fiscal resources.

One of the important decisions made by public leisure service organizations concerning the provision of programs has to do with the concept of equity as mentioned in Chapter 1. In particular, leisure service organizations are being required to look at the types of services and programs they are providing in relation to the social/economic status of the customers. Are the services provided by such organizations being distributed equitably? Are leisure services financially accessible to all groups served by the organization equally? Should the leisure services be differentiated by income and other variables to enhance

their equitability? These questions often involve decisions made within the context of the expenditures of fiscal resources available. They often require the leisure programmer to make decisions and establish priorities based upon the values of the organization and its target audience.

Communicates Program Plans to Various Parties

Budget and resource attainment plans also can serve as important tools that the leisure service programmer can use to communicate his or her intentions. Although most people view budgets and resource attainment plans as collections of uninteresting figures and numbers, these plans can be designed in such a way as to be very appealing graphically. As such they can be used to communicate the programmer's enthusiasm and excitement for a concept or idea. A budget can also be an effective tool in demonstrating the relationship between the benefits and costs of a leisure service.

Resource attainment plans in particular often require a great deal of creativity in their preparation and presentation. They are often established to encourage a more diversified and creative way of acquiring fiscal resources. They can become important communication devices featuring the more unique and appealing parts of a leisure service experience. In a sense, such communication devices are designed with the idea of merging the ideal with the real in an appealing fashion.

Provides a Historical Record

A leisure service organization's previous budget and resource attainment plans present the programmer with a starting point for the next fiscal cycle. Past budget and resource attainment plans provide a wealth of information that can help the programmer not only examine the past, but more importantly, prepare for the future. Viewed over an extended period of time (five to ten years), budgets and resource attainment plans can help the programmer identify trends and fads. Further, such analysis can be useful in projecting future needs based on program demands versus the amount of resources historically available to a program or organization.

With the advent of computers, a considerable amount of financial data can be stored and retrieved instantaneously for comparative purposes. Further, it is possible to integrate information concerning customer needs and levels of satisfaction with financial information to determine levels of performance and excellence within an organization. Such trends can be monitored continuously, which provides a historical record of the work of an organization and the relative success of its programs. Although we live in a constantly changing environment it is important for the leisure service programmer to have a clear awareness of previous financial commitments and their relative impact.

Commits the Organization to a Course of Action

Finally, budget and resource attainment plans are a tangible reflection of the goals and aspirations of individuals and organizations. As such they represent symbolically the course of action to which the organization and individuals within it have committed themselves. Budget and resource attainment plans reflects the hopes and aspirations that individuals hold for the work of the agency. People become committed to these ends. Budget and resource attainment plans, as a reflection of these goals, serves as a rallying point for action. The budget provides direction to the work of individuals and helps them better understand their work efforts within the context of broader organizational goals.

If budget and resource attainment plans are to provide direction to leisure service programmers, there must be mechanisms in place that encourage involvement in the processes that lead to their creation. Leisure service programmers must play an active role in the creation of the budget and in the monitoring of its implementation. The best way for a leisure service manager to instill a sense of ownership in the budget process is to make sure that programmers are a part of its development. Managers must be prepared to allow leisure service programmers not only to create, but also to manage their own budgets. Leisure service programmers must become familiar with the process and be prepared to assemble, work with, and monitor their budgets and resource attainment plans.

Cost (Expenditures) and Revenues

In general, the leisure service programmer will be concerned with two elements budgetarily—cost (expenditures) and revenues. We can think of expenditures as the costs involved in running an activity. In other words, expenditures reflect those fiscal resources that are spent to create or produce the leisure experience. Revenues are often thought of as the income that can be earned or generated, or that is available to a leisure service organization.

To produce a leisure experience there are costs involved in the creation and implementation of the activity or event. We call these *expenditures* in financial management terms. All organizations expend funds for such items as personnel, materials, and supplies. In the normal course of the operation of an agency, expenditures for such elements which contribute to the creation of a given leisure experience often occur on a regular basis. These types of expenditures or costs are known as *operating costs*. Leisure service organizations also expend funds for larger projects including the development of facilities, the acquisition of equipment, and so forth. Such expenditures are known as *capital expenditures* and usually are not made on a recurring basis.

Different types of leisure service organizations will depend on different sources of revenue. For example, in voluntary (nonprofit) organizations the major source of revenue comes from membership fees, program charges, contributions, and grants. In public agencies, revenues for program services come from taxes, fees and charges, contractual fees, and other forms of assistance, such as grants and entitlements.

Commercial leisure service organizations will generate their revenue almost exclusively from fees and charges, although there are opportunities for government subsidies in the form of tax breaks and other cooperative relationships.

Cost (Expenditure)

Rossman (1989: 306) suggests that costs (expenditures) are the resources used by the agency in developing a specific program. He notes that " . . . cost includes all dollars the agency uses in producing a program regardless of the source of the dollars." In other words, cost represents the resources that the organization will use to produce the program. There are several different costs that must be considered when calculating the total cost of a program. The initial costs are known as *direct and indirect*. A brief discussion of each of these follows.

Direct cost   Direct cost refers to those *costs that must be made to produce a specific program*. Such costs are not shared with other services and are brought directly to bear on the creation of a given leisure experience. For example, to operate a day camp you must have counselors who meet on a daily basis with those children they are serving. The cost of this leadership is a direct cost associated with producing the program. Without the leaders there would be no program. Other direct costs might include expenditures made for arts and crafts supplies, swimming pool rental, and transportation.

Indirect cost   Indirect cost can be thought of as those *services that are provided or exist within the organization that cannot be directly traced to a specific program*. As Rossman (1989) has written, " . . . indirect costs are those that the agency incurs regardless of whether or not it operates a specific program. They are created by two or more objectives and are therefore not traceable to a single cost objective." An example of an indirect cost for a leisure service organization is the expense paid for energy for a multipurpose community center housing several diverse programs. Indirect costs are also sometimes referred to as overhead costs and are charged as part of the general costs that are necessary to maintain an organization.

Calculating the total cost of a program is done by adding direct cost to indirect cost. Indirect costs are difficult to determine. Such costs are usually incurred for the services in support of direct services delivered to customers. Thus, indirect costs are calculated for such support services as clerical work, bookkeeping and accounting, and perhaps building upkeep and maintenance.

Later in the chapter, in the section on pricing, we will also refer to fixed and variable costs. Fixed costs refer to those expenditures that must be made regardless of the number of individuals participating in a given event or activity. Variable costs, on the other hand, can increase or decrease depending on the number of customers served by the event and/or the scope and size desired by the programmer. Again, these items will be discussed in more detail later in the chapter.

Revenues

Hemphill (1985: 35–36) in discussing sources of revenue for park and recreation systems, has developed an interesting taxonomy outlining various classifications of revenue. He suggests that *there are four separate classifications of revenue that may be found in leisure service organizations—compulsory resources, earned income, contractual receipts, and financial assistance.* The first classification, *compulsory resources,* refers to those cash and non-cash revenues that occur, according to Hemphill, as a result of the taxing and regulatory powers of a government agency. According to Deppe (1983), property tax, although a declining percentage of local revenues, accounts for one-third of the revenue collected by local governments.

The next category in Hemphill's classification system is earned income. *Earned income* refers to those cash revenues that are realized through fees and charges. Obviously, this is a very important category of income for leisure service organizations. It is not unusual for some fee and/or charge to be assessed for nearly every program activity and event operated by a given leisure service organization. It is the major course of revenue for programming leisure services. The most comprehensive classification system for *fees and charges* in the park and recreation field has been developed by Hines (1974: 101–103). He suggests that fees and charges may be classified as follows:

1. *Entrance Fees*—Fees charged to enter a large park, botanical garden, zoological garden, or other developed recreational area. The areas are usually well defined but are not necessarily enclosed. The entrance is the patron's first contact with the park. It may contain additional facilities or activities for which fees are charged.

2. *Admission Fees*—Charges made to enter a building, structure, or natural chamber are designated as admission fees. These locations usually offer an exhibit, show, ceremony, performance, demonstration, or special equipment. Entry and exit are normally controlled and attendance is regulated.

3. *Rental Fees*—A payment made for the privilege of exclusive use of tangible property of any kind is considered a rental fee. This fee gives the patron the right to enjoy all the advantages derived from the use of the property without consuming, destroying, or injuring it in any way. [Hennepin, Minnesota, Parks advertises its equipment, rental fees, and group services in a brochure (see Figure 11.1).]

4. *User Fees*—When a charge is made for the use of a facility, participation in an activity, or as a fare for controlled ride, it is referred to as a user fee. The patron usually enjoys the privilege simultaneously with others. It is not the exclusive right as in the case of the rental fee.

5. *Sales Revenues*—All revenue obtained from the operation of stores, concessions, restaurants, etc., and from the sale of merchandise or other property is included in this category. Unconditional ownership of the item must pass from the seller to the buyer with each sale.

6. *License and Permit Fees*—License and permit will be considered synonymous. A license is a written acknowledgment of consent to do some lawful thing without command; it grants a liberty or privilege and professes to tolerate all legal actions. It usually involves permission to perform an action. It seldom grants authority to occupy space or use property.

7. *Special Service Fees*—The charges made for extraordinary articles, commodities or services, or accommodation to the public are considered special service fees. Such accomodations must be unusual in character and are not normally considered a required governmental service.

The next classification in Hemphill's taxonomy is known as *contractual receipts*. Contractual receipts are cash revenues that accrue as a result of legal agreements between a park and recreation agency and other parties. Public/private ventures are an increasingly important

Figure 11.1 Equipment, Rental Fees & Group Services. (Hennepin (Minnesota) Parks.)

GIFT CATALOG

A guide to
community
giving

An opportunity to

Give A Gift
That Keeps Giving

City of Indianola

Parks & Recreation
Department
P.O. Box 299
Indianola, Iowa 50125

Figure 11.2   Gift Catalog. (Parks &
Recreation Department, Indianola, Iowa.)

way of creating mutually beneficial ways of
building cash revenues for both parties. Wesemann (1981) has written that contracting is valuable because it provides opportunities for
producing a specified output at a preagreed
price. In this way, the contractor bears the
burden of producing the service at a fixed cost
and the organization can benefit by maximizing
its revenue generation.

An example of a contracted service enhancing
the revenue position of an organization is the relationship that has been established between the
University of Northern Iowa and the United
States Army. The U.S. Army has contracted with
the University of Northern Iowa for a variety of
services for youth. A predetermined fixed price
is set between the University and the Army. The
Army in turn is free to establish a fee and charge
structure to recover costs as well as to produce
profit for the Morale, Welfare, and Recreation
Service Organization. The extensive line of youth
services under the trademark name of *Camp Adventure* ™ have provided a series of dynamic and
innovative youth services. The major benefit of
the program to the U.S. armed forces has been
access to highly qualified professionally trained
staff members and a program design that can be
implemented with great consistency and effectiveness at a variety of locations.

The last category established by Hemphill is
that of programs of *financial assistance*. The financial assistance category can be thought of as
external funds that come from grant sources, entitlements, donations, or other resources. An example of a gift catalog from the Parks and
Recreation Department, City of Indianola, Iowa,
is found in Figure 11.2. This gift catalog outlines
a variety of different suggestions for donations
or gifts that can benefit the park and recreation
system and in turn to citizens of this community.
Some of the suggestions made in the catalog include contributions that can be made to parks
(shelters, play equipment, trees, etc.), swimming

pools, the senior citizen center, the arts and crafts center, a softball complex, and to recreation equipment in general.

What is a Budget?

A budget can be thought of as a financial plan. It is a way of estimating the types and amounts of financial resources needed to implement a program for a specific period of time. Deppe (1983: 40) has written that "a budget is a plan for financing and conducting a program or service for a given period of time—usually a year." Edginton and Williams (1978: 280) have said that "a budget provides information as to what resources the organization will acquire and how they will be acquired, how these resources will be spent, and what services will result." Thus, a budget helps identify the events and activities the leisure service organization wishes to provide and helps state them in financial terms.

The process of budgeting is tied closely to program planning. As Wildavsky (1974: 2) writes, " . . . a budget may be characterized as a series of goals with price tags attached." A budget helps the leisure service programmer project future program needs and state them in financial terms. Thus, a budget helps the programmer think ahead and, in fact, develop a blueprint for his or her work in the future. A budget should serve the leisure service programmer. The budget should not drive the program, but rather the program should drive the budget.

Most, if not all, leisure service programmers are required to engage in the budgeting process. Although it is not unusual for a programmer to spend a large block of time developing a budget at one time of the year, budgeting should be viewed as an ongoing, continuous process. Most programmers will be responsible for developing a portion of their organization's budget. These budgetary plans, when integrated with ones from other programmers within the organization, will constitute the beginning of the development of an agency-wide budget. The work of a programmer in this stage of the process of budgeting requires an analysis of the services to be offered and the development of estimates of financial expenditures as well as potential revenues.

As mentioned, budgeting should also be viewed as an ongoing process. The programmer is not only responsible for the initial expenditures and revenues, but also will often be asked to monitor the extent to which these are realized. In other words, the programmer is given the responsibility of making sure that once a budget has been approved the expenditure of funds does not exceed the authorized amount. Further, the leisure service programmer will be charged with carefully monitoring the amount of revenues generated by a program to ensure that they are satisfactory. Leisure service programmers today are being challenged to ensure that expenditures are made at appropriate levels and that desired levels of revenues are produced. Many programs are self-supporting; that is, the programmer is responsible for generating enough revenue to cover the cost of a program.

Edginton and Williams (1978: 281) have also noted that the budget process may seem " . . . overwhelming, mysterious and complex. . . ." Certainly this may be the case for the novice leisure service programmer. However, with experience, the budgeting process can become simplified and can be viewed as a supportive programming aid. Again, as Edginton and Williams (1978) note, budgeting need not be complicated or complex. A well-organized budgeting system can be extremely important to the successful operation of any leisure program. The budget, in many respects, is a part of the program development program formula. It enables the programmer to express, in financial terms, the elements necessary to create the leisure event or activity.

Budget Types

Leisure service programmers will be exposed to a variety of types of budgets. Although there may be some standardization from agency to agency concerning the types of budgets found, (state regulatory laws often require local governments to follow a prescribed set of procedures) in general each individual leisure service organization will develop a unique set of internal budget procedures that will be followed. From a more global perspective, the types of budgets used by organizations have evolved over the last hundred years. This is especially the case in government, which will be the major focus of our discussion in this section. As the need for more diverse types of information has emerged over the past several decades, there has been an evolution in the sophistication of budgets.

When the concept of budgeting was first introduced the main concern was for improving control of funds. The creation of budgeting systems was basically a product of social reform that occurred during the Progressive Era. As complex organizations grew in government, voluntary, and commercial sectors, there was a need to provide more precise information, as well as to insure that fiscal operations were handled with integrity. Discussing the development of budgeting, Deppe (1983) has written that budgeting is primarily a twentieth-century innovation. He notes:

> It was not until 1906 that New York City, under the auspices of the newly established Bureau of Muncipal Research, organized a budgeting system that was designed around using an object of expenditure system for budgeting and accounting control. This began the so-called "traditional object of expenditure" type of budget which is still used by cities today. The idea of establishing a budget system spread rapidly to other cities, especially large ones, and by the mid-1920s most cities had adopted budgetary methods (Deppe 1983: 41).

The budget innovations that occurred in the early 1900s set the ground work for a host of innovations that were to occur over the next several decades. In more recent years, there has been attention focused on the development of budgets that link program activities and their resulting outcome with expenditures. A whole host of budget types and systems have been developed, including performance budgeting (late 1940s); program budgeting (1950s); Planning Program Budgeting System (1960s); and Zero Base Budget (1970s). Each of these types of budgeting systems is found in use in the United States and Canada in leisure service organizations. The programmer will be served well by having a firm understanding of the particulars of the philosophy and concepts of budgeting used by the organization within which he or she is employed. The following section provides a brief overview of budget types associated with leisure service organizations including *line-item, program, performance, PPBS,* and *zero-based budgeting.*

Line-item budget   This approach to budgeting is also known as object classification budgeting. It was developed in the early 1900s as a way of correcting problems that were associated with the mismanagement of funds in government. Prior to that time, the standard process was to pool all funds into one central account. Obviously, it was difficult to determine how funds were being spent. Thus, the line-item enabled professionals to identify the "object of the expenditure" and the cost for each object (Deppe 1983: 41). Slightly over half of the public recreation organizations in the United States report using this approach to budgeting (Schroth 1978).

The line-item approach to budgeting involves *identifying the cost of a particular function and then associating it with a budget classification.* In other words, a number of classifications, within the budget, and then the costs for these activities, are associated with these categories in a standard, systematic, and consistent fashion. Over the years, the line-item approach to budgeting has evolved to include a number of specific standardized categories. These are as follows:

Personnel Services—This classification includes the direct labor of individuals who are employed within the organization on either a regular or temporary basis and are paid on either an hourly wage basis or a fixed salary.

Contractual Services—This classification includes those services that are performed under an expressed or implied contract. The contractual arrangements of a leisure service organization range from postage, telephone, printing, and repairs, to the cost of heat, light, and power. A contractual arrangement between a leisure service agency and another organization would not only involve the use of that organization's equipment, but also the personnel necessary to implement said service.

Supplies—Supplies are commodities that are entirely consumed or show rapid depreciation in a short period of time. Examples would be fuel, office supplies, cleaning supplies, and turf-care products.

Materials—Materials are commodities that have a more permanent and lasting quality than supplies. They may include such things as materials used in construction and sports equipment.

Current Charges—This type of expenditure includes the cost of clothing allowances, insurance, rental of typewriters, dues, and any other charges that are contracted at the option of the organization.

Current Obligations—These consist of fixed charges that have resulted from previous financial transactions entered into by the organization. For example, the payment of the organization's share of social security (United States) or social insurance (Canada) and its contribution to its retirement or pension program would be in this classification. Also included may be the cost of interest on the organization's debts, which may result from borrowing money for capital improvements.

Properties—This classification includes the cost of improvements that are made to an organization's physical resources. It also includes the direct purchase cost of any new equipment or other physical resources; in other words, anything that is appreciable and has a calculated period of usefulness. This might include such things as playground equipment, machinery, office equipment, the cost of real estate, and any improvements made to existing properties.

Debt Payment—Debt payments may be distinguished from current obligations in that debt payments refer to the organization's payments on the principle of a given debt, rather than the interest (Edginton and Williams 1978: 302–303).

The line-item approach to budgeting is often combined with other types of budgets. The advantages of such a system are that it provides additional ways of producing financial information. Because the line-item approach to budgeting is so widespread, combining it with other types of budgets offers the programmer the opportunity for comparison and standardization. This can be useful when determining the relative cost of one program compared to another.

The drawbacks of using the line-item budget are that it does not link cost with performance measures and precludes the possibility of clustering all of the costs associated with producing a specifically identified event or activity. In other words, there may be costs that are involved in producing a given activity, but the object classification system prevents the clustering of these costs. Thus there is no way of formally determining the total cost of the program within the budget structure itself. Despite these disadvantages, the line-item approach to budgeting is a very important and often-used budgetary tool in leisure service organizations today.

Program budgets   Program budgets are a way of clustering together all associated costs for a given event, activity, or facility. A program budget is *a way of clustering all of the costs that are necessary* *for the creation of a program.* Again, Deppe (1983: 42) writes " . . . where object of expenditure budgets identified only the over-all agency, program budgets emphasize the programs and services offered by the agency." The program approach to budgeting allows for a recasting of the traditional line-item budget into specific programs and services. In this way, it is possible for a comparative analysis of the costs and perhaps benefits associated between programs.

A key to this approach to programming is the establishment of program decision-making packages. A program decision-making package can be thought of as a budgetary unit wherein the total of all the associated costs of that element are identified with that package. In other words, a program decision-making package would include the costs associated with personnel, contractual services, supplies, materials, current charges, current obligations, properties, and debt payment that are necessary to implement a given activity. Thus, each program decision-making package can be compared in terms of total costs with other ones.

An important part of program budgeting is the analysis and comparison of program decision-making packages. Much of the decision making that takes place concerning program packages will probably occur at management levels. However, there is a strong trend in leisure service organizations to encourage the participation of employees in the decision-making process. In developing and presenting program decision-making packages, programmers will want to keep in mind some basic questions regarding the factors that may influence how their ideas are evaluated.

In general terms, some of these questions are as follows:

1. What are the goals and objectives of this leisure service organization?
2. What leisure service programs are available and/or need to be created to move toward these goals and objectives?

3. What will each of these leisure service programs cost in human and material resources and what will each contribute toward accomplishing the desired goals and objectives?
4. Which of these leisure service programs should be implemented and to what extent?
5. Do we have a feasible plan for implementing them?
6. Can we evaluate at appropriate times the relationship between the proposed and actual accomplishments? (adapted from Feldman, 1973)

As one can see, these steps to developing and evaluating program decision-making packages create an opportunity for a more integrated approach to programming. Budgets can be established in light of organization goals and objectives and programs to be offered. The programs can be compared with one another to determine whether or not they are effective at fulfilling the goals of the organization and as a result meeting real needs. Program budgeting in a sense simplifies the process of budgeting as it enables the programmer to review his or her work (including the budgets that they may propose) in light of the work of the entire organization. This approach to budgeting enables the programmer to understand more specifically how their efforts contribute to the overall achievement of the organization's goals and objectives.

Performance budgeting Performance budgeting *attempts to link the amount of resources that are consumed in producing a program with its output.* The development of this approach to budgeting is a natural evolution of the need for more information for decision-making purposes. It stands to reason that leisure service programmers have the need to know what kind of impact their efforts have on those they are serving, and in turn, whether or not the investment of resources is an effective one.

The heart of performance budgeting is the identification of performance indicators. Performance indicators are the mechanism used by a leisure service organization to identify and measure its output. Howard and Crompton (1980: 284) have written that there are three types of performing indicators—workload measures, efficiency measures, and effectiveness measures. These approaches to measuring performance can be defined as follows:

1. *Workload Measures*—Workload measures refer to the volume of work that is being completed. A workload measure asks the question "how much is being completed?" In other words, workload measures focus on such questions as "How many hours of service activity are being provided?", "How many individuals are being served?", and so on.
2. *Efficiency Measures*—Efficiency measures refer to how well the resources of the organization are being consumed. Such measures are usually stated as a ratio of the amount of the resources invested and the amount of output produced. So, for example, the leisure service programmer might calculate the total number of hours available in a program and divide it by the program cost. This will provide a measure of the service per hour. This could also be calculated on the basis of individual participation and measure the cost of participation for each hour of involvement by each participant.
3. *Effectiveness Measures*—Effectiveness measures refer to the extent to which a program achieves its stated goals and objectives. A program might have skill attainment as its primary goal. Effectiveness measures would then focus on measuring the degree to which an individual has attained the skill. Effectiveness measures also are often concerned with customer satisfaction.

Performance budgets are often used in conjunction with line-item budgets. The information derived from budget analysis can be very useful to programmers in determining the relative impact of their efforts. Such knowledge can help guide the programmer in making recommendations and decisions about the types of services to be offered. The most important factor concerning program budgeting is that it provides a mechanism for leisure service programmers to think about the benefits that they are trying to produce.

Planning, programming, budgeting system (PPBS) budgets This approach to budgeting was developed in the 1960s in the U.S. Department of Defense. PPBS was later applied in a widespread fashion throughout the federal government. It has been employed as a budgeting system by many organizations and agencies, although today it is applied in a more conceptual sense. *The PPBS budget process focuses on the establishment of goals and objectives, long-range planning, and evaluation.* Deppe (1983: 43) has written that the PPBS system does the following:

1. Identifies overall system-wide goals and objectives and relates programs and services to those goals.
2. Places emphasis on long-range planning where the costs and scope of programs and services are projected over a period of time—generally five years.
3. Requires a systematic analysis of alternatives, as well as an evaluation of programs to determine those programs that best meet objectives.

How does PPBS work? The PPBS approach to budgeting is essentially a performance-oriented process. It attempts to link the goals and objectives of an organization with results. In order for this to occur, results must be quantified in some fashion, and further there must be a way of measuring the outputs of the program. Usually this involves the establishment of evaluative criteria or standards to measure acceptable levels of performance. Another feature of the PPBS process is that it attempts to provide information and control to individuals who are at the level of program production. In other words, not only does PPBS provide the programmer with fiscal resources, but all other resources to implement the program. This approach to budgeting requires that the programmer develop not only a financial plan but also a program statement detailing the extent to which that service meets the goals and objectives of the organization.

Zero-based budgeting First developed in private industry in the late 1960s and then adapted to government in the early 1970s, *zero-based budgeting forces an organization to rejustify its expenditures on a year-to-year basis.* It is not unusual in any organization for funds to be committed to a program or service year in and year out without considering whether or not that activity or event is actually meeting the needs of those it is intended to serve.

Zero-based budgeting asks the programmer to focus on two primary concerns. The first is to ask the question "Are current activities being implemented in an efficient manner?" The second question is to ask the programmer to consider "which current activities could be eliminated, or reduced, in order to support the development of other newer activities which might have greater potential of meeting customer needs." These two questions form the basis of the conceptual strategy used to implement the zero-based budgeting concept. They ask "Are we doing things well?" and "Can some of our activities be changed or eliminated in order to produce more efficient outcomes?"

Zero-based budgeting involves four basic steps. They are as follows:

1. *Establish Program Decision-Making Packages*—The establishment of program decision-making packages involves the identification of activities to be provided. Program decision-making packages can be built around a set of functions, facilities, or events. They might include the purpose of the activity, the costs and benefits, and the program's performance measures.
2. *Analyze Program Decision-Making Packages*—The next step in the process involves the evaluation

and rating of each program decision-making package for the purpose of funding. Basically the task here is to determine which of the program decision-making packages best meets the goals and decisions of the organization. In the case of similar programs the question would be which program package meets the needs of the organization in the most efficient way possible.
3. *Evaluate and Rank Program Decision-Making Packages*—This is the actual decision-making process. Once all of the analytical information has been presented and reviewed, decisions must be made as to which packages are to be funded. These are placed in rank order to create the priority system. The most important programs would be funded initially followed by those of lesser priority.
4. *Prepare a Financial Plan*—The last step in the process is the establishment of a budget for the programs identified within the process. This budget can then be reviewed by decision makers at other levels in order to determine how much money should be made available in order to implement proposed programs.

The zero-based approach to budgeting is a useful tool. It provides an opportunity for yearly evaluation and review of activities. It forces the programmer to rethink existing services and rejustify these in light of the goals (which may change) and available resources (which may also change). Conceptually, zero-based budgeting may be one of the most powerful tools available to programmers to help them stay current and up-to-date. Practically, it may require greater amounts of energy and time in preparing budgeting information, especially as it relates to establishing performance measures.

Budget Worksheets

Most leisure service organizations have developed a system that is used by programmers to provide financial information concerning activities and events. It is usually referred to as a "budget worksheet." The budget worksheet is prepared in conjunction with the "program information worksheet" as described in Chapter 9. The purpose of these two documents is to provide both program and financial information for decision-making purposes in a concise standardized fashion. The program worksheet, as previously mentioned, will often contain information about the objectives of the program, times, dates, and location. From this information, financial estimates can be prepared. *The purpose of the budget worksheet is to help the leisure service programmer project financial estimates.*

The budget worksheet is prepared with a great deal of attention to detail. Detailed consideration must be given to every aspect involved in the construction of the program. There will be financial costs associated with almost every aspect of the program. Leaders must be paid, supplies must be purchased, publicity must be developed, and other costs, such as those associated with transportation, postage, and rentals must be accounted for on the budget worksheet. Using a budget worksheet allows the programmer to identify in a systematic fashion those costs associated with the elements identified as necessary to creating a leisure experience.

What would be found on a budget worksheet? In general, *budget worksheets present three types of information—a description of the program, cost estimates, and potential revenues.* First, they provide a description of the program. In other words, budget worksheets provide the decision makers with an overview of the leisure event or activity. Often budget worksheets will detail who the program serves, location, dates, times, and a brief description of the content of the program. Second, a budget worksheet will present information concerning cost estimates. Cost estimates or expenditures will vary, but in general will be concerned with the cost of personnel, supplies and materials, and other miscellaneous expenses. Finally, budget worksheets provide information concerning potential revenues to be earned from the program. This might include revenue generated from fees, the sale of supplies and materials, and other sources.

Figure 11.3 presents a budget worksheet used by the Juneau, Alaska, Parks and Recreation Department. This budget worksheet is an excellent example of a document that has been created to detail the various items related to the financial management of an event or activity. The programmer is required to provide detailed information concerning: (1) the event or activity including its name, dates, times, locations, fees and ages; (2) the income to be generated from the event or activity (including the number of individuals registering, fees to be charged, and other income); and (3) the expenses (including salaries, benefits, manpower pool, travel expenses, mileage, telephone, printing, advertising, rentals, repairs, contractual services, office supplies, postage, materials, refunds, and miscellaneous items. The budget worksheet is also set up in such a way that the programmer may calculate the total revenue and the total expenses. The difference between these two budgetary items (total revenue minus expenses) provides information concerning the net income of the event or activity. As one can see from viewing the budget worksheet from the Juneau Parks and Recreation Department, net income can be calculated either positively or negatively.

The Juneau Parks and Recreation Department worksheet has an additional interesting feature. The flip side of the worksheet is a program information sheet. Thus, the programmers working in this agency are able to integrate program detail with budget information very easily. Obviously, this adds an element of convenience to programmers working in this agency and promotes greater working efficiency. Further, by having both budget and program information on a single form, it reduces the possibility of losing information or having to scramble for two or three different sheets of paper for information.

JUNEAU PARKS AND RECREATION
EVENT BUDGET SHEET

EVENT _____   LOCATION(S) _____

DATE(S) _____   FEE(S) _____

TIME(S) _____   AGE(S) _____

TOTAL INCOME:

    Registrations _____ x _____   = $_____
    Other   (fees) $_____
    Miscellaneous $_____

    Total Revenue $_____

EXPENSES:

		BUDGET	ACTUAL
110	Salaries – Regular	_____	_____
120	Benefits	_____	_____
140	Manpower Pool	_____	_____
200	Travel Expenses	_____	_____
201	Mileage	_____	_____
310	Telephone	_____	_____
320	Printing	_____	_____
	Advertising	_____	_____
330	Rentals	_____	_____
340	Repairs	_____	_____
390	Contractual Services	_____	_____
480	Office Supplies	_____	_____
481	Postage and Parcel Post	_____	_____
490	Materials and Commodities	_____	_____
		_____	_____
		_____	_____
	Refunds	_____	_____
	Miscellaneous	_____	_____

    Total Expenses $_____

Net Income $ ± _____

Prepared by: _____   Approved by: _____

Figure 11.3 Budget Worksheet. (Juneau (Alaska) Parks & Recreation.)

JUNEAU PARKS AND RECREATION
PROGRAM INFORMATION

I.   PROGRAM/EVENT

Title: _____

Supervisor: _____

II. ELIGIBILITY

Who: _____

III. REGISTRATION

Date: _____

Location: _____

Fee: _____ /team _____ /participant

Maximum Number of Teams _____ or Participants _____

IV. SCHEDULING

Game Days: _____

Game Times: _____

Game Locations: _____

Practice Begins: _____

League Games Begin: _____

Game Schedules Available: _____

V.   COMMENTS

_____

_____

_____

VI. ADDITIONAL INFORMATION

Please attach time line if applicable, including news releases, rule
revisions, registration information, agenda for meetings or clinics, etc.
Be sure to fill in the budget on the back of this form.

Figure 11.3   (continued)

Having program and budget details consolidated on one document is also valuable to managers and others reviewing such information. Managers like to have information presented in a clear, concise, and direct fashion.

Another example of the budget worksheet is found in Figure 11.4. This example was developed by the Grand Junction, Colorado, Parks and Recreation Department. This form is structured following the description of budget worksheets discussed above. It requests that the programmer completing the worksheet provide information concerning: (1) the event or activity (located at the top and bottom of the form); (2) the estimated expenditures (identified as salaries, supplies, other services/charges, and operating capital); and (3) information on the revenue, cost, and net income stated, negatively or positively, of the program. This form also presents financial information from previous years for comparative purposes. In addition, it requires the programmer to identify and list various account numbers used by this department's accounting system.

The budget worksheet is an important tool for the leisure service programmer. It often requires investigative work; that is, the programmer must call businesses or consult trade catalogs to determine the costs of supplies, equipment, and materials. It requires that the programmer understand the organization of the program, event, or activity to be offered in terms of required leadership, facility needs, or other factors that contribute to the success of a program. Creating an idea for a program is the imaginative, inspirational, and innovative part of the work of the programmer. Creating the budget detail for an event or service is the analytical portion of programming. The two cannot be separated. Excellent programmers are not only those individuals who can envision a creative program idea, but also those who can actually organize the event or activity. Developing the budget material to implement a budget program is an important part of the planning process in which successful leisure programmers engage.

Resource Attainment Plan

What is a resource attainment plan? In order to plan, organize and implement a leisure service experience, a variety of resources are required. When we discuss budgeting we are referring primarily to fiscal resources. However, the programmer must be concerned with not only fiscal resources, but other types of resources that have an impact on the creation of an event or activity. Thus, a resource attainment plan identifies in a broader sense the resources necessary for program development and implementation. We can think of a resource attainment plan as a *process directed toward the identification and procurement of resources other than those found in the budget*.

Edginton and Williams (1978: 305–306) have written that it is essential that organizations " . . . allocate not only fiscal resources, but all resources within the jurisdiction of the organization . . . [that are necessary for program development] . . . These include equipment, building space, work hours, inventory and all other resources that contribute to the accomplishment of goals and objectives." Thus, one can see that there are a variety of resources that can be found that are not contained within the budget proper. These resources can come from within or from without the organization. Often the leisure service programmer will be required to utilize many resources outside the budget to produce a program.

The importance of a resource attainment plan is that it focuses the attention of the leisure service programmer on all of the details related to program implementation. This allows needed resources to be presented in a framework wherein they can be systematically identified and pursued. Most of the efforts of programmers to identify needed resources outside of the budget are completed in a spontaneous rather than a systematic fashion. The development of a resource attainment plan requires the programmer to think and plan ahead regarding the types and numbers of other resources needed. More systematic thinking can create the opportunity for innovative and creative perspectives on resource attainment.

```
              GRAND JUNCTION PARKS AND RECREATION DEPARTMENT
                 RECREATION PROGRAM BUDGET WORK SHEET

PROGRAM_____

FUND_____ COST CENTER_____PROJECT_____BUDGET YEAR_____

SALARIES
CLASS TITLE       # OF STAFF   HOURLY WAGE        HOURS




                      SALARIES TOTAL_____
_____
SUPPLIES
LINE ITEM ACCT.        ITEM                        COST




                      SUPPLIES TOTAL_____
_____
OTHER SERVICES/CHARGES
LINE ITEM ACCT.        ITEM                        COST




                  SERVICES/CHARGES TOTAL_____
_____
OPERATING CAPITAL
LINE ITEM ACCT.        ITEM                        COST




                 OPERATING CAPITAL TOTAL_____
_____
                  ACTUAL     BUDGET    REVISED    REQUESTED
                   1988       1989       1989       1990
TOTAL PROGRAM
REVENUE           $_____  $_____  $_____  $_____

COST              $_____  $_____  $_____  $_____

NET               $_____  $_____  $_____  $_____
_____
PROGRAM DESCRIPTION   I.E. SESSIONS, CLASSES, PARTICIPANTS, FEES, ETC.
```

Figure 11.4 Budget Worksheet. (Grand Junction (Colorado) Parks & Recreation Department.)

One of the important features of a resource attainment plan is that it enables an organization to integrate its efforts with those of other agencies. Leisure service organizations and other agencies often work on a collaborative basis to produce programs. Many contributions are made on an in-kind basis. In other words, services are exchanged without the expenditure of fiscal resources. Often the exchange of such services reduces the charges associated with financial transactions. Locating and developing collaborative relationships often proves to be mutually beneficial to both parties.

What are the uses of a resource attainment plan? First, a resource attainment plan enables the programmer to identify the resources necessary to implement a program. This in turn presents the programmer with an opportunity to prioritize those resources which must be a part of the budget structure and those which can be obtained through alternative sources. A resource attainment plan allows for the identification of alternative sources. In this way the programmer has an "information bank" that can be tapped for both current and future use. For example, if the resource attainment plan identifies the use of volunteers to implement a program, a list of individuals willing to contribute their time, not only becomes available for current use but also for future use. Finally, a resource attainment plan enables the programmer to reconceptualize his or her resource base. The opportunity to acquire resources becomes much broader when viewed in the context of a total community, rather than just the budget of an organization.

Steps in Developing a Resource Attainment Plan

As indicated, the development of a resource attainment plan should be completed in a systematic fashion. Thoughtful attention should be given to the planning of a program and in turn the resources necessary to implement that program. It is important to remember that a budget is a finite resource but within any given community there are an infinite number of resources that can be tapped. It is not uncommon for leisure service organizations to be supported generously by the community.

Some of the steps that should be addressed in the development of a resource attainment plan are as follows:

1. Identify the goals and objectives of a specific activity.
2. Identify and define all of the human, physical, fiscal, and technological resources necessary to implement the program.
3. Determine which resources are contained within the organization's budget structure and document.
4. Determine all other resources necessary to implement the program and document.
5. Scan the environment to determine the availability of resources.
6. Coordinate with other agencies, institutions, and businesses to determine the availability of potential resources.
7. Identify which resources can be located on a short-term basis and which require more long-term procurement.
8. Develop strategies for securing resources outside the budget structure of the organization.
9. Locate resources found outside the budget structure and secure.
10. Evaluate the resource attainment plan on a periodic basis to determine its effectiveness in meeting its goals and objectives.

The development of a resource attainment plan follows the procedures used in other similar program activities. In general, the programmer first determines program detail and scans the environment to identify the resources that might be available to help in the process of program development and implementation. This is followed by actually securing of resources and then evaluating one's efforts.

Types of Alternative Resources

There are a number of alternative resources that are available to programmers. Although we cannot identify all of the categories of alternative resources, there are a number that should be considered by leisure service programmers.

Gifts and donations   A gift or donation is an outright contribution to an organization. Gifts and donations can be made for very specific items related to a particular program. It is not unusual for individuals to contribute a piece of equipment, a game, decorations, food, or other items in support of a progam. Gifts and donations can also be made in a cash form. They also do not have to be offered for any specific service. Gifts and donations can be given by an individual and/ or an organization on a nonspecific basis. That is, funds can be given and used at the discretion of the programmer to develop any portion that he or she sees fit.

In-kind contributions   As previously mentioned, in-kind contributions are those resources made available to a program by individuals and/ or organizations that require no financial transaction. Although in-kind contributions can include materials and supplies, they more than likely involve the sharing of labor, facilities, and/ or equipment. For example, a school district may work cooperatively with a leisure service organization by providing a gymnasium at no charge for a particular leisure service event or activity. The school district perceives the sharing of its gymnasium as a contribution to the community's welfare and as a support of its own effort of community service.

Sponsorship   It is commonplace among leisure service organizations to seek sponsorship for events and activities. Such sponsorships have historically been made by community service and fraternal organizations. Increasingly, businesses, especially corporations, have engaged in the sponsoring of leisure service events and programs. The Thunder Bay, Ontario, Park and Recreation Department annually seeks sponsorship of its "Summer in the Parks Concert Series" (see Figure 11.5). The series, serving over 12,000 individuals in 1989, was sponsored by CBQ–CBC Radio, Lakehead University, and the Thunder Bay Musicians Association. The City of Albany, Oregon, Parks and Recreation Department pro-

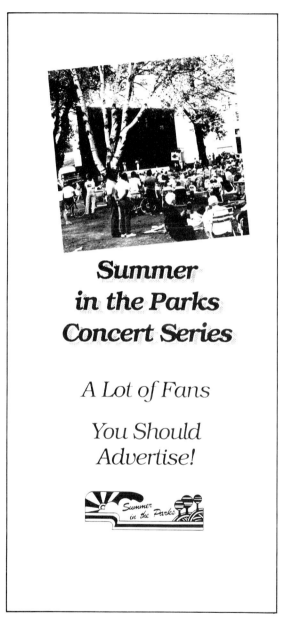

Figure 11.5   Summer in the Parks. (Thunder Bay (Ontario) Parks & Recreation.)

vides a similar type of music program. They receive corporate sponsorship from a variety of corporations such as Hewlett-Packard and Weyerhaeuser Forest Products Company.

Scrounging All programmers, to be successful, must be good at scrounging. Scrounging can be thought of as the adaptation or recycling of resources that are obtained usually gratis through some source. It involves the use of one's imagination and inventiveness to see discarded resources cast for potential use. One person's junk is another's treasure! *Camp Adventure* ™ staff members are legendary scroungers. Counselors from this program have taken discarded potato chip containers and reused them as decorated "Spirit Sticks." They have also saved the styrofoam packing from electronic components and used them for costume decorations in camp skits.

Partnerships When two or more organizations cooperate to provide a program, it can be said that they have entered into a partnership. Organizations often participate with one another sharing unique resources to produce programs that are mutually beneficial. Partnerships involve a joint sharing of human, physical, and fiscal resources. Not all partnerships are equal. In some cases, one organization may share more of its resources. Partnerships usually require a high level of trust between organizations and usually involve a strong commitment to producing a shared program of excellence.

An example of a partnership between two businesses is illustrated in Figure 11.6. In this case the Seattle Mariners Baseball Club has formed a partnership with Horizon Air to provide a package tour to a baseball game. Customers are invited to fly to Seattle to attend a Mariners baseball game; the package includes round-trip air transportation, overnight accommodations and box seats to the game. The advantages of this type of arrangement are obvious—the airlines benefit from increased travel, the hotel from increased patronage, and the Mariners are able to draw more fans to their games. Partnerships can be formed not only between commercial enterprises but also between public agencies. Further, they can be established between commercial and/or nonprofit organizations.

Volunteers Volunteers are the backbone of public and voluntary leisure service organizations. Without volunteers the programs of these organizations would be severely curtailed. The

Figure 11.6 Partnership between Seattle Mariners and Horizon Air.

recruitment, training, and recognition of volunteers requires a high level of management sophistication on the part of the programmer. Again, the Thunder Bay, Ontario, Park and Recreation Department's volunteer development program serves as an excellent resource. Their volunteer program operated in fourteen community centers equals the work of sixty-three full-time employees. This represents a value to the community conservatively estimated at $523,250. Over 570 volunteers in the Department's summer program contributed 4000 hours of time.

By no means are these the only types of alternative resources. Programmers should recognize that there are many other sources that can be tapped to help in the development and implementation of programs. The development of a resource attainment plan can provide the programmer with a systematic approach to identifying resources. The resource attainment plan provides the programmer with the opportunity to expand his or her resource base beyond the structure of a budget. In a sense the programmer is limited only by his or her imagination, individual effort, and desire to identify and locate alternative resources.

Pricing

As leisure service programmers have become increasingly responsible for generating revenues to support events and activities, the concept of pricing has become an important dimension to consider when designing the effort. In commercial leisure service organizations it is often possible for an organization not only to break even but also to generate a profit. In governmental and voluntary organizations programs are required to at minimum make back the direct cost of the event or activity. In either case, pricing has become an important dimension of the program planning process.

Rossman (1989: 307) suggests that a program price can be defined as follows: " . . . price is the dollar amount the agency charges . . . [customers] . . . to participate in a specific pro-

gram." In other words, the price is the cost that the customer must bear in order to participate in the program. The price of a program is usually stated in financial terms (dollars and cents) and is related to the demand for and value of the service. *The price that is established for a service not only reflects the costs, (both direct and indirect) of the program to the organization, but also often reflects the extent to which the service is sought by individuals.* Usually, the higher the status of the service, the greater the amount individuals are willing to pay. In other words if an individual customer values the benefits derived from a given leisure service it is possible that he or she would be willing to pay a higher amount.

A simple model can be applied to understand the concept of pricing as it relates to leisure programming. Four pricing factors are important in determining the actual price of the program or event—fixed direct, fixed indirect, variable direct, and market demand.

Direct and indirect costs were discussed earlier in this chapter. A *fixed* cost can be thought of as the amount of funds charged against a program that does not vary regardless of the number of customers participating in a given program; for example utility costs. *Variable costs* are those costs

Figure 11.7 Swimming Pool Coupon. (Lively Park Swim Center, Willamalane Park & Recreation District, Springfield (Oregon).)

that increase or decrease according to the number of customers participating in a program. *Market demand* factors are those related to the availability of similar services and the actual customer demands for those services. The assumption is that the greater the market demand for services the higher the price. Another way of looking at the market demand element is to relate it to the value that people place on the benefits derived from a leisure experience. The amount that individuals are willing to pay for a service may be a reflection of what they value. Sometimes higher-priced services are confirmation of a certain status and reflect the desire for individuals to associate themselves with a quality of program or service.

One of the strategies that leisure service organizations often use to attract consumers related to pricing is that of varying prices either to promote volume participation or to attract people to a new service. In the former case, the leisure service organization might create a family

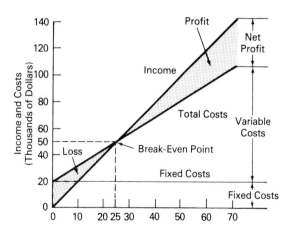

Figure 11.8 Break-Even Chart. (Weston, J. F., & Brigham, E. F. (1978). *Managerial Finance* 6th ed. Hinsdale, IL: The Dryden Press, 72.)

pass program. In the latter case, an organization might want to consider providing a free sample or low-cost fee for the first time that a person takes part in a service. Figure 11.7 presents a sample "free individual or family admission" to a Lively Park Swim Center, operated by the Willamalane Park and Recreation District, Springfield, Oregon.

Break-Even Analysis

One approach to determining the price of a program is through the use of a financial tool known as a break-even analysis. This analytical tool can be used to help the programmer to determine the point at which the revenues from an activity or event are sufficient to meet the expenditures. Bullaro and Edginton (1986: 278) have noted that a break-even analysis *calculates the point at which revenues generated from the sales of a service can meet expenses.* This provides the programmer with useful financial information to help understand the relationship of direct, indirect, fixed, and variable costs in calculating the price of a program.

Figure 11.8 presents an example of a break-even analysis for a leisure service activity. Fixed direct costs are those costs associated with the actual production of the program. These expenditures do not change or vary and must be attended to when establishing a program. One can think of fixed direct cost as the minimal cost to produce a program. When we think of fixed direct cost we are often talking about expenditures for a leader, promotion, and an area or facility needed to implement a program. Variable direct costs are those that change depending on the volume or number of customers participating. For example, the amount of arts and crafts supplies necessary to implement a program may increase or decrease depending on the number of customers participating. Interestingly, it is the control of variable fixed costs that often can produce the profit margins required by an organization. Control of variable direct costs should be a high concern of the leisure service programmer.

Fixed indirect costs in this model result from a variety of expenditures, including salaries paid to adminstrators and support staff, depreciation on buildings and equipment, and other factors. Fixed indirect costs, as indicated, do not change or vary depending on the number of customers participating in the program or activity. In other words, in calculating the cost of a program, an additional 20 to 40 percent is added onto the sum of the fixed direct and the variable direct cost of a program.

How do we calculate market demand? Howard and Crompton (1980: 28) note that there are two basic strategies that can be used to calculate prices when the cost of the program is not solely dependent on the direct or indirect cost. In other words, there are two general pricing methods that are available to leisure service programmers. These are known as *going rate pricing* and *demand-oriented pricing*. Going rate pricing can be thought of as the amount charged for a service when compared with prices charged by similar leisure service organizations offering similar services. Demand-oriented pricing is built on the assumption that the price should be established depending on what the customer is willing to pay. The demand for services concept in pricing is affected by the availability of services and the perceived quality of services. In other words, demand-oriented pricing can be affected by the amount of services to individuals and their perception of the quality or status of services.

Summary

Budgeting and resource attainment are two important elements that the leisure service programmer must consider in the design and implementation of leisure service programs and activities. It is important to recognize that budgets follow programs, not the reverse. That is, the leisure service programmer should design the program first and then create a budget to support the program's implementation. Today leisure service programmers are increasingly being held accountable for the financial aspects of service delivery. They are often required not only to produce revenues that meet basic program costs but also to generate revenues for other program services and organizational functions.

A budget and resource attainment plan can assist the programmer in a number of ways. In particular these tools help the programmer plan, implement, and control activities and events. Also, the budget and resource attainment plan are useful in helping the programmer translate program concepts into economic reality, establish program priorities, communicate program plans, establish a historical record, and build commitment to a course of action.

A budget can be thought of as a plan. Stated in financial terms, a budget helps estimate the types of fiscal resources necessary to implement a program. Budgets help the leisure service programmer identify what resources are required and also which methods will be used to locate and secure them. The budget helps the programmer think ahead and establish a blueprint of action for the future. There are several types of comprehensive budget systems that are available to leisure service programmers. These include line-item budgets, program budgets, performance budgets, PPBSs, and zero-based budgets.

A resource attainment plan identifies in a broader sense the resources necessary to organize and implement a program. A resource attainment plan is not only concerned with fiscal resources but other resources. A key to locating resources is to look for alternative sources outside the leisure service organization. Extraorganizational alternative resources include gifts and donations, in-kind contributions, sponsorships, scrounging, partnerships, and volunteers.

Discussion Questions and Exercises _____

1. Explain what the statement "budgets follow programs, not the reverse" means.

2. Identify and define eight trends that have an impact on the financial management of leisure service organizations.

3. Identify and define eight ways that a budget and resource attainment plan can impact on the work of a leisure service programmer.

4. Identify and define seven categories of earned income. Research and provide examples from the leisure service field for each of these categories.

5. Define the concept of budgeting. Identify and define five types of budget systems.

6. Select a leisure service organization of your choice from the commercial, voluntary, or governmental sector and locate a copy of that organization's budget. Analyze the budget in terms of total revenue and expenditures and type of budget employed and calculate the percentage of expenditures supported by earned income.

7. Using the budget worksheet in Figure 11.3, develop a budget scenario for an arts-and-crafts class for ten-year-old children. The class should be designed to meet two hours a week for ten weeks.

8. What is a resource attainment plan? How is it different from a budget?

9. Identify and discuss six categories of resources available to leisure service programmers that can be used to support the organization and implementation of leisure service activities and events.

10. Why is pricing important in leisure service programs? How can the break-even analysis be used to calculate the price of a service?

References

Bullaro, J. J. and C. R. Edginton. 1986. *Commercial leisure services.* New York. MacMillan.

Crompton, J. L. 1987. *Doing more with less in the delivery of recreation and park services.* State College, PA: Venture.

Deppe, T. R. 1983. *Management strategies in financing parks and recreation.* New York: Wiley & Sons.

Drucker, P. 1985. *Innovation and entrepreneurship.* New York: Harper & Row.

Edginton, C. R. and J. G. Williams. 1978. *Productive management of leisure service organizations.* New York: Wiley & Sons.

Feldman, S. 1973. *The administration of mental health services.* Springfield, IL: Thomas.

Hemphill, S. A. 1985. Revenue management: Beginning with basics. *Parks and Recreation* 20(12): 32–38.

Hines, T. I. 1974. *Revenue source management in parks and recreation.* Arlington, VA: National Recreation and Park Association.

Howard, D. R. and J. L. Crompton. 1980. *Financing, managing and marketing recreation and park resources.* Dubuque, IA: Wm. C. Brown.

Rossman, J. R. 1989. *Recreation programming: Designing leisure experiences.* Champaign, IL: Sagamore.

Schroth, R.J. 1978. Effects of local government structures on budgetary procedures of municipal park and/or recreation departments. Unpublished dissertation, Indiana University.

Wesemann, H. E. 1981. *Contracting for city services.* Pittsburgh, PA: Innovations Press.

Weston, J. F. and E. F. Brigham. 1978. *Managerial finance.* 6th ed. Hinsdale, IL: The Dryden Press.

Wildavsky, A. 1974. *The politics of the budgetary process.* 2nd ed. Boston MA: Little Brown.

12 | Delivering Leisure Programs

Learning Objectives

1. To provide the reader with an overview of *the importance of the customer/leader interface.*
2. To help the reader identify and define the various *types of interactions* that can be planned, organized, and taught to employees.
3. To identify and define *the hallmarks of excellence in customer/leader interactions.*
4. To provide an overview of *the roles and responsibilities of leisure service programmers* as supervisors.
5. To identify *strategies used in removing barriers* as a supervisory responsibility.
6. To provide an overview of procedures and approaches to *managing the flow of a leisure service program.*

Introduction

Connecting with the customer to provide fulfilling, rewarding leisure experiences is the primary purpose of any leisure service organization. The ability of front-line, direct, face-to-face leaders and leisure service programmers operating as supervisors to effectively deliver leisure experiences is essential to organizational success. Customers are very valuable to an organization. In delivering services, leisure service programmers must be responsive, courteous, and concerned about their customers' welfare.

The leisure service programmer often functions as a supervisor. In this role, he or she is responsible for ensuring that services are delivered effectively and efficiently. The programmer as a supervisor exists to help clarify and define organizational goals, and to remove the barriers that prevent the successful delivery of leisure services. Supervisors have a number of responsibilities, ranging from the production of services to the creation and maintenance of safe work and leisure environments.

Both front-line leisure service leaders and supervisors are involved in managing the flow of programs. Managing a program's flow involves structuring leisure environments to achieve desired goals. It can involve sequencing activities or arranging environmental conditions to produce the desired leisure experience(s). In this chapter, the broad concept of delivering leisure programs is presented. Initially, the customer/leader interface will be analyzed, with particular attention paid to the hallmarks of excellence in this area. The topic of supervising leisure service personnel also will be presented. And finally, a discussion of the procedures and methods used in managing program flow from both a practical and theoretical perspective will be briefly introduced.

The Customer/Leader Interface

The most important relationship in the process of programming leisure experiences is that of the customer/leader interface. In fact, in most cases the interaction that the leisure professional has with a given customer may very well be the pivotal point in the success or failure of the leisure experience. Further, both the short- and long-term success of any leisure service organization may be predicated upon the goodwill that is established between customers and leaders on a moment-to-moment basis. Thus, the interaction that occurs on either a formal or casual basis should be carefully thought out, and in fact planned, organized, and taught to members of a leisure service organization.

Albrecht and Zemke (1985: 106) have identified different types of service-oriented categories of employees within organizations. They have suggested that there are three types—primary service staff, secondary service staff and service support staff. Primary service staff are those individuals who have direct, planned contact with the customer. In other words, they are the people who are planning, organizing, and implementing programs and activities that result in leisure experiences. Secondary service staff are those individuals who have incidental contact with customers. They may be individuals conducting registration, providing information, and/or preparing equipment, supplies, or areas and facilities for primary service staff to conduct programs. Finally, support service staff are those individuals who provide supervisory or logistical support. For example, the leisure programmer in charge of primary staff members delivering services would be considered a support staff member. As Albrecht and Zemke (1985: 106) note, discussing this latter type of position, ". . . if you're not serving the customer, you better be serving someone who is."

In many leisure service organizations, programs and services are delivered by seasonal, or part-time or volunteer staff. Finding excellent individuals to occupy such positions is, indeed, a challenging task for any leisure service programmer. These front-line staff members, in all likelihood, make up the vast majority of personnel recruited and hired by leisure service organizations. Little is done to enhance their status within organizations and, as a result, with few exceptions, they do not remain with the organization over an extended period of time. Such individuals are often the lowest paid and receive the least amount of training and development.

The status of front-line staff members in leisure service organizations creates a dilemma. They are the vital link to the customer, and the primary contact point from the organization to those it serves. The first step in establishing a strong customer/leader interaction is to make sure that a leisure service organization's front-line people are its "bottom line." That is to say, the organization must invest in its front-line staff in terms of planning, training, and development. An organization must devote more of its resources to ensuring that its front-line people are knowledgeable and responsive to customer needs.

Front-line staff members should be able to represent the organization as well as the top-level managers. They should be in a position to act independently on behalf of the organization and commit its resources to solving problems. Behaviors that are responsive to customer needs and that are innovative and creative should be encouraged. For example, Federal Express empowers all of its professional staff, including its front-line staff, with the ability to act on behalf of the company to meet customer needs. One front-line staff member of Federal Express rented a helicopter to repair a power line in order to meet a delivery deadline when a snowstorm jeopardized the organization's service reputation.

The University of Northern Iowa's *Camp Adventure*™ makes its front-line leadership core a focus for its activities. As indicated in the program's "Values and Traditions" statement, "Our bottom line is our front-line leaders . . . We promote positive, caring child/leader interactions . . . Sincerity, genuineness and caring are our hallmarks . . . *Camp Adventure*™ staff are high on life, high on kids." These statements reflect the intention of the program in promoting the value of part-time/seasonal volunteer leaders and the type of interaction desired within the program. The standards established are high, the training provided is thorough and rigorous, and the results that are achieved are extraordinary. In the *Camp Adventure*™ program, all staff members, not just the management team, are trained for a minimum of three months.

An excellent example of the management of the interactions that take place between customers and professionals is found at Disney World and Disneyland. Nearly all forms of interaction are scripted. When an individual customer is greeted at the front gate, the entire process has been scripted, taught and rehearsed with employees. This is also the case with attractions such as the Jungle Boat Ride. In fact, even deviations from the script are identified so that there are no ad libbed activities. In addition the custodians are taught appropriate strategies for interacting with customers, called "guests," at both Disneyland and Disney World theme parks. The results of such a well-planned, well-coordinated effort are obvious. The Disney theme parks provide enjoyable, pleasant, and customer-friendly leisure experiences. One result of the Disney training effort is the consistency of their services across customers. Further, one can expect the same level of hospitality continuously and the same experience engineered on a consistent basis.

The effects of well-planned, well-organized and well-taught programs focused on customer/leader interactions are numerous. First, and perhaps most important, is the fact that they provide opportunities to promote customer satisfaction. The customer's satisfaction with the leisure experience should be the primary goal of any leisure service organization. Satisfied customers, in turn, develop a degree of loyalty and commitment to the organization. Individuals who have been successfully engaged in a leisure experience will more than likely return on a continuous basis to participate in the activities and programs provided by the organization. Still further, well-managed customer/leader interactions also produce a high degree of employee pride. Such pride often results in greater employee productivity, retention, morale, and, ultimately, excellence. In other words, when there are "good things happening" between customers and leaders, both parties are affected in positive ways.

What Types of Interactions Can Be Planned?

There are a number of types of interactions that can be planned, organized, and taught to employees of a leisure service organization. The types of interactions presented here are illustrative of the areas that can be identified and managed within leisure service organizations. They are, by and large, interactions that take place between individuals. This is not to diminish the importance of written or electronically communicated information, but the emphasis here is on the people-to-people interaction.

In any interaction that occurs within a leisure service organization between people, there are a number of factors that can be managed. The first is to acknowledge and recognize the impact of "body language." Body language, like other forms of communication, sends a message to customers. However, such communication is nonverbal in nature and is influenced by our gestures, body movement, facial expressions and so on. A front-line staff person can go through the motions of assisting a customer, but negative body language can convey a sense of impatience, hostility, exasperation, and other messages that tell customers that their patronage is not valued.

Another area that can be managed is that of the actual verbal interaction that takes place between the customer and the leisure service leader. Every customer deserves to be treated as a unique individual; every leisure experience, every occasion, needs to be presented in such a way as to ensure that the customer has a fully satisfactory experience. Often, continuous interaction with customers, or repetition, leads to "robotization" of the experience. Robotization of experience takes away feelings of freshness, genuineness, sincerity, and concern for the welfare of the individual. The leisure service leader must guard against treating individual customers like a number to be processed. Even if the same question is asked time and time again, each person must be treated as if his or her concerns are noteworthy and important.

A good example of robotization is the bureaucratic, red-tape responses that individuals give to customers requesting information on a program or activity. For example, staff may defer questions to others even though they could be of assistance if they really wanted to be. Or, they may use the guise of organizational rules, regulations, and procedures to avoid assisting customers when it would be possible to work within the system to solve a problem or help the customer achieve a goal. Leisure service programmers and leaders need to avoid this bureaucratic, red-tape cop-out—"I can't do it," "I can't respond," "That isn't my area," "That isn't in my job description." The staff within the organization should be willing to bend the rules (not break them) if it will help customers meet their needs.

Still another area of customer service that can be managed is how we engage the customer. Often, engaging the customer can be done in ways as simple as making eye contact, presenting a friendly smile, or saying hello. Most leisure services require involvement with the leader. The leader has a responsibility for bringing the customer into the experience. This may involve making an individual a part of a group, teaching a skill that requires feedback, or simply providing information to help a customer make a decision. In each of these cases, customers must be engaged in a way that makes them a part of the experience. Individuals need to be made to feel as if they are comfortable and that their involvement in the experience is important and desirable. Otherwise, they may sit on the sidelines and not become involved because they are not engaged by the leader.

Finally, every act by a leisure service leader is analyzed for its symbolic meaning. Customers look for meaning in the actions of leaders. Careful attention must be given to the behaviors exhibited by the leader to ensure that the intended message and values are being communicated effectively. Casual comments, as well as more formal pronouncements and directives, make a great impact on people. The leader must be careful to sensibly choose words, phrases, and comments to customers. This is especially important as many leisure service leaders are viewed as important role models. The youth coach, the teen leader, the after-school care leader, the senior citizen specialist, and other individuals in leadership roles have a great impact on those customers with whom they work.

The leisure service programmer should seek to clarify all potential interactions; no interaction is too small or too insignificant to be discounted. All forms of interaction that occur between staff and customers of a leisure service organization can be scripted out and taught to employees. Further, the interactions that occur between customers of a leisure service organization can also be managed. Some of the areas that can be planned, organized, and taught include the following.

Programs and activity interactions Programs and activity interactions are certainly an area in which leisure service programmers can script the dialogue. How we teach, how we interact with individuals in an instructional program, how we present information, as well as other program services, can be scripted to ensure that consistency and positive interactions with the customer occur.

Telephone interaction The manner in which staff interact with customers while on the telephone can have a great deal of impact on the image and effectiveness of the organization. Just the initial greeting that is offered sets the stage for the interaction that occurs. For example, thanking the customer for their interest in the organization sets a positive tone and should be a standard procedure.

Informational exchange It is surprising to note the number of organizations that do not train their staff to disperse information properly. Usually, when people want information from an organization, they want it to be accurate so that they will be able to make an informed decision. Leisure service organizations need to make sure that all individuals have full access to pertinent information or knowledge and/or are able to refer customers appropriately.

Registration interactions Registration procedures for programs can be incredibly frustrating for customers. These types of procedures can be reviewed in order to make sure that customers are given accurate, timely information, and that the exchange of money is documented and efficient. Registration interactions can be organized so that the procedures are made as convenient as possible for the customer. The organization staff should attempt to anticipate what will happen during the registration process and plan accordingly. If it is likely that there will be a greater volume of registrants at a particular time, ensure that extra staff are put on to handle the registration efficiently. Also anticipate the questions of registrants for other information about the organization and have materials available. The computer-generated registration form in Figure 12.1 attempts to anticipate the needs of customers by noting that they are to bring a painter's smock for Halloween ceramics.

Office interactions We often assume that the interactions that occur in an office situation are private and not observed by customers. This is far from the truth. Observations by customers of office interaction has a great impact on their perceptions of the leisure service organization.

Willamalane
PARK AND RECREATION DISTRICT
765 North A Street,
Springfield, OR 97477-4770
(503) 746-1669

DO YOU RECALL WHERE YOU FIRST HEARD ABOUT THIS PROGRAM? (Check one)
Quarterly Tabloid ☐ Family Members/Friends ☐
Willamalane Flyer ☐ Newspaper ☐
Radio ☐ Other ____

BRING A PAINTER'S SHIRT/SMOCK.

OFFICE USE ONLY
Dist. $3.50 Non-Dist. $5.25
Date ____ Initial ____
Receipt No. ____
Sig. Card Out ____ Ret'd. ____

Name ____ (LAST) (FIRST) (PLEASE PRESS FIRMLY)
Address ____
City ____ Zip Code ____
TLN 30132 Program HALLOWEEN CERAMICS (AGES 3-5)
Date(s) 10/30 (START) (END) Day(s) TU Time 3-4P
Doctor ____ Phone ____

Revenue # 000000000000000
Birthdate ____ Age ____
Home Phone ____
Emergency Phone ____
Work Phone ____
Instructor ____
Location YOLANDA ELEMENTARY
Insurance Company ____

Medical Information (Allergies, Asthma, etc.) ____

The undersigned releases Willamalane Park & Recreation District from all liability which may arise from participation of the undersigned in the said program. In the event the participant is under the age of 18, the undersigned agrees to hold the District harmless from any liability it may suffer through the participation of the child in said program. The undersigned hereby requests and permits any hospital emergency department physician, any other physicians he or she may wish to designate and any hospital personnel to render to the above named applicant any medical and/or surgical treatment he/she may require in my absence.

Signature ____ (PARENT OR GUARDIAN SIGNATURE IF APPLICANT UNDER 18) ____ RELATIONSHIP TO APPLICANT

Figure 12.1 Registration Form. (Willamalane Park and Recreation District, Springfield, Oregon.)

Office or organizational interactions should be carried on in a professional manner, recognizing that there is an audience.

The Hallmarks of Excellence in Customer/ Leader Interactions

What are the hallmarks of excellence in customer/leader interactions? What leader behaviors need to be taught, reinforced and encouraged within leisure service organizations? Can organizations recruit individuals who exemplify desired behaviors? It is important to remember that excellence in customer/leader interactions does not just occur; it takes the careful selection and nurturing of professional staff members in order to produce desired results. Positive customer/leader interactions do not occur by chance. When such behaviors are planned, organized, and taught to professional staff members, the result is usually superior performance.

Some of the behaviors that are desirable in promoting excellence in customer/leader interactions are as follows.

Anticipatory behavior It is not enough merely to respond to customer needs. Rather, effective leaders should anticipate customer needs in advance and then put into place strategies to meet these anticipated needs. The leader should put himself or herself in the place of the customer and attempt to determine what service would be desired.

Working knowledge of organization Informed leisure service leaders are better able to serve customers. Working knowledge of the organization implies that each person understands its vision and mission structure, personnel and, most importantly, programs and services. It is surprising how compartmentalized the work of individuals within many organizations is. Working knowledge of an organization can help solve customer problems and create a stronger image of the organization.

Attention to detail It is the little things that make the difference between a superior organizational effort and a mediocre performance. Attention to detail requires thought, planning, and a creative nature. As Zeithaml, Parasuraman, and Berry (1990: 6) note ". . . service leaders are interested in the details and nuances of service, seeing opportunities in small actions that competitors might consider trivial. They believe that how an organization handles the little things sets the tone for how it handles the big things. They also believe that the little things add up for the customer and make a big difference."

Competence The idea of competence is important to the delivery of leisure programs and activities from the standpoint of customer confidence as well as the ability to have the leader perform the function that has been promoted. Zeithaml et al. (1990: 21) have written that competence can be thought of as the possession of the required skills and knowledge to perform a service.

Sincerity In working with customers, sincere behavior is an important attribute to demonstrate. Sincere individuals are ones who operate without deceit, pretence, or hypocrisy. They are individuals who are straightforward in their interactions with the customer.

Friendliness Friendliness is a characteristic that is manifested in supportive, helping types of behaviors. A friendly person is thought to be one who acts in a kindly fashion and is not hostile in his or her behavior toward others. People who promote friendliness are those who have amiable, positive, supportive relationships with others.

Belief in the power and value of what you do
Perhaps there is nothing more powerful than the commitment that a professional makes to pursuing an ideal. For example, belief in the power and value of play is an ideal upon which professional practice is built. Believing in something creates a certain passion and commitment. This passion and commitment is often translated to the customer. Belief in what you do often results in pride. It shows up in details, such as the way that people are dressed, to more important issues, like the way customers are treated.

Courtesy Courtesy is the politeness or generosity demonstrated by the leader in interacting with the customer. Courteous behavior often involves making the customer feel comfortable, being kind, or showing special consideration for the unique needs of an individual.

Problem-solving orientation The ability to help customers solve problems is an important behavior to be exhibited by leisure service leaders. The ability of leaders to help customers overcome barriers to a satisfying leisure experience is essential. Having a problem-solving orientation means that you are concerned about the welfare of the customer and will try to find ways to resolve issues that stand in the way of successful participation.

High standards and a commitment to excellence Having high standards suggests a commitment to excellence. "True service leaders aspire to legendary service; they realize that good service may not be good enough to differentiate their organization from other organizations. Service leaders are zealous about implementing the service right the first time. They value that goal of zero defects. . . ." (Zeithaml et al. 1990: 6).

Integrity Integrity refers to an individual's uprightness, honesty, and sincerity. In the discussion of integrity, Zeithaml et al. (1990: 7) have remarked that ". . . one of the essential characteristics of service leaders is personal integrity.

The best leaders value doing the right things, even when inconvenient or costly. They place a premium on being fair, consistent, and truthful. . . ."

Enthusiasm/energy Enthusiasm is an essential element in providing positive customer/leader interactions. People who demonstrate enthusiasm are thought to be inspired and eagerly interested in others and their cause. Enthusiasm, like the commitment that one makes to an ideal, is contagious. Energetic people are often thought of as being very vigorous and dynamic. In the leisure service area, people with energy motivate or energize others to action.

Communications Effective communications are fundamental to successful customer/leader interactions. As Zeithaml et al. (1990: 22) have suggested, communication involves ". . . keeping customers informed in the language they understand and listening to them."

Generosity When we think of individuals who are generous, we think of people who are willing to give of themselves or share with others. Generous people are thought to be unselfish individuals who are willing to go the extra mile to ensure that the customer has a satisfying leisure experience.

Service orientation A service orientation can be thought of as the extent to which an individual focuses his or her attention on the needs of customers. As Rado (1989: 67) has noted, ". . . Customer service includes any activities that demonstrate an attention to customer needs and desires." Having a service orientation means attempting to understand the perception of the customer and placing the needs of the customer foremost.

Access Access can be thought of as the ability of the customer to approach and interact with the leader; it is the ease of contact that the customer has with the leader (Zeithaml et al. 1990: 22).

Care and concern Of all the qualities that are essential to creating excellence in customer/ leader interactions, care and concern are perhaps the most important. Care and concern for others implies having empathy—trying to understand their needs and relate to their welfare. When we say we are concerned with others, it means we are dedicated to helping them with compassion and interest.

Freedom from risk In most leisure service programs and activities there is an element of risk. Freedom from either psychological or physical risk can influence the success or failure of the leisure experience. Leaders should work to help customers relieve their fears and enhance their competence to participate in leisure events and activities.

Credibility The credibility of customer/leader interactions refers to the trustworthiness, believability, and honesty of the transaction that takes place (Zeithaml et al. 1990: 21). Usually the onus for establishing credibility rests upon the individual providing the service and/or is a manifestation of the value of the organization itself.

Striving for partnerships The relationship that should emerge between the customer and the leader is one of mutual benefit. Mutually beneficial relationships or partnerships are ones in which there are no losers, but rather the parties strive for a "win/win" situation. Partners have an equal commitment to the welfare of each other and are able to derive satisfaction from the interaction. The satisfaction for the customer is excellence in the leisure experience and for the leader it is personal satisfaction and/or organizational profit.

Appearance consistent with customer expectations The degree to which customers perceive the organization to be competent and well-organized may well be influenced by the physical appearance of the leader. A leader who is disheveled and has unkempt projects will have an unfavorable organizational image. By the same token, the leader who is dressed appropriately for the leisure experience and who takes pride in his or her appearance will convey a more professional and polished image.

Consistency No matter how many times the leisure service leader has successfully implemented a given service, he or she should approach each new customer and each new situation with the same level of intensity. Once excellence has been achieved, consistency is the next goal. To be consistently excellent in the provision of a service from one situation to the next is the hallmark of outstanding customer/ leader interactions.

Reliability Zeithaml et al. (1990: 21) have written that reliability can be thought of as the ability to perform the promised service dependably and accurately. Crompton and MacKay (1989: 367) have studied the importance of service quality dimensions in selected public recreation programs. They found that reliability consistently emerged across programs as the most important dimension of service quality (1989: 367). Further, MacKay and Crompton (1990) have also reported that perceptions of the importance of various service quality dimensions vary according to type of activity.

Positive attitude One's attitude toward the customer can have a great impact on the reception of the program or activity. Upbeat, direct, and encouraging interactions with customers usually reflect a positive attitude. The positiveness in this attitude can be transmitted to other individuals.

Responsiveness This can be thought of as the desire and willingness to help customers and to be prompt in providing programs and services (Zeithaml et al. 1990: 21). Individuals like to feel that when they communicate their needs the leader is attentive. People hate to be ignored and made to feel that their needs are not important.

Being responsive is attending to people's needs in such a way that they are made to feel important and special.

Establishing a positive physical climate
Zeithaml et al. (1990: 21) have noted that the appearance of physical facilities, equipment, personnel, and communication materials can influence the extent to which customers view a service as being of high quality. Leisure service organizations can establish a climate that promotes positive customer service. Both the physical environment and the service environment should communicate to the customer that their patronage is desired. The physical environment can have an impact on the perceptions of customers of whether or not the organization is customer friendly. A clean, well-organized, well-worded, and warm environment communicates the intentions of a leisure service organization to its customers, as contrasted with a disorganized, cluttered, and cold environment.

Demonstrating appreciation   Individuals like to feel as if their business is valued and that they are appreciated. Thanking an individual for contributing to your organization's success is good business. The best way to thank individuals is to do it on a day-to-day basis via word of mouth; a word of thanks goes a long way.

Such behaviors must be taught, maintained, and reinforced on a continuous basis. Being customer-oriented means being attentive to those factors that make the leisure experience satisfying to the individual and make leisure areas and facilities hospitable and attractive. No organization should assume that its employees necessarily will be oriented toward its customers. Behaviors that lead to positive customer relations should be reinforced and individuals should be given continuous feedback (both positive and corrective) on their performance related to service behaviors. There is no secret in creating positive customer/leader interactions; it simply means

operating so the customer's ". . . current situation, frame of mind, and needs are addressed" (Albrecht and Zemke 1985: 32).

Supervising Leisure Service Personnel

By and large, most leisure service activities and events are implemented by seasonal, part-time, or volunteer staff. For example, in the organized camping field, there are over 300,000 seasonal staff members employed to serve as camp counselors, program specialists, and instructors (American Camping Association 1983). This is also the case with leisure services operated by government, such as municipal parks and recreation departments, voluntary organizations such as the YMCA, and commercial organizations such as theme parks. The supervision of seasonal and part-time employees is a very important part of the work of leisure service programmers.

Most professionals involved in programming positions in the leisure service field are in supervisory positions. In such positions, they are responsible for developing program ideas; promoting activities and events; recruiting, selecting, and developing staff; and supervising the work efforts of staff. Supervision can be thought of as a process of helping individuals to perform the tasks that they have been assigned. We often think of supervision as monitoring or controlling the work of others. However, in reality, the work of a supervisor is one of encouraging the efforts of others and ensuring that leisure service leaders have the opportunity to perform to their fullest capacity.

Supervision: A Working Definition
The term supervision has many meanings. Breaking the work into its two component parts—*super* and *vision*—we find that the term super implies "over and above," and vision means looking over or above or perceiving abstract images. Supervision has also been associated with

the terms *leader* or *master*. In most leisure service organizations, the supervisor can be thought of as the individual who oversees individuals who are involved in the direct delivery of services. A supervisor may also be responsible for overseeing a program area or facility and charged with the responsibility of developing and implementing a series of events or activities.

The U.S. government has provided a definition of supervisor. The Taft-Hartley Act of 1947 defines a supervisor as follows:

> Any individual having authority, in the interest of the employer, to hire, transfer, suspend, lay off, recall, promote, discharge, assign, reward, or discipline other employees, or responsibility to direct them, or to adjust their grievances, or to effectively recommend such action, if in conjunction with the foregoing exercise of such authority is not of a merely routine or clerical nature, but requires the use of independent judgement.

Thus, as one can discern from reviewing this all-encompassing definition, the work of the supervisor involves a wide variety of managerial functions related to human resources with leisure service organizations. Another perspective in defining supervision comes from Terry (1978: 6). He notes that ". . . supervision means achieving desired results through the efforts of others in a manner that provides challenge, interest, and satisfaction in the use of human talents." The emphasis in this definition is on effectively using human resources to achieve desired results. Terry (1978: 6) maintains that the supervisor ". . . suggests to the . . . [leisure service leader] . . . how to do it, create and maintain a work environment conducive to a person's personal development, encourage the growth of the person's abilities to their fullest potential, and aid in satisfying both the organizational and individual wants from the job efforts."

Most supervisors must have not only technical knowledge of the program activities or events that they are supervising, but obviously they must be able to work effectively with other people. Most supervisors of leisure service organizations have been in direct service roles and, as a result, often have first-hand knowledge of the problems that are associated with organizing and implementing leisure services. The work of the leisure service programmer as a supervisor is challenging and complex and is the focal point for the creation of most program efforts within leisure service organizations. Leisure service supervisors are often called upon to set standards, to create a work agenda, observe behavior, motivate employees and evaluate the impact of leisure experiences upon customers.

Roles and Responsibilities of the Leisure Service Supervisor

If one were to ask a hundred leisure service supervisors to identify their specific roles and responsibilities, one would probably receive a hundred different answers. Each leisure service organization, each job setting that a supervisor works within, and the individuals with whom the supervisor works, all create a great deal of diversity and situation-specific activity. Every supervisory job will be different and uniquely tailor-made for the needs of a given leisure service organization. However, there are a number of general roles and responsibilities that are often associated with the work of leisure service supervisors. According to Boyd (1984: 17–18), some of the *roles and responsibilities of the leisure service supervisors are production, quality, cost, methods, morale, training, and safety.* Below is a brief description of each of these facets of supervision.

Production Production, in terms of work within leisure service organizations, refers to the creation of leisure experiences and/or associated activities (such as the management of concession operations) that contribute to successful programming efforts. The work of the leisure service supervisor in this case is to ensure that leisure events and activities are created in a manner consistent with the vision, mission, goals, and objectives of the organization. It means identifying resources and bringing these resources to bear in a timely, prompt, and meaningful fashion. For example, this could involve the recruitment and selection of staff.

Quality Quality is a perception of excellence that is created or held within the mind of the customer. Today, customers expect high-quality leisure services. The leisure service supervisor can promote high quality by setting high standards, staying in touch with customers, and observing the way in which activities or events are implemented. Quality requires constant attention to the methods and procedures that are used in delivering services. Higher quality programs are produced when the supervisor and direct-service personnel work in harmony to produce leisure activities and events.

Cost Boyd (1984: 17) suggests that cost control and cost reduction are essential in profit, nonprofit, and government organizations. He suggests that supervisors should strive, through cost-control and cost-reduction measures, to enhance the profitability of commercial organizations, and in other types of organizations the highest quality services should be provided at the lowest possible expenditure of funds. According to Boyd (1984: 17), "supervisors can help employees understand that they, too, have a responsibility to contribute to cost control and cost reduction." Leisure service supervisors usually contribute to the development and control of budgets and resource attainment plans. In this way, they are able to contribute significantly to the management of finances within leisure service organizations and contribute directly to improving an organization's fiscal well-being.

Methods The specific methods and procedures used to conduct leisure events and activities usually falls under the direction of the leisure service supervisor. The methods and procedures employed all contribute to cost and quality control. Therefore, careful attention must be given to identifying and continuously reviewing the methods and procedures employed within leisure service organizations. Finding ways to improve work methods and procedures by identifying new technology, improved patterns of interactions with customers, and new management systems are all a part of the leisure service supervisor's roles and responsibilities. A new work method or procedure may very well spell the difference between success or failure within a program. Constant innovation, as well as thoughtful attention and investigation, is required in this area.

Morale Supervisors also have as a responsibility creating and maintaining positive morale within the leisure service organization. Morale can be thought of as the attitude that people have toward the work environment. It can be either positive or negative. Positive morale can reflect on the productivity of the organization. Positive morale can create espirt de corps and pride, and can instill a "can do" attitude among employees. Individuals and organizations today often look to their work environments for support. A positive, upbeat, friendly work environment that is conducive to good morale can be an important dimension in creating and maintaining excellent work situations.

Training There are three types of training—orientation, in-service, and developmental—that leisure service supervisors organize and implement. Orientation training is concerned with helping individuals learn about the organization's values and philosophy. In addition, orientation training often presents information about an organization's structure, roles, and methods and procedures for conducting business. In-service training is concerned with reinforcing previously taught information and upgrading existing skills and knowledge by introducing new technology or methods and procedures for conducting business, and brainstorming for solving existing and emerging organizational problems. Developmental training is focused on the enhancement of the human resources of an organization, with no specific task or job-related function in mind. The latter is concerned with helping individuals develop themselves with the assumption that as people within an organization improve the organization, as a whole, is enriched.

Safety management   Ensuring that leisure experiences are provided and maintained in a safe manner is an important role of the leisure service supervisor. The same can be said about work environments for employees. It is the supervisor's responsibility to ensure that physical work spaces and the procedures that are employed are safe for staff members. The Occupational Safety and Health Act (OSHA) places a strong responsibility upon leisure service organizations to maintain safe work environments. OSHA has established guidelines that can be reviewed and used to guide the development of supervisory activities in this area.

In addition to the above responsibilities and functions, supervisors also find themselves heavily involved in the appraisal of direct-service staff. Basically, the appraisal function is one of helping individuals understand the criteria to be used in the evaluation process, helping individuals establish goals for the future, providing feedback, and discussing ways in which individuals can change their work procedures and/or behaviors. Also, the leisure service supervisor may occasionally be involved in disciplinary actions. The key to effective handling of disciplinary actions is to keep employees well informed about shortcomings in their performance, let them know the

expectations for their performance, and allow them the opportunity to correct their performance. If these measures are not effective, more severe measures up to and including dismissal may be necessary.

Removing Barriers: A Supervisory Function of Leisure Service Programmers

One of the most important functions of a leisure service programmer is that of removing barriers that prevent individuals providing leisure services from implementing programs effectively. To paraphrase Peter Drucker (1985), ". . . the one and only responsibility of . . . [leisure service programmers as supervisors] . . . is to ensure that employees do what they get paid to do. The best way to help individuals do their jobs effectively, is to assist in the removal of barriers that prevent them from doing their work successfully.

What are some of the barriers that leisure service programmers can assist individuals in overcoming? There are probably numerous specific problems that emerge in any given leisure service setting. In fact, the removal of barriers is probably a day-to-day activity. However, some of the more general ones include the following:

Lack of knowledge of the vision and mission of the organization   How do individuals fit into an organization? What is the relationship of their effort to the total effort of the organization? What ends or aims is the organization working toward? How can the work of individuals delivering leisure services be integrated with the overarching goals of the leisure service organization? Clarification of these issues can serve to strengthen the work of individuals providing direct services. Lack of knowledge often creates a barrier to achieving the goals of the organization.

Lack of task and role clarity   One barrier to the delivery of services occurs when leaders do not have adequate knowledge of the tasks or roles that they are to perform. In other words, when people don't understand what is expected of them, they can become frustrated, perform poorly, and/or engage in inappropriate work activities. The leisure service programmer must have appropriate technical knowledge to be able to explain to individuals how a task is to be carried out and how the leader's work is related to other functions, people, and resources within the organization.

Fear of failure When individuals are criticized within organizations for trying new methods or new procedures, they will usually withdraw from further attempts to be innovative. The lack of such innovation reduces potential gains. One of the most important roles that the leisure service programmer can play is creating an environment where people are not afraid to try new methods. Such experimentation often leads to greater productivity, innovation and creativity. People will not risk failure if the consequences of failure are inordinately high. Robert Toalson, General Manager of the Champaign, Illinois, Park District, operates his organization using what he calls "the mistake philosophy: that is, if you are not making any mistakes, you are not trying anything new."

Lack of proper supplies, equipment, and materials The lack of proper resources—supplies, equipment, and materials—can be a great impediment to implementing successful leisure experiences. One of the great challenges faced by leisure service programmers is providing the right amount of resources at the right time and at the right place. People need the proper tools to do their jobs. Without adequate resources, it is extremely difficult to successfully implement events and activities. Often, providing supplies, equipment, and materials means that the leisure service programmer will have a working knowledge of the needs of a given program or service and create a distribution system that ensures the availability of these resources.

Excessive bureaucracy/red tape Work in most leisure service organizations is organized bureaucratically. This means that leisure service organizations have created rules, policies, and procedures to help achieve their goals. Such bureaucracy often becomes stifling, formidable, and difficult to understand. Most of all, it is frustrating. It is the function of leisure service programmers to humanize the rules, policies, and procedures of the organization so that they are reasonable, prudent, and applicable to various situations. Doing things by the book is important, but one of the functions of the leisure service programmer is to use common sense in interpreting rules, policies, and procedures to assist individuals in successfully implementing their leisure activities or events.

Lack of social/emotional support Individuals implementing leisure services are not unlike any other employee. They need support in a variety of forms. People seek approval and praise as well as empathy, from others in the work environment. They want to be supported in their efforts, socially and emotionally. Providing social/emotional support may involve giving encouragement, cheering the work of individuals, facilitating their efforts, and instilling confidence. Providing social/emotional support to individuals often serves to make the work environment more humane, less stressful, and more considerate.

Lack of recognition The lack of recognition of the efforts of individuals implementing services often produces feelings of apathy and frustration. Often, people develop the notion "if my leisure service superior doesn't care to recognize me for my efforts, why try harder?" There are many ways to recognize people for their contributions to the work of an organization. Recognition can occur formally or informally. It can be done on a casual basis, or it can be done in such a way as to bring attention and distinction to the work of an individual. Recognition of the efforts of most people is best accomplished by thanking them, showing them that they are appreciated, and reinforcing their own sense of self-worth. The glib, ''one-minute manager approach'' of methodically, mechanically dishing out praise is not sufficient; praise must be sincere, heartfelt, and genuine in order to be effective.

Lack of orientation, in-service, and developmental training Individuals need to be oriented in a formal way to the vision and mission of an organization. Further, such values need to be reinforced and promoted on a continuous basis. In addition, new approaches, strategies, and techniques for providing services should be discussed on an ongoing basis. Leisure service programmers can help direct-service providers by effectively orienting and training them prior to implementation of activities, and also by helping them to acquire new skills and knowledge. Training and development programs can also be established as a way of helping individuals to solve problems. In addition, such efforts can be directed at encouraging the creativity of individuals and energizing their efforts by providing stimulating challenges and other motivational activities. Often when people are grouped together for such training and development programs, synergy occurs, thereby encouraging the formulation of new ideas and ways of solving problems.

In order to help individuals implement leisure services effectively, the programmer must be careful to ensure that they have the autonomy and authority to carry out the task which has been assigned. One of the greatest barriers that is faced by individuals providing services is that of oversupervision. There is a fine line between offering appropriate supervisory suggestions and recommendations and stifling the work of individuals. The leisure service programmer has to be careful to make sure that values and assigned tasks are carried out, but not at the expense of individuals' creativity, spontaneity, and dignity. Subordinates might not do the job exactly as the

supervisor would do it; however, that is often part of the learning process. The leisure service programmer should establish high standards and challenge individuals to meet them, but also create a safety net that is supportive and prevents failure.

Managing the Program Flow

One of the most important elements in delivering leisure programs and services is to get people into and then hold them in a leisure experience. Posed as a question, how do we create environments that are compelling to individuals and then, once we have individuals within these environments, how do we ensure that we will accomplish the anticipated goals for the program? Or, still further, how do we create ''magic'' for our customers? ''Magic'' occurs when the reality of the leisure experience exceeds the expectations. These are, indeed, difficult and challenging questions with which leisure service programmers must deal. They speak to the need for paying attention to and managing the flow of customers as they move through a leisure experience.

In Chapter 2, we discussed the idea that programmers can manage the animation of an event as it moves through time. It is this animation to which we are referring when we speak of the program flow. In other words, program flow can be thought of as the movement from one activity to another throughout the life of a given leisure experience. Activities within a given leisure program can be coordinated and integrated with one another to produce an overall experience. Individuals can be encouraged and nurtured; their emotions can be heightened and lowered; their intellects and perceptions can be stimulated in a sequential format that produces desired program goal or goals. Further, individuals can be given very active roles in shaping their own leisure experiences. Choice can be introduced, control can be reduced, spontaneity and freedom can be encouraged.

The Social Recreation Curve

Perhaps the earliest recognition of the idea that program flow could be managed was in the formats applied to the management of social recreation activities. In producing a social recreation activity, it was thought that activities should start with ice-breakers, followed by mixers, and then more active recreational pursuits. As the program peaked, active activities were reduced and more passive ones introduced. In the literature of the leisure service field, this concept is known as the *social recreation curve.*

Perhaps the most complete discussion of the social recreation curve concept has been developed by Ford (1974: 81–94). Figure 12.2 presents Ford's model of the social recreation curve. Discussing this model, she notes that in planning programs there is a curve of action to follow. Ford writes:

> In social activities, the pitch of excitement is at a natural quiet or low level as the participants arrive and "start warming up" to the activities and each other. The planner wants the group to leave the event calmly and quietly also. This means that the leader plans through the social events and socialization, that the high pitch of the event will be mid-way through the time of the program (Ford 1974: 90).

The social recreation curve enables the programmer to engage customers immediately and cut the program at its emotional high. The assumption is that individuals can be guided through a process that will enhance social interaction and create memorable experiences. This approach to managing program flow works and has been successfully applied by leisure service programmers for years. It is a practical, hands-on mechanism for moving from one activity to another; activities are sequenced in relation to one another in a purposeful manner.

Managing the Autotelic Experience

Another example of managing the program flow that is more theoretical in nature suggests the same ends. Csikszentmihalyi (1975) has developed a concept known as the autotelic experience. He suggests that *leisure occurs when an individual experiences a loss of ego, a loss of self-consciousness, engages in self-forgetfulness, is engaged in the transcendence of individuality, and loses an awareness of self-construct.* In this state, the individual is in control of his or her actions and the environment. The individual has no active awareness of control, but is simply not worried by the possibility of the lack of control or failure. He or she feels a sense of personal power and control. When an individual reaches this state it is known as *flow.*

Figure 12.3 presents a model of the flow state. The implications of this theoretical model for leisure programming are relatively straightforward. The job of the leisure service programmer is to assist individuals in entering the state of flow. The programmer does this by matching the action opportunities or challenges with the individual's action capabilities or skills. In other words, the programmer attempts to match the customer's skill level with a challenge that will produce an experience that is stimulating, but not overwhelming.

Once the leisure service programmer has assisted the customer in entering the flow state, the goal is to keep the individual in the flow state by adjusting the degree of challenge of the activity and/or the skill level of the customer. If the challenge is too difficult or demanding for the customer's skills, he or she will experience stress or anxiety. On the other hand, when the customer's

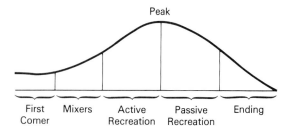

Figure 12.2 Social Recreation Curve. (From Ford, P.M. (1974). Informal Recreational Activities. Bradford Woods, IN: American Camping Association, p. 90.)

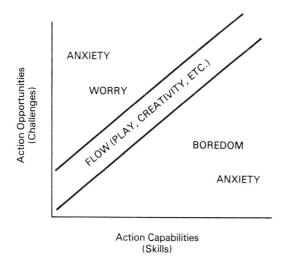

Figure 12.3 A Model of the Flow State. (From Csikszentmihalyi, M. (1975). Beyond Boredom & Anxiety.)

capabilities are higher but the challenge is still too demanding, he or she can become worried or concerned. Conversely, when the customer's skills are greater than the challenge presented, boredom results. This state may fade into anxiety when the ratio between the challenge and the skill level of the customer become too great. A state of flow is felt when opportunities for action are in balance with the individual's skills; thus the experience becomes autotelic.

Managing Program Animation

We can think of the *animation of a program as the action of the activity or event*. The leisure service programmer puts into motion an event or activity. He or she establishes and controls the animation of the program by ensuring that certain events occur in a timely and sequential pattern. Discussing the idea of program animation, Rossman (1988: 11) has written that the leisure service programmer ". . . anticipates and plans how the action sequences of a program will unfold and then puts in place the elements necessary to guide the interactions." In this approach, the programmer tries to ". . . anticipate and predict the outcomes of the interactions

within a program and the order in which the events will unfold" (Rossman 1988: 11).

Managing the action sequences or the animation of a program is analogous to writing and then conducting a symphony. The leisure service programmer plans each of the events and the way in which they are sequenced. As the event is actually implemented, the leisure service programmer will modify the action sequence established in order to produce the desired outcomes. One interesting fact in this approach to programming is that customers actually play a role in shaping the animation of a leisure experience. In other words, their reactions to events and activities can influence the animation of the leisure experience. They can interact with others and/or the environment to change the way that the program is sequenced. The opportunity for such action provides for a degree of spontaneity, individuality, and personalization of leisure programs.

In the implementation of programs there is often a reconfiguration of events in order to meet the needs of the moment. As the design of the program changes, the leisure service programmer must react to emerging needs and conditions. This makes the program process very dynamic, requiring great sensitivity to the way in which customers are responding to various stimuli in the environment. It requires the leisure service programmer to anticipate changes and be prepared to respond with contingent strategies.

Program Life Cycle

In Chapter 2, the concept of the product life cycle was introduced. Programs also have a life cycle. *The concept of the program life cycle suggests that events and activities have a life span.* Basically, this life span can be identified, anticipated and managed. All programs have a take-off point, reach their saturation, and then decline. If modifications are not made (perhaps increasing the challenge or complexity, or enhancing the novelty of the activity for the customer), interest in the program will diminish.

As a program is implemented, it is important for the leisure service programmer to know where the activity is in the program life cycle. If the program is a new activity, it may appear very novel to customers. On the other hand, the lack of familiarity with the activity may decrease the level of involvement and commitment to the activity by customers. The programmer will want to make customers familiar with new activities, yet promote those program attributes that might be more attractive to them. When a program reaches the saturation point in terms of customers' interest, and becomes more or less routine, the leisure service programmer will want to make sure that the conditions that ensure success are held constant. Finally, as interest in the program declines, modifications in the way the program is packaged, priced, and promoted will be necessary in order to sustain interest. In fact, the service itself will have to be modified dramatically in order to maintain customer interest and involvement.

Registration

One of the most essential, but often least-considered methods or procedures required in the delivery of leisure service is that of registering customers. Registration involves creating a list or record of customers who wish to participate in a given program or service. Registration can be fraught with problems, such as misinformation, long lines, and/or confusing procedures. The registration process, like other procedures in the delivery of a program, should be managed carefully and with the needs and interests of the customer in mind.

What does the customer expect in a registration process? To answer this question, you need to place yourself in the customer's shoes. Individuals want a registration process that is convenient, accessible, easy to understand, orderly, efficient and well organized. Customers also will often desire more in-depth, on-the-spot information about programs, activities, and facilities.

They often desire written directions and colorful, highly visible graphics to direct them through the registration process. Customers want and demand accountability in terms of cash collection and accounting procedures. These things are givens and need to be present or provided.

However, an opportunity to present the organization in a very favorable light is offered by adding value to the registration process. Adding value includes, for example, refreshments, child care, an information table staffed by a knowledgeable employee, provision of adequate parking, and striking, high-visual-impact brochures about coming events to be offered by the leisure service organization and targeted to the market segment for which registration is being done. The organization can also give away at registration inexpensive novelty items imprinted with its logo, motto, or symbol, such as balloons, buttons, pencils, key chains, and so on. These types of activities, which are offered above and beyond the expectations of customers, make a great impression and offer an opportunity for extremely positive public relations. They also tell customers that their participation is valued. With a small effort, the registration can more effectively meet the customer's needs and actually exceed their expectations. The registration process in itself can become highly attractive, a pleasant and motivating experience that not only can stimulate interest in current programs and services, but build customer loyalty for the future.

Rossman (1989: 245–249) writes that there are five basic registration methods that can be used by leisure service organizations. These registration methods have to do with issues related to convenience and accessibility, and primarily deal with location of the registration procedure and the processes that are employed by the organization. They are as follows.

Central Location Method—In this approach to registration, the process is consolidated into a centralized facility. All of the information required for registration is contained within this unit and it is often advertised in such a way as to focus the registration activities at carefully controlled dates and times.

Program Location Method—This is a more decentralized approach, wherein registration occurs at the actual program site. It is more convenient for participants and creates opportunities for the customer to become familiar with the site and the program staff (Rossman 1989:246). One problem with this method is that customers have to go to several sites to register for multiple program options.

Mail-In Method—The mail-in method of registration involves completion of a registration form and payment mailed directly to the leisure service organization. This method is very convenient for the customer, although it does not allow for any personal interaction and feedback.

Telephone Method—The telephone method of registration is gaining in popularity. It can be handled in one of two ways. First, individuals can call in and talk directly with staff members who will take their registration and process necessary information. Second, it can be handled using the telephone and the computer. Computer registration systems using telephone access are gaining in popularity. These procedures are costly, but will offer more accessibility in the future to leisure service organizations of all sizes.

Combination of Methods—Many leisure service organizations use a combination of the above-mentioned methods. This is done to improve accessibility and convenience to the customer and out of a recognition that there are multiple ways of meeting people's needs.

The registration procedures used by the Indianola, Iowa, Parks and Recreation Department are found in Figure 12.4. This organization uses a combination of registration procedures. It advertises three basic ways of registering for programs—mail-in, after hours drop-off, and walk-in. In addition, it provides complete discussion of exactly how to sign up for programs so that the customer is provided with the basic information required to complete the procedure. An-

other example of registration is found in Figure 12.5 from the Burnaby, British Columbia, Parks and Recreation Department. The mail-in registration procedure used provides a simple and direct approach to this process.

The registration process can be made more efficient with the use of computers. There are a number of software programs that are available for use in the registration process. Such programs provide a variety of features and outputs. For example, they can provide up-to-date class lists of customers who have registered, demographic profile of customers, accounting information, and so on. Computer registrations can also be tied into the agency's mailing list and can provide information regarding customer interests for future mailings. Figure 12.6 is an example of a computerized registration receipt from the Programmed for Success, Inc., software company. This receipt provides a variety of types of information, including the organization's name, where to call for information, customer's name, address and phone, fee charges, activity enrolled in, starting date, and so on.

Managing Customer Concerns

No matter how well planned or organized, any given leisure experience is subject to the interpretation of the customers as to its value, quality, and effectiveness in meeting their needs. Further, sometimes the organization will make errors that have a negative impact on customers. How should the leisure service programmer deal with frustrated, upset, angry, and/or disappointed customers? The answer, quite simply is that the customer is always right.

It is important to remember that the leisure experience is an individually defined one. Customers have different expectations based on previous experiences that can affect their experiences as customers. Further, the demand for higher quality services is ongoing. The demand for excellence in service is greater today than it

REGISTRATION

1

MAIL-IN

Indianola Parks and
Recreation Department
Box 299
Indianola, IA 50125-0299

2

AFTER HOURS DROP-OFF

Place form and payment in a
sealed envelope and drop in
the Drop Box located on the
front of the Parks & Recreation
Office.   301 W. 2nd Avenue

3

WALK-IN

Walk-in Registration
will begin August 28 at
301 W. 2nd Avenue.

HOW TO SIGN UP

Please register early! If a class does not have sufficient numbers of participants registered by two working days prior to the beginning of the class, the class will be cancelled.

COMPLETE REGISTRATION FORM: Be sure all information is correct and the program numbers are included. Registration forms are available on the inside back cover.

ENCLOSE PAYMENT: Total all fees and make check payable to Indianola Recreation or charge the amount to your VISA or MasterCard. Do not send cash. All fees must be paid in full. Registrations with incorrect fees will be notified by telephone and held from processing until the correct fee has been received.

MAIL-IN, DROP-OFF, OR WALK-IN: Mail-in or drop-off registrations will be taken from the time registration information is mailed until the program begins or is filled.
Drop off box is located on the front of the Indianola Parks and Recreation Department Office, 301 W. 2nd. Indianola Parks and Recreation is not responsible for lost mail.
Walk-in registrations will be taken beginning August 28, 1989, at the Parks and Recreation Office, 301 W. 2nd, until the program begins or is filled. Mail-in and drop-off registrations will have priority before August 28, 1989. Registrations will be processed by random draw on the day they are received up to 5:00 p.m. Those received after 5:00 p.m. will be processed the next day. Only walk-ins will be processed immediately, after August 28, 1989.

CONFIRMATION: Drop-off and mail-in registrations will be sent back a confirmation receipt/verification in the mail.

REGISTRATION INFORMATION: If a class was filled before your registration was processed, you will automatically be placed on a waiting list. We will open additional sections of classes if possible. Our main goal is to meet your needs!
Use current age or grade unless otherwise listed. Use age at beginning of program.
Programs that are taxed are listed as such in the brochure. When entering the fee, please just list the total fee with taxes included.

NON-RESIDENT FEE: Non-residents need to add non-resident fees from each program.
No non-resident registration will be processed until the correct fees have been received.
Non-residents are those that reside outside the CITY LIMITS of Indianola.

REFUNDS: Refunds will only be given if a program is cancelled or a medical excuse from a doctor is presented. We reserve the right to cancel a program due to limited enrollment. A refund will be sent for cancelled programs.

IMPORTANT: By their very nature, many parks and recreation programs involve body contact, substantial physical exertion, emotional stress, and/or use of equipment which represents a certain risk to users. It is recommended that you check with your physician prior to participating in Parks and Recreation activities. Registrants in any program assume responsibility for any risk, implicit or direct, by participation in said activity or facility.

ADDITIONAL REGISTRATION FORMS: Additional Registration forms are available at the Parks and Recreation Office.

Figure 12.4   Registration Procedures for a Local Parks and Recreation Department. (Indianola (Iowa) Parks and Recreation Department.)

BURNABY PARKS AND RECREATION

REGISTRATION BY MAIL:

Please mail to:
Registration Clerk, Burnaby Parks & Recreation Department, 4949 Canada Way, Burnaby, B.C. V5G 1M2
Or mail to the registration locations listed above and on the previous page.

FEES

Full payment of fees must accompany your registration form. Make cheques payable to "The Corporation of the District of Burnaby". All courses are subject to cancellation if under enrolled. Participants are responsible for their own accident and medical coverage. If you are 65 years and over, program fees are half the adult rate.

REFUNDS

Full fees are refunded in cases where classes are cancelled due to insufficient registration. **No refunds** will be issued except for medical or exceptional circumstances. No refunds will be considered after one third of the program has taken place. Some Recreation for the Retired programs have a no refund policy. Check with the centres for the services affected. Requests for refunds must be made in writing to the:
Burnaby Parks and Recreation Department, 4949 Canada Way, Burnaby, B.C. V5G 1M2 and MUST INCLUDE THE ORIGINAL COURSE REGISTRATION RECEIPT. Medical reasons must be verified by doctor's certificate. A $3.00 service charge is deducted from all refunds, plus a prorated charge after the first session.

REGISTRATION FORM (For Parks and Recreation mail in registration only)

Course Name _____
Location of course _____
Day of Course _____ commencing date _____
Time of Course _____ Level _____ Set _____
Age (if child) _____ Senior Citizen _____ (please check)
Participants Name _____
Address _____
Postal Code _____ Phone (home) _____ (business) _____
Parents Initial (if child) _____ Registration Fee _____
Special Information

REGISTRATION FORM (For Parks and Recreation mail in registration only)

Course Name _____
Location of course _____
Day of Course _____ commencing date _____
Time of Course _____ Level _____ Set _____
Age (if child) _____ Senior Citizen _____ (please check)
Participants Name _____
Address _____
Postal Code _____ Phone (home) _____ (business) _____
Parents Initial (if child) _____ Registration Fee _____
Special Information

Figure 12.5 Mail-In Registration Form. (Burnaby (British Columbia) Parks and Recreation Department.)

was ten years ago. And ten years from now customers will demand an even higher level of service. The expression of customer concerns in the form of complaints or criticism of a given leisure service organization can provide valuable information. If organized and managed effectively, such feedback can provide information concerning the quality of customer/leader interaction, the viability of program structures, the appropriateness of areas and facilities, and the administrative procedures that are used to manage an organization. Customer concerns not only can be a source of information to the organization, but also can paradoxically serve to enhance the organization's relationship with its customers.

To emphasize this point, customer complaint studies conducted for the White House Office for Consumer Affairs by an organization known as Technical Assistance Research Programs, Inc., found that handling dissatisfied customers in a

pro-active fashion would help in resolving concerns and, in fact, reflect in a very positive fashion on an organization. Their findings were as follows:

1. The average business never hears from 96 percent of its unhappy customers. For every complaint received, the average company in fact has twenty-six customers with problems, six of which are serious problems.
2. Complainers are more likely than non-complainers to do business again with the company that upset them even if the problem isn't satisfactorily resolved.
3. Of the customers who register a complaint, between 54 and 70 percent will do business again with the organization if their complaint is resolved. That figure goes up a staggering 95 percent if the customer feels that the complaint was resolved quickly.
4. The average customer who has had a problem with an organization tells nine or ten people

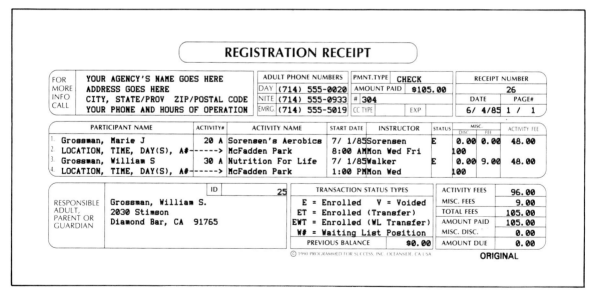

Figure 12.6 Computer-Generated Registration Form. (Programmed for Success, Inc., Oceanside, CA)

about it. Thirteen percent of people who have a problem with an organization recount the incident to more than twenty people.

5. Customers who have complained to an organization and had their complaints satisfactorily resolved tell an average of five people about the treatment they received (Albrecht and Zemke 1985: 6).

Thus, as one can see, immediate and prompt response to customer concerns can positively affect an organization in significant ways. Every attempt should be made to find ways to respond quickly, constructively, and positively to complaints and concerns expressed by customers.

Dealing with Individual Complaints

One of the key factors in quickly and satisfactorily responding to expressions of customer concern are the actions and behavior of front-line staff. Front-line staff should be empowered to handle problems. They should be schooled in principles of customer service, including procedures to be used in dealing with negative situations that might arise. Rules for dealing effectively with customers include having a problem-solving orientation, careful listening and communication, a sincere attempt to view things from the customers' perspective (it is important to remember that the logic of the customer is not always the same as the logic of the organization) and, most importantly, the ability to respond in a rapid, effective, and direct manner.

On the other hand, avoid patronizing, solicitous, non-supportive behaviors. Remember, very few customers want to have to complain, in fact many will avoid complaining and live with the problem. Therefore, the customer must feel very strongly about an issue if he or she takes the time, effort, and emotional energy necessary to confront an organization regarding poor services or products.

What specific steps should be taken to solve customer concerns? What actions should be taken in order to resolve complaints and issues that

emerge? Listed below are six steps that can be applied in situations that emerge in terms of customer complaints within leisure service organizations. They are as follows:

1. Acknowledge the importance of the problem immediately.
2. Gather all of the relevant information needed to answer the problem quickly. Use open-ended questions that require more than yes or no answers, such as: What is the problem and when did it first occur? What have you done about the problem to date? For more specific answers, use closed questions, such as, did you push the right button on the vending machine?
3. Once the problem and a plan of action have been determined, the customer should be told precisely what will happen, when and why. In customer-service situations, ignorance is most assuredly not bliss.
4. Review commitments. These commitments should be clearly stated to a customer and confirmed. If a customer expects a call in a week, and is called a month later instead, he or she will feel neglected, even if the problem has been solved.
5. Follow through on commitments. No one should ever make a promise for an organization that cannot be kept. Broken promises lead to irate customers.
6. Listen for non-service-related cues. Citizens will share a wealth of information when prompted. Your employees can often uncover needs for additional services or problem solutions this way. Employees can alert management to potential problems and opportunities.

Again, quick response, maintaining commitments, and understanding the customer's point of view are important elements in responding to concerns. The ability of frontline people to effectively manage the expectations of individuals, even when things have gone wrong, can have very dramatic effects on the success or failure of an organization.

Developing a Customer Concern System

Customer concerns should not be handled in a random, shotgun, haphazard fashion. Leisure service organizations need to develop a system for handling customer concerns. A customer concern system provides an opportunity for an individual to provide information to the organization concerning its services. Such a system, if organized in an effective manner not only provides an orderly, organized way for the customer to offer meaningful comments, but also for the organization to respond.

A customer concern system should have several objectives. First, the system should provide information to the organization in an organized way that allows for an orderly, well-thought-out response. Second, such a system provides a safety valve, or buffer, for customer complaints, enabling the organization to handle customer concerns at the earliest possible time, rather than later when the situation may be more volatile. Third, a customer concern system is in writing and is therefore more accurate and quantifiable. It should provide guidelines for staff behavior and information for decision making.

The Central Oregon Park and Recreation District, located in Redmond, Oregon, has adopted a policy statement entitled "User Concern System" as a guideline for receiving and acting upon comments, suggestions, and recommendations of the residents of this area. This policy, shown in Figure 12.7, presents the methods and procedures used by this organization to respond to customer concerns. Written documentation is recorded on a "User Concern" form. The information is distributed to appropriate parties and follow-up procedures are established. All information is analyzed on a biannual basis in order to follow trends.

Figure 12.8 is an example of a "Resident Comment Form" developed by the Willamalane (OR) Park and Recreation District. This form is available at the various programs and facilities operated by this organization and can be mailed by customers directly to the superintendent of the district. Every complaint, concern, suggestion, and/or compliment is reported to the superintendent of the district, the marketing director and the supervisor of the program or facility affected. Customers making comments are guaranteed a telephone call within two days. Every effort is made to resolve the concern as soon as possible.

At a minimum, every leisure service organization should attempt to respond in writing to comments that have been made by customers. While letters of apology cannot rectify problems, they do attempt to extend the goodwill of the organization to the dissatisfied customer.

Observational Program

In addition to routine supervision by leisure service programmers and customer complaint/concern forms, the organization can implement an observation of its programs and staff. This type of quality control program places observers appearing as customers in key program settings. These observers evaluate services and staff, in order to provide both positive feedback as well as constructive criticism. Walt Disney World employs this type of program within its theme parks, calling it a "shopper program." The focus of the program is to provide information about programs and services from the guest's point of view. The program does not attempt to test the staff members through harassment or other difficult behavior, but to simply observe the situation in terms of courtesy and service, employee appearance, cleanliness of facilities and areas, telephone interaction, quality of merchandise and food, and so on.

Observation of staff, services, programs, and other factors should be based on predetermined objectives and criteria. Some of the considerations that should be considered when implementing such a program follow:

1. Define the goal of the shopper program—what are you monitoring?
2. Determine who can request the service and for what purpose.

CENTRAL OREGON PARK AND RECREATION DISTRICT

USER CONCERN SYSTEM

Section 1. PURPOSE OF THE USER CONCERN SYSTEM: The comments, suggestions and recommendations of the users of the Central Oregon Park and Recreation District can serve to strengthen, enhance, and identify areas needed for improvement. This policy sets forth, in a systematic fashion, methods and procedures for dealing with comments, suggestions and recommendations made by users. It provides for a structured means of input and review by the professional staff and the Board of Directors. This will encourage responsive action on the part of the professional staff and the Board of Directors as a whole.

Section 2. DEFINITIONS OF USER CONCERNS: A user concern is often framed in a negative sense. That is, it is viewed as a complaint rather than as an opportunity for improvement of the operations, leadership and areas and facilities of the District. Some of the areas that might be commented upon by users could include the following:

A.   Areas and Facilities. Suggestions might be made concerningthe cleanliness, design and functional aspects of areas and facilities.

B.   Programs. Activities offered by the District can result in expressions of concern.

C.   Leadership. The personal interaction that a leader has with a user can be an area of concern.

D.   Operational Procedures. Registration, program costs, methods of publicity, as well as others, can all be areas of concern.

E.   Other.

Section 3. PROCEDURES TO BE EMPLOYED IN THE USER CONCERN SYSTEM: Often-times, expressions of concern will come to individuals serving as elected or appointed members of the District. The following procedure shall be employed by all individuals, including members of the Board of Directors, the General Manager, full-time permanent employees and temporary employees. Then receiving comments, all individuals are to be courteous and willing to listen to individuals and assist them in completing proper forms.

A.   Written Documentation. All expressions of concern shall be recorded on the Central Oregon Park and Recreation District User Concern Form. This form asks for the name, address and telephone number of the individual and a description of the comment, suggestion or recommendation made.

B.   Distribution Procedures. All comments shall be recorded by the Administrative Services Coordinator for bi-weekly distribution to the Board of Directors and all permanent full-time staff members.

C.   Disposition or Action Procedures. All suggestions that must be acted on immediately because of safety shall be the responsibility of the individual and/or supervisor receiving the user concern. All other routine comments or suggestions shall be acted upon by the appropriate individual within the organization. The resulting action shall be recorded on the user concern form and become a part of the bi-weekly report made to the Board of Directors and all other staff members.

D.   Response to User Concerns. An acknowledgement in the form of a letter and/or phone call will be made to all individuals completing a user concern form. This letter will thank the individual for their input and suggest the procedures of review that will be employed. If action is taken on the concern at a later date, an additional follow-up letter shall be written.

E.   Bi-Annual Report. On a bi-annual basis, an analysis will be made of all concerns, suggestions and recommendations offered by users to the District. This will be undertaken, in order to determine trends and other areas of concern that may impact upon the operations of the District.

Figure 12.7   User Concern Policy Statement. (Central Oregon (Redmond, OR) Park and Recreation District.)

Dear Residents:

The Willamalane Park & Recreation District strives to serve the leisure needs of all its residents. It is the sincere pledge of the staff to provide the best in park and recreation facilities and services to the residents of the District. We value those that we serve. Your comments, suggestions, and input regarding our facilities and services are important to us. If we have not lived up to your expectations, we would appreciate feedback from you. It is our intent to respond to your needs in a timely and responsive fashion; your feedback will help us to better serve you.

Please complete this form and mail it to me or contact our administrative office at (503) 726-4335. Office hours are Monday through Friday, 8:00 a.m. to 5:00 p.m. Thank you.

Daniel R Plaza

Daniel R. Plaza
Superintendent

Tear Here

RESIDENT COMMENT FORM

Your Comments Are Welcome.

SERVICE QUALITY

	Excellent	Satisfactory	Improvement	Unacceptable
Staff Courtesy	☐	☐	☐	☐
Program	☐	☐	☐	☐
Convenience	☐	☐	☐	☐
Registration	☐	☐	☐	☐

FACILITY QUALITY

Appearance	☐	☐	☐	☐
Cleanliness	☐	☐	☐	☐

What other facilities or services would you like to see the Willamalane Park & Recreation District provide?

_____

_____

_____

_____

What particular facility/service is this comment directed toward? _____

_____

Date: / / Time of day: _____

(Optional Information)

Name: _____
Address: _____
City/State/Zip: _____
Telephone: _____

Your Input Helps Us Improve.

Willamalane
Park & Recreation District

RESIDENT COMMENT FORM

Willamalane
Park & Recreation District

FIRST CLASS

BUSINESS REPLY MAIL
PERMIT NO. 40   SPRINGFIELD, OR

POSTAGE WILL BE PAID BY ADDRESSEE:

DANIEL R PLAZA SUPERINTENDENT
ADMINISTRATION BUILDING
WILLAMALANE PARK & RECREATION DISTRICT
151 NORTH FOURTH STREET
SPRINGFIELD OR 97477-5498

NO POSTAGE
NECESSARY
IF MAILED
IN THE
UNITED STATES

Figure 12.8   Resident Comment Form. (Willamalane (Springfield, OR) Park and Recreation District.)

3. Have the normal customer/guest situation.
4. Have the shopper look and act like an average customer.
5. Do NOT have the shopper harass the employee.
6. Note variables of the setting (time of day, day of week, season, attendance—best to shop the person several times).
7. Educate the shopper. List specific procedures or interactions to observe.
8. Use the service for positive feedback to employees as well as suggestions for improvement.
9. Be specific in your observations and suggestions. (Telling someone he or she is not courteous is not specific enough.)
10. Develop a standard form for the shopper to use. (The Disney Approach to People Management, n.d.).

An observational program can be invaluable to a leisure programmer. It can provide methods of seeing the program or service through the eyes of the customer and thereby provide unique information that may not be possible to obtain in other ways. An observational program can be helpful in determining more effective ways to interact with the customer and thereby more effectively anticipating problems.

Summary

Perhaps one of the most important areas of leisure service programming is the actual delivery of activities or events. It is in the delivery of programs where the customer and the leader interact and the leisure experience is created and appreciated. The ability of frontline leisure service leaders and supervisors to deal effectively with customers is an essential element in this phase of program planning. The ability of leisure service organizations to create positive relations and interactions between customers and professional staff members may very well spell the difference between organizational success and failure.

The customer/leader interface is the pivotal point in the delivery of most leisure services. Leisure service organizations employ many primary

service professional staff members who have direct contact with customers. In addition, there are many individuals in leisure service organizations who serve in secondary and support roles in which contact with customers is incidental, yet still important.

Customer/leader interactions can be planned and managed. For example, organizations can plan program and activity interactions, telephone interactions, information exchanges, registration interactions, office interactions, and casual conversations. Excellent customer/leader interactions are usually reflected in attention given to a variety of behaviors including but not limited to a professional staff member's sincerity, attention to detail, courtesy, integrity, access, generosity, consistency, reliability, and responsiveness.

Since many of the professional staff members delivering leisure services are often seasonal and/or part-time employees, the supervision of such individuals is important. Supervisory activities usually involve the development of program ideas, promotion of programs, recruitment, selection and development of staff, and the control of work efforts. There are a number of specific roles and responsibilities in which leisure service supervisors engage. Some of these include attention to production, quality, cost, methods, morale, training, and safety.

An important dimension managed by frontline leaders and supervisors is the flow of an activity or event. Program flow can be thought of as the animation of an event or activity as it moves through time. Any given leisure program can be organized and delivered in such a way as to ensure satisfaction with the experience. Events and activities can be organized to produce difference emotional states and benefits for customers.

The registration procedure involves placing the names of individuals on lists for programs or services. It can be enhanced dramatically by adding value to the process selected. There are five basic methods of registration—central location, program location, mail-in, telephone, and

370

Categories of Evaluative Questions

Purpose	Goals	Strategies	Program Elements	Results
To Aid in Account-ability	What goals were chosen? What goals were considered, then rejected? What alternative goals might have been considered? What evidence exists to justify the goals that were chosen? How defensible is this evidence? How well have the goals been translated into objectives? Overall, what is the merit of the goals that were chosen?	What strategy was chosen? What alternative strategies were considered? What other strategies might have been considered? What evidence exists to justify the strategy that was chosen? How defensible is this evidence? How well was the chosen strategy translated into an operational design? Overall, what is the merit of the chosen strategy?	What was the operational design? To what extent was it implemented? What were the strengths and weaknesses of the design under operating conditions? What was the quality of the effort to implement it? What was the actual design that was implemented? Overall, what is the merit of the process that was actually carried out?	What results were achieved? Were the stated objectives achieved? What were the positive and negative side effects? What impact was made on the target audience? What long-term effects may be predicted? What is the relation of costs to benefits? Overall, how valuable were the results and impacts of this effort?

Figure 13.1 A Matrix for Identifying and Analyzing Evaluative Questions. (From Stufflebeam, D. L. (1974). *Meta-Evaluation*. Kalamazoo, MI: The Evaluation Center, 18.)

Often the question is raised, "Who should conduct the evaluation?" Another question addresses the issue of who is best qualified to conduct an evaluation—trained versus untrained personnel or internal versus external personnel. Usually a "professional" evaluation refers to one that is conducted by someone from outside the organization. Conversely, an "amateur" evaluator is usually identified as someone within the organization designated to conduct the evaluation. Essentially, it is an agency's decision whether or not to utilize an individual with specialized knowledge of design, data collection, and analysis. In addition, the advantages of using an outside evaluator may be that (1) bias-free judgment is provided, (2) a fresh view of operations is offered, and (3) objectivity regarding the program may be obtained.

Although the inside evaluator (member of program staff) may not have the precise training and expertise of the outside evaluator, he or she may be considered to have more first-hand knowledge of the overall program, be accepted by the staff, and function in a less obtrusive manner in conducting the evaluation. Possibly, his or her biases and knowledge of less obvious intervening variables may hinder objectivity. In addition, using an evaluator unskilled in evaluation techniques may render the findings null and void from the outset.

Perhaps a compromise is to provide opportunities for program staff to receive training in evaluation procedures and processes. This would enable the organization to have a so-called "expert" on staff, with the potential to train additional staff through in-service training efforts. It is important that whoever is selected for the evaluator's role understands the characteristics of evaluation to include utility, objectivity, judgment, action, and standardization (rather than scholarship, creativity, or pure research).

It is important to delineate what components of the recreation and leisure service delivery system are to be evaluated. Virtually every aspect of the operation is subject to evaluation if the organization is to understand its progress toward goals, objectives, standards, or more efficient decision making. Generally, items for evaluation can be divided into these areas:

1. *Personnel*—Direct face-to-face leaders or programmers, supervisory and administrative personnel, and support personnel—maintenance, fiscal, clerical, secretarial; includes the phenomenon of leadership.
2. *Program/Operations*—All activity and programmatic efforts including subcategories of (a) programs—visual arts, new arts, performing arts (drama, dance, and music), social recreation, hobbies and collecting, sports, games and athletics, literary arts, aquatics, volunteer services, aquatics wellness and outdoor recreation—and (b) operations—fiscal, maintenance, and supportive tasks carried out to support or promote programs, areas, facilities, or administration of the overall delivery system.
3. *Policy Dimensions/Administration*—Includes policies, rules, regulations, standards, guidelines, legislative mandates, contracts, and other dimensions establishing parameters for the organization, its personnel, and customers; the function of administration and supervision of the organization in relation to established standards, goals, or objectives.
4. *Customers*—Those individuals who participate in offerings of the recreation and leisure service delivery system on a regular or intermittent basis; potentially includes full spectrum involvement from individuals representing all age levels and both sexes; a variety of ethnic, religious, and cultural groups; individuals of varying abilities and socioeconomic levels.
5. *Physical and Fiscal Resources*—All fiscal and physical holdings of the agency, including the subject buildings; developed and undeveloped areas; land masses and water areas; equipment, materials, and supplies used in the program.

The evaluation of programs will include each of the five areas mentioned. These categories are not evaluated entirely independent of each other; there is an interaction among and between each of them. When evaluating customers' outputs, the programmer will undoubtedly examine programs, operations, administration, supervision and leadership, physical and fiscal resources, and the specific personnel who provided the programs.

The comprehensive nature of evaluation is evident. With this in mind, it is important to view the evaluation effort in a holistic sense. In other words, do not evaluate personnel in a vacuum. Many other components, variables, or ingredients are necessary before decisions can be made regarding a course of action or a summative evaluation is provided.

Common Hazards in Evaluation

In any evaluation process, there may be pitfalls, problems, or hazards. Some may be minute and pass with time or a timely strategy for eradication. Others, if allowed to go unnoticed, will post imminent hazards that will affect the success of the overall evaluation effort. The programmer, evaluator, and others engaged in the evaluation process should heed the following warning signs.

Claiming much, providing evidence of little Leisure programmers must be cautious not to overexaggerate what they have really accomplished. A good example is the "turnstile" approach—where hundreds may attend a particular activity or event. It could be claimed that it was a roaring success purely on a quantitative basis. However, the question must be asked, what evidence exists to indicate any qualitative change in attitudes, behavior, or need?

Selecting measurement instruments not logically related to the intervention In some instances, the leisure programmer may choose to upgrade the quality of the instrument being used to assess change. In the zeal to use "standardized instruments," the programmer may overlook the appropriateness of the instrument or its power to draw out the necessary information or data.

Use of norm-referenced as opposed to criterion-referenced scores or data Though we may be enamored of natural norms, we rarely have the opportunity to use them in leisure programs and services. The closest approximation is that of the psychomotor domain. Sometimes using national norms to determine fitness or other life qualities is not desirable. One tends to generalize findings, which does little to assist the individual in focusing on increasing his developmental level. Since there are few instruments available, it is desirable to evaluate individuals on the basis of where they are in relation to a developmental continuum (criterion referencing).

The careless collection of data The end result of the evaluation process may mean someone's job, increased costs or waste of money, and inappropriate use of resources. For these reasons, it is imperative that collected data be accurate, organized, and verified. Careless handling and coding of data may have serious repercussions in the future.

Having limited skills and knowledge of evaluation procedures and instrumentation An evaluator who has limited knowledge and skills in evaluation procedures, methodology, and instrumentation severely hampers the potential contribution evaluation may make to the agency, its program, and its personnel. It is important for any one assuming the role of evaluator to obtain skills in evaluation protocol, procedures, methods, and data collection so as to ensure high-quality information as a result of the evaluation process.

Allowing bias, prejudice, preconceived perceptions, or friendship to influence the evaluation outcomes Some evaluation situations may require the evaluator to come with a prepared decision. This may seriously challenge the credibility not only of the evaluator but also of the evaluation process employed. Whatever the situation, the evaluator should not be constrained or otherwise unduly influenced by political situations, innuendo, gossip, friends, or the biases and prejudices common to everyone.

Using either internal or external evaluators exclusively It is hazardous to rely solely on either an internal or external evaluator. The primary reasons are that: (1) the internal evaluator may be too close to the situation to be objective (although he or she does have a better grasp of the dynamic interactions and mood of the organization); (2) the external evaluator may, on the other hand, not be able to place all the parts of the picture together (perhaps having just arrived or possibly only being assigned to review parts of the entire operation or program). A better approach might be to maintain some semblance of balance by relying on different internal evaluators as well as periodically engaging an outside team of experts to evaluate the program.

Not planning the evaluation effort If the purpose of a particular evaluation effort is not known, it is difficult at best to forecast what impact or meaning it will have to those who hold decision-making positions. Additionally, the organization or evaluator must have a detailed evaluation plan to illustrate what the plan's purpose is, its scheduled events, approach, requirements, and deliverables or outputs (Nadler 1969: 125).

Scheduling evaluation as a cumulative or summative process Evaluation is an ongoing process, but many individuals perceive it to be what happens *after* you complete a program. Evaluation should not be relegated to a summative position. As programs are planned, developed, and implemented the process of formative evaluation must take place (Tallmadge 1977: 61–71; Bannon 1976: 267).

Ethical Considerations
Whether an individual serves as an internal or external evaluator, there are certain ethical considerations he or she must address. Although the evaluator may never stoop to the level of "payoffs" for a favorable evaluation, there is a gray area where it is difficult to determine ethically whether you should "agree or disagree," "accept or refuse," or "call attention to or overlook" a particular situation. Each individual evaluator will enter the evaluation process with a different background and different skills, values, and perceptions of right or wrong. As such, one person's decision may not necessarily be another's.

Anderson and Ball (1978: 148–149) suggest the following positions regarding ethics in evaluation:

1. The evaluator's responsibility transcends simple competence in the work of evaluation. It includes not promising too much at the outset, ensuring that role relationships are proper and secure before work begins, and insisting on appropriate warnings about the limitations of the evaluation in all reports of the results.
2. The evaluator must assume loyalties other than those to the program. These include loyalties to the profession of program evaluation and to the public, which ultimately provides the authority for both program and evaluation. Thus, the evaluator has the responsibility to refuse to perform any evaluation services demanded by a program director or funding agent that he deems unethical.
3. Evaluations should be as open as possible, within the constraints of the privacy of the participants, the confidentiality of individual data, the contractual obligations, and the smooth working of program and evaluation. When the evaluation is open, germs like suspected evaluator bias and undue program pressure do not thrive as readily.

The evaluator has specific ethical responsibilities to the individual or agency who commissions the evaluation. Above all, individuals who engage in the evaluation process must consider the ramifications of their work. The slightest deviation, error, or miscalculation in either data collection, observation, recollection, or written or oral communication could have considerable implications for the future of an agency, program, or individual employee. The evaluator should respect evaluation but never fear either the process or outcome.

Quality Assurance

A recently emerging concept, quality assurance, is related to the assessment and evaluation process. Used extensively in the medical profession, quality assurance has historically been directed toward improving health care by improving the quality of care provided. Applied in settings where therapeutic recreation services are provided, the notion of quality assurance has the potential for broader applications for other leisure service organizations. *Quality assurance can be thought of as a formal management mechanism that helps regulate services with an eye toward improving procedures that, in turn, result in a higher quality of services to customers.*

Quality assurance programs have emerged for a variety of reasons. One of the most important factors influencing the rise of quality assurance programs has been the increase in cost for services. The issue here is one of determining ways of maintaining quality while containing or even reducing costs. Another facet influencing the rise of quality assurance programs has been the dramatic change in the demand for leisure services and also the types of leisure services required in today's society. Because the field is changing rapidly, there is a need to systematically ensure that quality programs and services are provided in the face of rapidly shifting societal leisure preferences. A third reason why quality assurance has emerged as an important mechanism is the fact that leisure services, in some cases, are perceived to be of poor quality, delivered in a shoddy and unreliable manner. We live in a society that values quality and will accept only those services that produce the highest value and satisfaction; we live in a world where people have high expectations. Increased expectations often lead to dissatisfied, critical, and even litigious customers.

Our society is service-oriented. The measurement of services is difficult, challenging, and demanding. Because of the expansion of leisure services in all segments of society, there has also been, in some cases, a deterioration in the quality of services. Those leisure service organizations that address the need to maintain and/or improve levels of quality are developing uniquely defined niches in society. Quality services occur because of the careful monitoring and management of the routine, day-to-day activities of an organization as well as an awareness of the perceptions of those receiving services. Quality assurance programs demand that organizations manage their programs with excellence, in a cost-effective manner, and maintain a strong customer orientation.

According to Richards and Rathbun (1983) the essential components of a sound quality assurance program should involve several distinct elements. We have modified their recommendations from the medical profession to apply in a broader sense to the delivery of leisure services. They are as follows:

1. *Identification of Problems*—Identification of important or potential problems, or related concerns, in the leisure functioning of customers.
2. *Assessment*—Objective assessment of the cause or scope of problems or concerns. Basically, this involves determination of the reasons why problems are occurring. It is one thing to identify a problem; it is another matter to know why the situation emerged.
3. *Development of Priorities*—The next step in the process is the establishment of priorities. Priorities should be established on the assumption that the resolution/prevention of problems and enhancements in services will have a positive impact on leisure functioning of customers. Conversely, priorities can be set on the basis of the predicted impact on customers if the problems identified are not resolved.
4. *Implementation*—This step in the process involves implementation of the quality assurance program. In other words, at this point, steps are taken that deal with the quality assurance problems identified.
5. *Monitoring*—This step in the process involves keeping track of activities that have been developed to ensure that the desired quality of services has been achieved and then sustained.
6. *Documentation*—The last step in the quality assurance process is one of ensuring that appropriate records and other documents related to accountability are maintained.

Quality assurance activities have been mandated for health programs by federal health legislation. Quality assurance activities help ensure accountability to regulatory agencies, funding sources, and consumers of services (Woy et al. 1978). Quality assurance and evaluation activities are clearly linked to each other. Both are concerned with accountability. Basically, the notion of accountability has emerged as a mechanism to control the impact and cost of activities. While this idea is not new in the management of leisure service businesses, it has not been addressed forcefully in the management of political/governmental and/or voluntary leisure service organizations.

Key Concepts of Quality Assurance

A number of key concepts emerge that are related to the idea of quality assurance. First is the idea that quality assurance activities rely extensively on peer review, rather than on internal management analysis. Second, quality assurance programs are focused on the needs and welfare of the customer and not the agency. In other words, they are customer specific rather than organizationally oriented. Next, quality assurance programs are organized in such a way as to identify appropriate and adequate levels of service delivery. Quality assurance programs demand that service levels are compared to costs and, in turn, to appropriate indicators of quality. In other words, a key concept is the cost-quality trade-off; quality should be adequate but not excessive. Finally, quality assurance activities require the development of specific service plans and the planning of the transactions that are to take place between customers and leaders.

Some of the more important definitions and terms associated with the quality assurance concept are as follows:

> *Quality Assessment*—Quality assessment refers to a process directed toward measuring quality. It does not involve any attempt to change or improve levels of leisure functioning and/or program or service delivery.

> *Quality Assurance*—Quality assurance has a dual purpose. Like quality assessment, quality assurance is concerned with measuring quality. However, quality assurance is also directed toward finding mechanisms that improve the quality of services offered to customers when necessary.

> *Structural Assessment*—Structural assessments in a quality assurance program involve making judgments as to whether or not the conditions that are present provide for excellence. Structural assessments may include the number and size of buildings, the ratio of customers to staff, types of equipment, financial support, and staff management.

> *Process Assessments*—This component refers to the need for reviewing what happens to an individual during the course of participation in a leisure experience. In other words, how do we interact and handle customers that desire information about our programs, participate in them, or have some other involvement or relationship with the leisure service organization.

> *Outcome Assessment*—Outcome assessment refers to the analysis of the skill to which customers exhibit behaviors, attitudes, and skills that are desired or planned as a result of participation in a leisure experience. It can also refer to the level of leisure functioning following participation in a leisure activity.

> *Efficacy*—The concept of efficacy refers to the degree to which the customer achieves or does not achieve benefit from leisure programs and services under ideal circumstances. Whereas efficiency refers to the benefits derived under average circumstances, efficacy asks the question "What benefits can be obtained when a leisure service is delivered in circumstances that are *most advantageous* to both the customer and the service provider?"

> *Technical Care*—Another concept refers to the measurement of technical care. Technical care, especially in therapeutic recreation settings, refers to the diagnostic procedures used and methods and treatment techniques in terms of their appropriateness.

> *Art-of-Care*—Whereas technical care is concerned with the procedures used in delivering

services, art-of-care focuses on the measurement of the quality of interaction between the providers of leisure services and customers. Measurements might include communication patterns, leadership behavior and style, and ethical practices (confidentiality, integrity, honesty, and so on).

In assessing quality within leisure service organizations, there are two variables that can be examined—*program elements and desired outcomes*. In Chapter 2, we discussed six elements that could be manipulated in order to produce a leisure program. In general, these six elements deal with such concerns as the soundness of the physical structures within a leisure service organization, the types of objects present, the rules used to govern interactions, and the process or ordering of the leisure service program or event itself. For example, one of the key elements in assuring quality is to make sure that the interactions (transactions) that take place between a leader and a customer are positive. Often, this requires ensuring that individuals act in a courteous, positive, helpful, competent, and sincere fashion. When referring to outcomes as a way of assessing quality, we are referring to what actually happened to the customer, in terms of their level of leisure satisfaction, leisure functioning, and so on.

Evaluation and Quality Assurance: Similarities and Differences

Quality assurance and evaluation activities have similarities and differences. However, one thing is clear: both evaluation and quality assurance are concerned with accountability and control. Perhaps the most significant difference between evaluation and quality assurance is the focus of the analysis. In evaluating leisure programs, there is a tendency to analyze the performance of leisure programs and services in relation to the goals and objectives that have been established. In measuring the achievement of goals and objectives, an effort is made to determine the effectiveness and efficiency in meeting these ends. On

the other hand, quality assurance activities focus on issues that are customer-specific and related to the work of professionals in providing services. Often, evaluative criteria are established to measure performance. Thus, the focus in quality assurance is on what happens to people, rather than on whether or not the program is organized and constructed in an efficient and effective manner, as it is in program evaluation.

Table 13.1 points out the key differences between evaluation and quality assurance. Quality assurance programs, especially in medical settings (these would affect many therapeutic recreation programs) have been mandated by legislation. On the other hand, evaluation schemes adopted by leisure service organizations do not emerge because of legal mandates, but often are established as one of the steps in the programming process. Another difference is that quality assurance programs require extensive peer review, as contrasted with program evaluation, which relies primarily on administrative review. Other notable differences between these two processes are the methods that are used to gather information and draw conclusions about service delivery and customer satisfaction.

Approaches to Evaluation

There are a number of approaches and models that can be used to evaluate the five categories mentioned earlier in the chapter (personnel, program/operations, policy dimensions/administration, customers, physical and fiscal resources). This section provides seven selected approaches to evaluation, with representative models to illustrate their relationship to recreation programming. These selected approaches are not all inclusive but do provide the reader with basic tools with which to begin. Additionally, it should be noted that some of the methods and models require several years of training because of their sophistication or complexity. Overviews are provided to present the rudiments of each.

TABLE 13.1   Contrasting Characteristics between Program Evaluation and Quality Assurance

Key Variables	Program Evaluation	Quality Assurance
Legislative Sanctions	Minimal but increasing	Extensive—but only in the past 10 years
Reliance on Peer Review	Minimal	Extensive
Reliance on Administrative Review	Extensive	Minimal
Level of Analysis	Generalized and program-specific, focused on data-based judgments about program (or service modality) effort, efficiency, effectiveness, and relevance	Client- and service provider-specific and focused on quality of specific service delivery transactions through reliance on service/client records
Basic Objectives	• Maintain high levels of effort relative to program capacity for effort • Assess outcome and select most effective/efficient programs • Assess relevance and impact of total program effort with regard to service needs in a specified community	• Assure that individual clients receive appropriate care • Detect deficiencies and errors in service provider capacity • Control costs by preventing overutilization and ensuring that needed services are provided in a timely, efficient manner
Principal Methods	• Analysis of resource utilization, capacity for effort, and level of effort • Assessment of outcomes and the effectiveness of program effort • Assessment of program efficiency relative to effort and outcomes • Analysis of comparative cost-effectiveness • Analysis of program adequacy relative to needs for services	• Concurrent review —Admissions certification —Continued stay review —Utilization review and "length of stay" analysis • Retrospective review —Medical (clinical) care evaluation —profile monitoring

Atkisson et al. 1978: 413.

The seven selected approaches include (1) *goals, objectives, and discrepancy approach;* (2) *expert judgment approach;* (3) *systems planning and decision-oriented approach;* (4) *standards approach;* (5) *policy analysis approach;* (6) *research method approach;* and (7) *communicative and interactive approach.*

Goals, Objectives, and Discrepancy Approach

This particular approach to evaluation *involves identification of goals and objectives and then an assessment to determine the discrepancy between the expected performance/outcome and the actual or realized performance/outcome.* From a simple perspective, this approach to evaluation involves establishing a set of goals and objectives, organizing and implementing a program or service, determining the extent to which goals and objectives are actually attained, and then using this information

to change or modify the program offering. Figure 13.2 presents the basic process used in this type of evaluation.

The *goal attainment scaling model* serves to illustrate the goals, objectives, or discrepancy evaluative approach. Conceived as an evaluation scheme with the individual as the object of the analysis, goal attainment scaling has been adapted as a program evaluation model. A GAS model provides for "goal setting as a regular program activity and facilitates assessment of goal-method-outcome relationships" (Franklin and Thrasher 1976: 80).

The goal attainment scale requires that a number of goals be established which the organization or program wishes to attain. Each goal is assigned a weight relative to the other goals and the organization's status with regard to the goals at the beginning of the evaluation period. The gradients typically used are:

1. Most unfavorable outcome likely
2. Less than expected results
3. Expected level
4. More than expected
5. Best anticipated results

The most unfavorable outcome receives a score of 1 and the best anticipated results a score of 5. The goals might be to (1) introduce new

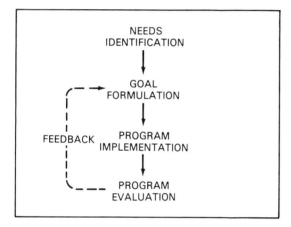

Figure 13.2   The Process of Program Evaluation.

			Weighted Value			
	10	10	15	10	5	10	10

programming, (2) improve existing programming, (3) improve physical facilities, (4) upgrade staff levels, (5) increase staff competence, (6) improve community relations, (7) obtain additional funding. These goals are then weighted according to importance. If goal 3 was considered to be the most important, it might be given a weight of 15; the least important goal might be given a weight of 5.

For each goal, five possible outcomes are established. For goal 3, improving physical facilities, the possible outcomes might be (from least favorable outcome to best results):

1. No improvement in physical facilities
2. Maintenance and repairs made on existing facilities
3. Existing facilities remodeled
4. Expand existing facilities to desired specifications
5. New physical facilities constructed

At the beginning of the evaluation period, the current level of functioning is determined by multiplying the weighted value by the program level of attainment for each goal and adding the scores. At the end of the evaluation period, the scores are recomputed to produce an *actual goal attainment score* (English n.d.).

In Figure 13.3, the actual goal attainment score is computed by multiplying 15 (weighted value) by 1 (level of attainment), 10 by 3, 10 by 3, 10 by 3, 10 by 2, 10 by 4, and 5 by 1 and adding these totals. The actual goal attainment score for this program is 170.

It is apparent from the description that GAS is one means of quantifying evaluative data and allows programs to be compared numerically with their previous levels. It is frequently useful to be able to present such data to lay people who may not be familiar with more traditional ways of evaluating program changes. Goal attainment scaling also allows one program to be compared with another within an organization or with similar programs in other organizations.

Figure 13.3   A Sample Goal Attainment Scale.

The function of the *discrepancy evaluation model* (DEM) is as follows:

> [A means of] comparison of what is, a performance (P), to an expectation of what should be, a standard (S). If a difference is found to exist between the standard and the performance, the difference is known as a discrepancy (D). If a performance exceeded the standard the discrepancy is positive. A negative discrepancy exists when the performance is less than the standard.
>
> In an established program, three types of evaluation are performed. Input evaluation seeks to determine whether the program has been instituted as it was planned. Process evaluation monitors the sequential accomplishment of enabling objectives. These two types are essentially aimed at program improvement. The third type of evaluation is output evaluation, designed to assess the program for achievement of terminal objectives and substantiate causation (Yavorsky, 1976: 5).

Since the DEM is based on the concept that performance must be compared to standards, the standards are formally represented in the program design, a part of which includes the objectives of the program. The program design should set forth input standards or resources to be used in the program. In the recreation setting, resources might include clients, staff, physical facilities, and equipment. Process standards should describe the means to be used to fulfill the program goals. Processes used in the recreation setting would be the recreation programming offered in a particular situation. Output standards are the goals the program seeks to achieve. In the case of recreation programming, probable outputs would be skills and attitudes. Output standards can also be called terminal performance objectives or enabling objectives.

Once the standards are established, it is possible to compare the program performance with them to see if discrepancies exist. If there are discrepancies, three types of action can be taken

to correct them: (1) performance can be controlled to a greater extent to produce conformity to the standard; (2) the standard can be redesigned to reflect the actual performance; or (3) the program can be terminated. In each case, the program design is affected. If the program begins anew, a new evaluation cycle is instituted with a new program design and a new plan for evaluation (see Figure 13.4).

The DEM is quite extensive and requires training to adequately conduct its intricate procedures. The positive side of DEM is that it provides a valid and reliable approach that can be used by internal evaluators. This avoids the high costs of using external evaluators or teams.

Another model to measure discrepancies between desired goals and objectives and outcomes is the *service hour evaluation model*. In this model, the leisure service programmer establishes a goal of the number of service hours a given event or activity should produce. According to Rossman (1989: 391) service hours can be determined by

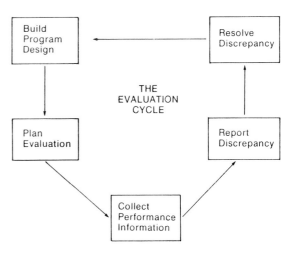

Figure 13.4   Discrepancy Evaluation Model. (From Yavorsky, D. K. (1976). *Discrepancy evaluation: A practitioner's guide.* Charlottesville, VA: Evaluation Research Center, 5.)

multiplying the length of time a program is offered times the number of customers. Rossman offers the following model:

$$C \times H = SH$$

In this formula, a service hour (SH) is equal to one customer (C) participating for one hour (H). This strategy can be linked to other variables such as age, gender, and geographic location, in order to provide information concerning the number of program service hours actually delivered to a target population. If a leisure service organization establishes a goal of providing a specific number of service hours to a target group then an analysis of the actual service hours can provide a basis for the discrepancy that might occur. Many leisure service organizations are concerned about the cost-effectiveness of programs. Establishing a common denominator to measure programs, such as service hours, can yield more precise and accurate information concerning costs.

Expert Judgment Approach

Sometimes it is necessary to obtain another opinion regarding the delivery of leisure programs. The *use of experts or consultants to evaluate parts of or an entire program* is common practice. The expert may choose to use some formal approach to evaluation but usually the individual's opinion or judgment is what is being sought by the individual or agency who commissions the evaluation.

The positive side of using the expert judgment approach is that the approach and results tend to be specific and void of complicated forms, processes, or statistical treatments. In addition, the expert may bring his reputation to bear on the outcome of the evaluation. The drawbacks to this approach include: (1) the expert's biases and prejudices; (2) the focus on one portion of the program rather than the entire effort; (3) the lack of a valid and reliable methodology; (4) subjective nature of the effort; and (5) the cost.

Individuals who can provide expert judgment oftentimes bring a fresh point of view to the evaluation process. They may view the program in an entirely different light. Using experts to pass judgments on a portion of a program does appear to be something of a luxury.

Systems Designs and Decision-Oriented Approach

Systems designs, as applied to the provision of leisure services, *involve a step-by-step analysis of the procedures and events used in organizing and delivering programs.* Subsequently, an analysis of the extent to which these procedural models produce desired outcomes allows for evaluation to occur. Like the goal discrepancy model of evaluation, systems designs enable the programmer to gauge the extent to which a particular preconceived approach to organizing a program produces desired outcomes. Thus, systems designs guide planning activities, implementation activities, and serve as a basis for review and control of programs.

Three techniques are particularly useful in evaluating leisure services and serve to illustrate the application of systems designs to the evaluation process. These are *program evaluation review technique* (PERT), *critical path method* (CPM), and *management by objectives* (MBO).

PERT is an event-oriented technique, which focuses on the planning, scheduling, and controlling of events in a quantitative manner. Its primary analytical device is a network or flow chart, which illustrates how the programmer moves toward achieving a stated goal or objective. In the PERT chart, major events are noted, with activity linkage between events. Time estimated to complete the event is listed between the events. This estimate of time is expressed in the following manner:

1. *Optimistic Time (to)*—Length of time required without complications or unforeseen difficulties arising in the activity.

2. *Most Likely Time (tm)*—Length of time in which the activity is most likely to be completed; estimated under "normal" conditions.
3. *Pessimistic Time (tp)*—Length of time required if unusual complications or unforeseen difficulties occur (Williams 1972: 17–18).

As is indicated in Figure 13.5, the time to complete a particular activity is estimated to be optimistic (three hours), most likely (six hours), and pessimistic (nine hours).

PERT can be used in a variety of ways, including research and development, program planning, construction, maintenance, staff development, and building or area operations. There are six distinct advantages to using PERT:

1. Creation of a realistic, detailed, easy-to-communicate plan, which greatly improves the chances for attainment of project objectives.
2. Prediction of time and uncertainties of performance.
3. Attention focused on parts of a project that are most likely to impede or delay its achievement.
4. Information provided about project resources that are not being fully utilized.
5. Simulation of alternative plans and schedules.
6. Provision of thorough and frequent project status reports.

PERT requires training in order to be used effectively as a technique in parks and recreation. More sophisticated aspects, including computer application, require additional training in computer programming.

The first step in PERT is to establish the program or project objective. Once the objective is identified, the programmer needs to delineate all tasks or activities necessary to accomplish the objective. The next step is to actually plot the information on a Gantt or bar chart (see Figure 13.6) or a network.

PERT incorporates the critical path method (CPM) in that each activity is graphically illustrated, so that the least restrictive, most expeditious path is taken to ensure maximum return and efficiency in program delivery.

Mittelstaedt and Berger (1972) illustrate the CPM and its application to program or activity execution. In Figure 13.7 the steps required to produce or sponsor a dramatic show are illustrated.

The advantage of using PERT/CPM as an evaluative approach is its contribution to the systematic planning and execution of proposed objectives. Through logical and sequential systems planning, the programmer can improve the efficiency with which programs are delivered. In addition, it is an excellent model for formative evaluation. The major drawback is that PERT/CPM focuses primarily on quantitative measurements of performance. It does not attempt to analyze the qualitative aspects of a program.

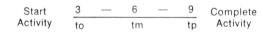

Figure 13.5   PERT Estimate of Time.

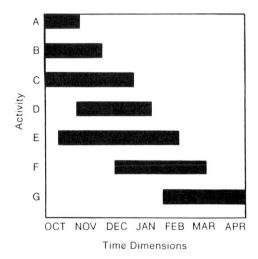

Figure 13.6   Sample Gantt or Bar Chart.

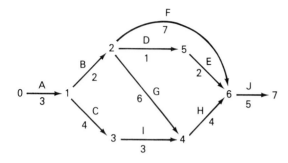

Task		Time

Task A	Choose and obtain play and director
Task B	Cast actors
Task C	Select staff
Task D	Prepare scenery and props
Task E	Install scenery and props
Task F	Advertise play
Task G	Rehearse actors
Task H	Prepare costuming and effects
Task I	Print tickets and programs
Task J	Dress rehearsal

Figure 13.7 CPM for a Drama Presentation. (Mittelesteadt, A. H. & Berger, H. A. (1972). The critical path method: A management tool for recreation. *Parks & Recreation* 8(7), 14–15.)

Additional benefits of PERT/CPM, as cited below, indicate that it will:

1. encourage a logical discipline in the planning, scheduling, and control of projects;
2. encourage more long-range and detailed planning of projects;
3. provide a standard method of documenting and communicating project plans, schedules, and time and cost performance;
4. identify the most critical elements in the plan, focusing management attention on the 10 to 20 percent of the project that is most constraining on the schedule; and
5. illustrate the effects of technical and procedural changes on the overall schedule (Moder and Phillips 1964: 5–6).

Although there are several key proponents of MBO, there are almost as many definitions as there are proponents. McConkey (1975: 10–11) defines MBO as

A systems approach to managing an organization . . . . It is not a technique, or just another program, or a narrow area of the process of managing . . . it encompasses budgetary (but goes far beyond). First, those accountable for directing the organization determine where they want to take the organization or what they want it to achieve during a particular period . . . . Second, all key managerial, professional, and administrative personnel are required, permitted, and encouraged to contribute their maximum efforts to achieving the overall objectives. Third, the planned achievements (results) of all key personnel are blended and balanced to promote and realize the greater total results for the organization as a whole. Fourth, a control mechanism is established to monitor progress compared to objectives and feed the results back to those accountable at all levels.

Utilizing the systems approach to planning and decision making, MBO is composed of five components: objectives; plan; managerial direction, and action; control (monitoring); and feedback.

The basic elements of MBO are illustrated in Figure 13.8. Notice that the foundation of the managing cycle is measuring results (evaluation).

Standards Approach
Another avenue for evaluation is the standards approach, in which *a set of local, state, national, program-specific, or federal standards are applied to the existing program or operations of an agency*. This is the most frequently used approach in the park and recreation field and may be appealing because of the checklist nature of data collection.

Bannon (1976: 268) notes that as proponents of the use of standards suggest, the checklists employed require few of the research skills typically associated with evaluative research. The

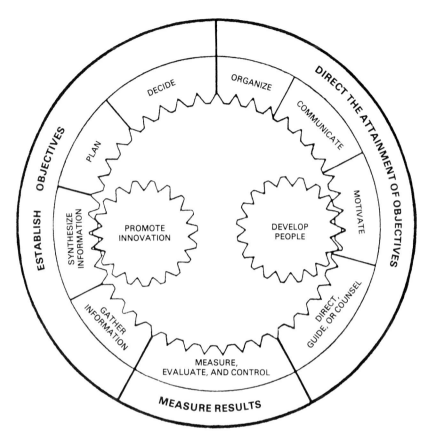

Figure 13.8 MBO and the Managing Process. (From McConkey, D. D. (1975). MBO for nonprofit organizations. NY: American Management Association, 16.)

checklist approach is relatively inexpensive. The standards approach permits some comparison across programs. This approach also provides the administrator with a chance to look closely at his or her program; in fact the greatest strength of this approach may be not the evaluation itself, but the process of self-appraisal.

There are a number of prominent standards in the park and recreation field, including: Van der Smissen, "Evaluation and Self Study of Public Recreation and Park Agencies"; American Camping Association (ACA) national standards for camps; Joint Commission on Accreditation of Hospitals (and affiliate committees); national standards for long-term care facilities; Intermediate Care Facilities for the Mentally Retarded;

psychiatric facilities standards; and normalization standard entitled Program Analysis of Service Systems (PASS), developed by Wolfsenberger. All of these establish standards that may be used to compare actual practice.

One major drawback of the standards approach is that what may be an appropriate standard for one system may be obsolete, outdated, or inappropriate for another. As Bannon (1976: 269) indicates:

> Reliance on national standards or guidelines may mask the necessity to identify the needs and desires of the population to be served. Furthermore, evaluating through checklists and schedules seldom requires the description of the

impact of program activity on the community or participant. The judgement of program effectiveness is often limited to one person. Collective judgments are seldom tapped, and the self-appraisal nature of the approach is clearly subject to bias.

Closely associated with the standards approach is the notion of accreditation, certification, licensure, or registration. Usually the agency or individual is examined in relation to a set of a priori standards or criteria and judged as to whether or not it meets the minimums established by a review board. Such is the case with the National Recreation and Park Association/American Association for Leisure and Recreation (NRPA/AALR) Accreditation Standards for park and recreation curricula. In addition, states may have certification, registration, or licensure programs by which personnel are identified as having achieved a certain set of criteria, standards, or score on an examination.

These programs of professional evaluation, when applied correctly, are helpful in screening out unprepared or unqualified persons in the field. As is the case in many other professions, the criteria are oftentimes broad or weak and coupled with grandfather clauses, and offer little assurance of quality or performance.

In addition to the standards and accreditation, certification, and licensure or registration approaches is the *investigative* approach. This approach is usually problem-oriented and commissioned by an outside agency, controlling board, or administrative authority. Central to the investigative approach is the need to identify the source of an existing problem, take immediate corrective action and monitor any mandates of the investigative team. Usually the investigative team is composed of individuals with administrative, legal, or enforcement authority. Such an approach is rarely pleasant. The results are also sometimes punitive and devastating to both personnel and programs.

The advantage of the investigative approach may lie in its focus on a specific problem with the intent that the problem be resolved immediately. The drawbacks are that it is usually perceived as being negative by both the evaluator/investigator and the individual or individuals being investigated.

Policy Analysis Approach

The policy analysis is yet another way to evaluate leisure programs. In order to provide leisure services, organizations, agencies, and businesses promulgate policies, procedures, and practices to guide their work. Analyzing organizational policies prior to their implementation attempts to predict: (1) What effects would be produced if the policy were implemented? or (2) What effects would be produced if the policy were not implemented? The difference between these two courses of action would indicate the predicted effect of the policy. Conversely, analyzing policies after they have been implemented can help the organization determine the degree to which the policy and consequent program have had the intended effect. *The policy analysis approach focuses on the examination of agency policies with the intent that thorough examination and evaluation will result in them being retained, reformulated, or discarded.*

There are four basic approaches to policy analysis that can be employed by leisure service organizations. These are (1) impact analysis, (2) cost benefit analysis, (3) implementation analysis, and (4) political analysis. Following is a brief discussion of each of these approaches to policy analysis.

Impact analysis Impact analysis attempts to determine what societal change will occur if a policy is implemented. It involves the construction of a systematic plan to collect and analyze data in order to attempt to predict the impact on society of a given program. A given policy may have an economical, political, social, cultural, and/or environmental impact on individuals, institutions, communities, and social systems.

Cost-benefit analysis Cost-benefit analysis attempts to weigh the resources that would be committed to implement a given policy against the predicted policy outcomes. It is a process for structuring a decision-making framework to evaluate alternatives and select the best course of action. Cost-benefit analysis is particularly useful when trying to decide between two programs or projects that achieve the same objectives.

Implementation analysis This method of policy analysis focuses on the feasibility of procedures, methods, and practices associated with a given policy. Basically, this approach asks the questions, "Can the agency carry out the policy?" Just because a policy is established it doesn't guarantee that an organization has the capacity or ability to implement it. Organizations often don't produce the impact that is desired because of lack of resources, not because the policy is not a good idea.

Political analysis The last method of policy analysis attempts to determine whether or not a policy will be acceptable to decision makers. If decision makers are not willing to support a policy, it is not likely that it will be implemented. Therefore, this is an important aspect of policy analysis.

The examination of policies is an often overlooked practice in the evaluation of programs and services. This approach helps us determine the feasibility and desirability of policies that exist within organizations. This approach to evaluation is especially useful in political/governmental organizations and voluntary organizations. However, it is not confined or limited to either of these two sectors.

Research Method Approach

Formalized research comprises much of the evaluation being done in the field of leisure today. There are a variety of research models that have been adapted for use in program evaluation.

Table 13.2 lists *nine basic methods of research* and briefly describes their purposes and how they might be used.

Basic to all these methods is the need to plan the research well. This requires that the problem area is identified and the literature relating to it is thoroughly surveyed. The actual problem to be investigated must be defined clearly and specifically. Then a hypothesis must be formulated—one that is possible to test—and the variables and concepts defined. The research design is then developed to maximize the internal and external validity. In other words, were any changes in results attributable to the treatment in question, and can the results of this research be generalized to populations other than those actually involved in the research?

While these steps are desirable in conducting formal research, it is possible for research to be done effectively but in a less-structured fashion. Action research is carried on in the setting in which the results are to be applied—i.e., the classroom or recreation center. The problem is defined and a general procedure for the conduct of the research is formulated prior to the start of the study. In casual or "common sense" approach research, there is even less formalization of the research process. A problem is identified but not specifically defined; procedures are loosely planned, and changes are noted by informal observation of the planned treatment.

Research is a useful evaluative tool in that the results are quantifiable and thus more easily interpreted by those outside the field. Because research designs seek to provide both reliability and validity there is a high degree of confidence in the results of the study.

However, it is also true that many research designs require a high degree of expertise on the part of the evaluator in designing the research and in interpreting the results, and may be costly in terms of time and money. In applying research designs to ongoing programs, it is difficult to build in the types of controls required in true research, and certain ethical questions arise

TABLE 13.2 Nine Basic Methods of Research

Method	Purpose	Examples
Historical	To reconstruct the past objectively and accurately, often in relation to the tenability of a hypothesis.	A study reconstructing practices in the teaching of spelling in the United States during the past fifty years; tracing the history of civil rights in U.S. education since the Civil War; testing the hypothesis that Francis Bacon is the real author of the works of William Shakespeare.
Descriptive	To describe systematically a situation or area of interest factually and accurately.	Population census studies, public opinion surveys, fact-finding surveys, status studies, task analysis studies, questionnaire and interview studies, observation studies, job descriptions, surveys of the literature, documentary analyses, anecdotal records, critical incident reports, test score analyses, and normative data.
Developmental	To investigate patterns and sequences of growth and/or change as a function of time.	A longitudinal growth study following an initial sample of 200 children from six months of age to adulthood; a cross-sectional growth study investigating changing patterns of intelligence by sampling groups of children at ten different age levels; a trend study projecting the future growth and educational needs of a community from past trends and recent building estimates.
Case and Field	To study intensively the background, current status, and environmental interactions of a given social unit: an individual, group, institution, or community.	The case history of a child with an above average IQ but with severe learning disabilities; an intensive study of a group of teenage youngsters on probation for drug abuse; an intensive study of a typical suburban community in the Midwest in terms of its socioeconomic characteristics.
Correlational	To investigate the extent to which variations in one factor correspond with variations in one or more other factors based on correlation coefficients.	Investigation of relationships between reading achievement scores and one or more other variables of interest; a factor-analytic study of several intelligence tests; a study to predict success in college based on intercorrelation patterns between college grades and selected high school variables.
Causal-Comparative or Ex Post Facto	To investigate possible cause-and-effect relationships by observing some existing consequence and searching back through the data for plausible causal factors.	Identification of factors related to the drop-out problem in a particular high school using data from records over the past ten years; to investigate similarities and differences between such groups as smokers and nonsmokers, readers and nonreaders, or delinquents and nondelinquents, using data on file.

TABLE 13.2   Nine Basic Methods of Research—*Continued*

Method	Purpose	Examples
True Experimental	To investigate possible cause-and-effect relationships by exposing one or more experimental groups to one or more treatment conditions and comparing the results to one or more control groups not receiving the treatment (random assignment being essential).	Investigation of the effectiveness of three methods of teaching reading to first grade children using random assignments of children and teachers to groups and methods; to investigate the effects of a specific tranquilizing drug on the learning behavior of boys identified as hyperactive using random assignment to groups receiving three different levels of the drug and two control groups with and without a placebo, respectively.
Quasi-Experimental	To approximate the conditions of the true experiment in a setting which does not allow the control and/or manipulation of all relevant variables. The researcher must clearly understand what compromises exist in the internal and external validity of his or her design and proceed within these limitations.	Most so-called field experiments, operational research, and even the more sophisticated forms of action research which attempt to get at causal factors in real life settings where only partial control is possible; e.g., an investigation of the effectiveness of any method or treatment condition where random assignment of subjects to methods or conditions is not possible.
Action	To develop new skills or new approaches and to solve problems with direct application to the classroom or other applied setting.	An in-service training program to help teachers develop new skills in facilitating class discussions; to experiment with new approaches to teaching reading to bilingual children; to develop more effective counseling techniques for underachievers.

Isacc and Michale 1971: 14.

in the withholding of beneficial treatments from a segment of a test population merely for purposes of research.

Communicative and Interactive Approach

As in the needs identification and assessment process, *the communicative interactive approach is based on the involvement of individuals, community groups, special interest groups, and focus groups to gather information before the planning of a program.* Likewise, it is often useful to work with individual customers and customer groups on a face-to-face basis while they are participating in a leisure experience and at its conclusion. The strategies described in Chapter 5, Needs Identification and Assessment, can be applied effectively in the evaluation process.

The major advantage of this approach to evaluation is getting direct and sometimes even immediate feedback from the actual customer who has participated in the service. Communicative and interactive approaches to evaluation often provide an opportunity for the professional to have a dialogue with the customer. The process is interactive; this implies that a two-way exchange is taking place. Thus, the professional is able to explore further the attitudes, values, and behavior states of the customer. This enables the leisure service professional to probe below the surface to gain more in-depth knowledge and understanding of the customer's response to a given leisure experience.

The communicative and interactive approach demands attention to high ethical standards.

Confidentiality must often be maintained when discussing the impact of the organization's work upon the customer. Further, care must be taken to ensure that the leisure service professional does not abuse the relationship of trust that is established with the customer. Withstanding these concerns the communicative and interactive approach to evaluation holds great promise for more fully understanding the ways in which programs affect customers. The amount of information that can be generated from this type of evaluation approach is staggering.

This approach to evaluation also lends itself to qualitative as well as quantitative analysis. Qualitative evaluation focuses more on factors that are difficult to assign numbers to. As Kraus and Allen (1987: 24) have written, qualitative evaluation ". . . examples might include behavioral styles, aesthetic qualities, personality traits or feelings . . . ." Understanding these factors may be central to determining the extent to which an organization has satisfactorily provided a meaningful leisure experience. By communicating and interacting with people, we can gauge more effectively their personal responses and feelings about a particular leisure experience or event. Ultimately, if we are to measure the true impact of our professional efforts, we must begin to understand what happens to individuals subjectively when they experience leisure.

Data Collection: An Overview of Instruments

Earlier in the chapter, it was stated there were five categories of items to be evaluated (personnel, program/operations, policy dimensions/administration, customers, and physical and fiscal resources). In order to evaluate any one or all of these categories, the leisure service programmer selects an appropriate model or approach. Some of the approaches that can be used to measure these factors are *attitude and rating scales, case and field studies, checklists, importance performance analysis approach,* and *questionnaires.* However,

before data collection can take place, the programmer must first know what is to be evaluated and what approach is to be taken in collecting the required information or data.

This section presents an overview of several methods of data collection. The programmer should be cautious when selecting a measuring instrument. Farrell and Lundegren (1983: 222–223) suggest *twelve attributes of a good measuring instrument:*

1. The first attribute and the most important one is that the test should possess reliability, validity, and objectivity. If these qualities are missing, then there is almost no need to judge it further—it is not adequate.
2. The tool should measure the important factors. What these factors are should be determined by the objectives of the program or its sub-parts.
3. It should be appropriate to the participants evaluated in terms of such things as age, sex, and special factors (e.g., reading level). For example, the Tennessee Self-Concept Scale requires a sixth-grade reading level and is therefore inappropriate for young children.
4. It should discriminate between those people, programs, or facilities that possess the trait being measured and those who do not have it, and be sensitive enough to identify a real difference if one exists.
5. It should be given in a reasonable length of time. For example, a questionnaire that takes one-and-one-half hours to administer would not be the tool of choice at the formative evaluation stage of a new crafts program.
6. A good test should be easy to prepare and administer—the less complex the better, providing it still does what it is purported to do.
7. Availability of norms and standards should be considered, as they serve to strengthen interpretation of test results.
8. There should be clear, concise directions.
9. The scores should be readily interpretable.
10. The attribute that is measured should be clearly delineated so that it is clear specifically what was lacking in performance and what type of modification is needed. For example, if a campsite

in a state park were rated on a score of one to ten, and it received a four, what does the park superintendent know in terms of modifying the sites in order to receive a ten? The person receiving the evaluation should gain some idea of what to change. Feedback should be provided by the instrument.

11. Tested scoring directions should be provided.
12. It should measure unique data that have not already been gained in some other way.

Attitude and Rating Scales

The *measurement of an individual's attitude* is usually difficult. Several data collection approaches and instruments can be used to obtain quantitative measures. Attitude scales generally attempt to overcome errors obtained from using rating scales. Pelegrino (1979) indicates that two criteria are commonly used in selecting items for inclusion in a scale.

> First, the items must elicit responses that are psychologically related to the attitudes being measured. Secondly, the scale must differentiate among people who are at different points concerning the dimension being measured. To differentiate among such individuals, items that are discriminated at different points on the scale are usually included (1979: 158).

There are basically three types of attitude scales including: (1) the Likert (summation scale), (2) equal appearing intervals (Thurstone), and (3) the cumulative scale (Guttman).

The most popular and widely used attitude scale in recreation is the Likert scale. This data collection technique is a scale of five items ranging from (5) strongly agree to (1) strongly disagree. Other points on the scale include (4) agree, (3) undecided, and (2) disagree. The ability to assign a numerical value to each category allows for statistical treatment. An example of the Likert scale is provided in Table 13.3.

An additional attitude measurement that is frequently used in leisure studies is the semantic

differential technique. The essence of this technique is the establishment of bipolar objective pairs (e.g., leisure-work) and a scale in between where the respondent can select a position. Neulinger (1974: 175–176) incorporates this technique in his study of leisure. An example is presented in Table 13.4.

TABLE 13.3 Example of Likert Scale

Below are listed a number of free-time activities. Using the scale values given, indicate what in your opinion society's position regarding these activities should be.

This Activity Should Be:	Scale Values
Very strongly encouraged	7
Strongly encouraged	6
Encouraged	5
Neither encouraged nor discouraged	4
Discouraged	3
Strongly discouraged	2
Very strongly discouraged	1

Free-Time Activities:	Your Position
a—Activities emphasizing mental endeavors such as studying, taking adult education courses, etc.	_____ (1)
b—Activities involving the taking of habit-forming drugs	_____ (2)
c—Activities that consist basically of doing nothing, being idle, "hanging around," etc.	_____ (3)
d—Activities involving active participation in social affairs, such as volunteer work, club activities, etc. ...	_____ (4)
e—Activities that consist basically of doing nothing, efforts, such as writing, painting, or playing an instrument.	_____ (5)
f—Activities involving the consumption of alcohol	_____ (6)
g—Activities involving productive efforts, such as certain hobbies like woodworking, leather tooling, sewing, etc.	_____ (7)
h—Activities involving physical exercise, such as sports and calisthenics, hunting and fishing, or just walking.	_____ (8)

Neulinger 1974: 176.

TABLE 13.4 Example of Semantic Differential Scale

Below are sixteen 7-point scales each referring to a word pair. Use these scales to describe what *leisure* means to you. The scale points indicate the following:

1 = Extremely
2 = Quite
3 = Slightly
4 = Neutral or unrelated
5 = Slightly
6 = Quite
7 = Extremely

Put a check mark at that point on the scale which best describes what leisure means to you.

For example, if the word pair is
  beautiful   1   ✓   3   4   5   6   7   ugly

and you feel that leisure is *quite* beautiful, you would check 2 on the scale; on the other hand, if you feel that leisure is *extremely* ugly, you would have checked 7 on the scale.

Word Pairs

Leisure Is:

boring	1 2 3 4 5 6 7	interesting	(51)
solitary	1 2 3 4 5 6 7	sociable	(52)
honest	1 2 3 4 5 6 7	dishonest	(53)
empty	1 2 3 4 5 6 7	full	(54)
desirable	1 2 3 4 5 6 7	undesirable	(55)
necessary	1 2 3 4 5 6 7	unnecessary	(56)
powerful	1 2 3 4 5 6 7	powerless	(57)
mature	1 2 3 4 5 6 7	developing	(58)
valuable	1 2 3 4 5 6 7	worthless	(59)
meaningful	1 2 3 4 5 6 7	meaningless	(60)
passive	1 2 3 4 5 6 7	active	(61)
satisfying	1 2 3 4 5 6 7	unsatisfying	(62)
thin	1 2 3 4 5 6 7	thick	(63)
good	1 2 3 4 5 6 7	bad	(64)
refreshing	1 2 3 4 5 6 7	tiring	(65)
pleasant	1 2 3 4 5 6 7	unpleasant	(66)

Neulinger 1974: *The psychology of leisure*. Springfield, Ill.: Thomas, 175–176.

Gunn and Peterson (1978: 257) provide another type of scale, referred to as a *rating scale*. The intent of the rating scale is to determine the level of performance of an individual during a specific observation period. This is usually done in relation to selected behavioral objectives. Table 13.5 provides information on a hypothetical course in drama and the performance of each class member.

Each of these measurement tools is appropriate to use in collecting data on personnel, program/operations, policy dimensions/administration, customers, and physical/fiscal resources.

Case and Field Study

Case studies are *in-depth investigations of an individual, unit, organization, or agency.* The data is organized in a manner that presents not only a historical perspective, but also detailed data regarding the individual or unit. Depending on the purpose, the programmer will study a portion or entire life of an individual. Case studies are written in a narrative fashion with certain points highlighted or illustrated in the body of the report.

The data collected in the case study are particularly useful as background information for planning in-depth investigations. Usually because of its intensive nature, the case study will

TABLE 13.5 Rating Performance Score Sheet

X = Able to perform before instruction
O = Unable to perform before instruction
① = Unable to perform after instruction
⊗ = Able to perform after instruction

	TPO 1: EO 1—Voice Projection	EO 2—Voice Inflection	EO 3—Facial Expression	EO 4—Eye Contact	EO 5—Gestures	EO 6—Gracefulness	TPO 2: EO 1—Charm	EO 2—Beauty	EO 3—Versatility
1. Charming, Prince	⊗	⊗	⊗	⊗	⊗	⊗	⊗	⊗	①
2. Ella, Cinder	⊗	⊗	⊗	⊗	⊗	⊗	⊗	⊗	⊗
3. Fudd, Elmer	⊗	⊗	⊗	⊗	⊗	⊗	①	①	⊗
4. Hood, Robin	⊗	⊗	⊗	⊗	⊗	⊗	⊗	⊗	⊗
5. Mouse, Minnie	⊗	①	⊗	⊗	⊗	⊗	⊗	⊗	①
6. Ridinghood, Red	⊗	⊗	⊗	⊗	⊗	⊗	⊗	⊗	⊗
7. Robin, Christopher	⊗	⊗	⊗	⊗	⊗	⊗	⊗	⊗	①
8. Oyl, Olive	⊗	⊗	⊗	⊗	⊗	①	①	①	⊗
9. Vanwinkle, Rip	①	①	①	①	①	①	①	①	①
10. White, Snow	⊗	⊗	⊗	⊗	⊗	⊗	⊗	⊗	⊗
11. Zel, Rapun	⊗	⊗	⊗	⊗	⊗	⊗	⊗	⊗	⊗

Term: *Fall*
Course: *Drama*
Instructor: *Brothers, Warner*

Gunn and Peterson 1978: 257.

reveal much more than an ordinary investigation or review. The weakness of the case study is in its numbers. There are very few statistical treatments that are capable of dealing with the small sample size used in this data collection method.

According to Farrell and Lundegren (1983: 239), the general steps in the case study approach are:

1. Identify the focus of the investigation. Is it the behavior of an individual, a study of a community, or is it a program with a larger structure?
2. Identify the nature of what needs to be studied in regard to this focus. Is it in the affective, the cognitive, or the psychomotor domain? For example, evaluation of the leader may be in the affective domain, the participant in the psychomotor, and the agency in the cognitive.
3. Select the measurement tools to collect the appropriate data. The tools used are such things as questionnaires, rating scales, anecdotal records, logs, diaries, attitude scales, life history or biographical forms, and various sociometric instruments.
4. Collect the data in a planned, systematic way (see specifics under the individual methods described earlier), optimizing the available evaluators to get the most usable data in a reasonable time frame.
5. Collect and present the data in a logical way.
6. Interpret data in a manner appropriate both to the situation studied and to the audience to whom the report is directed.
7. On the basis of the findings, prepare solutions to problems and make general recommendations.

Case studies as a data collection tool are limited in their application. The primary application would be to personnel and consumers. In some instances this approach could be used to describe a program or operations, policy dimensions, or administration of a particular effort.

Checklists

Probably one of the most frequently used data collection instruments in recreation and leisure fields is the checklist. This approach is simply *a*

listing of items to be checked off by a programmer, leader, supervisor, or support personnel. The varieties of checklists are as abundant as the varieties of processes to collect information.

The use of checklists is somewhat limited in terms of their application to quantitative measurement. The programmer will be able to obtain a frequency indication regarding the particular item being evaluated but the data does not lend itself to higher levels of statistical treatment. Checklists come in many varieties. Table 13.6 provides an example of the structure of a checklist used in the maintenance of a program area.

Importance Performance Analysis Approach

A potentially useful approach that can be applied in this area is known as importance-performance analysis. This model of evaluation

TABLE 13.6 Maintenance Checklist for Crafts Room

						Tudor Recreation Center Daily Maintenance Checklist (Crafts Room) (To be filled out and initialed each day)
M	T	W	Th	F	S	
□	□	□	□	□	□	1. Oven unplugged
□	□	□	□	□	□	2. All water turned off
□	□	□	□	□	□	3. Table tops cleared
□	□	□	□	□	□	4. Storage cabinets locked
□	□	□	□	□	□	5. Tool rack inspected; all tools accounted for
□	□	□	□	□	□	6. Floor swept
□	□	□	□	□	□	7. Trash emptied into large dumpster outside
□	□	□	□	□	□	8. Floor mopped
□	□	□	□	□	□	9. Lights turned out
□	□	□	□	□	□	10. Windows secured
□	□	□	□	□	□	11. Doors locked
						Thank you.

WEEK OF _____

SIGNED _____

_____

provides *a method for soliciting input from customers* to help a leisure service organization determine how effectively it performed in delivering potential program benefits. The importance-performance analysis involves a pre-test and post-test. Initially customers are asked to identify those program benefits which they perceive as being most desirable. After they have participated in the program, customers are asked to indicate how effectively the leisure service organization has accomplished the identified program benefits.

The results of these tests (both the pre- and post-perceptions of benefits) are graphically displayed on a two-dimensional matrix. As seen in Figure 13.9 the vertical axis on the matrix illustrates responses to pre-test inquiries concerning the importance of various program attributes. The horizontal axis shows the distribution of responses to post-test scores dealing with performance in producing desired program benefits.

The importance-performance analysis approach is of value to leisure service organizations because it provides a measure of customer satisfaction. It enables customers to not only indicate to an organization what benefits they desire from a leisure experience, but how effectively the organization has produced them. It also enables an organization to focus on those areas that need improvement and/or should be emphasized more in the design or manipulation of program elements. Rossman (1989: 387) notes that ". . . this technique is particularly useful for formative evaluation of new, developing program services or evaluation of existing services whose attendance may have dwindled." Rossman goes on to note that the importance-performance analysis approach may not be as valuable in the area of summative evaluation.

Questionnaires

The most frequently used method of data collection is the questionnaire—either a paper and pencil type in which the respondent fills in the answers or an interview schedule in which an interviewer asks the questions and the respondent

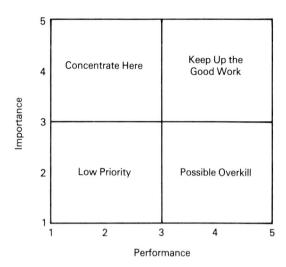

Figure 13.9 Importance-Performance Grid.

gives an oral reply. *Questionnaires can obtain descriptive information about the sample population,* or can attempt to assess their attitudes or can provide data to explain their behavior. The types of questionnaires used may depend on the type of information needed, the time and money available for the survey, and the population to be sampled.

Questions may be phrased in different ways, depending on the amount of information desired and the amount of flexibility the questioner wishes to allow. The most structured questionnaire is the fixed alternative type. The question is asked and the respondent must select an answer from among alternatives offered by the questioner (e.g., yes/no, true/false, multiple choice, checklist, rank order). Because the number of responses is limited, this type of questionnaire is the easiest to administer and process but tends to provide the most superficial responses; this is because there is no avenue by which the respondent can express opinions that differ from the responses offered.

Open-ended questionnaires are the most flexible because the respondent is free to supply whatever answer he or she thinks is appropriate.

They are the most effective at getting in-depth responses and true beliefs and may even reveal new possibilities not considered by the questioner. However, because such a wide range of responses is permitted, it is more difficult to process and analyze the results. Persons with poor oral or written communication skills may have difficulty with such a questionnaire. Scale items are a special type of fixed alternative format that presents a statement and asks the respondent to express his degree of agreement or disagreement with it. Construction of the questionnaire, whatever its format, will have much to do with its success at securing the desired information. It is advisable to consult a textbook or research technique for guidance in this area.

Summary

The leisure programmer must address the issue of evaluation daily in the delivery of services. In an era of accountability, it is imperative that the programmer is cognizant of and competent in the various approaches to program evaluation. The future will demand not only quantitative but also qualitative data to support the continuation of programs.

Evaluation basically involves making value judgments. The purposes of evaluation are many and can be viewed from three different orientations: customer, program, and organization. Customer-oriented evaluation focuses on customer satisfaction and the leisure behavior of the customer and provides mechanisms that encourage input. From the perspective of designing programs, evaluation helps in the arrangement of elements related to organizing and implementing a program. Further, it enables the programmer to handle more effectively the transactions that occur between customers and professional staff. From an organizational perspective, evaluation assists in establishing priorities, objectives, budget allocations, and control of services.

In conducting the evaluation, the leisure service programmer will have to determine who will actually do the evaluation—an internal or external person. In addition, the evaluator and the agency sponsoring the evaluation must review all ethical aspects of the evaluative process before engaging in the actual evaluation. There are several components of the leisure service organization that can be categorized for evaluation purposes. These include: (1) personnel; (2) programs/operations; (3) policy dimensions/administration; (4) customers; and (5) physical and fiscal resources. Each agency should have a comprehensive evaluation plan that covers all aspects of its operations. The most useful approach is a dynamic system evaluation plan, one that uses feedback loops.

In the past several decades a new concept known as quality assurance has emerged that is related to evaluation. Quality assurance involves the measuring of services against standards and then the development of strategies to improve services in order to ensure that an appropriate level of service delivery is achieved. Quality assurance is related to evaluation in that both are concerned with accountability and control. However, the major difference between the two is that evaluation tends to focus on program components and elements, while quality assurance focuses on issues that are customer-specific. In other words, quality assurance deals more with customer satisfaction, care, and transactions that occur between customers and leisure service programmers.

There are several approaches and models for evaluation, which provide the recreation and leisure programmer with various options that can be applied to selected situations. Seven major approaches to evaluation include: (1) goals, objectives, and discrepancy approach; (2) expert judgment approach; (3) systems design and decision-oriented approach; (4) standards approach; (5) policy analysis approach; (6) research method approach; and (7) communicative and interactive approach.

An overview of several data collection instruments was provided. The leisure service programmer should be able to synthesize

information and select approaches on a contingency basis. No one approach or instrument will satisfy the demands of all situations. Evaluation should be viewed as an ongoing process that enables the leisure service organization to make better judgments about how to serve its customers and how to use its resources. Unfortunately, evaluation is often undervalued and/or not approached in a comprehensive fashion within leisure service organizations.

Discussion Questions and Exercises

1. Define evaluation. Discuss how evaluation involves making value judgments within leisure service organizations.

2. Why is evaluation important? Discuss this from three perspectives—those of the customer, the program, and the organization.

3. What is the difference between formative and summative evaluation? What is measurement?

4. Identify five areas in which evaluation can occur within leisure service organizations.

5. What are the hazards in program evaluation? Identify and discuss at least five that have an impact on the work of leisure service organizations.

6. What kinds of ethical responsibilities do leisure service programmers have in the evaluation process?

7. Define quality assurance. Discuss how quality assurance programs are customer-specific as opposed to program-oriented.

8. Identify seven approaches to evaluation. Give an example of each one. Locate a leisure service organization and determine what approach is most prevalent in the agency you select.

9. What are the benefits of policy analysis in evaluating the programs within leisure service organizations? Compare and contrast these benefits with other approaches to evaluation.

10. Develop a program to evaluate a leisure service activity. Include in your plan a discussion of the approach to be used and the instruments that will be necessary to collect relevant information.

References

American Institutes for Research 1970. *Evaluative research.* Pittsburgh, PA.

Anderson, S. B. and S. Ball. 1978. *The profession and practice or program evaluation.* San Francisco: Jossey-Bass.

Attkisson, C. C., W. A. Hargreaves, N. J. Horowitz, and J. E. Sorensen, eds. 1978. *Evaluation of human service programs.* New York: Academic Press.

Bannon, J. J. 1976. *Leisure resources: Its comprehensive planning.* Englewood Cliffs, NJ: Prentice-Hall, Inc.

English, J. n.d. *Goal attainment scaling.* Dallas, TX: South Central Regional Center for Services to Deaf Blind Children.

Farrell, P. and H. Lundegren. 1983. *The process of recreation programming: Theory and technique.* 2nd ed. New York: John Wiley & Sons.

Fink, A. and J. Kosecoff. 1978. *An evaluation primer.* Beverly Hills, CA: Sage Publications.

Franklin, J. L. and J. H. Thrasher. 1976. *An introduction to program evaluation.* New York: John Wiley & Sons.

Gunn, S. L. and C. A. Peterson. 1978. *Therapeutic recreation program design.* Englewood Cliffs, NJ: Prentice-Hall.

Isacc, S. and W. B. Michale. 1971. *Handbook in research and evaluation.* San Diego: Knapp.

Kraus, R. and L. Allen. 1984. *Research and evaluation in recreation, parks, and leisure studies.* Columbus, OH: Publishing Horizons.

Mayer, W. 1975. *Planning curriculum development.* Boulder, CO: Biological Sciences Curriculum Study.

McConkey, D. D. 1975. *MBO for non-profit organizations.* New York: American Management Associations.

Mittelesteadt, A. H. and H. A. Berger. 1972. The critical path method: A management tool for recreation. *Parks & Recreation* 8(7): 14–15.

Moder, J. J. and C. R. Phillips. 1964. *Project management with CPM & PERT.* New York: Reinhold Publishing Corporation.

Nadler, G. 1969. A universal approach to complex systems design. *The Engineering Manager.* Montreal: The Engineering Institute of Canada.

Neulinger, J. 1974. *The psychology of leisure.* Springfield, IL.

Pelegrino, D. A. 1979. *Research methods for recreation and leisure: A theoretical and practical guide.* Dubuque, IA: Wm. C. Brown.

Richard, S. III, E. P. and K. C. Rathbun. 1983. *Medical risk management: Preventative legal strategies for health care providers.* Rockville, MD: Aspen Systems Corporation.

Rossman, J. R. 1989. *Recreation programming: Designing leisure experiences.* Champaign, IL: Sagamore Publishing.

Stufflebeam, D. L. 1974. *Meta-evaluation.* Kalamazoo, MI: The Evaluation Center.

Tallmadge, G. K. 1977. *The joint dissemination review panel: Ideabook.* Washington, DC: Superintendent of Documents.

Van der Simissen, B. 1972. *Evaluation and self-study of park and recreation agencies: A guide with standards and evaluative criteria.* Arlington, VA: National Recreation and Park Association.

Williams, John G. 1972. Try PERT for meeting deadlines. *Park Maintenance* 25 (9): 17–18.

Woy, J. R., D. A. Lund, and C. C. Attkisson. 1978. Quality assurance in human service program evaluation. In Attkisson, C. C., W. A. Hargreaves, N. J. Horowitz, and V. E. Sorensen, eds. *Evaluation of Human Service Programs.* New York: Academic Press.

Yavorsky, D. K. 1976. *Discrepancy evaluation: A practitioner's guide.* Charlottesville, VA: Evaluation Research Center, University of Virginia.

14 | Facilitating Leisure Behavior

Learning Objectives

1. To help the reader *understand the need for facilitating leisure behavior.*
2. To provide the reader with information concerning *barriers to successful leisure participation.*
3. To help the reader gain knowledge of *leisure education models.*
4. To provide the reader with examples of the application of *information dissemination models.*
5. To help the reader gain knowledge of *leisure counseling models.*
6. To provide the reader with information concerning *leisure facilitation techniques and theories.*

Introduction

Why is it necessary to discuss the facilitation of leisure behavior? Simply stated, North Americans are ill-prepared to handle their leisure. Not only do many individuals often lack knowledge of available resources, but may even lack the skills necessary to participate in leisure in meaningful ways. Further, North American culture still has a strong work ethic, but does not have a complementary leisure ethic that provides a balance in lifestyle. Our educational systems do little to prepare us for leisure and, as a result, leisure experiences may be unsatisfying.

It is interesting to note that North Americans today seemingly are taking their leisure more seriously. There has been a greater emphasis on pursuing healthy, active lifestyles as reflected in individual efforts directed toward stress reduction, better nutrition, weight control, and improvement of overall fitness. Leisure is an area in which individual customers can profit from greater knowledge of services, as well as an exploration of attitudes that shape and have an impact on one's lifestyle. People seek meaningful leisure experiences today and have a desire to develop the appropriate skills, knowledge, and attitudes that are required for successful participation. Leisure service programmers can assist customers by helping them access information, make decisions, and clarify leisure-related values, as well as through traditional strategies such as providing instructional programs and services.

In this chapter, a discussion of two approaches that are designed to facilitate the development of leisure behavior—leisure education and leisure counseling—are presented. In addition, the methods by which information is collected, sorted, and disseminated in a number of recreation and leisure service organizations are described in detail. These approaches have been included in this chapter since they represent another specific type of program service that can be organized and delivered by leisure service organizations. The focus of leisure education, leisure counseling, and information dissemination, which are mechanisms of service delivery, is on the acquisition of the skills, knowledge, and attitudes required for a fulfilling leisure experience.

Toward Optimum Leisure Development

In order for an individual to have an opportunity to reach his or her highest leisure potential, the educational process must start in the earliest stages of life. It is important to note that several key elements must be present in order for optimum leisure development to take place. These include:

> *Skills*—Each individual must develop a repertoire of play skills that are built on cognitive, affective, and psychomotor competencies.
>
> *Knowledge*—It is critical for the individual to develop an understanding of the vast array of leisure activity options available; in addition, the individual consumer must know what equipment, materials, and supplies are required for a specific activity (as well as where it is located, when it is offered, and so forth.)
>
> *Experience*—The opportunity to experience leisure activities will increase the individual's confidence to explore other dimensions of leisure and to perfect skills, and will add to overall leisure fulfillment and development.
>
> *Attitudes, Values, and Appreciation*—The individual consumer must develop a positive perception of leisure. . . . One's attitude toward the commodity of leisure plays an important role in determining the value of the leisure experience.

Barriers to Leisure Fulfillment

It is important to know that many individuals are ill-prepared to deal with the leisure phenomenon. Lack of preparatory leisure development is only one of several barriers that may eventually prevent an individual from achieving a quality of life or leisure fulfillment. The *following nine categories of barriers* are indicative of the difficulties faced daily by individuals in their quest for a high-quality leisure lifestyle.

1. *Attitudinal Barriers*—These types of barriers refer to a customer's thoughts about real or imagined factors that hinder participation. An example of an attitudinal barrier might be the commitment that one makes to maintaining a strong work ethic.

2. *Communicative Barriers*—Communicative barriers either can be personal or may exist on a broader organizational level. On an organizational level, communicative barriers relate to the ability of an agency to provide clear, accurate, and meaningful information concerning program offerings. On a personal level, such barriers focus on the individual's ability to receive and send messages clearly.

3. *Consumptive Barriers*—Consumptive barriers refer to the tendency of individuals to "purchase" experiences based on what is thought to be in vogue rather than what is right for the individual. Pursuing leisure needs based on a false agenda can be a barrier to meaningful and fulfilling leisure involvement.

4. *Temporal Barriers*—Not having enough time or quality time in which to pursue leisure interests can be a barrier. Today, not only is available leisure time for white-collar workers shrinking, but also the distribution of time (twelve-month school years, flex time, four-day work weeks, time deepening) is creating barriers that call for new approaches to address customer's leisure concerns.

5. *Social Cultural Barriers*—We live in an era of incredible diversity—racial, ethnic, social, economic, political, and cultural. Such pluralism requires an equally diverse approach to providing programs and services. Without attention to diversity, barriers emerge that prevent full development of one's leisure lifestyle.

6. *Economic Barriers*—Lack of access to discretionary income can have an impact on one's

ability to experience leisure. This is especially true in a society that has a fully developed commercial leisure service system and continues to reduce more accessible public and nonprofit leisure services. Also, economics produces perceived barriers, because individuals often relate the value and quality of a service to its cost.

7. *Health Barriers*—Major traumas, accidents, and illnesses can prevent customers from full leisure participation. We live in a culture that places great emphasis on the individual's physical and mental well-being. People are encouraged to maintain a high level of fitness and social/emotional wellness in order to enjoy life. If circumstances prevent total wellness, health factors can become a barrier to full participation.

8. *Experiential Barriers*—A lack of previous experience with, or orientation to, a leisure activity can be a major barrier. People will participate more often in familiar activities, rather than unfamiliar activities. We often avoid what we don't know.

9. *Lack of Leisure Awareness*—One of the major barriers that individuals experience today is that of acquiring and maintaining a "leisure ethic." They are unaware of the value of leisure experiences and have been conditioned by the Protestant work ethic. Further, individuals lack knowledge of the leisure skills and leisure resources needed to participate in meaningful leisure programs and services.

In the literature, the terms *nonparticipation, nonuse,* and *constraints to participation* have emerged in discussions on the topic of barriers. Although the literature in this area is not substantial, there have been a number of researchers who have addressed this topic (Boothby et al. 1981; Godbey 1985; Francken and van Raiij 1981; Jackson 1983; Jackson and Searle 1983; Romsa and Hoffman 1980; Searle and Jackson 1984; Searle and Jackson 1985; and Witt and Goodale 1981). Jackson (1983) identifies barriers viewing nine categories of recreation and leisure service activity. The study conducted by Witt and Goodale (1981) views the relationship between eighteen barriers to leisure enjoyment and family stage. Boothby et al. (1981) studied why individuals cease their participation in sporting events and activities. Francken and van Raiij (1981) looked at the relationships between barriers and leisure satisfaction while identifying associated social and economic antecedents.

Two of the more recent studies concerning barriers to participation have been conducted by Godbey (1985) and Searle and Jackson (1985). Godbey has developed a model to measure non-participation in public leisure services. He finds that lack of awareness of services was a major factor leading to nonparticipation. However, when viewing the reasons for nonparticipation in specific leisure services, he finds that location, lack of interest, lack of time, personal health reasons, and the use of an alternative facility or programs were the most highly ranked reasons for nonparticipation. These results are found in Table 14.1.

Searle and Jackson (1985) studied barriers to participation among 1240 respondents in the Province of Alberta. Each of the respondents was asked "Is there any recreation activity that you don't take part in now but would like to start regularly?" Those individuals desiring a new activity were asked to determine whether or not fifteen predetermined reasons were perceived as presenting a barrier. They found that the highest-ranked barrier was work commitments, followed by overcrowded facilities or areas, problems in locating others to recreate with, lack of opportunity to participate near one's home, and family commitments. Their findings present insight into barriers associated with participation in leisure activities (see Table 14.2).

It seems in reviewing the literature, that time, family and work commitments, and location are perhaps the most significant barriers to participation in leisure services. Interestingly, many of the studies conducted have not found economics/cost as a major barrier to participation. As leisure service programmers, it may be that ensuring that services are offered in convenient locations and at convenient times are two of the

most important factors to address. And these variables are often within the control or influence of the leisure service programmer. On the other hand, family or work commitments and some other barriers may require more long-term strategies that influence customers' attitudes, values, and opinions. In other words, strategies

TABLE 14.1 Reasons for Nonparticipation in Specific Leisure Services in City A by Rank and Frequency

Rank	Reason	N
1	Site Location Inconvenient	47
2	Lack of Sufficient Interest	43
3	Lack of Time	40
4	Personal Health Reasons	37
5	Use Alternative Facility or Program	32
6	Fear of Crime at Site	28
7	Lack of Skill—Don't Know How To Do Activity	18
8	Site Too Crowded	16
9	Lack of Transportation—No Car	15
10	Lack of Money	12
11	Lack of Public Transportation	9
11	Fear of Crime Traveling To and From Site	9
13	Site Poorly Maintained	8
14	Don't Know Enough About Site	7
14	Too Old	7
16	Site Hours of Operation Inconvenient	4
17	Site Polluted	3
17	Don't Know Anyone at Facility or Program	3
17	Don't Have Other People To Do Activity With	3
17	Don't Like Program Leader or Staff	3
21	Activities Not Interesting	1

Godbey 1985.

*Reasons given by those respondents who knew of the existence of the specific leisure service in question indicated they wished to participate but were prevented from doing so. More than one reason could be given.

TABLE 14.2 The Relative Importance of Barriers to Participation

Rank	Barrier	% Perceiving Barrier as "Often" or "Sometimes a Problem"
1.	Work commitments	71.7
2.	The recreational facilities or areas are overcrowded	64.4
3.	It is difficult to find others with whom to participate	58.3
4.	There is no opportunity to participate near my home	57.2
5.	Family commitments	56.2
6.	The price of recreational equipment	53.1
7.	Admission fees and charges to use recreational facilities	45.3
8.	I don't know where I can participate in this activity	43.1
9.	I don't know where I can learn the activity	31.6
10.	I am shy about participating in public	28.7
11.	Present price of gasoline	26.3
12.	Not having the physical abilities	20.0
13.	Lack of transportation	17.2
14.	Not having artistic or creative abilities	16.0
15.	I am physically unable to participate	9.7

Searle and Jackson 1985.

that are focused more on attitudinal, value, and consumptive behaviors may help to overcome barriers related to these factors.

Strategies for Removal of Barriers to Leisure Fulfillment

In most leisure service organizations it is difficult to identify barriers to leisure fulfillment, pinpoint the causes, and develop strategies for their removal. During the next few years, it will be imperative for the profession and for professionals to identify specific strategies for removal of the barriers. Identification of the strategies is not sufficient; we will need to test the strategies, document their effectiveness, and validate the procedures. If we are able to collect a set of effective strategies, we could potentially increase leisure awareness and satisfaction in the consumer significantly.

The *barriers identified in the previous section can be reduced or removed through several general strategies* that enhance the delivery system. These strategies are primarily related to increased two-way communication between the consumer and

the leisure service professional. The list of strategies that follows is by no means exhaustive.

1. Identify consumer needs, values, and leisure behavior.
2. Provide multi-faceted communication media efforts to insure awareness.
3. Use the latest audio, video, and computer technology to penetrate the agency's large target markets.
4. Analyze participation and user satisfaction, and use the data to plan future offerings.
5. Conduct adult, continuing, and outreach educational efforts to promote understanding, awareness, and evaluation.

The challenge to leisure service professionals is to identify the consumer's current and past leisure behavior and to help in bringing that individual into contact with leisure resources and opportunities. It is incumbent upon the professional to use strategies that are pertinent to and compatible with the individual's lifestyle and leisure needs.

Leisure Education, Information Dissemination, and Leisure Counseling: What's the Difference?

Leisure education and leisure counseling have often been thought of as synonymous. They are not. *Leisure education* focuses on giving information to individuals so that they may more effectively choose appropriate leisure activities. *Leisure counseling*, on the other hand, focuses more on helping individuals learn more about themselves with an eye toward enhancing their personal growth and development through leisure. Although these distinctions may appear to be slight, the work of the leisure service programmer and the implications for each customer can be dramatic. At one extreme, leisure education in its simplest form is providing resource information to individuals. At the other extreme, leisure counseling may involve therapy that leads to change in an individual's leisure functioning. The purpose of leisure counseling is to change an individual's leisure behavior by increasing, for one, an individual's decision-making ability. *Leisure information dissemination* models are systems that have been established to collect, sort, and disseminate information about programs and services.

An excellent model describing the differences between leisure education and leisure counseling has been formulated by Tinsley and Tinsley (1984: 81) and is shown in Figure 14.1. Basically, Tinsley and Tinsley view leisure education as an information-giving process, with the purpose of helping individuals attain new information in a cognitive manner. They also view the counseling function as being concerned with new information, but the means of intervention are dramatically different and may foster greater personal growth. In other words, leisure counseling deals not only with providing information, but also with promoting distinct changes in the behavior of individuals.

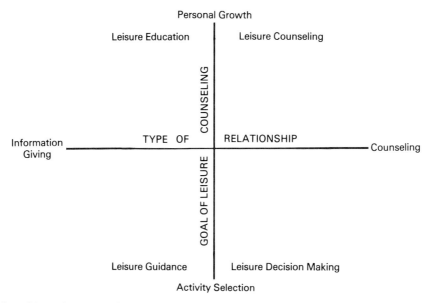

Figure 14.1 Classification of Leisure Education and Leisure Counseling Models by Function. (From Tinsley, E. A. and Tinsley, D. J. *Leisure counseling models.* In Dowd, E.T. (1984). *Leisure Counseling.* Springfield, IL: Thomas.)

In the past several decades several leisure education models have emerged. The focus of these has been primarily to provide information to individuals to aid in the selection of leisure activities and events. Edwards (1977: 17), for example, has developed an interview format to assess individual interests. She has developed and uses the constructive leisure interview sheet to identify demographic information, leisure activity preferences, and personal interests. Other leisure education models include those developed by Dickason (1972), McKechnie (1974), Burke (1976), Fain (1973), Connolly (1977), and Johnson and Zoreink (1977). Each of these models has, in general, focused on providing information to individuals enabling them to choose leisure activities or events wisely.

At the same time that leisure education models were being developed, there were also leisure counseling models that were established. These models go beyond merely giving information to customers, but rather focus on helping them alter or shape their decision-making posture. In particular, leisure counseling models developed by Montagnes (1976), Hayes (1977), McDowell (1976), Remple (1977), Gunn and Peterson (1978), and Overs et al. (1974) all have emphasized decision-making elements and providing information. In addition, the models by Remple (1977), Gunn and Peterson (1978), Overs et al. (1974), and Loesch and Wheeler (1982) have emphasized the establishment of a counseling relationship that emphasizes a process of counseling that contributes to the self-actualization of the individual (Tinsley and Tinsley 1984: 88).

In the following section, leisure education, information dissemination and leisure counseling models will be presented and discussed.

Leisure Education Models

An overview of several approaches used in education for leisure is presented in this section. Some are well developed and have been field-tested, while others are merely conceptual or philosophical. Most models are applicable in several settings and should not be perceived in a limited sense—e.g., LEAP (described below) which is used in the public school system.

Leisure Education Curriculum—National Recreation and Park Association

The National Recreation and Park Association (NRPA) with support from the Lilly Endowment, Inc. (Indianapolis, Indiana), has developed *leisure education curriculum materials for grades K through 12.* The purpose of the grant, as a research effort, was to delineate the components of leisure education—determining the state of the art and creating a specific curriculum model plus accompanying materials to be field-tested. The project was identified as the Leisure Education Advancement Project (LEAP).

The approach taken in the LEAP curriculum model was one of developing positive attitudes toward leisure. In other words, the curriculum materials do more than merely help the teacher develop leisure activity skills; they are directed toward helping people understand leisure phenomena and develop leisure values. *The approach of LEAP is based on the central premise that as leisure becomes more important in a person's life, each individual will need to develop skills, abilities, and attitudes in order to have a satisfying leisure experience.* Again, the LEAP curriculum materials should not be thought of simply as activity guides for skill development but, rather, as a model program for developing attitudes necessary for understanding leisure as well as for promoting quality of life through satisfying leisure experiences.

The major purpose of this curriculum model was to assist public schools in instructing students to:

1. Appreciate the use of leisure time (discretionary time) as an avenue for personal satisfaction and enrichment;
2. Understand the array of valuable opportunities available in leisure time;

3. Understand the significant impact that leisure time has, and will have, on society or appreciate natural resources and their relationship to discretionary time and the quality of life; and
4. Make decisions regarding their own leisure behavior (NRPA 1977: 10).

The LEAP curriculum was designed to be infused into the existing school curriculum. The intent was not to provide an additional content area but to complement and enrich the existing curricular materials toward the achievement of eight basic leisure goals, called *targets*. Targets, written in terms of objectives to guide curriculum development, were as follows:

1. The student will understand that most life experiences can be leisure experiences. They can be active or passive, alone or with others, physical or mental, planned or spontaneous, anticipatory or reflective.
2. The student will understand that . . . leisure as well as work must be viewed as a very important source of self-worth and dignity. It also influences the quality of life, even actual survival.
3. The student will understand the affect that the dynamic interaction of natural and physical environment, social institutions, and individual lifestyles has on leisure opportunities, choices, and behavior.
4. The student will identify, understand, and evaluate leisure resources available in the community, state, and nation; the student will develop appreciation of various modes that individuals have of utilizing these resources.
5. The student will recognize that leisure experiences are neither good nor bad. The value assigned is a matter of personal and societal judgment. The student will recognize that leisure experiences are chosen because they seem appropriate to the individual, limited by social control.
6. The student will appreciate those intangible qualities of leisure experiences which transcend an individual's physical existence but are experienced on the emotional and spiritual plane.

7. The student will recognize and evaluate the consequences each person's use of leisure has on human, social, constructed, and natural environments. The student will recognize that each person is ultimately responsible for his own leisure as well as for influencing the community to suggest leisure opportunities.
8. The student will understand that leisure, as well as work, family, and other social roles can help develop a life plan to insure personal growth and satisfaction (NRPA 1977: 10).

The curriculum centers on the eight target statements (general objectives) and presents detailed illustrations of how the teacher, community leisure service programmer, therapeutic recreator, leisure counselor, and youth worker could use the materials to facilitate leisure development. For each target statement, there is a corresponding rationale statement that provides background information in support of the general objectives. In addition, observable behaviors are delineated, so that the facilitator can measure the outcomes of participation and objective achievements. Furthermore, the materials provide *focus points*, which enable the facilitator to break down the observable behaviors into discrete activities (referred to as *building blocks and milestones*) that, in turn, enable the student participant to achieve the stated objectives.

An additional feature of the materials is that they provide further task delineation by offering beginning, intermediate, and advanced levels of the focus points. It is important to note that the facilitator may select many target statements to use in the facilitation of leisure development and is not duty bound to present the material in sequential order—for example, target statements 1 through 8. One might use target statement 1:

The student will understand that most life experiences can be leisure experiences. They can be active or passive, alone or with others, physical or mental, planned or spontaneous, anticipatory or reflective.

Which focuses on leisure as a phenomenon, but then follow this with target statement 4:

The student will identify, understand, and evaluate leisure resources available in the community, state, and nation; the student will develop appreciation of various modes that individuals have of utilizing these resources.

Which focuses on resources—including people, places, and programs.

The contribution of the LEAP curriculum materials is significant in that since 1981 the National Education Association has advocated (in its statement of "Cardinal Principles of Secondary Education") that the education for the worthy use of leisure time is an important objective in the total educational process; however, the thrust for leisure education in American schools has been borne by the National Recreation and Park Association and its branch, the Society for Park and Recreation Educators. The LEAP materials serve as the first tangible evidence that a leisure education curriculum not only can be developed but also can contribute significantly to the education of elementary and secondary schoolchildren. The model curriculum synthesizes the dimensions and values of leisure for the first time into a fully integrated and developed set of curriculum materials. Prior to this effort, there had not been a totally unified set of curriculum materials available for teaching the discrete dimensions of leisure. The curriculum materials represent a primary effort on the part of the NRPA. In essence, what LEAP has done is to provide the following:

> . . . A quantum "leap" in the availability of materials for the development of leisure education curricula throughout the nation. The initial survey of leisure education programs conducted by NRPA staff, based on data from forty-seven states and the District of Columbia, indicated that only two states reported "an operational leisure philosophy and programs which focused upon more than skills and activities" (Ball 1973: 5).

The efforts of the National Park and Recreation Association in raising the consciousness of public education toward the value of leisure education must be continued through the implementation and review nationwide of the LEAP curriculum materials.

Leisure service professionals should not only incorporate elements of the curriculum into their own organization's leisure education development program but should also serve the advancement of leisure pursuits by advocating the adoption of the curriculum and educational systems within their service area. The leisure service professional should assume roles that allow him or her to be more than a tender or "referee" of leisure activities. Leisure education should not be construed as the sole property of the public education system. It is incumbent upon the professional recreator, regardless of the setting or constituency, to assume the role of the leisure educator.

This role finds the professional engaged in new arenas outside the common domain of activity provision and facility management. The authors feel that the LEAP materials could be modified to serve as a basis for program development and enrichment through a broadening of the agency's purpose. It is obvious that the economy will not allow full-scale development of leisure education programs in the nation's school systems. It is therefore incumbent upon recreation and leisure systems to adopt an expanded mode of service delivery incorporating leisure education.

Systems Approaches to Leisure Education
There are several interesting leisure education models utilizing general systems theory. Among the more significant contributions have been systems designs developed by Mundy and Odum (1974)—"A Systems Approach to Leisure Education"—and one developed by Leisure Information Service (1976) (a private Washington D.C.–based consultant firm—"A Systems Model for Developing a Leisure Education Program for Handicapped Children and Youth (K–12).)"

In order to understand these various models, a brief review of general systems theory is necessary. *General systems theory can be thought of as a method for explaining how various component parts within the total environment are related and inter-related.* Systems theory as applied to leisure education models include two basic systems. These two systems, which have been employed by leisure service delivery systems theorists, are used to explain the component parts of these delivery systems. The *static system*—where inputs are identified (e.g., consumer leisure service personnel and environment) and used as the basis for determining a *process* for delivering leisure services and subsequently *outputs*—is one of the two systems. Figure 14.2 illustrates how the linear flow functions. The drawback to the static system is that outputs are not reviewed prior to determining the process by which these services are delivered. The second approach is the *dynamic system* design. In this approach, the same flow of information design is used as in the static system—with one important modification. The outputs are carefully reviewed; and through a feedback loop, one is able to modify the process in order to achieve greater output (see Figure 14.3). Together with the process of flow charting, one is able to discretely analyze each component of a system. The resulting effect is that one is able to both task-analyze the approach and arrange these tasks in some developmental sequence. This process enables an individual to objectify and know precisely what tasks produce the outcomes of the design—in the case of leisure education models, the outcomes produced by a given leisure education model. The following is an analysis of the aforementioned leisure education models.

The Mundy and Odum systems model As indicated in Figure 14.4, Mundy and Odum (1974) conceived the process of leisure education as including five components: leisure awareness (1.0); self-awareness (2.0); decision making (3.0); leisure skills (4.0); and social interaction (5.0). The focus of the process mode is on the process of (3.0) decision making. The individual is initially made aware of leisure and its concomitant properties and is prompted to develop a degree of self-awareness, which culminates in a statement of personal needs and leisure goals. The process continues through an individual's development of leisure skills and subsequent social interaction in which a leisure lifestyle is developed. *The essence of the process mode is to heighten one's leisure awareness and self-awareness and promote a higher quality of life.* The model then presents representative outputs in terms of the individual. The following outputs are suggested by Mundy and Odum:

1. Uses his or her knowledge of leisure and leisure experiences in order to enhance the quality of his or her life during leisure.
2. Is able to use knowledge about himself or herself in making leisure decisions which enhance the quality of his or her life during leisure.
3. Is competent to direct his or her own leisure experiences toward qualitative goals through realistic planning.
4. Uses leisure skills to reach his or her leisure goals.
5. Interacts with and relates to others during leisure in a manner compatible with his or her leisure goals (Mundy and Odum 1974: 54).

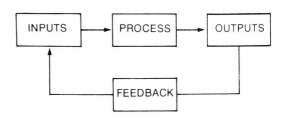

Figure 14.3   A Dynamic System.

Figure 14.2   A Static System.

It is interesting to note that Mundy and Odum consider leisure education from a specific viewpoint. They suggest that leisure education is not:

1. Attempting to replace one set of values with another set of values.
2. A new name for recreation or recreation services.
3. A watered-down, simplified version of a recreational leisure professional preparation program.
4. A focus on the value of recreation or the recreation profession.
5. A focus on getting people to participate more in recreational activities.
6. Imparting standards of what is "good" or "bad" use of leisure.
7. Relating every school subject to leisure.
8. A course or series of courses.
9. Restricted to the educational system.
10. Restricted to what educators should do but not what leisure service personnel do.
11. A program to undermine the work ethic (Mundy and Odum 1974: 55–56).

On the other hand, according to Mundy and Odum, leisure education can be thought of as:

1. A process enabling the individual to identify and clarify his or her own leisure values and goals.
2. An approach enabling an individual to enhance the quality of his or her life during leisure.
3. Deciding for oneself what place leisure has in life.

INPUT

AN INDIVIDUAL

LEISURE SERVICES PERSONNEL WHO CAN DESIGN LEARNING EXPERIENCES TO REACH THE ULTIMATE OUTCOMES OF LEISURE EDUCATION

PROCESS
LEISURE EDUCATION

OUTPUT

AN INDIVIDUAL WHO:

USES HIS/HER KNOWLEDGE OF LEISURE AND LEISURE EXPERIENCES IN ORDER TO ENHANCE THE QUALITY OF HIS/HER LIFE DURING LEISURE.

IS ABLE TO USE KNOWLEDGE ABOUT HIM/HERSELF IN MAKING LEISURE DECISIONS WHICH ENHANCE THE QUALITY OF HIS/HER LIFE DURING LEISURE.

IS COMPETENT TO DIRECT HIS/HER OWN LEISURE EXPERIENCES TO QUALITATIVE GOALS THROUGH REALISTIC PLANNING.

USES LEISURE SKILLS TO REACH HIS/HER LEISURE GOALS.

INTERACTS WITH AND RELATES TO OTHERS DURING LEISURE COMPATIBLE WITH HIS/HER LEISURE GOALS.

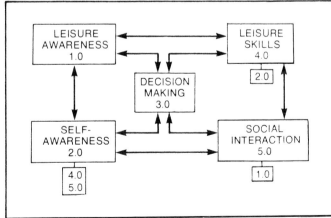

Figure 14.4 A Systems Approach to Leisure Education. (From Mundy, J. and Odum, L. (1979). *Leisure education: Theory and practice.* New York, John Wiley and Sons, p. 54.)

4. Coming to know oneself in relation to leisure.
5. A lifelong continuous process.
6. Relating one's own needs, values, and capabilities to leisure and leisure experiences.
7. Increasing the individual's options for satisfying quality experiences in leisure (Mundy and Odum 1979: 2–4).

The Mundy and Odum model appears to be one of the first schematic models that analyzes the component parts of a leisure education process. Its significance may lie in the interactive approach—blending leisure awareness and skill development with self-awareness and social interaction in the quest for a quality of life. At the locus of Mundy and Odum's model is the process of decision making. It is important to note that this process places the decision for leisure awareness, development, outcomes, and consequences in the hands of the consumer—where it rightly belongs. The decision-making process reflects a clear understanding of social theory, and its emphasis is on independent, self-actualizing behavior. It is important to remember that the voluntary nature of involvement by individuals in consuming leisure experiences is dependent on their ability to discriminate and choose among a variety of sources in fulfilling their leisure needs. Without the awareness to discriminate between potential experiences, decision-making capabilities are limited. An additional feature of Mundy and Odum's approaches is their presentation of parameters concerning what constitutes leisure education. This is important because of the confusion existing among professionals about such terms as *leisure counseling, recreation, leisure facilitation, leisure development,* and *lifelong leisure development.*

The interaction approach suggested by Mundy and Odum treats the entire process in a holistic sense. As such, each component of the entire process is dependent on the others. One's leisure awareness concept, in turn, affects one's self-awareness and self-concept. This, in turn, also affects the ability to determine the level of social interaction desired and shape societal normal and expectations. These components are all dependent on the extent to which an individual has developed his or her leisure skills.

Leisure Information Service systems model
In conjunction with a grant from the U.S. Office of Education (Bureau of Education for the Handicapped under PL 91–230, Title VI—Education for the Handicapped Act in 1975), Leisure Information Service (LIS) prepared *a systems model for leisure education of handicapped children.* The systems model addressed four basic points:

1. The use of recreative activity as an instrument of self-realization.
2. Development of a program plan that includes exploration, orientation, and skill development in and for the use of discretionary time to ensure that handicapped youngsters realize the value of discretionary time.
3. Development of a program plan for utilizing educational, community, and human resources to enable handicapped youth to participate in recreational activity suitable to their needs.
4. Changing the attitudes of both the handicapped and the public by training in and exposure to the discretionary time potential (Leisure Information Service 1976: 8).

As a research effort, the development of the systems model curriculum focused on several major tasks including:

1. Analysis of the rationale for the statement that education for leisure, as discussed by educators, recreators, and philosophers is a worthy and appropriate goal.
2. Analysis of the techniques and materials developed during the last decade which related to leisure time education for the handicapped.
3. Analysis of the instrumentation available for assessing leisure education. Consideration was given to criterion-referenced and norm-referenced tests.
4. Development of a systems model for leisure education for the handicapped. This model included:
   a. A rationale based on relevant theory and research.

b. Objectives based on needs of the handicapped for leisure time education.
c. Techniques appropriate to objectives and needs of handicapped persons.
d. Appropriate instrumentation to assess accomplishments of the proposed objectives (Leisure Information Service 1976: 9).

The systems approach used by the LIS viewed leisure education as a broad effort with numerous components. Figure 14.5 illustrates the components of the leisure education systems model.

The overall curriculum developed by LIS is competency-based. *The major program areas consist of (1) awareness and understanding, (2) assessment and planning, and (3) activity exploration.* Each of the major program areas is separated into two *strands*. The first program area, awareness and understanding, is divided into categories reflecting one's ability to engage in leisure decision making. The second major program area strands are focused on developing abilities to establish lifelong leisure goals. The third program area strands address skill development and application. These assist the individual student in engaging in leisure pursuits in the home, school, and community.

To further delineate the curriculum, the LIS project subdivided strands into *areas.* The areas represent specificity of skills needed within the strand. Beyond the areas the curriculum included from two to seven topics in each area. In all, the curriculum presents thirty-one topics, ranging from 1.1.0 (reasons people differ), to 4.3.0 (leisure selection) and specific activity areas, such as 10.6.0 (sports and games).

The taxonomy chart shown in Figure 14.6 provides an overview of the entire curriculum. Although the curriculum appears to be quite complex, the example in Table 14.3 may illustrate how a goal related to bowling can be implemented in the classroom or community-based program.

Community Education Model

The community education movement has emerged over the past few years as a viable alternative to the public schools' role as "9:00 A.M. to 3:00 P.M." educators. *Community education is a broad philosophical concept, intent on improving the responsiveness of a community to its constituents' needs through optimum utilizing and planning of its resources.* Its focus is to bring the citizenry together with its resources and effective problem solving.

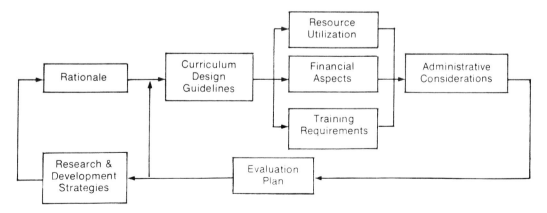

Figure 14.5   The Components of a Leisure Education Systems Design. (From Leisure Information Service (1976). *A systems model for developing a leisure education program for handicapped children and youth.* Washington, D.C.: Hawkins and Associates, Inc., p. 11.)

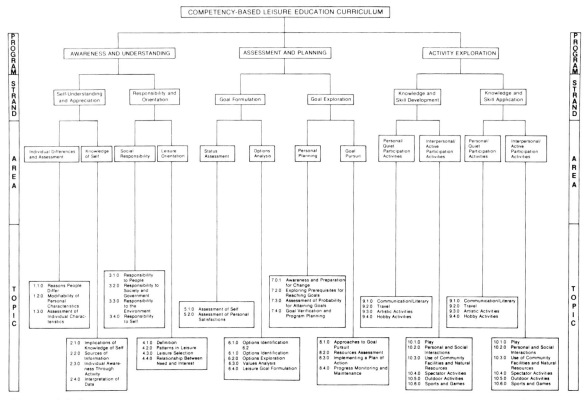

Figure 14.6 Taxonomy Chart. (From Leisure Information Service: *A systems model for developing a leisure education program for handicapped children and youth.* Washington, D.C.: Hawkins and Associates, 1976, p. 50.)

The National Community Education Association, as quoted in Godbey (1978), states:

> ". . . Community education is philosophy that pervades all segments of education programming and directs the thrust of each of them towards the needs of the community. The community school serves as a catalytic agent by providing leadership to mobilize community resources to solve identified community problems . . . affects all children, youth, and adults directly and helps to create an atmosphere and environment which sees its schools as an integral part of community life (Godbey 1978: 218).

Established in 1936 by Frank J. Manley (a public school director of health and physical education in Flint, Michigan), and funded by philanthropist Charles Stewart Mott, the community

school concept grew rapidly. With Flint, Michigan, serving as a national model, communities across the nation responded to the need for broad-based community leisure education. The movement has been given support by a number of national professional organizations including:

United States Jaycees

Big Brothers of America

National Congress of Parents and Teachers

National Community Education Association

National Recreation and Park Association

American Alliance for Health, Physical Education, Recreation and Dance

Society of State Directors of Health, Physical Education and Recreation

TABLE 14.3   Illustration of Behavioral Objectives for a Leisure Education Topic

Illustration of Behavioral Objectives for a Particular Leisure Education Topic

Program III
Activity exploration
 Knowledge and skill development

 Area 10.0.0
 Interpersonal/active participatory activities

  Topic 10.6.0
  Sports and games

   Goal 10.6.3.0
   Demonstrates knowledge/skills necessary to participate in a bowling activity

    Objectives
    10.6.3.1   Identifies location of bowling alley
    10.6.3.2   Phones to establish session times
    10.6.3.3   Determines transportation
    10.6.3.4   Dresses appropriately
    10.6.3.5   Travels to bowling alley
    10.6.3.6   Selects correct size of shoes
    10.6.3.7   Manages money for shoe rental
    10.6.3.8   Manages personal belongings
    10.6.3.9   Bowls using appropriate form
    10.6.3.10   Bowls with accuracy
    10.6.3.11   Scans pins
    10.6.3.12   Scores game
    10.6.3.13   Practices bowling-establishment etiquette
    10.6.3.14   Manages money for number of frames bowled

Leisure Information Service 1976: 52.

American Association of School Administrators

National Association for Public Continuing and Adult Education

National Association of Elementary Principals

National Association of Secondary School Principals

Association of Supervision and Curriculum Development

National School Boards Association

National Education Association

International Association of Community Educators, Inc. (Godbey 1978: 220)

Major strides were made toward achieving articulation on community-school recreation issues by the establishment of the National Steering Committee on Community Schools—Community Education in the 1970s. The Steering Committee was composed of representatives from the National Recreation and Park Association, the American Association for Leisure and Recreation, and the National Community Education Association.

Although much attention in the community school movement has been paid to the *cooperative use* concept, its strength may lie in its broad appeal to community residents who need continuing leisure education opportunities regardless of age, sex, ethnic background, or ability. The intent of community education is to provide its citizenry with ongoing educational outlets that promote a quality of life. Obviously, this does not cease when an individual receives a high school diploma—in fact, it may just begin!

Work-Leisure Model

Another unique approach is used by many foreign countries and by some industries in the United States. In Holland, for example, *education for leisure is infused into the job for young workers* between the ages of sixteen and eighteen. The Dutch refer to the schools that prepare young workers for life in society as *levenscholen*. These schools have been operable since the early 1950s. Deraeck and Ballaert (1976) describe the process of education for life that takes place in the centers:

> They are centers of education where young workers take part in an educational process on an inductive basis, arranged mostly around handicrafts, sports, and outdoor life, as well as an introduction to the technology of mass media. This takes place one or two days a week, while work at regular jobs goes on the rest of the week. These centers of education are now compulsory for all workers under eighteen for two days a week, fulfilling their part-time educational obligations. This is totally different from traditional education. Furthermore, vocational training is not even included in the curriculum (Deraeck and Ballaert 1976: 14).

The Belgian educational system, which ends its compulsory component at age fourteen, has also addressed the need for leisure education through its occupational force. Evening classes are provided for both blue- and white-collar workers under age forty in order to develop a critical and creative attitude toward life. The individual may spend up to 50 percent of the normal working time in the evening credit hour classes, in which the Minister of Employment includes leisure education.

In addition to the credit hour approach to leisure education, the Belgian educational system addresses the issue of lifelong education. Through a program entitled "Vacation for Socio-Cultural Promotion," all workers between ages sixteen and twenty-five received the opportunity to be absent from work for five or six days a year to attend educational courses. Other programs similar to this were also developed in the Netherlands but have met with some problems concerning employers and subsidies for the program.

A recent upsurge in comprehensive recreation and leisure program opportunities offered by American industrial firms leads one to believe that soon North American workers will give the leisure phenomenon a different look. Heretofore, there has been little connection between the work ethic advocates and the rather tangential activity programs of industry. Current trends, led by the phenomenal attention to physical and cardiovascular fitness, are changing the structure of corporate North America. Many industries and corporations are now moving rapidly to establish on-site fitness and recreation centers for employees and their families, although this is not a new concept. The recent flurry of involvement has resulted from a nation's concern over its physical fitness and the rise of one lifelong leisure pursuit—jogging!

Although the recent interest is commendable, Americans are still afflicted by the malignancy of the work ethic. Stress, anxiety, overwork, and ergomania (compulsion to work) still dominate North American society. Only when industry adopts the European and Eastern countries' concept of blending work and leisure will we achieve the quality of life we desire.

Edwards' Constructive Leisure Inc. Model

One model that has served another need is the commercial venture of Constructive Leisure, Inc., of Los Angeles, California. The approach taken by this organization is *to provide leisure education and interest identification to individuals or groups who may not get satisfaction from their current leisure* (Edwards 1977). The target population is usually general in nature but is directed at those over junior high school age.

Individuals or groups pay a fee for lectures, interest identification, discussion, and assistance from associates of Constructive Leisure, Inc. Advertised as an "avocational counseling" venture, the services include:

1. Interest testing and referral
2. Group testing
3. Publications (books and articles)
4. Lectures and speeches
5. Courses in the practical use of leisure
6. Radio and television
7. Counseling services
8. Counselor training and counseling supplies

Operated since 1968 as a private enterprise, the Edwards model offers another approach to facilitating leisure development. Many graduates in recreation, leisure studies, and counseling may be interested in pursuing this innovative career as traditional job markets change in their complexion.

Sponsorship of Leisure Education

Although leisure education is commonly associated with public school systems, it is becoming increasingly evident that the responsibility for its existence transcends the established or formal educational systems. The nature of the leisure experience makes it difficult, if not impossible, to relegate its function to a single agency. Several additional *factors support the notion that leisure education is the responsibility of a multitude of agencies and individuals.* These factors include:

1. *Lifelong Learning*—The learning process does not cease when one graduates from school but continues throughout life.
2. *Semiformal Learning Environment*—The home, community, office, and industry all serve as semiformal centers for learning.
3. *Community and Adult Education Movements*—Both of these movements have been based on the concept that learning can take place in the community in a semistructured manner and can address the singular or collective educational needs of the individual. In addition, the multi-use of

our community centers and schools during hours outside of the traditional school hours is part of an overall cost-effective utilization of public facilities.

4. *Life's Laboratory*—Although skills and simulated situations may be developed in the classroom, their application in everyday life situations is paramount. This necessitates having the individual practice leisure skills and develop his or her total leisure *life-space* in the community, in the neighborhood, or at home.
5. *Other agencies*—Youth serving agencies (YMCA, YWCA, 4-H, Boy Scouts, CYO, Camp Fire), religious agencies, private enterprises (National Outdoor Leadership School, American Youth Hostels, Inc.), and federal agencies (U.S. Department of the Interior, U.S. Department of Education, U.S. Department of Health and Human Services, Canadian Ministry of Amateur Sports and Physical Fitness) all provide forms of leisure education.
6. *Public schools*—For the most part, public schools address only a small segment of our society and only for nine months of the year. After school hours and summer months are usually spent in some form of leisure pursuit or play experience.

In order to clearly articulate and heighten the opportunities for individuals to develop "leisure literacy," it is the responsibility of the home, school, and community agencies to provide leisure education as well as opportunities for leisure.

Information and Dissemination Models

Leisure service organizations must become involved in the comprehensive collection and dissemination of leisure service information if they are to meet the vast changes in society relating to leisure consumption. For some agencies, this will not be a new function; however, for many others this task will involve a challenging new effort. Leisure service organizations attempting to view their constituents in a holistic manner recognize that their own resources are limited and, in the best interest of the customer, need to be supplemented with the resources of other organizations or agencies. In order to effectively meet the leisure needs of individuals cooperatively with other agencies, it is necessary to establish *a system that allows the organization to collect, sort, and disseminate information concerning all leisure opportunities within a given service area.* In this section of the chapter, the way in which four systems (National Park Service; Etobicoke, Ontario; Fremont, California; and Milwaukee, Wisconsin) have approached the new and important function of information collection and dissemination will be discussed.

Touch-Sensitive Computer Information Systems, National Park Service

Touch-sensitive computer information systems have been applied to help customers gain access to information about a variety of leisure services. For example, passengers arriving at San Francisco International Airport have access to touch-sensitive computers that enable them to access such information as cultural activities, historical points of interest, and park resources. A person would locate on the computer menu the general area of interest, e.g., park resources, by touching the computer screen. The menu is then further delineated, specifying types of park resources and geographic locations. The consumer is able to pinpoint very specifically the park's hours of operation, its resources, and directions for accessing it.

Hultsman (1988: 1–11) has studied the application of touch-sensitive computers in the National Park Service. In her study, touch-sensitive computers (TCS) were used to study how visitors to the park interact with the computer. The TCS computer program enabled participants to specify three activities in which they would like to participate. Basically, Hultsman found that the use of such programs reduced orientation programs by getting information to users quickly.

They are valuable to customers and may provide benefits by:

1. Indicating availability of activities in areas that have the greatest appeal to visitors, thereby matching interests with activity options.
2. Decreasing wandering by directing visitors to desired areas, thus reducing time, effort, and fuel consumption.
3. Aiding visitors in planning multiple attraction routes efficiently, thus accommodating the preferences of a greater number of party members with visits to diverse attractions along a single computer-designed route.
4. Reducing congestion by informing visitors about peak use periods, road closures, and alternative routes, particularly in high-use areas with limited road access to key attractions. A program that provides current status conditions, as well as possible substitute activities during heavy-use periods may help reduce frustration that could could result from unexpected delays (Hultsman 1988: 8).

TSC systems can be useful in displaying information and reducing problems associated with program changes or other variables. TSC systems are excellent ways of storing large amounts of information and helping the customer sort the information according to his or her needs. In this way, TSC systems are helping individuals identify programs and services that are uniquely related to their needs. Further, such systems reduce the amount of time it takes individuals to access programs and presents opportunities to increase the efficiency of interaction between a leisure service organization and those it serves.

Etobicoke, Ontario, Parks and Recreation Department

This park and recreation service *prepares a brochure that lists hundreds of extra organizational services.* The brochure listings include the names of extra organizational programs/organizations and resource persons to contact regarding the given services and their phone numbers. The programs and services listed in the sections of the brochure generally are not those created directly by the Etobicoke agency. Rather, they reflect the organization's concern for working cooperatively and collaboratively with other community organizations to effectively meet the needs of individuals by providing them with comprehensive information regarding leisure service opportunities in their service area. Not only is information listed concerning traditional leisure activities (such as sports, arts, and programs for senior citizens) but also other community service agencies that have a more indirect bearing on leisure pursuits (e.g., health services, single-parent groups, family service associations, etc.). The philosophy is perhaps best reflected in a statement included in their brochure, which reads as follows:

> One of the most recent and momentous changes in our community has been the rise and growth of community organizations. This is reflected in the number of groups and organizations which have arisen in recent years for the purpose of adding weight and giving voice to a variety of community projects and issues.
>
> The Etobicoke Parks and Recreation Department is no exception to this phenomenon and many of its services are the result of direct and indirect community planning and participation. It is becoming increasingly difficult to find an area of society which has not had an effect on its daily operation. Changing attitudes, life styles, and the growing focus on leisure are factors which have been a significant impact on the changing face of recreation. Cooperation, coordination, and involvement are indispensable to our Department's mode of operation. Besides its affiliation with Federal, Provincial, and Metro Toronto bodies, it maintains a close rapport with most local groups.
>
> The Etobicoke Parks and Recreation Services Department, through its staff in the community, is always available for consultation, guidance, and assistance to help local groups and organizations achieve their goals.

The organization of Etobicoke is decentralized, so that service involves more direct contact and interaction between the professional staff and the citizens of the community. As a result, it has moved from the direct provider role to a more indirect enabling approach. This new philosophy and approach encourages the organization to assume a posture whereby the collection and dissemination of information is an important component of its operation. In point of fact, the decentralization of services necessitates a formalized system for the collection and dissemination of information. In a hierarchically organized system, interested in promoting only its own services and facilities, the collection and dissemination of information is relatively simplistic. The need for a more sophisticated systemized approach, in which large numbers of individuals must be involved, arises with an organization's movement toward the Etobicoke decentralized model.

The Etobicoke model of information dissemination exemplifies a written approach to comprehensive information dissemination of recreation and leisure services for a given service area. Further discussion of the Etobicoke approach to brochure construction has been included in Chapter 10.

Leisure Service Information Bureau, Fremont, California

One of the first direct person-to-person information dissemination systems was established by the Department of Recreation and Leisure Services in Fremont, California. This innovative service was *established to disseminate area leisure information, especially via the telephone.* Not only was information available concerning the department's own activities and services, but information was also distributed regarding other public and private agencies' recreation and leisure services in and around the San Francisco Bay area.

Basically, the system was operated by one individual who also served as a secretary/receptionist for the Department. Information concerning various recreation and leisure service opportunities was researched and stored in an index-type file. The phone number for the system was advertised through the departmental brochure. Individual requests for information were made primarily via direct telephone contact between the participant and the information service system. For example, a person interested in the location of a particular park within the community could phone in and receive that information; an individual interested in the hours of operation of a given facility (e.g., the San Francisco Planetarium) could gain such knowledge through the utilization of information dissemination systems, in season, information could also be obtained concerning snow conditions at area resorts in the California Sierra Nevada.

The direct person-to-person information dissemination system can be implemented at little additional cost in most recreation and leisure systems. The idea of a community information dissemination system has been widely accepted throughout the United States. Federal programs have supported the establishment of these types of systems; however, many of these federally supported systems have not maximized their potential in terms of collecting and disseminating recreation and leisure service information.

Most community parks and recreation systems have recognized the importance of providing information to their clients concerning the vast leisure opportunities available in their given area. As noted, a municipal parks and recreation department will often use its brochure (distributed quarterly or semiannually) to publicize not only its own leisure activities but also those of other public and private agencies in the area.

Division of Municipal Recreation and Adult Education, Milwaukee, Wisconsin, Public Schools

An interesting approach to the collection and sorting of leisure information that utilizes the computer has been developed by the Division of Municipal, Recreation and Adult Education in the Milwaukee, Wisconsin, Public School System. This organization, over a six-year period of time, established a *computer leisure counseling service model*. The complete counseling model will be discussed later in the chapter; at this point, two components of the model—the *systems activity file* and the *inventory file*—will be discussed relative to the collection of information, as will the use of the computer to store information.

As indicated, two files are used to identify community recreation and leisure service activities. The activities file includes detailed and comprehensive information concerning given activities on separate file cards. The information available about a given activity may range from rules and equipment needed, to psychological ramifications and limitations for individuals with various physical and mental impairments. In addition, specifics regarding activities offered by the Division of Municipal Recreation and Adult Education are included.

The inventory file attempts to identify and catalog all available information concerning recreation and leisure opportunities in the area. Sources of information include brochures, newspaper articles, promotional literature, catalogs, and other sources describing recreation and leisure opportunities, programs, and services. Both files (activity and inventory) are coded into nine activity categories. The activity categories include: (1) games; (2) sports; (3) nature; (4) collection; (5) homemaking/homecraft; (6) art and music; (7) educational, entertainment, and cultural; (8) volunteer; and (9) organizational. These nine categories are further subdivided, so that up to 999 activities can be cataloged in this system. In addition, these two primary files are cross-referenced with one another—enabling one, for example, to determine the place, time, and cost for all nature activities in the area.

A program has been written, so that a computer stores the above information concerning the various activities as well as the geographic location and other relevant information of given activities. Thus, information concerning a given set of activities throughout the entire service area can be obtained quickly and then tailored very specifically to individual needs. The implications of the computer model are profound. Consider, for example, the possibilities of providing information to a consumer for comparative purposes—geographic location, quality of leadership, cost, and so on. Consider also the implications for recreation and leisure organizations, since this approach eliminates the element of ignorance of area activities. Community citizens with access to this type of system do not have to depend on hearsay, receipt of brochures, or media advertisements in order to become aware of leisure opportunities. In most cases, the latter types of information come to the consumer as a result of chance and in a fragmented fashion. The information that the consumer does receive is likely to be incomplete; all possibilities in this area are not likely to be drawn to his or her attention.

Again, the Milwaukee computerized system is an approach that can serve as a model for other communities. If no computer is available, the operation could be scaled down.

Models for Leisure Counseling

Several interesting, innovative, and diverse approaches to providing leisure counseling have emerged over the past few years as previously indicated. This section provides a brief review of some of the representative models—including the *Gunn and Peterson* leisure counseling model, *Milwaukee* leisure counseling model, *Hayes* leisure education–leisure counseling model, and the *triangulation* leisure counseling model. The following descriptions provide a brief synopsis of each model and its major proponents.

Gunn and Peterson Leisure Counseling Model

Using a systems approach to the development of their model, Gunn and Peterson (1978) view leisure counseling as:

> . . . A helping process which uses specific verbal facilitation techniques to promote and

increase self-awareness, awareness of leisure attitudes, values, and feelings, as well as the development of decision-making and problem-solving skills related to leisure participation with self, others, and environmental factors (Gunn and Peterson 1978: 214).

The Gunn and Peterson model provides specific information regarding (1) the general requirements (inputs) for leisure counseling, (2) the process for implementing a leisure counseling program, and (3) the general outcomes (outputs) of the counseling program. In the model, emphasis is placed on ensuring that an individual receives an assessment prior to embarking on a counseling program. It is also imperative that a professionally trained leisure counselor staff the program. *The process consists of assessment, goal determination, program planning, program implementation, evaluation, and post-programming* as described in Figure 14.7. As a result of the leisure counseling process, specific outputs can be identified. The purpose of the counseling effort is to increase leisure awareness, self-awareness, decision making, problem solving, and personal satisfaction regarding one's leisure lifestyle.

Milwaukee Leisure Counseling Model

Begun as the Milwaukee Avocational (vis-a-vis Vocational) Guidance Leisure Counseling Model, the Milwaukee Leisure Counseling Model became the nation's first community-based leisure counseling effort. Magulski Hirsch-Faull, and Rutkowski (1977) indicate that the Milwaukee model grew in response to three needs:

1. To help people in the mainstream of life who want to raise the level of their potential through recreational activities;
2. To provide counseling for the sheltered, including prison inmates, hospital patients, and alcoholics; and
3. To help special populations, the aged, culturally disadvantaged, and handicapped to develop a sense of worth to themselves and their community (Magulski, Hirsch-Faull, and Rutkowski 1977: 25–26).

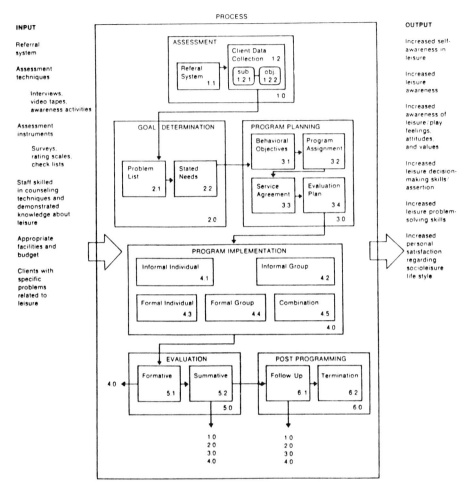

Figure 14.7 A Systems Approach to Leisure Counseling. (From Gunn, S. L. and Peterson, C. A. (1978). *Therapeutic recreation program design.* Englewood Cliffs, NJ: Prentice-Hall, p. 220.)

Overall, the Milwaukee model was intent on *assisting individuals in determining their leisure interests and matching them with community-based leisure pursuits.* The major contribution of the Milwaukee model was its development of several key methods of collecting and storing data regarding leisure opportunities in Milwaukee. The model resulted in one of the first scientifically based activity classification systems. Identified as the *avocational activities file,* it provided three levels of categorization, including specific numbers for activities. Based on the Library of Congress classification system, it provides a delineation of some 900 categories of leisure activities and leaves room for additional activities to be added.

In addition to the classification system, an inventory of all leisure pursuits in the community was developed. This data constantly changed; but the basic system for scanning, identifying, and classifying activities has remained intact. A modernization of the earlier approach to placing the inventory on index cards, through computerization, was later developed.

A leisure interest finder was also developed by the Milwaukee model and, more specifically, by

Dr. Joseph Mirenda. Called the Mirenda Leisure Interest Finder, the questionnaire provides the opportunity for the individual to react to a list of ninety activities representative of Milwaukee's services with a Likert-type (one to five) rating scale. An accompanying profile sheet allows the counselor to chart the individual's interest in selected categories of leisure and make appropriate referrals.

With the computerization of the interest inventory and data bank of activities, each individual can be processed in a short period of time. Precision in analyzing the ratings is provided, and costs of the service are minimal.

Actually, the Milwaukee model is one of the few information and counseling systems in operation in the nation. This revolutionary model was far ahead of its time and continues to influence leisure service delivery.

Hayes Model for Leisure Education/Leisure Counseling

Table 14.4—the Hayes (1977) model for leisure education and recreation counseling in therapeutic recreation—*provides a detailed view of the process for assisting individuals in leisure lifestyle development*. This model promotes an individualized approach to treating individuals in a therapeutic setting. The primary contribution that the Hayes model makes is its resolution of the major issues surrounding leisure education and leisure counseling. Hayes fuses the two concepts and illustrates how they are related. Another major contribution of the Hayes model is the attention paid to transition of the patient from the counseling (and rather dependent) setting to his or her return into the community setting. Finally, the Hayes model endorses a "developmental and preventive concern" in promoting leisure lifestyle development.

Triangulation Leisure Counseling Model

The triangulation leisure counseling model was developed by Loesch and Wheeler (1982). This model of leisure counseling is built on the assumption that leisure is a potentially unique human endeavor and is highly complex. *Its foundation is tied to three dimensions of human function—affective, behavioral, and cognitive.* In this process, the leisure service programmer, as a counselor, would identify the customer's preferred mode of functioning, either affective, behavioral, or cognitive, as it relates to leisure. The model is unique in that most models look at one dimension of individual functioning, whereas in this model all three aspects of the individual's functioning are considered simultaneously.

According to Loesch and Wheeler, the triangulation leisure counseling model has four distinct goals. They are:

1. To enable leisure counselors and their clients to establish mutually acceptable, appropriate, and effective counseling relationships.
2. To enable leisure counseling clients to be aware of and to understand their own affective, behavioral, and cognitive dimensions as they relate to current and potential leisure activities.
3. To help leisure counseling clients develop effective awareness and decision-making skills applicable to their current and potential leisure activities.
4. To help leisure counseling clients achieve the maximum possible satisfaction from their leisure activities.

Assessment using this model would include gaining knowledge about the customer's feelings about various leisure activities and values (affective), the customer's knowledge of leisure and leisure resources (cognitive), and the customer's skill level and prior participation in various leisure activities (behavioral). A program plan is then designed to address all identified problems in the customer's leisure lifestyle.

Instrumentation for Leisure Facilitation

Although there are very few valid and reliable instruments to specifically assess leisure functioning, many new approaches, applications, and instruments have been developed over the past few years.

TABLE 14.4 Hayes Model for Leisure Education and Counseling

Phase I—Individual's Involvement in Therapeutic Recreation Service (TRS) Program

Admission to Institution, Facility, or Program	Initial Interview by Therapeutic Recreation Specialist; Give Activity Interest Inventory	Therapeutic Recreation Specialist Consults with the Treatment or Rehabilitation Team or Its Equivalent	Development of Individualized Therapeutic Recreation Service (TRS) Program to Enhance Individual and Group Skills in Appropriate Activities	Obtain Consensus on Prediction of Discharge Date and Discharge Location

Task I	Task II
Principal goals are to establish rapport; discover ourselves and each other; getting acquainted; and discover the needs and interests of the patients.	Principal goals include developing individualized T.R.S. program to enhance individual and group skills that will assist the individual's successful reintegration into appropriate leisure living in the community.
Objectives	Objectives
1. To establish lines of communication with each patient. 2. To establish a casual atmosphere during individual and group sessions. 3. To make yourself known to everyone in the group. 4. To establish the group in the appropriate configuration. 5. To establish and maintain an appropriate amount of discipline. 6. To stay attuned to each person's interests and interjections. 7. To encourage all group members to become involved. 8. To discover the needs and interests of the patients.	1. To develop a close complementary working relationship with other members of the treatment team. 2. To provide consultation to, and to receive consultation from, the treatment team. 3. To develop goals and objectives for the patients based on assessed patient needs and interests. 4. To evaluate the patient's current level of functioning. 5. To involve the patient in T.R.S. activities as well as individual and/or group facilitation sessions. 6. To determine the responsibilities of the T.R. Specialist. 7. Evaluate the effectiveness of the T.R.S. activities and program and the leisure education and recreation counseling sessions. 8. To obtain consensus on prediction of discharge date and location.

TABLE 14.4   Hayes Model for Leisure Education and Counseling—*Continued*

Phase II—Leisure Education and Recreation Counseling Process

Therapeutic Recreation Service Involves Individual in Leisure Education
and Recreation Counseling Program Including

Task III

Principal goals would include involvement in activities with carry-over value and appropriate costs; and involvement in community activities with supervision.

Objectives

1. Assist the individual in determining what is carry-over value and what are appropriate activities for him.
2. Determine if the client's interests are in concert with the established treatment and/or training goals.
3. Helping the individual or group determine the value of trips into the community.
4. Assist the individual in determining the type and nature of community activity involvement he/she wants or needs.
5. The T.R. Specialist must develop relationship, interaction and cooperation with community recreation and leisure agencies.

Task IV

Principal goals would include discussion, instruction and facilitation of related necessary activities for successful involvement in total community living.

Objectives

1. To facilitate appropriate patterns of dress and behavior.
2. To assist with budgeting money for life activities and for recreation and leisure use.
3. To discuss value, importance and relationship of successful vocational adjustment.
4. To assist in the development of a proper program of nutrition, rest, sleep, and exercise.
5. To facilitate verbal and nonverbal expression of feelings, emotions, and attitudes.
6. Assist with understanding methods of utilizing public transportation and other pubic services and facilities.
7. Assist with understanding how to locate possible recreation and leisure resources.
8. To assist with understanding procedures for joining programs, paying fees, etc.
9. To facilitate making intelligent decisions and choices and initiating appropriate action.

Task V

Principal goals would include discussion and facilitation sessions concerning the development of positive feelings toward self and toward community leisure living.

Objectives

1. Discussions concerning the concept of the leisure-work ethic in our society.
2. Discussion and facilitation sessions concerning the budgeting of time for work, personal use and for leisure time use (conduct a time-budget analysis).
3. Assist with the development of positive feelings toward self in relationship to others and community.
4. Assist in understanding the relationship of leisure and recreation to total community living.

Task VI

Principal goals would include developing articulation and correspondence with community liaison persons; developing a familiarity of the discharge location and involvement in community recreation and leisure service activities and experiences without supervision on a small group and individual basis.

Objectives

1. To help the patient become familiar with the discharge location in terms of the leisure resource potential.
2. To develop a series of specifically designed pre-discharge sessions.
3. To assist in determining when the patient is ready for separation from the protective environment and ready for independent functioning.
4. To reevaluate the patient's leisure and recreation interests (using same interest inventory).
5. To assist patients in clarifying value received from leisure experience.

TABLE 14.4   Hayes Model for Leisure Education and Counseling—*Continued*

Phase III—Individual's Increasing Involvement in Community Leisure Experiences

Pre-discharge Interviews with Individual; May Have Sessions with Previously Discharged Individuals Residing in the Community; Sessions May Include a Community Liaison Person.	Follow-up Assistance Given by the T.R Specialist; Visitations Made to the Individual by the T.R. Specialist; Follow-up with the Community Liaison Person.	Evaluation of Level of Development of the Individual in Terms of His/Her Adjustment to Total Community Living with Emphasis on Leisure.	Assist in Development of Remedial or Alternative Course of Action for Improving Chances for Successful Community Adjustment if Necessary.	Determining When Follow-up and Evaluation Should Cease—in Cooperation with the Treatment Team and Individual.

<table>
<tr><td align="center">Task VII</td><td align="center">Task VIII</td></tr>
<tr><td>Principal goals would include establishing a post-discharge plan, establish follow-up assistance procedures by the T.R. Specialist.</td><td>Principal goals would include the evaluation of the development of individual's adjustment to total community living, developing remedial plan and termination of LERC process.</td></tr>
<tr><td align="center">Objectives</td><td align="center">Objectives</td></tr>
<tr><td>

1. To establish, in cooperation with the treatment team and the client, a post-discharge plan which will enable the client to actualize knowledge, skills, and experiences from the leisure education and recreation counseling process.
2. To assist in discussion concerning the value of experiences gained in LERC process in adjusting to the vocational and leisure situations to be encountered by the client.
3. To familiarize patient with any leisure information-dissemination system and the procedures for utilizing the system for his/her personal benefit. (Use LERC file "Guide to Leisure Resources" and "Resource Map" showing location of all resources.
4. To develop a correlation between the hospital and community-based recreation and leisure opportunities.
5. To develop procedures for follow-up visitations and evaluation.

</td><td>

1. To visit the individual in the community on a predetermined basis.
2. To assist the individual in self-evaluation in terms of:
   a- social interaction
   b- dress and behavior
   c- appropriate activity involvement
   d- budgeting time and money
   e- work adjustment
   f- verbal and nonverbal expression
   g- activity skill acquisition
3. To share results with the treatment team.
4. To develop a plan, in cooperation with the treatment team and the individual for remedial or alternative courses of action.
5. Continue to follow up with the individual until the decision is made by T.R. Specialist, treatment team, and the individual to terminate the process.

</td></tr>
</table>

McDowell 1976: 18–21.

Most instruments in leisure facilitation center on identifying, classifying, and analyzing leisure interest. Using widely varying classification systems and constructs, several instruments have been developed to assess leisure interest. Witt and Groom (1979: 28) indicate that the new interest in leisure counseling has led to a rash of leisure interest finders as tools in assessing leisure func-tion. The authors present an interesting schematic of the distinction, relationship, and interrelationship of needs, wants, and interests that they contend must be understood prior to the application of an interest finder. Figure 14.8 clearly illustrates the complex nature of identifying leisure interests and behavior. The problems of definition and measurement of need have

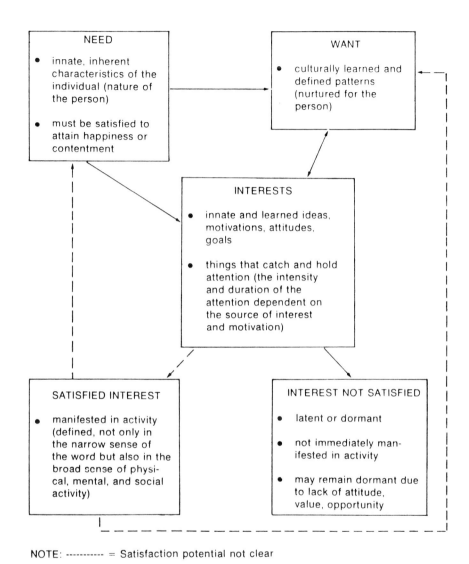

NOTE: ----------- = Satisfaction potential not clear

Figure 14.8   The Relationship of Needs, Wants, and Interest. (From Witt, P.A. & Groom, R. (1979). Damages and problems associated with current approaches to developing leisure interest finders. *Therapeutic Recreation Journal* 13(1), p. 23.)

been addressed through the establishment of four different levels of interest.

The first type of interest is labeled expressed interest—a verbal expression of interest in an activity; the second is manifest interest which is synonymous with participation in an activity; the third type is tested interest, interest as measured by objective tests, as differentiated from inventories based on subjective self-estimates. (Assumption being that interest will manifest itself in some form of increased knowledge about the activity, or any other relevant information); the fourth type is called inventoried interest, assessed by means of lists of activities similar to those in expressed interest except that each response is given an experimentally determined weight. The score then represents not a single subjective estimate but a pattern of interests, which research has shown to be rather stable (Witt and Groom 1979: 24).

Witt and Groom (1979) suggest that:

"Test constructors are aware of the problems . . . but test users are not always as careful when interpreting and making inferences about the test results." It might even be ventured that in the case of some leisure interest finders, even some of the "constructors" aren't fully aware of some of the shortcomings or limitations of the theory on which a particular interest finder is based or the way it is proposed to be used! Most users are unaware of these problems and as a result may end up utilizing instruments constructed for one purpose under conditions or in settings where they don't apply (Witt and Groom 1979: 28).

Probably the most well-developed and scientifically documented instrument available is the leisure activities blank (LAB) developed by McKechnie (1974). The instrument is used to determine an individual's past and future leisure behavior in seven activity categories. Correlated with demographic variables such as age, sex, and income, the instrument provides a simple self-administered fifteen-to-twenty-minute test. Walshe (1977: 110–111), in a review of the LAB, indicates:

The LAB is based on 120 recreation activities judged to have high participation rates in the United States. The respondent indicates the extent of past involvement in each activity and the extent of expected future participation, thus tapping actual behavior and intentionality. The client places the number corresponding to the extent of past participation beside each activity on side one of the answer sheet as follows: "never engaged in the activity," "tried it once or a few

times," "did it regularly but no longer," and "currently engage in it regularly." Indicating his/her future activity intentions in the same manner on side two, the client decides if he or she "expects to do it in the future," "is uncertain or doesn't know," or "expects to do it sometime in the future."

Scales for past and future responses are developed according to factor analysis. Two validity scales—frequent past and frequent future—determine if the respondent is answering the LAB in a purposeful and accurate manner. The test is scored using superimposed scoring templates.

It is suggested that the interpreter of the LAB needs adequate knowledge of basic inferential statistics and familiarity with leisure activities. He or she should have expertise in personality testing and assessment and related psychological fields; supervised experience in diagnostic work; and an up-to-date knowledge of the validation literature on the LAB itself. Preferably, the interpreter should have a Ph.D. degree in clinical or personality psychology.

It is obvious from Table 14.5 that much development and scientific research must take place in order for the field to advance. The table presents a matrix of information on the type of instrument, developer, format, target, training, source, reliability, validity, strengths, and weaknesses.

Facilitation Techniques and Theories

The primary element in the counseling or facilitative process is the relationship established between the individual facilitator/counselor and the client/consumer. Not only does the facilitator/counselor's personality, background, and other intervening variables have to be accounted for, but also it is imperative that he or she identify and utilize sound theoretical approaches in the delivery of service. Trained in selected facilitation techniques, the facilitator/counselor should be able to select the approach appropriate to the individual consumer's needs.

Whether the technique or theory is drawn from the affective, cognitive, behavioral, or potpourri category is incidental. What matters is that the facilitator/counselor should be trained in the technique, that he or she knows when and how to apply it, and that the person is flexible enough to modify or shift as the situation demands. Table 14.6 provides an overview of several major theories that have been or can be used in the leisure facilitation process.

Techniques and theories derived from existing models of psychological therapy can be used effectively as a part of the leisure counseling and facilitation process. The following section provides a glimpse of selected techniques such as *Gestalt awareness, life space interviewing, rational-emotive therapy, assertive training, behavior therapy, values clarification, transactional analysis, client-centered therapy, relaxation therapy and systematic desensitization, and reality therapy.* It is not the authors' intent to provide information that will lead untrained or unskilled individuals out of the classroom and into practice. It is important to note that individuals who want to pursue a career as a leisure counselor should gain extensive training in the counseling field before setting up practice.

Gestalt awareness A therapeutic approach developed by Frederick S. Perls, Gestalt awareness has its origins in psychoanalysis, European phenomenology, existentialism, and Gestalt psychology—all of which deal with perceptions, awareness, and knowledge of reality. Perls felt that many people had personalities lacking wholeness. His therapeutic approach aimed to remedy this problem by *helping clients to become aware of their intellects, emotions, creativity, body feelings, and behaviors.* A variety of techniques are used to achieve these goals—including a number of art forms such as singing, drawing, and sculpting. The use of such media allows the client to express himself symbolically and nonverbally. Emphasis is placed on the here and now, immediacy of experience, the process of personal growth, and the human potential. Clients are asked to focus on the "now" behaviors they would like to change rather than on events in the past. They are encouraged to learn more about themselves and their feelings. Such knowledge is considered essential if the fragmented personality parts are to be made whole. The client learns to recognize blocks in awareness and behavior as they manifest themselves in his life.

In Gestalt therapy, the therapist listens and observes, then tries to understand and help the client to express what is his interpretation of the interaction of events. The client is taught to express his feelings in the "I" language—"I don't have to do what I don't want to do; I don't have to give in to your demands." As a leisure-counseling technique, Gestalt awareness can be used as a way of helping the individual to identify and remove blocks to successful leisure behavior. Some such blocks according to Gunn would be fear of making mistakes, lack of experience or knowledge, or admonitions toward safety. Some awareness techniques that are especially helpful are role-playing, music, poetry, and art (Gunn 1977: 22).

Life space interviewing Fritz Redl developed the techniques of life space interviewing in his work with aggressive, emotionally disturbed children. In dealing with such children, he found that traditional psychiatric techniques—the interview in a setting isolated from the child's living environment—were inadequate to handle crisis situations or behavioral episodes. Unless the behavior was interpreted to the child in an on-the-spot intervention, it was too likely to become distorted or lost entirely.

Therefore Redl proposed life space interviewing to handle life events in close proximity to the time and place where they occurred in order to offer ego support on the spot or to exploit a child's life experiences for some specific educational gain (Newman 1974: 250). Life space interviewing in contrast to delving into the past to bring about changes in present behavior or

TABLE 14.5   Instrumentation Matrix

Instrument	Developer	Format	Target	Training
Avocational Activities Interest Finder	Natalie D'Agostini	Checks one or two (Interest)	—	—
Avocational Counseling in Milwaukee	Robert P. Overs Sharon Taylor Catherine Adkins	Card Sort (Interest)	Handicapped	
Computer Research Avocational Guidance Program (not available)	Lawrence C. Hartlage	Forced Choice (Interest)	—	Little
Constructive Leisure Activity Survey (CLAS)	Patsy Edwards	"Tried" "Would like to try" "No interest" (Interest)	Over junior high age	Suggest professional group & individual counseling/imagination, ingenuity, common sense
Leisure Activities Blank (LAB)	George E. McKechnie	Extent of past & expected participation (Interest)	Between 15 and 20	Statistics; personality assessment. Ph.D. in clinical psychology recommended
Leisure Interest Inventory (LII)	Edwina E. Hubert	Forced Choice (Interest)	Not specified	Familiarity with statistics, tests, & measurement, & LII constructs
Milwaukee Model	George T. Wilson Robert P. Overs Joseph Mirenda	(Interest)	—	Little
Taylor-Johnson Temperament Analysis	William J. Beausay	(Personality)	Athletes	—
Walshe Temperament Survey (WTS)	Willoughby Ann Walshe	True-False (Personality)	Questionnaire over 18; trained counselor can use basic concepts for observation of child	Understanding of four temperaments

Adapted from Walshe 1977: 116–117.

personality, attempts to provide ego support in time of stress. Rather than focusing on perceptions of past conflicts and the unconscious, life space interviewing attempts to examine feelings and impulses relating to a real behavioral incident.

Life space interviewing can occur anywhere—i.e., where the client is. The interviewer can be anyone who naturally participates in that client's environment and with whom the client has a trusting relationship. Often in a group setting the interviewer is an authority figure, caregiver, or leader. Certain behavioral issues are selected as targets for interviewing, and all potential interviewers in the environment are aware of these specific issues. The most obvious behaviors are chosen for intervention. Timing of the interview is crucial; the more immediate the conduct of the interview to the behavioral incident, the more effective the treatment.

TABLE 14.5 Instrumentation Matrix—*Continued*

Source	Reliability	Validity	Strengths	Weaknesses
—	—	—	Detailed (545 items)	Unknown
Extensive ''sorts'' & files developed from libraries and research	Test-retest High to very high	Assumed; is direct interest approach	Achieved very positive results: as much time spent on each client	Needs further assessment of reliability and validity
—	—	—	Computerized; gives quick answers	Unknown
—	Inferred from broad, successful experience	Assumed; is direct interest approach	The ''pioneer'' has enjoyed wide experience & good results	Needs further assessment of reliability and validity
Factor analysis of 120 recreational activities	Acceptable—needs more testing	High due to factor analysis method	Most sophisticated; best use of statistical methods	Limited high middle-class sample
Kaplan's 5 typologies	High correlation	Assumed on basis of constructs & jury assessment	Tightly-knit construction	5 typologies seem to overlap somewhat, e.g., mobile and immobile games
—	—	Assumed; is direct interest approach	Computerized; gives quick answers	Needs assessment of reliability and validity
Experience of athletes	—	—	An interesting approach; compares percentiles of athletes with population groups	Unknown
Galen's four temperaments	Work being done in this area	Assumed; questions directly reflect characteristics of four temperaments	Helps client know self; can be applied to all areas of life	Currently assessing reliability and validity

The goals of life space interviewing are: to help the client to be more sensitive to the feelings of others and to help him or her to observe and monitor his or her own behavior. It helps the client to develop a sense of right and wrong—helping the participant to become aware of a sense of values. The interviewer attempts to assist the client in seeing alternatives to his or her behavior and to maintain his or her own ego boundaries.

Life space interviewing helps to defuse some of the volatile feelings involved in a behavioral incident, because the interviewer absorbs some of the hostility and frustration and helps the client to share his or her feelings of panic, fury, and guilt. The interviewer helps the client maintain communication in a situation from which he or she might prefer to withdraw. The interviewer

TABLE 14.6 Summary of Counseling Theories

Theory	Human Nature	Belief
(1) Dynamic Psychology/Psycho-analysis (Freud)	Internal, unconscious forces. Tension reduction; regression, repetition, self-elimination, and alienation. Unfilled needs: sex and aggression.	Behavior is product of past. Recapture emotions for cure. Resistance/transference important. Control through self-disclosure.
(2) Analytic Psychology (Jung)	Self-actualization. Future-striving. Turn from darkness. Inner/outer conflicts. Collective unconscious.	Neurotic: unaware of problems; should work on them. Unconscious; rich source of causes of repression.
(3) Client-centered Therapy (Rogers)	People have positive direction. Accept new if no anxiety. Mental health; aware, self-searching. Life changes; nothing is fixed.	Repression leads to emotional disturbance. Aspects of self are dissociated. Counselor fully accepts client; counselor reflects client; client accepts self.
(4) Gestalt Therapy (Perls)	Organism seeks wholeness; needs to keep in balance. Disown unliked parts of self. Today's nature is neurotic.	Whole greater than sum of parts. Awareness curative. "I" now and how vital. Avoidance; symptom of hole.
(5) Behaviorism (Skinner)	Passive. No free will. Genes and environment control. Client can be manipulated through cause and effect.	Counselor can change client's behavior by changing environment. Behaviorists can change the world.
(6) Transactional Analysis (Berne)	All have multiple nature. Nature has three parts; Child, Parent, and Adult appear in transactions.	Each is responsible for own future. Can change position when it is understood what part of self is communicating.
(7) Humanistic Existentialism	Existence precedes essence. We avoid reality/responsibility for own choices. Self-deception equals neurosis.	Each act reveals whole self. No unconscious/resistance/transference. Emotions are deliberate. Psychological health equals acceptance of responsibility.
(8) Reality Therapy (Glasser)	Basic needs; relatedness and respect from self/others. Do what gives the feeling of worth to self/others.	All psychological problems alike. People are ill because they act irresponsibly and deny reality. Bad to study the unconscious.
(9) Transcendental Meditation (Maharishi)	Real brain-work below conscious level. Instruction needed to reach it. Nervous system is self-ordering.	Pure awareness is good for physical/psychological health. Awareness comes from body-rest with mind alert.
(10) Primal Therapy (Janov)	Human brain stores childhood pain.	Stored pain is deeply buried pain of birth, childhood, etc. If there is an open path to pain, health is achieved.

Edwards 1977: 116–117.

is able to intervene to remind the client of appropriate behavior in situations in which he or she is flooded with impulses and emotions. The interviewer may intervene for the client by exerting external controls in a crisis.

Life space interviewing, then, is useful to clarify and put events into perspective; it is disciplinary in that it attempts to change behavior, and it aims to help the client to understand his feelings. Life space interviewing can be used as a leisure counseling technique, if the counselor is willing to become an active participant in the

TABLE 14.6   Summary of Counseling Theories—*Continued*

Goal	Treatment	
Change client. Fill in gaps in memory. Lift repressive defenses. Control internal forces.	Master-slave relationship. Client uses free association. Reports childhood and dreams. Counselor shows causes of neurosis.	
Liberate unconscious. Remove repression. Change client and integrate. Maintain integrated person.	Search for meaning/self. Counseling is mutual process. Recall at certain age. Dream interpretation.	
Client changes basic personality; integrates self. Client develops self-love, fully-functioning personality.	Counselor shows positive regard and real self. Counselor is quiet; client talks. Counselor accepts/reflects client. Counselor clarifies, and client gains self-knowledge.	
No change; make whole and live better inside/outside. Get back disowned parts. Responsible for self and growth.	Continual awareness. Frustrate client so that he/she solves own problems in "now." Acts out dreams; fills in holes.	
Motivate client to seek socially acceptable behavior. Gain knowledge of "why" of human conduct.	Reward/reinforce good behavior. Punish/deprive to stop bad behavior.	
TA is tool to use to get at the basis for behavior and feeling. Change client for better and therefore change the course of the world.	TA better in groups. Counselor and client have a mutual relationship. Analyze give and take in transactions. Encourage adult.	
Cast light on whole client. Client comes to awareness/reality. Client sees/knows self; no fear. Counselor does not change client.	No set treatment ideas. Mutual counselor/client relationship. Counselor is authentic. No history or interpretation.	
Client should be realistic, responsible, right, and moral. Deal with real world. Support conscience.	Individual or in groups. Counselor is involved with client. Examines daily actions. Counselor rejects bad behavior, not client.	
Reduce stress, expand conscious awareness and client withstands fatigues and daily life.	Course of instruction. Groups, with individual consulting. Mantra selected. Meditates twice daily by self.	
Feel comfortably alive. Become open and express emotions.	Regular set program. Individual and group therapy. Relieve early pain: Scream. Give vent to feelings.	

leisure pursuits of the client or if the counselor is involved in the natural environment of the client (such as a milieu therapy setting in an inpatient psychiatric facility). Obviously in these situations, the therapist could observe target leisure behaviors and use life space interviewing to deal with the behaviors as they occur.

Rational-emotive therapy   Albert Ellis, a psychoanalyst, developed a method for speeding up time-consuming and often frustrating Freudian analysis and called it rational-emotive therapy. His goal was *to actively direct patients to analyze and solve their problems rationally rather than to approach them illogically and emotionally.*

He hypothesized that behavior has three components—an activating event (A); the irrational beliefs of the individual (B); and an emotional consequence(C) that is unpleasant or aversive to the individual and leads him or her to seek counseling but is not a result of (A)—it is a result of (B). Ellis believed that in therapy—point (D)—these beliefs would be confronted and disputed; and the result—point (E)—would be a change in the behavior of the individual.

Ellis described eleven irrational beliefs: (1) it is essential to be approved or loved by virtually everyone; (2) one must be competent, adequate, and achieving to be worthwhile; (3) some people are bad, wicked, or villainous and deserve punishment; (4) it is a terrible catastrophe for things to be different than one would like; (5) unhappiness is caused by outside individuals and is outside the control of the individual; (6) dangerous or fearsome things should be a constant source of anxiety; (7) it is easier to avoid difficulties and responsibilities than to face them; (8) one should be dependent on others who are stronger; (9) past experiences and events determine present behavior; (10) one should be quite upset over other people's problems and disturbances; (11) there is always a right or perfect solution to every problem (Ellis 1976: 73). Ellis felt that these beliefs are accepted almost universally within our society, and when accepted into the A-B-C personality system, lead to emotional upset. He emphasized that one's attitudes and beliefs about events, circumstances, or behaviors are more important than the events themselves.

Rational-emotive therapy follows a basic systematic pattern to teach a client to think rationally. First, the client recognizes a problem and seeks help to overcome it. The counselor helps the client to discover the cognitive pattern that is generating the disturbed feeling; the disturbed feeling is attacked; the old, maladaptive behavior is replaced with new realistic thought patterns; and in a final step the client tries out his or her new attitudes in more fulfilling behaviors.

Rational-emotive therapy has produced successful results with a wide variety of populations, but it is limited to those who thought processes are relatively intact. Because the techniques used to achieve the goals of this form of therapy are relatively nonspecific, it is highly reliant on the skill and creativity of the counselor to bring about successful changes in behavior. Because the counselor is highly directive, he or she puts the client in the undesirable position of dependency, and, at the same time, leads the client to accept the counselor's values rather than to develop his or her own values.

Rational-emotive therapy methods are compatible with leisure counseling as pointed out by McDowell (1976), who states:

> It is suggested that a leisure counseling approach which uses rational problem-solving and decision-making processes can help the client resolve his leisure problems, or create an atmosphere for personal inquiry and leisure education (McDowell 1976: 53).

The client's attitudes, values, and beliefs about leisure and leisure pursuits can be analyzed, and the irrational ones can be replaced by more realistic ones. This should lead to new behaviors that can then be tried out and lead to a more satisfying mode of leisure behavior.

Assertiveness training Assertiveness training is an increasingly popular behavior modification technique aimed at changing nonassertive behavior patterns learned in childhood. Nonassertive behavior is considered to be self-denying; it allows others to make choices for the individual; it does not lead to achievement of goals, and it leaves the individual feeling anxious and hurt.

A more desirable pattern of behavior, *assertive behavior, is self-enhancing, represents the individual's own choices, is more likely to achieve his or her goals, and leaves the individual and others feeling satisfied.* Assertive behavior is seen to be different from aggressive behavior, which is self-enhancing at the expense of others, achieves its goals by hurting others, and opens the individual to acts of revenge by victims of his or her behavior.

One way in which assertive behavior can be learned is through the use of sample situations, dialogues, and exercises that may be practiced alone or with others. Such practice helps the individual to identify situations in which he or she behaves in a nonassertive manner and helps him or her learn new types of responses, which are assertive rather than aggressive. A basic component of assertiveness training is the concept of *assertive human rights*—i.e., all persons are created equal on a human-to-human plane and deserve the privilege of expressing these rights. Each person is the ultimate judge of his or her own behavior; he or she can express his or her feelings about a situation but cannot judge others. One has the right to express oneself and feel good about doing so but may not hurt others in the process. Nonverbal cues (such as voice tone and control, eye contact, posture, physical distance, and gestures) are seen as important components of assertive behavior.

Nonassertive behaviors are thought to result from an increase in anxiety that prevents normal actions. To determine the assertion level of the individual, a variety of assertiveness inventories are available in which the individual is asked how he or she would react in given situations. Once assertion levels are determined, a hierarchy of anxiety-causing situations is developed to establish goals for assertive behavior.

Individual problem situations may then be designed so that the individual may rehearse specific behaviors to fit each situation. When the situation is role-played, the individual gains confidence and gets some idea of the probable results of his or her actions, with a resultant decrease in anxiety. Feedback to the individual through discussion or taping is an important part of the process, as it helps support his or her

strengths and encourages him or her to continue attacking weaknesses. Another useful technique is to have the counselor model the assertive response to a particular situation, to have the individual imagine the situation and his or her response, and to suggest changes before the situation is role-played. It may be helpful to write out a script and act it out until the individual feels comfortable with it.

Studies have shown that assertiveness training seems to be primarily situation-specific. In other words, the assertive behavior was increased only in those situations for which it has been rehearsed. Therefore, it is recommended that a wide variety of situations be practiced with the individual—including close interpersonal relationships, consumer problems, employment, social situations, the initiating of actions, and the denying of unreasonable requests.

Assertiveness training has been used extensively by women's groups to counter the childhood training of women that leads many of them to be overly submissive; it also has been used in a variety of clinical settings. It is more effective with a population having a level of understanding that allows transfer of the learned behavior to new situations and recognizes that a choice of behaviors is available to the individual.

Some authorities are skeptical as to the value of assertiveness training. It has occasionally resulted in negative behavior changes in the individual—especially a tendency to become overly aggressive. The individual's new behaviors may jeopardize some interpersonal relationships, or may falsely lead the individual to expect that this new ability to be assertive will bring wholesale positive changes in all aspects of his or her life. One aspect of the technique that has yet to be fully researched is the longevity of the training. Does it become a permanent part of the individual's behavior repertoire?

The technique of assertiveness training may be useful in leisure counseling in helping individuals to resist those who might try to impose their leisure interests and values on them against their real desires. They may become more forceful in participating in those leisure activities they prefer and may gain a realization that their leisure interests are equally as important as those of spouse, family members, and friends. Assertiveness training may also be helpful to the individual who expresses interest in certain activities but is reluctant to participate because of fears of meeting new people—whether embarrassed about a lack of knowledge or uncomfortable in new situations.

Behavior therapy Popularly known as "behavior modification," behavior therapy is based on the theory that all behavior, good or bad, is learned. Therefore, behavior modification can be defined as the attempt to apply learning and other experimentally derived psychological principles to problem behavior. In a behavioral therapy approach, a functional analysis is constructed that details the frequency with which the problem behavior occurs, the situations in which it occurs, and the consequences of the behavior. This becomes the baseline by which progress can be measured.

The therapist then determines the desired behavioral goals or "terminal behaviors" that he or she wishes to achieve through therapy. Contingency management is the tool used to attempt to alter behavior—referring to "the process of *changing behavioral responses by controlling the consequences of that response*" (Krumholtz and Krumholtz 1972: 119).

This can be done in several ways. Positive reinforcement is used to increase a person's performance of a certain behavior by rewarding the individual immediately upon completion of a correct response. The reward must follow the behavior immediately to establish a connection between the behavior and the reward. Negative reinforcement seeks to decrease the frequency of a behavior by calling attention to a particular undesirable consequence of that behavior. This type of reinforcement usually appears in the form of a threat.

Punishment is a way of decreasing the frequency of the response it follows. It usually involves physical or emotional pain to the individual or a loss in status or privilege. Punishment is a powerful reinforcer and, in some cases, acts to reinforce rather than to extinguish the inappropriate behavior (i.e., a student who is reprimanded by a teacher for talking in class may actually be rewarded by the attention). It may also cause long-lasting fears and anxieties and encourages the person to seek a means of escaping rather than to deal with the consequences. Occasionally, self-monitored punishment can be an effective technique. In this situation, the person seeking to effect the behavior change would administer his or her own punishment when the undesirable behavior occurred.

To stimulate certain behaviors an individual may never have exhibited previously, it may be necessary to reward successive steps that will ultimately lead to the desired behavior. However, the steps must be identified with the subject prior to beginning the treatment. Conditioned reinforcers (such as tokens or money) can be dispensed at the time a behavior occurs. These conditioned reinforcers must be linked with and signal the delivery of other reinforcers that will be dispensed at a future time.

In order to maintain a desired behavior over a long period of time, an intermittent schedule of reinforcement is used, so that the frequency of rewards for proper behavior decreases as the behavior appears to have been learned. In eliciting a desired response in the early phases of behavior therapy, cueing for the correct performance before the action is performed may speed the learning process. Modeling may increase the person's incentive to learn the behavior by allowing him or her to observe a prestigious person performing the behavior. Parents are usually the first natural models; but teachers, friends, siblings, or entertainment figures may also be considered worthy of emulation. Other techniques that have proven effective in changing behavior are to allow a person to continue the undesirable behavior until he or she tires of it; to not reward the undesired act; to reward a behavior incompatible with the undesired act; or to terminate a mildly aversive situation when the subject's behavior improves.

Attention is a powerful reinforcer; by ignoring an undesirable behavior, it may be effectively reduced. Negative reinforcement is probably the least desirable method of stopping inappropriate behavior, while the most desirable would be to find an acceptable substitute behavior and reward it. In a behavior-oriented approach to leisure counseling, one would attempt to identify the person's problem behavior, determine alternative behaviors that could be learned in place of the problem behavior, and substitute these more desired behaviors through a system of reinforcement. Such an approach has been found to be especially useful in working with children.

Values clarification   Values clarification is a teaching technique developed primarily to assist classroom teachers in *guiding individuals into understanding, developing, and ranking values.* The technique attempts to involve the participant in learning by doing or by discovery. The teacher acts as a facilitator who achieves the desired goals through skillful questioning rather than lecturing. This technique helps the student to arrive at his or her own answers rather than to unquestioningly accept answers provided by others.

According to Raths, Harmin, and Simon (1966: 85) the process of valuing consists of seven parts:

1. Prizing one's beliefs and behavior
2. Publicly affirming these
3. Choosing consciously from alternatives
4. Choosing after consideration of consequences
5. Choosing freely for one's self
6. Acting on the chosen belief
7. Repeating the behavior consistently

The counselor should be aware of and sensitive to the process of valuing and act in such a way as to stimulate the process. One way for the counselor to provide such a stimulus is by questioning the student. The questions should stimulate the student to think about and clarify his or her own values and should not convey the judgments or values of the questioner. There is no predetermined answer, and the questions are carefully phrased to avoid prejudicing the respondent into providing a particularly "good" answer. The questions may stimulate a short discussion, but the primary goal is to stimulate the student to form his or her own opinions. Typical questions might be: What do you believe? What do you think? How did that make you feel? What outcome would that have? Would you stand up and affirm that in a public place?

Values clarification can be particularly useful in the leisure counseling process because it is a way of encouraging a person to examine his or her lifestyle and the relationship of work and leisure within that lifestyle. A variety of exercises may be used to help the individual, either alone or in a group, to identify and rank his or her values regarding work and leisure. For example, the individual might be presented with a long list of activities (both life-sustaining and optional) and then asked to note how much time he or she would devote to each activity weekly. The importance or value placed on each activity by the individual could then be determined by the amount of time allotted to it, providing a convenient means for ranking these activities. Such exercises are useful in stimulating thought and discussion about leisure and work and may be combined with the values clarification questioning mentioned earlier in this discussion.

Transactional analysis   Transactional analysis is a psychotherapeutic technique developed by Eric Berne. He felt that client *behavior is characterized by three ego states—parent, adult, and child*—which he defined as memory events based on previous experiences and behaviors of the individual. The child ego state is seen as preserved behavior from childhood prior to nine years of age. Perception is syncretic, and thinking is at a prelogical or preoperational level of development. The adult state is essentially a data gathering and processing function, isolated from emotion but necessary to observe and predict reality. The parent state is, for the most part, neither perceptive nor cognitive; rather, it is based on behavior copied from parents or other authority figures and is the repository of tradition and values of society.

Berne developed a complex theory to explain behavior based on transactional analysis—the stimulus and response between the various ego states. Transactional analysis groups devoted much of their time to exploring behavior of group members in terms of transactions between the various ego states—particularly in the playing of games or the ways in which such games obstructed the achievement of real intimacy. Berne described a game as "a series of ulterior transactions with a gimmick leading to a usually well-concealed, but well-defined payoff (Berne 1973: 370–393). The payoffs may be *strokes,* which is Berne's term for verbal recognition or improvement—solidifying the person's social position. Games are used to help fulfill the person's life plan. Berne theorized that a person establishes this plan early in life; thus, it is firmly lodged in the child ego state. As a result, the person spends his whole life in predetermined ways based on decisions made as a child.

Transactional analysis has as a goal the "cure" of the presenting symptoms and the freeing up of the adult, so that the individual may choose freely—unhampered by the influences of the past. The "cure" is precisely defined as the contrast between the patient and the therapist established early in the treatment. Berne outlined several therapeutic approaches that may be employed by the therapist. The therapist is direct and active. He or she may confront, explain, confirm, interpret, support, or persuade—all in terms of the transactions occurring in the client's behavior.

Transactional analysis offers the advantage of using colloquialisms—a special transactional analysis language that allows for more effective communication between therapist and client. The "words have the same meaning by definition for everyone who uses them." The patient is encouraged to engage in understanding, observing, and verifying behavior and is given the language to communicate his or her observations and understandings to others. Transactional analysis can be applied in leisure counseling to help the client understand the origins of his or her particular attitudes and values concerning leisure. Game analysis also may be useful in helping a client to understand his or her leisure behavior.

Client-centered therapy Psychotherapist Carl Rogers developed the theory of client-centered therapy, which is *based on the hypothesis that a relationship between the client and therapist should reflect and communicate the realness, caring, sensitivity, and nonjudgmental understanding of the helping person.* He theorizes that each person acts rationally according to his or her perception of the world, and it is the responsibility of the therapist to understand these perceptions.

Rogers believes that the personality seeks self-actualization, or wholeness "which serves to maintain or enhance the organism" (Rogers 1959: 169). A basic component of the actualizing process is keeping a self-concept congruent with an individual's experiences. This congruency occurs when self-experiences are accurately symbolized and included in the self-concept in the "accurately symbolized" form. Society forces the individual to curb some of his or her impulses toward achieving self-actualization, but the individual feels them; thus, a state of incongruence is created. Therapy helps the individual to achieve congruence and to acknowledge his or her self-actualizing urges (Rogers and Meador 1973: 226).

Rogers feels that client-centered therapy helps the client experience personality changes if the therapist is congruent and integrated in the relationship and is able to communicate his or her understanding and empathy to the client. In order to be effective, the therapist must be genuine—aware of his or her own feelings and able to expose them to the client. He or she must be capable of empathetic understanding—able to listen and understand the world as the client sees it. He or she responds to the client with positive regard. The counselor avoids judgmental behavior and, instead, provides caring that is not an approval/disapproval basis.

Rogers identified seven stages of behavior change in the therapeutic relationship. The first stage involves communication about external things and unwillingness to talk about oneself. In the second stage, feelings are described, but in a distant way, and problems are seen as external to the person. In the third stage, feelings and experiences that are described as unacceptable predominate, but most feelings are described in the past tense. The present is described freely in the fourth stage, and clients begin to realize that feelings previously denied are close to the surface. They experience some fear as well as some realization of their own responsibility for problems. In the fifth stage, such feelings are freely expressed and assumed by the individual. In the sixth stage, previously denied feelings are experienced with immediacy and acceptance. In the seventh stage, the person experiences his or her feelings more comfortably and confidently.

Client-centered therapy has been criticized for theoretical reasons and for the demands it makes on a therapist. Many people in the field do not agree with Rogers' theory of the self-actualizing tendency, while others feel he sets forth too many criteria or necessary conditions for psychological changes to occur. However, client-centered therapy does place the responsibility for behavior change on the individual in the present time. The past is not explored, since present emotions are considered to determine how the individual functions.

The client-centered approach may be used in leisure counseling to help the client to become more aware of his or her attitudes and values concerning leisure. The client-therapist relationship can help the client achieve self-actualizing leisure behavior. Leisure counseling has been defined as "a helping process which facilitates interpretive, affective, and/or behavioral changes in others toward the attainment of their total leisure well-being " (McDowell 1976: 9). Gunn (1977: 23) defines leisure counseling as the following:

> . . . [A] helping process utilizing verbal facilitation techniques to promote an increase in self-awareness, awareness of leisure attitudes, values, and feelings and the development of decision-making and problem-solving skills related to leisure participation with self—others and environmental factors.

Both of these definitions seem to focus on a client-centered approach to the leisure-counseling process. The client-centered approach is important to leisure counseling for its emphasis on understanding, caring, trust, and respect in the client-counselor relationship.

Relaxation therapy and systematic desensitization Relaxation therapy is frequently used in conjunction with systematic desensitization (both forms of behavior-therapy) as a *solution to alleviating anxiety and learned fears.* Some of the uncomfortable consequences of anxiety are physical changes in the body (such as high blood pressure, rapid breathing, quickened heartbeat, and changes in skin temperature). Progressive relaxation is one technique used to help an individual overcome these physical responses to anxiety.

The relaxation technique usually begins by tensing various muscle groups within the body tightly, maintaining the tension for a few moments, then releasing and experiencing the change—at the same time attempting to keep the rest of the body muscles relaxed. With repeated experience of the relaxed sensation and practice at techniques to achieve it, a total relaxation regimen for the whole body takes five to ten minutes—for example, to relax the hands, arms, and shoulders, there are four steps taking four to six minutes initially:

1. Tighten the right hand into a fist, building up tension in your hand and forearm. Relax. Repeat once.
2. Repeat step one using the left hand.
3. Bend your right elbow, making your right hand into a fist and tensing your forearm and upper arm. Relax. Repeat once.
4. Repeat step three using the left arm.

When a specific situation or stimulus that causes a person to feel anxious can be identified, the situation is presented to the individual in graded steps and the person is taught to overcome his or her anxiety symptoms with the learned techniques of muscular relaxation. For instance, if a person were afraid of public speaking, a hierarchy of anxiety-producing situations might be developed in which the person first spoke to a group of children, then to a group of friends, then to a group of adults with no special knowledge of the subject matter, then to a group of professionals in the subject area. When fear was experienced, in each situation the person would consciously use his or her learned relaxation techniques to counter the fear.

The desensitization process can be used in various ways. Rather than actually participating in the anxiety-producing situation, some individuals are able to imagine the situation and the fear and then apply the relaxation techniques. In other instances, fear stimuli have been presented through media such as pictures, slides, videotapes, or recordings. In order for such a program to be successful, the client must be highly motivated and the anxiety fairly specific to object or theme. Some individuals are not able to relax enough to rid themselves of the fear, and other therapeutic techniques may be used with greater success.

These techniques may be useful in leisure counseling in order to help an individual achieve a level of relaxation and relief from tension that will make participation in leisure activities more enjoyable. Relaxation therapy gives one a feeling of self-control and success in dealing with personal problems and behaviors. It is possible that systematic desensitization might have some effectiveness in helping an individual to overcome fear and anxiety related to present or potential leisure pursuits.

Reality therapy   Reality therapy, as developed by Dr. William Glasser, is highly opposed to the conventional psychoanalytic techniques based on Freudian theory. Rather than delving into the unconscious and focusing on the past, *the reality therapist is concerned with present behavior. The reality therapist believes that unrealistic and irresponsible behavior results from unfulfilled needs.* The reality therapist becomes personally involved with his or her client—in contrast to the psychoanalytic therapist, who remains aloof and impartial. The reality therapist deals with the question of morality (moral behavior being defined as "that in which a man gives and receives love, and feels worthwhile to himself and others" [Glasser 1965: 57]. Glasser feels that morality—the need to love and be loved—and the need to feel worthwhile to ourselves and to others are basic psychologic needs.

The first step in reality therapy is involvement. The therapist and the client establish a warm, personal, caring relationship; in this stage, the focus is not on the client's problems but on the building of a trusting relationship. Once this involvement becomes strong enough, present behavior is discussed, emphasizing the fact that the client chooses his or her own behavior. Feelings are considered less important than behavior and will not change until behavior changes (Glasser 1965: 57).

The therapist then seeks to have the client evaluate his or her behavior—whether it is good for the client or for people he or she cares about and whether it is socially acceptable in his or her community. The therapist does not make value judgments but encourages the client to do so and to try to change those behaviors the client judges to be negative to self or to others (Glasser 1965: 57).

The therapist helps the client to engage in more positive behavior. Change is planned in small steps in order to minimize the chance for failure. The client is asked to make a written or verbal commitment to pursue the plan. If the client does not keep his or her commitment, the value judgment and plan are reevaluated. The therapist emphasizes the value of the commitment and the necessity for fulfilling it; he or she does not accept excuses as to why the commitments are not fulfilled and does not use punishment if the client does not achieve his or her goals. Offering praise when commitments are kept is a much more desirable way of promoting responsible behavior.

Reality therapy can be used with virtually any client population because people seeking help have a basic factor in common—they have failed to behave in such a manner as to fulfill their basic needs and must learn different behaviors that will lead to need fulfillment. The leisure counselor can assist a client to evaluate leisure behavior in terms of its morality, as the word is used in reality therapy. Once the negative behaviors are identified, the counselor can help the client to formulate a plan to change those behaviors. The leisure counselor should be a motivational force in helping the client to fulfill the commitment to positively alter his or her leisure behavior.

Because reality therapy is based on present rather than past behavior, it is more easily learned than some of the other therapeutic techniques. Because of the necessary personal involvement of the counselor, this technique requires someone with a strong, warm personality to serve as therapist—someone who is willing to establish a stable, accepting relationship with his or her client.

Summary

It has been noted that the leisure consumer is often ill-prepared to deal with factors such as an abundance of leisure time, the ever-increasing complexity of choice, early retirement, and retrenchment from a work-oriented society. The increasing interest in leisure education as a vehicle for the preparation for leisure should continue. In an era of fiscal conservatism, it is even more important that professionals in the leisure service field promote the need for leisure education.

In discussing the concept of leisure education, the authors maintain that education for leisure should be the responsibility of many agencies and organizations. It should pervade the home, school, and community throughout the entire lifespan of an individual. Significant leisure education models such as LEAP should be advocated and implemented and other leisure education models should also be developed and evaluated.

If an individual is having difficulty in overcoming certain barriers to leisure fulfillment, the leisure service professional should be in a position to facilitate the removal of the barrier or barriers. In this chapter, nine such barriers were identified; and general strategies for their removal were presented. Through the removal of the barriers to leisure fulfillment, the leisure service professional may facilitate opportunities for human development. It is hoped that this will have a positive effect on the total life space of the individual.

Discussion Questions and Exercises

1. Why is the facilitation of leisure behavior a responsibility of leisure service organizations and professionals?

2. Discuss the current leisure lifestyles of North Americans. How are they similar? Different? What factors influence leisure behavior?

3. Identify nine barriers to leisure fulfillment and suggest strategies for overcoming each.

4. Provide a rationale for instituting a leisure education curriculum in the public schools, in a community leisure service agency, and in adult and continuing education centers.

5. Identify and define two major leisure education models.

6. Establish a rationale for leisure service organizations for establishing, collecting, and sorting information on programs.

7. Investigate public, private nonprofit, and commercial leisure service organizations to determine how they disseminate information related to leisure.

8. Define leisure counseling and illustrate the role it serves in facilitating leisure behavior.

9. Identify and describe three counseling techniques and discuss how they could be used with individuals who have significant barriers to leisure fulfillment.

10. What ethical factors should be considered when selecting a given leisure counseling facilitation technique?

References

Ball, E. 1973. *Draft rationale statement for leisure education.* Unpublished; prepared for the Leisure Education Advancement Project, National Recreation and Park Association.

Berne, Eric, C. M. Steiner, and J. M. Dusay, "Transactional/Analysis." In Ratibor, Ray, M. Zurjevich (ed.), *Direct Psychotherapy*, Vol. I, Coral Gables, FL: University of Miami Press, 1973), pp. 370–393.

Boothby, J., M. F. Tungatt, and A. R. Townsend. 1981. Ceasing participation in sports activity: Reported reasons and their implications. *Journal of Leisure Research* 13(1).

Burke, G. 1975. A community-based model for the delivery of leisure counseling services to special populations. In McDowell, C. F. 1976. *Leisure Counseling.* Eugene, OR: Center for Leisure Studies.

Compton, D. M. and J. E. Goldstein, eds. 1977. *Perspectives of leisure counseling.* Arlington, VA: National Recreation and Park Association.

Connolly, M. L. 1977. Leisure counseling: A values clarification and assertive training approach. In Epperson, A., P. A. Witt, and G. Hitzhusen. 1977. *Leisure Counseling.* Springfield, IL: Thomas.

Deraeck, G. and L. Ballaert. 1976. Education permanente' of young workers in leisure time and on the job. *Leisure Today,* October.

Dickason, J. G. 1972. Approaches and techniques of recreation counseling. *Therapeutic Recreation Journal* 6.

Edwards, P. B. 1977. *Leisure counseling techniques.* Los Angeles: University Publishers.

Ellis, A. 1976. Requisite conditions for basic personality change. *Journal of Consulting Psychology* 23(6).

Fain, G. 1973. Leisure counseling: Translating needs into action. *Therapeutic Recreation Journal* 7.

Francken, D. A. and W. F. van Raiij. 1981. *The process of recreation programming.* New York: John Wiley and Sons.

Glasser, W. 1965. *Reality therapy.* New York: Harper and Row.

Godbey, G. 1978. *Recreation, park and leisure services: Foundations, organizations, administration.* Philadelphia: W. B. Saunders.

Godbey, G. 1985. Nonuse of public lcisure services: A model. *Journal of Park and Recreation Administration* 3(2).

Gunn, S. L. 1977. The relationship of leisure counseling to selected counseling theories. In Compton, D.M. and J. E. Goldstein, eds. *Perspectives of Leisure Counseling.* Arlington, VA: National Recreation and Park Association.

Gunn, S. L. and C. A. Peterson. 1978. *Therapeutic recreation program design.* Englewood Cliffs, NJ: Prentice-Hall.

Hayes, G. A. 1977. Leisure education and recreation counseling. In Epperson, A. P. A. Witt, and G. Hitzhusen. 1977. *Leisure Counseling.* Springfield, IL: Thomas.

Hultsman, W. Z. 1988. Application of a touch-sensitive computer in park settings: Activity alternatives and visitor information. *Journal of Park and Recreation Administration* 6(1).

Jackson, E. L. 1983. Activity-specific barriers to recreation participation. *Leisure Sciences* 6(1).

Jackson, E. L. and M. S. Searle. 1983. Recreation non-participation: Variables related to the desire for new recreation activities. *Recreation Research Review* 10(2).

Johnson, L. P. and D. A. Zoreink. 1977. The development and implementation of a leisure counseling program with female psychiatric patients based on value clarification techniques. In Epperson, A., P. A. Witt, and G. Hitzhusen. 1977. *Leisure counseling.* Springfield, IL: Thomas.

Krumholtz, J. D. and H. B. Krumholtz. 1972. *Changing children's behavior.* Englewood Cliffs, NJ: Prentice-Hall.

Leisure Information Service. 1976. *A systems model for developing a leisure education program for handicapped children and youth.* Washington, DC: Hawkins and Associates, Inc.

Loesch, L. C. and P. T. Wheeler. 1982. *Principles of leisure counseling.* Minneapolis: Educational Media Corp.

Magulski, M., V. Hirsch-Faull, and B. Rutkowski. 1977. The Milwaukee leisure counseling model. *Leisure Today* April.

McDowell, C. F. 1976. *Leisure counseling.* Eugene, OR: Center for Leisure Studies.

McDowell, C. F. An analysis of leisure counseling orientations and models and their integrative possibilities. In Compton, D. M. and J. E. Goldstein, eds. 1977. *Perspectives of leisure counseling.* Arlington, VA: National Recreation and Park Association.

McKechnie, G. E. 1974. The psychological structure of leisure: Past behavior. *Journal of Leisure Research* 6.

Montagnes, J. A. 1976. Reality therapy approach to leisure counseling. *Journal of Leisureability* 3.

Mundy, J. and L. Odum. 1979. *Leisure education: Theory and practice.* New York: John Wiley and Sons.

NRPA. 1977. *Kangaroo kit: Leisure education curriculum* Vol. 2. Arlington, VA: National Recreation and Park Association.

Newman, R. G. 1974. *Groups in school.* New York: Simon and Schuster.

Overs, R. P., S. Taylor, and C. Adkins. 1974. *Avocational counseling in Milwaukee.* Milwaukee: Curative Workshop of Milwaukee.

Raths, L. M. Harmin, and S. B. Simon. 1966. *Values and teaching.* Columbus, OH: Merrill Publishing.

Remple, J. 1977. A community-based experiment in leisure counseling. In Epperson, A., P. A. Witt, and G. Hitzhusen. *Leisure Counseling.* Springfield, IL: Thomas.

Rogers, C. 1959. A theory of therapy, personality and interpersonal relations as developed in the client centered framework. In S. Roch, ed. *Psychology: A Study of Science* 3. New York: McGraw-Hill.

Rogers, C. and B. D. Meador. 1973. Client-centered therapy. In R. Corsini, ed. *Current Psychotherapies.* Itasca, IL: F. E. Peacock Publishers.

Romsa, G. and W. Hoffman. 1980. An application of non-participation data in recreation research: Testing the opportunity theory. *Journal of Leisure Research* 12(4).

Searle, M. S. and E. L. Jackson. 1984. Recreation non-participation: Socio-economic variables in perceived barriers to participation. *Leisure Sciences,* in press.

Searle, M. S. and E. L. Jackson. 1985. Recreation non-participation and barriers to participation: Considerations for the management of recreation delivery systems. *Journal of Park and Recreation Administration* 3(2).

Tinsley, E. A. and D. J. Tinsley. 1984. Leisure counseling models. In Dowd, E. T. *Leisure Counseling.* Springfield, IL: Thomas.

Walshe, W. A. 1977. Leisure counseling instrumentation. In Compton, D. M. and J. E. Goldstein, eds. *Perspectives of Leisure Counseling.* Arlington, VA: National Recreation and Park Association.

Witt, P. A. and T. L. Goodale. 1981. The relationship between barriers to leisure enjoyment and family stages. *Leisure Sciences* 4(1).

Witt, P. A. and R. Groom. 1979. Damages and problems associated with current approaches to developing leisure interest finders. *Therapeutic Recreation Journal* 13(1):23.

15 | Future Trends and Professional Issues

Learning Objectives

1. To assist the student in understanding *the role of change in the provision of leisure services.*
2. To help the student identify *factors that are influencing the delivery of leisure services in a changing society.*
3. To acquaint individuals with the strategies and methods that can be employed by the leisure service programmer in *understanding and shaping the future.*
4. To provide information concerning *demographic, technological, economic, and social and cultural trends influencing leisure.*
5. To provide information concerning *professional issues influencing the delivery of leisure services.*

Introduction

All leisure service professionals are challenged with the future. Change is a dominant factor influencing societal leisure values and practices. The leisure market is constantly evolving and new ways of experiencing leisure are being sought by people. Change is an element which the leisure service professional may or may not successfully understand. Changes occurring in our environment today have tremendous impact on how we will operate in the future.

Leisure service programmers can have two orientations to the change process. One is a passive, noninteractive, reactive approach to change; the other is to be involved as a contributor to activities of the future. The passive, noninteractive, reactive approach to change finds the professional waiting for events to have an impact on his or her organization and then reacting to these events. The leisure service professional assuming this posture does not attempt to anticipate change, but rather scurries to keep pace with the emergence of new patterns of leisure behavior and activity. The question often posed by an individual professional operating from this perspective is "What *is* occurring?" rather than "What *may* occur?"

The second orientation to the change process is to see oneself as a participator in the creation of the future. As Tindall (1984) has noted, " . . . the ability to understand and keep pace with change, as well as to create innovative responses that can impact its direction is the one theme most central to prolonged vitality for any profession or business of the future." She further notes that the leisure service professional must become " . . . a master of change and innovation, as opposed to its victim." In the same vein, Brauer (1984) has noted that leisure service organizations must " . . . choose between being leaders, victims, or survivors . . . " in this era of dramatic and rapid change.

In this chapter, we will explore some of the factors that influence the work of the leisure service professional in leading in an era of change.

We will explore basic orientations toward change. In addition, a number of tools and strategies that can be used to identify changes will be presented. Several trends—demographic, technological, economic, social, and cultural—will be reviewed. Finally, some areas of future direction will be identified.

Living in an Era of Change

It is perhaps trite to suggest that we live in one of the most change-oriented periods in the history of humankind. Changes that have occurred economically, technologically, socially, and politically in the past several decades are staggering, as has been the rate of these changes. There have been more inventions in the last two decades than in the previous 100 years. We have moved in just a short period of time from a society in which the emphasis was on mass production and centralization to one which emphasizes the more unique needs of individuals in a decentralized fashion.

Brauer (1984) further suggests that there will be more ambiguity and the potential for less understanding and acceptance of basic concepts. This will occur because of both the diversity of interests emerging during the present era and the rate of change. In discussing change, he has noted that there are several different perspectives that have emerged. They are as follows:

1. Change will be constant, rather than the exception to long periods of sameness.
2. Change is basic and substantive: New definitions (of *family, work, health care*); male-female roles/relationships; diminishing resources / increasing toxic wastes; eroding social cements under increased stress.
3. Change is pervasive/persistent/worldwide/self-generated; an interdependent/interconnected world eliminates isolation (1984: 58).

As one can see, there are a number of perspectives concerning change. Change will be constant, substantial, pervasive, persistent. In other words, change will be with us and in order to succeed as leisure service professionals, we will have to understand change, become adept at reading and predicting trends toward change and provide visionary leadership to meet the challenges of the future.

The Information Era

In order to understand this period of change in which we currently live, it is useful to explore changing ideas and concepts as they have emerged in the past. To develop a foundation for understanding this period of change, it is essential to review history for the past several thousand years. Toffler (1980), in his book *The Third Wave,* has suggested that the history of humankind can be divided into four segments—precivilized society, the agricultural revolution, the industrial revolution, and the technological revolution (or the information era). Each of these changes in the history of humankind represents a major shift influencing the thinking, values, attitudes, and behavior of individuals. Ferguson (1980), author of *The Aquarian Conspiracy,* calls these changes *paradigm shifts.* They are major changes shaping the way we live all aspects of our lives.

The *information era* (also known as *post-industrial society* and the *technological revolution*) emerged as a result of technological advances and changes in the type and nature of work engaged in by individuals. We are witnessing enormous changes as the industrial society gives way to a new society emphasizing the creation and distribution of information and services. The information era is built on a new set of assumptions and will require new ideas, new concepts, and new strategies in response to the new values that currently exist and will continue to emerge.

The information era is challenging leisure service programmers to develop new paradigms or new ways of solving new problems. The information era is built on a different set of assumptions than the industrial era. For example, in the industrial era there was an effort directed toward standardizing and mass-producing goods and services. This followed the assumption that people were not necessarily unique and that their needs could be met in a systematic, uniform fashion. On the other hand, the information era recognizes the need for uniquely designed and organized services that cater to individual needs, more specifically suited to individual tastes, values, and behavior.

As we shift from an industrial society to an information society, there will be several factors that will have a direct impact on leisure service organizations. Some of the important trends, drawn from a variety of sources include the following.

1. *Cultural Pluralism*—We live in a diverse society, where personal choice is a major factor in determining leisure preferences. As leisure service programmers, we must cater to different ethnic, racial, social, and geographic tastes.
2. *Rural vs. Urban Society*—Worldwide, we are becoming more concentrated, dense, and urban in our spatial arrangements with one another. This means that there will be emphasis on the use of buildings, rooms, mass media, as well as a need for finding ways of continuing to incorporate natural beauty in our everyday lives.
3. *Increasing Democracy*—Participation in the affairs and events that affect people's lives is being demanded. People are seeking freedom worldwide. Freedom and involvement in control of one's destiny are central concepts of the leisure experience.
4. *Multiple Options*—Individuals seek tailor-made services that reflect their needs and preferences. We will no longer be able to produce one type of service, but will need many variations on the theme.
5. *Emphasis on Human Resources*—The information era places great value on human resources. Leisure can be used to help develop human resources to reach their potential. Creativity, thinking, and positive human relations can be developed through leisure.
6. *Technology*—New technology has an impact on leisure, as well as other areas of social life, including the structure and nature of work, the labor market, education, and government. As Naisbitt (1982) maintains, we are moving toward

a "high-tech, high touch" society—a society where for every technological innovation introduced, there will be a need for a counterbalance in human response.

7. *Emphasis on Spiritual/Personal Fulfillment*—As material needs are met and work and leisure are fused, greater emphasis will be placed on personal fulfillment and life satisfaction. Leisure provides a means, in this context, to engage individuals to explore their spiritual, intellectual, and moral development.

8. *Enhanced Communications*—We are able to communicate via computers and satellites much more rapidly than ever before. Social and political events unfolding worldwide are transmitted instantaneously throughout the globe. This allows rapid dissemination of information regarding leisure trends and a more socially and politically aware population.

9. *Rapid Mobility*—People seek freedom to travel from one location to another. With the advent of air, rail, and other forms of transportation, travel is made easy, accessible, and affordable, thereby increasing leisure opportunities for the masses.

10. *Movement from Institutional Help to Self-Help*—Self-help suggests the ability of people to manage their own affairs more effectively. This could result in changing the nature of service delivery to one more indirect and could find people taking greater individual control of their leisure lifestyles.

These factors will provide great challenges to leisure service programmers. They will call for a redefinition of the orientation and strategies used by leisure service delivery systems. Not only will leisure service professionals be challenged to cope with change, but there will be an increasing level of complexity in their professional environments. There are more variables that will need to be considered when planning leisure programs. Not only will individual needs be considered, but also broader social, economic, technical, and political factors will be brought to bear on the delivery of services.

A New Paradigm for Leisure Service Delivery

The leisure service profession must break new ground. The profession must seek a new paradigm for defining itself, its relationships to those it serves, and the services it provides. It is important to recognize that the information era is built on a different set of assumptions from those of the previous era. Most of our existing leisure service delivery systems are built on assumptions of the past. These assumptions may no longer be relevant or useful in helping define future leisure programs and services.

Designing a new paradigm for the leisure service profession will be challenging. Consider the fact that most leisure service organizations have their historical roots in the industrial era. Municipal parks (ca. 1850s), playgrounds (ca. 1880s), organized camping (ca. 1860s), recreation centers (ca. early 1900s), national parks (ca. 1870s), state parks (ca. 1860s) and youth-serving organizations (ca. late 1800s and early 1900s) all emerged during the Industrial Revolution. Although many of these organizations have continued to evolve, it may be that there is a need for other institutions to be created in response to changes in the information era.

Over the past several decades, there has been considerable effort made to open the leisure service profession to new and different ways of thinking. For example, a much greater emphasis has been placed on the potential interaction between the public and commercial sectors. New emphasis has been placed not only on defining leisure, but also on assisting leisure service organizations in measuring their impact in terms of economic and social factors.

Perhaps one of the most dramatic changes that is occurring concerns the way in which social issues and individual values are addressed in the information era. The basic assumptions concerning the productive capacity of government in particular are being challenged. Lack of public confidence as reflected in referendums directed at reducing property taxes, lack of confidence in government officials, and a decline in the quality of services is forcing a readjustment of our thinking in terms of the ways in which leisure services are delivered.

As we move from a centralized to a decentralized society, a number of fundamental changes have occurred. For example, we have shifted from an era in which political activism was a stronger determinant than the marketplace. In the present era, we are shifting back to a situation in which individual values and social choice may be more fully acted out in the marketplace rather than on a political stage. We have found that government does not have the productive capacity to generate sufficient economic resources for meeting social needs. Heretofore, our political system was capable of evolving internally to accommodate changes and to create new social forms and institutions to meet emerging challenges.

It may be that governmental systems will continue to evolve and be responsive to social needs. However, it appears that the action will be in the marketplace in the future and not in centralized bureaucratic organizations. If this scenario is an accurate one, individuals involved in the creation and delivery of leisure services will need a different set of skills. They will need the knowledge of the mechanisms that are essential in the analysis of a market and the free enterprise system. In other words, the skills and knowledge of future leisure service programmers must focus on marketing, entrepreneurship, calculated risk-taking, vision, and knowledge of people and their behavior.

In viewing this major transformation, it is important to remember that while we search for new, economical ways to meet social needs, our methods must at the same time be ethical and confirm the basic underlying values of the profession—conservation and preservation of natural resources, promotion and protection of human dignity, and the wise use of leisure. The window for innovation is a narrow one; most of the conditions that will serve as a basis for change have already been put in place. Many new, innovative, and creative concepts have been put in place to meet changing social conditions. The competitive marketplace will sort out those who can meet human needs in the most efficient and effective manner possible. However, there are still opportunities for individuals and organizations to provide fundamental redirection to the movement by creating new strategies to meet newly emerging leisure needs and conditions.

Discussing the need for a fundamental reorientation for public leisure service delivery systems, Grey (1984) has provided an outline for redirection in the information era. He writes that this is a time of great concern, uncertainty, ambivalence, and ambiguity. He suggests that public recreation, in particular, is being challenged to respond with a new paradigm of service delivery. He notes that the paradigm of the past governed the thinking of leisure service professionals in the public sector for nearly a half century. Grey calls for a new paradigm built on a new set of assumptions that reflect present and potential future conditions.

Grey's paradigm is found in Table 15.1. This model presents a discussion of the changing role sought by public leisure service organizations. As one can see, the information on the left-hand side of the table presents the traditional approach to providing services. There are some dramatic differences in terms of the role of leisure service programmers, interaction with customers, and the way in which services are financed and evaluated. For example, in the traditional paradigm, the emphasis is on providing programs consisting of activities and acting as a direct service provider. In the emerging paradigm, the emphasis is on programs that meet social and economic needs rather than being generated from a list of leisure activities, and the work of the professional involves acting as a community organizer and catalyst.

TABLE 15.1 A Paradigm of the Future

Traditional Paradigm	Emerging Paradigm
• Provide equal services to all the citizens. • Provide programs consisting of a series of activities selected from a restricted list of recreation pursuits. • Act as a direct-service provider. • Offer programs in department facilities. • Provide staff leadership of activities. • Fund basic services from tax sources. • Plan by updating the past. • Plan programs with the staff. • Encourage participation by publicity. • Evaluate results primarily in terms of attendance. • Motivate the staff to work for the people. • Justify budgets in terms of historical precedent. • Require financial accountability. • Achieve the ultimate goals of a fine recreation program.	• Provide services based on social and economic need. • Provide programs of human service that may go far beyond traditional recreation activities. • Act as a community organizer and catalyst in matching community resources to citizen need. • Offer programs anywhere in the community. • Use staff resources to coach citizens until they can provide their own leadership. • Fund service from a variety of sources, including fee-for-service, contract arrangements, barter, agency partnerships, and cooperation with the private sector, as well as tax resources. • Organize services around client groups in response to participants' felt needs and a careful community-wide needs analysis. • Plan by anticipating a preferred future. Plan with potential clients, community informants, other agencies, political figures and corporations as well as staff. • Develop a marketing approach to operations. • Evaluate services in terms of human consequences. • Motivate the staff to work with the people. • Justify budgets in terms of social need and program results. • Require financial and program accountability. • Achieve the ultimate goal of human development and community organization.

Gray 1984: 48–49.

Futuring: Strategies and Methods

There are a number of strategies and methods that can be employed by the leisure service professional in helping understand and/or shape the future. Tindall (1984) has suggested that the process of *futuring* is both an art and a science. She notes that to be successful, the leisure service professional must develop both " . . . one's ability to be both artist and scientist in preparing for the future" (Tindall 1984: 13). Futuring involves not only projecting future trends and issues, but also directing the future by having a vision of a possible, realistic, attainable mission for the leisure service organization.

Data-Based Strategies and Methods

There are a number of specific strategies that can be employed by leisure service professionals in planning for the future. Most of these strategies

involve an understanding of the environment as it evolves. Such strategies usually involve careful analysis of demographic changes, social/cultural trends, economic factors, and environmental changes. As Tindall (1984) notes, statistical analysis can be undertaken to determine changes in " . . . housing, population growth, employment, age groupings, ethnicity, earning and spending patterns, overall economic growth or decline, household or family composition, work and leisure lifestyle patterns, and what people value and how they spend their leisure time." There are a number of specific strategies and methods that can be used in the planning process. These include the following.

1. *Strategic Planning*—Strategic planning focuses on developing a management process that helps establish and maintain a balance between the leisure service organization and the external environment. The function of a strategic plan is to ensure that an organization's resources are

brought to bear in a timely fashion to meet opportunities or needs that arise. It is a process directed toward planning that takes into consideration potential changes in the environment.

2. *Market Information System*—A market information system is a strategy directed at gathering information related to customers in an organized and systematic fashion on a regular basis. Figure 15.1 presents a customer inquiry card in the form of a sample questionnaire for the Milton Bradley Company. It asks a variety of questions to obtain information about customers. A marketing information system may involve using both primary and secondary sources of data and/or by directly interacting with individuals in customer focus groups. Often, a marketing information system involves predicting the demand for a service; this is known as forecasting.

3. *Short- and Long-Range Plans*—Most organizations have plans. Short-range plans usually spell out ends desired by the leisure service organization on a one- to three-year basis. Long-range plans spell out goals for a longer period of time, usually ten years or longer. Most leisure service organizations have plans relating to land acquisition and facility development. On the other hand, few leisure service organizations have plans that spell out development activities for leisure programs and services.

In gathering information to plan for the future a variety of strategies can be used by the leisure service programmer. Secondary sources provide opportunities for the analysis of *demographic characteristics*, usually obtainable from U.S. census data. In addition, leisure service professionals can engage in *environmental scanning*, which involves an analysis of changes in conditions in social, political, economic, cultural, or other elements that can influence the work of an organization. Another mechanism for gathering information is known as *trend or content analysis*. This involves collecting information from various sources, such as newspapers, magazines, etc., to determine the emergence of fads or trends in the environment that might have an impact on the delivery of leisure services. For example, a scan of popular weekly news magazines suggests that there is a

rise in interest in physical fitness in the past decade. Finally, *social indices* can be monitored and provide information that can be useful in planning services. For example, changes in discretionary income, employment rate, and so forth can be useful in developing strategies for providing services. The United Way organization regularly gathers information and conducts media scans to identify emerging trends in the nation. It offers several publications that report the results of its efforts.

Artistic Strategies and Methods

Artistic strategies and methods for identifying future directions refer to the use of one's intuitive and creative abilities to build toward the future. As Hitt (1988) notes, there are two kinds of leadership—transactional and transformational. Transactional leaders exchange benefits (money, recognition, status, etc.) for effort. Transformational leaders have the ability to create a vision for the future and inspire individuals to a higher ideal. The principle theme of transformational leadership is lifting people into their better selves. This is done by leaders who have the ability to transform their vision, or the organization's vision into a significant reality.

The literature today is replete with references to the need for transformational leadership. Authors such as Peters (1987), Bennis and Nanus (1985), Naisbett and Aburdeen (1985), and Hitt (1988) call for visionary managerial leaders. As Hitt notes:

> Formulating a clear vision of a desired future may be the most important leadership function. Without a clear vision, we might be satisfied that we were doing things right, but we would not know if we were doing the right things. The ability to create a clear vision is the key attribute that separates managers from leaders (Hitt 1988: 42–43).

Tindall (1984) suggests that there are a number of strategies that can be employed to help deal with the complexities of the changing

MB MILTON BRADLEY
CUSTOMER INQUIRY CARD

DEAR CUSTOMER,

CONGRATULATIONS ON PURCHASING A QUALITY MILTON BRADLEY GAME. YOU MADE AN EXCELLENT CHOICE. PLEASE COMPLETE AND RETURN THIS CARD WITHIN THE NEXT 10 DAYS. THE INFORMATION REQUESTED WILL HELP US DEVELOP NEW GAMES THAT MEET THE DESIRES OF YOU AND YOUR FRIENDS/FAMILY. IT WILL ALSO ALLOW MILTON BRADLEY TO KEEP YOU INFORMED ABOUT THESE GAMES AS THEY BECOME AVAILABLE. THANK YOU VERY MUCH FOR YOUR HELP.

1. Your First Name   M.I.   Last Name

Street   Apt. No.

City   State   Zip

Telephone

2. Date of Purchase:
Month   Day   Year

3. Was this product a gift or a self purchase?
- [ ] Self purchase
- [ ] Surprise gift
- [ ] Gift that was requested by the user

4. Are you . . . .
- [ ] The purchaser
- [ ] The recipient
- [ ] Both the purchaser and user

5. Was this game . . .
- [ ] Better than expected
- [ ] As good as expected
- [ ] Not as good as expected

6. Is this game played with . . .
- [ ] Family members including children under 18 yrs.
- [ ] Family of adults over 18 yrs.
- [ ] Children only under 18 yrs.
- [ ] Other (Please explain)

7. Where was this game purchased?
- [ ] Toy Store
- [ ] Department Store
- [ ] General Merchandise (Sear's, Penney's, etc.)
- [ ] Drug Store
- [ ] Mail Order
- [ ] Discount Store
- [ ] Received as a Gift
- [ ] Catalog Showroom
- [ ] Other (Specify)

8. This game was purchased for. . .
- [ ] Children under 18
- [ ] Adults
- [ ] Both children under 18 and adults.

9. How did you first become aware of this product?
- [ ] TV Commercial
- [ ] Newspaper Ad
- [ ] Friend/Relative
- [ ] Store display
- [ ] Played with it before
- [ ] It was recommended
- [ ] Others

10. Did you plan to purchase this game before entering the store?
A. [ ] Yes   [ ] No

B. If **No** on 10A, what made you finally decide on this game?
- [ ] Salesperson's recommendation
- [ ] Price
- [ ] In-store display/literature
- [ ] Only brand available
- [ ] Packaging

11. Please check your level of agreement with the following statements about this game:

	Agree	Disagree
Is a fun family game	[ ]	[ ]
Is fun entertainment with my friends	[ ]	[ ]
Is a good value for the money	[ ]	[ ]
Too simple of a game	[ ]	[ ]
Too difficult of a game	[ ]	[ ]
Just right as a game	[ ]	[ ]

12. Of the following games, please check which ones you own and play often:

	Own	Play Often
Trivial Pursuit	[ ]	[ ]
Monopoly	[ ]	[ ]
Pictionary	[ ]	[ ]
Win, Lose or Draw	[ ]	[ ]
Scruples	[ ]	[ ]
Yahtzee	[ ]	[ ]
Secrets	[ ]	[ ]
Balderdash	[ ]	[ ]

13. What games have you purchased in the past year?

Game	Age of Primary User/Receiver

14. How old are you?
_____ Years Old

15. Marital Status:
- [ ] Married
- [ ] Divorced/Separated
- [ ] Widowed
- [ ] Single/Never married

16. Are you . . . .
- [ ] A Student
- [ ] Employed-full time
- [ ] Retired
- [ ] Employed-part time

17. Which group describes your annual family income:
- [ ] Under $14,999
- [ ] $15,000 - $24,999
- [ ] $25,000 - $34,999
- [ ] $35,000 - $44,999
- [ ] $45,000 - $54,999
- [ ] $55,000 - $64,999
- [ ] $65,000 - $75,999
- [ ] $75,000 - and over.

18. What magazines do you read on a regular basis?

Figure 15.1 Example of a Customer Inquiry Card Included with Milton Bradley Company Games.

nature of our society. She suggests several strategies that can be employed. Among the most applicable are the following:

1. *Change-Making*—The term change-making is derived from the theme of the book *The Change Masters* (Kanter 1983). Kanter writes " . . . the individuals who will succeed and flourish in the times ahead will be masters of change; adept at reorienting their own and others' activities in untried directions to bring about higher levels of achievement" (1983: 65). Change-making involves four basic steps: (1) thriving on novelty, (2) inspiring others to a clear vision, (3) working through terms to promote decision-making, and (4) promoting self-esteem by encouraging others.

2. *Visionary Leadership*—Providing visionary leadership involves setting a new direction for an organization in times of chaos, turbulence, and uncertainty. Hitt (1988) suggests that it is not only necessary to create the vision, but to determine steps and methods to implement it. A vision without action is useless. Visions empower people. As Bennis and Nanus (1985: 90) note, " . . . when the organization has a clear sense of its purpose, direction, and desired future state, and this image is widely shared, individuals . . . " are empowered.

3. *Entrepreneurship/Intrepreneurship*—We live in a society where the need for social innovation and change is great. *Entrepreneurship*, according to Drucker (1985), is a process of innovation. It involves the creation of new institutions, programs, or services that meet societal needs. When accomplished within the context of an existing organization, it is known as *intrepreneurship*. Entrepreneurs are individuals who are risk-oriented, visionary, inner-directed, and often achievement-oriented. Entrepreneurship provides a mechanism to bring various resources together to create new programs, services, and organizational structures. Entrepreneurs often have to break with tradition to develop creative and innovative products and services, even though conventional wisdom suggests a more cautious posture. Entrepreneurs are able to analyze and see things in new and bold ways (Bullaro and Edginton 1986: 21).

The above-mentioned strategies and methods involve having the leisure service professional operate in a pro-active posture. The purpose of these strategies use one's intuitive and managerial abilities in order to bring about change. They involve creating or managing a vision and, as a result, bringing about change and an ordering of the future. As Drucker (1985: 35) notes, successful innovation " . . . consists in the purposeful and organized search for changes and in the systematic analysis of opportunities such changes might offer for economic or social innovation." He notes that the search for change and innovation can be done in a diagnostic and disciplined fashion, and can lead to what he calls "innovative opportunity."

Population Dynamics: Trends

Leisure service programmers must be attuned to the customers or populations they serve. Scanning trends in demography, technology, human resources, and economic, social, and cultural factors can provide key information to assist in the creation and development of leisure experiences. North American society and culture is constantly undergoing change. Although some of these changes cannot be predicted in advance and can only be responded to as they occur, others can be determined. For example, we know that as the baby boom generation moves through its life span it will have enormous impact on society. When the mean age of the baby boom was younger, products and services were largely geared to this age grouping. As the baby boom generation matures, advertising for products and services has also tended to reflect this older age grouping.

Demographic Trends

Jones (1980) has suggested that no single generation will have a greater impact on our society than the baby boom generation. Underhill (1981) has dramatically depicted the movement of the baby boom generation for the decades of 1970–1990. The greater percentage of the population will be between the ages of twenty and sixty-four. This can be contrasted with population figures for 1970, in which 59 percent of the population was between the ages of one and thirty-four.

At the same time, the generation following the baby boom generation, known as the *baby bust* generation, is significantly smaller. For example, by the year 2000, the baby bust generation will comprise only 34 percent of the work force. The smaller generation following the "baby boom" generation will lead to an increase in the median age of individuals living in North America. It is estimated that by 1995 the median age of the workforce will be thirty-seven, as contrasted with the early 1980s, when the median age was thirty-five. Clearly, we will be dealing with an aging population and the programming focus of leisure service organizations may very well expand to include more services for middle-aged adults and older adults. Godbey (1986) notes that ". . . the over-sixty-five population will increase from 12 percent of the population to between 18 percent and 24 percent by the year 2030."

Another very significant change is that of the structure of North American families. The idealized family of the working husband and the wife as a full-time homemaker is now a myth. In the 1950s, about 70 percent of all families were structured in this traditional, idealized manner. Today, however, such an arrangement exists only in approximately 19 percent of families (Godbey 1986). In fact, it is estimated that 46 percent of all children born in the late 1970s will spend some portion of their youth in single-family households (Godbey 1986). Over 60 percent of all married women are now in the work force. The number of double income families has increased from 36 percent to 49 percent in the last twenty years.

In addition to the fact that there are more dual income families, there are also more single-parent households. Again, Godbey (1986) writes, ". . . in 1910, the average household consisted of 4.5 persons; that number has now shrunk to 2.7 and is likely to decline still further. Over 30 percent of all households are headed by one individual,

and a large percentage (nearly 70 percent) of these individuals are in the work force. This has strong implications for leisure programming. Perhaps there will be an increased need for latchkey leisure services and other types of programs that cater to individuals living in single-parent households. It is interesting to note that 20–30 percent of children under the age of eighteen are now being raised in one-parent households.

Another factor influencing changes in the nature of households in North America is the number of units that do not fit either traditional or single-parent models. These units are referred to as non-family households. According to Godbey, in the mid-1980s, such households accounted for 23 percent of family units and by the 1990s are projected to approach 30 percent of all households. Such units are made up of individuals who are living together and not yet married or between marriages. In addition, it includes people living together as a unit, such as the elderly.

Leisure experiences are often viewed as compensatory opportunities for individuals who find dissatisfaction in their occupation. When designing leisure experiences, there is often a need to have a thorough understanding of an individual's work experience. One of the dramatic changes that has occurred in the last three decades has been the distribution of the work force. Today, nearly 75 percent of the work force are engaged in information and service-based occupations (as contrasted with 3 percent of the work force in agricultural and 13 percent in manufacturing occupations). The challenge to leisure service programmers will be to design leisure experiences that meet the needs of information and service-based workers. Such individuals may have occupational pressures, values, and needs that are unique because of the intense and oftentimes sedentary nature of their work.

The racial and ethnic composition of North America is changing rapidly. In the 1970s blacks constituted the largest racial or ethnic minority in the United States. By the mid-1980s, however, Hispanics constituted the largest racial or ethnic minority grouping. Hispanics immigrating from Mexico, Central America, and the Caribbean have increased dramatically in the last decade. In addition, large immigrations from Asian countries have changed the ethnic and racial composition of the country dramatically in recent years. These changes in ethnicity and racial composition may influence patterns of leisure programming. Leisure programming must be made relevant for ethnic and racial groupings to reflect the unique cultural and social needs of these populations.

Technological Trends

The technological changes that occur in society will have a profound effect on the creation and delivery of leisure services. The personal computer has only been a force in the marketplace for a short period of time. The computer and other electronic media are transforming the way that we process and use information. We are moving from a written culture to an electronic culture that will increase our ability to use words and numbers in terms of speed and volume.

One of the most significant changes related to technology is that of telecommunications. We now have the ability to interact with one another rapidly via telephone—including teleconferencing and FAX services. Telecommunications enable us to travel to distant locations, arranging lodging, transportation, and tours to points of interest. Telecommunications also provide opportunities to bring leisure experiences directly to us at our own locations. We are able, for example, to vote for our favorite plays on Monday Night Football, to receive information from our favorite baseball players, and to be connected to a variety of other services.

The personal computer is also significant as a leisure opportunity in itself. Computers can be fun and people can spend hours learning about the computer by playing games and interacting with it. The computer can facilitate flexible work schedules that influence how people use their

leisure in the future. Individuals may be able to complete their work at home on a computer, in a manner that complements their life rhythms. Thus, they may be able to work intensely and productively and then use their leisure in ways that are more satisfying and valuable to them as individuals.

Economic Trends

Trends in the economic environment will have a direct bearing on leisure in North America. The economy will have a direct impact on the amount of discretionary income available to individuals. It appears that, in fact, there will be more discretionary income and that the purchase and consumption of leisure products and services will continue to have an impact on our gross national product. There are several economic factors that appear to support the continued emergence of a strong leisure service industry.

First, as mentioned, there is a shift from an industrial-based economy to an information/service-based economy. Interestingly, many of the new jobs that will be available come from the leisure service sector, especially hotels and restaurants. It is estimated that by the year 2000, 80 percent of all jobs will be in the service sector. The growth of the leisure service industry has been unparalleled as an economic force in the last two decades. It is estimated that expenditures for leisure services in the United States will exceed those for housing construction and defense combined.

The second factor is the rate of change of economic cycles. In other words, product and service life cycles in our society are becoming much shorter and, as a result, the economy will cycle more rapidly. This means that leisure service programmers must be prepared for rapid changes in service delivery. As people's tastes change, fads will emerge, mature, and fade quickly. Further, advances in technology will spin off new product and service developments. In order to remain responsive and competitive, leisure service organizations will have to hone their research and marketing efforts.

Social and Cultural Trends

There are a number of social and cultural changes that have an impact on leisure programming. Three are worthy of discussion—the leisure and work ethic, ideological differences across generations, and women's rights. Yankelovich (1982) has written that the " . . . leisure ethic has become institutionalized in society." In other words, we have moved into an era where the leisure ethic is a strong determinant and shaper of culture. Leisure is expected and often viewed as a measure of social status. As Godbey (1986) notes, leisure is associated with "the good life" and as Yankelovich (1982) notes it is viewed as an "entitlement."

While leisure is valued, is there more leisure time available to individuals? The answer to this question at first glance is "yes." However, in reviewing time-budget studies, it appears that individuals have less leisure time today than they did in past years. In 1975, the median workweek length was 43.1 hours (Godbey 1986). By 1984, the median workweek length increased to 47.3 hours. It could be that the changing nature of occupations has had much to do with the expansion of the workweek. There apparently is also a decline in the amount of leisure available to individuals. Godbey (1986) reports that " . . . the median time for leisure was down from 24.3 hours in 1975 to 18.1 hours in 1984." Additionally, women have less hours of leisure per week (15.6) than men (20.3) (Godbey 1986). Obviously the demands on the working women (work, as well as greater responsibility for household chores and child care) has a bearing on her amount of leisure time.

Another social/cultural trend is related to the generational groupings that exist in North America today. There are at least three different societal generations with differing perceptions, values, and life experiences. Each generation operates from a different ideological perspective, although each subsequent generation inherits part of the intellectual, social, and cultural values of the previous generation. However, often the various generation groupings come in direct conflict with one another.

The first generation, now in their sixties or beyond, were often the sons and daughters of immigrants. This group survived the Great Depression. They married late or not at all, had small families when they did marry, and a large proportion of them lived in rural areas. Many forms of recreation and leisure were prohibited due to economic constraint and prevailing norms and mores. Idleness was suspect. Upward mobility was a central goal in life and hard work was the key to success. Behavior patterns were inflexible. The nuclear family, with a husband who was the sole provider at the head of the family and the mother as homemaker and housewife, was the norm. A future orientation and self-denial were common as was conformity in dress and lifestyle. " . . . Most men worked a fifty-hour week and had two weeks' vacation" (Yankelovich 1982).

The second generation was born during the baby boom era at the end of World War II. They moved, when they could, from the cities to the suburbs. The percentage of people defined as middle class rose to 70 percent of the population in 1960. This generation married young and bought big houses and cars. The baby boom generation, which was huge, reshaped every aspect of American life as it passed through successive age groups. It was characterized by great optimism about the future, a belief in science, and the gradual acceptance of the belief that the future orientation of their parents could be short cut. According to Yankelovich (1982) this generation developed the *psychology of entitlement.* Emphasis changed from *we to me* in their decision making. Nonetheless, this generation exhibited great idealism and made strides in combating racism, environmental degradation, and other social issues. In regard to recreation and leisure, during the first fifteen years after World War II, emphasis was on owning material goods and equipment which could be used during leisure. Slowly the emphasis shifted from *having* to *doing.*

Leisure was increasingly viewed as personal, and fulfillment and "experientialism" either replaced or developed alongside of materialism.

The third generation, now in their twenties and thirties, are marrying later or not at all which, historically, had been the custom until the baby boom generation. This generation has moved from the suburbs back into city centers or to small towns. Leisure is viewed as a right, although this group is less fortunate economically. They are becoming somewhat more conservative in redeveloping a future orientation. They are not, however, prepared to minimize the importance of leisure (Godbey 1986: 1–2).

Thus, as one can see, in reading the above material, there are definitive ideological shifts that have occurred in North American society. Each generation grouping is influenced by a number of societal events and, in turn, develops an ideological orientation to life. These ideological orientations influence the perceptions that individuals develop concerning major social institutions, including work, family, religion, and leisure. Again, leisure service programmers must be cognizant of what kind of impact these different orientations and values will have on their ability to find satisfaction in their leisure programs and activities.

Women's rights have emerged in the last several decades as a growing social/cultural force. Restructuring of the work force has no doubt had a significant impact on the emergence of women's rights. However, other issues dealing with equity have forced a reorientation not only of work but also of leisure environments. A significant example is the revamping of collegiate sports to reflect the need for equal participation in non-revenue-generating activities. This has trickled down to the public leisure service organizations, where there has been a growth of sports programs for women of all ages. Reducing the inequity that exists in the provision of leisure experiences between men and women will be a major challenge for leisure service programmers.

Future Leisure Programming Directions and Professional Issues

In this section of the book a number of projections concerning leisure programming will be presented. In addition, several professional issues related to leisure programming will be addressed.

Future Directions

A review of the professional literature in the leisure service field, as well as an analysis of demographic, economic, technological, and social and cultural trends and changes serves as a basis for this section of the book. It is interesting to note that the leisure service field has gone through many changes in the past two decades. Increased demand for leisure and changing leisure preferences have changed the scope and nature of leisure experiences available to North Americans. Some of the future directions that may influence leisure programs are as follows.

1. *Multiple-Option Programming*—Sheffield (1984) has suggested that leisure professionals must engage in multiple-option programming. She notes that various activities can be organized in ways that promote either cooperation, competition, or individualization. The challenge to the leisure service programmer is in creating diverse opportunities that meet a multitude of needs in the marketplace.

2. *Planned, Deliberate Leisure Programming*—Godbey (1986) suggests that conditions of economic restraint as well as the aging of the population and a more highly educated customer will require more planned and deliberate leisure programming. As people become more sophisticated and are required to pay more for services, they will become more selective and demanding in their choices. Thus, greater care will be required in creating and delivering leisure services.

3. *Quality and Value*—Quality and value are, and will continue to be, important in the creation and delivery of leisure services. Again, as the population becomes more sophisticated in the selection of leisure experiences, quality and value will

be important dimensions that will influence customer decision making. As Godbey (1986) notes, the critical leisure customer will increasingly seek higher quality in both leisure products and the leisure experience.

4. *Risk Recreation*—There is an increase in the desire for leisure services that have an element of perceived risk. At the same time, leisure service organizations are being challenged to determine ways to manage leisure environments in such a way as to reduce risk. In fact, concerns over potentially litigious situations are forcing the closure of some leisure service organizations. One challenge of the future will be to balance customers' desire for risk in their leisure experiences while at the same time ensuring that there are safe conditions.

5. *New Populations, New Programs*—Changing demographic conditions will create opportunities for new leisure services. For example, single-parent households increase opportunities for services for children in latchkey-type activities. Maturity of the baby boom generation creates opportunities for greater leisure programming for middle-aged adults. The aging of the population presents opportunities for increased programming to older adults.

6. *Wellness and Fitness Programs*—There has been a sustained and continued interest in wellness and fitness programs during the past decade. This will continue into the next decade and leisure service organizations will be provided with opportunities to further develop program concepts in this area. The wellness and fitness area is largely a response by the baby boom generation to concerns for health, status as reflected in appearance, and aging. In the fitness area we are likely to see further development of the "machine fitness age." There will be increased emphasis on use of exercise equipment such as computerized stationary bikes and treadmills. Aerobic programs will find new ways to attract individuals and there will be a continued emphasis on low-impact activities. Swimming, water aerobics, and water workouts will increase. Walking and hiking will gain further popularity with an emphasis on interacting with the environment.

7. *Culturally Based Programming*—North America is becoming more culturally diverse. As a result, there will be a need to develop leisure programs and services that meet the needs of different racial, cultural and ethnic groupings. Perhaps the largest increases in numbers among ethnic groups has occurred as a result of immigrations of Hispanics and Asians. There will be opportunities for the creation of festivals, special events, sports, arts and crafts programs, and other services that reflect the cultural backgrounds of such groupings.

8. *Immediacy and Convenience*—North Americans are in a hurry and they value expedience. They desire to have services delivered to them in a timely and convenient fashion. The location and timing of a service is critical to its success. We live in a society that demands that leisure service programmers be responsive to the need to have programs and activities packaged and organized in such a way that they are easily accessible and delivered when customers desire to have them (usually now).

9. *Leisure and the Arts*—Will there be a renaissance in the arts? Naisbitt and Aburdeen (1990: 62) in discussing changes in the 1990s have written, "The arts will gradually replace sports as society's primary leisure activity." They suggest that ". . . there will be a fundamental and revolutionary shift in leisure time and spending priorities."

10. *Time Distribution*—One of the more interesting trends emerging is that of the reconceptualization or distribution of time. The information era presents new ways of viewing work and leisure. Flex time, flex place (the worksite), and the need for more efficient use of public and private resources are all contributing to new ways of how we use our time. For example, many school districts are considering operating on a twelve-month basis. This means that school-age children will be taking their vacations at times different from the normal nine-month cycle. Further, individuals are working different configurations of hours, thereby providing them with extended periods of leisure. Finally, technology such as computers, fax machines, etc., are providing individuals with an opportunity to

define their own space and location. In other words it is no longer necessary to go to one's work place, or to follow a schedule. This opens up opportunities for different ways of approaching one's leisure. One of the results of this is that there is going to be a loss of leisure time. In fact, since the 1970s there has been a 30 percent loss of leisure, approximately eight hours per week. Time constraints will mean that leisure programs will have to be provided at accessible and convenient times.

11. *Packaging or Bundling Services*—The concept of packaging or bundling services suggests that leisure programmers organize a total service concept. The packaging or bundling concept suggests that as time constraints become a greater factor, there will be a need to cluster services that enable one to have a quality leisure experience. A scenario for the future might be one in which the needs of the entire family are met under one roof. The kids swim while the mother engages in aerobic activities and the father jogs. Child care, food concessions, and other services might all be found at one convenient location.

12. *Simpler, More Convenient Services*—People will seek simpler, more convenient leisure experiences. The demand for such services is a reflection of an aging society, greater time constraints, less discretionary income, less open space, compacted housing conditions, and increases in energy cost. Interestingly, during the 1990s, home-based activities will continue to be central leisure activities. More families are spending a larger percentage of time at home aided by their video machines and home entertainment units. Single-parent families will look to leisure as a way of reinforcing values in an inexpensive, simple, and convenient manner.

Professional Issues

Leisure service programmers must be responsive to a number of emerging professional issues that have a potential impact on the quality of programs and services. Some of these concerns are moral and ethical, whereas others are managerial and administrative in nature. Sensitivity to

such professional issues can assist the leisure service programmer in responding in an appropriate manner in an environment of great change. Some major professional issues relating to leisure service programming include the following.

1. *Accessibility*—Accessibility refers to both physical and social access to leisure services that prevent individuals from participating in leisure opportunities. Work toward the elimination of physical barriers has progressed in the past several decades, although much still needs to be done. The 1990 Americans with Disabilities Act (ADA) will impact all areas of leisure service programming and delivery. Social barriers are more complex and, hence, more difficult to remove. Often, individuals misunderstand or distort information, creating a barrier between the leisure service programmer and the customer.

2. *Equity*—Equity was discussed in Chapter 1 and is concerned with whether or not leisure services are dispersed in a fair manner. Issues of equity, as indicated, require the leisure service programmer to make political, social, and moral judgments. One serious issue of equity is whether or not individuals are deprived of the opportunity to participate in a leisure service because of the cost. The question becomes one of determining ways to make fees and charges to programs reasonable so that their impact as a barrier to participation is minimized.

3. *Ethical Behavior*—North Americans demand ethical behavior. Integrity, confidentiality, and community citizenship are hallmarks of ethical professional behavior. Customers expect professionals to operate in an objective and honest manner. They also expect that their interactions with professionals be maintained in a confidential fashion. Further, customers expect that professionals, exhibit citizenship by participating in the affairs of the community, contributing to its economic, social, and environmental development and well-being.

4. *Excellence and Innovation*—Leisure service professionals are being challenged to operate with a high degree of excellence. In today's society, people demand quality and also require that professionals pursue their work with a high degree of productivity. To be excellent means that one's work always meets or exceeds the standards established by the profession. Innovation requires forward thinking that is continually creative and focused on the development of new, novel approaches to leisure service delivery. Innovative programmers are not satisfied to maintain the status quo; they are always trying to find better ways to provide services.

5. *Anticipatory Behavior*—Because of the rapid changes in product life cycles and economic cycles in North American culture, the effective leisure service programmer will have to engage in anticipatory behavior. It will not be enough to react to changes; it will be necessary to lead by creating a vision of the future. Anticipation of needs can refer to the needs of the organization or the needs of customers. This process can be bold and visionary, directing the work of the organization, or it can be the routine interactions with customers to make their leisure experience more satisfying and worthwhile.

6. *Development of Human Resources*—The majority of leisure programs are delivered by part-time or seasonal staff. This is a need to elevate the status of such individuals so that they receive appropriate orientation, training, and development. Often the lowest-paid individuals are those that are actually delivering the services to the customer. There is a need to make those involved in service delivery full partners in the process of meeting the leisure needs of a given constituency. Of critical importance is the transference of organizational values, traditions, and expectations for interacting with customers.

7. *Renewal of Infrastructures*—In order to make the leisure experience meaningful and relevant to individuals, the areas and facilities and other resources must be maintained in a contemporary and up-to-date manner. There is a need to rebuild many leisure service delivery systems. There are many outdated, poorly maintained, and ineffectively designed areas and facilities that need to be updated, rebuilt, or augmented. The public leisure service delivery system, in particular, is in great need of renewal.

8. *Accountability*—Leisure service programmers are increasingly being held accountable for the use of organizational resources. As resources have become more limited, organizations are requiring individual programmers to demonstrate the benefits derived from involvement in programs and activities. Accountability requires programmers to be responsive and provide relevant programs and services that meet real needs. The issue of accountability will increase rather than decrease in the future.

Summary

The future will be challenging to leisure service professionals. We live in a period of time in which change is constant and pervasive. In order to succeed, leisure service professionals will need to become adept at anticipating and dealing with change. Currently, we are experiencing a major transformation (known as a paradigm shift) in the thinking and behavior of humankind. This shift from the industrial era to the information era will require new approaches to providing leisure services and new ways of meeting and responding to emerging human needs.

There are a number of major factors that will have an impact on the delivery of leisure services in the future. Some of these include: cultural pluralism; living in a dense urban environment; increasing democracy; multiple options; emphasis on human resources; technology; emphasis on spiritual and personal fulfillment; enhanced communications; rapid mobility; and movement from institutional help to self-help. These factors will require a new paradigm for the delivery of leisure services. For example, in the public leisure service arena there may be a movement from direct-service delivery to enabling of services. Greater skills in marketing and entrepreneurship will be valued in all sectors in which leisure services are created.

Knowledge of population dynamics and other trends will be essential in future success. There are significant demographic changes occurring that will influence the delivery of leisure services. The population is becoming older. The family structure is changing dramatically. Technology is influencing the way we communicate with one another and our ability to process complex information rapidly and in great volume. The economic environment emphasizing more service-oriented occupations, changing the nature of work with the concomitant effects on the way in which leisure is pursued. Leisure is increasingly valued, but time to pursue leisure is declining.

Leisure service programmers will be faced with a number of challenges. These challenges will not only affect the nature and types of leisure service programs provided, but also the way in which the leisure service programmer operates. Our future appears to be dynamic and exciting. The challenges of tomorrow will enrich the work of professionals and also provide opportunities to significantly influence the lives of North Americans.

Discussion Questions and Exercises

1. We live in an era of change. What are some of the factors that have contributed to this change?

2. Change can be perceived from several different perspectives. What are they? Provide examples of change that a local leisure service organization has undergone in the last decade.

3. What current paradigm shift is influencing the work of leisure service programmers in North America?

4. Why is there a need to create new programs, services and institutions as a result of a paradigm shift?

5. Identify ten factors related to change that have a direct impact on leisure service organizations today.

6. Discuss how Grey's model for public leisure service organizations might result in new and different types of leisure programs and services. What roles would leisure programmers play in this paradigm for the future?

7. Identify six strategies and methods that can be used by leisure service programmers in understanding and shaping the future.

8. What role do emerging demographic, technological, economic, and social and cultural trends play in the development of leisure services?

9. Identify eight or more future directions that have a direct impact on leisure programmers and leisure programming.

10. Identify eight or more professional issues that must be addressed by leisure service programmers.

References

Bennis, W. and B. Nanus. 1985. *Leaders.* New York: Harper and Row.

Brauer, D. G. 1984. Survival in the information era. *Parks and Recreation* 19(5): 58–59.

Bullaro, J. J. and C. R. Edginton. 1986. *Commercial leisure services.* New York: MacMillan.

Drucker, P. 1985. *Innovation and entrepreneurship.* New York: Harper and Row.

Ferguson, M. 1980. *The aquarian conspiracy.* Los Angeles: Tarcher.

Godbey, G. 1986. Some selected societal trends and their impact on recreation and leisure. *A Literature Review—The President's Commission on American Outdoors.* Washington, DC: Superintendent of Documents.

Grey, D. 1984. Managing our way to a preferred future. *Parks & Recreation* 19(5): 47–49.

Hitt, W. D. 1988. *The leader-manager.* Columbus, OH: Battelle Press.

Jones, L. Y. 1980. *Great Expectations.* New York: Ballentine.

Kanter, R. M. 1983. *The change masters.* New York: Simon and Schuster.

Naisbitt, J. 1982. *Megatrends.* New York: Warner.

Naisbitt, J. and P. Aburdeen. 1985. *Re-inventing the corporation.* New York: Warner.

Naisbitt, J. and P. Aburdeen. 1990. *Megatrends 2000.* New York: Morrow.

Perry, James L. 1989. "The Effective Public Administrator" in James L. Perry, *Handbook of Public Administration.* San Francisco: Jossey Bass.

Peters, T. 1987. *Thriving on chaos.* New York: Knopf.

Sheffield, E. 1984. Are you providing multiple-option programming? *Parks and Recreation* 19(5): 56–57.

Stencel, S. 1980. Workers' changing expectations. *Life in the 1980s: Editorial Research Reports* October 31.

Tindall, J. P. 1984. Planning with vision: The art and science of futuring. *California Parks and Recreation:* 13.

Toffler, A. 1980. *The third wave.* New York: Morrow.

Underbull, A. H. 1981. Population dynamics and demography. *Journal of Physical Education, Recreation, and Dance.* October.

Yankelovich, D. 1982. *New rules.* New York: Bantam.

Appendix A
Market Survey
Bend, Oregon, Metro Park and
Recreation District

Bend Metro Park and Recreation District
Marketing Survey
Telephone Interview Questions

1. When we talk of leisure or free time, some people immediately think of parks and playgrounds, or sports such as football or tennis; others think of very different things, such as working on their car, visiting friends, sewing, cooking, or other hobbies. When you think of the things you do with your free time, what sorts of things do you think of?

   1. _____
   2. _____
   3. _____
   4. _____

2. What kinds of things do you do in your free time on weekdays?

   1. Stay home
   2. Go shopping
   3. Visit friends
   4. Attend a park and recreation program
   5. Attend night school
   6. Go to a private athletic club
   7. Visit a park
   8. Other _____
   9. No response

3. What kinds of things do you do in your free time on weekends?

   1. Stay home
   2. Go shopping
   3. Visit friends
   4. Attend a park and recreation program
   5. Go to a private athletic club
   6. Visit a park
   7. Other _____
   8. No response

4. How many hours of free time do you have on an average weekday?

   1. 1–3 hours
   2. 4–6 hours
   3. 7–10 hours
   4. Varies
   5. Don't know
   6. No response

5. How many hours of free time do you have on weekends?

   1. 1–3 hours
   2. 4–6 hours
   3. 7–10 hours
   4. Varies
   5. Don't know
   6. No response

6. What specific parks and recreation facilities do you use in the district? Please indicate about how often you use the facilities.

Location	Once a Month	Not at All	Almost Daily
1. Community parks i.e. Juniper	1	2	3
2. Neighborhood parks i.e. Stover	1	2	3
3. Juniper Aquatic & Fitness Center	1	2	3
4. Gyms	1	2	3
5. Organized athletics	1	2	3
6. Senior center	1	2	3
7. Tennis courts	1	2	3
8. Other _____	1	2	3
9. None			

7. Why don't you use the parks and services of Bend Metro Park and Recreation District?

 1. Fees
 2. Lack of leisure time
 3. Not safe
 4. Too far away
 5. Programs not interesting
 6. No family facilities
 7. Other _____
 8. No response

8. Have you had any problems with employees at any of the Bend Metro Park and Recreation District facilities?

 1. Yes
 2. No

9. What kinds of problems did you have?

 1. _____
 2. _____
 3. _____
 4. _____

10. What, if any, clubs, groups, or organizations do you belong to?

 1. Golf clubs
 2. Private health club
 3. Special interest club (skiing, RV's, tennis, art, etc.)
 4. Other _____
 5. None

11. Do you feel all of your leisure needs are being met by the clubs, groups, or organizations to which you belong?

 1. Yes
 2. No
 3. No opinion

12. Do you feel that your leisure needs are being met by the programs and facilities available through BMP&RD?

 1. Yes
 2. No
 3. No response
 4. If no, why? _____

13. How many activities and services have you or your family been involved with in the Bend Metro Park and Recreation District in the last 12 months?

 1. One
 2. Two
 3. Three
 4. Four or more
 5. No program involvement (skip to question 15)
 6. Don't recall

14. When making your decision to participate in district program(s), how important were the following factors?

	Very Important	Important	Not Important
1. Price	1	2	3
2. Location	1	2	3
3. Time of day	1	2	3
4. Social interaction	1	2	3
5. The instructor	1	2	3
6. Past experience with BMP&RD	1	2	3
7. Other _____	1	2	3

15. How would you describe the quality of services provided by the Bend Metro Park and Recreation District?

 1. Excellent
 2. Satisfactory
 3. Less than satisfactory (why?) _____
 4. No opinion

16. Do you think there are sufficient recreation areas, facilities, and programs in the district?

 1. Yes
 2. No (where can we improve?) _____
 3. No opinion

17. During the past six months a citizen's committee of thirteen people developed a comprehensive plan for the district. As part of this plan, the committee recommended certain improvements to existing facilities and additional facilities which they felt should be built as soon as possible. The cost of these recommendations would be $1.1 million dollars.

    Would you be willing to pay for these improvements by increasing your taxes by $24.00 per year, for the next three years? This assumes you own a $60,000 home in Bend.

    1. Yes
    2. No
    3. No opinion

18. In addition to the above improvements and additions, the Comp Plan's Citizen Advisory Committee has recommended that the district, as a long range goal, study the possibility of constructing a large multi-purpose community center.

    Do you believe that such a facility is needed in Bend? If so, what type of uses would you prefer the building be used for?

    1. Yes   Uses: 1) _____
    2. No   2) _____
    3. No opinion   3) _____

19. Should users' fees be increased to pay more of the total cost for the services provided?

    1. Yes
    2. No
    3. No opinion

20. Is having parks or recreational facilities provided by the BMP&RD within a 5–10-minute walk from home very important, somewhat important, or not important to you?

    1. Very important
    2. Somewhat important
    3. Not important

21. What are the three most important recreational opportunities (programs and/or facilities) provided by the BMP&RD that you particularly enjoy doing?

    1. _____
    2. _____
    3. _____

22. What are three activities or programs that you would like to participate in that are not currently available?

    1. _____
    2. _____
    3. _____

23. For statistical purposes, could you please indicate your age?

    1. 15–24
    2. 25–34
    3. 35–44
    4. 45–54
    5. 55–64
    6. 65 and over
    7. No response

24. How long have you lived within the Bend Metro Park and Recreation District boundaries?

    1. Less than 1 year
    2. 6–10 years
    3. 1–5 years
    4. More than 10 years
    5. Not aware that I live within the district

25. Are you a:

    1. Homeowner
    2. Renter

Appendix B
Market Survey
Eugene, Oregon Parks
and Recreation Department

Let Us Hear From You

Dear Patron:

Eugene Parks and Recreation Department staff is interested in what you have to say about parks and recreation services in Eugene in order to continue to offer programs to meet the leisure needs of our community. Your answers are very important to us even if you are not an active user of our services. We hope you will take a few minutes to fill out the survey below.

1. How long have you been a resident of Eugene? _____ (no. of years). Zip code _____

2. Which facilities have you or members of your household visited during the past 12 months, and how often?

	Not at all	2 times or less	3–8 times	More than 8 times
COMMUNITY POOLS:				
Amazon Pool				
Echo Hollow Pool				
Sheldon Pool				
COMMUNITY CTRS.:				
Amazon Center				
Petersen Barn Center				
Sheldon Center				
Westmoreland Center				
PROGRAM AREAS:				
Specialized Recreation				
Outdoor Program				
Athletics				

	Not at all	2 times or less	3–8 times	More than 8 times
SENIOR CENTERS:				
Kaufman Center				
Campbell Center				
PARKS:				
Skinner Butte Park				
Hendricks Park				
Owens Rose Garden				
Spencer Butte Park				
So. Ridgeline Trail				
Amazon Park				

4. Do you or members of your family recall registering for any Eugene Parks and Recreation classes/programs within the last year? If yes, please list:

Class	Time of Year	Location	Repeat Participant?
_____	_____	_____	(yes) ___ (no) ___
_____	_____	_____	___ ___

5. How important are the following factors in considering to participate in a program/class? (Most Important: 4; Important: 3; Not Important: 2; Least Important: 1):
   Location: _____ Price _____ Time of Day _____ Instructor _____

6. Overall, how satisfied are you with the way Eugene Parks and Recreation Department is providing program services? (Please circle).

   Satisfied   Dissatisfied
   Very Satisfied   Very Dissatisfied

7. Overall, how satisfied are you with current levels of maintenance (general upkeep, cleanliness, etc.) in city parks and facilities?

   Satisfied   Dissatisfied
   Very Satisfied   Very Dissatisfied

8. Please tell us the leisure/recreation activities in which you most often participate; i.e., passive activities, art/drama, sports, outdoors, crafts, etc.

   _____ _____ _____ _____

9. If you had time to participate in any recreation activity, what would it be?

   _____ _____ _____ _____

   (Please circle)
   Time of Day:
   Morning Afternoon Evening No Preference
   Time of Year:
   Fall   Winter   Spring   Summer

10. What programs would you like to see offered for children?

    _____ _____ _____ _____

    (Please circle)
    Time of Day:
    Morning Afternoon Evening No Preference
    Time of Year:
    Fall   Winter   Spring   Summer

11. Which factors would prevent you or members of your household from participating in Eugene Parks and Recreation programs? (If any of these apply, please circle the appropriate letter.)

    a. I don't have access to a car.
    b. My personal health prevents participation.
    c. Too busy with household responsibilities.
    d. Not really interested in Parks/Rec. programs.
    e. Lack of available parking.
    f. My work schedule prevents participation.
    g. Already involved with other activities: i.e., church, school, etc.
    h. I'm reluctant to go out at night.
    i. Don't feel safe when visiting parks.
    j. It costs too much to participate.
    k. Lack awareness of Parks/Rec. programs.
    l. Don't have anyone to go with.
    m. Lack child care.
    n. I never really considered participating.

12. To what extent would you support each of the following projects through a bond or serial levy? (Strongly Support: 4; Somewhat Supportive: 3; Right Now Reluctant: 2; Would Oppose: 1.)

    Indoor Pool: ☐   Sports Fields ☐   18-Hole Golf Course ☐   Delta Ponds Canoeway ☐ Amphitheatre Improvements ☐

13. How important do you believe parks and recreation are to the "quality of life" in Eugene? (Please circle)

    Important   Not Important
    Very Important   No Opinion

14. Can you tell us the age(s) of the people living in your household?
    Yourself _____ , Other adults (spouse, room-mate, etc.) _____ , Children _____ , _____ , _____ , _____ , _____ , _____

15. Are you a homeowner _____ or renter _____ ?

16. Do you/members of your household own a video-recorder (V.C.R.) or betamax?
    Yes _____ No _____

17. Are you a single parent? Yes _____ No _____

18. Which income category closely describes your total household income?

    _____ Under $6,000   _____ $20,000 to
    _____ $ 6,001 to $25,000
          $10,000   _____ $25,001 to
    _____ $10,001 to $35,000
          $15,000   _____ $35,001 to
    _____ $15,001 to $50,000
          $20,000   _____ Over $50,000

19. Do you/members of your family belong to a fitness club, health spa, etc. If yes, which one?

    _____

**You may take this survey to any Eugene Parks and Recreation facility, or mail to: Eugene Parks and Recreation Department, 777 High Street, Suite 102, Eugene, OR 97401.

AUTHOR INDEX

SUBJECT INDEX